P9-DCX-510

SUPPLEMENT III, Part 1
John Ashbery to Walker Percy

AMERICAN WRITERS
A Collection of Literary Biographies

LEA BAECHLER

A. WALTON LITZ

General Editors

SUPPLEMENT III, Part 1
John Ashbery to Walker Percy

Charles Scribner's Sons / New York

Maxwell Macmillan Canada / Toronto

Maxwell Macmillan International / New York Oxford Singapore Sydney

Library of Congress Cataloging-in-Publication Data

American writers: a collection of literary biographies.

Suppl. 3 edited by Lea Baechler and A. Walton Litz.
The 4-vol. main set consists of 97 of the pamphlets originally published as the University of Minnesota pamphlets on American writers; some have been rev. and updated. The supplements cover writers not included in the original series.
Includes bibliographies.
Contents: v. 1. Henry Adams to T.S. Eliot — v. 2. Ralph Waldo Emerson to Carson McCullers — [etc.] — Supplement[s] — [etc.] — 3, pt. 1. John Ashbery to Walker Percy. 3, pt. 2. Philip Roth to Louis Zukofsky.
1. American Literature — History and criticism. 2. American literature — Bio-bibliography. 3. Authors, American — Biography. I. Unger, Leonard, ed. II. Baechler, Lea. III. Litz, A. Walton. IV. University of Minnesota. Pamphlets on American writers.
PS129.A55 810'.9 73-1759
ISBN 0-684-19196-2 (Set)
ISBN 0-684-19356-6 (Part 1)
ISBN 0-684-19357-4 (Part 2)

Charles Scribner's Sons
Macmillan Publishing Company
866 Third Avenue
New York, New York 10022

Maxwell Macmillan Canada, Inc.
1200 Eglinton Avenue East
Suite 200
Don Mills, Ontario M3C 3N1

Macmillan Publishing Company is part of the Maxwell Communication Group of Companies.

Impression

1 2 3 4 5 6 7 8 9 10

PRINTED IN THE UNITED STATES OF AMERICA

Acknowledgment is gratefully made to those publishers and individuals who have permitted the use of the following materials in copyright.

"John Ashbery"
Excerpts from "A Wave," "As One Put Drunk into the Packet-Boat," "At North Farm," "Down by the Station, Early in the Morning," "Fantasia," "Litany," "Paradoxes and Oxymorons," "The Pursuit of Happiness," "Scheherazade," "Syringa," "Tapestry," and "Worsening Situation," from *Selected Poems* by John Ashbery. Copyright © 1973, 1974, 1975, 1979, 1980, 1981, 1983, 1984 by John Ashbery. Reprinted by permission of Viking Penguin, a division of Penguin Books USA Inc. and Carcanet Press, Ltd. Excerpts from "Self-Portrait in a Convex Mirror," copyright © 1974 by John Ashbery, from *Self-Portrait in a Convex Mirror* by John Ashbery; and excerpt from "The Ice Storm," from *April Galleons* by John Ashbery. Copyright © 1984, 1985, 1986, 1987 by John Ashbery. Used by permission of Viking Penguin, a division of Penguin Books USA Inc. and from *Selected Poems* by John Ashbery by permission of Carcanet Press, Ltd. Excerpts from "The Instruction Manual," "The Painter," "Some Trees," and "Two Scenes" from *Some*

Trees. Copyright © 1956 by John Ashbery. Excerpts from "Decoy," "Farm Implements and Rutabagas in a Landscape," "Fragment," "Soonest Mended," from *The Double Dream of Spring.* Copyright © 1970, 1969, 1967, 1966 by John Ashbery. Excerpts from "Clepsydra," and "The Skaters" from *Rivers & Mountains.* Copyright © 1962 by John Ashbery. Reprinted by permission of Georges Borchardt, Inc. for the author, and Carcanet Press, Ltd. Excerpts from "A Last World" and "Europe," Copyright © 1962 by John Ashbery. Reprinted from *The Tennis Court Oath* by permission of University Press of New England. Excerpt of interview from "John Ashbery (1976)," by Richard Kostelanetz, in *The Old Poetries and the New* (University of Michigan, 1981), by permission of the author (P.O. Box 444, Prince Street, New York, NY 10012-0008), copyright © 1976, 1981 by Richard Kostelanetz. Quote by John Ashbery from "John Ashbery" by A. Poulin, Jr. from a prose transcription of a videotape interview in October, 1969, sponsored by the Brockport Writers Forum, Department of English, State University College, Brockport, N.Y. 14420. All rights reserved, State University of New York. Reprinted by permission of A. Poulin, Jr., and John Ashbery.

"Djuna Barnes"

Excerpts from "From Fifth Avenue Up" and "Suicide" from *Selected Works* by Djuna Barnes. © The Author's League Fund, 234 West 44th Street, New York, NY 10036 as literary executor of the Estate of Djuna Barnes.

"Louise Bogan"

Excerpts from *The Blue Estuaries* by Louise Bogan. Copyright © 1968 by Louise Bogan. Reprinted by permission of Farrar, Straus and Giroux, Inc.

"Gwendolyn Brooks"

Excerpts from "The Anniad," "The Artists' & Models' Ball," "A Bronzeville Mother . . . ," "The Bean Eaters," "The Chicago Picasso," "In Honor of David Anderson Brooks," "The Lovers of the Poor," *Maud Martha,* "The Murder," "The Progress," "Riot," "Speech to the Young," "The Sundays of Satin Legs . . . ," "To the Young," and "The Wall." All verse by Gwendolyn Brooks, copyright 1987. Published in *Blacks* by The David Company, Chicago, Illinois 60619. Reprinted by permission of the author.

"William S. Burroughs"

Excerpts from *Naked Lunch* by William S. Burroughs. Copyright © 1959 by William S. Burroughs, renewed copyright © 1987, 1990 by William S. Burroughs. Used by permission of Grove Press, Inc. Excerpts from *Queer* by William S. Burroughs. Copyright © 1985 by William S. Burroughs. Used by permission of Viking Penguin, a division of Penguin Books USA Inc. Excerpts of interview with William S. Burroughs by Conrad Knickerbocker from *Writers at Work, Third Series* edited by George Plimpton. Copyright © 1967 by The Paris Review. Used by permission of Viking Penguin, a Division of Penguin Books USA Inc. Excerpts of letters from William S. Burroughs in *Letters to Allen Ginsberg.* Copyright © 1982 by William S. Burroughs. Reprinted by permission of Wylie, Aitken & Stone, Inc.

"Raymond Carver"

Excerpts from "Miracle" and "On an Old Photograph of My Son" from *A New Path to the Waterfall* by Raymond Carver. Copyright © 1989 by the estate of Raymond Carver. Used with permission of Atlantic Monthly Press.

"Jack Kerouac"

Excerpt from *Mexico City Blues* by Jack Kerouac. Copyright © 1959 by Jack Kerouac; copyright renewed © 1987 by Jan Kerouac. Used by permission of Grove Press, Inc. "Rimbaud" from *Scattered Poems* by Jack Kerouac. Copyright© 1970, 1971 by The Estate of Jack Kerouac. Reprinted by permission of City Lights Books.

"Galway Kinnell"

"Another Night in the Ruins," "The Bear," "How Many Nights," "The Last River," and "Vapor Trail Reflected in the Frog Pond" from *Body Rags* by Galway Kinnell. Copyright © 1965, 1966, 1967 by Galway Kinnell. Excerpts from "The Hen Flower," "Lastness," "Little Sleep's-Head Harouting Hair in the Moonlight," "The Shoes of Wandering," and "Under the Maud Moon" from *The Book of Nightmares* by Galway Kinnell. Copyright © 1971 by Galway Kinnell. Excerpts from "The Feast" from *First Poems 1946–1954* in *Selected Poems* by Galway Kinnell. Copyright © 1982 by Galway Kinnell. Excerpts from "The Apple," "Blackberry Eating," "52 Oswald Street," "Flying Home," "The Last Hiding Place of Snow," "The Sadness of Brothers," "The Still Time," and "There are Things I tell to No one" from *Mortal Acts, Mortal Words* by Galway Kinnell. Copyright © 1980 by Galway Kinnell. Excerpts from "The Frog Pond," "The Past," and "The Waking" from *The Past* by Galway Kinnell. Copyright © 1985 by Galway Kinnell. Reprinted by permission of Houghton Mifflin Co. Excerpts from "The River That Is East," from *Flower Herding on Mount Monadnock* by Galway Kinnell. Copyright © 1984 by Galway Kinnell. Excerpts from "The Avenue Bearing the Initials of Christ into the World," and "Freedom, New Hampshire" from *What A Kingdom It Was* by Galway Kinnell. Copyright © 1960 by Galway Kinnell. Copyright © 1988 by Galway Kinnell. Reprinted by permission of Houghton Mifflin Co. and Andrew Deutsch, Ltd. Excerpt of interview with Galway Kinnell by Louis Smith Brady from *New York Woman* Magazine. Copyright 1990 by New York Woman Magazine. Excerpt from "Approaching Home Ground: Galway Kinnell's *Mortal Acts, Mortal Words*" by Lorrie Goldensohn, *Massachusetts Review,* Summer 1984. Reprinted from *The Massachusetts Review,* © 1985 The Massachusetts Review, Inc. Excerpts of interviews with Galway Kinnell by Wayne Dodd and Stanley Plumly in *The Ohio Review,* Fall 1972. Reprinted by permission of Wayne Dodd, Stanley Plumly, and *The Ohio Review.* Excerpt from "Galway Kinnell" by Charles G. Bell in *Contemporary Poets,* 3rd Edition, edited by James Vinson. Reprinted by permission of St. Martin's Press, Inc. Excerpts from interview with Galway Kinnell by A. Poulin Jr. and Stan S. Rubin; and excerpt of interview with Galway Kinnell by William Heyen and Gregory Fitz Gerald from a prose transcription of a videotape interview in October, 1969, sponsored by the Brockport Writers Forum, Department of English, State University College, Brockport, N.Y. 14420. All rights reserved, State University of New York. Excerpt from "A Winter Daybreak Above Vence" from *This Journey* by James Wright. Copyright © 1980 by Anne Wright, Executrix of the Estate of James Wright. Reprinted by permission of Random House, Inc.

"Stanley Kunitz"

Excerpts from "The Crystal Cage," "King of the River," "The Layers," "The Portrait," "Quinnapoxet," "River Road," "The Testing-Tree," "The Way Down" from *The Poems of Stanley Kunitz 1928-1978* by Stanley Kunitz. Copyright © 1957, 1966, 1968, 1970, 1971, 1978, 1979 by Stanley Kunitz. Excerpts from "The Approach to Thebes," "Father and Son," "For the Word is Flesh," "No Word," "Open the Gates," "Poem," "Welcome the Wrath" from

Selected Poems, 1928-1958 by Stanley Kunitz. Copyright 1929, 1930, 1944, copyright © 1957 by Stanley Kunitz. Excerpt from "Of 'Father and Son' " from *A Kind of Order, A Kind of Folly* by Stanley Kunitz. By permission of Little, Brown and Company. Excerpt from "The Snakes of September" from *Next-to-Last Things* by Stanley Kunitz. Copyright © 1985 by Stanley Kunitz. Used by permission of Atlantic Monthly Press. Excerpt from "The Wellfleet Whale" from *The Wellfleet Whale and Companion Poems* by Stanley Kunitz. Copyright © 1944 by Stanley Kunitz. Reprinted by permission of the author. Excerpts from interviews with Stanley Kunitz from *The Paris Review.* Copyright © 1977, by *The Paris Review* and in 1985 by Stanley Kunitz. Reprinted by permission of *The Paris Review* and the author.

"Denise Levertov"
Excerpt from "Midnight Gladness" from *A Door in the Hive.* Copyright © 1984, 1987, 1988, 1989 by Denise Levertov. Excerpt from "Variations on a Theme by Rilke" from *Breathing the Water.* Copyright © 1984, 1985, 1986, 1987 by Denise Levertov. Excerpts from "Mass for the Day of St. Thomas Didymus" from *Candles in Babylon.* Copyright © 1978, 1979, 1980, 1981, 1982 by Denise Levertov. Excerpts from "Christmas 1944," "The Dogwood," "Jackson Square," "To The Snake," and "With Eyes at the Back of our Heads" from *Collected Earlier Poems 1940–1960.* Copyright © 1958, 1959, 1960, 1961, 1979 by Denise Levertov. "To the Reader" and excerpts from "The Altar in the Street," "Eros at Temple Stream," "The Jacob's Ladder," "The Olga Poems," "A Place to Live," and "To Stay Alive" from *Collected Poems 1968–1972.* Copyright © 1958, 1959, 1960, 1961, 1962, 1963, 1964, 1965, 1966 by Denise Levertov. Reprinted by permission of New Directions Publishing Corporation.

"James Merrill"
Excerpts from "Days of 1964," "Dream About Clothes," "The Emerald," and "Up and Down" from *Braving the Elements;* excerpt from "Lost in Translation" from *Divine Comedies;* excerpts from "Another August," "The Friend of the Fourth Decade," and "Mornings in a New House," from *The Fire Screen;* excerpt from a poem beginning "I must begin . . ." from *First Poems;* excerpt from a poem beginning "The message hardly needs . . . ," from *Mirabell: Books of Number;* excerpt from "The Thousand and Second Night," from *Nights and Days;* excerpt from a poem beginning "Giving up its whole . . ." from *Scripts for the Pageant;* excerpt from a poem beginning "We were not tough- . . ." from *The Changing Light at Sandover;* excerpts from "Fire Poem," "Scenes of Childhood," "A Tenancy," and "An Urban Convalescence," from *Water Street.* Reprinted by permission of James Merrill. Excerpt from a poem beginning "Humbly our old poets . . ." from *The Inner Room* by James Merrill. Copyright © 1988 by James Merrill. Reprinted by permission of Alfred, A. Knopf, Inc.

"W. S. Merwin"
Excerpts from "The Approaches," "Elegy," "Homeland," "In the Time of the Blossoms," "Lackawana," and "Presidents" from *The Carrier of Ladders.* Copyright © 1967, 1968, 1969, 1970 by W. S. Merwin. Excerpts from "East of the Sun and West of the Moon" and "Fable" from *The Dancing Bears.* Copyright © 1954, 1975 by W. S. Merwin. Excerpt from "The Portland Going Out" from *The Drunk in the Furnace.* Copyright © 1956, 1957, 1958, 1959, 1960, 1975 by W. S. Merwin. Excerpts from "The Animals," and "The Hydra" from *The Lice.* Copyright © 1963, 1964, 1965, 1966, 1967 by W. S. Merwin. Excerpts from "Anabasis (II)" and "A Poem for Dorothy" from *A Mask for Janus.* Copyright © 1952, 1975 by W. S. Merwin. Excerpts from "The Crossroads of the World etc," "The Man Who Writes Ants," and "Recognition" from *The Moving Target.* Copyright © 1960, 1961, 1962, 1963 by W. S. Merwin. Excerpts from "Berryman," "A Pause by the Water," and "Talking" from *Opening the Hand.* Copyright © 1983 by W. S. Merwin. Excerpt from "The Silence Before Harvest" from *Writings to an Unfinished Accompaniment.* Copyright © 1969, 1970, 1971, 1972, 1973 by W. S. Merwin. Reprinted by permission of Georges Borchardt Inc. for the author. Excerpts from "The Archaic Maker," "Losing a Language," "Night Above the Avenue" "Sight," "The Solstice," "Summer '82," "Term" and "West Wall," from *The Rain in the Trees* by W. S. Merwin. Copyright © 1988 by W. S. Merwin. Reprinted by permission of Alfred A. Knopf, Inc. Quote from Ezra Pound in postcard to W. S. Merwin. Copyright © 1991 by the Ezra Pound Literary Property Trust.

"Philip Roth"
Excerpts from *The Anatomy Lesson,* copyright © 1983, 1988 by Philip Roth; *The Counterlife,* copyright © 1986 by Philip Roth; *The Facts,* copyright © 1989 by Philip Roth; *The Ghost Writer,* copyright © 1979 by Philip Roth; *The Great American Novel,* copyright © 1973 by Philip Roth; *The Professor of Desire,* copyright © 1977 by Philip Roth; *Reading Myself and Others,* copyright © 1975 by Philip Roth; *Zuckerman Bound,* copyright © 1979 by Philip Roth; *Zuckerman Unbound,* copyright © 1981 by Philip Roth. Reprinted by permission of Farrar, Straus and Giroux, Inc.

"Susan Sontag"
Excerpts from *Styles of Radical Will,* copyright © 1969 by Susan Sontag; *A Trip to Hanoi,* copyright © 1968 by Susan Sontag; and *Under the Sign of Saturn,* copyright © 1980 by Susan Sontag. Reprinted by permission of Farrar, Straus and Giroux, Inc. Excerpts from *Against Interpretation,* copyright © 1966 by Susan Sontag. Reprinted by permission of Farrar, Straus and Giroux, Inc. and Andrew Deutsch Ltd. Excerpts from *Aids and Its Metaphors,* copyright © 1989 by Susan Sontag; *Illness as Metaphor,* copyright © 1978 by Susan Sontag; *On Photography,* copyright 1977 by Susan Sontag; and *Susan Sontag Reader,* copyright © 1982 by Susan Sontag. Reprinted by permission of Farrar, Straus and Giroux, Inc. and Penguin Books Ltd. Excerpts of interview with Susan Sontag by Paul Brennan in *London Magazine,* March/April 1979. Reprinted by permission of the author and London Magazine Editions. Excerpt from "Sontag's Urbanity" by D. A. Miller in *October,* Vol. 49, Summer 1989. Reprinted by permission of The MIT Press and the author. Excerpts of interview with Susan Sontag by Geoffrey Movius, reprinted by permission of Geoffrey Movius from the *New Boston Reveiw,* 1975. Excerpts from "Radical Styles" by William Phillips first appeared in the *Partisan Review,* vol. 36, no. 3, 1969. Copyright © 1969 by the Partisan Review Inc. Excerpt of interview with Susan Sontag in *Salmagundi,* 1975. Reprinted by permission. Excerpt from article by Richard Bernstein, *The New York Times,* January 26, 1989. Copyright © 1989 by The New York Times Company. Reprinted by permission. Excerpt from "High Prophetess of High Fashion" by George P. Elliott, in *The Times Literary Supplement,* March 17, 1978. Reprinted by permission of The Times Literary Supplement.

"Jean Toomer"
The lines from "Karintha," "Song of the Son," and "Seventh Street" are reprinted from *Cane* by Jean Toomer by permission of

Liveright Publishing Corporation. Copyright 1923 by Boni Liveright. Copyright renewed 1951 by Jean Toomer. From poem beginning "Above my sleep . . ." Reprinted by permission of The Estate of Jean Toomer.

"Alice Walker"
"Women" from *Revolutionary Petunias and Other Poems*, copyright © 1970 by Alice Walker, reprinted by permission of Harcourt Brace Jovanovich, Inc.

"Richard Wilbur"
Excerpts from "Advice to a Prophet," "A Hole in the Floor," "Someone Talking to Himself," and "The Undead," in *Advice to a Prophet and Other Poems*, copyright © 1961 and renewed 1989 by Richard Wilbur; excerpts from "The Mind-Reader" in *The Mind-Reader: New Poems*, copyright © 1976 by Richard Wilbur; excerpts from "The Lilacs" in *Walking to Sleep*, copyright © 1963 by Richard Wilbur; excerpts from "On the Marginal Way" in *Walking to Sleep*, copyright © 1956 by Richard Wilbur; reprinted by permission of Harcourt Bace Jovanovich, Inc. and Faber and Faber Ltd. Excerpts from "Beautiful Changes," "First Snow at Alsace," "Mind Country," "Praise in Summer," and "Water Walker" in *The Beautiful Changes and Other Poems*, copyright 1947 and renewed 1975 by Richard Wilbur; excerpts from "Ceremony," "Conjuration," "A glance from the Bridge," and "Part of a Letter," in *Ceremony and Other Poems*, copyright 1950 and renewed 1978 by Richard Wilbur; excerpts from "Alatus," All that Is," "Hamlen Brook," "Shad-Time," and "Trolling for Blues" in *New and Collected Poems*, copyright © 1988 by Richard Wilbur; excerpts from "A Baroque Wall-fountain in the Villa Sciarra" in *Things of This World*, copyright 1955 and renewed 1983 by Richard Wilbur; excerpts from "An Event" and "Love Calls Us to the Things of this World" in *Things of This World*, copyright © 1956 and renewed 1984 by Richard Wilbur. Reprinted by permission of Harcourt Brace Jovanovich Inc.

"James Wright"
Excerpts from "The Accusation," "All the Beautiful are Blameless," "At the Executed Murderer's Grave," "A Blessing," "But Only Mine," "A Christmas Greeting," "A Fit Against the Country," "A Horse," "Having Lost My sons, I Confront the Wreckage of the Moon: Christmas, 1960," "In Response to a Rumor that the Oldest Whorehouse in Wheeling, West Virginia, Has Been Condemned," "Lying in a Hammock at William Duffy's Farm in Pine Island, Minnesota," "The Minneapolis Poem," "The Morality of Poetry," "On the Skeleton of a Hound," "An Offering for Mr. Bluehart," "Old Man Drunk," "A Poem about George Doty in the Death House," "A Song for the Middle of the Night," "to a Defeated Savior," and "To the Muse." Reprinted from *Collected Poems* by James Wright. © 1971 by James Wright. Wesleyan University Press, by permission of the University Press of New England. Excerpt from "The Journey" from *This Journey* by James Wright. Copyright © 1982 by Anne Wright, Executrix of the Estate of James Wright. Reprinted by permission of Random House, Inc. Excerpts from *Above the River* by James Wright. Copyright © 1990 by Anne Wright. Reprinted by permission of Farrar, Straus and Giroux, Inc. Excerpts from "Poem" and "To Justify My Singing" reprinted from the Winter 1990 issue of *The Gettysburg Review* by permission of the editor.

"Louis Zukofsky"
Excerpts from "A-6" and "A-12" from *"A"* by Louis Zukofsky. Copyright © 1979 Celia and Louis Zukofsky. Reprinted by permission of The University of California Press. Postcard from the Gotham Book Mart advertising "A"-9, reprinted by permission of the Gotham Book Mart. Excerpt from review of Paul Zukofsky, *The New York Times*, December 1956. Copyright © 1956 by The New York Times Company. Reprinted by permission. Excerpt of review by Michael Steinberg, *The Boston Globe*, 1965. Reprinted courtesy of The Boston Globe. Excerpt from "After Reading *Barely and Widely*" by Robert Duncan from *The Opening of the Field*. Copyright © 1960 by Robert Duncan. Reprinted by permission of New Directions Publishing Corporation. Excerpt from review, " 'An Extraordinary Sensitivity': Zukofsky's 55 Poems" by William Carlos Williams. Copyright © 1991 by William Eric and Paul H. Williams. Reprinted by permission of New Directions Publishing Corporation. Excerpts of letters from Ezra Pound to Harriet Monroe, and excerpt of wire from Ezra Pound to Floss Williams © 1991 by the Trustees of the Ezra Pound Literary Property Trust. Reprinted by permission of New Directions Publishing Corporation, agents. Excerpt of letter from Harriet Monroe to Ezra Pound, Yale Collection of American Literature, Beinecke Library. Reprinted by permission of Mrs. John Arnold Howe. Excerpt of letter from H.B. Lathrop to Ezra Pound, Yale Collection of American Literature, Beinecke Library.

Introduction

The original four volumes of *American Writers: A Collection of Literary Biographies* (1974) assembled the ninety-seven essays that had first appeared between 1959 and 1972 as the University of Minnesota Pamphlets on American Writers, a series of "introductory essays . . . aimed at people (general readers here and abroad, college students, etc.) . . . interested in the writers concerned, but not highly familiar with their work." Characteristically, however, the essays of the initial series and the subsequent supplementary volumes have successfully integrated criticism with biographical detail in such a way as to address and to inform both the general reader and the specialist.

Like the essays in *Supplement I* (2 vols., 1979) and *Supplement II* (2 vols., 1981), the twenty-nine essays in this third supplement maintain the original goals of the series, each providing—for students in secondary and advanced education, librarians, scholars, critics, and teachers—a comprehensive treatment of the work and life of each author. And while the essay on Louis Zukofsky bears special mention as the first intensive examination of that poet's literary life and canon, a number of the essays in *Supplement III* offer the fullest biographical/critical accounts of their subjects to date. This feature of the present supplement is, to some extent, due to the volumes' responsiveness to contemporary writers who in the last several decades have clearly established the lasting import of their literary contributions. The essay on Raymond Carver is a particular case in point, for with it, in light of Carver's early death in August 1988, readers will encounter a thorough penetration of Carver's lifetime work.

Written by recognized experts, young scholars, and poet-critics, the essays collected here also reflect the range and variety of approach exhibited in recent literary study: balancing cultural history and literary biography with thorough analyses of individual major works, these essays are characterized, where appropriate, by their engagement of literary theory, feminist and Afro-American interpretations, and the political or aesthetic ideologies of their subjects. Continuing the tradition set forth in the previous supplements, these two volumes are attentive to women writers, emphasizing both writers who have recently enjoyed revived critical and popular attention—Louise Bogan, Djuna Barnes, Gwendolyn Brooks, Susan Glaspell—and contemporary women authors who have established their reputations as writers and maintained that status with continued and significant literary output, among them Denise Levertov and Toni Morrison. Also well-represented are African American writers, including Jean Toomer, Alice Walker, and Frederick Douglass, and an impressive number of social, historical, and cultural writers and critics.

In fact, *Supplement III* is distinguished by a table of contents that includes writers and critics as diverse as William S. Burroughs and Lionel Trilling, John McPhee and Susan Sontag, Jack Kerouac and Sam Shepard, Truman Capote and Philip Roth, Elizabeth Hardwick and Tom Wolfe, John Ashbery and James Wright. An eclectic collection, these two volumes are also notable for the number of essays devoted to poets, often contemporary ones, and their presence here reflects the richly various poetic undertakings of writers from the second half of this century. Besides those already mentioned, the poets presented in these two volumes include a number who came to maturity in the last two decades—among them Galway Kinnell, James Merrill, W. S. Merwin, Richard Wilbur—and Stanley Kunitz, whose literary activity as both a poet and teacher for over sixty years has influenced and engaged several generations of writers and readers.

As with the essays of the original series, *Supplement III* offers expertly conceived and informative essays on writers who portray the rich diversity of our literary heritage. These writers remind us, by their disparate yet bold endeavors of the literary life, that the readers of each generation must continue to reevaluate the impact and influence of particular writers and their major works in order to maintain the vitality of that heritage.

It is appropriate, at this point, to mention two writers who died before this work was brought to completion: the novelist Walker Percy (May 1916 – May 1990), whose novels explore universal questions within a solidly American tradition, and David Craig Austin (August 1961 – March 1991), poet and essayist, who contributed valuable editorial assistance on several Scribner reference projects, and who wrote two essays in a companion volume (*Modern American Women Writers*) to the series, along with the piece on James Wright in this book.

LEA BAECHLER
A. WALTON LITZ

Editorial Staff

Managing Editor

SYLVIA K. MILLER

Assistant Editor

VIDA PETRONIS

Copyeditors

JONATHAN ARETAKIS
MELISSA DOBSON
EMILY GARLIN
GRETCHEN GORDON
ERIC HARALSON
PATTERSON LAMB
KAREN READY
LUCY RINEHART
ELIZABETH WILSON

Proofreaders

JONATHAN ARETAKIS
DEBRA FEUERBERG
JERILYN FAMIGHETTI
CAROL HOLMES
SUSAN CONVERSE WINSLOW

Indexer

ASTOR INDEXERS

Publisher

KAREN DAY

Contents

Part 1

Part 2

Contributors

David Craig Austin. Poet and writer. Contributor to Scribner's *Modern American Women Writers.* JAMES WRIGHT

Brian A. Bremen. Assistant Professor of English, University of Texas, Austin. Author of essays on James Joyce and William Carlos Williams and of conference papers on the development of ethnic identities in the twentieth century. JEAN TOOMER

James M. Buzard. Junior Fellow, Society of Fellows, Harvard University. Author of articles on E. M. Forster, John le Carre, Byron, and William Morris. LIONEL TRILLING

Ann Charters. Professor of English, University of Connecticut. Author of *Kerouac: a Biography; Olson/Melville: A Study in Affinity;* and *Beats & Company: Portrait of a Literary Generation.* Editor of *Scattered Poems* by Jack Kerouac; *Three Lives* and *Q. E. D.* by Gertrude Stein; *The Beats: Literary Bohemians in Postwar America;* and *The Story and Its Writer.* JACK KEROUAC

Peter Cooper. Examiner, Educational Testing Service. Author of *Thomas Pynchon and the Contemporary World,* articles, and research reports. PHILIP ROTH

C. K. Doreski. Assistant Professor of English, Emmanuel College. Author of numerous articles; co-author of *How to Read and Interpret Poetry.* GWENDOLYN BROOKS

William Doreski. Associate Professor of English, Keene State College. Author of *The Years of Our Friendship: Robert Lowell and Allen Tate,* and of articles and reviews in various journals. DENISE LEVERTOV

Noël Riley Fitch. Visiting lecturer, University of Southern California, Los Angeles. Author of *Sylvia Beach and the Lost Generation: A History of Literary Paris in the Twenties and Thirties; Literary Cafes of Paris; Hemingway in Paris;* and numerous journal articles and chapters in books. Co-editor of *Faith and Imagination.* DJUNA BARNES

J. Ellen Gainor. Assistant Professor of Theatre, Cornell University. Author of *Shaw's Daughters: Dramatic and Narrative Constructions of Gender,* and articles on Bernard Shaw and Susan Glaspell. SAM SHEPARD

Celeste Goodridge. Assistant Professor of English, Bowdoin College. Author of *Hints and Disguises: Marianne Moore and her Contemporaries.* SUSAN SONTAG; GALWAY KINNELL

Janet Gray. Graduate student in English, Princeton University. ELIZABETH HARDWICK; ALICE WALKER

Wendy Hirsch. Graduate student, Columbia University. Review in *The American Scholar.* Editorial contributor to the Prentice-Hall *Twentieth-Century American Literature.* LOUISE BOGAN

James Kraus. Associate Professor of English, Chaminade University. Author of *The Biopoetics of Gary Snyder: A Study of the Poet as Ecologist,* as well as essays and poetry in such journals as *Virginia Quarterly Review; San Marcos Review;* and *Chaminade Literary Review.* W. S. MERWIN

Milton I. Levin. Professor Emeritus, English, Trenton State College. Author of *Noël Coward;*

co-author of *A Student's Guide to Fifty American Plays;* contributor to *The Reader's Encyclopedia of World Drama.* SUSAN GLASPELL

Mason I. Lowance, Jr. Professor of English, University of Massachusetts, Amherst. Author of *Increase Mather; Massachusetts Broadsides of the American Revolution; The Language of Canaan: Metaphor and Symbol in New England from the Puritans to the Transcendentalists,* and numerous articles on American culture, 1600–1900. Guggenheim Fellow. FREDERICK DOUGLASS

Veronica Makowsky. Associate Professor of English, Louisiana State University. Author of *Caroline Gordon: A Biography,* and of various articles and reviews on R. P. Blackmur, southern literature, and women's biography. Editor of R. P. Blackmur's *Henry Adams* and *Studies in Henry James.* Co-editor of *The Henry James Review.* WALKER PERCY

Randy Malamud. Assistant Professor of English, Georgia State University. Author of *The Language of Modernism.* TRUMAN CAPOTE

J. D. McClatchy. Visiting Lecturer, Creative Writing Program, Princeton University. Author of *Scenes from Another Life; Stars Principal; The Rest of the Way;* and *White Paper.* Editor of *Anne Sexton: The Artist and Her Critics; Recitative: Prose by James Merrill; Poets on Painters;* and *The Vintage Book of Contemporary American Poetry.* JAMES MERRILL

Vincent Passaro. Adjunct Professor of English/Creative Writing, Hofstra University. His fiction and criticism have appeared in *Harper's; Esquire; 7 Days;* and other journals. WILLIAM S. BURROUGHS

Michelle Preston. Writer and editor residing in Princeton, New Jersey. TOM WOLFE

Tim Redman. Assistant Professor of Literary Studies, School of Arts and Humanities, University of Texas, Dallas. Author of *Ezra Pound and Italian Fascism,* and numerous articles and papers on literature and rhetoric. LOUIS ZUKOFSKY

Peter Sacks. Professor of English and Creative Writing, The Johns Hopkins University. Author of *The English Elegy: Studies in the Genre from Spenser to Yeats;* and *In These Mountains* and *Promised Lands* (both collections of poems). RICHARD WILBUR

Grace Schulman. Poet; Professor of English, Baruch College, City University of New York. Author of *Burn Down the Icons* and *Hemispheres* (both collections of poems); and of *Marianne Moore: The Poetry of Engagement.* Translator of T. Carmi's *At the Stone of Losses;* and, with Ann Zavala, of Pablo Antonio Cuadra's *Songs of Cifar.* Poetry Editor, *The Nation;* former Director, 92nd Street Y Poetry Center. STANLEY KUNITZ

John Shoptaw. Assistant Professor of English, Princeton University. Author of *On the Outside Looking Out: The Poetry of John Ashbery.* JOHN ASHBERY

Norman Sims. Associate Professor of Journalism, University of Massachusetts, Amherst. Editor of *The Literary Journalists* and *Literary Journalism in the Twentieth Century.* JOHN MCPHEE

Valerie Smith. Associate Professor of English, University of California, Los Angeles. Author of *Self-Discovery and Authority in Afro-American Narrative;* and articles on race, gender, culture, and narrative. TONI MORRISON

Gary Williams. Professor of English, University of Idaho. RAYMOND CARVER

John Ashbery

1927–

IN A 1983 interview with John Koethe, John Ashbery offered the following explanation of his poetry by way of advice: "You should try to make your poem as representative as possible." Ashbery's own poetry is representative in several ways. First, he will choose particulars for their typical or representative quality. Ashbery told Ross Labrie that *The Vermont Notebook* (1975), for example, was written largely "on buses traveling through New England, though not Vermont. Generally speaking I guess it's a catalogue of a number of things that could be found in the state of Vermont, as well as almost everywhere else." Second, he will use details characteristic of some literary or nonliterary convention. We need not know who the newlywed is in the opening lines of "More Pleasant Adventures" (from *A Wave,* 1984) in order to recognize it as oral autobiography: "The first year was like icing. / Then the cake started to show through." As the poem exclaims, "Heck, it's anybody's story." But Ashbery commonly writes of personal experiences with details drawn from other lives. In an interview with John Murphy, he described "Soonest Mended" (from *The Double Dream of Spring,* 1970), for instance, as "my 'One-size-fits-all confessional poem,' which is about my youth and maturing but also about anybody else's." Third, Ashbery's "concrete particulars" are representative because they function in relations rather than as isolated terms. In "At North Farm," the opening poem of *A Wave,* the relational, representative character of Ashbery's poetics is immediately apparent:

Somewhere someone is traveling furiously toward you,
At incredible speed, traveling day and night,
Through blizzards and desert heat, across torrents, through narrow passes.
But will he know where to find you,
Recognize you when he sees you,
Give you the thing he has for you?

Hardly anything grows here,
Yet the granaries are bursting with meal,
The sacks of meal piled to the rafters.
The streams run with sweetness, fattening fish;
Birds darken the sky. Is it enough
That the dish of milk is set out at night,
That we think of him sometines,
Sometimes and always, with mixed feelings?

This lucid but indeterminate poem, crowded with indefinites, may leave readers with a host of questions: Who or what is traveling toward "you"? Does "you" mean "us" or "me"? Where is "here"? What is this poem *really* talking about? Rather than simply maintaining that the poem means just what it says, or doesn't mean anything, we may read "At North Farm," and any Ashbery poem, by attending to terms in their relations. The key relation in ''At North Farm,'' as the allusion to the postal carrier's motto (''Neither rain nor snow nor gloom of night . . .'') suggests, is the postal system, requiring a messenger (or sender), a message, and a receiver. We generate different readings of ''At North Farm'' depending on what terms we plug into the relational system. We can read the poem self-reflexively as the advent of the poem or new book of poems, amorously as the approach of a new lover, theologically as the coming of Christ (as Santa), autobiographically as the warding off of death, and so on. But ''At North Farm'' sustains no single meaning throughout.

At a further remove, ''sacks of meal'' (rather than grain) echoes ''sacks of mail,'' ''mail'' being strangely absent from this postal poem. Ashbery discussed this kind of cryptic revision in an interview with Richard Jackson: ''I just wrote a poem this morning in which I used the word 'borders' but changed it to 'boarders.' The original word literally had a marginal existence and isn't spoken, is perhaps what you might call a crypt word.'' All poets compose, consciously or unconsciously, by means of underlying ''crypt words,'' but in Ashbery's poetry the relations between missing words and those marking their absence take on an added significance. As Ashbery maintains in *Three Poems* (1972), ''the word that everything hinged on is buried back there. . . . It is doing the organizing, the guidelines radiate from its control.'' Reading Ashbery's poetry, then, involves hearing words in relation to missing words, and taking particulars in relation to the kind of thing or language they represent.

Born on July 28, 1927, John Lawrence Ashbery was raised in Sodus, New York, a small town near Lake Ontario in western New York State. His father, Chester Ashbery, operated a fruit farm, where Ashbery worked for several summers canning cherries, a sticky job he does not remember fondly. His mother, Helen Lawrence Ashbery, had taught biology in high school before she married, and it was in her father's house that Ashbery began reading literature, primarily Victorian novels. Fascinated by a 1937 article in *Life* on the surrealist exhibit at the Museum of Modern Art, he decided to try his own hand at the visual arts and took painting classes at the art museum in Rochester from the ages of eleven to fifteen. Some still lifes from this period survive. When Ashbery was thirteen, his nine-year-old only brother died of leukemia. At fifteen, Ashbery won a *Time* current-events award, selecting for his prize Louis Untermeyer's anthology of modern American poetry, which started him writing poetry. He remembers admiring the poetry of Elinor Wylie early on, but not being able to make much of either Wallace Stevens or W. H. Auden. Before he left home in 1943 for two years at Deerfield Academy, Ashbery declared his homosexuality to his mother. He published his first poems in the *Deerfield Scroll,* but was shocked to learn, at Harvard in 1945, that two of his poems had been stolen by a supposed friend of his at Deerfield and published in *Poetry* under the name Joel Michael Symington. His first credited publication of poetry, apart from poems in the *Deerfield Scroll* and the *Harvard Advocate,* would be in *Furioso* in 1949.

At Harvard, Ashbery majored in English, and, along with Robert Creeley and John Hawkes, studied poetry with Theodore Spencer. In 1947, with the help of Kenneth Koch, Ashbery joined the editorial board of the *Harvard Advocate,* which published ''Some Trees,'' among others of his poems. He collaborated with Fred Amory on a collage for one of the magazine's covers, and in his last semester at Harvard he met Frank O'Hara. In ''A Reminiscence,'' in *Homage to Frank O'Hara* (1988), Ashbery recalls being struck by the uncanny similarity of their accents:

> Though we grew up in widely separate regions of the east, . . . we both inherited the same flat, nasal twang, a hick accent so out of keeping with the roles we were trying to play that it seems to me we probably exaggerated it, later on, in hopes of making it seem intentional.

Ashbery wrote his senior thesis on Auden's poetry up to *The Sea and the Mirror* (1944), a book that influenced his own *Three Poems.* He met Auden at a reading at Harvard and got to know him through a mutual friend, James Schuyler, in New York. While an undergraduate, Ashbery also heard Wallace Stevens at Harvard give one of his rare poetry readings.

After he was turned down for graduate study in English at Harvard and accepted at Columbia, Ashbery moved to New York in the summer of 1949. Kenneth Koch, who had graduated the year before and was encouraging him to move, let him stay in his apartment for the summer. There he met Koch's upstairs neighbor, the painter Jane Freilicher, who became a lifelong friend. She introduced Ashbery to Larry Rivers, another friend for life, and to the world of abstract expressionism. Freilicher illustrated Ashbery's first, small collection of poetry, *Turandot and Other Poems* (1953). His play *The Heroes* (an Audenesque assemblage of Theseus, Patroclus, Achilles, Circe, and others in "a living room of an undeterminable period") premiered at the Living Theatre in 1952. That year, Ashbery also completed a master's thesis on the novels of Henry Green, a dialogue novelist in vogue at the time. During the same busy year, Ashbery and his constant friend James Schuyler began writing their own dialogue novel, *A Nest of Ninnies,* which they finished and published in 1969.

In comparison with the New York school of painting, the academic school of poetry seemed tame. The tradition of Robert Lowell, John Berryman, Allen Tate, and Randall Jarrell held little interest for Ashbery. His favorite poets during the late 1940's and early 1950's included Marianne Moore, Elizabeth Bishop, Wallace Stevens, William Carlos Williams, Delmore Schwartz, and F. T. Prince. Ashbery didn't care for much of Auden's self-consciously colloquial American poetry (*The Sea and the Mirror* excepted), and his taste for T. S. Eliot would not develop until later. He also began avidly reading the now-neglected poets David Schubert, Laura Riding, John Wheelwright, and the French poet and novelist Raymond Roussel, all of whom he would showcase as "An Other Tradition" in the Charles Eliot Norton lectures he was asked to deliver at Harvard in the 1989–1990 academic year. In 1956 he and O'Hara both submitted poetry manuscripts to the Yale Younger Poets competition, judged by Auden, and both were rejected in the preliminary round. When Auden complained that he did not like any of the manuscripts submitted to him, someone (possibly Auden's companion, Chester Kallman) told him about Ashbery's and O'Hara's rejected submissions. Auden asked to see the manuscripts and chose Ashbery's *Some Trees,* which O'Hara, in a typically generous review, hailed as the best first volume of poems since Stevens' *Harmonium* (1923).

Some Trees (1956), which included new work and nearly all the poems from *Turandot,* is as remarkable for what it excludes or slights as for what it presents. There is little detailed description of the world; few of the poems rely on close observation. New York passes unmentioned. Only "Some Trees" and the last section of "The Picture of Little J. A. in a Prospect of Flowers" employ anything like a lyric "I." Nor will the readers of Ashbery's later work find here the prosaic rhythms of speech or the cascading images of the purportedly indistinguishable "Ashbery poem." What we do find in *Some Trees* are poems of polished, often elevated or archaic diction, high sonic resonance, and high linear definition. Composing more by the line than by the sentence and proceeding more by sound than by sense, Ashbery creates poems that disassemble into their components, each of which collapses into itself, like a self-fulfilling prophecy. Consider the opening lines of "Two Scenes":

We see us as we truly behave:
From every corner comes a distinctive offering.
The train comes bearing joy;
The sparks it strikes illuminate the table.
Destiny guides the water-pilot, and it is destiny.
For long we hadn't heard so much news, such
noise.
The day was warm and pleasant.
"We see you in your hair,
Air resting around the tips of mountains."

Each line echoes itself, and creates, for its duration, a distinct sonic environment. Though syntactically fragmented, the fifth line centers the Miltonic "water-pilot" within his "destiny." And the tight weave of assonance and consonance in the first line submerges the idiomatic wish to "see ourselves as others see us." This folk adage or moral injunction ("If you could see yourself!"), however garbled, nevertheless organizes this scene of being seen. The news of who or how we are arrives by rail, sea, or over the wireless as the news and weather. But as the sonic slippage of "so much news, such noise" suggests, these bulletins carry little more than the ring of truth. "But who / Knows anything about our behavior?" Ashbery will ask thirty years later in *A Wave*; neither in life nor in art does the mask or guard come down.

Some Trees is a network of echoes, silences, secrets, ambiguous signs, defenses, and imminent revelations. "The Grapevine," for instance, begins with a sonorously convoluted warning: "Of who we and all they are / You all now know." The secrecy, evasiveness, and self-protectiveness that have become a trademark of Ashbery's poetry bear some relation to his necessarily covert homosexual lifestyle throughout the 1940's. Even the often-anthologized, limpid love lyric "Some Trees," which Ashbery wrote at Harvard in 1948 to one of his male classmates, betrays the caution necessary when behavior is shadowy and unsanctioned:

These are amazing: each
Joining a neighbor, as though speech
Were a still performance.
Arranging by chance

To meet as far this morning
From the world as agreeing
With it, you and I
Are suddenly what the trees try

To tell us we are:
That their merely being there
Means something; that soon
We may touch, love, explain.

Certainly this description of imminent love (such as was prophesied in "Two Scenes") is "anybody's story." And the brilliance of Ashbery's keeping what Charles Baudelaire called a "forest of symbols" to the horizontal, emotional plane of correspondences amazes. Yet this love is unaccompanied by open gestures, even though by mutual agreement the lovers have retreated from the world. The joy of the poem consists in the lovers' being surrounded by the nonjudgmental presences of the trees. Even so, this still performance cannot last, and the guarded time of self-reflection resumes:

Placed in a puzzling light, and moving,
Our days put on such reticence
These accents seem their own defense.

In the early 1950's, the United States was embroiled in the Korean War and grappling with the rise of Senator Joseph McCarthy, whose truly reductive imagination equated homosexuals with Communists. It was a time of lists, purges, drafts, and raids on suspicious bars. Ashbery told Richard Kostelanetz:

In the early 50's, I went through a period of intense depression and doubt. I couldn't write for a couple of years. . . . It did coincide with the beginnings of the Korean War, the Rosenberg case, and McCarthyism. . . . I was jolted out of this by going with Frank O'Hara—I think it was New Year's Day, 1952—to a concert by David Tudor of John Cage's *Music of Changes*.

With Cage's changes ringing in his ears, the young Ashbery's response to this repressive climate was neither fight nor flight but a resourceful evasive action. In "The Thinnest Shadow" the poet counsels himself (with a disturbingly paternal tone) to make himself a thin, moving target: "A face looks from the mirror / As if to say, / 'Be supple, young man, / Since you can't be gay,' " advice playing on the latent meaning of "gay" that Ashbery first learned in the mid-1940's. In "A Boy," Ashbery evades both the paternal repression of gays and the patriarchal oppression of the Korean War. Written in 1951, after Ashbery saw John Huston's mangled film version of Stephen Crane's *The Red Badge of Courage,* "A Boy" ends with a dire bulletin:

They're throwing up behind the lines.
Dry fields of lightning rise to receive
The observer, the mincing flag. *An unendurable age*.

The crypt phrase "the mincing fag" determines the conclusion. The decade of Ashbery's twenties, after World War II and during the Korean War (neither of which Ashbery fought in), was indeed unendurable.

One popular poem in which the artist goes his own way is the flawless sestina "The Painter," the only other Harvard poem included in *Some Trees*. As in "Some Trees," the enjambed tetrameters of "The Painter" keep to an effortless syntax and a colorless vocabulary, including the poem's end words ("buildings," "portrait," "prayer," "subject," "brush," "canvas"). It is remarkable, for instance, that the only color word appearing in "The Painter" is "white." With its fixed form and sustained irony, "The Painter" raises the issue of flawlessness. Yet the poem relies on a productive incongruity between its formal perfection and its Romantic subject matter, the painter in sublime confrontation with the ocean. No Vincent van Gogh or Jackson Pollock, Ashbery's painter is more of a Prufrockian artist who does not think the sea will sit for him. One key model for "The Painter" (as for Eliot's "The Love Song of J. Alfred Prufrock") is Robert Browning's "Andrea del Sarto (Called 'The Faultless Painter')." With its source material in Giorgio Vasari, long verse paragraphs, and extended apostrophe, and especially with its exploration of the aesthetics and psychology of perfection, "Andrea del Sarto" is also an important model for Ashbery's "Self-Portrait in a Convex Mirror," for which "The Painter" becomes the preliminary sketch. Like Ashbery's "perfectly white" sestina, Browning's Andrea del Sarto painting is colorless and finished: "All is silver-gray / Placid and perfect with my art." Andrea painstakingly paints his wife, and settles for technical excellence while chafing at the flawed soulful paintings of his rivals Michelangelo and Raphael:

Their works drop groundward, but themselves, I know,
Reach many a time a heaven that's shut to me,
Enter and take their place there sure enough,
Though they come back and cannot tell the world.

Ashbery literalized these dropping paintings, now thrown seaward by the rival painters, in the concluding tercet of "The Painter":

They tossed him, the portrait, from the tallest of the buildings;
And the sea devoured the canvas and the brush
As if his subject had decided to remain a prayer.

The most malleable of the end words in ''The Painting'' is ''subject,'' meaning subject matter, self, and subjection. To paint his ''self-portrait,'' Ashbery's painter masters his ego (as he had his model wife) and dips his brush into the sea, subjecting his conscious perfections to his oceanic ''soul.'' The paradoxically passive self-expression of abstract expressionism (''Imagine a painter crucified by his subject!'') was already in Browning's post-Romantic reading of the Renaissance. ''My soul,'' Ashbery's painter prays (with an implicit pun on ''canvas'' and ''sail''), ''when I paint this next portrait / Let it be you who wrecks the canvas.'' As though drawn on sand, the painting's ambiguous ''subject'' fails to survive:

> Finally all indications of a subject
> Began to fade, leaving the canvas
> Perfectly white.

But ''The Painter'' succeeds by drawing the mock-heroic proportions of the subject's subjection.

Along with ''Some Trees'' and ''The Painter,'' the most anthologized poem in *Some Trees* is ''The Instruction Manual,'' written in 1955. Unlike the collage narratives of such poems as ''Popular Songs'' or ''A Long Novel,'' ''The Instruction Manual'' follows a single narrator and a single, simple story from the beginning to an abbreviated end. A harassed, dreamy functionary, under a deadline to ''write the instruction manual on the uses of a new metal,'' gazes out the window and fancies he visits ''dim Guadalajara! City of rose-colored flowers! / City I wanted most to see, and most did not see, in Mexico!'' There is a special nostalgia, Baudelaire tells us in ''Invitation to a Voyage,'' for the ''country one does not know.'' But whereas Baudelaire's imaginary country is richly textured, recessed, and exotic, the ''local colors'' of Ashbery's Guadalajara are taken from Bishop's and Stevens' elementary palates:

> Around stand the flower girls, handing out rose- and lemon-colored flowers,
> Each attractive in her rose-and-blue striped dress (Oh! such shades of rose and blue),
> And nearby is the little white booth where women in green serve you green and yellow fruit.

In an interview with Sue Gangle in 1977, Ashbery provides a fascinating backdrop to this travelogue:

> I wrote [''The Instruction Manual''] actually when I was working for a publisher [McGraw-Hill], writing and editing college textbooks. . . . The poem . . . is probably about the dissatisfaction with the work I was doing at the time. And my lack of success in seeing the city I wanted most to see, when I was in Mexico. The long lines in the poem were suggested by Whitman. . . . Also the French poet, Raymond Roussel, whom I later studied in France.

Several things are interesting about Ashbery's retrospective sense of ''The Instruction Manual.'' First, unlike the speaker in lyrics such as those from Lowell's *Life Studies* or Whitman's apostrophe to the Suez Canal, Ashbery's persona is as cartoonish as the characters he imagines (''And, as my way is, I begin to dream''). He takes the reader on a walking tour of Guadalajara, the Proustian place-name (''Here you may see one of those white houses with green trim / That are so popular here. Look—I told you!''), and in fact appears as little more than an embodiment of the discourse of a travelogue. The reduced narrator, his generic observations, the languid (more than ecstatic Whitmanian) long lines, and the pleasant confusion of narrative levels in which we never really leave the frame for the picture, or the world for the map, are all strongly reminiscent of Bishop, whom Ashbery had begun to read in the 1940's.

By the time Ashbery had written ''The Instruction Manual,'' he had received a Fulbright Fellowship to write a thesis on Raymond Roussel in France, where, with some interruptions, he would spend the next decade of his life. Although he did not fulfill his intention of writing a dissertation on Roussel, Ashbery did publish a few articles on him, and even discovered the missing first chapter to Roussel's last, unfinished novel. Not long after his arrival Ashbery met Pierre Martory, an art and music critic for *Paris Match,* with whom he lived for the next nine years. Ashbery dedicated his second book of poetry, *The Tennis Court Oath* (1962), to Martory, and—in an unusual tribute—mentions his name as the fellow viewer of Parmigianino's *Self-Portrait in a Convex Mirror* in his best-known poem, of the same title: ''Vienna where the painting is today, where / I saw it with Pierre in the summer of 1959.'' In 1957 Ashbery began writing art reviews for *Art News,* and in 1960, through the help of Frank O'Hara, Ashbery became an art reviewer for the *New York Herald Tribune* in Paris.

The next year, Ashbery and Harry Matthews, a novelist whom he had met in France, enlisted Kenneth Koch and James Schuyler as coeditors of the Francophile literary review *Locust Solus* (named for one of Roussel's novels), which ran for two years. Also in 1961, John Myers coined the term ''New York school of poetry.'' Ashbery sees more differences than similarities in the poets of this ''school'' (from which he was absent at the time it was named). As he explained in 1981 to A. Poulin:

I think that Frank O'Hara's life was the subject of his poetry in a way that mine isn't. Although many of his poems are about things that happened to him, people that he knew, events he experienced, these were a kind of springboard for getting into something wider, more poetic. Kenneth Koch is at the opposite extreme, I think, because his work is involved much more deeply with just words, which are the end result he's after. Really words, rather than a transcending of them, which is what I have always felt I had to do. I might stand halfway between these two, because I don't feel that words are the end of thought and yet I don't feel that experience has to be transformed by words.

And Schuyler, Ashbery told Piotr Sommer, ''is really much more of a classical poet, I mean he's somebody more resembling Elizabeth Bishop whose work is very clear in structure.'' Though there were no qualities shared by the New York school of poetry other than a spirit of experimentation, there did exist a family relation of shared experiences, attitudes (a dislike, for instance, of the academic poetry being written in the 1950's), and projects. Ashbery collaborated with Schuyler, Koch, and O'Hara on various short plays and poems.

In 1962, to Ashbery's surprise, Wesleyan University Press (with Donald Hall on the board) agreed to publish a collection of his experimental poems written mostly in France, *The Tennis Court Oath.* The book disappointed critics, who felt shut out from its isolated words and phrases, but, significantly, this volume was singled out for praise by the ''language poets'' (another ill-fitting but adhesive label) for its relentless attack on conventional grammar, syntax, voice, and diction. Ashbery himself has expressed mixed feelings about this misshapen offspring. He told Richard Kostelanetz that much of the work was little more than an attempt to break away from the style of *Some Trees*: ''I didn't want to write the poetry that was coming naturally to me then, . . . and I succeeded in writing something that wasn't the poetry I didn't want to write, and yet was not the poetry I wanted to write.'' Probably no poem of Ashbery's has sent more readers' hands into the air than his detective epic, ''Europe,'' in which Ashbery collaged passages from a British detective novel, *Beryl of the Bi-*

plane (1917), written by William Le Queux during World War I. Le Queux's novel, set almost entirely in England, concerns the exploits of the ace pilots Ronald Pryor and his beloved, Beryl (compare ''Ash*bery*'') Gaselee, who fly ''The Hornet,'' an experimental flying machine (like Ashbery's ''Europe'') equipped with a top-secret ''silencer,'' which allows the pilots to creep up on their prey undetected. The deadly couple work not for the RAF but as undercover agents to protect England from ''the enemy within.'' The book is filled with the mechanisms of detection: Morse and other codes, disguises, and double agents. These doublings, in which the enemy looks and acts ''just like you and me,'' produce a paranoid atmosphere most immediately resembling the McCarthyism of the early 1950's. To see how representative this repressive paranoia is, we need only substitute ''Communists,'' ''homosexuals,'' ''Jews,'' or ''obscene artists'' for ''Germans.'' Though McCarthy had fallen and America was now an ocean away, Ashbery must have seen poetic possibilities both in the self-reflexively detective and in the sociopolitical dimensions of Le Queux's grim little novel:

> The engine had stopped, for, half the propeller
> being broken, the other half had embedded
> itself deeply into the ground. Collins came
> running up, half frantic with fear, but was soon
> reassured by the pair of intrepid aviators, who
> unstrapped themselves and quickly climbed out
> of the wreckage. Ere long a flare was lit and the
> broken wing carefully examined; it was soon
> discovered that ''The Hornet'' had been tampered with, one of the steel bolts having been
> replaced by a painted one of wood!
> ''This is the work of the enemy!'' remarked
> Ronnie thoughtfully. ''They cannot obtain sight
> of the silencer, therefore there has been a
> dastardly
> plot to kill both of us. We must be a little more
> wary in future, dear.''

Juxtaposing the above passage from page 61 of *Beryl* (which preserves the line breaks of the original) with a few of the 111 stanzas from ''Europe'' will give us an idea of Ashbery's own procedures:

104.

blaze			aviators
	out		dastardly

105.

We must be a little more wary in
    future, dear

106.

she was trying to make sense of
what was quick laugh
hotel—cheap for them
caverns the bed

box of cereal

Ere long a flare was lit
I don't understand wreckage

107.

blue smoke?	The steel bolts
It was as though	having been replaced
She had	by a painting of
the river	one of wood!
above the water	Ronnie, thoughtfully
	of the silencer

plot to kill both of us, dear.
pet
oh

it that she was there

These stanzas from ''Europe'' are dotted with the representative conventions of detective fiction. We know what to make of clues such as ''steel bolts'' or ''box of cereal,'' signs such as ''a flare'' or ''blue smoke?,'' or self-reflexive statements like ''she was trying to make sense of,'' whether or not we know their source. We also find romantic conventions, such as Ronnie's unintentionally hilarious, patronizing caution to Beryl. The ''wreckage'' of Ronnie and Beryl's airplane becomes a figure for ''Europe,'' another postwar wasteland. In stanza 104, the generically descriptive ''aviators,'' ''blaze,'' and ''dastardly,'' along with the colorless ''out,'' litter the open field of the poem in a mannered parody of William Carlos Williams or Charles Olson. In 107, the two-columned wreckage of the poem anticipates the long, double-columned ''Litany'' of *As We Know* (1979). On the left wing, we note that Ashbery has slightly altered Le Queux's prose to create the surrealist joke of a steel bolt being replaced by ''a painting of'' (rather than ''a painted'') one in wood. The lines ''Ronnie, thoughtfully / of the silencer'' duplicate the fracturing of the original prose as determined by the left margin of the published text, whose accidental features Ashbery preserves. And the final isolated words and phrases strewn about are reminiscent both of Anton von Webern's music and the erasures and splatters of Robert Rauschenberg and Jackson Pollock. Ashbery's ungrammatical fragments exceed the always grammatical experiments in ''automatic writing'' undertaken by surrealists such as André Breton and Guillaume Apollinaire. The problem with ''Europe'' is not its obscurity but its clarity. We ''get the idea'' of ''Europe'' too quickly and completely for the poem to keep satisfying us. Still, we are fortunate that Ashbery earned his wings of sustained lyric flight with ''Europe'' rather than, for example, with the moving but sober and essayistic ''Self-Portrait in a Convex Mirror.'' With ''Europe,'' Ashbery carved out an immense lyric space and dispersed a universe of poetic fragments that would take years to explore and to recollect.

The most ambitious and prospective poem in *The Tennis Court Oath* is ''A Last World,'' which in its mythological scope rivals *The Waste Land* and anticipates Ashbery's own long poem ''A Wave.'' The expansive, consecutive lines of ''A Last World'' culminate what Ashbery, in an interview with Piotr Sommer, has called ''the compromise style'' of *The Tennis Court Oath*: the poem is more disjunct than the poems in *Some Trees* but less fragmented than poems such as ''Europe.'' Like *The Waste Land,* ''A Last World'' diagnoses the sexual disorders of the Western world, in which ''passions are locked away, and states of creation are used instead, that is to say synonyms are used.'' Yet this repressive modern world in which love cannot speak its name is the only one in which poetry, speaking in synonyms, is possible. ''A Last World'' ends with a wonderfully sentimental apocalypse:

Everything is being blown away;
A little horse trots up with a letter in its mouth,
    which is read with eagerness
As we gallop into the flame.

Once we recognize that the crypt word for ''flame'' is ''sunset,'' the genre of the western (comically apt for a poem on the Western world) with its prairie winds, its pony express, its rocking-horse young readers, and its society of men riding off together, swings into view. Within the context of the poem, the horse is also the Trojan Horse, which leads to the burning of Troy. But Ashbery's flame is not simply destruction, or even Eliotic purgation, but the flame of desire, which renews private and fuels public life. With its scope, beauty, and intelligence, ''A Last World'' becomes the most important poem Ashbery had written thus far in his career.

Ashbery returned to New York for good in 1965, after his father died of a heart attack. (Frank O'Hara died the following year.) Also in 1965, Ashbery became an executive editor at *Art News,* where one of his duties was to recruit other poets to do art reviews. The following year, Ashbery published his third major volume of poems, *Rivers and Mountains,* which marked a return in some ways to the poetry of his first two volumes but also paved the way for many projects to come. "The Skaters," for instance, marks a clear advance over the austere discontinuities of "Europe" and in fact has more "personality" (livelier masks) than do any of Ashbery's earlier poems. The same disquieting muses of "The Instruction Manual"—Roussel, Marcel Proust, and Bishop—watch over "The Skaters" (the desert island passage in part three seems to have influenced Bishop's "Crusoe in England" [1976]). And much of "The Skaters" is involved with Proustian places never visited, typical boyhoods never experienced. Yet in many ways "The Skaters" is a kind of farewell to the New York school, as well as to his collage poems. Other playful collages will follow, but not on this romping scale. Ashbery told Kostelanetz that with "The Skaters" he wanted to "put everything in, rather than, as in 'Europe,' leaving things out." As with "Europe," "The Skaters" reproduces passages from another book, this time a British children's book titled *Three Hundred Things a Bright Boy Can Do* (1911). But the splintered, mysterious lines and stanzas of "Europe" have been replaced by long, easygoing lines reminiscent of "The Instruction Manual." The "instruction manual" *Three Hundred Things a Bright Boy Can Do* allowed Ashbery to sketch out a representative rather than a reminiscent childhood:

Fire Designs.—This is very simple, amusing, and effective. Make a saturated solution of nitrate of potash (common nitre or saltpetre), by dissolving the substance in warm water, until no more will dissolve; then draw with a smooth stick of wood any design or wording on sheets of white tissue paper, let it thoroughly dry, and the drawing will become invisible. By means of a spark from a smouldering match ignite the potassium nitrate at any part of the drawing, first laying the paper on a plate or tray in the darkened room. The fire will smoulder along the line of the invisible drawing until the design is complete.

With its self-reflexive imagery of secrecy, *Three Hundred Things a Bright Boy Can Do* probably appealed to Ashbery for the same reasons as did *Beryl of the Biplane*; but the way the text is adapted in "The Skaters" is quite different:

In my day we used to make "fire designs," using a saturated solution of nitrate of potash.
Then we used to take a smooth stick, and using the solution as ink, draw with it on sheets of white tissue paper.
Once it was thoroughly dry, the writing would be invisible.
By means of a spark from a smoldering match ignite the potassium nitrate at any part of the drawing,
First laying the paper on a plate or tray in a darkened room.
The fire will smolder along the line of the invisible drawing until the design is complete.

Ashbery does not mount or preserve this passage as a ruin of language or culture (as in "Europe" or Eliot's *The Waste Land*). Rather, he allows it to devour itself as a self-consuming, protean artifact. This temporal, more than spatial, "leaving-out business" produces here the sudden transformation from clichéd reminiscence ("In my day") to instruction manual ("ignite the potassium nitrate"). But with its discrete stanzas (verse paragraphs, quatrains, indented lyrics) and abrupt shifts in style and persona, "The Skaters" was not really well-equipped for the seamless or fluid transformations described above. Ashbery came closer in "Clepsydra," the watershed poem of *Rivers and Mountains*. "Clepsydra" was written in the spring of 1965, roughly a year after "The Skaters" was finished and a few months after "Fragment," the long poem of *The Double Dream of Spring*. The actual chronology of these three poems is important in charting Ashbery's progress as a poet. Before considering "Clepsydra," then, I will turn briefly to the ironically titled "Fragment" (not "Fragment*s*" but a piece from a vaster puzzle).

"Fragment" is a monumentally meditative poem, composed of fifty ten-line stanzas, or dizains, inspired by Maurice Scève's *Délie* (1544; "délie" is an anagram for "l'idée" or "idea"), which apparently leaves nothing out. "Fragment" was first handsomely published by Black Sparrow Press as a volume dedicated to James Schuyler, with two dizains per page facing the "illustrations" (like the emblems of *Délie*) of the cool realist Alex Katz. The first dizain of "Fragment" illustrates both its limitations and its power:

The last block is closed in April. You
See the intrusions clouding over her face
As in the memory given you of older
Permissiveness which dies in the
Falling back toward recondite ends,
The sympathy of yellow flowers.
Never mentioned in the signs of the oblong day
The saw-toothed flames and point of other
Space not given, and yet not withdrawn
And never yet imagined: a moment's
commandment.

It is helpful to place this block in the context of Ashbery's personal history. This stanza was written in December 1964, soon after Ashbery's father died. The mausoleum of "Fragment" opens with its "last block" being fitted into place. With the decorous "sympathy" of flowers, the grief that clouds the face of the mother and blots the memory of her former permissiveness from the wayward "son" (compare the "saw-toothed flames" of the child's drawn daisy "sun") commanded to honor his parents is never mentioned. This "moment's monument," as Dante Gabriel Rossetti called the sonnet form, sustains its meditative intensity for fifty stanzas, erotically extending its immediate grief with the memory of romantic separations. Yet the intensity of "Fragment" is achieved at the cost of variation. The childhood experience here is related in the same patient, ruminative language of thought as the mother's grief. Nor are the ungrieving signs of the times in the oblong daily news given in journalese. The consolatory "idea" of "Fragment," the absent yet latent moment of the past, means a lot to Ashbery. But it is difficult for the romantic momentum of "and yet not withdrawn / And never yet imagined" to overcome the inertia of "and point of other / Space not given." Or perhaps "Fragment" transcends its words and discourses too completely in its sanctuary of feelings and ideas.

Ashbery's language begins to thaw and coalesce in "Clepsydra," which Ashbery himself sees as a pivotal poem. As he told Kostelanetz:

After my analytic period, I wanted to get into a synthetic period. I wanted to write a new kind of poetry after my dismembering of language. Wouldn't it be nice, I said to myself, to do a long poem that would be a long extended argument, but would have the beauty of a single word? "Clepsydra" is really a meditation on how time feels as it is passing. The title means a water clock as used in ancient Greece and China. There are a lot of images of water in that poem. It's all of a piece, like a stream.

This newfound style, more "synthetic" than Pablo Picasso's reconstructions, seems in fact to be one of the topics of "Clepsydra":

The half-meant, half-perceived
Motions of fronds out of idle depths that are
Summer. And expansion into little draughts.
The reply wakens easily, darting from
Untruth to willed moment, scarcely called into
being

Before it swells, the way a waterfall
Drums at different levels. Each moment
Of utterance is the true one; likewise none are
true,
Only is the bounding from air to air, a serpentine
Gesture which hides the truth behind a congruent
Message, the way air hides the sky, is, in fact,
Tearing it limb from limb this very moment: but
The sky has pleaded already and this is about
As graceful a kind of non-absence as either
Has a right to expect: *whether* it's the form of
Some creator who has momentarily turned away,
Marrying detachment with respect, so that the
pieces
Are seen as parts of a spectrum, independent
Yet symbolic of their spaced-out times of arrival;
Whether on the other hand all of it is to be
Seen as no luck. [italics added]

The cascading, serpentine sentence, descending from William Wordsworth's "Lines Composed a Few Miles Above Tintern Abbey" and "Ode: Intimations of Immortality," from Stevens' "The Auroras of Autumn," and from Proust, has displaced the linear integrity of *Some Trees* and *The Tennis Court Oath.* In "Clepsydra" the enjambments seem "half-meant, half-perceived" pauses along the way. Only in retrospect do the end words sound their momentous ideas (cause, being, time, truth, etc.). The language of philosophical assertion and of argument takes its place alongside that of spontaneous, stream-of-consciousness description—something that was ruled out, for example, in "The Instruction Manual." The "I," who in "The Skaters" was not ready to explain, is brimming with justifications in "Clepsydra," though the first-person "I am" is withheld for about five pages. The diction of "Clepsydra" is idiomatic ("the way," "in fact") as well as lyrical, and the tone serious. Perhaps one limitation of "Clepsydra" is that it aims too carefully at being the "Intimations Ode" of its day (Wordsworth is better known for his wisdom than his wit). The humor in "Clepsydra" is wry rather than coy and evasive. And the wordplay ("whether" hides "weather," which translates "les temps") is self-effacing. A water clock, the clepsydra was used to time the arguments of lawyers in court. Ashbery's "Clepsydra" is itself a monumental argument: a philosopher's system, a lawyer's case, a plot summary, and a lovers' quarrel. The case tried is a divorce: that of the past from the present, the poem from the poet, and one lover from another. The question of "Clepsydra" may be put in romantic terms: "If our love has failed, was it false or unreal?" But the possibility that he "dreamt the whole thing," made up his past and his love, is ruled out in his wakeful end: "It is not a question, then, / Of having not lived in vain." Ashbery wakes in an uneasy assurance of the outside world: that of his apartment, and his past, which is realized in his own day and poem:

What is meant is that this distant
Image of you, the way you really are, is the test
Of how you see yourself, and regardless of
whether or not
You hesitate, it may be assumed that you have
won, that this
Wooden and external representation
Returns the full echo of what you meant
With nothing left over, from that circumference
now alight
With ex-possibilities become present fact, [. . .]

In our postdeconstructive world, we may find it difficult to believe in this world poem without supplement. But at least we find it easier to understand the blind faith in the weather, the story of life in the world, to which we sooner or later return.

The lyrics of *The Double Dream of Spring,* which include a sestina, a collage poem, a ballad, and translations, match the formal variety of *Some Trees,* but also exhibit a new discursive range. Consider the antic opening from the sestina "Farm Implements and Rutabagas in a Landscape":

The first of the undecoded messages read: "Popeye sits in thunder,
Unthought of. From that shoebox of an apartment,
From livid curtain's hue, a tangram emerges: a country."
Meanwhile the Sea Hag was relaxing on a green couch: "How pleasant
To spend one's vacation *en la casa de Popeye,*" she scratched
Her cleft chin's solitary hair. She remembered spinach. [. . .]

With its antic shifts in diction, "Farm Implements" is a far cry from the mannered formality of Ashbery's early sestina "The Painter." Ashbery's source for "Farm Implements" was a Spanish cartoon strip of *Popeye* in which the Sea Hag, like Circe, changes Swee'pea into a pig. Here the only metamorphoses are the familiar one of Popeye, sitting like a Miltonic God in thunder, whose spinach restores his omnipotence. But the Sea Hag adjusts to Popeye's mood swings: "If this is all we need fear from spinach / Then I don't mind so much."

In "Soonest Mended," the most popular poem in *The Double Dream of Spring,* the antic mixtures of "Europe" and "The Skaters" are themselves mixed in with the meditative argumentation of "Fragment" and "Clepsydra" in a poem with an easygoing pathos that we will recognize as characteristic of many of Ashbery's best later poems. Consider the fatal recognition that we are only end words in someone else's wacky sestina, only dice thrown in the game:

These then were some hazards of the course,
Yet though we knew the course *was* hazards and nothing else
It was still a shock when, almost a quarter of a century later,
The clarity of the rules dawned on you for the first time.
They were the players, and we who had struggled at the game
Were merely spectators, though subject to its vicissitudes
And moving with it out of the tearful stadium, borne on shoulders, at last.

The humor of this passage plays off its pathos. The counters aren't those of academic poetry, "they" and "I," the conventional world and the poet, but "they" and "we," those powers that be and "we" ordinary citizens who have little to say about our destiny. Twenty years earlier, in a review of Gertrude Stein's epic poem on "them," *Stanzas in Meditation,* the poet in exile praised the absence of the inclusive personal pronoun: "What a pleasant change from the eternal 'we' with which so many modern poets automatically begin each sentence, and which gives the impression that the author is sharing his every sensation with some invisible Kim Novak" (*Poetry,* 1957). By *The Double Dream of Spring* the middle-aged poet, once again part of the United States, has found a new interest in writing (rather than collaging) common American language and public discourses.

"Decoy," another more serious piece of resistance, begins with the "we" of the Declaration of Independence, whose own truths have divorced themselves from America's dream:

We hold these truths to be self-evident:
That ostracism, both political and moral, has
Its place in the twentieth-century scheme of things;
That urban chaos is the problem we have been seeing into and seeing into,
For the factory, deadpanned by its very existence into a
Descending code of values, has moved right across the road from total financial upheaval
And caught regression head-on.

This nation under God, which still ostracizes those of different sexual orientation, has descended into its own moral chaos. Ashbery's adoption of public, nonlyrical discourse marks an important advance in the career of the repatriated American poet. This hybrid, confrontational style, which has left its mark on the language poets, makes its poetry not by reshaping the world but by reforming the clichés of its daily, official life (''looking into,'' ''destined by its very nature to''). This democratization of language will lead to the sermonic history of Ashbery's declaration of poetic interdependence, ''The System,'' in *Three Poems.*

Three Poems is Ashbery's favorite book. It is also his most important book both in the sense that it continues his project of revitalizing (not parodying) ordinary languages for the purposes of prose poetry and because it spells out, hesitantly, Ashbery's ''philosophy of life and writing.'' *Three Poems* marks the poet's most extended and fruitful experiments with prose poetry. There are all kinds of speech and writing going on in these 118 pages: clichéd conversation, business diction, journalese, history, philosophy, sermon, graduation poetry, and so on. Moreover, the style moves from the Proustian Romantic narratives of ''The New Spirit'' to the more public history and homily of ''The System'' and the urgent reconciliations of ''The Recital.'' Ashbery has mentioned Arthur Rimbaud, St.-John Perse, Thomas Traherne, Auden, Proust, Giorgio de Chirico, and the later Henry James as stylistic influences on these poems. Although these authors all developed endless, protean sentences, none of their work really prepares the reader for the particular excitement and pleasure that *Three Poems* brings.

Three Poems consists of two fifty-page works, ''The New Spirit'' and ''The System,'' and a ten-page summation, ''The Recital.'' ''The New Spirit'' is written in unindented prose blocks and prosaic verse, ''The System'' in prose blocks, and ''The Recital'' in prose paragraphs. Within *Three Poems* itself, there are a number of nearly resolved dialectical oppositions: new and old, part and whole, present and past, private and public, and physical and spiritual love. After an initial consideration of the problem of poetic selection, ''The New Spirit'' moves into reflections on a love affair. This reminiscence is itself reminiscent of ''Clepsydra'' and ''Fragment,'' both in style and in subject matter, but it is more successful and diverse than either poem in that it modulates its language of private thought with the languages of public communication. Near the end of ''The New Spirit,'' these reflections coalesce into a character called ''the Ram,'' or simply ''he,'' who in ''The System'' takes the podium, or pulpit, offering a religious history of the 1960's and a sermon on living out one's destiny. In ''The Recital,'' which begins ''All right. The problem is that there is no new problem,'' an insistent, dark argument resolves itself:

> The point was the synthesis of very simple elements in a new and strong, as opposed to old and weak, relation to one another. Why hadn't this been possible in the earlier days of experimentation, of bleak, barren living that didn't seem to be leading anywhere and it couldn't have mattered less? Probably because not enough of what made it up had taken on that look of worn familiarity, like pebbles polished over and over again by the sea. . . .

For Ashbery, the collages of *The Tennis Court Oath* perhaps announced themselves too insistently as avant-garde, to the exclusion of subsequent explorations. In *Three Poems,* the prosaic, demotic elements, such as the worn simile of the pebbles, are not erased but blended into Ashbery's argument so that it is impossible to separate the public from the individual spirit.

The ''system'' of *Three Poems* represents the physical, political, and discursive systems that determine our lives: computer systems, the solar system, the circulatory system, the traffic system, the system of government, a philosophical or religious system, and so on. Ashbery's response is not to drop out but to work and write within and against the system. The historian who opens "The System" tells us that there was a subversive principle at work: "There was, however, a residue, a kind of fiction that developed parallel to the classic truths of daily life. . . . It is this 'other tradition' which we propose to explore." The oratorical turns of phrase here mark the clearest departure in style of "The System" from the personally charged reflections of "The New Spirit." But no clear and safe distinction may be drawn between the languages of the establishment and that of the non-establishment poet. "The Other Tradition" democratizes the poetry of "the Tradition."

To represent the other tradition, Ashbery replaces the historian's discourse with the pastor's. Ashbery's preacher of the gospel of love makes an important distinction, virtually the only one in Ashbery's poetry, between "the frontal and the latent" forms of happiness. Frontal happiness, he tells us, "is experienced as a kind of sense of immediacy, even urgency; . . . Its sudden balm suffuses the soul without warning, as a kind of bloom or grace." We recognize this kind of happiness as the privileged or involuntary moments of Wordsworth or Proust. The problem with these moments is that they don't last. What follows, and what Ashbery ultimately comes to prefer, is latent happiness. If "frontal" suggests "frontal assault" or "frontal pose," "latent" seems drawn from the mysteriously autobiographical final lines of Roussel's "The View":

> Thanks to the intensity suddenly increased
> of a memory long-lived and hidden ["vivace et
> latent"] of a summer
> Already dead, already far from me, suddenly carried away.

Latent happiness means, first, the feeling that the past bliss is about to return, like summer:

> We all know those periods of balmy weather in early spring, sometimes even before spring has officially begun: days or even a few hours when the air seems suffused with an unearthly tenderness, as though love were about to start, now, at this moment, on an endless journey put off since the beginning of time.

Ashbery in fact fell in love with David Kermani, who has remained his companion, while writing "The System." This Eliotic "mid-winter spring" may also be taken as the traces and influences of the lost moment that have permeated the text of the present. In the following tumultuous rhetorical question of "The System," Ashbery's preacher presents us with his article of faith:

> For they never would have been able to capture the emanations from that special point of life if they were not meant to do something with them, weave them into the pattern of the days that come after, sunlit or plunged in shadow as they may be, but each with the identifying scarlet thread that runs through the whole warp and woof of the design . . .

The claim that "this second kind of happiness is merely a fleshed-out, realized version of that ideal first kind . . ." is borne out most strongly in *Three Poems* itself, which is a brilliantly fleshed-out version of "Clepsydra." As "the faithful reflection of the idealistic concept that started us along this path, but a reflection which is truer than the original because more suited to us, and whose shining perspectives we can feel and hold," the full-blown latent happiness points forward to Ashbery's self-portrait in the convex mirror of the globe. The superiority of this model of latent happiness, whether or not one subscribes to Proustian or Wordsworthian consolations of the past, is that it is worldly and textual, rather than visionary and hyperlinguistic. Ashbery's romanticism is a means to an encompassing realism by which we make sense of ourselves in the context of the world.

In 1972, after new owners took over *Art News,* Ashbery found himself without a job as an art critic. He took a teaching job at Brooklyn College in 1974. But the ending (or interruption) of his career as an art critic encouraged Ashbery to "realize" his art criticism into poetry. The result was his best-known long poem, "Self-Portrait in a Convex Mirror." The volume containing the title poem, dedicated to Kermani, won Ashbery three major poetry prizes upon its appearance in 1975—the Pulitzer Prize, the National Book Award, and the National Book Critics Circle Award—and moved Ashbery, in many people's eyes, from "the other tradition" into "*the* tradition." Ashbery himself does not like the poem, which he finds too conventional—the apparently clear antipodes to the apparently obscure "Europe." He began "Self-Portrait" in Provincetown in February 1973, and finished in what he told me was "three months of not very inspired writing." Nevertheless, the unemployed art critic succeeded perfectly at what he set out to accomplish.

Part of Ashbery's difficulty with the poem is its pretext or premise. "Self-Portrait in a Convex Mirror" reads like a critical essay, a reflection on a small but remarkable painting by Parmigianino, an early mannerist whose distortions anticipated the surrealists. In his *Self-Portrait in a Convex Mirror* (1523–1524), Parmigianino painted his reflection in a convex barber's mirror onto a ball of wood so that his head, at the virtual center of the round painting, is framed by the elongated hand in the foreground or at the circumference. As Parmigianino's painting mirrors his reflection, Ashbery's poem reflects Parmigianino's painting. When Ashbery first saw the painting in 1959, he was studying Roussel, whose long poem "La Vue" (The View), with its immensely detailed and extended description of a convex scene depicted in the "ball of glass" on a pen holder, must have encouraged Ashbery's elongated meditation on Parmigianino's ten-inch painting. Ashbery begins the poem as an art critic:

As Parmigianino did it, the right hand
Bigger than the head, thrust at the viewer
And swerving easily away, as though to protect
What it advertises.

Ashbery "does it" here by eliding his grammatical subject ("[I want to do it] as Parmigianino did it . . .") in favor of an adverb, the grammatical indicator of "manner" (from "manus": hand). "As," the manner, protects the matter, the nearly erased "As[hbery]." Unlike the erasures of "Europe," this elision passes almost undetected. The poem and painting illustrate a paradox: the head moves the hand that draws the head. All the important relations in "Self-Portrait in a Convex Mirror" align themselves around the central head and the circumferential hand: depth and surface, matter and manner, signified and signifiers, whole and parts, past and present, present and future, and self and other. In fact, we may align more of the fluid images of "Self-Portrait" with either the head or the hand: "light [head] behind windblown fog and sand [hand]"; "The city [head] falling with its beautiful suburbs [hand]"; "There is room for one bullet [head] in the chamber [hand]."

Ashbery probes the otherness, or convexity, of the self-portrait in six stanzas or globes, which cover topics deliberately, like a well-shaped essay: (1) the confining present, (2) the receding past, (3) the convex future, (4) the otherness of the painting, (5) the otherness of the city and history, (6) and the otherness of creation itself. For Ashbery, the self exists only in the convex mirror of the world, understood spatially as other people, or temporally as the history of one's frustrated projects. Each stanza break ruptures the mannered world of the poem. Consider the break between the first and second globes:

You will stay on, restive, serene in
Your gesture which is neither embrace nor
 warning
But which holds something of both in pure
Affirmation that doesn't affirm anything.

The balloon pops, the attention
Turns dully away. Clouds
In the puddle stir up into sawtoothed fragments.
I think of the friends
Who came to see me, of what yesterday
Was like. [. . .]

The opening stanza, which concerns the imprisonment of the self within its self-portrayals, ends with a self-reflexive doctrine of "pure poetry," that the only subject matter of a poem is itself. In *An Apologie for Poetrie,* Sir Philip Sidney said that the poet "never affirmeth" since he never makes the reader take his fictions for the truth. But with this negative affirmation the boredom of incomprehension sets in. With the introduction of a new subject, the seamless global stanza bursts. Ashbery here puns on "pop art," particularly that of Roy Lichtenstein, who enlarged, or "blew up," the comic strip with its balloons of speech and clouds of thought. Each stanza break, each new "subject" in "Self-Portrait in a Convex Mirror," means the death of the old. In this mannered, perfect world, the only changes possible are violent.

In the last, longest globe, the critical patience has run out in an exasperated, impassioned recognition of the otherness of anybody's self-image:

 Is there anything
To be serious about beyond this otherness
That gets included in the most ordinary
Forms of daily activity, changing everything
Slightly and profoundly, and tearing the matter
Of creation, any creation, not just artistic
 creation
Out of our hands, to install it on some
 monstrous, near
Peak, too close to ignore, too far
For one to intervene? This otherness, this
"Not-being-us" is all there is to look at
In the mirror. [. . .]

The adverbs of manner ("Slightly and profoundly"), one line's triplication of "creation," the pregnant end words ("otherness," "everything," "matter," "this"), the imagery ("Peak" as the hand), the wordplay ("monstrous" means "sign"), and the final response with its existential vocabulary, all charge this passage with Ashbery's tragic eloquence. Any reader skeptical of Ashbery's "merit," or convinced of his "willful obscurity," may very well be converted by "Self-Portrait in a Convex Mirror." Despite the monochromatic limits of its ironic and elegiac tone, the poem is capable of both power and subtlety, and succeeds in both its conceptions and its manners.

While there is little formal variety in the free-verse lyrics of *Self-Portrait in a Convex Mirror,* there is a pleasant range of styles, such as the following narrative from "Worsening Situation":

 One day a man called while I was out
And left this message: "You got the whole thing
 wrong
From start to finish. Luckily, there's still time
To correct the situation, but you must act fast.
See me at your earliest convenience. And please
Tell no one of this. Much besides your life de-
 pends on it."
I thought nothing of it at the time. Lately
I've been looking at old-fashioned plaids,
 fingering
Starched white collars, wondering whether
 there's a way
To get them really white again. My wife

Thinks I'm in Oslo—Oslo, France, that is.

The coy figure skater of "The Skaters" and the explaining prophet of "The System" are both upended by this deadpan speaker, benumbed with capitalist anxiety. Deities here communicate through answering machines rather than burning bushes. The anticonfessional poet's hilarious final confession is doubly nonreferential: both "Oslo, France" and the gay poet's "wife" are off the map. This confidentiality, much like Robinson Crusoe's wish that Friday were a woman in Elizabeth Bishop's "Crusoe in England," is as good a self-portrait as anything in the volume.

The opening poem of *Self-Portrait in a Convex Mirror,* "As One Put Drunk into the Packet-Boat" (the title is taken from Andrew Marvell), introduces a new musicality into Ashbery's verse (the accents have been added; the ellipsis is Ashbery's):

I tríed each thíng, only sóme were immórtal and
 frée.
Élsewhere wé are as sítting ín a pláce where
 súnlight
Fílters dówn, a líttle át a tíme,
Wáiting for sómeone to cóme. Hársh wórds are
 spóken,
As the sún yéllows the gréen of the máple
 trée. . . .

The delicate interweaving of two- and three-beat measures marks a departure from the prosaic cadences of *Three Poems.* In fact, Ashbery's ellipses reveal that this first stanza should be read as a written fragment of this new style, as the next lines confirm: "So this was all, but obscurely / I felt the stirrings of new breath in the pages." This documentary distancing, which Ashbery developed in "Europe," now occurs without calling too much attention to itself.

At the other stylistic extreme, "Scheherazade" begins with a shorthand, gnarled scene description:

Unsupported by reason's enigma
Water collects in squared stone catch basins.
The land is dry. Under it moves
The water. Fish live in the wells. The leaves,
A concerned green, are scrawled on the light.
 Bad
Bindweed and rank ragweed somehow forget to
 flourish here.
An inexhaustible wardrobe has been placed at
 the disposal
Of each new occurrence. It can be itself now.

Unlike the natural, seasonal music of "As One Put Drunk into the Packet-Boat," these lines are strikingly artificial. The sentences seem too short or too long for the lines. The discordant intrusion of "Bad / Bindweed and rank ragweed" registers its absence. The Audenesque allegorical abstractions ("Unsupported by reason's enigma" and "at the disposal / Of each new occurrence") and the minimalist enigma ("It can be itself now") suspend our visualization of the landscape. No luxurious fairy-tale kingdom, this scene offers meager fare for the reader's eyes and ears. Yet the messy style of these lines is more experimental and ambitious than the free-verse opening of "As One Put Drunk into the Packet-Boat."

Houseboat Days (1977) contains some of Ashbery's best short poems to date. "Street Musicians," which opens the book, is a moving elegy; "Wet Casements" (my own favorite) is a protest by the now-famous poet against his encroaching publicity; "The Other Tradition" supplements the history of the avant-garde given in "The System"; "Pyrography," commissioned by the U.S. Department of the Interior for its bicentennial exhibition, explores America's westward expansion, burning its way across the continent; the antic "Daffy Duck in Hollywood" sketches the cartoonlike world of American materialism;

"And *Ut Pictura Poesis* Is Her Name" (borrowing Horace's dictum that a poem is like a painting) and "What Is Poetry" respond to creative-writing students, whom Ashbery had begun to teach, who want to know what poetry is, now, and how to write it, now. "Syringa" mythologizes the origin and the loss of song.

The only relative disappointment of the volume is, surprisingly, its long poem "Fantasia on 'The Nut-Brown Maid.' " Ashbery's "Fantasia" follows the fifteenth-century anonymous ballad stanza for stanza, often incorporating the language of its mannered debate. "The Nut-Brown Maid" is a courtly ballad in which He and She debate the legendary unfaithfulness of women by assuming the respective roles of the banished lover and his faithful nut-brown maid. The argument of "Fantasia," as in the ballad, is intricate and incremental—much like that of Ashbery's earlier amorous argument, "Fragment." It is a clear departure or retreat from the fluent mannerisms of "Self-Portrait in a Convex Mirror." A stanza from "Fantasia" will illustrate how little Ashbery is willing to trade on his patented fluid style:

Be it right or wrong, these men among
Others in the park, all those years in the cold,
Are a plain kind of thing: bands
Of acanthus and figpeckers. At
The afternoon closing you walk out
Of the dream crowding the walls and out
Of life or whatever filled up
Those days and seemed to be life
You borrowed its colors, the drab ones
That are so popular now, though only
For a minute, and extracted a fashion
That wasn't really there. You are
Going, I from your thought rapidly
To the green wood go, alone, a banished man.

By the time we reach the stubborn, vaguely pornographic syllables "bands / Of acanthus and figpeckers," we know we are no longer listening to the seductive rhythms of "Self-Portrait": "thrust at the viewer / And swerving easily away." It doesn't necessarily follow that "Fantasia" is inferior to "Self-Portrait," rather that it will not be preferred by the same readers or enjoyed for the same reasons. "Fantasia" is another world, a diversion from the relentless topicality of much contemporary poetry. Those who fancy the medieval and Renaissance subtleties of dialogue and argument will prefer "Fragment" and "Fantasia"; those who love propelled Romantic meditations will choose "Self-Portrait in a Convex Mirror" and "A Wave."

If no readers have thus far championed "Fantasia," many have applauded the short poems of *Houseboat Days*. The seductively resistant "Wet Casements," for instance, attracts readers by the very force of the writer's demand for privacy. The poem begins with a rare epigraph taken from Franz Kafka's unfinished story "Wedding Preparations in the Country" (1951): "When Eduard Raban, coming along the passage, walked into the open doorway, he saw that it was raining. It was not raining much." What interests Ashbery about this "passage" is that the reader sees through Raban's eyes. This voyeuristic pleasure can turn sour when the defining gaze of another is turned on us, so that we see ourselves as merely someone else's "correct impressions" of us. Many labels—"intentionally obscure," "fraudulent," "New York school poet," "canonical"—have been attached to the name Ashbery. Once an "Ashbery" poem slips out of the poet's grasp, it may be kept, read, and evaluated by any stranger who "carried that name around in his wallet / For years as the wallet crumbled and bills slid in / And out of it." Ashbery's response to this vicissitude of publication is anger and determination:

I want that information very much today,

Can't have it, and this makes me angry.
I shall use my anger to build a bridge like that

Of Avignon, on which people may dance for the feeling
Of dancing on a bridge. I shall at last see my complete face
Reflected not in the water but in the worn stone floor of my bridge.

I shall keep to myself.
I shall not repeat others' comments about me.

The bridge at Avignon, like Kafka's story, is unfinished. So too, the critical commentary on Ashbery will remain incomplete. For the time being, people may dance to his music. But the "complete face," still under construction, is for Ashbery's eyes alone. Even the final, seemingly confessional couplet is in the discourse of a journal resolution in which the doubled "I" remains apart from "myself" and "me." "Wet Casements" covers the same territory as "Self-Portrait in a Convex Mirror" more briefly and with more power.

"Syringa" (compare Pan's syrinx), arguably Ashbery's best lyric, tells the story of Orpheus in the mannered style of Ovid (or Jean Cocteau) rather than in the tragic style of Virgil. The poem begins casually:

Orpheus liked the glad personal quality
Of the things beneath the sky. Of course, Eurydice was a part
Of this. Then one day, everything changed. He rends
Rocks into fissures with lament. Gullies, hummocks
Can't withstand it. The sky shudders from one horizon
To the other, almost ready to give up wholeness.
Then Apollo quietly told him: "Leave it all on earth.
Your lute, what point? Why pick at a dull pavan few care to
Follow, except a few birds of dusty feather,
Not vivid performances of the past." But why not?
All other things must change too.

Eurydice is taken for granted here in this seriocomic apocalypse, which reminds one that Ovid's Orpheus, who taught men how to love young boys, was the mythical inventor not only of elegy but of homosexuality. The real test is not the absence of Eurydice but the presence of Apollo, who reminds the songster of the burden of the past. Harold Bloom had used "Fragment" in *The Anxiety of Influence* (1973) to illustrate how the Stevens of "Le Monocle de Mon Oncle" (1918) sounded more like Ashbery than vice versa, and had placed Ashbery in his canon of "strong poets" along with Whitman, Stevens, and Hart Crane. Ashbery's response, again, is that the past—whether it is a memory or a tradition—is latent in the present. The mistake is to try to recapture the past (in the manner of Orpheus or of Proust), as either a memory or a style, since the past will soon enough capture us:

Stellification
Is for the few, and comes about much later
When all record of these people and their lives
Has disappeared into libraries, onto microfilm.
A few are still interested in them. "But what about
So-and-so?" is still asked on occasion. But they lie
Frozen and out of touch until an arbitrary chorus
Speaks of a totally different incident with a similar name
In whose tale are hidden syllables
Of what happened so long before that
In some small town, one indifferent summer.

This wonderful passage (I have quoted only a fragment) illustrates the intelligence, clarity, humor, and nostalgic mystery of Ashbery at his best. Long gone into the technologized library crypts, only a few poets surface, and even then anonymously, from oblivion: "But what about / So-and-so?" As Ashbery instructs: "You can't say it that way any more." The old songs reverberate without royalties in current numbers, as Ashbery's representative summer echoes, again, the final lines of Roussel's "The View." Canonization is arbitrary (why Ashbery and not Roussel?) and for the few. But Ashbery's work is so diverse partly because he has not confined his reading (or criticism) to those on top of the charts. We should take the same approach in our reading of his own rich work.

In 1978 "Syringa" was set to music by Elliott Carter, one of Ashbery's favorite composers. Ashbery's poem, sung by a female mezzo-soprano, was scored along with various Greek fragments on the myth of Orpheus, sung by a male bass. The conversational, competitive simultaneity of this piece is characteristic of Carter's work, which influenced Ashbery's "Litany," the opening poem of *As We Know.* "Litany" runs for seventy pages in two parallel columns. The beginning stanzas illustrate the added dimensions of this parallelism:

For someone like me The simple things Like having toast or Going to church are Kept in one place.	*So this must be a hole* *Of cloud* *Mandate or trap* *But haze that casts* *The milk of enchantment*
Like having wine and cheese. The parents of the town Pissing elegantly escape knowledge Once and for all. The Snapdragons consumed in a wind Of fire and rage far over The streets as they end. The casual purring of a donkey Rouses me from my accounts: What given, what gifts. The air Stands straight up like a tail.	*Over the whole town,* *Its scenery, whatever* *Could be happening* *Behind tall hedges* *Of dark, lissome knowledge.*
He spat on the flowers.	*The brown lines persist* *In explicit sex* *Matters like these* *No one can care about,* *"Noone." That is I've said it* *Before and no one* *Remembers except that elf.*

The visionary obliquity of the right-hand, italicized column slants away from the upstanding, plainspoken intimacy of "someone like me" in the left column. The voices, however, soon become indistinguishable, like those of "Fantasia." The short lines of either side result in surprising, ominous pauses, as though they were running up against an invisible wall. The scene, depicted by the appearance of the poem on the page, is Main Street, U.S.A., with the town parents "pissing" (or "passing") elegantly and ritually along the middle blank space while escaping the carnal knowledge of the hedges of print on either side. The two-columned poem has various analogues or parallels: the two eyes or ears, consciousness and self-consciousness, text and commentary or translation, twin phalluses or columns of figures, newspaper or Bible columns of print, "simultaneous but independent monologues" (as Ashbery describes them in an introductory note), and so on. Ashbery told Peter Stitt, "I once half-jokingly said that my object was to direct the reader's attention to the white space between the columns." This white space at the core of the poem represents ineffable, unspeakable knowledge that keeps conversations and texts from intersecting. Following the terminology of "The System," we may think of the "*hole / Of Cloud*" as a frontal moment that has absconded like an "*elf*" (compare self) into the past but that still exerts its latent pressure. It may also mark the eclipse or absence of

God. Ashbery originally titled this poem ''The Great Litany,'' after Thomas Cranmer's Episcopal service in the Book of Common Prayer, where the minister's supplications and congregational responses are printed in italic and roman type respectively.

All the poems in *As We Know* are preoccupied with place or space. A series of one-liners, the diminutive counterpoints to ''Litany,'' make the most of their seven-by-nine-inch pages:

> I HAD THOUGHT THINGS
> WERE GOING ALONG WELL
>
> But I was mistaken.

The sobering visual and narrative humor of this poem relies on a double afterthought: that correcting one's mistaken projection about how things were going is also a mistake, since one's knowledge of ''things'' in the universal vacuum is so paltry that nothing can be concluded. The lyrics in *As We Know* are generally conducted in hushed tones that avoid the gregariousness of ''Litany.'' There is a sense of time running out in these haunted poems that results in a minimalist domestic economy, as in these lines from the volume's title poem:

> The light that was shadowed then
> Was seen to be our lives,
> Everything about us that love might wish to
> examine,
> Then put away for a certain length of time, until
> The whole is to be reviewed, and we turned
> Toward each other, to each other.
> The way we had come was all we could see
> And it crept up on us, embarrassed
> That there is so much to tell now, really now.

This intimate new style is minimal in discursive range, narration (''then,'' ''until''), vocabulary, figure (''it crept up on us'': age, a ghost), play (''reviewed'' book), and revision. In this tacit manner, the smallest and commonest words take on philosophical and religious import, such as ''all'' for totality, ''as'' and ''way'' for our manner of speaking and behaving, and ''it'' for latent presence. Aside from ''As We Know,'' there are several endearing and fascinating poems in the volume, including ''Many Wagons Ago,'' ''Haunted Landscape,'' ''Flowering Death,'' ''Knocking Around,'' ''Train Rising Out of the Sea,'' and ''This Configuration.'' Although the interior mode of the poems in *As We Know* makes it difficult for them to rival either the ringing periods of ''Clepsydra'' or ''Syringa,'' at least one poem in this volume, ''Tapestry,'' ranks among Ashbery's best:

> It is difficult to separate the tapestry
> From the room or loom which takes precedence
> over it.
> For it must always be frontal and yet to one side.
>
> It insists on this picture of ''history''
> In the making, because there is no way out of the
> punishment
> It proposes: sight blinded by sunlight.
> The seeing taken in with what is seen
> In an explosion of sudden awareness of its formal splendor.

The best-known tapestry for depicting '' 'history' in the making,'' the seventy-meter-long Bayeux Tapestry (ca. 1082), which Ashbery had seen in France, narrates the Norman Conquest, climaxing in the Battle of Hastings, where Harold is shown blinded by an arrow stitch to the eye. It is as difficult, now, to separate the Norman Conquest from its depiction as it is to separate the tapestry (and ''Tapestry'') from our responses to it—''The seeing taken in with what is seen.'' ''Tapestry'' is a dazzling display of Ashbery's ability to compose on several fronts simultaneously: self-reflexive, aesthetic, political, philosophical (Plato's cave), and personal. This twenty-two line poem, like the twenty-page ''Self-Portrait in a Convex Mirror,'' examines what art means, and only a poet who has studied and written about art for years could have written it.

Ashbery resumed writing art criticism in 1979, for *New York* magazine, and in the early 1980's he also wrote for *Newsweek*. Around this time, Ashbery purchased a Victorian-era house in Hudson, a small town in his native eastern New York State. These previously inhabited rooms seem to lend their own atmosphere to his next volume, *Shadow Train* (1981), a boxlike sequence of fifty poems, four quatrains each. These qua*trains* are "frontal and yet to one side" in that, unlike the sestets of sonnet sequences, they evade closure. What was "latent happiness" now looks more like anxiety in these poems. "The Pursuit of Happiness," for instance, ominously foreshadows some event that never happens:

It came about that there was no way of passing
Between the twin partitions that presented
A unified façade, that of a suburban shopping
 mall
In April. One turned, as one does, to other
 interests

Such as the tides in the Bay of Fundy. Meanwhile there was one
Who all unseen came creeping at this scale of
 visions
Like the gigantic specter of a cat towering over
 tiny mice
About to adjourn the town meeting due to the
 shadow,

The talismanic words of *As We Know*—"It came about," "way," "one"—are still in force. What is different here is the long-shot perspective, which takes in both the "gigantic specter" of the storm cloud and the "tiny" suburban Americans pursuing shelter. This perspective results in an ironically distanced narrative in which "one," rather than "we," "you," or "I," remains aloof as the cat. The vast scale of these stanzas removes us from the intimacy of *As We Know*. The humor of the tale is similarly "overshadowed" by its ominousness, as is its political discourse. "The Pursuit of Happiness" is a chilling declaration of dependence, but it may move us no more than it has moved its narrator.

The eerie objectivity of these minimalist building blocks can sometimes produce some fascinating special effects, as in "Paradoxes and Oxymorons":

This poem is concerned with language on a very
 plain level.
Look at it talking to you. You look out a window
Or pretend to fidget. You have it but you don't
 have it.
You miss it, it misses you. You miss each other.

The poem is sad because it wants to be yours,
 and cannot.
What's a plain level? It is that and other things,
Bringing a system of them into play. Play?
Well, actually, yes, but I consider play to be

A deeper outside thing, a dreamed role-pattern,
As in the division of grace these long August
 days
Without proof. Open-ended. And before you
 know
It gets lost in the stream and chatter of typewriters.

It has been played once more. I think you exist
 only
To tease me into doing it, on your level, and then
 you aren't there
Or have adopted a different attitude. And the
 poem
Has set me softly down beside you. The poem is
 you.

It is easy to see why this wonderful poem has been frequently anthologized. Here, the mixture of discourses—pedantic, romantic, sentimental, conversational—adds dimension after dimension to its plain levels. The author himself enters the poem, paradoxically, for a brief interview. What charges this poem, however, is its playful lover's discourse. A substitution of "I" or "me" for "it" will disclose "Paradoxes and Oxymorons" for the love song it is. Ashbery is often reserved and defensive, as when addressing the "critic," but he is equally persuasive and moving when dreaming of the "reader," his erotic double. Although *Shadow Train* is dwarfed by earlier volumes such as *Three Poems* or *As We Know,* it may be the right place to begin for the reader who wants to learn Ashbery's alphabet.

In the spring of 1982 Ashbery underwent major surgery for a nearly fatal spinal infection, and for a few years afterward he walked with a cane. Around the end of that year Ashbery began "A Wave," which he finished in about two months. This long title poem helped make *A Wave* Ashbery's best book since *Self-Portrait in a Convex Mirror*. Of Ashbery's long poems, "A Wave," with its surging free-verse stanzas, resembles "Self-Portrait" most closely, but it is free from the "subject matter" that, although merely a meditative pretext, confines the tone of "Self-Portrait in a Convex Mirror" within relatively narrow parameters. A wave is a fluid convexity ("wave" and "convex" are cognates), and that fluidity circulates through recurrent phases within the poem, from wake to wave to wait to wave again, as we see from the beginning:

To pass through pain and not know it,
A car door slamming in the night.
To emerge on an invisible terrain.

So the luck of speaking out
A little too late came to be worshipped in various guises:
A mute actor, a future saint intoxicated with the idea of martyrdom;
And our landscape came to be as it is today:
Partially out of focus, some of it too near, the middle distance
A haven of serenity and unreachable, with all kinds of nice
People and plants waking and stretching, calling
Attention to themselves with every artifice of which the human
Genre is capable. And they called it our home.

No one came to take advantage of these early
Reverses, no doorbell rang;
Yet each day of the week, once it had arrived, seemed the threshold
Of love and desperation again. At night it sang
In the black trees: *My mindless, oh my mindless, oh.*
And it could be that it was Tuesday, with dark, restless clouds
And puffs of white smoke against them, and below, the wet streets
That seem so permanent, and all of a sudden the scene changes:
It's another idea, a new conception, something submitted
A long time ago, that only now seems about to work
To destroy at last the ancient network
Of letters, diaries, ads for civilization.

The poem passes through a complete cycle here, with each new phase bringing a new scene and cast. The first unfinished sentence, with its Dickinsonian infinitives, presents us with the climactic end of an affair and its immediate wake. The next stanza gives us not the "morning after" but the dawn of civilization, an allegorical fair field, or landscape painting, full of folk. With the third stanza, we find ourselves in a protracted wait, along with the lover on the rebound. When the doorbell rings, however, the wave appears not as a lover but as a conceptual revolution that swamps our current ways of seeing the world. A wave may be a new (or renewed) love, a childhood crisis, a way of thinking, a brush with death, a new president, poem, or artistic movement. Ashbery did not consciously compose "A Wave" by phases, but the second-natured phases of this rapidly written poem must have allowed him to concentrate on the differences in manner that each transition brings. As we might expect, we miss the playful wit of "The Skaters" or "Litany," but we find in its place an unparalleled adventuresomeness in Ashbery's coming to terms with art, life, and love. The swelling crest of "A Wave" contains Ashbery's most moving writing since "Syringa."

The best lyrics of *A Wave* think through American discourses and languages rather than simply parody them, as in the powerful "Down by the Station, Early in the Morning":

It all wears out. I keep telling myself this, but
I can never believe me, though others do. Even
    things do.
And the things they do. Like the rasp of silk, or
    a certain
Glottal stop in your voice as you are telling me
    how you
Didn't have time to brush your teeth but gargled
    with Listerine
Instead. Each is a base one might wish to touch
    once more.

Before dying.

As the only alternative to toothpaste is Listerine, there is no way out of threadbare conversations, which nevertheless may be as charged with meaning as a Proustian rasp of silk. The intimate meditative minimalism of *As We Know* ("It all wears out"; "And the things they do") is here enlivened by the idiomatic undertones of *Three Poems*. Ashbery makes the worn-out figure of touching all the bases of a topic his own with the sentimental fragment "want to touch once more" and the suddenly frank "Before dying." Like "A Wave," "Down by the Station" (the title is from a children's train song) involves a cathartic interruption, which is also (like Listerine) a purification. The purgative third and last stanza dazzles with a moving economy:

As the wrecking ball burst through the wall with
    the bookshelves
Scattering the works of famous authors as well as
    those
Of more obscure ones, and books with no au-
    thor, letting in
Space, and an extraneous babble from the street
Confirming the new value the hollow core has
    again, the light
From the lighthouse that protects as it pushes us
    away.

The shocking rupture of the wrecking ball, after the second devastating stanza "break," upends but purifies the library with the languages of the tribe. The marker, "babble," gathers the crypt words "Babel," "bubble," "rabble," and "rubble," all of which speak their piece. The convex "hollow core," emptied by this catharsis (opening an apartment window onto the noisy street), sends out its own protective light, the "shield of a greeting," as Ashbery described Parmigianino's stylish gesture. The difficulty we have in fixing the stance of this passage—apocalyptic, moving, optimistic, and reflexive—is compounded by the split perspective of the reader / writer both inside the apartment and outside on the street. But this split perspective is characteristic of Ashbery's homey privacy. Ashbery has set us down beside him—"On the outside looking out," he says in a preceding poem ("But What is the Reader to Make of This?").

A Wave won Yale's Bollingen Prize in 1984, and the next year Ashbery received a MacArthur Prize Fellowship, which allowed him the leisure of writing for several years without teaching. Also in 1985, Ashbery published *Selected Po-*

ems, retrieving from among nearly forty years of poetry the work he wished to be remembered by. Ashbery then sold a vanload of his surviving papers to the Houghton Library at Harvard, some of which were gathered from the basement of his recently deceased mother's home in Sodus. These cumulative savings, in the face of losses, helped fund Ashbery's next published volume, *April Galleons* (1987).

Though there is no long poem in *April Galleons,* several of its lyrics equal those of *A Wave* in the pleasure they afford the reader: "April Galleons," "Finnish Rhapsody," "Vetiver," "Dreams of Adulthood," "Winter Weather Advisory," and "One Coat of Paint." In the Thoreauvian prose poem "The Ice Storm," Ashbery finds another way to make prose new. The allegory of the [p]rose at the center of this I-storm is lucidly unassuming:

Today I found a rose in full bloom in the wreck of the garden, all the living and sentience but also the sententiousness drained out of it. What remained was like a small flower in the woods, too pale and sickly to notice. No, sickly isn't the right word, the thing was normal and healthy by its own standards, and thriving merrily along its allotted path toward death. Only we hold it up to some real and abject notion of what a living organism ought to be and paint it as a scarecrow that frightens birds away (presumably) but isn't able to frighten itself away. Oh, no, it's far too clever for that! But our flower, the one we saw, really had no need of us to justify its blooming where it did. So we ought to think about our own position on the path. Will it ever be anything more than that of pebble? I wonder.

As the former minister Ralph Waldo Emerson said of the rhodora, "Beauty is its own excuse for being." Ashbery's message is that commentators (on roses or prose poems) are as self-reliantly transient as their subjects. This lay preacher, who (as in the later poems of Auden or Eliot) has been speaking regularly in Ashbery's later poetry, has here the garrulousness and self-betraying obstinacy of "Litany," which domesticates the Proustian character of *Three Poems.*

"Obviously," the narrator of the title poem of *April Galleons* concludes, "It was time to be off, in another / Direction." Since *April Galleons,* Ashbery has written the longest verse poem of his career, "Flowchart," and another volume's worth of short poems. He gave the Charles Eliot Norton lectures at Harvard during the 1989–1990 academic year, and also read his poetry in Japan, Sweden, and the Soviet Union. He edited an eclectic anthology of poetry, *The Best American Poetry: 1988,* which includes language poets alongside Iowa creative-writing graduates. Ashbery has resumed teaching, this time at Bard College, near his home in Hudson.

In the prose coda to "Fantasia," Ashbery offers us one good reason for living: "Always there was something to see, something going on, *for the historical past owed it to itself, our historical present.*" The historical present of Ashbery's ongoing work has been marked by changes. His less-popular books, *The Tennis Court Oath* and *Shadow Train,* were each followed by successful departures from their norms, *Rivers and Mountains* and *A Wave.* More significantly, Ashbery has resisted the temptation to reproduce his popular favorite, "Self-Portrait in a Convex Mirror." Yet nobody in American literature has written so many fine long poems. Rather than settling for an essayistic familiarity (as the later Auden often did), Ashbery has continued to experiment, and his work maintains a productive difficulty. The many changes in Ashbery's poetry, however, were not dictated merely by his own or by other poets' work. As powerfully as any poet of his generation, Ashbery has both represented and resisted postwar American history from the vantage point of someone on the outside looking out. We owe it to ourselves, in turn, to keep reading Ashbery's prospective representations.

Selected Bibliography

WORKS OF JOHN ASHBERY

POETRY

Turandot and Other Poems. New York: Tibor de Nagy Gallery, 1953.

Some Trees. New Haven, Conn.: Yale University Press, 1956.

The Tennis Court Oath. Middletown, Conn.: Wesleyan University Press, 1962.

Rivers and Mountains. New York: Holt, Rinehart, and Winston, 1966.

The Double Dream of Spring. New York: E. P. Dutton, 1970.

Three Poems. New York: Viking Press, 1972.

Self-Portrait in a Convex Mirror. New York: Viking Press, 1975.

The Vermont Notebook. Santa Barbara, Calif.: Black Sparrow Press, 1975.

Houseboat Days. New York: Viking Press, 1977.

As We Know. New York: Viking Press, 1979.

Shadow Train. New York: Viking Press, 1981.

A Wave. New York: Viking Press, 1984.

Selected Poems. New York: Viking Penguin, 1985.

April Galleons. New York: Viking Penguin, 1987.

OTHER WORKS

A Nest of Ninnies. With James Schuyler. New York: E. P. Dutton, 1969.

Three Plays. Calais, Vt.: Z Press, 1978.

The Best American Poetry, 1988. Edited by John Ashbery. New York: Macmillan, 1988.

"A Reminiscence," in *Homage to Frank O'Hara.* Edited by Bill Berkson and Joe LeSueur. Bolinas, Calif.: Big Sky Bolinas, 1988.

Reported Sightings: Art Chronicles, 1957–1987. Edited by David Bergman. New York: Alfred A. Knopf, 1989.

BIBLIOGRAPHY

Kermani, David. *John Ashbery: A Comprehensive Bibliography.* New York: Garland, 1976.

MANUSCRIPT PAPERS

The Houghton Library, Harvard University, Cambridge, Massachusetts, is currently cataloging Ashbery's manuscripts and correspondence through 1985.

BIOGRAPHICAL AND CRITICAL STUDIES

Altieri, Charles. "John Ashbery: Discursive Rhetoric Within a Poetics of Thinking." In his *Self and Sensibility in Contemporary American Poetry.* Cambridge: Cambridge University Press, 1984. Pp. 132–165.

Auden, W. H. "Foreword." In *Some Trees.* New Haven: Yale University Press, 1956. Pp. 11–16.

Blasing, Mutlu Konuk. "John Ashbery: Parodying the Paradox." In *American Poetry: The Rhetoric of Its Forms.* New Haven: Yale University Press, 1987. Pp. 200–213.

Bloom, Harold. "The Breaking of Form." In his *Deconstruction & Criticism.* New York: Continuum, 1979. Pp. 1–38.

———. "Measuring the Canon: John Ashbery's 'Wet Casements' and 'Tapestry.' " In his *Agon: Towards a Theory of Revisionism.* New York: Oxford University Press, 1982. Pp. 270–289.

———. *Modern Critical Views: John Ashbery.* New York: Chelsea House, 1985.

Bromwich, David. "John Ashbery." *Raritan,* 5:36–58 (Spring 1986).

Breslin, Paul. "Warpless and Woofless Subtleties: John Ashbery and 'Bourgeois Discourse.' " In his *The Psycho-Political Muse: American Poetry Since the Fifties.* Chicago: University of Chicago Press, 1987. Pp. 211–235.

Costello, Bonnie. "John Ashbery and the Idea of the

Reader.'' *Contemporary Literature,* 23:493–514 (Fall 1982).

Davidson, Michael. ''Languages of Post-Modernism.'' *Chicago Review,* 27:11–22 (Summer 1975).

Donoghue, Denis. ''John Ashbery.'' In his *Reading America: Essays on American Literature.* New York: Alfred A. Knopf, 1987. Pp. 302–319.

Fredman, Stephen. '' 'He Chose to Include': John Ashbery's *Three Poems.*'' In his *Poet's Prose: The Crisis in American Verse.* New York: Cambridge University Press, 1983. Pp. 99–133.

Holden, Jonathan. ''Syntax and the Poetry of John Ashbery.'' In his *The Rhetoric of the Contemporary Lyric.* Bloomington: Indiana University Press, 1980. Pp. 98–111.

Hollander, John. ''The Poetry of Restitution.'' *Yale Review,* 70:161–186 (Winter 1981).

Howard, Richard. ''John Ashbery.'' In his *Alone with America: Essays on the Art of Poetry in the United States Since 1950.* New York: Atheneum, 1980. Pp. 25–56.

Kalstone, David. ''John Ashbery: 'Self-Portrait in a Convex Mirror.' '' In his *Five Temperaments.* New York: Oxford University Press, 1977. Pp. 170–199.

Keller, Lynn. '' 'Thinkers without final thoughts': the continuity between Stevens and Ashbery'' and '' 'We must, we must be moving on': Ashbery's divergence from Stevens and modernism.'' In her *Re-making It New: Contemporary American Poetry and the Modernist Tradition.* New York: Cambridge University Press, 1987. Pp. 15–78.

Lehman, David, ed. *Beyond Amazement: New Essays on John Ashbery.* Ithaca, N.Y.: Cornell University Press, 1980.

McClatchy, J. D. ''Weaving and Unweaving,'' *Poetry,* 145:301–306 (February 1985).

Mohanty, S. P., and Jonathan Monroe. ''John Ashbery and the Articulation of the Social.'' *Diacritics,* 17:37–63 (Summer 1987).

Molesworth, Charles. '' 'This Leaving-Out Business': The Poetry of John Ashbery.'' In his *The Fierce Embrace: A Study of Contemporary American Poetry.* Columbia: University of Missouri Press, 1979. Pp. 163–183.

O'Hara, Frank. ''Rare Modern.'' *Poetry,* 89:307–316 (February 1957).

Perkins, David. ''Meditations of the Solitary Mind: John Ashbery and A. R. Ammons.'' In his *A History of Modern Poetry: Modernism and After.* Vol. 2. Cambridge, Mass.: Harvard University Press, Belknap Press, 1987. Pp. 614–633.

Perloff, Marjorie. '' 'Mysteries of Construction': The Dream Songs of John Ashbery.'' In her *The Poetics of Indeterminacy: Rimbaud to Cage.* Princeton: Princeton University Press, 1981. Pp. 248–287.

Ross, Andrew. ''Doubting John Thomas.'' In his *The Failure of Modernism: Symptoms of American Poetry.* New York: Columbia University Press, 1986. Pp. 159–208.

Shapiro, David. *John Ashbery: An Introduction to the Poetry.* New York: Columbia University Press, 1979.

Shoptaw, John. ''Saving Appearances: On John Ashbery.'' *Temblor,* no. 7:172–177 (Spring 1988).

Vendler, Helen. ''Making It New: *A Wave.*'' *New York Review of Books,* July 14, 1984. Pp. 32–35.

———. ''John Ashbery, Louise Glück.'' In her *The Music of What Happens: Poems, Poets, Critics.* Cambridge, Mass.: Harvard University Press, 1988. Pp. 224–261.

Von Hallberg, Robert. ''Robert Creeley and John Ashbery: Systems.'' In his *American Poetry and Culture, 1945–1980.* Cambridge, Mass.: Harvard University Press, 1985. Pp. 36–61.

Williamson, Alan. ''The Diffracting Diamond: Ashbery, Romanticism, and Anti-Art.'' In his *Introspection and Contemporary Poetry.* Cambridge, Mass.: Harvard University Press, 1984. Pp. 116–148.

INTERVIEWS

Bloom, Janet, and Robert Losada. ''Craft Interview with John Ashbery.'' *New York Quarterly,* no. 9:11–33 (Winter 1972).

Gangel, Sue. ''An Interview with John Ashbery.'' *San Francisco Review of Books,* 3:12 (November 1977).

Jackson, Richard. ''The Imminence of a Revelation.'' In his *Acts of Mind: Conversations with Contemporary Poets.* University: University of Alabama Press, 1983. Pp. 69–76.

John Ashbery and Kenneth Koch: A Conversation. Tucson, Ariz.: Interview Press, 1965.

Koethe, John. ''An Interview with John Ashbery.'' *SubStance,* 37–38:178–186 (1983).

Kostelanetz, Richard. ''How to Be a Difficult Poet.''

New York Times Magazine, May 23, 1976. Pp. 18–22.

Labrie, Ross. "John Ashbery." *American Poetry Review,* 13:29–33 (May–June 1984).

Lehman, David. "John Ashbery: The Pleasures of Poetry." *New York Times Magazine,* December 16, 1984, pp. 62–92.

Murphy, John. "John Ashbery." *Poetry Review,* 75:20–25 (August 1985).

Osti, Louis. "The Craft of John Ashbery." *Confrontation,* 9:84–96 (Fall 1974).

Poulin, A., Jr. "John Ashbery." *Michigan Quarterly Review,* 20:243–255 (Summer 1981).

Sommer, Piotr. "An Interview in Warsaw." In *Code of Signals: Recent Writings in Poetics.* Edited by Michael Palmer. Berkeley, Calif.: North Atlantic Books, 1983.

Stitt, Peter. "The Art of Poetry 33: John Ashbery." *Paris Review,* no. 90:30–59 (Winter 1983).

—JOHN SHOPTAW

Djuna Barnes

1892–1982

THE MOST ENIGMATIC figure among the famous women who made Paris home between the world wars was a tall, angular, auburn-haired beauty with a quick wit. Djuna Barnes was a short-story writer, poet, playwright, newspaper-woman, theater columnist, portrait painter, and illustrator of her own work. Her work was not voluminous, but she has been called "a writer's writer," as if to explain why she is more revered than read.

Barnes is best known for *Nightwood* (1936), a daring and complex poetic novel for which T. S. Eliot wrote the introduction. The difficulty of her prose, which depends upon thematic juxtaposition rather than chronological plot, as well as her black humor, fascination with the decadent, and frank discussion of female sexuality, has kept her outside the American literary mainstream. Yet the number of her serious and devoted readers continues to grow, as does the persistent legend of her eccentric, glamorous, and bisexual life abroad.

When Barnes's first novel, *Ryder,* appeared in 1928, an acquaintance from her Greenwich Village days reviewed it in *American Mercury* in words that describe both Barnes and her work:

Djuna Barnes has written a book that is all that she was, and must still be—vulgar, beautiful, defiant, witty, poetic, and a little mad—a bewildering hodge-podge of the obscene and virginal, of satire and wistfulness, of the grossest humor and the most delicate sadness—a book that absolutely baffles classification, but that surely is a most amazing thing to have come from a woman's hand.

Certainly the men were amazed. Walter Winchell remarked that she could "hit a cuspidor twenty feet away"; Robert McAlmon said she was "very haughty"; Ezra Pound said she "weren't too cuddly." But in the same breath they praised her beauty, confounded by her commensurate talent. Her friend Janet Flanner admired her for fearing no man.

But the daring of Barnes's subject matter and style belied the shy and private woman who is portrayed in the most famous photograph of her, which is in profile, half her face hidden. Her posture is erect, making her seem formal and prim, her hat and clothes dramatic, her thin nose and high cheekbones accented by red lips and nails. One friend said that her mouth "forms an immobile ellipse, a trifle Hapsburg." Natalie Clifford Barney, one of her most important friends during the Paris years, said:

Her mouth has an irresistible laugh. . . . Her appearance is most singular: she has a nose as sharply angled as an Eversharp pencil. . . . One can see in the bone structure of her large hands that she rides horses. . . . She is tall and slender, and her clothes fall at sharp angles against her powerful legs.

As Shari Benstock has noted, Barnes was ambivalent about her physical self: extremely vain and careful about her appearance and dress, yet resentful of any notice of her looks and often posing for photographs in profile. The vulnerability and indirection are features of her literary style as well, and a central trope in *Nightwood.* When Robin Vote is introduced in *Nightwood,* she is described lying in bed at the Hôtel Récamier: "In a moment of threatened consciousness she had turned her head."

Barnes was educated at home by her father, Henry Budington (who had changed his name to Wald Barnes when his parents divorced), and her paternal grandmother, Zadel Barnes Gustafson. Her mother, Elizabeth Chappell, her father's mistress, Fanny Faulkner (whom her father married in 1912), and their combined seven children lived under the same roof. Her grandmother, a powerful influence on Djuna's life, had been a journalist and had conducted a salon in London that included Elizabeth Cady Stanton and Lady Wilde, mother of Oscar Wilde. This unorthodox "family" lived first in Cornwall-on-Hudson, New York, where Djuna Chappell Barnes was born on June 12, 1892, and later in Huntington Township, Long Island.

These family relationships were treated in Barnes's later writings. Recent biographical research shows that at age eighteen Barnes lived for two or three months with fifty-two-year-old Percy Faulkner, the brother of her father's mistress, following an unofficial family ceremony in the farmhouse. She had many lovers in the next few years, including Courtenay Lemon, a scriptwriter with whom she lived in Greenwich Village for two years (1917–1919).

By the age of twenty Barnes was in New York City, studying at the Pratt Institute of Art and the Art Students League. Her Beardsleyesque drawings and pastels were shown in the Greenwich Village garret of Guido Bruno, the publisher of *Bruno's Weekly.* The following year she launched her journalistic career, contributing illustrated articles and stories to the *Brooklyn Daily Eagle,* the *New York Morning Telegraph* and the *New York Herald,* and later to magazines such as *Theatre Guild* and *Vanity Fair.*

Barnes's early journalistic career was accelerated by economic necessity, an unorthodox family life, and youthful sexual emancipation. She learned temerity and independence. Her grandmother, after all, had covered temperance and feminist crusades for *Harper's Monthly* in the 1880's. Djuna showed her own daring and involvement by having herself force-fed in order to write with understanding about the British suffragists. She continued to write realistic journalism for many years, supporting her mother (now separated from Djuna's father), her three brothers, and her ill grandmother. Although Barnes later denigrated her journalistic essays as "utterly wasteful," they are perceptive and original in focus and style. In 1985 forty of her best interviews (from Coco Chanel and Billy Sunday to Alfred Stieglitz and James Joyce) and twenty-three of her drawings, dating from 1913 to 1931, were published. Evident in her journalism, as in her fiction, is a criticism of American middle-class vulgarity ("mink-trimmed minds and seal-edged morals") and a sense of the superiority of the artist.

Though Barnes once called herself naive during this period, her writing certainly was not. Her satiric pieces occasionally focused on young girls full of illusions and vanity. Her reputation for hard and original prose and a keen mind added to the emerging legend of the young woman who dressed in a long opera cape and savored life. Her friends and associates in Greenwich Village included Edmund Wilson; Edna St.

Vincent Millay; Peggy Guggenheim and Lawrence Vail, whose colorful and dramatic personae matched Barnes's; Mary Pyne, an actress who was her best friend; the painter Marsden Hartley; and Guido Bruno, an entrepreneur and profiteer of poetry.

The work that Barnes valued was her poetry, which was characterized by its satire of middle-class values and an interest in death. Her first poems appeared in *Harper's Weekly* (1911). Guido Bruno published her first collection of poetry and explicit illustrations, a slip chapbook entitled *The Book of Repulsive Women* (1915), which revealed her interest in the grotesque. At the time it was seen as typical of a certain Greenwich Village bohemianism and decadence, though feminist critical thought now reads it as a critique of woman's place in Western society.

The portrayal of women in *The Book of Repulsive Women* is occasionally macabre, and it implies, according to Benstock, a clear relationship between the physical and psychological states of women. The degeneration of age is juxtaposed with "degenerate" acts of lesbian lovemaking. The woman in "Seen from the 'L' " is "chain-stitched" and "Slipping through the stitch of virtue, / Into crime." The woman in "From Fifth Avenue Up" is described as "strangled," "leaning," and "oozing." The body of one woman in Barnes's last poem, "Suicide," is given "hurried shoves":

> Her body shock-abbreviated
> As a city cat.
> She lay out listlessly like some small mug
> Of beer gone flat.

The drawings that illustrate this volume of poetry emphasize the "disjointed, grotesque, and abstract."

Barnes's first short stories, or "tales," appeared in 1914 ("The Terrible Peacock") and 1915 ("Paprika Johnson"). The contrived and complicated plots that end with a twist soon gave way to stories with a more modern and psychological focus. She continued writing short stories for fifteen years, publishing about thirty, which she revised and reissued through the years. Scholars consider the short stories "dark" and "comfortless." Louis F. Kannenstine writes that they present "the terror of the impossibility of being," James B. Scott that they "show *how* and *why* death can be the only real affirmation in a meaningless universe," Cheryl Plumb that they "set out the abundant inadequacies of life" and reveal that human consciousness is "fragile" and meaning "elusive."

An excellent illustration of these themes is "A Night Among the Horses," perhaps her most famous short story and the one for which she won the O. Henry Prize in 1918. At first glance this story appears to be a social or class struggle between John, a hostler ("I *like* being common"), and his betrothed, Freda Buckler, a cultured and traveled woman:

> She spread maps, and with a long hat-pin dragging across mountains and ditches, pointed to "just where she had been." Like a dry snail the point wandered the coast, when abruptly, sticking the steel in, she cried *"Borgia!"* and stood there, jangling a circle of ancient keys.

Freda tells him, "[I] will make you a gentleman. . . . You will rise to govenour—general—well, to inspector—." Beyond this class tension is a darker vision, for both the world of the ballroom, where John deserts Freda, and the world of horses, where he is at home, are tangled and confused, dark and deceptive. At the masked ball, with its "tipsy" revelers and a fat lady dancer "grunting in cascades of plaited tulle," he comes to "a sudden stop" on the dance floor, backs out of the French doors, and flees. Crawling under the fence in his tails and top hat, he seeks the horses, who are "tearing up the sod, galloping about as though in their own ball-room." Thinking that this world of "tangled branches" and horses with "legs rising and falling like savage needles taking purposeless stitches" is the world in which he belongs, he blames Freda for changing him so that the horses do not "know him":

Wheeling, manes up, nostrils flaring, blasting out steam as they came on, they passed him in a whinnying flood, and he damned them in horror, but what he shouted was "Bitch!", and found himself swallowing fire from his heart, lying on his face, sobbing, "I *can* do it, damn everything, I can get on with it; I can make a mark!"

The upraised hooves of the first horse missed him, second did not.

Presently the horses drew apart, nibbling and swishing their tails, avoiding a patch of tall grass.

With this sudden conclusion, Barnes is suggesting "the impossibility of returning to a state of innocence," says Plumb. But Barnes is also revealing the futility of self-achievement in either the indifferent natural world or the corrupt and materialistic social world. Both worlds are hostile to the human spirit.

Several elements of this story are typical of Barnes's fiction. She often uses animals or insects, as she did in another excellent story, "The Rabbit" (1917), in which an Armenian suitor steals and strangles a rabbit to prove to his love that he can be a hero. The horses of "A Night Among the Horses" reflect Barnes's interest in riding, for she was an equestrian and often dreamed about animals. Placing her characters close to death, suggesting the triumph of death, and satirizing middle-class manners are other elements found throughout her fiction.

During the decade in which Barnes began writing and publishing her artwork, poetic fiction, and journalism, she also wrote one-act plays, most of which appeared between 1916 and 1923. Three of these plays were staged by the Provincetown Players in 1919 and 1920, when she worked with Eugene O'Neill, who encouraged her work. Others were published in various periodicals, including the *Little Review,* the *Dial, Charm,* and the *Smart Set* (the first two helped to place her name among the avant-garde; the second two puzzled their popular readership).

The external action of Barnes's plays seems important only as it reveals the consciousness of her characters. Yet certain themes run throughout the plays: her concern with morality, social conformity, sexual repression, and self-deception. In *At the Root of Stars* (1917), *The Death of Life* (1916), and *Kurzy of the Sea* (1920), Barnes shows the artist or an outsider confronting middle-class attitudes. Occasionally she uses Irish dialect in her plays, a direct reflection of the influence of John Millington Synge (*The Playboy of the Western World,* 1907). "Synge first touched the Irish in me," she said.

Barnes's plays were occasionally praised but not often understood. Though Heywood Broun called *An Irish Triangle* (1920) one of "the best of the new one-act pieces," Lawrence Langner in *The Magic Curtain* (1951) noted that her plays "combined a startling sense of dramatic values with an incoherence of expression that made everything she wrote exciting and baffling at the same time."

After tasting the pleasures of Greenwich Village at its peak during the second decade of the twentieth century, Barnes sailed for Paris in 1920 (she later had difficulty remembering the date), presumably to report on expatriate life for *McCall's* magazine. Paris had historically drawn American artists—from Benjamin Franklin to Henry James. "Writing in Paris is one of the oldest American customs," wrote Van Wyck Brooks. "It all but antedates, with Franklin, the founding of the republic." Natalie Clifford Barney had arrived in 1902, Gertrude Stein in 1903, Edith Wharton in 1906, and Sylvia Beach in 1916. During the fertile period of literature between the world wars, Paris was the cultural capital. Djuna Barnes and Ezra Pound arrived in 1920, Ernest Hemingway in

1921; the momentum would peak at mid-decade.

When Barnes checked into the Hôtel Jacob et d'Angleterre at 44, rue Jacob, she joined many former residents of Greenwich Village, including Alfred Kreymborg, who was in the lobby when she arrived, and Harold Loeb, editor of the literary magazine *Broom.* She continued to support herself with journalism, using the pen name Lydia Steptoe for her most satiric pieces, which she wrote while propped up in her bed.

Paris was the best address for writers of the 1920's, and Barnes's arrival coincided with a major migration of Americans to the Left Bank. Here was an international intelligentsia, the avant-garde of modernism: Pablo Picasso, Gertrude Stein, Ezra Pound, and James Joyce. Like the other talented women of this period who had chosen the freedom and beauty of Paris (H.D. preferred Switzerland and Virginia Woolf England), Barnes savored the availability of alcohol and the leisurely café life as well as the quiet of the churches:

—And so it was I came to Paris, and a few hours later was leaning out of my window in the Rue Jacob, and thinking in my heart of all unknown churches, and so thinking, I put on my cloak and went to Notre Dame in the sad, falling twilight, and wandered under the trees. . .

When Notre Dame left her "comparatively untouched," Barnes concluded that her neighborhood church of Saint-Germain-des-Prés was "more possible," for "here one takes one's tears, leaving them unshed, to count the thin candles that rise about the feet of the Virgin like flowers of fire." She wrote about the city in her short stories and articles.

Despite the number of celebrities and eccentrics on the Left Bank, Barnes stood out. She appeared in most of the dozens of memoirs of the period, described in a solitary pose or with a group of daring women. Her work soon appeared in all the little journals, among them *Transatlantic Review, This Quarter,* and *transition.* Although she attended the notable events of the decade, including George Antheil's riotous *Ballet mécanique* in 1926, she chose her friends carefully and cherished her privacy. As one journalist noted, "She met all advances with a defiant vulgarity that confused utterly."

One friend she chose was another very private writer, the Irishman James Joyce. Among her interviews for *Vanity Fair* was one (April 1922) that emphasized Joyce the singer:

There are men in Dublin who will tell you that out of Ireland a great voice has gone; and there are a few women, lost to youth, who will add: "One night he was singing and next he wasn't, and there's been no silence the like of it!" For the singing voice of James Joyce, author of *A Portrait of the Artist as a Young Man* and of *Ulysses,* is said to have been second to none.

She writes of having talked to him often, "of artists and of Ireland," particularly in the Café aux Deux Magots. She wisely did not ask him questions and waited through his silences. Janet Flanner (Genêt) claimed that Barnes was the only friend in Paris who dared to call Joyce "Jim." Although she declared when his *Ulysses* appeared, "I shall never write another line. Who has the nerve to after this!," she did continue to write and draw.

In 1921 Barnes joined the group from Greenwich Village—which included Marsden Hartley, Berenice Abbott, Man Ray, and Robert McAlmon and his group—that moved briefly from Paris to Germany, where the dollar was stronger than in France. They were joined by Isadora Duncan and Charles Chaplin, who were in Berlin at that time. Barnes visited Budapest and Vienna, and sampled the drugs and decadence of postwar Berlin—an atmosphere that would find its way into *Nightwood* and foreshadow the milieu of World War II Berlin.

After returning from Berlin in late 1921 or early 1922, Barnes moved into an apartment at 173, boulevard Saint-Germain, just up the boulevard from the Café aux Deux Magots, on the same side of the boulevard as the Brasserie Lipp. She preferred the 6th arrondissement and was often seen drinking in its cafés, a pile of saucers on her table. In his column in the *Paris Tribune,* Harold Stearns wrote of seeing her often at Deux Magots. She dressed dramatically, kept her own counsel, and was admired for her talent, particularly after *A Book* (1923) appeared.

A Book included three one-act plays, twelve short and sparse stories, eleven lyrical poems, and six drawings. Two of the short stories, "Cassation" (originally entitled "A Little Girl Tells a Story to a Lady") and "The Grande Malade" (published in *This Quarter I* as "The Little Girl Continues"), are set in Paris cafés. Their "textual shadows," according to Carolyn Allen, reveal "a fictional seduction of the older 'Madame' by the younger narrator." These two stories, as well as "The Passion," are also interpreted as dealing with the nature of the artist and her relationship to the external world. Generally, the stories reveal a restlessness and an estrangement from society that characterize the expatriate literature of the period.

Barnes gained a reputation for her black humor and quotable observations. Matthew Josephson reported that she declared, "I came to Europe to get culture. Is this culture? . . . I might as well go back to Greenwich Village and rot there." One of the most memorable descriptions of Barnes came from her friend Kathryn Hulme (who would later write *The Nun's Story*), who remembered often seeing Barnes with her friends Janet Flanner and Solita Solano drinking martinis in a café, each dressed in a black tailored suit and white gloves, looking like three elegant Fates. Expatriate gossip columns liked to report on her with tongue in cheek: "Djuna Barnes, who, according to her publishers, is that legendary personality that has dominated the intellectual night-life of Europe for a century."

What particularly titillated the expatriate men was that this beauty was in love with Thelma Wood, a tall silverpoint artist from St. Louis given to the consumption of alcohol and wandering the streets of Montparnasse. For several years they lived in Barnes's apartment on boulevard Saint-Germain, then in an apartment at 9, rue St.-Romain that was filled with religious paintings and objects, a decadent reversal of the moral code that must have pleased Barnes. In all, they lived together for eight sometimes stormy years (1923–1931), and maintained a relationship that would later find artistic expression in *Nightwood,* with Wood the prototype of Robin Vote.

Barnes published "Aller et Retour" and "The Passion" in all the right expatriate little magazines. Ford Madox Ford published her work in his *Transatlantic Review* and held a party for her at the salon of Natalie Barney. She also appeared in *transition*, edited by Eugène Jolas, who trumpeted the language of the night and the subconscious. Jolas' *transition* is best known for its serialization of Joyce's *Work in Progress,* later to become *Finnegans Wake*. Not surprisingly, Jolas was eager to publish Barnes's "Rape and Repining," a chapter from her soon-to-be-published first novel, *Ryder,* which bears the unmistakable influence of Joyce.

In sharp contrast to Barnes's earlier terse/spare prose style, *Ryder* is copious, fantastic, ornamental, picaresque, and symbolic. In Joycean fashion she experimented with literary styles, using a pastiche of the epic, the Bible, the fable, the epistolary novel, and the couplet. Simply explained, it is a mock-Elizabethan chronicle of the Ryder (or Barnes) family—a social satire of conformity and sexual repression, with characters called Laura Twelvetree, Molly Dance, and Lady Bertha Bridesleep. It is complex in part because Barnes ignores chronological plot development and narrative progression in favor of thematic relationships. If the style is Joycean, the bleak wasteland view is T. S. Eliot's. *The American Mercury* called it "a piece of rubbish"; *The Argonaut* called it "vulgar, beautiful, witty, poetic, and a little mad"; other reviewers echoed one another with words such as "lusty," "plotless," and "amazing."

Feminist critics, as well as Barnes's biographer Andrew Field, emphasize the biographical parallels—although any suggestion of a narrative line is misleading and mocks this complex tour de force. Wendell Ryder (based on Barnes's father) lives polygamously, sleeping between his wife (the religious and long-suffering Amelia) and his mistress (the fertile and indifferent Kate-Careless) in a two-room cabin. Amid sexual innuendos and puns (certainly his name is one), the women fight for his body and soul. Unable to reconcile them, and harassed by his neighbors, he sends his wife away, despairing of the ideal. The question "And whom should he disappoint now?" echoes throughout the final chapter.

The theme of *Ryder,* argues James Scott, is that "disjointed and peculiar as Ryder's life appears, it is closer to nature than more conventional lives," and thus is "more spontaneous, more joyous, and far more productive of beauty." Yet Cheryl Plumb, who acknowledges Barnes's satire of middle-class sexual repressiveness, believes that Barnes intended "to present the perpetual conflict between physical nature and the human spirit in terms of the . . . egotism of Wendell Ryder." Other recent critics see an implied attack on Ryder, whose philosophy is essentially bourgeois. Their evidence is that his actions are comic and foolish, and that Barnes's imagery connects him with indecision and death. Through O'Connor (the homosexual doctor who would later play a major role in *Nightwood*) Barnes provides an alternative to Ryder—that is, a balance between physical nature and the human spirit. This interpretation is bolstered by the words of Molly Dance, who says that original sin is man's, not woman's: "It was an apple, surely, but man it was who snapped it up, scattering the seeds, and these he uses to this day to get his sons by."

Ryder, like Gertrude Stein's *The Making of Americans* (1925), was accused of being a "plotless" exercise. Both women, Benstock points out, were "chastized for being significantly different from their Paris colleagues and for failing to master the Modernist enterprise." Barnes was accused of being arcane and inaccessible, Stein of being repetitious and boring. They also shared, according to Benstock, an interest in focusing their work on their female forebears, "exposing the ways women are made to suffer for the patriarchy."

Ryder was dedicated to "T.W." (Thelma Wood), and the proceeds of the novel, together with money from *McCall's,* enabled Barnes to buy a fifth-floor flat in rue Saint-Romain at the end of 1928. Here she and Wood lived in one of two new brick buildings set back from the quiet, narrow street.

The imagination of the Left Bank expatriates was captured by the small book that Barnes next wrote and illustrated. *Ladies Almanack* (1928) is a kind of chapbook or broadsheet satirizing and celebrating the lesbians of Montparnasse—all disguised by names punning and mocking Elizabethan language. It was privately printed in a limited edition of 1,050 copies by Darantière of Dijon, arranged and paid for by Robert McAlmon, according to Barnes. The author was identified as "a Lady of Fashion." Barnes (who had hand-colored the first fifty numbered copies) and her friends sold it in the streets of Montparnasse. It remained an underground favorite until it was reprinted in 1972.

The humor and explicit sexuality of the drawings and subject matter of *Ladies Almanack* both shocked and satirized middle-class sensibilities. The antiquarian language enhances rather than diminishes the shock value. The book focuses on an aristocratic society of women in a garden of Venus, their rituals and credos, their erotic intrigues and crusades. The central figure is Dame Evangeline Musset—Saint Musset, whose religion is love. The book is organized into twelve short monthly sections, using the almanac format and paralleling seasonal time with the stages of life. In December Musset dies peacefully and unrepentantly at the age of ninety-nine.

As some on the Left Bank knew, Dame Musset was a portrait of Natalie Clifford Barney (1876–1972) and some members of her celebrated literary salon at 20, rue Jacob. Barney, originally from Dayton, Ohio, was a legendary figure in France, and the Amazon to whom Rémy de Gourmont addressed his *Lettres à l'Amazone* (1914). She wrote poetry in French, and her women lovers were many. Barney was a lesbian without ambivalence; she rejected religion, sentimentality, and monogamy, and believed that American women were born with Bibles in their mouths. For sixty years her Friday salon was an international center for leading writers and artists. In 1927 she organized the Académie des Femmes as a counterpart to the venerable male Académie Française.

Barney, who did much to encourage the artistic careers of other women, was particularly fond of Barnes, with whom she had a brief affair during the younger woman's first summer in Paris. Barnes was even forgiven when she appeared drunk at one of Barney's Friday salons. Barney presented her to the French literary circle and described that evening in her *Aventures de l'esprit* (1929):

Djuna Barnes, upright, unsullied, unpolished, grew pale at the insolence of honour being accorded her. . . . I had never introduced an author more awkward and less capable of serving her own cause. . . . Barnes possesses a candour and a sense of humour which passes through Cervantes and goes right back to Rabelais.

Barnes's wit had full play in the portrayal of the circle of Musset. Tilly Tweed-in-Blood was based, some guessed, on the English novelist Radclyffe Hall, author of the notorious lesbian work *The Well of Loneliness* (1929). Lady Bulk-and-Balk was based on Una, Lady Troubridge. Other characters include Daisy Downpour (who has not been identified), Doll Furious (Dolly Wilde), and Patience Scalpel (the only heterosexual figure, based, in part, on Mina Loy). Nip and Tuck were based on Janet Flanner and Solita Solano. These women encircle Evangeline Musset, who had developed in the womb as a boy who "came forth an Inch or so less than this." Her mission is to give sexual relief to young girls "for the Pursuance, the Relief and the Distraction, of such Girls as in their Hinder Parts, and their Fore Parts, and in whatsoever Parts did suffer them most. . . ."

The humor of *Ladies Almanack* ranges from satire of middle-class ideas of sexuality to loose parody of the Left Bank lesbians and pure laughter and verbal wit for the amusement of the reader, such as the puns on penetration / understanding and on tongues. While Scott, Kannestine, and Field believe that Barnes is censuring the promiscuity of lesbianism, specifically the lesbians of the Left Bank in the 1920's, feminist critics disagree. Plumb calls *Ladies Almanack* "a counterpoint to *Ryder*," and Susan Sniader Lanser says it is a "mock epic of proselytizing." These contradictory interpretations are a result of Barnes's elliptical and ambiguous prose, yet all agree that Barnes portrays lesbianism as having the same faults as heterosexual love. Karla Jay adds that Barnes's nonprivileged economic status made her able to stand outside the circle, much as Patience Scalpel does, and to criticize; indeed, the book reveals, as in her fiction, the limitations of all physical love.

Ladies Almanack argues for the place of women in society, but at the same time it laments their limitations. Barnes confirmed this bias when she declared, "I am writing the female Tom Jones." While some critics see the book as a celebration of lesbian pleasures, or, in Lanser's words, as "an inside joke" for Barney and her lesbian friends (Barney was very proud of the book), others—such as Jay—read harsh irony in the portrayal of Barney as a "conscienceless nymphomaniac"; Barnes, Jay claims, "bit the very hands that brought *Ladies Almanack* into existence."

The book laments less the choice of lesbianism than "Loneliness estranged" and the "very Condition of Women so subject to Hazard, so complex, and so grievous. . . ." It portrays instead the limitations of all earthly love: jealousy, unfaithfulness, egotism, time, and decay. The garden of Venus is subject to all of these:

We trouble the Earth awhile with our Fury; our Sorrow is flesh thick, and we shall not cease to eat of it until the easing Bone. Our Peace is not skin deep, but to the Marrow, we are not wise this side of *rigor mortis*; we go down to no River of Wisdom, but swim alone in Jordan. We have few Philosophers among us, for our Blood was stewed too thick to bear up Wisdom, which is a little Craft, and floats only when the way is prepared, and the Winds are calm.

This bawdy and salacious work, with its Banesian darkness, was followed by *A Night Among the Horses* (1929), a collection of short stories that included three new pieces and rewritten stories from *A Book*. Barnes continued to write feature pieces for periodicals, focusing on decay and pretense, and on the lack of moral concern in art. She needed the journalism money, though she disparaged this work as "bottom of the barrel."

Barnes's serious writing was hampered by her destructive personal life. "I am not a lesbian. I just loved Thelma," she declared. But the pain was outweighing the love. Despite their domesticity, their affair was dramatized by public scenes (often in the middle of the night, after Barnes had gone looking for Wood in the bars and cafés) and drunkenness. The affair was essentially over by 1928, though Thelma would visit her occasionally in Paris and during Barnes's trips to Greenwich Village between 1929 and 1931. Barnes immediately began writing a second novel she called "Bow Down" (later renamed *Nightwood*). When Barnes had surgery, Charles Henri Ford, a young friend she had met in Greenwich Village, moved into her apartment to care for her. Later he took her with him to Tangier (April–June 1933), where he typed a draft of her manuscript. She returned to Paris for an abortion after learning that she was pregnant by Jean Oberle, a French painter with whom she had had a brief affair.

There was "nothing left but a big crowd" in Montparnasse, Barnes remarked to Wambly Bald, columnist for the *Paris Tribune*. Utilizing her reputation for wit, Bald wrote a humorous interview in which they "rested their heads on each other's shoulders and wept for a minute" on the demise of the Left Bank: "We agreed that it was all over."

Perhaps it was no surprise to her friends when, in 1931 or 1932, Barnes left Paris for England with Peggy Guggenheim. Off and on for six or seven years she lived with the Guggenheim group, which included the novelists Emily Holmes Coleman, who did a great deal to help Barnes complete her next novel, and Antonia White, as well as various men, including John Holms, Guggenheim's lover. They lived in the countryside in a large rented castle (the most ornate and gloomy room was given to Barnes because it fitted her personality), Hayford Hall, called Hangover Hall. Although Field maintains that Holms was the center of the household, Mary Lynn Broe has argued that the settlement was an ideal for the women, a "revised ideology of family" and a "domestic haven." The Guggenheim money held the castle together and supported Barnes at forty dollars a month (by the time of Guggenheim's death in 1979, the monthly allowance had reached a high of three hundred dollars, where it remained until Barnes's death three years later). Her housing and the allowance from Guggenheim, together with the support of Coleman, allowed Barnes to finish *Nightwood,* which she dedicated "to Peggy Guggenheim and John Ferrar Holms."

Nightwood, cut down to a third of its original length, was first published in England in 1936. Its title suggests the surrealistic world of night and dreams that so concerned the surrealists in Paris (among the numerous titles that used the word "night" were those of works by Louis Aragon, Philippe Soupault, Max Jacob, Robert Desnos, and Paul Éluard). It also shows the influence of Barnes's association with Jolas and his journal *transition,* which trumpeted Jungian-inspired interest in dreams and an attack on rigid logic and linear time.

Whatever happens in the novel can best be summarized by the question "How does Robin Vote affect the lives of four people whom she meets in Paris in the 1920's?" All five characters are expatriates living in Paris; four are Americans. After marrying Felix Volkbein, an alienated Austrian Jew and a baron with a false pedigree, and bearing his child, Robin leaves him for Nora Flood, an American journalist. Nora tries to remake or domesticate Robin—to catch her in patriarchal norms, say the feminist critics—and thereby loses her to Jenny Petherbridge, a "dealer in second-hand . . . emotions," who "appropriated the most passionate love that she knew, Nora's for Robin." Abandoned, Nora looks to Matthew O'Connor, a brilliant transvestite psychoanalyst. He fails to ease her suffering ("I'll never understand her—I'll always be miserable—just like this"), and their relationship brings about his own spiritual collapse. Felix reappears, now devoted to caring for his son. In the final pages of the novel, Robin confronts Nora in a chapel at her American estate, yet they remain estranged.

Place Saint-Sulpice (in the 6th arrondissement) is the setting of the chapter "La Somnambule" and part of the chapter "Go Down, Matthew." Here, on either side of the church of Saint-Sulpice, are the Hôtel Récamier, where Robin Vote lives (and where Thelma Wood lived before she moved in with Barnes), and the Café de la Mairie, where Matthew O'Connor drinks until he is "drunk and telling the world" of its doom:

> He began to scream with sobbing laughter. "Talking to me—all of them—sitting on me as heavy as a truck horse—talking! Love falling buttered side down, fate falling arse up! . . . Now that you have all heard what you wanted to hear, can't you let me loose now, let me go? . . . Everything's over, and nobody knows it but me—drunk as a fiddler's bitch. . . . Now," he said, "the end—mark my words—now *nothing, but wrath and weeping!*"

Part of the difficulty in reading *Nightwood* lies in its structure, which rejects linear plot development in favor of eight sections that are not related in time or place. Joseph Frank calls the structure "spatial form," another critic "tableaux." It is like viewing a family album in which the photographs are arranged by memory association, not by chronology or any law of perceivable relationship. Though the first chapter seems to be tied to historical time, with Felix's birth in 1880 and the manufactured account of his ancestry, chronology disappears in 1920, when he arrives in Paris. Henceforth the characters seem to exist in the realm of night and sleep, where rational perceptions and time end. According to Jane Marcus, even the social order is inverted by introducing outsiders: Jews, lesbians, blacks, transvestites, circus people.

Robin Vote is introduced in the chapter "La Somnambule":

Her movements were slightly headlong and sideways; slow, clumsy and yet graceful, the ample gait of the night-watch. . . . She was gracious and yet fading, like an old statue in a garden, that symbolizes the weather through which it has endured, and is not so much the work of man as the work of wind and rain and the herd of the seasons, and though formed in man's image is a figure of doom.

Robin moves through the novel and through the lives of others with mystery and flux—characteristics that make her irresistible and fascinating to others. Whether or not she is physically present, her influence is felt in all actions, dialogues, and descriptions: "Robin was outside the 'human type'—a wild thing caught in a woman's skin, monstrously alone, monstrously vain," yet she is the central reality, dictating the form and poetry of the novel. She seems intangible—indeed, a mixture of two worlds: both boy and girl, "newly ancient," both innocent and depraved, both beast and human. Marcus calls her "Our Lady of the Wild Things, savage Diana the huntress with her deer and dogs, the virgin Artemis roaming the woods with her Band of Women." Biographers claim that Robin is a portrait of Thelma Wood and that the novel is for Barnes an exorcism of their relationship.

Nora, the wandering expatriate from America, is drawn to Robin's perversity; Robin represents Nora's unconscious, repressed self. According to Benstock, Nora is trapped in the Puritan ethic of her past and tries to domesticate Robin. She is, in O'Connor's words, "beating her head against her heart, sprung over, her mind closing her life up like a wheel on a fan, rotten to the bone of love for Robin." Nora is described as "a Westerner" and "an early Christian" who "robbed herself for everyone." In the chapter "Night Watch" she is presented in the image of a tree:

She was broad and tall, and though her skin was the skin of a child, there could be seen coming, early in her life, the design that was to be the weather-beaten grain of her face, that wood in the work; the coming forward in her, an undocumented record of time.

When she meets Robin, "they were so 'haunted' of each other that separation was impossible."

Like Robin, Matthew O'Connor is caught between waking and dreaming and damnation and grace, and his similarity to Robin may account in part for Nora's seeking his counsel when Robin abandons her. In the chapter "Watchman, What of the Night?" he tells Nora:

Well, I, Dr. Matthew-Mighty-grain-of-salt-Dante-O'Connor, will tell you how the day and the night are related by their division. The very constitution of twilight is a fabulous reconstruction of fear, fear bottom-out and wrong side up. Every day is thought upon and calculated, but the night is not premeditated. The Bible lies the one way, but the night-gown the other. The night, "Beware of that dark door!"

Matthew is the central prophetic voice of the novel, serving as both the chorus and the androgynous Tiresias of Greek tragedy and Eliot's *The Waste Land*. His monologues are brilliant and "torrential." He articulates a central theme of the novel:

Man was born damned and innocent from the start, and wretchedly—as he must—on those two themes—whistles his tune.

The evil and the good know themselves only by giving up their secret face to face. . . . The face of the one tells the face of the other the half of the story they both forgot.

The combination of beauty and barbarity, innocence and corruption, the human and the bestial, day and night, the demonic and the saintly, form the tropes of the novel, as do sexual difference and sameness. The central trope in *Nightwood*—as in *Ladies Almanack* and *Ryder* (Wendell Ryder is "much mixed . . . of woman and man")—is androgyny. To be caught between unattainable extremes of existence is a kind of hell.

The short final chapter, "The Possessed," is set in America. Robin has been sleeping in the woods of upstate New York and finally moves into a decayed chapel on Nora's estate. When her dog begins to bark, Nora opens the windows and unlocks the doors of her house, sensing Robin's presence. She goes to the chapel, where she discovers a makeshift altar of lighted candles, flowers, and toys arranged before the Madonna. Robin is soon on all fours facing the dog, which she meets forehead to forehead. The dog springs back, whimpering; Robin is "grinning and whimpering," backing the dog into a corner. When the dog barks and circles her, Robin responds by "barking in a fit of laughter, obscene and touching," pursuing the dog until they are both exhausted and "lying out" flat on the floor. Failing in her final attempt at communion with something living, Robin lies fallen and bestial.

Nightwood's appeal would be "primarily to readers of poetry," claimed Eliot in his introduction to the American edition of the novel. It is "so good a novel," he explains, "that only sensibilities trained on poetry can wholly appreciate it." He praises it for "the great achievement of style, the beauty of phrasing, the brilliance of wit and characterisation, and a quality of horror very nearly related to that of Elizabethan tragedy." Another poet, Dylan Thomas, was an enthusiast of *Nightwood,* calling it, with an unintended slur, "one of the three great prose books ever written by a woman." In style, the novel is a collage of shifting metaphors and language from the Old Testament, the Elizabethan and Jacobean periods, the metaphysical poets, early-eighteenth-century novels, late-nineteenth-century poetry, symbolism, and surrealism. In short, its style is baroque. Joseph Frank and Wallace Fowlie have demonstrated that the novel's structure is based upon poetic association, circular or arabesque patterns, and musical configurations such as the fugue.

Though *Nightwood* is generally considered Barnes's best-organized and most intensely written book, scholars are unable to agree on its classification, and interpretations of its meaning differ widely. Kannenstine calls it "a distillation of the despair and estrangement of expatriation." Marcus refers to it as "a kind of anarchist-feminist call for freedom from fascism." Benstock insists that it presents a world in which "the patriarchal vision" has estranged women "from themselves" and "from their appetites," causing their sexuality to become depraved.

The events that in part obscured the advent of this great experimental novel also drove Barnes out of England. Suffering from severe alcoholism, she had moved sometime in August 1932 from Hayford Hall to a Gothic abode in London that her friends called Nightmare Abbey. During a final trip to Paris, in 1939, she sold her apartment. When Peggy Guggenheim and Helen Joyce sent her to New York City in November 1939, the move was probably a rescue more from alcoholic oblivion than from the war in Europe.

Barnes's transient life after Paris was like that of several other women expatriates, including Nancy Cunard (1896–1965), the British publisher who owned Hours Press. In the 1930's both women were without a home, physically ill, and emotionally unstable. While Cunard chose political involvement, Barnes chose retreat and obscurity. In this withdrawal she can be compared with another British fiction writer, Jean Rhys (1894–1979), who disappeared into the English countryside until she and her work were rediscovered shortly before her death.

During the 1930's, when most literature was politically engaged, three important expatriate women writers insisted on writing about dreams and the female secret life: Barnes in *Nightwood,* Jean Rhys in *Good Morning, Midnight* (1930), and Anaïs Nin (1903–1977) in her multivolume diary and in *House of Incest* (1947). In this novel Nin uses some of the subject matter and imagery of *Nightwood,* which she admired; she also uses the name Djuna for a character in several of her works, including the first novelette of the 1939 edition of *The Winter of Artifice*. Barnes, Rhys, and Nin—who were all international wanderers—addressed in their fiction the question of woman's relation to her body. Though these women seem extremely vulnerable and out of step with the 1930's, their fiction has been favorably reevaluated. Though they refused to address political issues directly, says Benstock, the "psychopathology of the female spirit" that is the subject of their works "reflects a larger cultural paranoia and self-hatred."

Patchin Place in Greenwich Village was the setting for the second half of Barnes's life, what she called her "Trappist" period. She lived in increasing isolation and retreat. Her drinking led to a series of "breakdowns," as she referred to her alcoholism. E. E. Cummings, a neighbor, would occasionally call out of his window, "Are you still alive, Djuna?" Guggenheim and Barney, among others, sent her money. She wrote poetry and illustrated a brief bestiary, *Creatures in an Alphabet* (1982), but during this time she published only one major new work, *The Antiphon* (1958).

The Antiphon is a verse play about a mother and daughter, victims of a cruel and sexually aggressive husband and father, working out their anger. It is set in 1940, when Germany was bombarding England, at the ancestral home, Burley Hall, whose damage symbolizes the destruction of the family and its traditions as well as hostile world conditions. The house is filled with "wasteland" artifacts and prophecies of a totalitarian world and of the destruction of civilization. During a macabre scene that takes place during a family reunion, two brothers, one in a pig's mask and one an ass's mask, bungle a physical attack on their sister and mother. This family of the deceased Titus Higby Hobbs is essentially the family of Wendell Ryder, humorously dramatized in *Ryder*: both men espouse polygamy and free love; both have mothers who conducted salons; both men break up their homes. The allusions to Barnes's life have been noted by many critics. *The Antiphon*'s Miranda, for example, is a writer who is called "Queen of the Night" (suggesting the author of *Nightwood*).

The Antiphon went through twenty-nine drafts before publication and is clearly Barnes's most complex work, full of archaisms, compacted syntax, obscure allusions, dualisms, and timelessness. Eliot, as senior editor of Faber & Faber, had advised her to cut scenes, including one in Act II in which the father, Titus, unable to have his daughter for himself, barters her virginity for the price of a goat, to a man three times her age. Eliot's recommendations finally reduced the play to a third of its original size, but his bewilderment was echoed by a great number of critics, who used words such as "enigma" and "encrustation."

An anonymous reviewer in London's *Listener* claimed to be confused by what he called a "very obscure play" that "reads like *The Family Reunion* rewritten by Christopher Fry after studying Ivy Compton-Burnett." Praise came from American poets Richard Eberhart ("her eccentric diction may be timeless") and Howard Nemerov, and from her longtime friend Edwin Muir, who had convinced Eliot of the value of publishing *The Antiphon* and who said that hers was "the only prose by a living writer which can be compared with that of Joyce."

Muir arranged a reading of the play at Harvard. Both Barnes and Eliot attended. The reading was disappointing, but a more successful production was its 1962 premiere at the Royal Dramatic Theater of Stockholm in a translation by Dag Hammarskjöld and Karl Gierow. More recent critics, such as Lynda Curry, have reevaluated this work, and with the publication of *Silence and Power,* essays that examine Barnes's work from a sociopolitical perspective, *The Antiphon* is finally being fully analyzed.

In 1962 Barnes issued a rewritten collection of her short stories. Although *Spillway* does not include the stories that treat death in *A Book* and *A Night Among the Horses,* it does include the stories about "individual integrity and human mortality." Also in 1962 the *Selected Works of Djuna Barnes* appeared, with some works, such as *The Antiphon,* extensively revised. By the mid-1970's scholarly books about Barnes's work had begun to appear. The myths about her persisted, fueled by the public's renewed interest in expatriate Paris, by rumors of her alcoholism (although she did, by the end of her life, give up drinking), by her isolation (twice she was placed, against her will, in a sanatorium and a nursing home), and by her acerbic wit and stubborn opinions. In print, others called her an "embittered relic" and an "enigmatic neo-Gothic figure." Her bitterness came in part from what she called "this flesh laid on us like a wrinkled glove," for she detested "the physical debility of old age," according to Benstock. "The red-headed bohemian" was now gray. On June 18, 1982, she died at ninety years of age.

The critical assessment of Barnes's work has moved far beyond the initial praise of Eliot and the bewilderment of Pound, who said she "wrote like a baboon," to Field's claim that she is, along with Eliot and Joyce, "a major writer of our time" and that "Colette, Woolf, and Barnes" should be nominated for placement on Parnassus. Her admirers included Samuel Beckett, Anaïs Nin, and Dag Hammarskjöld.

This profound and complex writer was essentially moral in her struggle with the conflict between physical nature and the human spirit. Though Barnes probably abhorred both feminists and scholars, it is the feminist critics, those conducting the closest rereadings, who are making her works more accessible and attempting to respond to the challenge posed by the prophetic lines of her poem "From Fifth Avenue Up":

> Someday beneath some hard
> Capricious star,
> Spreading its light a little
> Over far
> We'll know you for the woman
> That you are. . . .

Selected Bibliography

WORKS OF DJUNA BARNES

BOOKS

The Book of Repulsive Women: 8 Rhythms and 5 Drawings. New York: Bruno Chap, 1915; Yonkers, N.Y.: Alicat Bookshop, 1948.

A Book. New York: Boni & Liveright, 1923; London: Faber & Faber, 1958.

Ladies Almanack. Dijon: Darantière, 1928; New York: Harper & Row, 1972.

Ryder. New York: Liveright, 1928; New York: St. Martin's, 1979.

A Night Among the Horses. New York: Horace Liveright, 1929.

Nightwood. London: Faber & Faber, 1936; New York: Harcourt, Brace, 1937.

The Antiphon: A Play. New York: Farrar, Straus & Cudahy, 1958; London: Faber & Faber, 1958.

Creatures in an Alphabet. New York: Dial, 1982.

COLLECTED WORKS

The Selected Works of Djuna Barnes. New York: Farrar, Straus & Cudahy, 1962.

Spillway. London: Faber & Faber, 1962; New York: Harper & Row, 1972.

Smoke and Other Early Stories. Edited by Douglas

Messerli. College Park, Md.: Sun & Moon Press, 1982.

Djuna Barnes Interviews. Edited by Alyce Barry. Foreword and commentary by Douglas Messerli. College Park, Md.: Sun & Moon Press, 1985.

New York—Djuna Barnes. Edited with commentary by Alyce Barry. Foreword by Douglas Messerli. Los Angeles: Sun & Moon Press, 1985.

Cold Comfort: A Biographical Portrait of Djuna Barnes in Letters. Edited by Mary Lynn Broe and Frances McCullough. New York: Random House, forthcoming.

The early one-act plays, some of which appeared in contemporary periodicals, have not yet been collected.

BIBLIOGRAPHY

Messerli, Douglas. *Djuna Barnes: A Bibliography.* Rhinebeck, N.Y.: David Lewis, 1975. For 1975–1989 works see Janice Thom and Kevin Engel's bibliography in Mary Lynn Broe, ed., *Silence and Power.* Carbondale: Southern Illinois University Press, 1990.

MANUSCRIPT PAPERS

The Djuna Barnes Papers are in the McKeldin Library, University of Maryland at College Park. Also of value are the Emily Coleman Papers, in the library of the University of Delaware at Newark, and the Natalie Clifford Barney Papers, in the Bibliothèque Littéraire Jacques Doucet, University of Paris.

BIOGRAPHICAL AND CRITICAL STUDIES

Allen, Carolyn. " 'Dressing the Unknowable in the Garments of the Known': The Style of Djuna Barnes' *Nightwood.*" In *Women's Language and Style.* Edited by Douglas Butturff and Edmund L. Epstein. Akron, Ohio: L. & S. Books, 1978. Pp. 106–118.

———. "Writing Toward *Nightwood*: Djuna Barnes' Seduction Stories." In *Silence and Power.* Edited by Mary Lynn Broe. Carbondale: Southern Illinois University Press, 1991. Pp. 54–66.

Benstock, Shari. *Women of the Left Bank: Paris, 1900–1940.* Austin: University of Texas Press, 1986.

Blankley, Elyse Marie. "Daughters' Exile: Renée Vivien, Gertrude Stein, and Djuna Barnes in Paris." Ph.D. dissertation, University of California at Davis, 1984.

Broe, Mary Lynn. "My Art Belongs to Daddy: Incest as Exile—The Textual Economics of Hayford Hall." In *Women's Writing in Exile.* Edited by Mary Lynn Broe and Angela Ingram. Chapel Hill: University of North Carolina Press, 1989. Pp. 41–86.

———, ed. *Silence and Power: A Reevaluation of Djuna Barnes.* Carbondale: Southern Illinois University Press, 1991.

Broun, Heywood. "Short Plays at Provincetown in Good Bill: *An Irish Triangle,* by Djuna Barnes, Is Best of the New York One-Act Pieces Now Presented." *New York Tribune,* January 15, 1920. Pp. 12.

Burke, Kenneth. "Version, Con-, Per-, and In-: Thoughts on Djuna Barnes' Novel *Nightwood.*" *Southern Review,* n.s. 2:329–346 (April 1966).

Curry, Lynda C. "The Second Metamorphosis: A Study of the Development of *The Antiphon* by Djuna Barnes." Ph.D. dissertation, Miami University (Ohio), 1978. Abridged as " 'Tom, Take Mercy': Djuna Barnes' Drafts of *The Antiphon.*" In *Silence and Power: A Reevaluation of Djuna Barnes.* Edited by Mary Lynn Broe. Carbondale: Southern Illinois University Press, 1991. Pp. 286–299.

Davis, Isabel. "The People in Djuna Barnes's *Nightwood.*" Ph.D. dissertation, State University of New York at Stony Brook, 1978.

Ferguson, Suzanne C. "Djuna Barnes's Short Stories: An Estrangement of the Heart." *Southern Review,* n.s. 5:26–41 (January 1969).

Field, Andrew. *Djuna: The Life and Times of Djuna Barnes.* New York: Putnam, 1983. Rev. ed., *Djuna: The Formidable Miss Barnes.* Austin: University of Texas Press, 1985.

Fowlie, Wallace. "Woman: *Nightwood* of Djuna Barnes." In his *Clown's Grail: A Study of Love in Its Literary Experience.* London: Dobson, 1948. Pp. 139–146. Reprinted in his *Love in Literature: Studies in Symbolic Expression.* Plainview, N.Y.: Books for Libraries, 1972. Pp. 139–146.

Frank, Joseph. "Spatial Form in Modern Literature,

Part II.'' *Sewanee Review,* 53:433–456 (1945). Reprinted in his *The Widening Gyre.* New Brunswick, N.J.: Rutgers University Press, 1963. Pp. 25–49.

Gildzen, Alex, ed. *A Festschrift for Djuna Barnes on Her Eightieth Birthday.* Kent, Ohio: Kent State University Libraries, 1972.

Greiner, Donald J. ''Djuna Barnes' *Nightwood* and the Origins of Black Humor.'' *Critique: Studies in Modern Fiction,* 17, no. 1:41–54 (1975).

Guggenheim, Peggy. *Out of This Century.* New York: Dial, 1946.

Herring, Phillip F. *Djuna Barnes: A Biography.* New York: Viking, forthcoming.

Hirschmann, Jack A. ''The Orchestrated Novel: A Study of Poetic Devices in the Novels of Djuna Barnes and Hermann Broch, and the Influence of the Works of James Joyce upon Them.'' Ph.D. dissertation, Indiana University, 1962.

Jay, Karla. ''The Outsider Among the Expatriates: Djuna Barnes's Satire on the Ladies of the *Almanack.*'' In *Lesbian Texts and Contexts: Radical Revisions.* Edited by Karla Jay and Joanne Glasgow. New York: New York University Press, 1990. Pp. 204–216.

Kannenstine, Louis F. *The Art of Djuna Barnes: Duality and Damnation.* New York: New York University Press, 1977.

Lanser, Susan Sniader. ''Speaking in Tongues: *Ladies Almanack* and the Language of Celebration.'' *Frontiers: A Journal of Woman's Studies,* 4:39–46 (Fall 1979).

Marcus, Jane. ''Carnival of the Animals.'' *Women's Review of Books,* 8:6–7 (May 1984).

———. ''Laughing at Leviticus: *Nightwood* as Woman's Circus Epic.'' In *Silence and Power: A Reevaluation of Djuna Barnes.* Edited by Mary Lynn Broe. Carbondale: Southern Illinois University Press, 1991. Pp. 221–250.

Plumb, Cheryl J. *Fancy's Craft: Art and Identity in the Early Works of Djuna Barnes.* Selinsgrove, Pa.: Susquehanna University Press, 1986.

Raymont, Henry. ''From the Avant-Garde of the Thirties: Djuna Barnes.'' *New York Times,* May 24, 1971, p. 24.

Scott, James B. *Djuna Barnes.* Boston: Twayne, 1976.

Thomas, Dylan. ''*Nightwood.*'' *Light and Dark,* March 1937, pp. 27–29.

Weisstein, Ulrich. ''Beast, Doll, and Woman: Djuna Barnes' Human Bestiary.'' *Renascence,* 15:3–11 (Fall 1962).

Williamson, Alan. ''The Divided Image: The Quest for Identity in the Works of Djuna Barnes.'' *Critique: Studies in Modern Fiction,* 7:58–74 (Spring 1964).

—NOËL RILEY FITCH

Louise Bogan

1897–1970

"MY AIM," WROTE Louise Bogan in a 1937 letter to Theodore Roethke, "is to sound so pure and so liquid that travelers will take me across the desert with them." The purity and fluidity that Bogan sought in her work, and more often than not achieved, have been recognized by only a few readers, most of whom have been poets. Bogan has been, both during her career and since, a poet's poet, appealing to those attuned to her technical virtuosity and sensitive to her lyric cries. With the 1980 publication of *Journey Around My Room: The Autobiography of Louise Bogan—A Mosaic,* and the 1985 publication by Elizabeth Frank of *Louise Bogan: A Portrait,* however, readers have been captured by the intensely feeling woman portrayed in both books, and consequently have been drawn to the poetry.

Bogan would have despaired over this fascination with the life and the subsequent interest in the work. If she is known for anything, it is for her reticence and control. In *Journey Around My Room* she writes:

> The poet represses the outright narrative of his life. He absorbs it, along with life itself. The repressed becomes the poem. Actually I have written down my experiences in the closest detail. But the rough and vulgar facts are not there.

We thrive on "rough and vulgar facts" about one another's lives; with writers we yearn to draw correspondences between the lives and the work, but Bogan would have none of it.

Bogan began her career at the outset of high modernism, publishing her first book, *Body of This Death: Poems,* in 1923, one year after T. S. Eliot's *The Waste Land* appeared. Although considered a modernist (she wrote most of her poems during the 1920's and 1930's), Bogan was unlike the other poets of her generation in a number of ways. She never created a public persona, like Dylan Thomas, for example, whose poetry readings became grand performances; she had difficulty promoting her own work, unlike Ezra Pound and Roethke, who did not hesitate to call in literary favors and made sure their work was constantly in the public eye; and she wrote little poetry, even declining to publish in volumes individual poems that had appeared in magazines.

Bogan wrote poetry throughout the 1930's but refused to compromise her art in response to the political pressures of that decade, and when, in the 1940's, she turned her energies to criticism, she scorned the proponents and philosophy of New Criticism. Most of the modernists were extraordinarily conscious of being modern, while Bogan was not. A traditionalist, she had no desire to break new poetic ground; she was too busy competing with Dante. She wanted to tell the emotional truths she had gleaned from her life, and she wanted to do so in a very conventional way—through formal, metrical, rhymed verse. In the 1950's and 1960's her formal lyrics seemed out of place to a public craving looser, more open verse, and she felt her peculiarity. Yet Bogan did leave a last volume of collected work. Published in 1968, *The Blue Estuaries: Poems, 1923–1968,* preserves 103 of the poems she thought valuable, and the sound and consistent voice of her criticism has helped to shape our literary sensibility, if only in a small way. Despite these achievements and the numerous awards she received for her work, Bogan felt alone and odd, even in the last years before her death in 1970.

Bogan was born on August 11, 1897, in Livermore Falls, Maine. She and her family moved frequently, usually from one small mill town in the Northeast to another. The Bogan family, though poor and Irish Catholic, invariably lived in the Protestant section of town. Her childhood, and that of her brother, Charles, was wildly unsteady. Her parents, May Murphy Shields and Daniel Joseph Bogan, fought frequently and violently. Her mother, who was convinced she had married beneath herself, often left the family mysteriously and reappeared just as mysteriously—calmer, kinder, for a while. Louise was haunted years later by memories of being taken to hotels by her mother and waiting in the hallway outside a man's room. In *Journey Around My Room,* Bogan recalls with adoration the order she found at the home of a family named Gardner, where the Bogans boarded for a few months in 1904. Everything was in its place, everything was quiet, and meals were served on time. But this was someone else's home, and the Bogans soon left.

Bogan's artistic awakening is unusually clearly marked. She was visiting her mother in the hospital, she writes in *Journey Around My Room,* when she turned from her mother's bedside to a vase of marigolds:

> Suddenly I *recognized* something at once simple and full of the utmost richness of design and contrast that was mine. A whole world, in a moment, opened up: a world of design and simplicity; a kind of rightness, a kind of taste and knowingness, that shot me forward. . . .

The "sudden marigolds," as she calls them, shocked her into a new way of perceiving her world. She had glimpsed an internal order, truth, and beauty. She began to write poetry at the age of fourteen, when "the life-saving process" began.

At this time the literary scene in America was dramatically changed by Harriet Monroe's founding of *Poetry: A Magazine of Verse* in Chicago in 1912. For the first time in a consistent way, contemporary poetry of high quality was being published. Eliot, Pound, Wallace Stevens, and H.D. (Hilda Doolittle) all published early work in this journal and read each other's work in it. The following year, the American art world was ripped open at the Armory Show in New York, where Marcel Duchamp and others revealed a disjunction of images in art that paralleled movements in the literary world. New possibilities in the making of literature and art and a new audience for these productions gave a twofold strength to the modernist movement.

During these important moments in the life of modernism, Bogan was studying in Boston at Girls' Latin School, gaining a rigorous education in the classics, and writing steadily, piling up pages and pages of manuscript. She read *Poetry* from its first issue and regularly submitted poems and prose to the school's literary magazine. Bogan remarks in *Journey Around My Room* that by the age of eighteen she had learned "every essential of [her] trade." In large part this is true—she did not significantly vary her style or subjects throughout her career, but instead worked on refining a technical and musical skill that played itself out on a few themes. She occasionally experimented with free verse, but mainly she perfected the metrical melodies that sustain her songs about love, grief, and, above all, time.

In 1915 Bogan entered Boston University. The following year she declined a scholarship to Radcliffe in order to marry Curt Alexander, an army man whom she followed to the Panama Canal Zone in 1917. She was pregnant and miserable, having found that she had nothing in common with either the other army wives or her husband. She left him in May 1918, taking their infant daughter, Mathilde (called Maidie), to Boston. Her brother was killed in France a few months later, just before the end of World War I. She reconciled briefly with her husband in 1919, and the family lived together for a few months; then she separated from him again. He died of pneumonia in 1920.

Bogan's first marriage had been a disaster, and all her romantic hopes of love and escape and enduring comfort were destroyed. In the early poem "Betrothed" (in *Body of This Death*), Bogan writes:

What have I thought of love?
I have said, "It is beauty and sorrow."
I have thought that it would bring me lost delights, and splendor
As wind out of old time. . . .

These lines are unusual for Bogan in that they are about a specific, named experience (marriage) and are formally uncharacteristic: long, irregular, and unrhymed. They are typical, though, in that they set forth a persistent trope of paired polarities—emotions, images, or perceptions—here, beauty and sorrow. The pairing seems inevitable, as do the tensions between the two—tensions often form the basis on which the poems are structured.

While coping with romantic disillusionment, Bogan was trying to make a living and raise her child. For long periods she left her daughter in Massachusetts with her parents, visiting on weekends and living during the week in New York's Greenwich Village, where she soon became part of the literary community. In the 1910's the Village had become a bohemia where inexpensive rents and abundant housing attracted artists and writers. In 1919 Prohibition changed the residential character of the Village through the proliferation of speakeasies. By the early 1920's Bogan had met William Carlos Williams, Malcolm Cowley, Lola Ridge, John Reed, Louise Bryant, Mina Loy, and Edmund Wilson, who was one of her first friends in New York. She and Wilson kept up a long and lively friendship throughout their lives, drinking together, writing verse jointly, studying German, and discussing in late evenings and long letters the literary world and its inhabitants.

A brief affair during this period with a young radical named John Coffey (a thief who claimed that he stole in order to be arrested and, at his trial, use the courtroom as a forum in which to gain attention for the plight of the poor) would disturb her in later years because she believed that the literary community was scandalized and would never forget the incident. At this time she was immersed in Village life and, according to Frank, her biographer, was reading Jules LaForgue (a major symbolist poet), as were Hart Crane, Allen Tate, Rolfe Humphries, and Yvor Winters. In 1921 her work first appeared in *Poetry,* which printed five of her poems. Bogan was only twenty-four. She had already published poetry in *The New Republic, Others, Vanity Fair, Voices, The Measure,* and several other little magazines.

When Eliot shocked the literary world with the publication of *The Waste Land* in 1922, Bogan was writing some of the poems printed in her first book even as she was fighting bouts of depression. She began seeing a psychiatrist, and would continue to do so for much of her life. She had been working at various branches of the New

York Public Library, and at one of them she met Marianne Moore, with whom she later became friends. In the spring she traveled to Paris and Vienna, intending to write and study the piano for several months. Although she had completed only a few poems when she returned in September, the next year Bogan published her first book of poetry, *Body of This Death.*

The collection was well received, although most reviewers found the poetry obscure, which was a complaint that would persist in reviews of later volumes. Mark Van Doren, in a favorable review written for *The Nation,* states that ''one can be sure that experience of some ultimate sort is behind this writing,'' but he does not attempt to name the experience. A poet himself, Van Doren praises the ''pure poetry'' and ''sheer eloquence'' in Bogan's lyrics, and ventures that the book ''may be a classic.''

The volume is brief, containing barely thirty poems, and opens, as her later volumes would, with ''A Tale.'' In it, a young boy ''cuts what holds his days together,'' in search of ''a light that waits / Still as a lamp upon a shelf.''

> But he will find that nothing dares
> To be enduring, save where, south
> Of hidden deserts, torn fire glares
> On beauty with a rusted mouth,—

The youth here, and the women and other voices in the later poems, search for something innocent and lasting, yet find ''beauty with a rusted mouth,— / Where something dreadful and another / Look quietly upon each other.'' Though the boy desires some kind of freedom and something beyond permanence, the specific object of his search remains elusive, the landscape mysterious, and the ''dreadful something'' enigmatic. In the silence of the poem's resolute and fearless conclusion is the first taste of disillusionment, the knowledge that what lasts is terrible and patient and sometimes beautiful.

Several of the poems in the volume mention a broken, stilled world: ''a bell hung ready to strike'' (''Medusa''); ''your lips, closed over all that love cannot say'' (''Betrothed''). Landscapes conjure a world so still and desolate that it seems dead: ''Life moves no more'' (''Ad Castitatem''); ''beauty breaks and falls asunder'' (''Juan's Song''); ''so the year broke and vanished on the screen'' (''The Romantic''); ''in the withered arbor, like the arrested wind'' the statue stands (''Statue and Birds''); ''like a thing gone dead and still'' (''Men Loved Wholly Beyond Wisdom''); ''she is a stem long hardened'' (''The Crows''). The unnamed yet distinct landscape is a dangerous, comfortless place where not lovers, but love itself, betrays. Again and again, the failure of love and its consequent grief erupt from the pages of these poems. The question that forms the last line of ''Juan's Song''—''Who is it, then, that love deceives?''—is asked and answered in remarkable variations throughout the volume.

The title of the volume, which comes from Paul's cry (Romans 7:24) ''Who shall deliver me from the body of this death?'' points to a recurrent theme in the book. With the betrayal of love and the relentless, empty landscape, the people are left trapped and yearning for escape. In ''The Alchemist,'' the speaker says:

> I burned my life, that I might find
> A passion wholly of the mind,
> Thought divorced from eye and bone,
> Ecstasy come to breath alone.
> I broke my life, to seek relief
> From the flawed light of love and grief.

The alchemist fails, of course, and is left with ''unmysterious flesh.'' The speaker cannot escape the body and its dangerous passions and desires. Other ways of escape are useless. Chastity is invoked in ''Ad Castitatem,'' and the speaker is left with ''beautiful futility.'' The almost dead voice in ''Chanson un Peu Naïve'' asks, ''What body can be ploughed, / Sown, and broken yearly?'' It is hers, time and time again.

The speakers are left to endure in an indifferent landscape. As in ''A Tale,'' when the youth is somewhere ''south / of hidden deserts,'' in ''Medusa'' the speaker stands ''like a shadow / Under the great balanced day''; in ''Betrothed'' she has ''only the evening here, / and the sound of willows''; in ''The Crows'' there is ''only bitter / Winter-burning in the fields''; and in ''Fifteenth Farewell,'' there are ''only / Levels of evening, now, behind a hill, / Or a late cockcrow from the darkening farms.'' In each case there is ''only'' the dreadful, independent landscape. The voices are alone and apart, each trapped in a cumbersome body and set in isolation in a world that is dark and aloof.

The poems are for the most part written in short, metrical rhyming stanzas; even when Bogan ranges into free verse, the lyrics are stanzaic, resonant with internal rhyme, and tightly controlled in their rhythms. From the very first, reviews of Bogan's work have praised her technical expertise. To be sure, some have said that is all there is—technique, plus a dash of obscurity and bitterness. Adamant throughout her life that form is integral to beauty in art, Bogan aimed for formal integrity in both her poetry and her prose, and demanded it of others in her criticism.

In the 1953 essay ''The Pleasures of Formal Poetry,'' Bogan confronts the two most common objections to form—that it restricts and that it is old-fashioned and bereft of possibility. Although she acknowledges that some formal verse patterns are indeed out of date, she suggests that the modern captivation with experimental form is too exclusive and that ''experimental'' poets need not neglect the surprising possibilities available in formal verse. Bogan argues that the modern discomfort with form derives from moral bias; that is, some poets avoid writing formal poetry because they think there is something wrong with it, that constraints of formal verse betray the inner individual self. Bogan believed that rhythm is inherent in nature. When she began teaching in the late 1940's, she started each of her courses by asking her students to list rhythmic tasks and activities, and, most important, bodily rhythms, pointing out that the human pulse and breath give us a sense of time. That sense of time is the point from which the pleasure of formal poetry begins.

About the time *Body of This Death* was published, Bogan met Raymond Holden, who was to become her second husband. (Frank writes that Holden was, in fact, responsible for its publication.) He was separated from his wife and family, and soon he and Bogan began to live together. In a 1924 letter to John Peale Bishop, Edmund Wilson describes Holden as ''an amiable mediocrity.'' Holden was from a wealthy old New York family and had studied at Princeton (where he met Wilson) before he began working as a writer, publishing poems in several magazines. He eventually wrote a novel, *Chance Has a Whip* (1935), which fictionalizes his early life with Bogan.

In 1925 Holden, Bogan, and her daughter, Maidie, moved to Boston, where Holden had a job editing a travel magazine. On July 10 of that year they were married. The initial period of their life together was fairly quiet and productive. Bogan had days alone to write while Holden was at the office and Maidie was at school. Tensions between the two emerged, however, and the competition between two writers aggravated existing insecurities. Bogan continued producing her hard-wrought poems, and in 1926 she was invited to the Yaddo writers' colony, where she wrote ''Dark Summer,'' which would become the title poem of her second collection. In the fall the family moved back to New York City. Holden became ill, so they traveled to Santa Fe, where he could recuperate. There they met the writers Arthur Davison Ficke, Janet Lewis, and Yvor Winters. Winters, a restrained poet and scathing critic, would later characterize Bogan as one of the rare lights among the poets of his day.

In 1927 the couple decided to purchase a farm in the New York countryside and in Hillsdale found a house they could refurbish. They divided their time between working on the house and on their writing. Several of Bogan's poems from their first years together (collected in *Dark Summer: Poems*) continue the themes of love, entrapment, and grief, and add images of hidden things. The bird in "Winter Swan" appears with its "long throat bent back, and the eyes in hiding"; in "If We Take All Gold," the gold or sorrow is "hid away / Lost under dark heaped ground"; and in "For a Marriage," the husband sees "deep-hidden, / The sullen other blade." Things are not simply closed, covered, stilled, or forgotten; here they are deliberately hidden from sight and silenced from speech.

Bogan eventually had enough poems for another collection, and in 1928 she met John Hall Wheelock, who was to become the editor of her second, third, and fourth books, and a friend for the remainder of her life. Wheelock was himself a poet, and several of her letters to him reveal the strong impact he had on her work. To him she brought up the idea of writing a novel using autobiographical pieces, which was tentatively titled, with various spellings, "Laura Dailey's Story." Bogan worked intermittently on the prose work throughout her life but never completed it. Portions of it were published in *The New Yorker,* and several sections are collected in *Journey Around My Room.* Bogan wrote several short stories, most of which were published in *The New Yorker* and all of which remain uncollected. They are brief vignettes of searing revelation in a character's life. Little critical attention has been given to the fiction, but Bogan never claimed to be a fiction writer. She was always a poet who wrote criticism for a living and fiction when she could not write poetry.

Although "the long prose thing," as she called it, never materialized, a second volume of poetry did: *Dark Summer* was published in 1929. The book included only thirty-six poems, eleven of which had appeared in *Body of This Death.* The reviewers again praised the craft and remarked upon the obscurity of the poems. Bogan began to be compared in earnest with other women poets of the day, and gender-laden adjectives were used to describe her verse. Several reviews of this book and the others, collected in Martha Collins' *Critical Essays on Louise Bogan* (1984), tell as much about the period as they do about Bogan's work. Louis Untermeyer wrote of her "chastely composed pages," and Eda Lou Walton described her "immaculate spirit." Clearly these critics were uncomfortable with the declarations of love's devastation offered in controlled, precise words. It is never popular for a woman to reject love; it conflicts with central beliefs about who women are.

A few critics noticed the poems' preoccupation with the passage of time, and others commented on their metaphysical quality. In a review for *The New Republic,* Yvor Winters singled out "The Mark," "Come, Break with Time," and "Simple Autumnal," declaring that these poems "demand—and will bear—comparison with the best songs of the sixteenth and seventeenth centuries." They are songs, in the lyric sense of the word; in fact, many of the poems here and in other volumes have some version of "song" in their title. The comparison with English Renaissance verse is astute in two ways. First, Bogan's self-appointed task was to tell the truth of her existence, no matter how painful, in pure language. Second, her plain-style line resembles the style of metaphysical verse, especially that of John Donne and Ben Jonson. A tendency to use monosyllabic words prevails and greatly affects the rhythm, most often slowing the pace of the lines. In "Simple Autumnal," for example, the lines following are classic plain-style lines: "Because not last nor first, grief in its prime / Wakes in the day, and hears of life's intent." It is a complicated line to use, because the rhythm of the monosyllables must be sustained and directed by their individual weights and by the rest of the words in the poem. The lines begin in regular iambics and move after the caesura to variation; "grief" is thus emphasized both thematically and metrically. Following the comma after "day," the meter resumes regularity.

The landscapes of *Dark Summer* are, by and large, the indifferent ones of Bogan's first book. In "Late," for example, the earth is "harrowed and wild," the cliff is "sterile," and the sky is "pure," "cold," and "unchanged." And, as expected, the title poem radiates the negation that pervades the volume. The storm "is not yet heard"; the shaft and flash "are not yet found"; the rite is "not for our word"; and the kisses are "not for our mouths." Summer shadows the speaker with a sense of being out of place and season. This poem appears next to "Simple Autumnal," and both evoke a world of heaviness and delay.

Yet the poems are more than mere depictions of hard landscapes; there is always the presence, if not the voice, of someone grieving over what has happened or what is not to be. The cause may be unnamed, but the abiding feeling of abandonment, betrayal, and secrecy is always discernible. Emotion is at the heart of Bogan's verse, and emotional truths are the kind she struggled to understand and convey. In the haunting poem "The Cupola," for instance, we are brought inside an abandoned chamber where a mirror hangs, put there "for no reason" by a nameless "someone." The three stanzas are rich with images of drifted leaves reflected in the shuttered room, yet the poem evokes an utterly empty place, where what happens to be there does not matter. "Negligent death" is spilled randomly, yet in season, tied to some natural but foreign measure of time. The poem never specifies who was here, or why the person hung the mirror, or why death lingers, but a clear sense of abandonment is carefully conjured by the images of negation and the illusion of specificity.

When *Dark Summer* was published, Bogan and Holden were still dividing much of their time between New York City and Hillsdale. Bogan was regularly reviewing for *The New Republic* and had resumed the long process of composing poems. She visited with Edna St. Vincent Millay, who was a friend of Wilson's and was living in nearby Austerlitz. This full and productive period came to a shattering halt on the day after Christmas 1929. She and Holden had briefly been away from their home in Hillsdale when they received a phone call notifying them that it had burned down. All her manuscripts were destroyed; of them, she was able to save only a commonplace book from early school days and a journal she had written in Vienna. The family, devastated by their loss, moved back to New York City to begin again.

By this time Holden was managing editor of *The New Yorker* and Bogan was at home, suffering from depression. She was cheered, for a time, in 1930, when she received the John Reed Memorial Prize from *Poetry* magazine for her first two books. Recognition did not come abundantly to Bogan, although she won several major poetry prizes near the end of her career and was respected by her limited public throughout her life. She had a difficult time accepting her ambitious self, and she most often held back from promoting herself or asking for literary favors even from close friends. In an imaginary dialogue recounted in *Journey Around My Room,* a nameless speaker asks, "You had ambition?" Bogan answers, "I wished to live without apology." Her ambitions were most often explicitly personal or emotional, not professional. She, who fought depression and wild emotions her entire life, wanted above all to control them enough to live in peace from day to day.

Yet snatches of remarks about other writers, or asides tacked onto long letters about something else, reveal that Bogan did have a clear sense of her place in the poetry world. In 1936, after being plagiarized for the second time, she wrote angrily to Wheelock asking that something be done to fight the plagiarism or prevent it from being published: ''I am the one poet in America, with a definite note, who is almost unknown.'' Her pure lyric note, which she worked at sounding all her life, *was* overlooked by her contemporaries. She was respected and praised, but not understood, and she knew that signaled a limited audience. She was particularly sensitive at this time to what appeared to be her ''anonymity,'' for she was trying to remain steadfastly pure in terms of lyric focus, refusing to succumb to the rage for political literature.

To Roethke, Bogan had written the previous year, in encouragement as much to herself as to him, ''But if one is minor, one is minor: being good AND minor is something.'' She thought of herself as good and minor, not as good as Dante Alighieri, or Christina Rossetti—both of whom she wished to be like—but good and rare. Bogan saw her value in her brave fight to keep alive the uncontaminated lyric line that met truth, syllable by syllable. Her ambitions also were tempered by her ambivalent feelings about what a woman poet could and could not do: women could not write epics; women should not write sonnet sequences; women should keep ''small'' emotions out of their work.

Emotional truths should not be sentimental or ''mawkish,'' Bogan demanded. She excised poems (such as ''A Letter'') from early collections because they did not meet her increasingly severe standards for poetic utterance. Her detractors and even several of her admirers lament this delineation of emotions into the acceptable and unacceptable. The ''smaller'' emotions—those that might be sentimental without achieving poignancy—she banished from her poetry. Ruth Limmer, her friend and editor, wrote in her essay on Bogan printed in Collins' *Critical Essays* that Bogan's reticence ''alienated the larger audience . . . and had the effect of circumscribing her talent.'' Her reticence probably does account for Bogan's being overlooked and out of print during part of her career, since it sometimes made her poems difficult to grasp. And there is no doubt that the range of her talent was narrow. Nonetheless, the specific emotions—love and grief—that Bogan wrote about, and the large, encompassing theme of time, which holds much of her work together, attest to her willingness to confront directly these essential matters of human life.

Bogan did not think that matters of the American and European political and economic worlds were or should be within the scope of poetry. During the 1930's, when the mood of the nation swung according to the fluctuations of the Great Depression, as American economic and political structures came to be less secure, many looked to socialism and communism for an answer. When her friend Edmund Wilson, who was attracted to the hope of communism, traveled to the Soviet Union in 1935, Bogan wrote to Rolfe Humphries, ''I have always thought that the pure artist had his place, and should stick right in it, being as productive as possible and as pure as hell, whatever was going on outside.'' Bogan, who aimed to be a pure artist and write pure poetry, scorned those who enthusiastically embraced the Communist party as if it were ''the answer''; she knew there was no ready-made solution to any problem, and that emotional honesty and hard work were as close to an answer as one could get. Politics was beside the point; life and art were what mattered.

Further, Bogan saw the defection of her friends and colleagues (besides Wilson, Humphries, Léonie Adams, Genevieve Taggard, and Millay all for some time turned left) as a sign of intellectual and emotional weakness. She believed that their work began to be directed outside the important inner life, and that it failed in its inclination to an authority besides the self. This failure of loyalty to oneself damaged creativity by making it inauthentic and dishonest. Bogan was particularly riled by the activities and pronouncements of the poet Archibald MacLeish, who, following his move to the literary left, generated several antagonistic declamations of literary criteria. After one such speech, Bogan wrote to Humphries in 1938: "I STILL THINK THAT POETRY HAS SOMETHING TO DO WITH THE IMAGINATION; I STILL THINK IT OUGHT TO BE WELL-WRITTEN. I STILL THINK IT IS PRIVATE FEELING, NOT PUBLIC SPEECH." Her emphasis here, as elsewhere, is on truth of feeling and its expression in well-written language.

During the 1930's Bogan's life did change, however, in terms of her career, marriage, personal finances, and emotional health. Prompted by Wilson, Bogan began in 1931 to review poetry for *The New Yorker,* and she continued to do so for thirty-eight years. Aside from many short notices throughout the years, she wrote two yearly omnibus reviews on the poetry of the season, as well as several longer pieces on individual poets such as Edna St. Vincent Millay, William Butler Yeats, and Robert Penn Warren. In a letter to the editor William Shawn, written in 1941, in which she asks for a raise, she mentions W. H. Auden's praise of her work (he thought her the best critic of poetry in America), and suggests that she "did something toward keeping the flag flying . . . during the darkest days of political pressures upon writing." She did, as she notes, make the verse department "step by step, into a real influence." In her reviews, several of which are collected in *A Poet's Alphabet: Reflections on the Literary Art and Vocation* (1970), she details the strengths and weaknesses of the major and minor writers of the day in clear, sometimes biting prose.

The job gave Bogan some financial security, since she was salaried, but the money was hardly enough to live on. Moreover, the struggle to write the reviews came to be onerous, and she would often feel overwhelmed by the books arriving daily, demanding her attention. To be sure, Bogan ignored some verse that she did not like, and she was sparing in her reviews of women poets, but the reviews that she did write helped in some measure to shape our taste today, since those who were noticed were those who were read, and those who were read were those who were anthologized and discussed and included in classroom syllabi. For example, she did not write about Laura Riding or Gwendolyn Brooks and all but ignored May Sarton's many volumes of poetry, but she did write guarded praise of Emily Dickinson, Elizabeth Bishop, and Marianne Moore. *The New Yorker* became a force through the stern and flammable leadership of Harold Ross, and was transformed into a mainstream magazine with a reputation for publishing work of high quality.

Reviewing gave Bogan a steady, if burdensome, outlet for articulating her critical acumen during a time when she was finding it increasingly hard to write poetry. She wrote the bulk of her fiction during the 1930's; five stories were published in *The New Yorker* in 1931, and eight more between 1933 and 1935. As would happen repeatedly in her life, however, positive career moves were coupled with emotional upheavals. In 1931 Bogan suffered a breakdown. She and Holden had become a popular couple, entertaining frequently in New York, often gathering writers and artists from *The New Yorker* as well as their old friends from the Village. At the same time, however, Bogan became convinced that Holden was having affairs, and many arguments ensued. After a visit to her family in March of that year, she suffered a breakdown in April and entered the Neurological Institute in New York. Later that month she moved to a sanatorium in Connecticut, where she managed to write "Hypocrite Swift" (collected in *The Sleeping Fury:*

Poems), and in June she returned to Holden in New York.

A period of relative stability followed, and in 1932, encouraged by a friend, the writer Morton Zabel, Bogan applied for a Guggenheim Fellowship for a year of travel abroad. Reluctantly she sought supporters; Robert Frost, Monroe, Millay, and several others wrote letters of recommendation. The fellowship was awarded and Bogan sailed for Genoa in April 1933, expecting that her daughter would join her in the summer. Her journal from this time records her enthusiasm for simply seeing—Genoa, Naples, Palermo, Sicily—and she loved Italy, at first. In Rome she was bombarded with letters from Holden, who complained of his poor health and his lack of a job, and steadfastly claimed fidelity. His letters then turned ambiguous, alluding to another woman; hysterical letters from Bogan raged across the ocean in response. Bogan continued to travel and write (journal pieces and poetry), and in France she met friends from Santa Fe. She visited with John Dos Passos, Henri Matisse, and Ford Madox Ford. Her daughter came in July, and the two traveled to Italy and Austria. The value of the dollar was dropping and her funds were running out, and she was still tortured by suspicions about her husband. She and her daughter returned home in September to find her apartment rearranged by Holden's mistress. A second breakdown followed, during which Bogan again abjured romantic dreams and tried to unravel her painful life. She did separate from Holden, but not until 1934; they were divorced in 1937.

Bogan's spirits were lifted in 1935, when she began an affair with Roethke, with whom (she said to Wheelock) she fell "mildly in love." Poems from this period include "Roman Fountain," "Baroque Comment," "Single Sonnet," and "Evening Star." Their amorous relationship was brief, but they subsequently exchanged letters, Bogan generally urging him to let himself suffer and "*look* at things until you don't know whether you are they or they are you" if he wanted to write lyric poetry. She became a mentor of sorts to him, encouraging but refusing to coddle him. She was invited several times to lecture at the University of Michigan, where he held an appointment, and filled in for him when he was on leave.

Bogan's finances toppled in 1935, and she was evicted from her apartment when Holden stopped sending the payments specified in their separation agreement. Despite spirited disclaimers to the contrary, the crisis hit Bogan hard, and she scrambled to set herself up again. She did, and then had to cope with the death of her mother in 1936. Despite personal tragedy, Bogan found the resilience to continue her work on a third collection, *The Sleeping Fury,* which was published in 1937.

The collection, containing twenty-five poems, was dedicated to Wilson. To open the volume she used lines from Rainer Maria Rilke as an epigraph, one she would use for the rest of her books: "Wie ist das klein, womit wir ringen; / Was mit uns ringt, wie ist das gros." ("How small is that with which we struggle; / How great is that which struggles with us.") These poems were written during the period from 1930 to 1936, when her second marriage disintegrated and she suffered two emotional breakdowns. The book was well received where it was reviewed (the poet Kenneth Rexroth's review is an exception), but not all the important journals of the time gave it attention. As Martha Collins notes in the introduction to her *Critical Essays,* comparisons of Bogan with the metaphysical poets were frequent and the emphasis on obscurity decreased somewhat.

Critics (and friends) like Zabel and Ford remarked upon Bogan's "accent and austerity of poetic truth" (Zabel) and her "authentic" poetry (Ford). Allen Tate, a poet, a critic, and a friend, gave her the peculiar compliment of praising her for being "a craftsman in the masculine mode," by which, one assumes, he meant that he was impressed by her sure technique and expert control of sound and sense. Getting at the truth with a steady hand was what she wanted to do, and Bogan was pleased by the reviews, though disappointed that the range of notice was so limited.

Of any of the volumes that lose something by being collected with the others in *The Blue Estuaries, The Sleeping Fury* perhaps suffers the most. Its movement and integrity are experienced best in the long-out-of-print individual volume. Bogan, in a half-jesting summary in a letter to Zabel, written as she was preparing the collection for publication, says that the poems move from the period of "despair, neurosis, and alcoholism" to further despair, then to "the period of Beautiful Males (ending with 'Man Alone'). Then the spiritual side begins. . . . All ends on a note of calm: me and the landscape clasped in each other's arms." This third volume is her last full collection; later ones offer some new poems but primarily reprint older work.

Formally, Bogan varies the structure of some of the poems. The metered verse appears in shorter lines (from five stresses in *Dark Summer* she moves to several poems with three stresses per line). The free-verse poems still appear in longer lines, but there are fewer lines in each poem. Also, *The Sleeping Fury* is the last volume for which she wrote sonnets. A standard poetic model in the tradition of Petrarch, Spenser, and Shakespeare, the sonnet as a vehicle for twentieth-century hearts and minds is a challenge not chosen by many modern poets. Yet Bogan thrives within its confines, as she exclaims in "Single Sonnet": "Bend to my will, for I must give you love: / The weight in the heart that breathes, but cannot move. . . ." This exhortation nicely glosses her prose statements on formal poetry, in that she couples form and love, and stasis and life, with the strict sonnet form and its capacity to liberate emotion.

A mature, resolute voice opens the volume and sets its tone in "Song": "It is not now I learn / To turn the heart away. . . ." She writes "the heart" and not "my heart," enlarging the poetic situation with the definite article; there is even distance between the voice and the heart, though both inhabit the same body. In the conclusion to this short poem, all in iambic trimeter, the "I" is lost or transformed into an "eye":

> It is not the heart that grieves.
> It is not the heart—the stock,
> The stone,—the deaf, the blind—
> That sees the birds in flock
> Steer narrowed to the wind.

The presence of grief is still keenly felt, though not by the betraying heart of the first two books. Bogan gives a familiar catalog of negation in monosyllables, the regular beats of which are broken in the last line. Who it is that feels the grief is never identified, though the determined flight of the birds is precisely rendered. The deliberation and braced patterning of the birds is easily a metaphor for the construction of this volume—the poems are individually written and collectively arranged against the force of time.

Time is as much a presence here as grief and love and beauty, especially since each is given shape and substance in the context of time. In "To Wine," for example, the speaker asks the cup to "Return to the vein / All that is worth / Grief. Give that beat again." Some lost warmth or passion is missed and wanted; the voice demands the "beat" of life. "Grief" is set off, a single word beginning the last line of the poem, followed by a period. The initial repeated "g" in "grief" and "give" emphasizes the beat, and the meter insists we attend to the grief. Life is signified by movement, here as in so many of Bogan's poems, and the motion is not random, but timed and in time.

And, as in so many of her poems, Bogan writes of enduring—lasting through time and past heartbreak. In ''Single Sonnet'' she writes of bearing things for too long, and ''The Sleeping Fury'' confronts the scourge endured for years. In ''To My Brother Killed: Haumont Wood: October, 1918,'' she addresses her brother directly and writes that ''all things endure / . . . Save of peace alone.'' Most of the poem is fleshed out within the ellipsis, where the list of all the things that do endure is ultimately undercut by the last sad and sure line. This poem moved Marianne Moore so much that several times she mentioned her gratitude to Bogan for having written it.

Bogan continues a habit of mind that pervades her first book, *Body of This Death*: the insistence on putting distance between grief and its cause. In that first volume, for example, she had collected the ironic ''Fifteenth Farewell'' (how many does it take?), which swears to ''forget the heart that loves.'' Although the lover is displaced, it is not the beloved who must be forgotten but, rather, the heart that loves. The struggle is turned inward, and it is the self that betrays. In *The Sleeping Fury* several poems take up a tone of resolution to break off memory, connection, and imprisonment. In the most explicit, ''Kept,'' the speaker asks, ''What are these rags we twist / Our hearts upon . . . ?'' and decides that it is time for ''the playthings of the young'' to ''Get broken, as they should.'' The unwelcome disillusionment voiced by the youths of the earlier volumes has become transformed: the speakers in several piercing poems of the third volume deliberately set about the business of growing up, even if that means relinquishing the heart.

One way of understanding the struggle that Bogan takes up again and again in her work is to look at a prominent pair of opposites in this volume: the tension between saying and not saying, between speech and silence. The lyrics themselves are of course artifacts of language; in them she does say things. But for a writer to write so often about the difficulty and danger of ''saying'' reveals much about that writer's relationship to her own work. These poems are all the more poignant since Bogan's letters reveal (as do some of her poems—witness ''The Daemon'') the terrible trial she experienced in trying to (and having to) piece together words.

In ''To Wine'' the dead are ''lipless,'' that is, the mark of death is to be incapable of speech. In ''Poem in Prose'' the speaker tries to write of the beloved but says she cannot (though of course she does in this poem), and all that issues from their fight of love is silence. Here and in the exquisite ''Italian Morning'' she is rendered speechless by love: ''(O bred to love, / Gathered to silence!).'' In ''Baroque Comment'' she lists a movement from some primitive world to artificial structures, heaping ornate words upon themselves, and ends with ''The turned eyes and opened mouth of love.'' In ''Poem in Prose,'' silence is a sign of death; in the rest, silence is a sign of life—to the lover but not to the poet.

The peace that Bogan described in her letter to Zabel about the sweep of this third volume is an uneasy one. In ''Exhortation'' (to the self), she derides the abuse of ''bastard joy'' and brings together the task of heart and hand: ''In the cold heart, as on a page, / Spell out the gentle syllable / That puts short limit to your rage. . . .'' In verse she tries both to articulate and to limit rage (or whatever emotion she is working with in a particular poem), and in her limitations and reticences we often meet silence. One wonders if the attempt to control rage in verse is one reason Bogan found it increasingly difficult to write, limiting herself to so little yet demanding so much.

Her main themes of disillusionment in love and the endurance of grief were soon challenged by a happy love affair. Bogan met this unidentified man in 1937, while returning home after a renewed Guggenheim grant had enabled her to travel to Ireland, where she had been plagued by fears that the old ''scandal''—as she thought of it—of her affair with Coffey was buzzing in literary circles. Her fears took other shapes, and she imagined she was being followed through the streets of Dublin. She thought much about William Butler Yeats during this short trip, especially his writings on masks, something very familiar to her and an idea she had incorporated into her poetry. Terrified of Dublin and horrified by the ugliness she encountered, Bogan cut short her trip and sailed home in a desperate condition two months after arriving. In New York, an electrician befriended her and nursed her back to health. Although the two maintained their relationship for eight years, Bogan did not write of him or introduce him to her friends.

She ceased a lifetime of moving from apartment to apartment when she returned to New York and found an apartment near the Neurological Institute in northern Manhattan. She had just turned forty—an age at which she had claimed there could be no new love for a woman. The 1930's were ending, and she had managed to last them out and find some stability in her personal and domestic life. Although they were divorced, she kept Holden's name on her apartment buzzer; except for a chance meeting, she never saw him again. Her daughter was living nearby and studying music at Juilliard. Bogan had for a time a steady love life, privacy, sufficient money, and peace of mind.

Perhaps she had gained enough security to change her long-standing rule against personal disclosure in public. She participated in the 1939 *Partisan Review* symposium "The Situation in American Writing," in which authors were asked to answer questions about influence and direction in their work and the larger cultural situation. As to her acknowledged literary influences, she cited her strong classical education, her reading of the French symbolists through the translations of Arthur Symons, and her reading of the English metaphysical poets, Yeats, and the Americans Edgar Allan Poe, Henry David Thoreau, Emily Dickinson, and Henry James. Her response to Yeats was complete: she thought he was the greatest poet of the modern period. She had been reading him seriously since 1916 and writing about him in the mid 1930's (Yeats died in 1939). For her, Yeats was the fighter who knew himself and gave his best to his art. He cared passionately and wrote exquisitely. In the essay "On the Death of Yeats" (1939) Bogan writes that his late work in particular "touched the borders where poetry becomes ultimate evocation, and the regions where religion rises from universal mystery." He was able to tap the source of the lyric cry that she claimed as her vocation.

As a more personal and earlier influence, Bogan briefly discussed what it was like to be a poor Irish Catholic, especially in a Protestant town. She was slapped with the nickname "Mick" and knew that mattered more than anything else. Surely her later love for Yeats was in some way tied to her Irish ancestry and the difficulty and shame it had caused her throughout her youth. She saw that he inspired the Irish out of their "artistic inertia" and gave them a literature to glory in and a history to reclaim.

Turning in the symposium to questions of generational influences, Bogan discussed the political situation of the 1930's and its detrimental effect on many writers of the time:

> The economic crisis occurred when that generation of young people was entering the thirties; and, instead of fighting out the personal ills attendant upon the transition from youth to middle age, they took refuge in closed systems of belief, and automatically (many of them) committed creative suicide.

According to Bogan, such writers fought the Great Depression outside themselves, the political and economic Depression, and did not have the courage or maturity to confront the inner demons. Bogan's arrogance was hard won; she had scraped herself off "the icy floor of the ninth circle of hell" (as she called it in a 1935 letter to Roethke) not once, but twice, yet had continued to write.

The poems were "given" to Bogan less and less, though, and her next book of verse, *Poems and New Poems* (1941), was a collection of previously printed work with only a few new poems. Bogan was reluctant to do the volume, but, prompted by Wheelock, she did. Her friend Zabel strongly disapproved of the lighter verse she included, and berated her in private and in public for publishing the poems. The two, who quarreled often, were this time both stubborn and angry enough to keep their distance for two years. Along with the lighter verse, which introduced a new tone in Bogan's work, she rearranged earlier sequences, deleted six poems, and added sixteen, most of which had been written in 1938.

Besides the lighter verse (examples are "Variation on a Sentence" and "Animal, Vegetable, and Mineral"), Bogan included two translations (from Jean-Pierre Jouve and Heinrich Heine); a two-line, one-sentence epigram ("At midnight tears / Run into your ears."); and the familiar formal verse and occasional free-verse experiment. It was harder for her to write, and she clearly was trying to broaden the range of her poetic material while remaining true to her conception of the pure lyric. Though two collected volumes would follow, this was the first to present the work Bogan wanted to preserve from two decades of writing, and it opened the way for critics to comment on her development. Were the new poems new?

Marianne Moore wrote a wonderfully detailed review in *The Nation* and, in her typically tilted style, called Bogan's work "compactness compacted." She discussed the relation of Bogan's poems to seventeenth-century verse and called Bogan "a workman," praising her deliberate craftsmanship and saying that her "forged rhetoric . . . nevertheless seems inevitable." Malcolm Cowley was one of the early critics to note that Bogan often wrote poems about poetry and about the process of writing, yet in his review in *The New Republic* he chided her for her narrow range of expression and lamented that she did not write faster and with less inhibition. Stanley Kunitz, too, complained (in *Poetry*) that some of the poems seemed overworked and could do with a dose of associative freedom, though in large part he admired her elegant lyrics. The reviewers on the whole praised the work but were impatient for more and different poetry.

A stirring exception was Auden, who took the occasion to discuss the problem of the artist's self-development within a demanding community and public that offered little encouragement. Writing in *Partisan Review,* he acknowledged "the price and reward for such a discipline," and noted that Bogan's acute insight did not come easily. He saw a gradual development of consciousness that allowed her to become more objective, not merely distant and afraid. Above all, he respected her decision to dare to "face the Furies" and remain loyal to herself, never pandering to the public.

Despite these reviews, Bogan despaired that her book was all but invisible to the indifferent literary world. And, despite Auden's public declaration of "the permanent value" of her work, she knew that not enough people felt this way and that her books might well be out of print before her death—which they were.

The subjects are, for the most part, the same here as in previous work: endurance, love, grief, and the difficulty of writing or speaking what matters. There are occasional glimpses of the more "objective" perspective that Auden describes, as in "Zone":

We have struck the regions wherein we are keel
    or reef.
The wind breaks over us,

And against high sharp angles almost splits into
    words,
And these are of fear or grief.

The last line of the poem quietly attests, "We have learned how to bear." The sharp landscape has been internalized and the unspoken but known words are "fear or grief." These words, not uttered, yet written here, are borne through time without defense or complaint. Because the context has been abstracted, what prompted the lesson is unknown, though the experience of it is strongly felt.

A very different poem, but one retaining an aura of objectivity, is "Evening in the Sanitarium." It is different for Bogan because it is peculiarly modern in setting, names characters besides the self or the absent lover, and moves from line to line by means of narration. Though she originally gave it the subtitle "Imitated from Auden," Bogan dropped the acknowledgment when she realized that the poem came, in fact, primarily from her own memory. Stylistically, perhaps, its modernity of place owes something to Auden, for Bogan rarely located her poems more specifically than by reference to a natural setting, deserted room, or half-mentioned bed. The poem's prose counterpart is her unpublished story "The Long Walk," which describes the daily afternoon walk of sanatorium patients accompanied by their nurse. Although the patients at first enjoy the freedom, they are soon jarred into the searing feelings of imprisonment and loneliness that brought them to the sanatorium.

No freedom or revelation happens in "Evening in the Sanitarium," in which Bogan narrates a third-person vignette about women "evening" out and dulling their hearts and minds. The women are cured of extremities: the academic's face is "blunted," the manic-depressive "levels off." The women are trapped in a moment of time, one defining moment that they cannot break out of but must learn to bear. "The period of the wildest weeping, the fiercest delusion, is over." For Bogan, her "wildest weeping" was calmed in her last stay at the Neurological Institute, but the uncontrollable tears would return at the end of her life, some twenty years later, and send her into despair.

"The Daemon," a very disturbing poem but one more formally typical of Bogan, is revealing about her poetic process, why it was so difficult for her to write and why she nevertheless struggled to do so her entire life. Her muse is not the familiar angelic figure—most often a woman—who inspires the writer to creativity. And, although Bogan would write in letters of how poems would be "given" or have "arrived," more often than not she recounts the painstaking process of culling from language its finest expression.

Her muse is a tyrant, evil and insatiable in its desire to extract the utmost from the exhausted self. The poem consists of three short quatrains, rhymes regularly and simply, and is connected by the first repeated words of each stanza, "Must I . . . ?" The speaker asks,

Must I tell again
In the words I know
For the ears of men
The flesh, the blow?

The words of the poem are almost entirely monosyllabic, and the lines are stressed with either two or three beats, the result of which is the pounding of the questions. The violence of the "blow," the "bruise," and the "halt," and the final quick, cruel answer, are each amplified. The speaker must tell and show and speak "to the lot / Who little bore"—again as before. To the request for abatement, the daemon relentlessly insists, "It said *Why not?* / It said *Once more.*" The speaker feels compelled to reveal the blows and bruises received, yet is hesitant to do so, instead obscuring the hurt by offering the grieving or stilled heart.

The compulsion to write and the misgivings about doing so imperfectly suddenly collided after the publication of this fourth volume. Bogan did not know what to do next, and for seven years she could not complete a poem. She had succeeded in silencing the daemon and went about the business of writing in ways that she could. Although she was not happy about the shift in focus, she concentrated on her critical writing, which she had been steadily producing along with the poetry for several years. Her reputation as a critic was as strong as, if not stronger than, her reputation as a poet, yet she drew scant comfort from the fact and felt overlooked by the public.

Poems and New Poems sold slowly, and Bogan was irritated with her publishers for not advertising the book. Her annoyance increased when her proposal for an anthology of lyrics was rejected. She, and several of her friends, had expected her book to win the Pulitzer Prize (she never did), and disappointment about that failure lingered. She had come to feel betrayed by her publishers, and so Bogan broke with Wheelock and Scribners, yet, through Wheelock's patience and loyalty, they maintained their friendship. He would later nominate her for honorary positions and write letters on her behalf to secure her place in the Academy of American Poets.

For the next years Bogan wrote criticism, taught, and helped a generation of writers by judging applications for grants. From just before the publication of *Poems and New Poems* until 1944, Bogan worked with William Maxwell on a manuscript. She had met him through *The New Yorker,* where he was poetry editor. He had already published two novels, and Bogan encouraged him to turn a short story he had written into a novel of adolescence, *The Folded Leaf,* helping him revise it at every stage of the work. Later (in 1953) Bogan would help another writer, the poet May Sarton, and encourage her to be stern and courageous in her poetry. The two eventually collaborated on translations from Paul Valéry that have never been collected but were published in various little magazines. Sarton has left a vivid memoir of Bogan from this period in *A World of Light: Portraits and Celebrations.* It is tinged with a trace of bitterness, however—Bogan never reviewed Sarton at length.

During this period, Bogan also began to meet with critical acclaim, however limited. In 1944 she was invited to judge applications for Guggenheim poetry fellowships and was elected a Fellow in American Letters at the Library of Congress—through Archibald MacLeish, against whom she had earlier railed. The following year she was appointed Consultant in Poetry at the Library of Congress and moved to Washington, D.C., for several months (while *The New Yorker* held her job open) to carry out her duties. While at the Library of Congress she gave a series of readings that were taped; they capture her deep, careful voice releasing one by one, in serious measures, the words she so struggled to write. In this period she was asked to judge the Harriet Monroe *Poetry* Award and to give the Hopwood Lecture at the University of Michigan.

"My 'ambition' is finished," she wrote in her journal at the time, as Frank relates. "Now I only ask for continued vigor, and the ability to see, interpret, and *move around.*" And Bogan did move around—giving readings and lectures, and serving on poetry-award committees. More and more she was becoming part of the public poetry world, not simply a writer alone in her apartment turning out a few volumes of verse. She reunited with old friends like Zabel and Tate, and met Moore again after twenty years. Her affair with "the mystery man" ended, seemingly without regrets or recriminations. Although she still could not write poetry, she found some satisfaction in her professional and personal life.

In 1948, as a Fellow in American Letters, Bogan met with other elected writers and came face to face with Eliot for the first time. She thought him beautiful. With the other fellows—including Léonie Adams, Auden, Conrad Aiken, Eliot, Robert Lowell, Katherine Anne Porter, and Karl Shapiro (who objected)—she voted to award the prestigious Bollingen Prize for poetry to Ezra Pound, for *The Pisan Cantos*. With the war ended and Pound accused of treason, though judged unfit to stand trial, a public furor raged over the decision. Although Bogan later came to regret her vote, at the time she believed that Pound's political beliefs did not mar the work.

Also in 1948 she began a project that would capture her imagination and open a new friendship. Through Auden she was introduced to Elizabeth Mayer, who was older than Bogan and who had known Rilke, whose work Bogan loved. The two collaborated on a translation of Goethe's *The Sorrows of Young Werther* (1971), which ended up, as Frank writes, more a rendering than a literal translation. Other work with Mayer followed, and together they translated Goethe's *Novella* (1971) and *Elective Affinities* (1963), as well as Ernst Jünger's *The Glass Bees* (1960).

Besides the translation projects with Mayer and Sarton, Bogan began a long stint (from the late 1940's to the early 1960's) of teaching at New York University, the University of Chicago, the University of Arkansas, and Brandeis University, among other places. Perhaps the most demanding course was one she offered at New York's 92nd Street Y in 1956—Marianne Moore, who had several books of poetry behind her and whose reputation was secure, registered for the course. Bogan had to rethink her syllabus because she regularly used one of Moore's poems to illustrate syllabic verse. Apparently Moore took copious notes and asked endless technical questions. Bogan took it in good spirits and went on to teach other classes, always emphasizing form in her analyses.

In 1951 Bogan was commissioned to write a summary of American poetry, published later that year as *Achievement in American Poetry, 1900–1950*. In it she does not mention herself. She discusses the first half of the century, from the strains of sentimental and genteel Victorianism to modern (midcentury) formalism and pessimism. She locates a shift of spirit with the symbolists and sees breakthroughs also occurring in Ireland with Yeats. She cites Edwin Arlington Robinson as a critical figure in American poetry and its turn from sentimentality toward modern psychological complexity and truth. In the same chapter she lauds women for keeping alive the line of poetic intensity. "Women's feeling," she writes, "at best is closely attached to the organic heart of life." She cites as an example Emily Dickinson, whose first volume was published posthumously in 1890, and whose later collections appeared at the turn of the century.

According to Bogan, the real breakthrough occurred in the first years of the century, when poets were influenced by realism in fiction and painting, by the closing gap between American and European art, and by America's new self-consciousness. Bogan discusses "the American Renaissance," its beginning marked by the founding of *Poetry*. For her, Vachel Lindsay, Edgar Lee Masters, Carl Sandburg, and Robert Frost are important figures in opening the range of poetic material by including subjects not usually considered poetic and by making these subjects more distinctly American. Of Eliot's work she remarks that *The Waste Land* is not a picture of despair, and that his early critical work was seminal in that it gave a historical perspective to modern literary criticism. Again she lists the fine women poets of the time—and is especially admiring of Elinor Wylie—this time adding an intellectual dimension to their special virtues.

Noteworthy events of the 1930's that catch her eye are Hart Crane's abbreviated career, Eliot's religious conversion, Yeats's later style, and the surge of critical work on literary theory. This chapter, covering the period of political and economic upheaval, is entitled "Ideology and Irrationalism." She never did understand or accept the reasons that her friends were attracted, if briefly, by Marxist dreams.

Although she did not write poetry between 1941 and 1948, Bogan says that poetry in general had become "broadly workable and capable of a variety of applications." Pound, Eliot, Auden, and others had given poetry new life, and the new formalists were producing interesting work. Younger poets she highlights are Randall Jarrell, Elizabeth Bishop, Robert Lowell, and Richard Wilbur. She concludes the study with a warning, urging her contemporaries, "in a period of general pessimism, [not to] dispense with inner joy."

Bogan had begun writing a few poems and sending them out once again to journals. She found a new publisher and planned a new volume, which came out in 1954 as *Collected Poems, 1923–1953*. In each of the three new poems included, a feeling of conclusion pervades, and allusions to death are strong. In "After the Persian" she writes, "Goodbye, goodbye! / There was so much to love, I could not love it all . . ."; in "Train Tune" the journey is backward, "Back through midnight"; the last poem is titled "Song for the Last Act," and each refrain, like "Now that I have your heart by heart, I see," gives a sense of finality and summation. Although Bogan was only in her late fifties when she published this book, poetry had become increasingly difficult for her to write, and she feared that it would probably be her last volume.

Critical reception was admiring, but quieter than usual, and except for a splendidly insightful piece by Léonie Adams, the reviews offered the familiar adjectives—"skillful," "restrained," "profound." The book won a Bollingen Prize shared with Adams (1955), which pleased Bogan, since she and Adams were old friends. Although Bogan wrote a few other poems after "Song for the Last Act," it was one of her best, and none thereafter would be as lovely or important. The refrain to the stanzas changes slightly, from "Now that I have your face by heart I look," to "Now that I have your voice by heart, I read," and finally to "Now that I have your heart by heart, I see." The progression from looking to reading to seeing focuses, at last, on the heart. The person to whom the poem is addressed is there and not there, having been incorporated into the speaker in the passage of time and the legacy of memory. Written in 1948, after her long silence, the poem illustrates that Bogan's gift was still alive, if dormant.

In 1955 her first collection of criticism, *Selected Criticism: Prose, Poetry,* was published; subsequently it was superseded by her posthumously published collection *A Poet's Alphabet*. Some of her magazine pieces remain uncollected, however, including her omnibus reviews for *The New Yorker*. As much as her criticism helped her through periods of poetic aridity, Bogan was uncertain if it had not in fact made "the creative side rather timid," as she wrote to her editor at *The New Yorker,* Katharine S. White, in 1948, just as she was beginning to write poetry again. Bogan, the perfectionist who began her literary career comparing herself to Dante and throughout the years developed strict criteria for what literature should be—truthful, heartfelt, formal, and daring—felt daunted by the standards she demanded. The language in any piece of literature must be exquisite and expected, yet startling in its beauty. Her critical voice is confident and authoritative, and her record of response to modern literature still yields insight and pleasure.

Bogan continued to lecture, teach, and travel through the 1950's, and in 1959 she was awarded five thousand dollars by the Academy of American Poets. Financial tensions eased late in her life, although she could never have been called affluent. She kept up her correspondence, as she had during her entire life; and her late letters, as witty and spirited as the early ones, allow us to glimpse the playful, feisty side of her, which rarely comes out in her poetry. In them she records the latest literary gossip, her immediate reactions to literary works, her advice to fellow writers, and her shifting sense of despair and delight.

Bogan returned to trying to write her memoirs—"the long prose thing"—and was able to recover several scenes from her childhood. She was by then spending time regularly at the MacDowell writers' colony, and pieces of memoirs and poetry surfaced. When in New York City she also continued translating and writing essays for publication and presentation. The honorary degrees she received meant much to her, since she had never earned a college degree and often felt wary of academics. Nonetheless, as Frank points out, she was adamant that criticism not be the province of specialists.

In 1962 Bogan gave a lecture at Bennington College that outlines the development of her thinking on the position of the woman writer. In the 1947 essay "The Heart and the Lyre" she had rehearsed remarks she used in *Achievement in American Poetry* on verse written by women in the United States, listing "the special virtues of women":

Women are forced to become adult. They must soon abandon sustained play, in art or life. They are not good at abstractions and their sense of structure is not large; but they often have the direct courage to be themselves.

The list continues, with the narrow range severely delineating women's potential. Bogan takes account, as she must, of the usual criticism of women's writing—that it too often lapses into romantic sentimentalities—and she challenges that notion, asserting that a woman's singular gift is her heart.

Before this essay, and between it and the Bennington lecture, Bogan had made scattered statements about a female aesthetic, most often in longer remarks on individual poets. She always maintained that women are different and write differently, drawing upon different strengths and fending off different weaknesses than men. Women can never write successful surrealist poetry, for example, because they are too wedded to the concrete and because their basic impulse is gentle and not given to shock effects. Bogan knew she was no feminist, and in fact was uneasy about the very word; and while she admitted to limiting the literary possibilities for women because of their limited nature, she tried to turn this by concentrating on "the special virtues" of women.

In the Bennington lecture Bogan intended to talk about several important women poets throughout the ages but ended up discussing women prose writers, placing them in the context of women from antiquity on. Underneath the often humorous essay we hear rumblings of discontent that make one question her belief in just how "special" women's virtues are. She writes of how women were vital parts of civilization even before their utterances were recorded, and of how "the harsher periods of masculine power" silenced them. Moving from cultural history to literary history, Bogan cites Dorothy Richardson, author of *Pilgrimage* (a series of novels published 1915–1967), as a crucial transitional figure, in a way more important than James Joyce, since her novel was the first to bring stream-of-consciousness writing to literature. She notes Richardson's awkwardness, then applauds her as a woman who sensed her own worth and displayed it grandly.

Bogan passes from Virginia Woolf, to whom she is not in the least generous, to Simone de Beauvoir, of whom she is deeply suspicious. Both are too angry and absolute for her tastes. The best women writers, she says, are the ones who tell their own truth, "both observed and suffered through." Her list of what women must not do in literature mostly includes strictures against attitude: the inclination to whine, to indulge in theatrics, and so forth. Women can, however, write about any subject and in any form (a point she had disputed in earlier days).

For the next two years Bogan continued to write criticism, and in 1964 she began a year's appointment in Boston, at Brandeis University. A light class schedule gave her much time to herself, and she received a fairly high salary, a situation for which she felt guilty afterward. The classes did not go as she had hoped, nor were the students as serious as she demanded; this, and being in a place filled with memories, contributed to her diminishing spirits. Physical problems aggravated her difficulties and added to her fatigue and loneliness. Depression beset her once again, and in the early summer of 1965 she checked into the Neurological Institute for several weeks. She tried to resume her life but often felt severe panic, so she went for help to the sanatorium in White Plains where she had been in the 1930's.

Months later she was home in New York City, but the depression lingered, especially in the mornings, when she would find herself crying. One of her last poems, "Little Lobelia's Song," describes a creature who seemed to haunt her with tears. This and some new poems (most written years earlier) were included in Bogan's final volume, *The Blue Estuaries*. While the collection does not contain everything she ever wrote or published, it does offer the best of her work that she wanted to preserve. Praise for the volume was high, if delayed, but Bogan was not cheered. Nor did the 1967 ten-thousand-dollar lifetime award from the National Endowment for the Arts lift her spirits.

A new writing block set in, and this time Bogan could not write anything, not even prose. She decided, at long last, to resign from *The New Yorker* in 1969 and felt immense relief after doing so. Yet the relief did not persist; once more the morning tears came and daytime struggles ensued. She had withdrawn from friends and spent most of her time alone, reading. Her health deteriorated and her depression would not abate. On February 4, 1970, she was discovered dead in her apartment by a friend; she had died of a heart attack.

At the close of her Bennington lecture, Bogan summarized the achievement of women writers by asking what women have said throughout time. She concluded that women have asked the same questions men have asked: "Who am I? From whence did I come? Is there a design in the universe of which I am a part? Do you love me? Shall I die forever?" And these, surely, are the questions that Bogan asked in her own work: Who was she? (How did her heart, mind, and flesh make up the person who loved and suffered?) Where did she come from? (What was her childhood really like, and how did that fit into the woman she became? Who were her literary ancestors, and how was she to come to terms with them?) Was there a design in the universe to which she belonged? (How did she fit in with her contemporaries? How did she lose the God of her Catholic youth?) Was she loved? (And, if not, how would she resolve the absence or betrayal of love?) Would she die forever? (Would her books come back into print? How would she be remembered?)

We remember Louise Bogan, through her writing, as an immensely complicated and compelling woman. She was rarely happy, yet sometimes joyful, and, more often than not, resolute in the face of personal trauma. She wanted to be healed, to endure whatever rakings of the heart were necessary to feel well again. In her poetry she confronted again and again her Fury, her Medusa, and her Daemon—figures no less intimidating on paper than they appeared in her nightmares. She explored her subjects—love, grief, and death—bravely and sensitively. And, for all of her writing life, she endeavored to tell the truth about her life, and to tell it plainly and beautifully.

Selected Bibliography

WORKS OF LOUISE BOGAN

POETRY

Body of This Death: Poems. New York: Robert M. McBride, 1923.

Dark Summer: Poems. New York: Scribners, 1929.

The Sleeping Fury: Poems. New York: Scribners, 1937.

Poems and New Poems. New York: Scribners, 1941.

Collected Poems, 1923–1953. New York: Noonday Press, 1954.

The Blue Estuaries: Poems, 1923–1968. New York: Farrar, Straus & Giroux, 1968; Ecco Press, 1977.

LITERARY CRITICISM

Achievement in American Poetry, 1900–1950. Chicago: Henry Regnery, 1951.

Selected Criticism: Prose, Poetry. New York: Noonday Press, 1955.

A Poet's Alphabet: Reflections on the Literary Art and Vocation. Edited by Robert Phelps and Ruth Limmer. New York: McGraw-Hill, 1970.

MANUSCRIPT PAPERS

The Louise Bogan Papers are at Amherst College. Some of her correspondence is at the American Academy and Institute of Arts and Letters; and the Henry W. and Albert A. Berg Collection, New York Public Library, Astor, Lenox, and Tilden Foundations.

CORRESPONDENCE AND MEMOIRS

What the Woman Lived: Selected Letters of Louise Bogan, 1920–1970. Edited by Ruth Limmer. New York: Harcourt Brace Jovanovich, 1973.

Journey Around My Room: The Autobiography of Louise Bogan—A Mosaic. Edited by Ruth Limmer. New York: Viking Press, 1980.

BIBLIOGRAPHIES

Couchman, Jane. "Louise Bogan: A Bibliography of Primary and Secondary Materials, 1915–1975." *Bulletin of Bibliography*, 33, no. 2:73–77, 104 (February–March 1976); 33, no. 3:111–126, 247 (April–June 1976); 33, no. 4:178–181 (July–September 1976).

Smith, William Jay. *Louise Bogan: A Woman's Words*. Washington, D.C.: Library of Congress, 1971.

TRANSLATED WORKS

The Glass Bees. By Ernst Jünger. New York: Noonday Press, 1960. With Elizabeth Mayer.

Elective Affinities. By Johann Wolfgang von Goethe. Chicago: Henry Regnery, 1963. With Elizabeth Mayer.

The Journal of Jules Renard. New York: George Braziller, 1964. With Elizabeth Roget.

The Sorrows of Young Werther and Novella. By Johann Wolfgang von Goethe. New York: Random House, 1971. With Elizabeth Mayer.

ANTHOLOGY

The Golden Journey: Poems for Young People. Chicago: Reilly & Lee, 1965. Compiled with William Jay Smith.

BIOGRAPHICAL AND CRITICAL STUDIES

Bawer, Bruce. "Louise Bogan's Angry Solitude." *New Criterion*, 3:25–31 (May 1985).

Bowles, Gloria. *Louise Bogan's Aesthetic of Limitation*. Bloomington: Indiana University Press, 1987.

Collins, Martha, ed. *Critical Essays on Louise Bogan*. Boston: G. K. Hall, 1984.

DeShazer, Mary. " 'My Scourge, My Sister': Louise Bogan's Muse." In *Coming to Light: American Women Poets in the Twentieth Century.* Edited by Diane Wood Middlebrook and Marilyn Yalom. Ann Arbor: University of Michigan Press, 1985. Pp. 92–104.

Dorian, Donna. "Knowledge Puffeth Up." *Parnassus: Poetry in Review,* 12–13:144–159 (Spring–Winter 1985). Review of *The Blue Estuaries.*

Frank, Elizabeth P. *Louise Bogan: A Portrait.* New York: Knopf, 1985.

Novack, Michael Paul. "Love and Influence: Louise Bogan, Rolfe Humphries, and Theodore Roethke." *Kenyon Review,* n.s. 7:9–20 (Summer 1985).

Peterson, Douglas L. "The Poetry of Louise Bogan." *Southern Review,* 19:73–87 (Winter 1983).

Ridgeway, Jacqueline. *Louise Bogan.* Boston: Twayne, 1984.

Sarton, May. *A World of Light: Portraits and Celebrations.* New York: W. W. Norton, 1976. Pp. 215–234.

—*WENDY HIRSCH*

Gwendolyn Brooks

1917–

AT THE AGE of seventy, with the publication of *Blacks,* Gwendolyn Brooks set the terms for any and all discussion of her career as an American poet. Within a blue-black flexible binding, the volume's competing typefaces reflect the trajectory of her publishing career from the white New York world of Harper & Row to the black independent presses of Detroit and Chicago: Dudley Randall's Broadside Press; Haki Madhubuti's (Don Lee's) Third World Press; and her own Chicago-based publishing house, The David Company, which she named after her father. Dedicated to her parents, this collection of poems represents the poet's aesthetic *and* political response to her public life. The austere volume requires the audience to reconsider the essential Brooks and to remember that, for her, "Blackness / is a going to essences and to unifyings" ("To Keorapetse," in *Family Pictures*). Those essences and unifyings inform her decision to publish her own work. As she explained in an interview with D. H. Mehlem:

> Satisfactions of publishing my own work: "complete" control over design, print, paper, binding, timing, and, not least, the capitalization of the word Black. . . . The current motion to make the phrase "African American" an official identification is cold and excluding. . . .
>
> The capitalized names *Black* and *Blacks* were appointed to compromise an open, wide-stretching, unifying, empowering umbrella.
>
> The freedom of self-publishing far outweighs what Brooks sees as the "Irks": "distribution, Storage, Printers."

To review her career is to recognize the consistency of her wide-stretching, empowering, "do-right" vision even as her style has contracted and relaxed to accommodate her perception of shifting audiences and social urgencies.

Heir to the expectations of the Harlem Renaissance, Brooks continues to register aesthetically the racial identity crises of the African American poets who continue to marvel at Countee Cullen's "curious thing": "To make a poet black, and bid him sing!" By the late 1960's she had earned the regard of a new generation of black poets as she proclaimed, "True black writers speak *as* blacks, *about* blacks, *to* blacks" ("The Message of Flowers and Fire and Flowers," in Madhubuti's *Say That the River Turns*). Her formative years seemed to her then "years of high poet-incense; the language flowers . . . thickly sweet. Those flowers whined and begged white folks to pick them, to find them lovable. Then— the Sixties: independent fire!" Her daughter, Nora Brooks Blakely, contends that her mother "more than anything else . . . is a 'mapper' . . . delineat[ing] and defin[ing] the scenery of now"

(''Three-Way Mirror,'' in Madhubuti's *Say That the River Turns*). Much of that present-tense scenery has remained remarkably constant as Brooks has charted the experience of being black in Chicago, in the United States (what she would finally call the Warpland).

Though Brooks saw the late 1960's as a time of political and artistic conversion—a time ''to write poems that will successfully 'call' . . . all black people . . . *not* always to 'teach' [but] to entertain, to illumine''—a review of her early expectations suggests that she has been about this all along. Brooks grows impatient with politically aware readers who miss these urgent observations in her early work. In an interview with Claudia Tate, Brooks challenged Tate's assessment that her earlier works lacked ''heightened political awareness.'' She explained:

> I'm fighting for myself a little bit here, but not overly so, because I certainly wrote no poem that sounds like Haki's [Don L. Lee's] ''Don't Cry, Scream''. . . . But I'm fighting for myself a little bit here because I believe it takes a little patience to sit down and find out that in 1945 I was saying what many of the young folks said in the sixties. But it's crowded back into language like this:
>
> *The pasts of his ancestors lean against*
> *Him. Crowd him. Fog out his identity.*
> *Hundreds of hungers mingle with his own,*
> *Hundreds of voices advise so dextrously*
> *He quite considers his reactions his,*
> *Judges he walks most powerfully alone,*
> *That everything is—simply what it is.*
>
> *''The Sundays of Satin-Legs Smith''*
>
> My works express rage and focus on *rage*.

In fact much rage is ''crowded back'' in every gathering of Brooks's poems. And since the expression of anger, if it is righteous anger, is seldom devoid of the redemptive qualities of honor, pride, humor, or love, the absence of these correlatives is notable in Brooks's poetry.

A Gwendolyn Brooks poem offers language or voice to her imagined constituency: the ''old-marrieds'' of Bronzeville who live speechless ''in the crowding darkness''; De Witt Williams; Mrs. Sallie, Pepita, and Melodie Mary in the Mecca; Lincoln West; the Near-Johannesburg Boy. She is at heart a partisan making audible the silent lives of her world: lives in Chicago and, later, Africa. She lends dignity to the individuals and their experiences by giving them names, descriptions—a place. ''I don't start with the landmarks,'' she insists. ''I start with the people'' (*Report from Part One*). Nora Brooks Blakely sees her mother's poems as ''entrances to the lives of people you might, otherwise, never know.''

Finding a poetry suitable to aesthetic *and* social needs has troubled Brooks throughout her career. In competing dedication poems in ''In the Mecca,'' ''The Chicago Picasso,'' and ''The Wall,'' she explores the primary tensions of her art and life not only as a black poet but also as a Chicago-based poet. Though all three are poems of commemoration, they nonetheless ask different and perhaps mutually exclusive questions of the poet. In ''The Chicago Picasso,'' written in August 1967, the Seiji Ozawa–Mayor Daley–Picasso event forces the poet into an uncomfortable relationship with ''Art'':

> Does Man love Art? Man visits Art, but
>   squirms.
> Art hurts. Art urges voyages—
> and it is easier to stay at home,
> the nice beer ready.
>   In commonrooms
> we belch, or sniff, or scratch.
> Are raw.

The monumental art at the center of this poem is set against our animal nature; rather than consoling, this art ''hurts.'' In fact, Brooks sees the folk as subservient to this overwhelming presentation of Culture: ''But we must cook ourselves and style ourselves for Art, who / is a requiring courtesan.'' In an anthropological twist, the civilized / ''the cooked'' devitalizes the primitive / ''the raw.'' This dedicatory poem offers an ultimately sterile, disconnected view of music, art, and politics. Contrary to Carl Sandburg's characterization of the city as a ''Hog Butcher'' in his poem ''Chicago'' (1916), Brooks describes a world of gloss and success where art puts people in their place.

''The Wall,'' also written in August 1967, arises organically from the voices of people not very unlike the folk population of Edgar Lee Masters or Sandburg—except for their powerful blackness. The humility inspired by The Wall supplants the artificial reverence commanded by the Chicago Picasso. Here the poet celebrates, with the rhythmic fervor of Vachel Lindsay, a community in the making, as a slum wall is transformed into an object of reverence and art (the Wall of Respect):

> A drumdrumdrum.
> Humbly we come.
> South of success and east of gloss and glass are sandals;
> flowercloth;
> grave hoops of wood or gold, pendant
> from black ears, brown ears, reddish-brown
> and ivory ears;
> . . . . .
> Women in wool hair chant their poetry.
> . . . .
> On Forty-third and Langly
> . . . .
> All
> worship the Wall.

This projection makes art a vital part of a community. In a curious way, Brooks has rerouted the magi and made their journey a solipsistic one. Here the object of reverence is culturally intrinsic; it is also worthy of respect. The Wall of Respect remains for Brooks an emblem of that historical moment when she recalled ''hot-breathing hope, clean planning, and sizable black cross-reference and reliance'' (interview in *Tri-Quarterly*).

Brooks retains from those years of revolution and protest ''something under-river; pride surviving, pride and self-respect surviving.'' In spite of the flight of many black writers to major white publishing houses, she stands firm in her commitment (born of a time of revolution and nourished in the intervening years) to write for and be published by blacks. She in fact champions a segregated literary criticism. She explained to Tate:

> I believe whites are going to say what they choose to say about us, whether it's right or wrong, or just say *nothing*. . . . We should ignore them. I can no longer decree that we must send our books to black publishers; I would like to say that. I have no intention of ever giving my books to another white publisher. But I do know black publishers are having a lot of trouble. . . .
>
> We must place an emphasis on ourselves and publish as best we can and not allow white critics to influence what we do.

Although she achieved great success at the hands of what she came to regard as an enslaving culture (the Pulitzer Prize in 1950; Guggenheim Fellowships in 1946 and 1947), Brooks no longer courts the white literary establishment or those who indulge in ''literary 'hair-straightening.' ''

Making poems into verbal analogues of the Wall of Respect has done little to ease the tension in Brooks's mind between the desired audience (her people) and her actual audience (the academics of the college classroom). Norris Clark (echoing George Kent) suggests in ''Gwendolyn Brooks and a Black Aesthetic,'' ''It is precisely because Brooks's poetry fails to appeal to the black masses that it appeals aesthetically to the 'blacks who go to college.' '' The political atmosphere of the late 1960's made a poem like ''Riot'' a historical curiosity that survives without context. As Langston Hughes knew all too well, "Politics can be the graveyard of the poet. And only poetry can be his resurrection."

The monumental collection *Blacks* suggests that poetry has always resurrected Brooks. These poems' renewing observations of experience and people are products of "one who distills experience—strains experience" (Brooks's description of the poet). Amid stylistic shifts and historical cataclysms, Brooks keeps her look, her identity. She is a poet, unawed by wonder and comfortable with the stunning quotidian, who knows that, as she says in "The Artists' and Models' Ball":

Wonders do not confuse. We call them that
And close the matter there. But common things
Surprise us. . . .

Even as her poems verbally enact what Brooks calls "brav[ing] our next small business," her life mimics her aesthetic credo: "Live in the along."

This lifelong habit of attending to the available particulars was instilled during Brooks's "sparkly childhood, with two fine parents and one brother, in a plain but warmly enclosing two-story gray house" (*Report from Part One*). For Brooks, "Home meant a quick-walking, careful Duty-Loving mother" and a "father, with kind eyes, songs, and tense recitations" for his children. In dedicating *Blacks* to the memory of her "plain but warmly enclosing" parents, she paid tribute to her family as the original and sustaining force in her life.

Though her parents lived in Chicago, Brooks was born in Topeka, Kansas, on June 7, 1917. Both parents were descendants of blacks who had migrated to Kansas at the end of the Civil War; her father was the son of Lucas Brooks, a runaway slave. Her mother, Keziah Corine Wims, had returned home to her native Kansas for the birth of her first child. Prior to her marriage, Keziah Wims had attended Emporia State Normal School and taught fifth grade at the Monroe School in Topeka. She met David Anderson Brooks during the summer of 1914; they married in July 1916. David Brooks, a native of Atchison, Kansas, had moved to Oklahoma City at the age of nine and remained there until he finished his schooling—of the twelve children in his family, he was the only one to complete high school. He "got up at five o'clock to feed horses and to do other chores, so [he] could go to school." He attended Fisk University in hopes of a medical career but found that family obligations necessitated full-time employment. He became a janitor at the McKinley Music Publishing Company in Chicago. Gwendolyn recalled that though "not many knew of [her] father's lowly calling . . . SOMETHING . . . stamped [her] 'beyond the pale.' " In 1918, when Gwendolyn was sixteen months old, her brother, Raymond, was born. When she was three, the family moved from cramped quarters in Hyde Park to an apartment at Fifty-sixth and Lake Park Avenue. Here Gwendolyn and Raymond could play in the garden plot their mother tilled.

From her father, Gwendolyn acquired a love of "fascinating poetry" and "jolly or haunting songs" that he sang; her favorite was "Asleep in the Deep." Her mother also loved music, played the piano, and was often heard singing "Brighten the Corner Where You Are." The Brooks family encouraged the familiar, the repeatable. Holidays were occasions for well-loved rituals of cooking, singing, and decoration. Gift-giving days necessitated "the bake-eve fun" of baking and wrapping. In particular, Christmas was a time when "certain things were done. Certain things were not done."

One of the things "not done" in the Brooks household was Mother working outside the home. Father furnished "All the Money." Shortfalls in the family account meant that they ate beans and "would have been quite content to entertain a beany diet every day, if necessary . . . if there could be, continuously, the almost musical Peace [they] had most of the time." Home was nourished by her father's "special practical wisdom," which unerringly held the family together. He was a father who "really took time with his children."

Childhood was a time of dancing and dreaming—and writing. School offered little in the way of sweet society. Ostracized because of her appearance (too dark), her shyness, and her inability to "sashay," Brooks retreated into her world of home and imagination. Though her mother recalls her "rhyming at seven," Brooks dates the start of her poetic activity to her eleventh year. Her natural diffidence and her distaste for school-age pastimes like "Post Office" and "Kiss the Pilla" led young Gwendolyn to a discovery of her "in-life."

If Brooks's solitary childhood nurtured her writing, then her encounter with *Writer's Digest* fostered an alternative society as the fledgling poet discovered "*oodles* of *other* writers" who "ached for the want of the right word—reckoned with mean nouns, virtueless adjectives." When Brooks was thirteen, her father gave her a desk "with many little compartments, with long drawers at the bottom, and a removable glass-protected shelf at the top, for books." Here was a place to work, to dream, to reach. Her presiding spirit was Paul Laurence Dunbar (Langston Hughes recalled that "almost every Negro home had a copy of Dunbar"); Brooks wrote a poem every day under his portrait and studied "the Complete Paul Laurence Dunbar." In fact, Keziah Brooks predicted that Gwendolyn would become "the lady Paul Laurence Dunbar."

Brooks wrote daily and read widely. Traces of John Keats and William Wordsworth coexist in her writing with the more dominant voices of the Chicago school (Sandburg, Masters) and the Harlem Renaissance (Dunbar, Hughes, and Cullen). Cullen's *Caroling Dusk: An Anthology of Verse by Negro Poets* (1927) and Hughes's *The Weary Blues* (1926) made Brooks realize that "writing about the ordinary aspects of black life was important." After having endured the "coldness of editors, spent too much money on postage," she experienced her first publishing triumph in 1930, at the age of thirteen: *American Childhood* published "Eventide." Within three years the *Chicago Defender* was regularly accepting Brooks's poems for its column "Lights and Shadows."

By 1934, the year of her high school graduation, Brooks had written to and actually met James Weldon Johnson—the meeting occurred at the insistence of her mother, secure in her belief in Gwendolyn's talent. Johnson did not recall receiving any poems from the young poet, claiming he got "so many of them." He did suggest, however, that her talent would be best served by reading the modern poets. Already secure in her understanding of Hughes and Cullen, she began to read T. S. Eliot, Ezra Pound, and E. E. Cummings. Later that year, Keziah engineered another meeting, this time with Hughes. She "brought a whole pack of stuff" to his reading at the Metropolitan Community Church. Far from dismissing Gwendolyn, Hughes "read [her poems] right there" and declared that she "must go on writing." Though several of her teachers had urged her to continue writing so that she might, one day, be a poet, no classroom encouragement inspired her as much as did Hughes's making time for her work.

Brooks's studies came to an end with her graduation from Wilson Junior College (now Kennedy-King College) in 1936, leaving her to confront the working world. As an educated woman, she was ill prepared for the harsh conditions and humiliating nature of service work. Her flight from her first job as a maid led her to the Illinois State Employment Service—and an even less tolerable position: secretary to Dr. E. N. French, a "spiritual adviser" who sold "Holy

Thunderbolts, charms, dusts of different kinds, love potions'' from the Mecca, the once ''splendid palace, a showplace of Chicago'' that was now ''a great gray hulk of brick.'' Nothing in her early years had prepared Brooks for such a concentration of misery. These experiences resisted fictional treatment and continued to preoccupy her until they surfaced as the poems of *In the Mecca* (1968).

Membership in the NAACP Youth Council offered Brooks more than a community organization, for it was during a meeting at the YWCA on Forty-sixth and South Park that ''the girl who wrote'' met ''a fella who wrote.'' Brooks writes that her ''first 'lover' was [her] husband,'' Henry Lowington Blakely II. Blakely recalls ''a shy brown girl . . . [with a] rich and deep [voice] . . . [whose] shining was inward . . . [and he] felt warm in that shining.'' On September 17, 1939, after ''a nice little wedding'' in her parents' home, Brooks felt ''bleak when . . . taken to [her] kitchenette apartment . . . [and] the cramped dreariness of the Tyson.'' But soon that forbidding atmosphere yielded to the company and the togetherness of ''mutual reading.'' A kitchenette was a place where a son could be ''suddenly born'' (as Henry Lowington Blakely III was on October 10, 1940), where that same son could ''contract broncho-pneumonia,'' or where mice would come out of the radiators ''in droves.'' For Brooks the kitchenette itself would become a controlling metaphor of her first collection of poems, *A Street in Bronzeville* (1945), as well as of her novel, *Maud Martha* (1953). Feeling that ''marriage should get most of a wife's attention,'' she ''scarcely put pen to paper'' for a year after her son's birth.

In 1940 Brooks submitted ''The Ballad of Pearl May Lee'' to the poetry contest of the Negro Exposition. Over the objections of Hughes, the judges awarded the prize to Melvin Tolson, considering Brooks's poem ''too militant.'' In 1941 Brooks and Blakely attended a poetry class at the South Side Community Art Center that was led by ''socially acceptable, wealthy, protected'' Inez Cunningham Stark. Stark wished to be considered ''a friend who loved poetry and respected [her students'] interest in it.'' A reader for *Poetry* magazine, she gave all students a one-year subscription to the journal and ''an education in modern poetry.'' The apprentice poets were serious and enchanted and diligent. And though some went home crying, many learned how to revise. Stark encouraged her students to read and study poetry, to avoid the easy technical device or cliché, to shun the obvious. Her critiques were ''cool, objective, frank.'' Several of Brooks's Bronzeville poems were written under her guidance.

After winning a workshop prize (S. I. Hayakawa was a judge), as well as the 1943 Midwestern Writers' Conference poetry award, Brooks was encouraged to submit her first poetry manuscript to Emily Morison of Alfred A. Knopf (Hughes's publisher). Morison was impressed enough to counsel expanding the number of ''Negro life'' poems. Though Brooks took Morison's advice, she did not resubmit to Knopf but instead sent her manuscript to Harper & Brothers. There an editor showed it to the novelist Richard Wright, who applauded its genuineness and suggested expanding the collection, perhaps by adding a long poem. With the addition of ''The Sundays of Satin-Legs Smith,'' *A Street in Bronzeville* was published in 1945.

In many ways the book marked the end of Brooks's innocent workshop years and the beginning of her career as a poet of national standing. From the generalizing indefinite article (*A*) and the subtitle (*Ballads and Blues*) to the closing sonnet sequence (''Gay Chaps at the Bar''), the poems both carry on the ''tradition'' and defy it. While the poems reflect the influence of the Harlem Renaissance writers and their use of dialect, they more often than not rely upon idiomatic expressions such as one might find in Robert

Frost. Like Frost, Brooks acts as a census-taker, recording the neighborhood's vital statistics and treating every entry with equal disinterest.

It is in this professional distance that Brooks's perceived realism resides. She charts the emotions without emotional display. The collection begins with a series of kitchenette vignettes, progresses to ballads and "The Sundays of Satin-Legs Smith," and ends with the sonnet sequence. More than a response to the South Side's kitchenette ethos or a continuation of the Chicago school of "folk nativist" poets (Sandburg, Masters, Edwin Arlington Robinson), *A Street in Bronzeville* begs for contextual examination as a 1945 reaction to a world of racial, class, and sexual tensions—and war. The black soldiers in these poems project more than masculine racial pride; they are a national challenge to racial relations.

Typical Bronzeville poems foreground the victims. Some are condemned to silence and "crowding darkness" ("the old-marrieds"), while others have life prematurely wrenched from them (the unborn of "the mother"; DeWitt Williams). Brooks is often relentless in the manner in which she captures the "fact" of Bronzeville, as in "the murder":

> This is where poor Percy died,
> Short of the age of one.
> His brother Brucie, with a grin,
> Burned him up for fun.
>
> No doubt, poor Percy watched the fire
> Chew on his baby dress
> With sweet delight, enjoying too
> His brother's happiness.
>
> No doubt, poor Percy looked around
> And wondered at the heat,
> Was worried, wanted Mother,
> Who gossiped down the street.
>
> . . . .
>
> No doubt, poor shrieking Percy died
> Loving Brucie still,
> Who could, with clean and open eye,
> Thoughtfully kill.
>
> Brucie has no playmates now.
> His mother mourns his lack.
> Brucie keeps on asking, "When
> Is Percy comin' back?"

Though the poem is devoid of conventionally realistic detail, the governing impression is one of unerring fidelity to truth. As Brooks jostles us with familiar and pleasing words made terrible—"grin," "fun," "chew"—the repeated chorus of "No doubt" leaves the impression that *here,* in Bronzeville, this is the quotidian.

Many of the poems coalesce into a sharp-edged cast of acquaintances: Matthew Cole "in / The door-locked dirtiness of his room"; Sadie, who "stayed at home" while Maud "went to college" (anticipating Toni Morrison's *Sula* [1973]); the hunchback girl "think[ing] of heaven" (feminizing Dylan Thomas' "The Hunchback in the Park" [1942]); Mrs. Martin's Booker T., "[who] ruined Rosa Brown"; Moe Belle Jackson, whose husband "whipped her good last night" (echoing Billie Holiday's "Ain't Nobody's Business"). Still others require heroes—or antiheroes. "Queen of the Blues" not only updates Hughes's "The Weary Blues" but also reacts to an entire tradition of sorrow songs and folk seculars. "Ballad of Pearl May Lee" provides an early rationale for Brooks's 1951 essay "Why Negro Women Leave Home." Its savage narrator shares the rage and humiliation black women feel when their men "grew up with bright skins on the brain." With "Gay Chaps at the Bar," Brooks forsakes characterization for the sonnet sequence. As Cullen and Claude McKay had done before her, she finds an opportunity for argument in the form itself. The formal shift, from ballads and blues to sonnets, is not jarring; rather, it effects a kind of recessional. Questions of race, identity, and love as they trouble those "home from the front" lack the resolution the narrative poems have. The volume concludes with unexpected irony:

And still we wear our uniforms, follow
The cracked cry of the bugles, comb and brush
Our pride and prejudice . . .

. . . .
For even if we come out standing up
How shall we smile, congratulate: and how
Settle in chairs? Listen, listen. The step
Of iron feet again. And again wild.

Patrons of poetry, familiar with Hughes and accustomed to Frost and Stephen Vincent Benét and Edna St. Vincent Millay, eagerly received the Bronzeville poems. Liberal readers, "comfortable" with the racial themes, neglected the harsh commentary that was contained within what Brooks herself called a "rather folksy narrative." *The New York Times Book Review* (November 4, 1945) found "the idiom . . . colloquial, the language . . . universal." *Poetry* (December 1945) praised her "capacity to marry the special qualities of her racial tradition with the best attainments of our poetic tradition"; *Saturday Review* (January 19, 1945) considered the poems to be a "poignant social document";
The New Yorker (September 22, 1945) praised the freshness of "her folk poetry of the city."

More important was the approbation of Brooks's peers. Cullen wrote to her on August 24, 1945, "I am glad to be able to say 'welcome' to you to that too small group of Negro poets, and to the larger group of American ones. No one can deny your place there." McKay followed with an equally congratulatory note on October 10: "[I] welcome you among the band of hard working poets who do have something to say." But it was Hughes's loving review in the *Chicago Defender* (September 1, 1946) that must have brought Brooks the greatest joy: "This book is just about the BIGGEST little two dollars worth of intriguing reading to be found in the bookshops these atomic days. It will give you something to talk about from now until Christmas." Critics such as Houston A. Baker, Jr., Gary Smith, and George Kent agree that many of these poems were revolutionary in the way they dealt with race and sexual relationships; they disagree on whether Brooks was seeking to universalize the plight of her subjects.

In addition to the local success of *A Street in Bronzeville*, the book garnered numerous prizes for the poet. By the time Brooks published *Annie Allen* (1949), she had won the *Mademoiselle* Merit Award (1945), Guggenheim Fellowships (1946, 1947), the American Academy of Arts and Letters Grant for Creative Writing (1946), and *Poetry*'s Eunice Tietjens Memorial Prize (1949). In the process she became a recognized writer and began to write reviews for the *Chicago Daily News* and the *Chicago Sun-Times*. This hometown work led to reviewing for Hoyt Fuller's *Negro Digest, The New York Times*, and the *New York Herald Tribune*. She "stopped reviewing because I decided that even a reviewer . . . should have read Everything." Brooks does recall that "while I Had At It, I was exuberant." Besides her excitement at receiving the packages of reviewer's copies, she relished the opportunity to share and support.

No matter how history recalls Brooks's literary contributions to the years 1941–1949, Brooks remembers the period as her "party era," a time when "party" became a verb. Unlike her solitary childhood and adolescent years, these were times when "merry Bronzevillians" put on the spread and "conversation was our 'mary jane.' " The best parties were at 623 East Sixty-third Street, Brooks's "most exciting kitchenette." Like Hughes, Brooks found her best material when "walking or running, fighting or screaming or singing" beneath her window. And as if to commemorate this shared vision, Hughes came to Brooks's exciting kitchenette for the party of the decade. Having finished at the Lab School in

Chicago, he chose her party for his farewell to Chicago and claimed that it was the ''*Best* party . . . I've ever been given!'' Brooks ''squeezed perhaps a hundred people into our Langston Hughes two-room kitchenette party. Langston was the merriest and the most colloquial of them all. . . . He enjoyed everyone; he enjoyed all the talk, all the phonograph blues, all the festivity in the crowded air.''

With *Annie Allen,* Brooks advanced beyond the loose vignettes and sonnets of the Bronzeville poems, preferring to trace the arc of a single character's life. Unable to ignore the war entirely, she dedicated the volume to Edward Bland, a friend whom she had first met in Inez Cunningham Stark's poetry class, and who had died in Germany in March 1945, and introduced it with the elegiac ''Memorial to Ed Bland.'' The dedication and poem appear before the table of contents, as though separate from the rest of the collection. The bold captions and headline-like titles turn the contents page into a poem itself and make it clear that the poet is responding to literary as well as reportorial instincts in this collection. The opening sequence, ''Notes from the Childhood and the Girlhood,'' though a bit more contracted than earlier poems, is familiar to readers of the Bronzeville collection. For these are poems where reality and imagination always collide. However ''pinchy'' the world, it ''prances nevertheless with gods and fairies.'' The central sequence, a mock epic titled ''The Anniad,'' contends with the literary world beyond the Chicago street noises. The hyperconscious lapidary language, the contracted lines, and the seven-line stanzas hurl Annie into an excessively ornamental and artificial world:

> Vaunting hands are now devoid.
> Hieroglyphics of her eyes
> Blink upon paradise
> Paralyzed and paranoid.
> But idea and body too
> Clamor ''Skirmishes can do.
> Then he will come back to you.''

Brooks, attempting a stylistic tour de force, seems to have tired of black vernacular structures and white strictures upon style and content. She succeeds on a stylistic level but overwhelms the ordinariness of her subject matter with that success. The work recovers in ''Appendix to 'The Anniad' '' and the final ''Womanhood'' sequences, where the narrative pulse is palpable and the style is Brooks's own. Mature Annie's laments—''People who have no children can be hard''; ''What shall I give my children? who are poor?''—complement the expanded focus of these final sonnets.

If Brooks expected more of her readers, she had expected much more of herself. With *Annie Allen,* she sought to identify herself both with and against the tradition. These conflicting needs confused reviewers. The complexity of the volume caused many readers to complain that these weren't Bronzeville poems. But Phyllis McGinley, in *The New York Times Book Review* (January 22, 1950), saw that as an advantage. Singling out ''The Anniad'' for special praise, she claimed that Brooks was best when she forgot ''her social conscience and her Guggenheim scholarship,'' thereby ''creating unbearable excitement.'' In spite of the mixed reception accorded the collection, it was awarded the Pulitzer Prize in 1950. Though Brooks was the first black writer to win a Pulitzer in any category, she did not establish a precedent, merely a referent. It would be thirty-three years before another black woman would win (Alice Walker in 1983).

Some critics see *Annie Allen* as Brooks's first important work. Baker situates the collection in the greater swirl of modernism; in the book's echoing of Ernest Hemingway, Eliot, and Pound, it ''join[ed] the mainstream of twentieth-century poetry in its treatment of the terrors of war.''

Haki Madhubuti (Don Lee) reads its importance in a different way:

> *Annie Allen* (1949), important? Yes. Read by blacks? No. *Annie Allen* more so than *A Street in Bronzeville* seems to have been written for whites. . . . [''The Anniad''] requires unusual concentrated study. . . .This poem is probably earth-shaking to some, but leaves me completely dry. . . .
>
> There is an over-abundance of the special appeal to the world-runners. . . .

By the late 1960's, Brooks would join Madhubuti in his assessment of this successful period of her career. But for the moment, the Pulitzer brought with it public recognition and a national reputation.

The birth of her daughter, Nora, on September 8, 1951, convinced Brooks to leave the Kalamazoo, Michigan, home to which the family had moved in 1948. In spite of their wish to escape the racial tensions and claustrophobic conditions of inner-city life, the family returned to Chicago and by 1953 had their own home, at 7428 South Evans Avenue, near the University of Chicago.

In ''How I Told My Child About Race'' (1951), however, Brooks recorded an unsettling experience. When she and her son were walking home, they were assaulted by stone-throwing young whites in that very ''university district, mecca of basic enlightenment and progressive education. . . . The buildings, with their delicate and inspiring spires, seemed . . . to leer, to crowd us with mutterings—'Oh no, you black bodies!—no sanctuary here.' '' This incident forced a mother to explain not what race is but why it is what it is. Long before Brooks would turn to the Pan-African movement for identity, she refused to drag ''the subject of 'race' down for frequent examination and hammering, because [she thought] that children should be helped to view the samenesses among themselves and others.''

In 1953 Brooks published her ''autobiographical novel,'' *Maud Martha*. Favoring the ''nuanceful, allowing'' form of the novel over the memoir, she nonetheless reads herself into every page. Here ''fact-meat'' combines with ''chunks of fancy'' to build a narrative familiar to readers of her earlier works. Lower-class, vignetted titles echo strategies from the Bronzeville poems and prepare us for the dailiness of the lives within. Known faces and circumstances crowd the story of Maud's coming of age and young married life. A larger cast of kitchenette folks—Binnie, Mrs. Teenie Thompson, Mr. and Mrs. Whitestripe—is ''real,'' as are many of the heroine's adventures. The slights and daily indignities (''the self-solace''), the masculine domination of Maud's every move, prompt what Brooks later called ''woman rage.'' In ''brotherly love,'' as she dresses a chicken, Maud's empathy is allowed to go beyond the human circumstances:

> But if the chicken were a man!—cold man with no head or feet and with all the little feather, hairs to be pulled, and the intestines loosened and beginning to ooze out, and the gizzard yet to be grabbed and the stench beginning to rise! And yet the chicken was a sort of person, a respectable individual, with its own kind of dignity. The difference was in the knowing. What was unreal to you, you could deal with violently.

Much later, as if anticipating the animal-rights movement, Brooks would reinforce this notion of chickens as ''people'': ''people, that is, in the sense that we conceive people to be: things of identity and response.''

Maud Martha received polite reviews that dismissed it with annoyance or faint praise. *The New Yorker* (October 10, 1953) complained that it was but a ''series of sketches''; the *Southern Review* (October 1953) found it an ''ingratiating first novel.'' Only the *Chicago Defender* (September 30, 1953) saw how the novel ''struck at the twisted roots of racial antagonisms.'' In the wake of feminist criticism, some contemporary critics (particularly Mary Helen Washington and Patricia and Vernon Lattin) see it as a revolutionary work. Washington, attacking earlier views of the work as full of "optimism and faith," sees it instead as a work straining to contain its "bitterness, rage, self-hatred, and silence." Rarely in Brooks's oeuvre is there such a challenge to work against the pleasures of the narrative line and decode the savage "woman rage" just underneath. Here she uses the homey story to mask its own meanings, forcing the reader to translate not merely the black cultural context but the feminist context as well.

The rest of the 1950's were mostly spent addressing the needs of Brooks's children at home—and in verse. In 1956 *Bronzeville Boys and Girls* was published. These poems, juvenile reductions of her "adult" poems, are serious considerations of poverty, racism, and loneliness. Though offset by the lively rhythms and sound patterns, the sober vision of this childhood world remains. Reviewers, comfortable with their Gwendolyn Brooks "slot," tended to see the poems as universal expressions, rhythmic and simple. The *New York Herald Tribune Book Review* (November 18, 1956) explained the secret of the book: "Because Miss Brooks is a Negro poet, she has called these *Bronzeville Boys and Girls,* but they are universal and will make friends anywhere, among grown-ups or among children from eight to ten."

With the death of her mentor, Inez Cunningham Stark, on August 19, 1957, and of her father, on November 21, 1959, Brooks assumed greater responsibilities in her life and art. She reconsidered early experiences in the hopes of writing another novel, the tale of an unfortunate, dark-skinned boy named Lincoln West. Though she published poetic versions of little Lincoln's life, she left the novel unfinished. She also hoped to tell the story of the Mecca and Dr. E. N. French but, like Lincoln's tale, this would have to await a poetic treatment. With two major collections behind her, and having achieved a certain celebrity, Brooks entered a new decade, one in which she would become mentor to yet another generation.

With *The Bean Eaters* (1960), Brooks advanced to a new level of technical and aesthetic power as well as of social conscience. Originally entitled "Bronzeville Men and Women," the collection takes seriously what Kent sees as its association with Vincent van Gogh's *The Potato Eaters.* The world of these poems is one of poverty, dim spirits, and truncated hopes. Rather than presenting "acceptable" vignettes of blacks, these poems "massage the hate-[she]-had" as they address the world. Much of the book's drama draws upon Brooks's father's presiding spirit, evident in the opening "In Honor of David Anderson Brooks, My Father":

> A dryness is upon the house
> My father loved and tended.
> Beyond his firm and sculptured door
> His light and lease have ended.
>
> . . . .
>
> He who was Goodness, Gentleness,
> And Dignity is free,
> Translated to public Love
> Old private charity.

"Goodness, Gentleness, / And Dignity" abound in the life moments of *The Bean Eaters,* expanding upon what Stanley Kunitz praised as "the warmly and generously human" side of *Annie Allen.*

The Bean Eaters depends less upon its cast of characters for effect and more upon the depth of social and moral decisions it gives voice to. In this collection, language pulses and despair intensifies as Brooks searches beyond Bronzeville for meaning in the black experience. The topicality of this collection does not depend upon the war, but advances to consider the civil-rights news from the South. As the opening poem, "The Explorer," suggests, the volume works "to find a still spot in the noise. . . . a satin peace somewhere.'' But in the end the poems derive their energy from ''Only spiraling, high human voices, / the scream of nervous affairs, / Wee griefs, / Grand griefs. And choices''—choices made, choices denied, choices ''that cried to be taken.'' For the couple in ''The Bean Eaters,'' the choice seems to have been one of acceptance of their lot:

They eat beans mostly, this old yellow pair.
Dinner is a casual affair.
Plain chipware on a plain and creaking
    wood,
Tin flatware.

Two who are Mostly Good.
Two who have lived their day,
But keep on putting on their clothes
And putting things away.

And remembering . . .
Remembering, with twinklings and twinges,
As they lean over the beans in their rented back
        room
    that is full of beads and receipts and
        dolls and cloths,
    tobacco crumbs, vases and fringes.

Brooks unassumingly intensifies the couple's poverty, relying upon the choral effect of ''mostly'' and the ''ing'' of participials and gerunds. However present-tense the action, the sheer routine of the couple draws the poem into memories of the detritus of their lives. While they seem never to have had any choices in their lives, they have endured. In startling contrast to this aged pair, the young toughs of ''We Real Cool'' opt for pool—and early death. Unlike the voice of Hughes's ''Motto'' (''I play it cool / and dig all the jive / That's the reason / I stay alive''), Brooks's pool players ''left school . . . sing sin . . . thin gin . . . die soon.'' ''Say the 'We' softly,'' says Brooks, because ''the boys have no accented sense of themselves, yet they are aware of a semi-defined personal importance'' (*Report from Part One*).

That ill-defined need for personal importance carries over to the topical poems ''A Bronzeville Mother Loiters in Mississippi. Meanwhile, a Mississippi Mother Burns Bacon'' and ''The *Chicago Defender* Sends a Man to Little Rock.'' Although Brooks had always been engaged in the race crisis in America, she found in the Emmett Till case a terrifyingly comprehensible extreme of what she had witnessed in Chicago. The Till case at first seems so horrible as to warrant a literary analogue: ''From the first it had been like a / Ballad.'' But, pursuing the literary whiteness and blackness, Brooks sees a literary and social worldview collapse as it relates to blacks:

    The fun was disturbed, then all but
    nullified
    When the Dark Villain was a blackish
    child
    Of fourteen, with eyes still too young
    to be dirty,
    And a mouth too young to have lost
    every reminder
    Of its infant softness.

With ''terrifying clarity'' the Till diptych reacts to both the murder and the acquittal of the accused murderer, exposing a world of racist inversions where ''white'' is ''black'' and ''grown-ups'' are ''bab[ies] full of tantrums.'' The poem itself becomes an agent of the ''meddling'' North with its ''pepper-words, 'bestiality,' and 'barbarism,' / and / 'Shocking.' '' As in earlier poems of ''woman rage,'' Brooks plumbs the distortion of sexuality in the case: chivalry as an excuse for murder. A chain of empathy is forged between women as the accused murderer's wife comes to hate the circumstances of her life:

Then a sickness heaved within her. Then
    courtroom Coca-Cola,
The courtroom beer and hate and sweat and
    drone,
Pushed like a wall against her. She wanted to
    bear it.
But his mouth would not go away and neither
    would the

Decapitated exclamation points in that Other
Woman's eyes.

The only poetic resolution for Brooks is to yield a severed, truncated verse—"The Last Quatrain of the Ballad of Emmett Till"—to Mrs. Till, a fellow Chicago mother: "She kisses her killed boy. / And she is sorry." As the *ks* collide, love, sexuality, and death seem inextricably linked.

The Chicago-Mississippi connections were part of Brooks's neighborhood sensibility. The *Defender,* in part responsible for the Great Migration of blacks from the rural South to Chicago after World War I, had made it a policy to keep Mississippi on its front page. Lynching was a metaphor for life in the South. For white America, the Till case was the horrible exception; for Brooks and readers of the *Defender,* it was the rule. These connections grew in generalization in "The *Chicago Defender* Sends a Man to Little Rock." The reporter discovers a place of families, baseball, concerts, hymns—where evil wears a human face. Like the "ballad" of Till, the "saga" of Little Rock is a "puzzle." The reporter unearths unmentionable news: " 'They are like people everywhere.' " In an unexpectedly Audenesque conclusion, Brooks declaims, "The loveliest lynchee was our Lord."

If *The Bean Eaters* was but a collection of "Negro poems," reviewers might have been more receptive. But in her extended poem "The Lovers of the Poor," Brooks challenges race, class, and "do-goodism." The ladies from the Ladies' Betterment League mean well but know little and care less about the root causes of the poverty and race enslavement of the "voiceless." They discover that

. . . it's all so bad! and entirely too
much for them.
The stench; the urine, cabbage, and dead
beans,
Dead porridges of assorted dusty grains,
The old smoke, *heavy* diapers, and they're
told,
Something called chitterlings. The darkness.
Drawn
Darkness, or dirty light. The soil that stirs.
. . . .

They've never seen such a make-do-ness as
Newspaper rugs before!

More accustomed to "the nice Art Institute," the ladies seek a less distressing project. Many readers, comfortable with the Southern civil-rights poems, felt somewhat abused as Brooks turned her lyric attack toward class indifference. Unlike Hughes's "Dinner Guest: Me" ("I know I am / the Negro Problem"), Brooks's "Lovers of the Poor" are forced to visit the "Problem."

Whether in the alleys and tenements of Chicago or in the red dirt roads and shacks of Mississippi, Brooks depicts a world where blacks are always at risk. Unlike many topical poems, these civil-rights pieces have survived their inspiration.

Reviewers, uneasy with the book's topicality, found comfort in identifying *The Bean Eaters* as a collection of "social" poems, as if the category ameliorated their unease. Retrospectively, critics have marveled at the way in which Brooks turned "raw materials" into "artistry"; Baker saw the Till sequence in a psychological and political light, claiming that it was "an evocation of the blood-guiltiness of the white psyche in an age of dying colonialism"; Jean Marie Miller, in "The World of Gwendolyn Brooks," claimed that "Brooks spans races in her poetry, not by reaching for a pre-existing Western universalism, but by exploring and digging deeply enough into the Black experience to touch that which is common to men everywhere." In 1972 Madhubuti saw the major weakness of the book as its "quiet confirmation of the 'Negro' as equal," failing to assess the enemies of blacks accurately.

The social turbulence of the 1960's asked much of Brooks. On the one hand, she had achieved fame as the most honored "Negro poetess" in America. On the other hand, the Pulitzer and Guggenheim awards came at the expense of her poems (who among her readers really heard the anger and despair?), and the success that seemed to be isolating her from her people concerned her on both a literary and a social level. As political challenges became more frequent, the media became increasingly chary in areas touching upon race. Early in 1962, Kent recounts in his biography of Brooks, New York radio station WNEW denied airtime to a musical setting of "Of De Witt Williams on His Way to Lincoln Cemetery" because of the word "black." The station's management claimed the reference would outrage "Negro" listeners. Brooks, following liberation movements in Africa, failed to believe that a word with such currency in Africa could give offense. At mid-career she saw this as an opportunity to emphasize her commitment to the greater political implications: "For seventeen years. Without ever detouring from my Business—which is being a writer. Many of the banners so brightly (and originally, they think) waved by today's youngsters I waved twenty years ago, and published sixteen years ago."

Brooks's need to share her work with the young led her to the classroom, informally at first and then professionally. Invited to read at the White House in 1962, Brooks used that and other public occasions to use fame for fortune so that she could fund programs and awards in creative writing. Her teaching career began in September 1963, when Mirron Alexandroff, president of Chicago's Columbia College, invited her to run a poetry workshop: "Do anything you want with it. . . . Take it outdoors. Take it to a restaurant—run it in a restaurant, a coffee shop. Do absolutely anything you want with it. *Anything!*" She accepted the challenge of trying "to enjoy this thing [she] had never done before." Appearing in her "new little professor's blue suit," she sought to communicate what Inez Cunningham Stark had given to her: "the knowledge, the magic, the definitions" (*Report from Part One*).

The workshop at Columbia College led to more teaching, at Elmhurst College (Illinois), Northeastern Illinois State College, the University of Wisconsin–Madison, Columbia University, and the City University of New York. She found the excitement and challenge of teaching, and the freedom to experiment, most gratifying. But after suffering a small heart-attack on Christmas Day of 1971, she bade the classroom a "final Goodbye." Though uncertain whether writing can be taught, Brooks nonetheless believed that teachers can "explain the wonders" of poetry and "oblige the writing student to write." She met students' protestations and pleas—"Can't do it. CanNOT do it"—with a refusal to reconsider her demanding assignments, "telling them they were insulting their college and their own intellects." She provided tickets to "deputized" students so that they could attend poetry readings and report back to the class. She discovered the shared secret of teaching: "Such activities . . . enabled *me* to enjoy a class—and when I enjoyed it, almost without exception so did my students."

Teaching, coupled with the "news at home," encouraged Brooks to re-envision the work included in *Selected Poems* (1963). This gathering of poems cemented Brooks's critical reputation. *The New York Times* felt confident enough to claim that "Miss Brooks won a Pulitzer Prize in 1950 and deserved it." Reviewers in *Poetry* and the *Saturday Review* praised her idiomatic language, claiming it was the key to her ability to universalize and empathize. The praise showered on the volume overlooked the topical addition of "Riders to the Blood-Red Wrath." Written in 1963, the poem commemorated the Freedom Rides of 1961. The subject matter fairly rips at the poem's formal fabric:

My proper prudence toward his proper probe
Astonished their ancestral seemliness.
It was a not-nice risk, a wrought risk, was
An indelicate risk, they thought. And an excess.

With *Selected Poems* Brooks seems to have willed a formal closure to "Part One" of her writing career. Her relationship with Harper & Row would not end until after the publication of *The World of Gwendolyn Brooks* (1971), but that collection would strain to contain *In the Mecca.* Though she could but dimly perceive the direction her career would take, Brooks knew that her poetry had already taken her far beyond what was acceptable for a "Negro" poet in America.

As early as August 1962, Brooks had written to her editor at Harper & Row about her "Mecca" poem: "I can't give up on the thing; it has a grip on me." Readings, teaching, and family matters kept her from a full commitment to this nagging project. But it was not until she attended the Second Fisk University Writers' Conference in April 1967 that the requisite inspiration and political fire came to her. Used to being "loved" at readings and lectures, Brooks discovered that here, among the "New Blacks," she was "coldly Respected." Here Imamu Amiri Baraka (LeRoi Jones) shouted, "Up against the wall, Brother! KILL 'EM ALL!" And here Brooks met blacks understood by *no* whites, especially "professional Negro understanders." On December 28, 1969, a tribute to Brooks at Chicago's Affro-Arts Theatre continued her induction in the world of "New Blacks" as well as provided the meeting ground for her future biographer, George Kent. Schooled now by her juniors, she "enter[ed] at least the kindergarten of new consciousness" (*Report from Part One*). A year before the assassination of Martin Luther King, Jr., these blacks recognized the imminent collapse of integration as a social idea. Brooks heard the cry of Madhubuti's "New Integrationist," who sought "integration / of / negroes / with / black / people." What did Brooks discover? Black pride? Cultural nationalism? "You may use any label you wish," she says (quoted in Kent, *A Life of Gwendolyn Brooks*). "All I know is when people started talking about Blacks loving, respecting, and helping one another, that was enough for me." The passive spectatorship of the Bronzeville poems was gone for good. It was no longer enough to share through description the circumstances of being black. Madhubuti writes, "Brooks' post 1967 poetry is fat-less. Her new work resembles a man getting off meat, turning to a vegetarian diet" (Preface to *Report from Part One*).

In the Mecca bears more than traces of the Fisk "fever." Buoyed by her poetry workshop with a Chicago street gang, the Blackstone Rangers, Brooks found the street energy necessary to complete her long-stalled "Mecca" work. The book-length poem is at once an indictment of racism and poverty symbolized by an apartment building, the "once splendid palace" at Thirty-fourth Street between State and Dearborn that had collapsed into a littered and dangerous ruin—and a mystery story. The narrative, "a mosaic of daily affairs," spins around the search for the lost Pepita, the youngest of Mrs. Sallie Smith's nine children. After a sharp-focused introduction to Mrs. Sallie's domestic sphere, the poem inches out into corridors of threat and dirt, dishonor and decay, tedium and nobility. Gangs threaten from without, poverty and craziness from within. Characters are at once particularized—we learn quickly to distinguish the voices of Loam Norton, Way-Out Morgan, Melodie Mary—and homogenized into a collective response to Mrs. Sallie's "Where Pepita?": "*Ain seen er I ain seen er I ain seen er* / Ain seen er I ain seen er I ain seen her."

Fractured narrative lines carry the news that many Meccans, as Melodie Mary knows, are as trapped as the rats and roaches that share their space. That Pepita has in fact been killed by a tenant, Jamaican Edward, seems at once incidental and central to the fury and frustrations of the Mecca: "Hateful things sometimes befall the hateful / but the hateful are not rendered lovable thereby." How like the aborted fetuses of "the mother"—those whose "births and . . . names . . . straight baby tears . . . and games" were stolen—is this "little woman [who] lies in dust with roaches"—who "never went to kindergarten . . . never learned that black is not beloved."

The "After Mecca" section both honors heroes, past and present, and severs ties with the old consciousness. Elegies for Medgar Evers and Malcolm X are celebrations of black manhood in the light of the new black nationalism. The monument of "The Wall" towers over that of "The Chicago Picasso" in terms of black pride and aesthetic significance. "Sermons on the Warpland" confronts the essence of Ron Karenga's assertion: "The fact that we are black is our ultimate reality."

Contemporary reviews reflect the ways in which Brooks's "blackening language" left many white readers uneasy and guilt-ridden. M. L. Rosenthal, in *The New York Times* (March 2, 1969), stunned by "the horrid predicament of real Americans whose everyday world haunts the nation's conscience intolerably," nonetheless found the poems (especially the title sequence) "overwrought." A reviewer in the *Virginia Quarterly* (Winter 1969) complained that Brooks was "more self-consciously a Negro than ever before. . . . It is a new manner and a new voice for Miss Brooks, better than her earlier work in its honesty, poorer in its loss of music and control." William Stafford in *Poetry* (March 1969) complained of excessively local references. Madhubuti saw value in this unease, claiming that "*In the Mecca* 'blacked' its way out of the National Book Award in 1968"—thereby creating a new aesthetic, a new identity, for Brooks (Preface, *Report from Part One*).

As poet laureate of Illinois (appointed in 1968), Brooks continued her creative-writing outreach programs for elementary and secondary students. Funding scholarships, prizes, and trips to Africa, she seemed intent upon making writing an agent of social change and black pride. In December 1969 she separated from her husband and "the hard, demanding state of marriage"; she saw the subsequent stage of her life as her "next future," in which she would write poems "that [would] somehow successfully 'call' . . . all black people: black people in taverns, black people in alleys, black people in gutters, schools, offices, factories, prisons, the consulate" (*Report from Part One*). Her husband, an ardent integrationist, failed to agree with "the new, young movements among blacks."

A year of nightmare inversions and violence, 1968 became the vortex of aesthetic and political conversion for many American poets. While Robert Lowell retreated into history and sonnets, Adrienne Rich shrugged off all formal constraints (marriage as well as poetic conventions) in search of a language capable of articulating the time. Rage of a lifetime, distilled in a year, led Brooks away from New York and Harper & Row to Detroit and Broadside Press. The relationship with Harper & Row had always been cordial, but as Madhubuti records, "Harper's never . . . pushed the work of Gwendolyn Brooks" (Preface, *Report from Part One*). *The World of Gwendolyn Brooks* (1971) ended her association with the white publishing world. She no longer believed that blacks could afford the individual acceptance proffered by white America; black success depended upon collective association and action.

Broadside Press brought the congenial editorial support of Dudley Randall as well as a radically different-looking Brooks book. *Riot* (1969), the dust jacket states, "is a poem in three parts . . . aris[ing] from the disturbances in Chicago after the assassination of Martin Luther King in 1968." The natural informality of the volume resides in the startling "Black Expression" frontispiece by

Jeff Donaldson, the open typeface and relaxed page layout, the manuscript-page insert—and the jacket photo of Brooks, "a sister who kept her natural." Never before had Brooks been as transparently confrontational as in "Riot," a poem where black anger is unleashed upon the "desperate" and wealthy John Cabot. Lacking the strong narrative fabric of such class-violence poems as "The Lovers of the Poor," "Riot" is pure revolt:

But, in a thrilling announcement, on It drove
and breathed on him: and touched him. In that
    breath
the fume of pig foot, chitterling and cheap chili,
malign, mocked John. And, in terrific touch, old
averted doubt jerked forward decently,
cried "Cabot! John! You are a desperate man,
and the desperate die expansively today."

John Cabot went down in the smoke and fire
and broken glass and blood, and he cried "Lord!
Forgive these nigguhs that know not what they
    do."

The class polarizations of the poem intensify the rage and poverty of the "sweaty and unpretty" blacks, the disgust and wealth of "John Cabot, out of Wilma, once a Wycliffe." Cabot serves as more than a class symbol; for Brooks, he is a failed white aesthetic. The "rightness" he represents might as well be the rightness of the Pulitzer committee, the Guggenheim jury, the editors at Harper & Row. "The Third Sermon on the Warpland," more deliberately topical than "Riot," seeks a local as well as a general sense of the riots.

A series of sharply focused chapbooks—*Family Pictures* (1970), *Aloneness* (1971), *Beckonings* (1975), and *Primer for Blacks* (1980)—record Brooks's swiftly evolving sense of African family identity. Her trips to East Africa (1971) and West Africa (1974) were a necessary completion of her developing appreciation for her African identity. In spite of her need for assimilation in Kenya, she recognized immediately that she came bearing her "own hot just-out-of-the-U.S. smile." The "African Fragment" of *Report from Part One* (1972) charts a discovery both joyous and sad, for in Africa, Brooks encountered the fact of her lost culture: language, clothes, pride stripped away by the "Jamestown experiment." In 1973, reunited with her husband, she traveled to England. In the summer of 1974 they visited Ghana, England, and France.

As if to compensate for a heritage of deprivation, Brooks redoubled her efforts on behalf of the young. Poetry contests, scholarships, teaching about Africa and African Americans, travel grants so that the young might visit the "homeland"—Brooks made history, language, poetry into a continuum of race pride. The spirit of the Fisk conference pulsed life into Brooks's rescue missions. No longer was she content to describe despair; the time had come to avert despair. Tutored by raging youths at mid-life, she discovered things urgent and life-sustaining. Now it was her turn to save the young. In "To the Young Who Want to Die," she writes:

Sit down. Inhale. Exhale.
The gun will wait. The lake will wait.
The tall gall in the small seductive vial
will wait will wait:
will wait a week: will wait through April.
You do not have to die this certain day.
Death will abide, will pamper your
    postponement.
I assure you death will wait. Death has
a lot of time. Death can
attend to you tomorrow. Or next week. Death is
just down the street; is most obliging neighbor;
can meet you any moment.

You need not die today.
Stay here—through pout or pain or peskyness.
Stay here. See what the news is going to be
    tomorrow.

Graves grow no green that you can use.
Remember, green's your color. You are Spring.

Many of the works dedicated to children and adolescents—*Aloneness, The Tiger Who Wore White Gloves; or, What You Are, You Are* (1974) *Family Pictures,* and *Young Poet's Primer* (1980)—are in fact celebrations of the black family. As she explained in her address at Madhubuti's Twentieth Anniversary Conference on Literature and Society (December 1987):

I believe that writers should be writing more about the Black family. The Black family is really being hounded and hounded these days, and I feel we ''ordinary'' Black people shouldn't leave all the assessments of our essence to the likes of Bill Moyers, nor to Alvin Poussaint. We have tongues. We have calculating eyes.

In spite of pressure from feminist critics, Brooks has held the subject of the integrity of the black family above women's rights. She explained in an interview with Ida Lewis:

Relations between men and women seem disordered to me. . . . I think Women's Lib is not for black women for the time being, because black men *need* their women beside them, supporting them in these very tempestuous days.

Family Pictures offers a plausible trajectory for this life of new Pan-African imagination. For Brooks the hope begins with the individual life—even if that individual is the ''Ugliest little boy / that everybody ever saw'' (''The Life of Lincoln West'')—and then, and only then, can it advance to heroes, young and old. Her message is consistent in ''Speech to the Young'':

> And remember:
> live not for the Battles Won.
> Live not for The-End-of-the-Song.
> Live in the along.

This commitment to a life of action rather than victory allows Brooks the freedom to savor the dedication of the Gwendolyn Brooks Junior High School (Elmhurst, Illinois) more than her reading at the White House. However pleasant the January 1980 reading with Robert Hayden and Stanley Kunitz, the November 1981 dedication was the very embodiment of her social program. As Madhubuti wrote, Brooks had become ''a consistent monument in the real, unaware of the beauty and strength she had radiated.'' Honorary consultant to the Library of Congress in 1973, she served as a poetry consultant in 1985–1986. Somewhat inadvertently Brooks became a necessary reference for black *and* white readers.

In *to disembark* (1981) and *The Near-Johannesburg Boy and Other Poems* (1986) Brooks shuffled new poems in with old, providing a historical context for a younger audience. At the age of seventy her message remained quite clear: stay alive long enough to learn who you are—and, unlike the tiger who wore white gloves, learn to appreciate the fact that ''what you are you are.'' Though she vehemently rejects the notion of ''universal'' elements in her work, preferring to see herself as an African poet writing for a global black audience, Brooks continues to attract a diverse readership.

She also continues to draw admiration and honors from old and new audiences. The larger American literary community has come around to Madhubuti's belief that Brooks is ''a Living National Treasure.'' In 1987 she was elected an honorary fellow of the Modern Language Association. Since compiling *Blacks,* she has published *Gottschalk and the Grande Tarantelle* (1988). The collection includes ''Winnie,'' a tribute to Winnie and Nelson Mandela, as well as the title-sequence ''snapshot'' of Louis Moreau Gottschalk. In an interview with Mehlem, Brooks explained the larger significance of the poem:

The title poem . . . does exactly what I wanted it to do. There—are—The—Slaves: you are aware of the horror of their crisis *and* you are aware of the fact that human beings *will* break away from ache to dance, to sing, to create, no matter how briefly, how intermittently.

In this poem Brooks sees herself as a "reporter," investigating the appropriation of black culture by greedy whites: "Gottschalk, Elvis Presley, George Gershwin, Stephen Foster, etc., have molded Black exhilaration and richness into money-making forms." She provides "the *scheduled* insinuation that other whites have done likewise."

Brooks maintains a schedule of readings, lectures, and workshops throughout the country. In addition, she is completing a book of poems about Mandela and seeing *Maud Martha* into a paperback edition and perhaps a film. She hopes to complete the second volume of her autobiography, *Report from Part Two*. In spite of current projects, *Blacks* remains the inevitable touchstone for Brooks's popular and academic audiences.

Feminists, black and white, hear in Brooks an early voice in the struggle for gender equality. Though citing her poems of "woman rage" and female circumstance, these critics are deaf to the poet's quarrels with their ideas. Black readers regard her work as generational and historically significant in that she bridges audiences from the Harlem Renaissance to the present. And to the broader general audience, introduced to her work by anthology pieces, Brooks represents a poet genuinely engaged in the urban family and class crises of the late twentieth century. Whether readers come to *Blacks* from the turmoil of race relationships in the United States or discover more about that unrest from her work, they will find a poet who, at the age of seventy-two, counseled herself, "Die / in use" ("Instruction to Myself").

Selected Bibliography

WORKS OF GWENDOLYN BROOKS

POETRY

A Street in Bronzeville. New York: Harper & Brothers, 1945.

Annie Allen. New York: Harper & Brothers, 1949.

Bronzeville Boys and Girls. New York: Harper & Brothers, 1956.

The Bean Eaters. New York: Harper & Row, 1960.

In the Mecca. New York: Harper & Row, 1968.

Riot. Detroit: Broadside Press, 1969.

Black Steel: Joe Frazier and Muhammad Ali. Detroit: Broadside Press, 1971.

Beckonings. Detroit: Broadside Press, 1975.

Primer for Blacks. Chicago: Black Position Press, 1980.

Black Love. Chicago: Brooks Press, 1981.

to disembark. Chicago: Third World Press, 1981.

Mayor Harold Washington and Chicago, the I Will City. Chicago: Brooks Press, 1983.

The Near-Johannesburg Boy and Other Poems. Chicago: David Company, 1986.

Gottschalk and the Grande Tarantelle. Chicago: David Company, 1988.

Winnie. Chicago: David Company, 1988.

PROSE

Maud Martha. New York: Harper & Brothers, 1953.

Report from Part One. Detroit: Broadside Press, 1972.

ESSAYS

"Poets Who Are Negroes." *Phylon*, 11:312 (December 1950).

"Why Negro Women Leave Home." *Negro Digest*, 9:26–28 (March 1951).

"How I Told My Child About Race." *Negro Digest*, 9:29–31 (June 1951).

"They Call It Bronzeville." *Holiday*, October 1951, pp. 60–64, 67, 112, 114, 116–117, 119–120.

"Perspectives." *Negro Digest*, 15:49–50 (July 1966).

"In Montgomery." *Ebony*, August 1971, pp. 42–48.

"Boys. Black: A Preachment." *Ebony,* August 1972, p. 45.

"Winnie." *Poetry,* 151:20 (October–November 1987).

"Keziah." *TriQuarterly,* 75:38–50 (Spring–Summer 1989).

WORKS FOR CHILDREN AND ADOLESCENTS

Family Pictures. Detroit: Broadside Press, 1970.

Aloneness. Detroit: Broadside Press, 1971.

The Tiger Who Wore White Gloves; or, What You Are, You Are. Chicago: Third World Press, 1974.

Young Poet's Primer. Chicago: Brooks Press, 1980.

COLLECTED WORKS

Selected Poems. New York: Harper & Row, 1963.

The World of Gwendolyn Brooks. New York: Harper & Row, 1971.

Blacks. Chicago: David Company, 1987.

EDITED WORKS

A Broadside Treasury. Detroit: Broadside Press, 1971.

Jump Bad: A New Chicago Anthology. Detroit: Broadside Press, 1971.

A Capsule Course in Black Poetry Writing. Detroit: Broadside Press, 1975. Edited by Brooks and others.

MANUSCRIPT PAPERS

The Gwendolyn Brooks Papers are at Atlanta University, Atlanta, Georgia.

BIBLIOGRAPHIES

Loff, Jon N. "Gwendolyn Brooks: A Bibliography." *CLA Journal,* 17:21–32 (September 1973).

Mahoney, Heidi L. "Selected Checklist of Material by and About Gwendolyn Brooks." *Negro American Literature Forum* 8:210–211. (Summer 1974).

Miller, R. Baxter. *Langston Hughes and Gwendolyn Brooks: A Reference Guide.* Boston: G. K. Hall, 1978.

BIOGRAPHICAL AND CRITICAL STUDIES

Baker, Houston A., Jr. "The Achievement of Gwendolyn Brooks." *CLA Journal,* 16:21–31 (September 1972). Reprinted in his *Singers of Daybreak: Studies in Black American Literature.* Washington, D.C.: Howard University Press, 1974. Pp. 43–51.

———. *Modernism and the Harlem Renaissance.* Chicago: University of Chicago Press, 1987.

Blakely, Henry. "How I Met Miss Brooks." In *Say That the River Turns.* Edited by Haki R. Madhubuti. Chicago: Third World Press, 1987. Pp. 4–6.

Blakely, Nora Brooks. "Three-Way Mirror." In *Say That the River Turns.* Edited by Haki R. Madhubuti. Chicago: Third World Press, 1987. Pp. 7–9.

Bloom, Harold, ed. *Contemporary Poets.* New York: Chelsea House, 1986.

Brooks, Keziah. *"The Voice" and Other Short Stories.* Detroit: Harlo Press, 1975.

Brown, Frank London. "Chicago's Great Lady of Poetry." *Negro Digest,* 10:53–57 (December 1961).

Christian, Barbara. "Nuance and the Novella: A Study of Gwendolyn Brooks's *Maud Martha.*" In her *Black Feminist Criticism: Perspectives on Black Women Writers.* New York: Pergamon Press, 1985. Pp. 127–241. Reprinted in *A Life Distilled.* Pp. 239–253.

———."Trajectories of Self-Definition: Placing Contemporary Afro-American Women's Fiction." In *Conjuring: Black Women, Fiction, and Literary Tradition.* Edited by Majorie Pryse and Hortense J. Spillers. Bloomington: Indiana University Press, 1985. Pp. 233–248.

Clark, Norris B. "Gwendolyn Brooks and a Black Aesthetic." In *A Life Distilled: Gwendolyn Brooks—Her Poetry and Fiction.* Edited by Maria K. Mootry and Gary Smith. Urbana: University of Illinois Press, 1987. Pp. 81–99.

Crockett, Jacqueline. "An Essay on Gwendolyn Brooks." *Negro History Bulletin,* 19:37–39 (November 1955).

Davis, Arthur P. "The Black-and-Tan Motif in the Poetry of Gwendolyn Brooks." *CLA Journal,* 6:90–97 (December 1962).

———. "Gwendolyn Brooks: Poet of the Unheroic." *CLA Journal,* 7:114–125 (December 1963).

Fuller, James A. "Notes on a Poet." *Negro Digest,* 11:50–59 (August 1962).

Garland, Phyl. "Gwendolyn Brooks, Poet Laureate." *Ebony,* July 1968, pp. 48–56.

Gayle, Addison, Jr., "Gwendolyn Brooks, Poet of the Whirlwind." In *Black Women Writers, 1950–1980: A Critical Evaluation.* Edited by Mari Evans. Garden City, N.Y.: Anchor/Doubleday, 1984. Pp. 79–87.

Gould, Jean. *Modern American Women Poets.* New York: Dodd, Mead, 1984. Pp. 176–209.

Hansell, William H. "Gwendolyn Brooks' 'In the Mecca': A Rebirth into Blackness." *Negro American Literature Forum,* 8:199–207 (Summer 1974).

Harriott, F. "Life of a Pulitzer Poet." *Negro Digest,* 8:14–16 (August 1950).

Hudson, Clenora F. "Racial Themes in the Poetry of Gwendolyn Brooks." *CLA Journal,* 17:16–20 (September 1973).

Huggins, Nathan Irvin. *Harlem Renaissance.* New York: Oxford University Press, 1971.

Johnson, James N. "Blacklisting Poets." *Ramparts,* December 14, 1968, pp. 48–54.

Juhasz, Suzanne. " 'A Sweet Inspiration . . . of My People': The Poetry of Gwendolyn Brooks and Nikki Giovanni." In her *Naked and Fiery Forms: Modern American Poetry by Women—A New Tradition.* New York: Octagon Books, 1976; New York: Harper Colophon Books, 1976. Pp. 144–155.

Kent, George E. *Blackness and the Adventure of Western Culture.* Chicago: Third World Press, 1972. Pp. 104–138.

———. "Gwendolyn Brooks' Poetic Realism: A Developmental Survey." In *Black Women Writers, 1950–1980: A Critical Evaluation.* Edited by Mari Evans. Garden City, N.Y.: Anchor/Doubleday, 1984. Pp. 88–105.

———. *A Life of Gwendolyn Brooks.* Lexington: University Press of Kentucky, 1990.

Kunitz, Stanley. "Bronze by Gold." *Poetry,* 76:52–56 (1950). (Review of *Annie Allen.*)

Lattin, Patricia H., and Vernon E. Lattin. "Vision in Gwendolyn Brooks's *Maud Martha.*" *Critique,* 25:180–188 (1984).

Levine, Lawrence W. *Black Culture and Black Consciousness: Afro-American Folk Thought from Slavery to Freedom.* New York: Oxford University Press, 1977.

Madhubuti, Haki R. "Gwendolyn Brooks: Beyond the Wordmaker—The Making of an African Poet." In Brooks's *Report from Part One.* Detroit: Broadside Press, 1972. Pp. 13–30.

———, ed. *Say That the River Turns: The Impact of Gwendolyn Brooks.* Chicago: Third World Press, 1987.

Mehlem, D. H. *Gwendolyn Brooks: Poetry and the Heroic Voice.* Lexington: University Press of Kentucky, 1987.

———. *Heroism in the New Black Poetry: Introductions and Interviews.* Lexington: University Press of Kentucky, 1990.

Miller, Jean-Marie A. "Gwendolyn Brooks, Poet Laureate of Bronzeville U.S.A." *Freedomways,* 10:63–75 (First Quarter 1970).

———. "The World of Gwendolyn Brooks." *Black World,* January 1972, pp. 51–52.

Miller, R. Baxter. "Define the Whirlwind: *In the Mecca*—Urban Setting, Shifting Narrator, and Redemptive Vision." *Obsidian,* 4:19–31 (Spring 1978).

Mootry, Maria K., and Gary Smith, eds. *A Life Distilled: Gwendolyn Brooks—Her Poetry and Fiction.* Urbana: University of Illinois Press, 1987.

Ostriker, Alicia Suskin. *Stealing the Language: The Emergence of Women's Poetry in America.* Boston: Beacon Press, 1986.

Rampersad, Arnold. *The Life of Langston Hughes.* Vol. 2, *I Dream a World.* New York: Oxford University Press, 1988.

Redmond, Eugene B. *Drumvoices: The Mission of Afro-American Poetry.* Garden City, N.Y.: Anchor/Doubleday, 1976. Pp. 270–284.

Rivers, Conrad Kent. "Poetry of Gwendolyn Brooks." *Negro Digest,* 13:67–69 (June 1964).

Shaw, Harry B. *Gwendolyn Brooks.* Boston: Twayne, 1980.

Smith, Gary. "Gwendolyn Brooks's *A Street in Bronzeville,* The Harlem Renaissance, and the Mythologies of the Black Woman." *Melus,* 9:33–46 (Fall 1983).

Spillers, Hortense J. " 'An Order of Constancy': Notes on Brooks and the Feminine." *Centennial Review,* 29:223–248 (1985).

Washington, Mary Helen. " 'Taming All That Anger Down': Rage and Silence in Gwendolyn Brooks' *Maud Martha.*" *Massachusetts Review,* 24:453–466 (1983).

Williams, Gladys Margaret. "Gwendolyn Brooks's Way with the Sonnet." *CLA Journal,* 26:215–240 (1982).

INTERVIEWS

Angle, Paul M. "We Asked Gwendolyn Brooks." Chicago: Illinois Bell Telephone, 1967. Reprinted in Brooks's *Report from Part One.* Pp. 131–146.

Brooks, Gwendolyn. "Interview." *TriQuarterly,* 60:405–410 (Spring–Summer 1984).

Hull, Gloria T., and Posey Gallagher. "Update on Part One: An Interview with Gwendolyn Brooks." *CLA Journal,* 21:19–40 (September 1977).

Lewis, Ida. "Conversation: Gwendolyn Brooks and Ida Lewis—'My People Are Black People.' " *Essence,* April 1971, pp. 27–31. Reprinted in Brooks's *Report from Part One.* Pp. 167–182.

Mehlem, D. H. "Humanism and Heroism." In her *Heroism in the New Black Poetry: Introductions and Interviews.* Lexington: University Press of Kentucky, 1990. Pp. 11–38.

Stavros, George. "An Interview with Gwendolyn Brooks." *Contemporary Literature,* 2:1–20 (Winter 1970). Reprinted in Brooks's *Report from Part One.* Pp. 147–166.

Tate, Claudia. "Gwendolyn Brooks." In her *Black Women Writers at Work.* New York: Continuum, 1983. Pp. 39–48.

— *CAROLE K. DORESKI*

William S. Burroughs

1914–

ENOUGH TIME HAS passed since the heady days of the Beat movement for its individual artists to be judged on the larger terrain of American literature. There are three writers whose names are linked with the Beat era and whose reputations, through the paring of time, critical appreciation, and, not least, commercial success, qualify them to be called major figures: Allen Ginsberg, Jack Kerouac, and William Burroughs. The associations we make among them are social and historical; their works are distinctly their own.

Of the three, Burroughs, in the substance of his work, its structural experimentations, its influences, and its message, stands further apart from Ginsberg and Kerouac than the latter two do from each other. Burroughs himself has objected to having his work limited to the Beat context, and has insisted that it shares little of the Beat "philosophy": "I don't associate myself with [the Beats] at all, and never have, either with their objectives or their literary style. I have some close personal friends among the Beat movement . . . but we're not doing the same thing, either in writing or in outlook."

Burroughs was substantially older than the other writers in the movement. The grandson of William Seward Burroughs, inventor of the adding machine, and the son of Laura Lee and Mortimer Burroughs, William Seward Burroughs II was born in Saint Louis, Missouri, February 5, 1914. He graduated from Harvard in 1936, then did graduate work in anthropology and medicine. He had served in the military, traveled widely, and read extensively in the major disciplines when Ginsberg and Kerouac met him during their undergraduate days at Columbia in 1943 and 1944 (Kerouac had dropped out of school by that time, but maintained his Columbia connections and lived near Columbia, in Morningside Heights, between stints in the merchant marine).

Certainly the three came to share in their work a common impulse to break through the barriers of literary conventions and to elevate the principle of individual freedom from the restrictions of social responsibility and traditional conformity. But while Ginsberg and Kerouac were the inheritors of an American strain of spiritual exuberance and life-affirming visions of joy traceable to Ralph Waldo Emerson, Henry David Thoreau, Walt Whitman, and Mark Twain, Burroughs' influences came from deeper underground. His literary forebears were the writers of the grisly pulp fiction of his youth, hardboiled detective writers such as Dashiell Hammett and Raymond Chandler, authors from the decidedly lowbrow science fiction genre, the melancholy fragmentations of T. S. Eliot, and the efforts toward anti-meaning undertaken by the dadaists and surrealists. Kerouac and Ginsberg, while innovative, are not nearly so challenging to read; they work within the modes of traditional narrative and literal word–image associations, even though they sought to open up those traditions to a new vocabulary, a new sound that did justice to their original musical and lyrical sensibilities. Burroughs' writings, on the other hand, exist in the symbolic hyperreality of dreams. Indeed, much of Burroughs' work challenges the notion of language itself, trying to liberate words from their meanings and images from the words that produce them. His driving themes are bleak: death, invasion, repulsion, and control.

Nevertheless, Burroughs did serve as a crucial mentor, giving the two younger writers edifying books to read at the same time he was introducing them to the carnival atmosphere of Times Square and the lurid underworld of small-time criminals and drug addicts whom he knew there. It was a connection Ginsberg, for one, may well have come to regret; Herbert Huncke (the man who introduced Burroughs to narcotics, and one of the petty thieves in Burroughs' Times Square crowd), began using Ginsberg's apartment as a drop for stolen merchandise, landing Ginsberg in jail. Ginsberg pleaded insanity and spent time at the Columbia Psychiatric Institute, where he met a fellow patient named Carl Solomon, whose uncle was the publisher A. A. Wyn. It was Solomon who published Burroughs' first novel, *Junkie: Confessions of an Unredeemed Drug Addict* (1953).

That Burroughs, even before he was writing, had a major, even catalytic, affect on the Beat movement cannot be denied. Kerouac called Burroughs "the most intelligent man in America," and used him as a character in a number of his novels, most notably as Old Bull Lee in *On the Road* (1957). Burroughs also appeared as a character in John Clellon Holmes's early Beat novel, *Go* (1952). Ginsberg dedicated *Howl* (1959) to him—as well as to Kerouac and Beat fellow-traveler Neal Cassady—with the words: "William Seward Burroughs, author of *Naked Lunch*, an endless novel which will drive everybody mad."

Despite Burroughs' objections, he in turn owes a good deal of his success to the solidarity of the writers who made up the Beat movement. Ginsberg shepherded *Junkie* through the process of writing and editing, convinced Carl Solomon to bring it out as an Ace Books paperback, and promoted Burroughs to other writers. Ginsberg and Kerouac together did massive amounts of typing and editing on various revisions of *Naked Lunch* in 1957 and 1958, when Burroughs was attempting to pull the book together from literally thousands of pages of notes he had made during his years of drug addiction and withdrawal. Ginsberg was instrumental in getting that novel published as well, showing it to Maurice Girodias, owner of the Olympia Press, who rejected it but published a subsequent draft. Ginsberg later testified at the book's obscenity trial in the United States. In fact, the enormous success of *Naked Lunch* stemmed in part from Burroughs' fame as a Beat having preceded the appearance of the book. By 1962, when *Naked Lunch* was finally published in the United States, the popularity of Ginsberg's *Howl* and Kerouac's *On the Road* had already set the stage, providing a ready-made, fervent audience for the book.

Yet, when Burroughs insists he is not a Beat writer, he is not simply being cranky. Part of the difference lies in his ambivalence toward writing at all, an attitude starkly opposed to the exuberant self-redemption Kerouac and Ginsberg found in art. For a large portion of Burroughs' adult life, including most of the early years of his friendships with Kerouac and Ginsberg, Burroughs was not a practicing writer and did not consider himself to be one. He had written a good deal as a youth, but stopped during his teens, when at the Los Alamos Ranch School for Boys (later the property of the U.S. government and the birthplace of the atomic bomb), he developed a crush on a fellow student, the emotional pangs of which he recorded in detail in his diary. This diary, he has written in an essay, "The Name Is Burroughs" (included in *The Adding Machine*, 1986),

> put me off writing for many years. . . . The act of writing had become embarrassing, disgusting, and above all *false*. It was not the sex in the diary that embarrassed me, it was the terrible falsity of the emotions expressed. . . . for years after that, the sight of my words written on a page hit me like the sharp smell of carrion when you turn over a dead dog with a stick, and this continued until 1938. I had written myself an eight-year sentence.

Interestingly, Burroughs' next two writing experiences were collaborative, a fact that seems to have freed him from the dread of himself and his emotions that he associated with other literary attempts. "The curse of the diary," he writes, "was temporarily broken by the act of collaboration." The first of these respites came in 1938, when he and a fellow Harvard graduate student and St. Louis boyhood friend, Kells Elvins, "had many talks about writing and started a detective story in the Dashiell Hammett / Raymond Chandler line." Eventually they produced "Twilight's Last Gleaming," a story about "a ship captain putting on women's clothes and rushing into the first lifeboat . . . which was later used almost verbatim in *Nova Express*" (under the title "Gave Proof Through the Night").

It is not at all certain that the piece in *Nova Express* (1964) was indeed little altered from the original. Burroughs is not fully reliable on such matters—for one thing, this would have meant that by 1938 he had already invented his ubiquitous alter ego, Dr. Benway; what is more, the passage as it appears in *Nova Express* shows his ironic style and formal idiosyncrasies already fully developed:

> CAPTAIN BAIRNS was arrested today in the murder at sea of Chicago—He was The Last Great American to see things from the front and kept laughing during the dark—Fade out
>
> S.S. America—Sea smooth as green glass—off Jersey Coast—An air-conditioned voice floats from microphones and ventilators—:
>
> "Keep your seats everyone—There is no cause for alarm—There has been a little accident in the boiler room but everything is now/"
>
> BLOOOMMM

The collaboration with Kells Elvins marks the first use of an important Burroughs compositional motif—short performances he called "routines." While writing "Twilight's Last Gleamings" he and Elvins "acted out every scene and often got on laughing jags." Routines initially acted for sheer entertainment later became the source of material in *Queer* (written in 1952–1953 but not published until 1985), as well as of what Eric Mottram has called the "tetralogy" of novels consisting of *Naked Lunch, The Soft Machine* (1961, rev. ed. 1966), *The Ticket That Exploded* (1962, rev. ed. 1967), and *Nova Express.* Even in later works routines continued to be an important source. The routine demands no particular narrative groundwork nor development, which accounts for the almost arbitrary episodic quality of much of Burroughs' writing. A very good example of Burroughs' tendency to create different personae for no reason in particular is a brief, humorous routine from the early days of the Burroughs–Kerouac–Ginsberg friendship, recounted by Ted Morgan in *Literary Outlaw* (1988): "Burroughs gave parties on Bedford Street, emerging on one occasion from the kitchen with a plate of razor blades and light bulbs, and saying, 'I've got something real nice in the way of delicacies my mother sent me this week, *hmf hmf hmf.*' " To the reader who knows something of Burroughs and his problematic relationship with his parents, this routine, like most of his more elaborate ones, strikes one as wildly (almost psychotically) imaginative while, at the same time, being deeply revealing on an autobiographical–symbolic level.

"Twilight's Last Gleaming" was, almost needless to say, rejected for publication. Burroughs did not attempt to write again until 1943, when he collaborated with Jack Kerouac on a novel based on the killing of Dave Kammerer by Lucien Carr, two men intimately involved with the Burroughs–Kerouac–Ginsberg circle. The novel was rejected by every publisher to which it was submitted, and Burroughs "Again . . . lost interest in writing." He did not take up his pen again until 1948, when he began work on the book that would become *Junkie*.

Not having outlets for his work became as important a factor in discouraging Burroughs' writing as the earlier revulsion at his false emotions. In 1954, after *Junkie* had been published and *Queer* and *The Yage Letters* (1963) had not, he wrote to Kerouac that he was having "serious difficulties" with *Naked Lunch*:

I tell you the novel form is completely inadequate to express what I have to say. I don't know if I can find a form. I am very gloomy as to prospects of publication. And I'm not like you, Jack, I need an audience. Of course, a small audience. But still I need publication for development. A writer can be ruined by too much or too little success.

The revulsion at his own writing, his sense of the inadequacy of the novel, and his need for an audience all combined to develop in Burroughs a trait that clearly separates him from his fellow Beat writers: a severe distrust of language, a strong impulse to do something as a writer that is other than writing. He has even gone so far as to say, a bit disingenuously, that when he "began" to write at age thirty-five, his only reason was "boredom," that he started recording his experiences because he had "nothing else to do." What he was trying to communicate here, I suspect, was that he wanted to bring to the process none of the writer's traditional reverence for the text. He has reused his own material time and again, revised and republished bits and pieces of his novels in new novels and smaller tracts, introduced unorthodox methods of composition, cut up his words, cut up the words of other writers and incorporated them into his own, broken up his work into interrelated columns on the page, used tape recorders and other electronic devices to cull material, and tried again and again to escape from the prison of meaning and association that words enforce on his images.

He has striven, Burroughs has said, for a literature of silence, a breaking down of the control pattern in which words subjugate the reader to the text. In this sense he wishes to purify (and disempower) the process of transmitting an image from the source of its inspiration (dream, vision, newspaper story, or whatever else) to the writer, and from the writer to the reader. He has often described his goal as a writer to be merely a passive medium, a "recurrent writer's dream of picking up a book and starting to read. . . . One day the book itself will hover over the typewriter as I copy the words already written there." He has defined his essential identity as a messenger or even a physician, diagnosing the world and prescribing the images that cure it, as well as an autobiographer, a recorder of experience, roles that have allowed him to experiment with forms and methods in ways a purely literary writer would not dare. As such, he stands far apart from his fellow Beats, and from almost every writer of his time.

It is often forgotten that Burroughs, despite his late beginnings as a writer, had completed three books by the time he began *Naked Lunch*—or four, if the still unpublished collaborative effort with Kerouac, "All the Hippos Were Boiled in Their Tanks," is counted.

Burroughs' first published novel was *Junkie: Confessions of an Unredeemed Drug Addict*, which came out under the Ace Books imprint. In many ways the original appearance of *Junkie* was something less than a true literary debut. As Allen Ginsberg remarks in his introduction to the unexpurgated 1977 edition, the 1953 version was "a shabby package," a drugstore pulp paperback written under the pseudonym William Lee (Lee was Burroughs' mother's maiden name). Critic Jennie Skerl, in *William S. Burroughs* (1985), describes the situation in succinct detail:

Because of the "drug fiend" hysteria of the times, Burroughs was asked to write a prologue about his respectable family background, and a few passages and one whole section were arbitrarily cut. [Carl] Solomon wrote a placating introduction explaining that the book should be read as a warning, and parenthetical editor's notes were inserted "to indicate where the author clearly departs from accepted medical fact or makes other unsubstantiated statements in an effort to justify his actions."

Further to insulate the publisher from charges of advocating drug addiction, *Junkie* was piggybacked onto another book (each was upside down from the other, beginning at opposite covers), the memoirs of a righteous lawman, Maurice Helbrant, entitled *Narcotic Agent*. Helbrant was a former agent of the Federal Bureau of Narcotics. *Narcotic Agent* had first been published in 1941 and was described in the Ace edition as "more thrilling than any fiction story"—a sales pitch that would have been more appropriate for Burroughs, who had produced a fairly straightforward (for Burroughs) autobiographical rendering of his years using drugs in New York, Texas, and Mexico. It was not until twenty-four years later, when Penguin issued the book under the title *Junky* (with an introduction by Ginsberg), that the novel appeared in the United States under Burroughs' own name.

As Skerl points out, *Junkie,* although largely ignored by critics and dismissed by Burroughs himself, lays the groundwork for many of his later themes and efforts:

Burroughs' descriptions of underworld characters in *Junkie* show how he arrived at the characterizations of *Naked Lunch* and the later novels. When people are reduced and molded by need, their identities reside in their functions. . . .

Junkie is a complex and ironic work, and it leaves the disturbing impression that the author has somehow tricked the reader into a realm where physical and social realities begin to shift and dissolve.

The sordid and exclusive universe of *Junkie* also predicts what Marshall McLuhan later described in "Notes on Burroughs" (1964), referring to all of Burroughs' work, as a world

in which there can be no spectators but only participants. All men are totally involved in the insides of all men. There is no privacy and no private parts. In a world in which we are all ingesting and digesting one another there can be no obscenity or pornography or decency.

These themes would be much elaborated and expanded in *Naked Lunch.*

However, two other books were written first, neither of them published until later. The first was *Queer,* another autobiographical account, this time of a frustrated romance with a young man Burroughs met in Mexico (Morgan's *Literary Outlaw* identifies him only by the name Burroughs gives him in *Queer*: Eugene Allerton). *Queer,* addressing as it does a largely unrequited homosexual love, albeit in a mature and complex way, markedly corresponds to the much-despised Los Alamos diary of Burroughs' teens. *Queer* was too graphic and overt in its homosexual themes for A. A. Wyn or anyone else to publish in the 1950's (Burroughs has written that Solomon "would go to jail if he ever published *Queer*"), but this alone does not account for the book's remaining unpublished until 1985. *Literary Outlaw* covers the events that led up to *Queer*'s finally being published, as part of a multi-book contract Burroughs signed in 1984. The deal caused much animosity, in that it involved Burroughs' leaving his longtime agent, Peter Matson, and his publisher, Richard Seaver, who had been his editor since the early 1960's, in favor of Andrew Wylie and Viking Penguin, respectively. Burroughs had told Seaver and others for years that *Queer* would never be released. It is interesting to speculate whether Burroughs' teenage misgivings, the echoes of his earlier self-horror, may have contributed at least partially to the years of silence surrounding the book.

There proved to be another very compelling reason for *Queer*'s suppression, one Burroughs did not realize or acknowledge until 1985, when he prepared the manuscript for publication. In his introduction, he writes that the motivation to write *Junky* was "comparatively simple: to put down in the most accurate and simple terms my experiences as an addict." His motivations in writing *Queer,* however, "were more complex, and are not clear to me at the present time. Why should I wish to chronicle so carefully these extremely painful and unpleasant and lacerating memories?" A few pages later, he begins to answer the question:

> When I started to write this companion text to *Queer,* I was paralyzed with a heavy reluctance, a writer's block like a straightjacket. . . . The reason for this reluctance becomes clearer as I force myself to look: the book is motivated and formed by an event which is never mentioned, in fact is carefully avoided: the accidental shooting death of my wife, Joan, in September 1951.

Burroughs describes the obsessive need of his novelistic counterpart, Lee, to score sexually with Allerton and other men. This is an effect of his withdrawal. During addiction the sex drive, he says, disappears almost completely, to return when addiction ends. Yet, he remarks, the quest for "a suitable sex object" in *Queer* is "curiously systematic and unsexual." The contact that Lee was really looking for was "an audience," an audience that later, "as he develops as writer . . . becomes internalized."

Whatever Burroughs was looking for, he was not looking for it in his wife, Joan Vollmer. According to Morgan, based on interviews with Burroughs, Ginsberg, and others, the attraction between Vollmer and Burroughs had always been intellectual. When they first began living together in New York, they were considered the most sophisticated and intelligent members of the group that included Ginsberg and Kerouac. According to those who knew her and to Burroughs himself, Vollmer, as Burroughs was coming out of his addiction in Mexico City, was distressed by his search for male sex partners and his abandonment of her—yet it is possible that the abandonment was as much intellectual as physical, a point that has not been much explored in the scanty material that addresses this crucial moment in Burroughs' life.

Burroughs shot his wife on September 6, 1951, shortly after returning from a trip to South America with Allerton, during which he had tried, and failed, to obtain a hallucinogenic plant called *yage*, rumored to bestow telepathic powers and used by Indian *brujos.* This is the trip described in *Queer*. Burroughs, Vollmer, Allerton, and another man were drinking in the apartment of a friend, waiting to meet a buyer to whom Burroughs hoped to sell one of his guns, a .380 automatic. At one point, with no preliminaries, Burroughs picked up the gun and said to Vollmer, "Well, Joan, it's about time for our William Tell act." Vollmer put her highball glass on top of her head, and Burroughs aimed and fired. The bullet hit her in the head and killed her.

Although there were reports at the time that the shooting had been a William Tell misplay,

Burroughs denied it for many years, stating, as he had to the Mexican police, that he had been cleaning the gun (or "checking it over," as he says in an interview with Conrad Knickerbocker) and it had accidentally fired. It was not until the film documentary *Burroughs,* made by Howard Brookner and released in 1983, that Burroughs admitted publicly that the shooting had occurred as it had, the result of a stunt he called "an absolute piece of insanity." He also described the scene to Morgan, "verifying" the William Tell story.

Nowhere but in the introduction to *Queer,* however, has Burroughs put the killing into a context that so powerfully explains his own work. Here he recognizes that the killing of his wife was the central fact out of which his subsequent writing and his theory of art emerged. In fact, the introduction to *Queer* is the only critical writing either by—or, more pertinently, *about*—Burroughs that recognizes the real impact of this crucial incident. Burroughs' critics (most of them men) have on the whole steered clear of discussing it at length or trying to see what connections or repercussions it may have had. According to Burroughs:

> The event towards which Lee [in *Queer*] feels himself inexorably driven is the death of his wife by his own hand, the knowledge of possession, a dead hand waiting to slip over his like a glove. So a smog of menace and evil rises from the pages, an evil that Lee, knowing and yet not knowing, tries to escape with frantic flights of fantasy: his routines, which set one's teeth on edge because of the ugly menace just behind or to one side of them, a presence palpable as a haze.
>
> Brion Gysin said to me in Paris: "For ugly spirit shot Joan because . . ." A bit of mediumistic message that was not completed—or was it? It doesn't need to be completed, if you read it: "ugly spirit shot Joan *to be cause*," that is, to maintain a hateful parasitic occupation. My concept of possession is closer to the medieval model than to modern psychological explanations, with their dogmatic insistence that such manifestations must come from within and never, never, never from without. . . . I mean a definite possessing entity. And indeed, the psychological concept might well have been devised by the possessing entities, since nothing is more dangerous to a possessor than being seen as a separate invading creature by the host it has invaded. . . .
>
> I am forced to the appalling conclusion that I would never have become a writer but for Joan's death, and to a realization of the extent to which this event has motivated and formulated my writing. I live with the constant threat of possession, and a constant need to escape from possession, from Control. So the death of Joan brought me in contact with the invader, the Ugly Spirit, and maneuvered me into a lifelong struggle, in which I have had no choice except to write my way out.

As his later writings have elaborated, this "Control" comes in many forms: invasions of the body and of the planet by forces that occupy and multiply invisibly; as addiction, whether to drugs or to power or to words; as images that multiply like viruses; words themselves, which he later came to see as actual viruses (see Odier's *The Job* [1970, rev. ed. 1974], *The Book of Breeething* [1975], *The Adding Machine,* and elsewhere) and whose power he subverts by employing new compositional and narrative techniques; or even as protoplasmic and violent sexuality. Such sexuality is common in *Naked Lunch* and the later books. An early prototype appears in *Queer*:

> Lee and Allerton went to see Cocteau's *Orpheus.* In the dark theater Lee could feel his body pull towards Allerton, an amoeboid protoplasmic projection, straining with a blind worm hunger to enter the other's body, to breathe with his lungs,

see with his eyes, learn the feel of his viscera and genitals. Allerton shifted in his seat.

Queer, not published until late in his career, must be read as a seminal work, a leap toward an absolutely imaginative and original method of self-rendering, self-discovery, and self-healing that has continued to sustain him.

Burroughs' next effort grew out of the search for *yage*, the beginnings of which were described in the account of the trip to the Amazon jungle in *Queer*. Subsequent trips for the same purpose in 1953 were chronicled in a series of letters Burroughs sent to Allen Ginsberg, which, Burroughs has said, "were typed out from handwritten notes in offices where you use a typewriter for so much per hour in Bogotá and Lima." In the fall of 1953, back in New York and prior to leaving for Tangier, where he would live until 1959, he edited the letters into an epistolary novella, "In Search of Yage." In 1963 this was published, along with a letter from Ginsberg to Burroughs written in 1960, when Ginsberg traveled to South America and tried *yage* himself; a letter in return from Burroughs, written in London, describing his recent experiments with the cut-up method; another statement from Ginsberg interpreting his *yage* experience; and a final piece from Burroughs, "I am Dying, Meester?," in which he employs the cut-up method to make a new text out of the earlier letters. This hodgepodge, which maintains a curious unity and is an essential Beat document, is titled *The Yage Letters*.

The letters in the first part of the book are more fluid and less oppressive in tone than *Queer*, which dealt with the same milieu. There are the same loneliness and sexual yearning, but with somewhat more comic results, as when a boy, whom Burroughs has paid for sex, in a moment of apparent tenderness encourages Burroughs to take off his shorts—only so that he can steal them. Burroughs' and Ginsberg's *yage* visions differed in the atmosphere of their retelling, but when combined, they form some of the best, and perhaps the earliest, writing about the hallucinogenic experience.

The book was to have included a routine called "Roosevelt After Inauguration," which Burroughs refers to in one of his letters, but this was not published until 1964, as a pamphlet. It subsequently appeared in book form, with three other pieces, under the title *Roosevelt After Inauguration And Other Atrocities* (1979), and may have been deleted from *The Yage Letters* for fear of prosecution: when it first appeared, in the magazine *Floating Bear* in 1961, copies were seized by the Postal Service for obscenity. The routine involved a fantasy about Roosevelt and his cabinet:

Immediately after the Inauguration Roosevelt appeared on the White House balcony dressed in the purple robes of a Roman Emperor and, leading a blind toothless lion on a gold chain, hog-called his constituents to come and get their appointments. The constituents rushed up grunting and squealing like the hogs they were.

An old queen, known to the Brooklyn Police as "Jerk Off Annie," was named to the Joint Chiefs of Staff, so that the younger staff officers were subject to unspeakable indignities in the lavatories of the Pentagon, to avoid which many set up field latrines in their offices.

The Burroughs "routine," first developed along fairly literal lines in *Queer*, was in full flower by 1953. It would become the dominant motif of his writing for the remainder of the decade, during which he gathered the material that would make up his next four novels.

Naked Lunch, published in Paris in 1959 (under the title *The Naked Lunch*), became the subject of much discussion and renown in the United States shortly thereafter, although only small portions of it were serialized there prior to 1962. In 1958 the *Chicago Review* published an excerpt, but was kept from doing so a second time by University of Chicago authorities. The editors of the *Review* then raised money and created an independent magazine, *Big Table*, in order to publish the second excerpt, along with other writings from the Beats to which university trustees and administrators had objected. Issues of this magazine were seized by the Postal Service for obscenity, as were copies of the Paris edition of the book mailed to the United States. U.S. Customs also seized copies of the Paris edition. Grove Press had bought the American rights from Maurice Girodias of the Olympia Press in Paris, but could not publish the book because it was involved in defending booksellers on obscenity charges arising out of its publishing an American edition of Henry Miller's *Tropic of Cancer* (1934). When *Naked Lunch* finally was published in the United States, obscenity charges quickly followed in Boston. It was cleared of the charges in 1966. In effect *Naked Lunch* was the last book of any literary merit to be suppressed by means of the obscenity laws, and its judicial clearance marked the end of an era of state censorship of literature.

Naked Lunch is the book that made Burroughs' fame, if not his fortune (the first preceding the second by some thirty years), and it remains his most widely read work. Beyond that, it holds a position of almost mythological proportions in American literature, in part because of its narrative innovations and the mad, violent, comic despair and the countervening genius at its core, but also because of two other fascinating issues surrounding its existence: the suppression outlined above and, no less, the travails of its composition.

Beginning during the period chronicled in *The Yage Letters*, and subsequently during the years of addiction in Tangier, roughly from 1953 to 1958, Burroughs began keeping voluminous, fragmentary notes about his addiction; his travels and his observations of life, particularly "low" life, in Mexico City, Tangier, and elsewhere; and his various routines. Interestingly, the routines by this time had grown almost into a form of dementia. He had developed them in part as a frantic method of seduction for Allerton, the unresponsive lover in *Queer*, but they seem to have stayed with him and to have grown into a continuing strategy for re-creating himself long after Allerton had departed. He described them in very revealing terms in a letter to Ginsberg in April 1954:

> Routines like habit. Without routines my life is chronic nightmare, gray horror of midwest suburb. (When I lived in St. Louis and drove home past the bare clay of subdivided lots, here and there houses set down on platforms of concrete in the mud, play-houses of children who look happy and healthy but empty horror and panic in clear gray-blue eyes, and when I drove by the subdivisions always felt impact in stomach of final loneliness and despair. This is part of Billy Bradshinkel story. I don't know whether it is parody or not.)
>
> I have to have receiver for routine. If there is no one there to receive it, routine turns back on me and tears me apart, grows more and more insane (literal growth like cancer) and impossible, and fragmentary like berserk pinball machine and I am screaming: "Stop it! Stop it!"
>
> I am trying to write novel. Attempt to organize material is more painful than anything I ever experienced.

Much of the psychic terrain of Burroughs' writing is laid out in this passage. The routine *is* writing, which in turn is the necessary working out of problems that infect Burroughs like a virus. But the working out, the writing itself, is also capable of becoming a virus if there is no audience, if it turns and feeds on the madness within. What Burroughs found in writing, especially in the higher plane toward which he embarked with *Naked Lunch,* was the extinction of personality that T. S. Eliot had made into a credo of art years before (see his "Tradition and the Individual Talent," 1919). There are fascinating corollaries between Burroughs and Eliot that will be explored in more detail below.

The routines, meanwhile, were making their way into Burroughs' notes and his letters to Ginsberg. These were years of heavy addiction, and attempts to secure his writing or organize his material into novel form proved fruitless. Finally, in 1956, Burroughs traveled to London to be treated by Dr. John Yerbury Dent, who used a nonaddicting morphine derivative called apomorphine to regulate the addict's metabolism through the painful process of withdrawal. Cured of his habit (he would begin using again in the late 1970's and early 1980's, and have to undergo methadone treatment to get free), Burroughs returned to Tangier and began to put together his novel, culling through what amounted to over a thousand pages of material. The scene is described by Paul Bowles in "Burroughs in Tangier" (included in *The Burroughs File*, 1984):

> The litter on his desk and under it, on the floor, was chaotic, but it consisted only of pages of *Naked Lunch*, at which he was constantly working. When he read aloud from it, at random (any sheet of paper he happened to grab would do) he laughed a good deal, as well he might, since it is very funny, but from reading he would suddenly (the paper still in hand) go into a bitter conversational attack upon whatever aspect of life had prompted the passage he had just read. . . . I've never heard him mention an experience that made him more than temporarily happy.

In fact, the difficulties of organizing these prodigious pages, strewn all about his room, proved to be both the challenge and, eventually, the innovative triumph of *Naked Lunch*. Burroughs was assisted in typing and editing the manuscript at various times in 1957 and 1958 by Kerouac, Ginsberg, Alan Ansen, and others.

The book is made up almost entirely of what in *Queer*, and more elaborately in *The Yage Letters*, had been only occasional routines. Here the routine as a method of self-examination takes over almost entirely. The routines are presented in a series of episodes arranged in no particular order—indeed, the order had been changed many times as the book was being prepared, often at random. The locale is a city called Interzone, a composite of the tawdriest and most corrupt aspects of Mexico City, Panama City (the Canal Zone), and Tangier, which until 1956 had been an "international zone" governed by a body of European powers called the Board of Control (which itself sounds like a Burroughs creation). The addict–writer Willy Lee narrates, but is a much more ephemeral presence than in the earlier books. There are naturalistic passages about Lee and his companion, Jane (the name of Paul Bowles's wife and, of course, very similar to his own wife's name, Joan), making their way from Texas to New Orleans to Mexico, re-creating the trip Burroughs and Vollmer made in 1949. Even these are tinged with a new air of unreality:

> Shooting PG [paregoric] is a terrible hassle, you have to burn out the alcohol first, then freeze out the camphor and draw this brown liquid off with a dropper—have to shoot it in the vein or you get an abscess, and usually end up with an abscess no matter where you shoot it. Best deal is to drink it with goof balls. . . . So we pour it in a Pernod bottle and start for New Orleans past iridescent lakes and orange gas flames, and swamps and garbage heaps, alligators crawling around in broken bottles and tin cans, neon arabesques of motels, marooned pimps scream obscenities at passing cars from islands of rubbish. . . .

Lee and Jane drive into Mexico, and within a page the narrative dissolved into a routine about Bradley the Buyer, addict of power, possessor of souls, and forerunner of the evil figure of later novels, Mr. Bradley Mr. Martin:

Well the Buyer comes to look more and more like a junky. He can't drink. He can't get it up. His teeth fall out. (Like pregnant women lose their teeth feeding the stranger, junkies lose their yellow fangs feeding the monkey.) He is all the time sucking on a candy bar. Baby Ruths he digs special. "It really disgust you to see the Buyer sucking on them candy bars so nasty," a cop says.

The Buyer takes on an ominous grey-green color. . . .

. . . a yen comes on him like a great black wind through the bones. So the Buyer hunts up a young junky and gives him a paper to make it.

"Oh all right," the boy says. "So what you want to make?"

"I just want to rub up against you and get fixed."

"Ugh . . . Well all right. . . . But why cancha just get physical like a human?"

Later the boy is sitting in a Waldorf with two colleagues dunking pound cake. "Most distasteful thing I ever stand still for," he says. "Some way he make himself all soft like a blob of jelly and surround me so nasty. Then he gets wet all over like with green slime. So I guess he come to some kinda awful climax. . . . I come near to wigging with that green stuff all over me, and he stink like a old rotten cantaloupe."

Eventually the Buyer is called in by his district supervisor and relieved of his duties: "You are lowering the entire tone of the industry. We are prepared to accept your immediate resignation." The Buyer begs for a reprieve. When the supervisor refuses, the Buyer engulfs him. He roams about the landscape, consuming junkies and agents, until finally he is "destroyed with a flame-thrower—the court of inquiry ruling that such means were justified in that the Buyer had lost his human citizenship and was, in consequence, a creature without species and a menace to the narcotics industry on all levels."

The Bradley the Buyer section is, on the one hand, a parody of the need of the narc, which equals that of the junkie, and a commentary on the corrupt motives of authority, but it is also an imaginative reconfiguration of the sexual yearnings examined in *Queer*. The protoplasmic element of Burroughs' sense of sexuality, rendered metaphorically in the earlier work, becomes a literal reality in *Naked Lunch*. An image that contains both this political satire and sexual revulsion becomes central in *Naked Lunch*, although Burroughs had used it earlier, in *Junkie*: the orgasm of the hanged man. The image is replayed endlessly in the book and becomes its own meaning, the final expression of hideous power and lust.

Eventually four groups emerge, all vying for power in the world of *Naked Lunch*. Referring to this and the subsequent novels on the same themes, Eric Mottram writes in *William Burroughs: The Algebra of Need* (1971): "Burroughs presents a loveless world whose control is entirely in the hands of capitalists, doctors, psychiatrists, con men, judges, police and military, whose aim it is to perpetuate mass infantilism, apathy and dependence." The central figure in Burroughs' fiction that best fits that description is Dr. Benway, who first appears here (although according to Burroughs, as discussed earlier, Benway had emerged many years before in the routines with Kells Elvins that led to "Twilight's Last Gleaming"; for further reference to this, see the Knickerbocker interview). Benway is the satiric epitome of the modern scientist and technocrat for hire, willing to perform any abomination on assignment. Through him Burroughs reveals the psychosexual terrain on which he perceives the conflict of guilt and authority in contemporary society:

Benway is a manipulator and coordinator of symbol systems, an expert on all phases of interrogation, brainwashing and control. I have not seen

Benway since his precipitate departure from Annexia, where his assignment had been T.D.—Total Demoralization. Benway's first act was to abolish concentration camps, mass arrest and, except under limited and special circumstances, the use of torture.

"I deplore brutality," he said. "It's not efficient. On the other hand, prolonged mistreatment, short of physical violence, gives rise, when skillfully applied, to anxiety and a feeling of special guilt. . . . The subject must not realize that the mistreatment is a deliberate attack of an anti-human enemy on his personal identity. He must be made to feel that he deserves *any* treatment he receives because there is something (never specified) horribly wrong with him. The naked need of the control addicts must be decently covered by an arbitrary and intricate bureaucracy so that the subject cannot contact his enemy direct."

There are three organized groups of such "control addicts" in *Naked Lunch*, and a fourth that seems to be opposed to the other three. The Liquefactionists are lead by Hassan, a figure of unspeakable evil described in "Hassan's Rumpus Room." Again we see the image of oozing possession: "(Liquefaction involves protein cleavage and reduction to liquid which is absorbed into someone else's protoplasmic being.)" The Divisionists attempt to flood the world with clones of themselves, and in this sense foreshadow the invading Nova Mob in later novels. The third group vying for power is the Senders, who attempt to tyrannize through telepathy, a theme Burroughs first explored in *Queer*, where Lee describes to Allerton how the Russians and Americans are researching the telepathic powers of *yage* in order to subjugate their citizens, and of course their enemies, more easily. In Burroughs' years in Mexico City he had studied the Mayan codices, and he came to believe that the Mayas controlled their large slave populations through telepathy, a process he also has Lee describe in *Queer*.

The fourth, and apparently beneficent, group is the Factualists, led by A.J, who reappears in later fiction. The Factualists are the group with whom Lee, the narrator, is aligned. As Skerl points out:

The Factualists are a radical group that represents anarchic individualism. . . . Factualist agents attempt to foil the plots of the villains simply by revealing them. In a way the entire novel can be seen as such a revelation. . . . Factualist revelation is equated with the murder of a villain and with the apomorphine cure for addiction. There is a flaw in the Factualist program, however. Since all the agents are human, they are all potential addicts who may succumb at any moment: "all Agents defect and all Resisters sell out." Thus the situation is never resolved.

The Factualist strategy, if there is such a thing, involves a free association of images which relieves the addictive need for narrative and which was much elaborated with Burroughs' subsequent use of the cut-up technique. In *Naked Lunch* he must rely on his own wandering imagination:

Pictures of men and women, boys and girls, animals, fish, birds, the copulating rhythm of the universe flows through the room, a great blue tide of life. Vibrating, soundless hum of deep forest—sudden quiet of cities when the junky copes. A moment of stillness and wonder. . . .

Hassan shrieks out: "This is your doing, A.J.! You poopa my party!"

A.J. looks at him, face remote as limestone: "Uppa your ass, you liquifying gook."

Ihab Hassan, a critic sympathetic to Burroughs' work despite the outrages committed by a character with his very name in Burroughs' fiction, points out in *The Dismemberment of Orpheus* (1971) that the later development of compositional techniques which disempower language (predicted, I believe, by the passage above with its soundlessness and silence) reveals that Burroughs' "true aim is to free man by making him bodiless and silencing his language." This is supported by the comments Burroughs makes in *The Job, The Book of Breeething*, and elsewhere, on his efforts to achieve silence in literature. In *The Job* he takes this theory so far as to describe how film images and tape recordings of sounds can be used as a kind of voodoo to hex the people recorded, a hearkening to Native American cultures, which believed that photographs stole their souls.

The Factualists' vulnerability to controlling forces, to which Skerl refers, derives from what Burroughs in the introduction to *Naked Lunch* calls "total need":

> The face of "evil" is always the face of total need. . . . In the words of total need: '*Wouldn't you?*' Yes you would. You would lie, cheat, inform on your friends, steal, do *anything* to satisfy total need. Because you would be in a state of total sickness, total possession, and not in a position to act in any other way.

This tendency toward addiction is what the forces of evil play upon in *Naked Lunch* and in most of the later novels. All three of the organized controlling powers in *Naked Lunch* are described in images associated with parasites and viruses. The escape from this virus, as we have seen in the introduction to *Queer*, is the central conflict of Burroughs' work.

Three novels appeared in quick succession in the five years after *Naked Lunch*: *The Soft Machine*, *The Ticket That Exploded*, and *Nova Express*. In 1963 he published *Dead Fingers Talk*, which was not really a new work but a selection of routines from *Naked Lunch* and the other three novels. The material for all of these books came from the notes and manuscripts Burroughs had written in Tangier—in 1958 he moved to Paris, where he lived in the famed Beat Hotel, and in 1960 to London, remaining there, with a few short exceptions, until 1974. Because many of the characters, images, and themes Burroughs handles in *Naked Lunch* are explored in the next three novels, Eric Mottram and others have said that the four books together form a tetralogy. Burroughs, however, has insisted for several important reasons that *Naked Lunch* is distinct from the three novels that followed, to which he refers as a trilogy.

The first and most important evolution between *Naked Lunch* and the subsequent novels occurred as a result of Burroughs' use of the cut-up technique, which a friend, the painter and writer Brion Gysin, had discovered one day while cutting mats for his artwork. When he lifted the mats, Gysin discovered that the newspaper he had laid beneath them had been sliced into strips he could rearrange with interesting effects. Burroughs became enamored of the process and began using it in his writing. He would cut up pages of his own prose and rearrange the parts to make new sentences. He went on to cut up pieces from other writers, newspapers, magazines, and other texts and insert them into his prose. He also developed a method he called the fold-in technique, where he folded a page of writing over to achieve similar effects. He gives his best defenses of the technique in his interview with Knickerbocker:

> Cutups establish new connections between images, and one's range of vision consequently expands. . . . Cutups make explicit a psychosensory process that is going on all the time anyway. Somebody is reading a newspaper, and his eye follows the column in the proper Aristotelian manner, one idea and sentence at a time. But subliminally he is reading the columns on either side and is aware of the person sitting next to him. That's a cutup. . . . For exercise, when I make a trip . . . I will record this in three columns

in a notebook I always take with me. One column will contain simply an account of the trip, what happened. . . . the next column presents my memories: that is, what I was thinking of at the time. . . . And the third column, which I call my reading column, gives quotations from any book that I take with me.

Burroughs came to believe that the cut-up, like his dreams (which he recorded in notebooks and used copiously in his fiction), could present words, images, and fragments which predicted distant or future events as well as explained old ones.

I remember a cut-up I made in Paris . . . : "Raw peeled winds of hate and mischance blew the shot." And for years I thought this referred to blowing a shot of junk, when the junk squirts out the side of the syringe or dropper owing to an obstruction. Brion Gysin pointed out the actual meaning: the shot that killed Joan.

Thus Burroughs believed that the cut-up, as well as dreams and other methods of nonlinear composition, such as use of tape recordings and hieroglyphs, tapped into a human unconscious capacity for space–time travel.

This movement from distant past to inexplicable future became a theme as well as a technique. The three novels following *Naked Lunch* introduce and elaborate a series of new elements in Burroughs' cosmology, reinforcing his assertion that they are to be kept distinct as a trilogy: the Nova Mob, Nova Police, the theories of Wilhelm Reich (inventor of the orgone box and formulator of radical theories linking modern psychological, social, sexual, and emotional behaviors to viruses and cancer, among other things), Scientology, science fiction and western stories (thus, future and past), sensory deprivation, tape and film *as reality* (the "Reality Studio" and "biological theater"), Mayan codices and myths, and the mythology of the medieval Persian assassins led by Hassan i Sabbah.

The most important of these elements for rudimentary "plot" purposes in the trilogy is the Nova Mob, who have controlled the planet for thousands of years by taking the form of parasitic viruses that "infect" humans and make them susceptible to addiction and control. They operate through the human need for word and image, drugs, sex, and power. The Nova Police fight the Nova Mob through alleviation of addiction (to drugs via apomorphine, to word and image via silence), and are themselves susceptible to an addiction: power. Elements of this battle change from novel to novel and scene to scene, it takes place over vast expanses of time and space, and there are many characters involved on both sides, some of whom appear repeatedly, some only once. The conflict, in typical Burroughs fashion, is never resolved. However, through the fragmented narrative of the three novels, the characters and images associated with the two vying groups provide a kind of unifying mythological element.

Generally, the novels are composed of nonsequential arrangements of routines, but the routines are much shorter than they were in *Naked Lunch.* This may be due in part to the cut-up method, which makes sustained narrative much more difficult to write *and* read. (For a helpful guide to the arrangement of scenes in these novels, consult Michael Goodman and Lemuel Coley's *William S. Burroughs. A Reference Guide*.)

In the Knickerbocker interview, Burroughs lists some of the writers whose texts he took as precedents for the cut-up method and those he had plundered in using the method:

Of course, when you think of it, "The Waste Land" was the first great cutup collage, and Tristan Tzara had done a bit along the same lines. Dos Passos used the same idea in "The Camera Eye" sequences in *U.S.A.* . . .

INTERVIEWER: *Nova Express* is a cutup of many writers?

BURROUGHS: Joyce is in there. Shakespeare, Rimbaud, some writers that people haven't heard about, someone named Jack Stern. There's Kerouac. . . . Genet, of course. . . . Also Kafka, Eliot, and one of my favorites is Joseph Conrad. My story, "They Just Fade Away" is a folding (instead of cutting, you fold) from *Lord Jim*. . . . Richard Hughes is another favorite of mine. And Graham Greene.

Edited and reshuffled a bit, the authors listed here provide an index to the varied literary influences on Burroughs. There is a line that runs from the symbolist poets (Arthur Rimbaud and Charles Baudelaire, among others) to the surrealists (especially Tristan Tzara), to Franz Kafka and Eliot, all of whom are strikingly similar to Burroughs, not only in method but also in intention. Marshall McLuhan has explored the symbolist connection:

There is no uniform and continuous character in the nonvisual modalities of space and time. The symbolists freed themselves from visual conditions into the visionary world of the iconic and the auditory. Their act, to the visually oriented man, seems haunted, magical and often incomprehensible.

The surrealist connection has been developed by Eric Mottram in *William Burroughs: The Algebra of Need.* Mottram and McLuhan both also investigate the significance of Kafka, who exploded the logical and linear expectations of narrative and who was, like Burroughs, a seeker of silence. Dos Passos, whose technical innovations clearly influenced Burroughs' work, based a major character in *U.S.A.* (1925–1936) on the legendary Rockefeller publicity man Ivy Lee, who, Burroughs mentions, is a relative on his mother's side. He refers to the publicity methods his uncle developed as having "created images." Alan Ansen has explored the influence of Pound and Eliot. Morgan, in *Literary Outlaw,* does a fascinating exegesis on the similarities between the scene in *Naked Lunch* in which Dr. Benway interrogates Carl Petersen, and the scene in Conrad's *Under Western Eyes* (1911) when Razumov is questioned by Councillor Mikulin.

Of all of these, the connection to Eliot is perhaps the most intriguing, because of eerie similarities between the two men's biographies. Both were born and raised in St. Louis; and their respectable, bourgeois families, they discovered, held values they did not share. Both graduated from Harvard (indeed, while Burroughs was a student, Eliot delivered the Norton Lectures there, which Burroughs attended). Each pursued but did not complete graduate studies there, and drifted to Europe in search of a more congenial milieu. Eliot spent the rest of his life as an expatriate; Burroughs, a substantial portion of his. Both had significant difficulties with their wives that came to shape the fundamental images and meanings of their literature. Both even shared an obsession with cats—Eliot's *Old Possum's Book of Practical Cats* (1939) has a direct parallel in Burroughs' *The Cat Inside* (1986).

Perhaps most important, like Eliot, Burroughs relied on a multitude of voices to achieve a collage effect and to convey the entire atmosphere of a situation or scene with just a few words or lines of spoken phrase. In this regard, it is particularly interesting to examine the original facsimile manuscript of *The Waste Land* (published in 1973), which was a very different poem before Ezra Pound got hold of it. The original title was, tellingly, "He Do the Police in Different Voices," which might well function as title for a good many sections in a good many Burroughs novels, and it is composed of a series of unmistakable routines. A few of these routines survive in much shorter form in the final version of the poem: Marie, Madame Sosostris, the pub scene (which culminates in "HURRY UP, PLEASE,

IT'S TIME,'' a phrase that appears repeatedly in Burroughs' work), and the scene in the voice of the woman, saying ''Speak, why do you not speak.'' There has been very little by way of extensive appraisals of these similarities. This relationship is rich fodder for critics in the making, and serious study of it could result in an elevation of Burroughs' reputation in the academy.

Burroughs spent much of the later 1960's and early 1970's investigating nonliterary modes of expression: recordings, photography, film, and painting, among others. He revised or cut up many sections of his earlier work, mixed it with new, short pieces, including essays and interview material in which he expanded on his ideas, and reprinted them as small press editions and pamphlets. A good deal of these appear with artwork or photography accompanying the text. Burroughs became very interested in Dutch Schultz, the 1930's gangster whose last words, as he was lying in a Newark, New Jersey, hospital room after being shot, were taken down by a police stenographer; this monologue became famous as a kind of feverish surrealist document. Burroughs of course saw many similarities here with his own cut-up techniques and used Schultz's language to experiment with tape loops and a film script (published in book form in 1975). According to Jennie Skerl, all of these can be seen as part of a unified creative effort:

Burroughs' achievement as a novelist is substantial, but to see Burroughs as a novelist only is to ignore his artistic purpose and much of his work. For Burroughs is the creator of an artwork that ignores genre distinctions. Briefly summarized, Burroughs' artwork defines art as the process of consciousness, which produces a series of fragmentary works whose goal is to change the consciousness of the reader. . . . If the reader accedes to this demand, he must, in some sense, alter his consciousness and therefore change his life. . . . Such an aesthetic theory can never produce a masterpiece in the conventional sense because it ignores genre and craftsmanship.

Meanwhile, with the appearance of *The Wild Boys: A Book of the Dead* in 1971, Burroughs embarked on a new narrative quest. The text still relies on some of the old mythologies, particularly Egyptian and Mayan material, and some of the characters from the world of Interzone. But the use of the cut-up is much restricted, and there is a good deal more material laid out in conventional narrative form, with particular reference to science fiction, pulp westerns, and detective stories. *The Wild Boys* involves a pack of young, homosexual boys who travel in time and space and take up guerrilla warfare against the standard Burroughs forces of control:

In Mexico, South and Central America guerrilla units are forming an army of liberation to free the United States. . . . Despite disparate aims and personnel of its constituent members the underground is agreed on basic objectives. We intend to march on the police machine everywhere. We intend to destroy the police machine and all its records. We intend to destroy all dogmatic verbal systems. The family unit and its cancerous expansion into tribes, countries, nations we will eradicate at its vegetable roots. We don't want to hear any more family talk, mother talk, father talk, cop talk, priest talk, country talk, *or* party talk. To put it country simple we have heard enough bullshit.

In *The Wild Boys,* the related *Port of Saints* (1975, rev. ed. 1980), and even more in the trilogy of ''western'' novels that followed—*Cities of the Red Night* (1981), *The Place of Dead Roads* (1983), and *The Western Lands* (1987)—Burroughs attempts to integrate the themes of his earlier fiction (gruesome psychosexual instruments of control, telepathy, and so on) with his new mythologies (western outlaws, pirates, and private eyes battling such forces of control). *The Wild Boys* and the western trilogy include an enormous amount of autobiographical material from his boyhood in St. Louis, conveyed through the character Audrey Carsons/ Kim Carsons and others. Of course, the world of sodomy, excrement, disease, and death is still present, but in a more expansive landscape and a more accessible prose.

Any study of Burroughs, finally has to deal with the droll peculiarities of his personality. A well-brought-up Harvard alumnus, he failed to find a career until he was almost forty years old, and then it had to be one that did not pay. In the interim he had served as an exterminator, a store detective, and a marijuana farmer. He was a notorious drug addict and pederast; although arrested on various charges in New York, Louisiana, and Mexico, he spent little time in jail. He was discharged (honorably) from the army for psychiatric reasons: he had chopped a joint off his little finger in order to make an impression on a man with whom he was at the time morbidly in love.

Despite the awful shooting of his wife, Burroughs remained a ferocious devotee of weapons, both standard and obscure. There is, in Howard Brookner's documentary film *Burroughs,* an amusing scene where he demonstrates a few of those he keeps in his possession, including a blowgun, various styles of truncheons, and a vicious-looking knife, all accompanied by ironic monologue ("You're having a conversation with a man and you don't like what he's saying—SWISH—right across the jugular. Cut him off in mid-sentence.").

Nevertheless, in 1983, Burroughs joined the ranks of the respected, the established, and the creaking among American writers when he was invited to become a member of the American Academy and Institute of Arts and Letters in New York, a city where once he had been wanted only by the police. He accepted, and when asked to send material that could be included in an exhibit of the work of new members, asked if they would be interested in *Gun Door,* an artwork created by hanging bags of paint on a plywood panel and using it for target practice. The Academy declined the offer.

In fact, this and other artworks became an important source of income for Burroughs in the "punk" art craze of the 1980's. His paintings and objects were given gallery shows in New York and Europe, often selling out. "Painting is a hell of a lot easier than writing," Burroughs said. "It's the only way to go."

Selected Bibliography

WORKS OF WILLIAM S. BURROUGHS

NOVELS

Junkie: Confessions of an Unredeemed Drug Addict. By "William Lee." New York: Ace Books, 1953. Bound with *Narcotic Agent,* by Maurice Helbrant. Reprinted with foreword by Carl Solomon. New York: Ace Books, 1964. Reissued, in an unexpurgated edition, with an introduction by Allen Ginsberg, as *Junky.* New York: Penguin, 1977.

The Naked Lunch. Paris: Olympia, 1959. Published in the United States as *Naked Lunch.* New York: Grove Press, 1962, 1966 (first Evergreen Black Cat ed. paperback), 1984 (*Naked Lunch: Twenty-fifth Anniversary Edition,* with introduction by Jennie Skerl).

The Soft Machine. Paris: Olympia Press, 1961. Rev. ed., New York: Grove Press, 1966, 1967 (first Evergreen Black Cat ed.).

The Ticket That Exploded. Paris: Olympia, 1962. Rev. ed. New York: Grove Press, 1967, 1968 (first Evergreen Black Cat ed.).

Dead Fingers Talk. London: John Calder, 1963.

Nova Express. New York: Grove Press, 1964, 1965 (first Evergreen Black Cat ed.).

The Wild Boys: A Book of the Dead. New York: Grove Press, 1971.

Port of Saints. London: Covent Garden, 1975. Rev. ed., Berkeley, Calif.: Blue Wind, 1980.
Cities of the Red Night. New York: Holt, Rinehart & Winston, 1981.
Three Novels. New York: Grove Press, 1981. Includes *The Soft Machine, Nova Express,* and *The Wild Boys*.
The Place of Dead Roads. New York: Holt, Rinehart & Winston, 1983.
Queer. New York: Viking Penguin, 1985.
The Western Lands. New York: Viking Penguin, 1987.

OTHER BOOKS AND PAMPHLETS/BROADSIDES

The Exterminator. With Brion Gysin. San Francisco: Auerhahn, 1960; San Francisco: Dave Haselwood Books, 1967.
Minutes to Go. With Sinclair Beiles, Gregory Corso, and Brion Gysin. Paris: Two Cities, 1960.
The Yage Letters. With Allen Ginsberg. San Francisco: City Lights, 1963.
Roosevelt After Inauguration. New York: Fuck You Press, 1964.
They Do Not Always Remember. New York: Delacorte Press, 1965.
Health Bulletin: APO-33. A Metabolic Regulator. New York: Fuck You Press, 1965 (pamphlet).
Time. New York: 'C' Press, 1965 (pamphlet).
Valentine's Day Reading. New York: American Theatre for Poets, 1965 (pamphlet).
APO-33: Bulletin, a Metabolic Regulator. San Francisco: City Lights, 1966.
So Who Owns Death TV? With Claude Pélieu and Carl Weissner. San Francisco: Beach Books, 1967 (pamphlet).
The Dead Star. San Francisco: Nova Broadcast Press, 1969 (broadside).
The Job. With Daniel Odier. New York: Grove Press, 1970. Rev. and enl. ed., New York: Grove Press, 1974. Repr., New York: Penguin, 1989.
Ali's Smile. Brighton, Sussex: Unicorn, 1971.
Electronic Revolution. Cambridge: Blackmoor Head, 1971.
Brion Gysin Let the Mice In. Edited by Jan Herman. West Glover, Vt.: Something Else Press, 1973. Includes "The Invisible Generation," "Word Authority More Habit Forming Than Heroin," and "Parenthetically 7 Hertz" by Burroughs.
Exterminator! New York: Viking, 1973.
Mayfair Acadamy Series More or Less. Brighton, Sussex: Urgency Press Rip-Off, 1973 (pamphlet).
White Subway. London: Aloes seolA, 1973.
The Book of Breeething. With illustrations by Robert F. Gales. Berkeley, Calif.: Blue Wind, 1975, 1980.
The Last Words of Dutch Schultz. A Fiction in the Form of a Film Script. New York: Viking/Seaver Books, 1975.
Sidetripping. With photographs by Charles Gatewood. New York: Strawberry Hill, 1975.
Cobble Stone Gardens. Baltimore: Cherry Valley Editions, 1976.
The Retreat Diaries. New York: City Moon, 1976.
The Third Mind. With Brion Gysin. New York: Viking, 1978.
Blade Runner: A Movie. Berkeley, Calif.: Blue Wind, 1979.
Dr. Benway: A Passage from The Naked Lunch. Santa Barbara, Calif.: Bradford Morrow, 1979.
Roosevelt After Inauguration And Other Atrocities. San Francisco: City Lights, 1979.
Where Naked Troubadours Shoot Snooty Baboons. Northridge, Calif.: Lord John Press, 1979.
Early Routines. Santa Barbara, Calif.: Cadmus, 1981.
The Streets of Chance. With illustrations by Howard Buchwald. New York: Red Ozier Press, 1981.
Ah Pook Is Here, and Other Texts. New York: Riverrun, 1982.
Letters to Allen Ginsberg, 1953–1957. With prefaces by Burroughs and Ginsberg. New York: Full Court, 1982.
Sinki's Sauna. New York: Pequod Press, 1982.
A William Burroughs Reader. Edited by John Calder. London: Pan Books/Picador, 1982.
The Burroughs File. San Francisco: City Lights, 1984. With introductory essays by James Grauerholz, Paul Bowles, and Alan Ansen.
The Adding Machine: Selected Essays. New York: Seaver Books, 1986.
The Cat Inside. With eight drawings by Brion Gysin. New York: Grenfell Press, 1986.
Interzone. Edited by James Grauerholz. New York: Viking, 1989.
New York. Paris: Editions du Rocher, 1989.
Tornado Alley. With illustrations by S. Clay Wilson. Cherry Valley, N.Y.: Cherry Valley Editions, 1989.

BIBLIOGRAPHIES

Goodman, Michael B. *William S. Burroughs: An Annotated Bibliography of His Works and Criticism.* New York: Garland, 1975.

Goodman, Michael B., with Lemuel B. Coley. *William S. Burroughs: A Reference Guide.* New York: Garland, 1990.

Maynard, Joe, and Barry Miles. *William S. Burroughs: A Bibliography, 1953–73.* Charlottesville: University Press of Virginia, 1978.

Miles Associates. *A Descriptive Catalogue of the William S. Burroughs Archive.* London: Covent Garden, 1973.

Skerl, Jennie. "A William S. Burroughs Bibliography." *Serif,* 11:12–20 (Summer 1974).

BIOGRAPHICAL AND CRITICAL STUDIES

Ansen, Alan. "William Burroughs: A Personal View." *Review of Contemporary Fiction,* 4:49–55 (Spring 1984).

Bryant, Jerry H. *The Open Decision: The Contemporary American Novel and Its Intellectual Background.* New York: The Free Press, 1970. Pp. 199–228.

Cook, Bruce. *The Beat Generation.* New York: Scribners, 1971. Pp. 165–184.

Goodman, Michael Barry. *Contemporary Literary Censorship: The Case History of Burroughs' Naked Lunch.* Metuchen, N.J.: Scarecrow, 1981.

Gysin, Brion. "Cut-ups: A Project for Disastrous Success." *Evergreen Review,* 32:56–61 (April–May 1964).

Hassan, Ihab. "The Subtracting Machine: The Work of William Burroughs." *Critique,* 6:4–23 (Spring 1963).

———. *The Dismemberment of Orpheus.* New York: Oxford University Press, 1971. Pp. 249–250.

Kostelanetz, Richard. "From Nightmare to Serendipity: A Retrospective Look at William Burroughs." *Twentieth Century Literature,* 9:123–130 (1965).

Lydenberg, Robin. "Beyond Good and Evil: 'How To' Read *Naked Lunch.*" *Review of Contemporary Fiction,* 4:75–85 (Spring 1984).

———. *Word Cultures: Radical Theory and Practice in William S. Burroughs' Fiction.* Urbana: University of Illinois Press, 1987.

Mailer, Norman. "Some Children of the Goddess." *Esquire,* July 1963, pp. 64–69, 105.

Malin, Irving. "Flashes of *Schultz.*" *Review of Contemporary Fiction,* 4:143–144 (Spring 1984).

McCarthy, Mary. "Burroughs' '*Naked Lunch.*' " *Encounter,* 20:92–98 (April 1963).

———. "Dejeuner sur l'Herbe: *The Naked Lunch.*" *The New York Review of Books,* 1 (1):4–5 (1963).

———. *The Writing on the Wall.* New York: Harcourt Brace, 1970. Pp. 42–53.

McLuhan, Marshall. "Notes on Burroughs." *Nation,* 199:517–519 (December 28, 1964).

McNally, Dennis. *Desolate Angel: Jack Kerouac, the Beat Generation, and America.* New York: Random House, 1979.

Morgan, Ted. *Literary Outlaw. The Life and Times of William Burroughs.* New York: Henry Holt, 1988.

Mottram, Eric. *William Burroughs: The Algebra of Need.* New York: Intrepid Press, 1971; London: Marion Boyars, 1977.

Sante, Luc. "The Invisible Man." *The New York Review of Books,* May 10, 1984, pp. 12–15.

Skerl, Jennie. "Freedom Through Fantasy in the Recent Novels of William S. Burroughs." *Review of Contemporary Fiction,* 4:124–130 (Spring 1984).

———. *William S. Burroughs.* Boston: Twayne, 1985.

Solotaroff, Theodore. *The Red Hot Vacuum, and Other Pieces on the Writing of the Sixties.* New York: Atheneum, 1970. Pp. 247–253.

Tanner, Tony. *City of Words: American Fiction 1950–1970.* New York: Harper & Row, 1971. Pp. 109–140.

Tytell, John. *Naked Angels: The Lives and Literature of the Beat Generation.* New York: McGraw-Hill, 1976.

INTERVIEWS

Bockris, Victor, ed. *With William Burroughs: A Report from the Bunker.* New York: Seaver, 1981.

Corso, Gregory, and Allen Ginsberg. "Interview with William Burroughs." *Journal for the Protection of All Beings* (San Francisco), no. 1:79–83 (1961).

Knickerbocker, Conrad. "William Burroughs." In *Writers at Work: The Paris Review Interviews, Third Series.* Edited by Alfred Kazin. New York: Viking, 1967. Pp. 141–174.

Malanga, Gerard. "An Interview with William Burroughs.'' In *The Beat Book.* Edited by Arthur Knight and Glee Knight. California, Pa.: the unspeakable visions of the individual series, 1974. Pp. 90–112.

Odier, Daniel. *The Job: Interviews with William S. Burroughs.* New York: Grove Press, 1970. Rev. and enl. ed., New York: Grove Press, 1974.

Palmer, Robert. ''Rolling Stone Interview: William Burroughs.'' *Rolling Stone,* May 11, 1972.

Skerl, Jennie. ''An Interview with William S. Burroughs.'' *Modern Language Studies,* 12:3–17 (Summer 1982).

Tytell, John. ''An Interview with William Burroughs.'' In *The Beat Diary.* Edited by Arthur Knight and Kit Knight. California, Pa.: the unspeakable visions of the individual series, 1977. Pp. 35–49.

—*VINCE PASSARO*

Truman Capote

1924–1984

IN LATE 1959, Truman Capote came upon a brief article in *The New York Times* about the slaughter of a Kansas farming family. He showed it to William Shawn, editor in chief of *The New Yorker,* who agreed with Capote that it would make an intriguing story. Bennett Cerf, the Random House editor who was one of Capote's literary and high-society chaperons, lined up introductions to the Kansas academic community, and Capote was off to the Midwest, with his friend Harper Lee (author of *To Kill a Mockingbird*) along for the adventure.

The thirty-five-year-old writer, a precocious media darling and star of Manhattan's glamorous smart set, spent the next six years traveling back and forth to Kansas, working on a chronicle that became his tour de force, the best-seller *In Cold Blood: A True Account of a Multiple Murder and Its Consequences,* published in 1966. He became obsessed with this murder of an innocent heartland family and the characters of the killers. Capote used the event and the stories it generated as the basis for an appraisal of the American dream: *In Cold Blood* was a report from the front, a mid-twentieth-century update on what we were made of, on how we thought of ourselves as opposed to what we really were. Capote investigated, and reported, the state of American values and the composition of that mythicized collective figure who had spent a score of previous generations questing, pioneering, creating new worlds—that American who is "us," proudly singing our self-reliance and ourselves. His findings were unsettling.

Who was Capote to take this task upon himself, to present himself as an omniscient moral and cultural arbiter of twentieth-century America? When the short, effete, squeaky-voiced New Yorker arrived in Holcomb, Kansas, in the wake of the uncertain fear generated by the inexplicable murders, a few natives thought the strange-looking Capote himself might be the murderer, according to his biographer Gerald Clarke. In their eyes, said Harper Lee, "he was like someone coming off the moon." Although the Kansans he encountered first greeted Capote as little more than a flamboyant freak, later, as he worked his way into their confidence and their lives, they embraced him. Perhaps he could make right, or at least make sense of, what had happened to their world. Perhaps he was a visionary—the kind of twisted person who could explain the twisted world in which they lived.

Truman Streckfus Persons was born in New Orleans on September 30, 1924. His parents' marriage was in a constant state of turmoil. Truman's father, Arch Persons, was a schemer whose plans were rarely successful. His mother, born Lillie Mae Faulk, had little use for Arch.

He was only minimally present while Truman was growing up; a series of his mother's lovers were more prominent. While Truman's parents were indulging in their own little affairs, the young boy was left with relatives, usually his mother's endearing family, the Faulks, in Monroeville, Alabama.

In 1931, Lillie Mae asked Arch for a divorce so that she could marry Joseph Garcia Capote, a businessman who was more stable than Arch, and whose surname Truman had taken by 1933. While Joe and Lillie Mae provided a somewhat more secure home than Truman had had as a young child, he was still to have traumatic associations with the institutions of home and family, both real and fictional, throughout his life.

The Capotes lived in Greenwich, Connecticut, and New York City when Truman was an adolescent; his love affair with what he thought the most glamorous and exciting city in the world began at this time. At the age of eighteen he entered the world of contemporary belles lettres by securing a job as a copyboy at *The New Yorker*. Over the next few years, Capote worked to earn recognition as a rising young writer on other magazines, and to find a place for himself in New York's literary rat race. He applied himself to his writing passionately and intensively. Capote made the most of his winning social skills and the force of his personality: he was invited to write in residence at the prestigious Yaddo literary and artistic colony at the age of twenty-one, and he had indisputably arrived on the scene with a highly publicized and controversial best-seller by the time he was twenty-four.

Over the next three and a half decades, Capote left his imprint across what he considered to be civilized society. Based in New York, he made extensive forays into the world's most exotic resorts. His career, begun in fiction, was similarly far-reaching in style and subject. His circle took in hundreds of the world's most famous celebrities, among whom he traveled sometimes triumphantly, but sometimes disastrously. His two most significant romantic associations were with the critic Newton Arvin, from 1946 until 1949, and with the writer Jack Dunphy, from 1949 until Capote's death.

By the time of his death (in Joanne Carson's Los Angeles mansion) on August 23, 1984, from severe debilitation caused by drugs, alcohol, and emotional exhaustion, he had established a persona, what might be called a media presence, that linked together his eclectic written works, and at the same time somehow transcended them. Capote's pathetic decline at the end of his life—when he found himself embittered, out of control, creatively blocked—reflects the devastating personal toll his work exacted and provides an ironic counterpoint to his meteoric rise in youth.

Truman Capote's writing taught Americans something about who we were. He wrote of the country's heroes (Marilyn Monroe, Marlon Brando, Humphrey Bogart) and of its common folk (the Kansans). He captured the American landscape—the Midwest, Manhattan, New Orleans—as well as the glamorous international scene—the Mediterranean, Moscow, Haiti—as they appear to the urbane American adventurer. He wrote of his childhood in the South, portraying a vivid sense of that region and its people, and at the same time offering a moving psychological portrait of modern American childhood and adolescence, with its anxiety, instability, hostility, and loneliness. Though Capote drew closely on his own childhood experiences—his unloving and abusive parents, the odd relatives he traveled among, trying to find a home—he parlayed this into a more generalized contemporary portrait of the vagaries and pain of the modern American family.

He wrote of American aspirations at their most elementally capitalist and consumerist, as he looked at Tiffany's, Fifth Avenue, the Upper East Side, and the Four Seasons, and at their most depraved and destructive, as he looked at death row, and also as he eavesdropped on what people were actually saying at the Four Seasons. He flitted within high society, entranced with the trappings of the elite and their culture, embracing them but then turning on them just as fiercely in vicious-spirited exposés of their hypocrisy and idiocy.

America affirmed, during a decades-long fascination with this character, that he did indeed know where to look to find its story. The public followed him wherever he went, devouring piece by piece his idiosyncratic dissection of contemporary society. Capote's own relationship with the public was both productive and destructive: he loved the clamoring approval of the crowds, the media, the glitterati, yet he was also susceptible to frequent breakdowns, to addictive and self-destructive behavior, to the fear of failing to live up to the public's expectations. He shared with his character Holly Golightly, in *Breakfast at Tiffany's* (1958), frequent susceptibility to "the mean reds": "You're afraid and you sweat like hell, but you don't know what you're afraid of. Except something bad is going to happen, only you don't know what it is." He was quite capable of humiliating himself in numerous ways, coast to coast, in front of millions.

Capote's success covered a realm extending from fiction to journalism, from books to magazines, from plays to musicals to movies to television documentaries, from serious literary efforts to black-tie parties that dominated the society pages. In the course of his eclectic literary and cultural career, the bizarre pervasive character of the writer himself always preceded him and infused whatever he was undertaking. Capote's mark on American letters is inseparable from the relationship of this writer-character to American culture at large—the extent to which the public trusted him (and the extent to which he was successful) at taking the American pulse, with a wider range and scope and in more multifaceted ways than any other writer, artist, or intellect had demonstrated.

Capote's canvas extended to wherever Capote himself wanted to go and could get in. He was commercially motivated to a certain extent, and he took on some dubious projects because the price was right. But he was more strongly drawn to novelty—novel venues from Kansas to Kyoto, and whatever might be for him a new way of capturing those venues—and to fame. In novels, novellas, fragments of novels, nonfiction, short stories, and magazine pieces—all copiously gathered into various published collections—as well as in his films, Capote mixed freely on his canvas parties, places, failed projects (scripts and ideas that otherwise never came to fruition), and, especially, people: family, lovers, tormentors, and many alter egos, people who were real or fictional, or fictional people who were thinly disguised real people. In his final literary effort, published in 1987 as *Answered Prayers: The Unfinished Novel,* he retells his own adventures, as he had done in his numerous travel pieces; he shares a lifetime of accumulated gossip, as he did in smaller doses with Monroe in "A Beautiful Child" (1955) or with Brando in "The Duke in His Domain" (1957); he explores the glamorous intrigues and seamy underside of the cosmopolitan life, as he had done in *Breakfast at Tiffany's* and numerous stories. The glittering people who compose the worthies of the world in Capote's eyes recur throughout his work: Eudora Welty, Colette, Jackie Kennedy, Greta Garbo, Jane Bowles, Cecil Beaton.

Capote, like many writers, was fond of telling the same story over and over, examining it each time from a slightly different approach or perspective, and that narrative is a strong connective force among his disparate undertakings. When he tells various versions of his life story, he always wrestles with the pervasive issue of his sexuality, its formation and development—he did this in his first published work, *Other Voices,*

Other Rooms (1948), and continually thereafter. The story that Capote retells is generated by, and is about, loneliness. It is the story of how a talented yet troubled man writes the world around him. ''I'm an alcoholic. I'm a drug addict. I'm homosexual. I'm a genius,'' was Capote's oft-repeated self-description, as resonant a mantra as Timothy Leary's ''Tune in, turn on, drop out.''

Capote's triumph was that he wrangled his Ur-story into a fascinating spectrum of smart reports from the cutting edge of American culture that his audience watched as eagerly as they watched Capote himself. He came across as a kind of freak, but never enough so that he repelled for long. His readers felt warmly toward him, as toward a mascot, and they were always ready to take him back into their hearts, to see what adventure he was up to next. He was not a writer-hero like Ernest Hemingway, Norman Mailer, or Jack Kerouac, with whom Americans vicariously identified; rather, his audience necessarily distanced themselves from him. One of his last incarnations, as the fey crime boss Lionel Twain in the tedious Neil Simon film *Murder by Death,* was his least dignified, his silliest; still, it only added to the mythic allure of his persona. Like Leary, and other cultural commentators such as Andy Warhol and John Lennon, Capote transcended the social stereotype of the writer-artist-intellectual, achieving a prominence that was transcultural and far-reaching.

Capote's far-flung aspirations translate into a career that defies simple summation. Charting the various phases, periods, genres, and manifestations of his work, his different focuses, would quickly result in a graphic confluence of arrows, overlaps, and free-floating escapades. Capote's work begins with his southern fiction: his first novel, *Other Voices, Other Rooms,* published when he was twenty-three, as well as *The Grass Harp* (1951), which he adapted as a musical, with little success, and an assortment of short stories such as ''My Side of the Matter'' (indebted to Eudora Welty's ''Why I Live at the P.O.''), ''Children on Their Birthdays,'' and ''A Tree of Night,'' collected in the 1949 *A Tree of Night and Other Stories.*

Capote's southern fiction, with its element of southern gothic and of a troubled South, is firmly in the tradition of Flannery O'Connor, Eudora Welty, Carson McCullers, and, less strikingly but still notably, of William Faulkner and Tennessee Williams. Capote's South is a land of haunting spaces and shadows. As Joel, the young protagonist of *Other Voices, Other Rooms,* first sees the landscape through which he will journey, he finds it ''lonesome country; and here in the swamplike hollows where tiger lilies bloom the size of a man's head, there are luminous green logs that shine under the dark marsh water like drowned corpses.'' A thick folkloric milieu of southern ghosts and tragic seers reinforces the pervasive gothic. The settings, Noon City and Skully's Landing, symbolically accentuate the boy's ''psychological journey from day into night, from the active aboveground world into the underground world of dreams,'' writes Clarke These dreams become nightmares as Joel settles in at Skully's Landing: Capote writes of his protagonist, ''At thirteen Joel was nearer a knowledge of death than in any year to come.''

The Grass Harp takes its name from the eerie atmosphere described by its narrator, Collin, at the beginning of that novel:

> [Past] a glaring hill of bonewhite slabs and brown burnt flowers [in the Baptist cemetery] begins the darkness of River Woods. It must have been on one of those September days when we were there in the woods gathering roots that Dolly said: Do you hear? that is the grass harp, always telling a story—it knows the stories of all the people on the hill, of all the people who ever lived, and when we are dead it will tell ours, too.

Capote's landscapes are evocative and fecundly storied. He begins to discover in his early writing, and will violently confirm by the time he gets through Kansas, that the American landscape is hostile, exciting but dangerous; it cannot be confidently controlled or navigated. It reveals the stories of the dead and of the horror of their deaths, of the unfulfilled chaotic lives that terminate in the certain bleak closure of these deaths which powerfully dominate the landscape.

Capote's gothic panorama is largely peopled by grotesques: Cousin Randolph in *Other Voices, Other Rooms* is the most resonant of these. Inhabiting a gaudy room of faded gold and tarnished silk that subtly sickens Joel ("It all made him feel as though he'd eaten too much candy"), Randolph lamely tries to imitate a Wildean decadent, but his actual experience is without any of the requisite trappings, except for a vague memory of an orgiastic Mardi Gras. His posturing appears hollow, even to the young Joel, and yet Randolph represents Joel's (and thus, Capote's) fate. Ihab Hassan writes, he has "all the unpredictability and perverted innocence which qualify him for becoming the mentor and lover of Joel" (*Radical Innocence: Studies in the Contemporary American Novel,* Princeton, N.J. [1961], p. 241). Eventually, Randolph is seen exposed, weakened, pathetically lonely. His onetime affiliation with prizefighter Pepe Alvarez provides a moment of potential greatness, a kind of homosexual (per)version of a Hemingway tableau, but Randolph's inability to connect, his uncomfortable fate as a social misfit, shatters that moment: "One night Pepe came to the house very drunk, and proceeded with the boldest abandon to a) beat Dolores [another member of a loosely organized "family" in which Randolph only temporarily belongs, whom Pepe loved as Randolph loved Pepe] with his belt, b) piss on the rug and on my paintings, c) call me horrible hurting names, d) break my nose, e and f and otherwise." Randolph's eventual incarnation is as a feeble transvestite, dressed as Dolores and pining after Pepe.

Capote's panorama of southern grotesques includes characters like Miss Roberta, who initiates Joel on his journey and points him toward Noon City: "She had long ape-like arms that were covered with dark fuzz, and there was a wart on her chin, and decorating this wart was a single antenna-like hair"; Zoo, the servant at the Noon City home, with an elongated neck that made her "almost a freak, a human giraffe," a magnet for horrific violence, knife assaults, and gang rape; a carnival freak show, with a four-legged chicken, a two-headed baby floating in a glass tank, and a Duck Boy flapping his webbed hands. In "My Side of the Matter," the narrator verbally assaults his wife's aunts, who have poisoned her mind against him: "Eunice is this big old fat thing with a behind that must weigh a tenth of a ton. . . . [Olivia-Ann] is a natural-born half-wit and ought really to be kept in somebody's attic. She's real pale and skinny and has a mustache." In "Children on Their Birthdays," the young protagonist Miss Bobbit lives in a boardinghouse with the alcoholic Mr. Henderson, who "would charge to the top of the stairs and bellow down to Mrs. Sawyer that there were midgets in the walls trying to get at his supply of toilet paper. They've already stolen fifteen cents' worth, he said." That story opens in the finest form of Capote's gothic grotesque: "Yesterday afternoon the six-o'clock bus ran over Miss Bobbit. I'm not sure what there is to be said about it."

Capote's grotesqueries are not absolute or immutable: in the wings, there are always, providing kindness, various incarnations of the character of Sook Faulk, a much older cousin of Capote's who, though seen by her family as childlike and simple, lavished loving companionship on the young boy when no one else did. There are also families, and a degree of caring that comes from these families, tentative and sometimes twisted though they are.

In *The Grass Harp,* this "family" includes a crotchety old judge and Riley, a charismatic young man, who are drawn to comfort and protect Collin and Dolly (the characters based on Capote and Sook); yet the group can exist together only when they flee up into a tree, removing themselves from society and living, literally, above it in a tree house. The sheriff and townspeople clamor beneath trying to disrupt and sunder this family. Eventually they succeed in bursting Capote's untraditional family, which had temporarily transcended the limitations of an imperfect social setting. Since Collin and Dolly are not allowed to live in the tree house, they must subsist in the mundane real world, where Dolly cannot endure. Collin needs Dolly as Capote needed Sook; the older woman is the one who hears and sees the supernatural beauty of things, like the stories from the grass harp. (Later, in *The Thanksgiving Visitor,* published in 1967, Sook tells the young Capote, "Chrysanthemums . . . are like lions. Kingly characters. I always expect them to *spring.* To turn on me with a growl and a roar." And Capote writes, "It was the kind of remark that caused people to wonder about Miss Sook, though I understood that only in retrospect, for I always knew just what she meant.") Capote badly needs this spirit, this companion. Sook saw that everyone, even young Truman, has a kind of specialness within him, the kind of specialness that materializes only up in the trees and only if there is a Dolly figure to bring it out, as she does for the Judge and Riley as well. Capote's fantasy vision in this novella approaches a surreal appraisal of what a boy must do to survive in the South. Collin's perspective sharply presents the lonely desperation of a young boy who must depend on the kindness of strangers (though Joel, like Capote himself, finds this kindness no more satisfying than did Blanche DuBois), and if not the kindness then the strangeness of strangers.

Capote retains fertile memories from his southern boyhood odyssey, and his southern world is one that scares, threatens, and represses the young boys who are trying to make sense of it, trying to discover their selves, their roles in life, amid a generally hostile or disquieting cast of characters. The hero is predominantly uncomfortable, embarrassed, awkward in this world where he does not fit. In *Other Voices, Other Rooms,* this sensibility is epitomized when Joel is asked, "Why are you so fidgety? Must you use the bathroom?" He replies, " 'Oh no.' He felt all at once as though he'd wet his pants in public. 'Oh no.' " The quintessential adolescent fear of being wrong and ridiculous permeates Capote's southern literature, and a similarly elemental fear resonates throughout his career.

That fear is closely linked with loneliness, which throughout Capote's writing generates a clear sense of otherness. The "other" of *Other Voices, Other Rooms* represents the people and places where Capote and his characters cannot live. Capote knows that comfortingly "normal" voices and rooms exist, but his sensibility cannot reach them. Little Sunshine, a bizarre hermit in that book, whose nickname reveals that not much hope peeks through and whose creation of "a charm guarantee no turrible happenins gonna happen" inflames Joel's desire for such an amulet, stays in his swampy gothic home in an abandoned hotel because "it was his rightful home. . . . If he went away, as he had once upon a time, other voices, other rooms, voices lost and clouded, strummed his dreams." William L. Nance writes in *The Worlds of Truman Capote,* "For Joel, as for Little Sunshine, home is a decayed and forbidding place, but it must be accepted, even if it should prove to be presided over by the devil-man." The otherness—an alternate and more palatable reality—is dimly perceived, but can never be attained.

Capote's protagonists are thus doomed to a spectrum of manifestations of lonely isolation. When Collin arrives to stay with his aunts in *The Grass Harp,* Dolly says, "I told Verena you would be lonesome.'' In ''Master Misery,'' Sylvia lives with her married sister, who asks her, ''Doesn't it make you lonesome seeing how happy we are?'' In ''Shut a Final Door,'' ''Walter was alone and very lonesome in New York.'' In ''Miriam,'' Mrs. H. T. Miller's ''interests were narrow, she had no friends to speak of.'' In *Breakfast at Tiffany's,* Holly Golightly receives letters from soldiers that ''were always torn into strips like bookmarks. . . . *Remember* and *miss you* and *rain* and *please write* and *damn* and *goddamn* were the words that recurred most often on these slips; those, and *lonesome* and *love.*'' However painful, lonely, or misfitting the grotesque reality may be, it is one that is destined to endure for Capote.

Not fitting, not belonging, is the tragic bane of all Capote's characters, from Joel and Collin to Holly and Perry Smith (one of the murderers from *In Cold Blood*). In ''Shut a Final Door,'' Walter is the New York urbane cosmopolitan manqué; after the failure of his personal relationships and his professional aspirations, he collapses in the arms of a fellow sufferer: '' 'Hold me,' he said, discovering he could still cry. 'Hold me, please.' 'Poor little boy,' she said, patting his back. 'My poor little boy: we're awfully alone in this world, aren't we?' '' These words might serve as an epigram to the whole of Capote's work, and to his life. ''Hold me'' is a plea Capote never stopped making. There were always characters in his writing and people in his life who could pat the lonely man's back and try to soothe him, but the soothing is never completely successful. Capote's heroes inescapably remain ''awfully alone.'' Capote's world of troubled Southerners—tormented crippled misfits, always at least bordering on the grotesque—resembles McCuller's world in *The Ballad of the Sad Cafe* (1943), or John Kennedy Toole's in *A Confederacy of Dunces* (1980). His characters are not as self-expository or voluble as those in many of Williams' or Faulkner's worlds, but they seek the same kind of communion (however tenuous and fragile) and family unity (which is somewhat achieved, but always tentatively).

Other Voices, Other Rooms is a bildungsroman: Joel travels to Skully's Landing incomplete, in search of his father and trying to find himself as well; but what does he learn? From Jesus Fever and Little Sunshine he tries to learn the ways of the South, its people, its gnosis; from Idabel and Florabel he tries to learn how to play with and interact with his peers; from Randolph, Miss Amy, and his paralyzed father he tries to learn his background, his family heritage; from Zoo he tries to learn how to be cared for. From this array of characters who are themselves very unstable, Joel attempts to wrench out some sense of meaning, some human connection. He needs to learn the archetypal human endeavors: how to go on a quest, however eerily unpromising it seems; how to recognize and attain an amulet; how to commune with one's father. Joel must learn these things, however unfulfilling and even irrelevant they may seem to the world around him. This learning is never completely successful—the others are too weird and too firmly limited in their own worlds, their own inadequacies. Nevertheless, one gets what one can from what is available; Joel, like Holly Golightly, like Kansas killer Perry Smith, and like Capote himself, learns how to scrounge for scraps.

Joel's adolescence is certainly not far removed from the twenty-three-year-old author's own. Capote, like Joel, was shunted around to various family members in the South as he was growing up, few of whom cared much for him or paid him much attention. Their distorted lives resembled, to a young boy, the ones he creates in his fiction. Joel's last name is changed from his father's, Sansom, to Knox, after his parents' divorce, making his search for his paternal legacy that much more difficult; this parallels Capote's name change in adolescence.

Adolescence, as depicted in the portrait of Joel, is certainly a scary prospect, but also, in a Joycean way, full of vast epic and artistic potential. Joel's fragmentary memories of youth are very much in the tempo of *A Portrait of the Artist as a Young Man* (1916):

He hadn't had a proper hour's rest since leaving New Orleans, for when he closed his eyes, as now, certain sickening memories slid through his mind. Of these, one in particular stood out: he was at a grocery counter, his mother waiting next to him, and outside in the street January rain was making icicles on the naked tree limbs. Together they left the store and walked silently along the wet pavement, he holding a calico umbrella above his mother, who carried a sack of tangerines. They passed a house where a piano was playing, and the music sounded sad in the grey afternoon, but his mother remarked what a pretty song. And when they reached home she was humming it, but she felt cold and went to bed, and the doctor came, and for over a month he came every day, but she was always cold, and Aunt Ellen was there, always smiling, and the doctor, always smiling, and the uneaten tangerines shriveled up in the icebox; and when it was over he went with Ellen to live in a dingy two-family house near Ponchartrain.

In spite of the dense gothic setting, and the oppressive forces of painful memory and an uncongenial present atmosphere, the adolescent sustains a degree of innocence that can lift him at least somewhat above this world; in spite of its decadence, the world is rich with character that can be potentially transmuted into art or, perhaps, repressed into art. In this bildungsroman Joel learns how to be Truman Capote when he grows up, just as the unpromising Stephen Dedalus must learn how to become James Joyce; Capote knows that this may not be a very comforting lesson, but it is one that embodies a kind of noble endurance. As he creates the characters of Joel, Idabel, and Randolph, Capote is locating himself somewhere among them—trying to define his sense of gender and sexuality, of goals and personality and relations to others. However tenuously, Capote works out in *Other Voices, Other Rooms* whatever strengths he will carry into his young adult life.

If the first item in Capote's oeuvre is southern fiction, item one-prime might be the author's later literature of nostalgic reminiscence. Even after Capote turned from writing about the South to writing about the chic, cosmopolitan world in which he moved as an adult, the powerful experiences of his southern childhood remained strong in his imagination. *The Thanksgiving Visitor* and *A Christmas Memory* (first published in 1956 and reissued as a boxed volume a decade later) are heavily influenced by the same southern voice of Capote's early fiction, but they are also importantly autobiographical, capturing the warmth of his relationship with his adored cousin Sook and also the anxiety of a young child who knows that he is terribly lonely and that he is fated to continue a lonely life because he does not fit in. These singular stories represent the essence of the Capote-as-character theme, which occupies much of his other work.

It is a bit hard to imagine Capote as his younger self in the episodes he describes from his rural Alabama childhood in *The Thanksgiving Visitor*: working on the farm, rising from bed at 5:30 A.M. for a breakfast of fried squirrel, fried catfish, and hominy grits. But the relationship between Truman and Sook rings true—again, an unlikely but vital affiliation. Another character, Capote's schoolmate Odd Henderson, is also an important type in Capote's writing. Odd is a tormenting bully, an underprivileged child whom Sook forces a reluctant Capote to invite for Thanksgiving. Odd, who repays Sook's kindness by trying to steal a cameo brooch from the bureau in her bathroom, seems much like the character of Dick Hickock, the meaner of the killers from *In Cold Blood.* Capote views this kind of personality as capable of enormous evil—the young Truman in *The Thanksgiving Visitor* has nightmares about Odd's meanness to him—but such a character nevertheless has a tender aspect: Sook tells Capote that Odd's mother views him as a tremendous help. (Hickock's parents, too, seem to have drawn strength from their son, however evil he was.)

This small portion of kindness is not meant to mitigate the dominant evil of the character, but, Capote knows, it is nonetheless something he must come to terms with. People are not unilaterally composed of any single characteristic—they are confusing bundles of contradictory traits. This story demonstrates Capote's vision of the complexity of morality and personality, especially cruel personalities. Odd represents the kind of character who is not just abstractly mean but specifically oppressive to Truman, reminding the young hero of his own deficient socialization; as troubled as Odd is, society is actually more likely to accept Odd than Truman:

> Once, when he had me pinned against a wall, I asked him straight out what I had done to make him dislike me so much; suddenly he relaxed, let me loose and said, "You're a sissy. I'm just straightening you out." He was right, I was a sissy of sorts, and the moment he said it, I realized there was nothing I could do to alter his judgment, other than toughen myself to accept and defend the fact.

Capote cannot condemn Odd for the torment he inflicts; self-debasingly, he seems to accept that the way of the world is to be subjected to such torment, given his own misfitting character. Odd speaks in the other voices from other rooms that are absolutely closed to Truman, and Truman's fascination with Odd echoes his obsession with the Kansas killers.

Still, despite the confusion that surrounds the young man, Sook is a respite. In *A Christmas Memory,* Capote depicts an episode of unmitigated warmth, as he tells how he and his cousin—referred to simply and touchingly only as "my friend"—collect nuts and berries in the woods and buy whiskey from the bootlegger Mr. Haha Jones for their annual ritual of making fruitcakes on a budget of $12.73 in loose change, carefully hoarded over the year. The portrait is uncharacteristically delightful: the elderly cousin and the seven-year-old boy get soused, as part of the ritual, drinking from jelly glasses the two inches of whiskey left over after the cakes are done. They distribute their thirty-one cakes in a way that reflects, again, the way Sook and Capote scrounged to form a makeshift network of "family":

> Who are they for?
>
> Friends. Not necessarily neighbor friends: indeed, the larger share is intended for persons we've met maybe once, perhaps not at all. People who've struck our fancy. Like President Roosevelt. Like the Reverend and Mrs. J. C. Lucey, Baptist missionaries to Borneo who lectured here last winter. Or the little knife grinder who comes through town twice a year. . . . Is it because my friend is shy with everyone *except* strangers that these strangers, and merest acquaintances, seem to us our truest friends? I think yes.

Even the gloomy Mr. Haha Jones softens in the face of this enterprise, and donates the whiskey in exchange for a fruitcake (with an extra cup of raisins in it as a reward). The pair wonders if Eleanor Roosevelt will serve the cake they sent her at dinner.

Breakfast at Tiffany's marked the beginning of Capote's literary fascination with wealth, parties, the elite, and the general atmosphere of panache that pervaded Manhattan, and it captures his equal fascination with the underside of this cosmopolitan world, the failure or absence of much that it promised, to which he was never oblivious. Gore Vidal asserted that Capote "abducted Isherwood's Sally Bowles for *Breakfast at Tiffany's*"; certainly, Capote creates an updated version of Berlin's famously cosmopolitan atmosphere. In a similar vein were Capote's continuing stream of New York stories (such as "Miriam," about the oppressive loneliness of Manhattan, and "Shut a Final Door," about proto-yuppies in Manhattan's fast lane, both in *A Tree of Night*) and such portraits as "New York" and "Brooklyn" in *Local Color* (1950); "A House on the Heights" in *The Dogs Bark: Public People and Private Places* (1973); and "Hello, Stranger," which details the fascinating stories of sordid humanity that come out over cocktails at the Four Seasons, and "A Day's Work," both in *Music for Chameleons* (1980).

Like Capote's southern writing, his cosmopolitan writing was drawn from a universe he knew intimately. While he was generally more successful in the sophisticated international world than in the South—famous and financially rewarded, more accepted, better (though certainly not perfectly) fitting—this writing retains a sense of Capote's lonely alienation and failure of human communion; perhaps this is an inescapable remnant of his youth. Holly Golightly represents a kind of transcendence for Capote's protagonists, because unlike Joel or Collin she is beautiful, gregarious, adored; she seems able to control her own life, which is filled with rich, exotic men (like the handsome Brazilian José Ybarra-Jaegar—intelligent, presentable, important) and the thrilling power brokers of the underworld (Sally Tomato, the crime boss who pays Holly a hundred dollars a week to visit him in Sing Sing and take back "weather reports" to his "lawyer") who seem willing to do anything for her. Money seems to materialize effortlessly for her: whatever she wants can be attained by taking a few trips to the powder room (financed luxuriantly by her escorts). For Holly, Tiffany's is a cosmopolitan refuge, a dazzling array of consumerist allure that, she believes, transcends sordid reality: "Nothing very bad could happen to you there, not with those kind men in their nice suits, and that lovely smell of silver and alligator wallets." She dreams of waking up one morning and having breakfast at Tiffany's—then she will know she has attained her version of nirvana.

Ultimately, though, Holly cannot write her own fantasy life, cannot escape her constraining past. Tiffany's is only a jewelry store—it doesn't serve breakfast, and it doesn't sell contentment. Holly's abandoned husband, Doc Golightly, materializes from Tulip, Texas, and unravels the image she has fabricated in Manhattan, showing that one cannot simply wish away one's dreary past and its responsibilities. Nor can she control the present—the Sally Tomato ploy turns out to be a conduit for drug-smuggling information, and the police catch up with Holly. After she is arrested, the media reports reflect the image Holly has created of chic cosmopolitan allure. DRUG RING EXPOSED, GLAMOUR GIRL HELD, read the tabloid headlines, with exotic stories about "the beautiful movie starlet and café society celebrity . . . highly publicized girl-about-New York . . . arrested in her luxurious apartment at a swank East Side address." But Holly's neighbor, the narrator, a struggling young writer entranced by her wild life—an incarnation of Capote, of course—sets the story straight, again, like Doc, exposing the distorted unreality of Holly's cosmopolitan facade: "She was not arrested in her 'luxurious apartment.' It took place in my own bathroom. . . . '*Here* she is: the wanted woman!' boomed Madame Spannela. . . . 'Look. What a whore she is.' "

Holly's world does not endure, though it was certainly exciting while it lasted, tingling with erotically sensual allure (which Audrey Hepburn toned down in the popular film version to a kind of teasing adolescent playfulness). Holly snags none of her dashing men; she cannot even sustain a relationship with her cat, which she refuses to name because that would imply responsibilities and permanence, and her life is not stable enough for that. She escapes from the law, from the clutches of society, running off to Buenos Aires in search of more rich men to sucker, but she has lost her allure, and she is far from Tiffany's; she looks more clearly like a moneygrubbing tramp. On the way to the airport, she abandons her cat in a rainstorm in Spanish Harlem. Having done this, though, she immediately realizes the pointlessness of leading her life as she has, with no connections. Unable to find the cat herself, she makes the narrator promise to return for it, which he does—finding it, after weeks of arduous searching, settled comfortably "in the window of a warm-looking room." He does not take care of the cat as he had pledged, since someone else, clearly, is already doing so. But simply by tracking down one of the loose ends Holly had left hanging, the narrator atones for at least a small part of his friend's reckless existence. Determined to ensure the cat's safety, he struggles to sustain a kind of communion and responsibility that Holly's hollow and emotionally barren cosmopolitanism did not allow.

In this story, Capote reflects on his own perceptions of his world. There is just a bit of Sook in Holly, in the sometimes uncritical rapport she establishes with the young man who is very different from herself, and in the loosely familial and supportive connection the two share. Holly, for a time, calls the narrator Fred—the name of the beloved brother she had abandoned in Texas. But more important, Holly is, at various times, both alter ego and ego for Capote. Though the narrator is only in the background of Holly's life, he is forcefully present as the recording and judgmental voyeur. Her careless adventure is not exactly his, but he does here confront the troubling morality, to which Holly is oblivious, of the cosmopolitan world. Unlike Holly, he will never be able to dispense with or repress its contradictions. Nance points to "the role of this story in Capote's gradual transition from fiction to nonfiction," writing that "he had moved from a private dream world to one that was identifiable, topical, even journalistic." *Breakfast at Tiffany's* does indeed embody the kind of journalism Capote takes up for the rest of his career: not because it has the same detached, objective perspective that characterizes his later style, but rather because of the author's role as a burrowing investigator out to get the story, out to expose what underlies the story he is reporting.

The cosmopolitan sensibility in *Breakfast at Tiffany's* evokes Capote's personal, extraliterary indulgence in the cosmopolitan life, his role as a publicity hound and social climber. Capote's courting of the public eye began with his first book, *Other Voices, Other Rooms,* or, more precisely, with the book's dust jacket. The boyish author lies supine on a sofa, oozing sensuality; later he told Lawrence Grobel, "I guess it assumes that I'm lying on the sofa and more or less beckoning somebody to climb on top of me." This "exotic photograph," he said, was "the start of a certain notoriety that has kept close step with me these many years." Capote's audience raised its eyebrows not simply at the photo or the book, but at the combination of the two. This set a pattern that was to endure throughout Capote's career—the writer's fascinating personality was always complexly intertwined with his text.

Cosmopolitanism, for Capote, manifested itself in a network of people and places. Clarke's biography meticulously describes how Capote sought out the best of these: the richest, the most socially alluring and well-connected, the most celebrated, the cutting edge. He lived in a symbiotic relationship with the people he latched onto: he traveled with them, visited their estates and retreats, flew with them on their private planes and cruised on their yachts, and parlayed connection into connection.

His modus operandi was to attach himself to glamorous, wealthy young women. He served as adviser and confidant; he was sensitive, understanding, nonthreatening, and they relished his companionship as a respite from the catty turmoil of their upper-class lives. Capote provided consolation, amusement, and sometimes even mentorship; he helped women improve their social skills and connections, and he had a good sense for women's fashion. Despite a calculating aspiration for social connections on Capote's part, often such attachments involved true and deep friendship as well. Sometimes Capote connected also with the husbands through the wives: the most famous example of this was his relationship with Barbara (''Babe'') Paley and her husband, CBS founder William S. Paley. Other famous people in his coterie included Lee Radziwill, her sister Jaqueline Kennedy (and, through her, her husband John), Joanne Carson (who was then married to Johnny Carson), Carol Marcus Saroyan Matthau (wife of William Saroyan and, later, Walter Matthau), Oona O'Neill Chaplin (Eugene O'Neill's daughter, who was married to Charlie Chaplin).

These people provided Capote with entrée to the beautiful places of the world. He drew on the energy of these locations, writing numerous shorter portraits of them and using them as backdrops for his larger efforts, but also seeming to have an almost compulsive need simply to *be* in such settings, in case something happened, to see who else was there. His haunts included the elite restaurant and hotel scene (the Four Seasons, Sardi's, the Plaza) in the 1950's and 1960's, the Hamptons and Palm Springs in the 1960's and 1970's, and later, perhaps most obsessively, the most fashionable New York bars and discos, especially Studio 54 (and inside that disco, the place of honor, the deejay's booth, where the crème de la crème congregated by special invitation), in the last frenzied years of his life.

Manhattan (annexing a slice of Brooklyn Heights) was the center of the universe by Capote's cosmopolitan standards and lent him a strong dose of creative energy. He wrote as a young man in ''New York'':

> It is a myth, the city, the rooms and windows, the steam-spitting streets, for anyone, everyone, a different myth, an idol-head with traffic-light eyes winking a tender green, a cynical red . . . a place to hide, to lose or discover oneself, to make a dream wherein you prove that perhaps after all you are not an ugly duckling, but wonderful, and worthy of love.

Capote had thoroughly exploited his childhood in the South for his early writing; in New York, he found a Pandora's box of new material. New York as a subject posed a bigger challenge, which later in his life often led to considerable writing blocks. The city sometimes forced him to flee, and eventually overwhelmed him, as it psychologically overwhelmed Mrs. H. T. Miller in ''Miriam.'' That short story, about an incomprehensible young girl (or an apparition of one) who haunts an Upper East Side widow, is one of the few instances in Capote's writing in which no communion—no connection, however tentative—can be achieved. New York, at its worst, can be omnipowerfully squelching. Still, it was the site of Capote's most vivid challenges and triumphs. Even *In Cold Blood,* his most famous work, though a story of Middle America, was commissioned by and first published in *The New Yorker*; it owes as much to the city that nurtured that magazine, and that nurtured Capote, as it does to small-town Kansas.

The Black and White Ball stands as a fantastic example of Capote's personal flair and his presence in the national spotlight. Capote threw the fabulously decadent affair for five hundred of his closest friends at the Plaza Hotel in November

1966. The list of invited guests, as printed in *The New York Times,* covered a range of celebrities including Sammy Davis, Jr., Jackie Kennedy, Mrs. W. Vincent Astor, Richard Burton, Oscar de la Renta, Noel Coward, Averell Harriman, Lillian Hellman, Christopher Isherwood, and the Baron and Baroness Guy de Rothschild, as well as some of the friends Capote had made in Holcomb, Kansas, like Alvin Dewey, the Kansas Bureau of Investigation's lead investigator on the Clutter murder case. The party was a real-life event but one that became transformed as it entered the national media into something that looked more like a scene out of Capote's fictional world of glitz. The American public devoured the spectacle: media reports of the ball were infused with ornate accounts of manners evocative of Edith Wharton's stylish turn-of-the-century affairs and intrigues.

Those who weren't invited were crushed. Those who did come flew in from all over the country and made a tremendous commotion over their hairdos, their costumes (black was prescribed for men, black or white for women), and their masks—Halston and Adolfo were deluged with orders for personalized masks, for which they charged hundreds of dollars. *Time* magazine reported that Capote boasted of having spent a mere thirty-nine cents on his mask, only to be undercut by Theodore Roosevelt's eighty-two-year-old daughter Alice Roosevelt Longworth, who had shopped around and paid thirty-five cents.

As Capote's cosmopolitan connections and literary success became stronger, he broadened his scope to take on projects such as adapting works for plays, musicals, and movies; he also wrote screenplays. Neither a 1954 musical based on his short story "House of Flowers" nor a 1952 play based on *The Grass Harp* were well received. His film adaptation (with William Archibald) of Henry James's *The Turn of the Screw,* titled *The Innocents* (1961), was disappointing, and his film scenario for *The Great Gatsby* was rejected. Film productions of *Breakfast at Tiffany's* and *In Cold Blood* were lucrative for Capote, and his publicized presence at the filming of *In Cold Blood,* on location in Kansas, heightened the connection between his roles as writer and media figure. Among his most successful ventures was his work on the offbeat John Huston film *Beat the Devil* (1954). In this film noir parody of the Graham Greene variety of spy film, Capote imbues his characters with an exotic Mediterranean flair, and Robert Morley, Humphrey Bogart, and Peter Lorre are amusingly insouciant in their roles. It was Capote's disclosure of his friendship with Bogart, dating from the production of the film, that broke the ice in his first interview with the murderer Perry Smith, who idolized the actor.

An important ingredient in the hodgepodge that constitutes Capote's cosmopolitan world is his sexuality. It is difficult to determine whether Capote's homosexuality is more pertinent as a biographical or as a literary issue; probably, as with most aspects of the writer, its role is intertwined in both the personal and literary spheres, and cannot be placed neatly on either side. Capote is one of America's most important authors to be openly gay throughout his career, and while his writing is by no means purely "gay literature," Capote's sexuality infused his writing to much the same degree that it defined his life. In his southern literature, this sexuality is a bit more closeted, probably reflecting some of Capote's own uncertainty and the confused hostility that his homosexuality encountered in the South. The young Capote had experienced numerous manifestations of homosexuality in himself and around him, like Joel Knox in *Other Voices, Other Rooms,* who, as a young boy, "had witnessed many peculiar spectacles, . . . most puzzling of all, two grown men standing in an ugly little room kissing each other." Joel is stereotypically effeminate, as was Capote himself: "He was too pretty, too delicate and fair-skinned, . . . a girlish tenderness softened his eyes, . . . his voice was uncommonly soft." Joel's relation to Cousin Randolph, who is flamboyantly gay, probably illustrates the young Capote's view of homosexuality: he sees that what he is destined to become will make him a target of scorn; he sees that gay life can be lonely and difficult, especially if one is flamboyant (as Capote must have known he would be) and surrounded by people who are already uncompassionate. While Randolph is the only person in Skully's Landing who serves as any kind of role model for Joel, he is a satirically caricatured model, and the others in the family attempt to repress Randolph's manifestations of his homosexuality in front of the boy (again, Capote knows what will be in store for him). As Randolph squeezes Joel's hand, Joel knows that if there is any communion to be gleaned in this family, it will have to involve Randolph; he accepts this communion on one level, but at the same time, "holding hands with Randolph was obscurely disagreeable, and Joel's fingers tensed with an impulse to dig his nails into the hot dry palm." Joel mirrors Capote's ambiguity about his sexuality: not about whether he is gay, of which there is no question, but about what it means to be gay.

The narrator in *Breakfast at Tiffany's* is able to remain essentially detached from Holly's world because it is heterosexual, and he is not. Much of Capote's writing from this period embodies a muted but unapologetic homosocial sensibility. In "A Diamond Guitar," one of three short stories published with *Breakfast at Tiffany's,* Mr. Schaeffer is the elder statesman of a prison farm to which a young Cuban named Tico Feo is brought:

Mr. Schaeffer glanced up at the boy and smiled. He smiled at him longer than he had meant to, for the boy had eyes like strips of sky. . . . Looking at him, Mr. Schaeffer thought of holidays and good times.

Such loaded glances are Capote's usual method of vaguely implying the love of men for men. Later in this story, Capote is more specific:

Soon Tico Feo was allowed the honor of having a bed near the stove and next to Mr. Schaeffer. . . . Except that they did not combine their bodies or think to do so, though such things were not unknown at the farm, they were as lovers.

In "Shut a Final Door," Walter's encounter is less kind:

I was in a bookshop, and a man was standing there and we began talking: a middle-aged man, rather nice, very intelligent. When I went outside he followed, a little ways behind: I crossed the street, he crossed the street, I walked fast, he walked fast. This kept up six or seven blocks, and when I finally figured out what was going on I felt tickled, I felt like kidding him on. So I stopped at the corner and hailed a cab; then I turned around and gave this guy a long, long look, and he came rushing up, all smiles. And I jumped in the cab, and slammed the door and leaned out the window and laughed out loud: the look on his face, it was awful, it was like Christ. I can't forget it.

Clearly, Walter has some kind of homosexual inclination, which he represses here. Still, Walter and Capote are aware of the suffering of the anonymous follower: he is a Christlike martyr to the world's cruelty. In nearly every one of Capote's stories can be found a moment of gay awareness, sometimes positive, often suppressed or crushed (as between Randolph and Pepe in *Other Voices, Other Rooms*), and, especially earlier in his career, frequently oblique (as with Vincent in "The Headless Hawk" [1946], who takes "rather female pride in his quarters").

In *In Cold Blood,* the sexuality of both killers is troubling. Dick Hickock is at least a potential rapist, child molester, and exhibitionist. Perry Smith seems, loosely, to have the same kind of attraction for Dick as described in Capote's early muted portraits of homosexuality; he is drawn to Dick (and frequently dreams of a life involving a strong tie with him), and jealously resentful of Dick's reckless heterosexuality. Capote himself seems to have a keen tenderness for Perry and his unresolved sexuality. Perry, on his way to the gallows, kissed Capote on the cheek and said, "Adios, amigo." Capote later reported that Perry said to him, "Good-bye. I love you and I always have."

By the time he published *Music for Chameleons,* Capote's references to homosexuality had become forthright and explicit. In "A Beautiful Child," he describes a one-night stand he had with Errol Flynn; in "Then It All Came Down," he reports uncensored his subject's vivid description of gay sex in prison; in "Hidden Gardens," his interviewee recounts a joke—the kind of gay humor that perhaps appeals to Capote's campy persona: Jesse James storms onto a train and shouts, " 'Hands up! We're gonna rob all the women and rape all the men.' So this one fellow says: 'Haven't you got that wrong, sir? Don't you mean you're gonna rob all the men and rape all the women?' But there was this sweet little fairy on the train, and he pipes up: 'Mind your own business! Mr. James knows how to rob a train.' " In *Answered Prayers* Capote offers an especially unfettered portrait of homosexuality in the world of the sophisticated set.

Capote was writing during a time when it was acceptable, marginally, for a gay man to discuss his sexuality, not in terms of general gay rights or acceptance, but as one eccentric artsy fag. A stereotypically capricious gay atmosphere was acceptable; the reality of the largely closeted and suppressed gay world was not. Homosexuality in Capote's writing is not very real—nor does it reflect the chaotic tribulations of Capote's love life: he had two long-term and relatively satisfying relationships, but numerous others that generally proved difficult and uncontrollable. Rather, Capote's sexuality is parodically distanced from what is assumed to be a "normal" (heterosexual) audience. As perhaps America's most prominent openly gay celebrity of the 1950's and 1960's, Capote might be criticized as too campy, too effete, too confirmative of prejudicial stereotypes about gays. His writing was probably not very helpful to the contemporary gay community, as was, for example, James Baldwin's more socially conscious *Giovanni's Room* (1956), nor did it ever attempt to provide a thorough overview of some part of the gay world, as did Hubert Selby's *Last Exit to Brooklyn* (1964). Capote does not pave the way for other homosexual writers or readers—in his writing, homosexuality is a fact, and accepted, but in a way that relates only to Capote himself. Still, he lived his life on his own terms, and underneath the cultivated facade of quivering, limp-wristed effeminacy was a core of strength that allowed him to act and be seen exactly as he wanted to be—never to mask his personality, however ridiculous it might seem.

Capote worked with two important photographers, Richard Avedon and Cecil Beaton. Capote wrote the text for Avedon's 1959 collection of celebrity photographs *Observations* (in which he appeared himself in a puckish pose), helping the photographer capture the personalities of such figures as Isak Dinesen, Ezra Pound, and Mae West. Beaton was a longtime close friend, and some of his masterful skill at capturing people's inner personalities with a photographically objective precision seems to have rubbed off on Capote; as Capote's work matured, he relied less on the grotesquely surreal personality portrait and more heavily on closely detailing the lives, the speech, the literal behavior of his subjects.

Such detailing is evident in the passage on Dinesen from *Observations*:

The Baroness, weighing a handful of feathers and fragile as a *coquillage* bouquet, entertains callers in a sparse, sparkling parlor sprinkled with sleeping dogs and warmed by a fireplace and a porcelain stove: a room where she, an imposing creation come forward from one of her own Gothic tales, sits bundled in bristling wolfskins and British tweeds, her feet fur-booted, her legs, thin as the thighs of an ortolan, encased in woolen hose, and her neck, round which a ring could fit, looped with frail lilac scarves.

Capote was working harder, more carefully, to evoke a vision that was not simply a psychologically internalized memory, but one that could stand as a public statement—one that was still, of course, imbued with a subjectively judgmental atmosphere, but an atmosphere that was meant to be shared more widely, more accessibly. In portraits of celebrities such as Louis Armstrong, Marilyn Monroe, and Humphrey Bogart, Capote presents (with a bit of his own recasting) what these people look like, or should look like, to the world at large. His choice of subjects in *Observations* reflects his cosmopolitanism, and this combined with the power he saw in photography moved Capote on to another important phase of his writing, that of nonfiction prose.

Two extremely successful journalistic enterprises in 1956 set the stage for Capote's best-known work, *In Cold Blood.* Both *The Muses Are Heard* and "The Duke in His Domain" were commissioned for *The New Yorker. The Muses Are Heard* is a meticulous account of a touring production of *Porgy and Bess* behind the iron curtain, the first of its kind ever undertaken by an American company. In the preface to *Music for Chameleons* he wrote:

I conceived of the whole adventure as a short comic "non-fiction novel," the first. For several years I had been increasingly drawn toward journalism as an art form in itself. . . . Journalism as art was almost virgin terrain, for the simple reason that very few literary artists ever wrote narrative journalism.

In his description of the traveling, the rehearsals, the interpersonal relationships and squabbles of the actors, the behind-the-scenes diplomatic and theatrical arrangements, there is nothing stylistically fascinating or overwhelming. In places, Capote's prose clearly has been whipped into line by the hand of a *New Yorker* editor, to conform with the magazine's timelessly immutable style. But Capote's report is eloquent, careful, sharply paced. What he must have gotten out of the exercise was simply the experience of writing about real people, their characters, their interplay, their small but compelling intrigues: the discovery that there *is* a story sitting right out there in real life.

In "The Duke in His Domain," Capote refines his journalism with an extended close focus on one character, Marlon Brando. Capote shows himself adept at getting a personally revealing interview out of an actor notorious for his unwillingness to sit for such portraits. He captures Brando as a spoiled tyrant, egotistical, rambling disconnectedly, unusually confessional ("The last eight, nine years I've been pretty mixed up, a mess pretty much"), and protectively isolated, like a duke in his domain, from the outside world.

In both these reports Capote is present, somewhat more forcefully than is the background narrator in *Breakfast at Tiffany's.* He refines the character of author as insightful voyeur, the canny recorder who sets out for his readers, with just a small dose of guidance, the artifacts that compose whatever cultural milieu he chooses to define. In the 1950's and 1960's, he wrote nonfiction pieces in many of the same magazines in which he had earlier published short stories, thus establishing a connection between the two kinds of writing and the different voices he used for each. He wrote essays, travel pieces, and profiles for popular magazines—*Life, Harper's Bazaar, Mademoiselle, Redbook, Vogue, Esquire*—that people read in beauty shops and in their living rooms, magazines that purported to capture the life and times of contemporary America and Americans. Seemingly effortlessly, he turned out the vintage portraits and insights that could come only from a man who had soaked up life as he had, and, like Hemingway and Fitzgerald, Capote could not help inscribing himself in his writing as a character somehow more interesting than anyone else he wrote about. His style is marked by a kind of subtle omniscience, a savoir faire that is almost, but not quite, pompous, elitist, cosmopolitan. It is clear to his readers that his writing *could be* all these things, but that it is purposely, though not condescendingly, tailored to appeal to the curiosity of the middle-class masses.

In the preface to *Music for Chameleons* he said that writing *In Cold Blood* was "like playing high-stakes poker; for six nerve-shattering years I didn't know whether I had a book or not." In 1966, Capote found himself with a book that burst into the national consciousness. Two cold-blooded killers, Dick Hickock and Perry Smith, fascinated the writer and his audience in the same way that Milton's Satan fascinated Romantic readers: in their evilness, they stand out as immensely more compelling than their victims, four members of a comfortable Kansas farming family who, as Capote inspects them, end up looking like caricatures of a hackneyed ideal. Herb Clutter is a bourgeois petty tyrant, running his farm with an outdated puritanical rule. He forbids the use of tobacco, but his children sneak cigarettes; he ruthlessly fires any workers on his farm found with alcohol. Capote, himself an alcoholic and a drug addict, is drily but insistently sarcastic about what pass for Mr. Clutter's upstanding, noble virtues. Capote exploits the dark irony of the Clutters' lives with almost comic shamelessness. He describes pillows in Nancy's room bearing the legends HAPPY? and YOU DON'T HAVE TO BE CRAZY TO LIVE HERE BUT IT HELPS; as Mr. Clutter takes out a life-insurance policy on the day he will die, Capote records the insurance agent telling him, "From the looks of you, from what the medical report tells us, we're likely to have you around a couple of weeks more."

Clutter makes a show of pluralist tolerance, but intrusively and domineeringly forces his daughter Nancy to ease out of her relationship with her boyfriend, Bobby Rupp, because he is Catholic. Mrs. Clutter is psychologically frail; the details are not precise, but she resembles a nineteenth-century "neurasthenic," spending her days a virtual invalid in bed, while the rest of the family tiptoes around the house and tries not to jar her nerves or confront her condition. Mr. Clutter, who no longer sleeps with his wife, seems vaguely responsible for her condition.

Kenyon and Nancy are all-American kids, riding horses, active in 4-H; on the day of their deaths, Nancy takes time out from an activity-filled day to teach a younger neighbor how to bake a cherry pie; the night before, she had starred as Becky Thatcher in a student production of *Tom Sawyer*. They live in a home that Capote finds sterile, tacky, homogeneous, as he dissects it:

> spongy displays of liver-colored carpet intermittently abolishing the glare of varnished, resounding floors; an immense modernistic living-room couch covered in nubby fabric interwoven with glittery strands of silver metal; a breakfast alcove featuring a banquette upholstered in blue-and-white plastic. This sort of furnishing was what Mr. and Mrs. Clutter liked, as did the majority of their acquaintances, whose homes, by and large, were similarly furnished.

As Capote inspects and reconstructs their lives, their wholesomely American sensibilities seem like a mask for a crumbling inner world. Mr. Clutter plants a grove of fruit trees on his farm, an emblem of "the paradise, the green, apple-scented Eden" that, Capote informs us, the farmer strove to create. That image sets up Capote's pervasive irony, for *In Cold Blood* is about the failure of this paradise, about the brutal expulsion from this Eden—for the Clutters and, symbolically, for the American audience that envisioned the Clutters as the consummate representatives of themselves. While the portrait of prelapsarian life in Holcomb is steeped in the smug comfort of 1950's America, Capote is filtering his narrative through the much more cynical perspective of the 1960's—after the Kennedy assassination, in the throes of cold war paranoia. In the postmortem that he conducts on the Clutter family, the mass murder seems almost a secondary cause of death. Primarily, the American dream has become malignant; the murders are almost a symptom, rather than the cause, of the Clutters' demise.

In the early sections of the book, Capote perversely juxtaposes the lives of the Clutters and their killers. He introduces the killers by writing, "Like Mr. Clutter, the young man [Perry Smith] breakfasting in a café called the Little Jewel never drank coffee." With macabre insistence, Capote's narrative repeatedly jumps back and forth from the Holcomb family to the killers on their adventure to murder the Clutters. Capote forcibly conjoins their fates as he describes the central event of the story, the "four shotgun blasts that, all told, ended six human lives." His underlying thesis is that Dick and Perry are as integral a part of the American dream as are the Clutters, if not more so. *In Cold Blood* captured the American imagination in its methodical analysis of the disintegration of the American dream. The Clutters may surround themselves with the outward trappings of this dream, but they are slaughtered on page 72, and Capote's story has hundreds of pages to go.

The place to look for that story, Capote finds, is with the people who smashed the dream, Dick and Perry. They are, simply, more exciting than the Clutters; they are the people we must inspect to understand the future of American society, its hopes and values. Though the dream has gone bad for them, they are excellent practitioners (or perhaps victims) of some fundamental American sensibilities. They are daring, imaginative questers journeying through rough but challenging territory—across the Kansas heartland to kill the Clutters, and then all across America as they flee. The American landscape as mediated by the Clutters and their farm community is classically noble ("a white cluster of grain elevators rising as gracefully as Greek temples are visible long before a traveler reaches them"), but is brought to life only by the killers: "Until one morning in mid-November of 1959 [the day of the murders], few Americans—in fact, few Kansans—had ever heard of Holcomb." Capote writes that, in 1959, "the last seven years have been years of droughtless beneficence"; the rejoinder is implicit: seven years of lean will follow—the seven years in which the killers are caught, tried, and then await execution; the seven years in which Capote, with Dick and Perry's assistance, works on capturing their story and exploring its implications. The landscape is charged, and at its most vital, as Capote follows Dick and Perry through it, foraging for equipment for the murder and later escaping into its complex labyrinth as they flee from Kansas. Dick and Perry can read the land, can live off the land; the Clutters' physical environment is stagnant—cluttered.

Time and again, the two killers demonstrate how versatile their understanding of the local country is: Dick schemes elaborately and cunningly to cash bad checks to finance their journey, playing confidence games on shopkeepers and locals; in one instance, Perry poses as a bridegroom, with Dick as best man, to win the confidence of a clothing-store clerk—a calculating, untraditional re-creation of the American ''family.'' The epitome of Dick and Perry's fruitful interaction with the landscape comes in a touching scene involving two hitchhikers the killers pick up while they are on the lam: a young boy and his frail grandfather, on a torturous quest of their own to find their family and a place to settle. The two ''couples'' join together briefly and get along well. The boy and his grandfather finance their journey as resourcefully as do Dick and Perry: they collect bottles from the roadside and redeem them for the refund money. Contrary to what one might expect of cold-blooded murderers running from the police, Dick and Perry eagerly assist and join in the search for bottles, driving slowly through the vast Texas countryside and stopping to pick up empties:

> Dick was amused, but he was also interested, and when next the boy commanded him to halt, he at once obeyed. The commands came so frequently that it took them an hour to travel five miles, but it was worth it. The kid had an ''honest-to-God genius'' for spotting, amid the roadside rocks and grassy rubble, and the brown glow of thrown-away beer bottles, the emerald daubs that had once held 7-Up and Canada Dry. Perry soon developed his own personal gift for spying out bottles. . . . It was all ''pretty silly,'' just ''kid stuff.'' Nevertheless, the game generated a treasure-hunt excitement, and presently [Dick], too, succumbed to the fun, the fervor of this quest for refundable empties.

Capote shows in this scene the challenge of mining the landscape, and its fecundity—the quartet eventually comes up with $12.60 (coincidentally close to the $12.73 Capote and Sook scrounged in *A Christmas Memory*), which they split, and which provides the starving questers with a banquet at a roadside restaurant. The travelers are living off litter, the dregs of the landscape; but with its ''brown glow'' and ''emerald daubs,'' this landscape can be as evocative, as beneficent, as any nineteenth-century transcendentalist landscape portrait. As in James Fenimore Cooper's or Walt Whitman's visions of untamed country offering up plenty and adventure, Capote's adventurers, on the margin of society, appreciate and exploit the treasures of a familiar territory that has itself become marginal. The boy teaches the murderers some scavenging tricks, just as Natty Bumppo and the Indians shared with each other the secrets of the land, and this sharing, this appreciation and understanding of nature, becomes the basis of human communion.

Perry and Dick, in fact, exhaust the American landscape they have been milking: their ultimate goal is a home in Mexico. Perry fantasizes about living in Cozumel, which is, according to a magazine article he had committed to memory, ''a hold-out against social, economic, and political pressure. No official pushes any private person around on *this* island.'' From his memories of John Huston's movie *The Treasure of the Sierra Madre*, Perry has latched onto the notion of prospecting for gold in Mexico. Ironically, Perry realizes that one must forsake America if one is to attain the quintessentially American fantasies of individualism and instant self-made wealth in the mid twentieth century.

Dick and Perry have vivid hopes and dreams—unrealizable, but for that reason all the more dramatic and enthusiastic. They seek to control their own destinies through their own initiative. Their approach may be demented and evil, but Capote essentially eschews any moralistic sensibility as he probes for the archetypal American narrative he sees lurking in these events. The moral vacuum of Capote's story (perhaps a legacy of his southern gothic and grotesque vision) evoked a stunned and furious reaction on the part of some: Stanley Kauffmann wrote in *The New Republic* (January 22, 1966):

It is ridiculous in judgment and debasing to all of us to call this book literature. Are we so bankrupt, so avid for novelty that, merely because a famous writer produces an amplified magazine crime-feature, the result is automatically elevated to serious literature?

Hilton Kramer, in the *New Leader* (January 31, 1966), wrote that the book "is not what the language of fiction, the medium of a significant art, always is: the refraction of a serious moral imagination"; this "deficiency . . . stands out on every page." But most readers devoured the story, affirming it as compelling and important without stopping to think of its moral implications. This itself is a sign that Capote was right about the devolution, or irrelevance, of American morality.

Perry's mother is a full-blooded Indian, Capote notes—perhaps the author sees this story as the Indians' revenge on the white usurpers. In any event, Capote seems to imply that the American ideal is catching up with itself, destroying itself, and that a society capable of producing people like Dick and Perry deserves what it gets. Their fantasies, after all, are simply those ingrained by their society: they go on their crime and murder spree because they want a little money, a good life, a way to celebrate themselves. Perry, especially, wants family and human communion, which elude him as, Capote implies, it had eluded the Clutters. If anything, Capote seems to view Perry as more thoughtful than the Clutters, because Perry at least realizes the nature of his deprivation and takes steps to do something about it. He dreams of setting up a kind of home with a friend—at times he thinks about doing this with his sister's family or with other friends from prison, but eventually he settles on Dick. Perry is doing exactly what Capote had always had to do—to search for some sense of communion, however untraditional, to overcome the bad hand that society had dealt him. Capote's sympathies are with Perry, who is physically deformed (from leg injuries he received in a motorcycle accident) and who feels condemned to remain a social misfit. Capote has denied many critics' suggestion that on some level he was in love with Perry, having spent years visiting and corresponding with him before his execution. "I didn't love either one of them, but I had a great understanding for both of them, and for Perry I had a tremendous amount of sympathy," Capote told Lawrence Grobel. In his reportage, Capote scrutinizes the killers' letters, diaries, and psychiatric reports, trying to get as deeply inside their minds as he can, because he knows that this is where the story is, the journalistic scoop on the state of the American dream. Capote visits the two devotedly on death row, bringing back to the world their observations and impressions and seeming to envision them as the gurus, or philosophers, of their age.

The Black and White Ball of 1966, which Capote organized as a celebration of the end of his seven years of work on *In Cold Blood,* marks an important climax in Capote's life. He had been catapulted into the public eye, where he would remain prominently for the rest of his life, unchallenged as a public icon and with his character firmly set. At the same time, his writing never again reached the heights it had up to that point; this realization made him increasingly depressed and self-destructive, psychologically and physically, as his addictions escalated out of control. Bruce Bawer, in "Capote's Children," explains the disappointment many in the literary establishment felt about Capote's writing after *In Cold Blood*:

The appeal of much of this work has relatively little to do with its literary merits. Capote, in his zeal to write "nonfiction novels" and "nonfiction short stories," may well have thought that he was being faithful to "what is *really* true," but all he was doing, in actuality, was neglecting his obligation as a literary artist to create, to order, and thereby to serve not merely personal and superficial truths but universal ones. It is an obligation to which Capote was attentive for so long, and which he fulfilled with such distinction, that his ultimate renunciation of it (manifestly well-intentioned though it may have been) is particularly disheartening.

The author of *In Cold Blood* became a kind of popular media expert on crime and the mind of the criminal—"Then It All Came Down," an interesting short profile of Robert Beausoleil, a member of the Manson clan, features the same kind of incisive rapport with the murderer that marked *In Cold Blood.* In *Handcarved Coffins,* collected in *Music for Chameleons,* Capote revisits the territory he mapped out in *In Cold Blood,* exploring a series of unsolved murders. The pervasive compulsion (of the criminals, and of the detectives as well) is familiar ground. These murder cases are more intriguing and complex than the Clutter case, but the detective work is less successfully captured than in Capote's masterwork. Though *Handcarved Coffins* is subtitled *A Nonfiction Account of an American Crime,* Capote errs by contriving to bring this narrative closer to the realm of mystery fiction; his crisply eerie buildup milks the suspense of the crime drama, but what Capote misses here are the much more fascinating real-life implications of murderous evil that he had earlier captured so deftly. Capote's credentials as an authority on crime were also exploited in his collaboration on a 1972 television prison drama, *The Glass House,* and in a documentary on capital punishment, *Death Row, U.S.A.*, which was so grim that ABC decided not to air it.

To match the success of *In Cold Blood,* Capote had an idea for a different sort of masterpiece, a final tour de force that would stun the American audience. What endures of this idea is a loose but provocative story, published in installments in *Esquire* in the 1970's and then posthumously as the unfinished novel *Answered Prayers.* For this undertaking, Capote turned to his favorite subject, himself—the character of the writer in the fast world of Manhattan, the New York publishing scene, and the arena of the cosmopolitan elite. Some critical opinion holds that the work would have been devastatingly and resoundingly successful. James Michener predicted that Capote would be well remembered into the twenty-first century if he ever finished the book. Clarke wrote that the fragments "contain some of the best writing he ever produced," and Max Lerner asserted in the *New York Post* (April 28, 1976) that Capote writes, in what appeared of the novel, "as if he were the Saint-Simon of our times, writing the annals not of the Court of the Sun God at Versailles, but of New York and Paris, of the salons and hotels and the Left Bank. 'This is how it was,' he seems to be saying to later generations."

What came to be published of this work are three chapters (out of a projected eight or more) and a bizarre series of publishing anecdotes reflecting Capote's diminishing grasp on his life and his talent. To placate the demands of publishers for whom Capote missed over a decade of deadlines, he offered incredible accounts of lost or stolen chapters (Joseph Fox, his editor, speculates that Capote may have destroyed drafts of some chapters), and sometimes claimed to have finished the book and handed it over to Random House.

The fragments that were published, in any case, were quite enough to cause a well-publicized furor among those members of Capote's smart set whose lives were ruthlessly exposed, parodied, and dissected in the catty and contemptuous roman à clef. Capote in fact maintained in an interview with Grobel that the stories were "not intended as any ordinary roman à clef, a form where facts are disguised as fiction. My intentions are the reverse: to remove disguises, not manufacture them.'' Many of his closest friends cut him out of their lives, never to reestablish ties. Grobel writes that they ''were suddenly slapped awake with the realization that a writer among them—especially one as sharp and perceptive as Capote—was dangerous. Doors he had spent a lifetime prying open were now beginning to close on him.'' In a loose picaresque narrative focused on a very Capote-like young writer, P. B. Jones, and a glamorous society star, Kate McCloud (a composite portrait of Capote's rich confidantes), *Answered Prayers* presents luridly detailed and smutty stories of male prostitution, cheap sexual encounters, literary politics, international social warfare, and celebrity foibles.

In the decade before his death in 1984, Capote published two more collections of essays and stories that were competent and well received: *The Dogs Bark* and *Music for Chameleons*. Both feature the standard mix of cosmopolitan atmosphere, nonfiction portraits and essays, finely worked stories, and additional snippets of Capoteana; some of these were new; more were recycled. *Music for Chameleons* ends with an ''intervew'' by Truman Capote of Truman Capote, about the personality and experiences of, naturally, Truman Capote. The writer, at the end of his career, believes more firmly than ever that he has become his most interesting creation; the character he has created embodies everything else he has written. But Capote is not oblivious to the weaknesses inherent in the self-obsession he has nurtured. The interviewer tells the subject at the end, ''I love you''. The subject replies, ''I love you, too.'' And then,

TC: Zzzzzzz
TC: Zzzzzzzzz
TC and TC: Zzzzzzzzzzz

The interviewer falls asleep. The subject falls asleep. TC and TC, interviewer and subject, merge into the composite figure of ''Truman Capote.'' Public and private faces of the author-character, conjoined finally in one unified entity, as they tended to do throughout Capote's career, drift peacefully and harmlessly off to sleep, exhaustedly out of the limelight.

Selected Bibliography

WORKS OF TRUMAN CAPOTE

PROSE

Other Voices, Other Rooms. New York: Random House, 1948.
A Tree of Night and Other Stories. New York: Random House, 1949.
Local Color. New York: Random House, 1950.
The Grass Harp. New York: Random House, 1951.
The Muses Are Heard. New York: Random House, 1956.
Breakfast at Tiffany's: A Short Novel and Three Stories. New York: Random House, 1958.
Observations: Photographs by Richard Avedon; Comments by Truman Capote. New York: Simon & Schuster, 1959.
A Christmas Memory. New York: Random House, 1966. First published in 1956.
In Cold Blood: A True Account of a Multiple Murder and Its Consequences. New York: Random House, 1966.
The Thanksgiving Visitor. New York: Random House, 1968. First published in 1967.
One Christmas. New York: Random House, 1983.
Answered Prayers: The Unfinished Novel. New York: Random House, 1987. Separate chapters first published in 1975 and 1976.

ANTHOLOGIES

Selected Writings. New York: Random House, 1963.
The Dogs Bark: Public People and Private Places. New York: Random House, 1973.
Music for Chameleons. New York: Random House, 1980.
A Capote Reader. New York: Random House, 1987.

DRAMA

The Grass Harp. New York: Random House, 1952.

House of Flowers. New York: Random House, 1968. With Harold Arlen.

Trilogy. New York: Macmillan, 1969. With Eleanor Perry and Frank Perry.

FILMS

Beat the Devil. Columbia Pictures, 1954. Screenplay by Capote.

The Innocents. 1961. Screenplay by Capote and William Archibald.

Truman Capote's Trilogy. Allied Artists, 1969.

Murder by Death. Columbia Pictures, 1976. Featuring Capote.

WRITING FOR TELEVISION

The Glass House. CBS, February 4, 1972.

Truman Capote Behind Prison Walls. ABC, December 7, 1972.

Crimewatch. ABC, May 8, 1973, and June 21, 1973.

BIBLIOGRAPHIES

Bryer, Jackson R. "Truman Capote: A Bibliography." In *Truman Capote's "In Cold Blood": A Critical Handbook*, edited by Irving Malin. Belmont, Calif.: Wadsworth, 1968.

Stanton, Robert K. *Truman Capote, A Primary and Secondary Bibliography*. Boston: G. K. Hall, 1980.

BIOGRAPHICAL AND CRITICAL STUDIES

Bawer, Bruce. "Capote's Children." *The New Criterion*, 3, no. 10:39–44 (June 1985).

Clarke, Gerald. *Capote: A Biography*. New York: Simon & Schuster, 1988.

Garson, Helen S. *Truman Capote*. New York: Frederick Ungar, 1980.

Grobel, Lawrence. *Conversations with Capote*. New York: New American Library, 1985.

Heyne, Eric. "Toward a Theory of Literary Nonfiction." *Modern Fiction Studies*, 33, no. 3:479–490 (Autumn 1987).

Inge, M. Thomas, ed. *Truman Capote: Conversations*. Jackson: University Press of Mississippi, 1987.

Malin, Irving, ed. *Truman Capote's "In Cold Blood": A Critical Handbook*. Belmont, Calif.: Wadsworth, 1968.

Nance, William L. *The Worlds of Truman Capote*. New York: Stein & Day, 1970.

Reed, Kenneth T. *Truman Capote*. Boston: Twayne, 1981.

Siegle, Robert. "Capote's *Handcarved Coffins* and the Nonfiction Novel." *Contemporary Literature*, 25, no. 4:437–451 (Winter 1984).

—*RANDY MALAMUD*

Raymond Carver

1938–1988

AT THE TIME of his death in 1988, Raymond Carver was widely acknowledged as one of his age's finest crafters of short stories. Carver's work, which began to reach a national audience when *Esquire* published "Neighbors" in June 1971, was the product of a shy, sometimes self-destructive sensibility that drew its vision from the lives of the working poor among whom Carver grew up—and whose mode of perceiving he never fully left behind, despite the comfort and acclaim he enjoyed in the last decade of his life.

Raymond Carver was born May 25, 1938, in Clatskanie, Oregon, a lumber town about sixty miles downriver from Portland. His father, Clevie Raymond ("C.R.") Carver, had migrated to the Northwest from Arkansas about four years earlier and had drifted around, finding work where he could, including a stint as a laborer on the Grand Coulee Dam. In 1937 C.R. had returned to Arkansas briefly, where he married Ella Beatrice Casey. The "big, tall country girl and the farmhand-turned-construction-worker"—eventually to be joined by all of C.R.'s extended family—returned to the Northwest for work.

In 1941 the family moved across the Cascades to Yakima, Washington, a fruit-growing region and center for the timber industry, where Carver's father found work as a saw filer in the lumber mill. Carver's mother worked sporadically as a retail clerk or waitress, but never stayed long in any one job. He recalled her taking a couple of tablespoons of "nerve medicine" every morning from a bottle stowed beneath the kitchen sink. Home was a series of little two-bedroom rented houses, not all of which had indoor plumbing. Carver and his younger brother spent much of their time outdoors, fishing and hunting. This was Carver's milieu during his youth and adolescence, images that provide the core of a number of poems and early stories.

In an interview with Larry McCaffery and Sinda Gregory in the mid 1980's, Carver called his childhood "fairly conventional in many respects":

> We were a poor family, didn't have a car for the longest while, but I didn't miss having a car. My parents worked and struggled and finally became what I guess you'd call lower-middle class.
>
> . . . We didn't have much of anything in the way of material goods, or spiritual goods or values either. But I didn't have to go out and work in the fields when I was ten years old or anything of that sort. Mainly I just wanted to fish and hunt and ride around in cars with other guys.

Carver's father told him stories about his Arkansas ancestors and also read Zane Grey to him. When he was old enough to seek out his own reading material, Carver took pleasure from magazines such as *Sports Afield, Argosy, Outdoor Life,* and *Field & Stream.* In junior high and high school he went weekly to the public library to check out whatever struck his fancy—books on the Spanish conquistadores, historical novels, books on shipbuilding, Thomas B. Costain, Mickey Spillane, Edgar Rice Burroughs.

Although it was assumed that he would work at the lumber mill after graduation, Carver dreamed early of becoming a writer. At one point he wrote a story about fishing, and his mother rented a typewriter to help him get it into shape to mail out. Although nothing came of this first effort, Carver remembered the pleasure of imagining his manuscript out in the world, being read by somebody other than his mother. In high school Carver responded to a *Writer's Digest* ad for the Palmer Institute of Authorship, a correspondence course that he worked on diligently for a few months. Boredom eventually set in, and he never finished the course, but he received a certificate of completion anyway after talking his parents into paying the balance of the fee.

In 1956, the year Carver finished high school, his father took a job at a mill in Chester, California. Carver worked with his father for about six months before returning to Yakima to be with, and soon after to marry, his girlfriend, Maryann Burk. By the time he was twenty, Carver was the father of two children (Christine, born in 1957, and Vance, born in 1958) and had begun the phase of his life in which he "always worked some crap job or another, and my wife did the same." In the essay "Fires" (1982, included in *Fires,* 1983), Carver writes of this period as the real beginning of his life, at least his life as a writer:

> Most of what now strikes me as story "material" presented itself to me after I was twenty. I really don't remember much about my life before I became a parent. I really don't feel that anything happened in my life until I was twenty and married and had the kids.

Added to the difficulties of trying to provide for a family was the determination of both Carver and Maryann to get an education. Their first step toward this goal came in 1958, when they moved to California so that Carver could enroll at Chico State College. Carver's hunger for education had been intense since, while working as a delivery boy the previous year, he had caught a glimpse of the literary life in the person of "an alert but very elderly man" who gave him copies of *Poetry* and *The Little Review Anthology.* "Bleary from reading," Carver wrote later, "I had the distinct feeling my life was in the process of being altered in some significant and even, forgive me, magnificent way." It was a moment "when the very thing I needed most in my life—call it a polestar—was casually, generously given to me."

Just as potent was the impact of one of his teachers at Chico State—John Gardner, not yet a published writer himself, but with boxes of manuscripts and a passion for nurturing young talent. Carver's essay "John Gardner: The Writer As Teacher" first published in the *Georgia Review* in 1983 and reprinted in *Fires,* is a celebration of Gardner's willingness to offer line-by-line criticism and of his insistence on honesty of expression. Then and later Carver saw himself as "the luckiest of men to have had [Gardner's] criticism and his generous encouragement." Gardner gave him books to read—Hemingway, Faulkner, Chekhov, Flaubert, Joyce, Gass, Dinesen—and Carver felt "wild with discovery." "I tell you Maryann," he wrote in a quietly ecstatic poem ("Highway 99E from Chico," reprinted in *Fires*), that surely took shape during an exhilarated drive home after classes at Chico State, "I am happy."

With Gardner's help, Carver founded a student literary magazine called *Selection,* and in 1960—after Carver had transferred to Humboldt State

College—*Selection* published Carver's first story to appear in print, "The Furious Seasons" (republished in 1977, very slightly revised, as the title story in his second collection of fiction). At Humboldt, Carver worked with two other writers who recognized and encouraged his talent, Richard Day and Dennis Schmitz. They helped him found another magazine, *Toyon,* in which "The Father" appeared in the spring of 1961. Carver published three other stories in *Toyon* (made accessible by William Stull in *Studies in Short Fiction* in 1988)—"The Aficionados," "Poseidon and Company," and "The Hair"—but by the time they appeared he had already placed a story in a nationally circulated publication, the *Western Humanities Review* (Winter 1963). The story was "Pastoral," later revised as "The Cabin" in *Fires.* In interviews Carver frequently recalled the day he learned that "Pastoral" had been accepted (the same day he placed a poem, "The Brass Ring," in an Arizona magazine): "It was a terrific day! Maybe one of the best days ever. My wife and I drove around town and showed the letters of acceptance to all of our friends. It gave some much-needed validation to our lives."

Carver graduated from Humboldt State in 1963 and, with the meager assistance of a five-hundred-dollar scholarship, enrolled in the Iowa Writers Workshop. After a year, however, he was back in California, working as a night janitor in a Sacramento hospital and trying to write during the days. "When I went home at night," he wrote later in "The Autopsy Room" in *Ultramarine* (1986),

my wife would say,
'Sugar, it's going to be all right. We'll trade
this life in for another.' But it wasn't
that easy. . . . Nothing
was happening. Everything was happening. Life
was a stone, grinding and sharpening.

These were the years Carver characterized in the essay "Fires" as "ravenous," adding that he would rather take poison than have to relive that period. Driven to write and yet kept from it by the "ferocious" demands of parenting and the need to bring in money, Carver concluded that "if I wanted to write anything, and finish it, and if ever I wanted to take satisfaction out of finished work, I was going to have to stick to stories and poems." The work accumulated very slowly, taking form whenever Carver was able to grab an hour or two for writing, frequently in a car parked in the driveway.

The first significant fruit of this period was the story "Will You Please Be Quiet, Please?," published in the Chicago-based magazine *December* in 1966 and selected by Martha Foley for inclusion in *The Best American Short Stories 1967.* That year also brought a measure of relief from years of minimum-wage drudgery: Carver landed an editing job at Science Research Associates (SRA) in Palo Alto and moved his family into a house with a converted garage, where he could occasionally escape to write. In the spring of 1968 his wife received a stipend to study in Tel Aviv, so the whole family spent six months in the Middle East, and Carver absorbed material for the poems that appear in the third section of *Fires.*

The attention that accrued as a result of his selection for the Foley collection, coupled with the publication in 1968 of a collection of poems (*Near Klamath,* issued by the English Club of Sacramento State), only strengthened Carver's conviction that he was warranted in giving time to writing. Yet by 1968, almost as if in rejection of these long-sought signs of success, Carver had given himself over to a mode of behavior that would nearly kill him before he was able to control it. "Alcohol became a problem," he told Mona Simpson during an interview for the *Paris Review* in the summer of 1983 (included in *Fires*). Saddled with an old car, a rented house, and serious debt—as well as the perennial "wagonload of frustration" from having neither privacy nor leisure to write—he "more or less gave up, threw in the towel, and took to full-time drinking as a serious pursuit."

A great many of Carver's stories and poems offer a view of life as experienced through an alcohol-induced haze; he is, in fact, one of the finest chroniclers of lives wrecked by booze, from the hopeless and self-deluded speaker of "Cheers" ("They don't understand; I'm fine, / just fine where I am, for any day now / I shall be, I shall be, I shall be . . .") to the dead-ended couple in "Gazebo," all of whose important decisions have been "figured out" while drinking ("Even when we talked about having to cut back on our drinking, we'd be sitting at the kitchen table or out at the picnic table with a six-pack or whiskey") to the hapless guzzler of cheap champagne in "Careful" who must rely on his ex-wife to relieve him of his earwax. There is sometimes a certain despairing humor in these portraits, but beneath it is always the feeling that real ugliness can erupt suddenly, without provocation, as it does in the stories "Tell the Women We're Going," "A Serious Talk," "One More Thing," "The Bridle," "Vitamins," and in such poems as "Union Street: San Francisco, Summer 1975," and "From the East, Light" from *Ultramarine*. One of the most clear-sighted and devastating of these narratives is "Wine," a poem from the posthumous *A New Path to the Waterfall* (1989) about Alexander the Great's burning of Persepolis and drunken, impulsive murder of his friend Cletus. Carver's tone is sorrowful, perplexed, yet his gaze is unblinking as Alexander rises from his bed of grief to drink himself oblivious at Cletus' funeral.

Carver frequently insisted to interviewers that his work was not autobiographical in a direct sense. Yet he acknowledged in "Fires" that most of his stories "bear a resemblance, however faint, to certain life occurrences or situations." He also indicated to Mona Simpson his preference for work, "whether it's Tolstoi's fiction, Chekhov, Barry Hannah, Richard Ford, Hemingway, Isaac Babel, Ann Beattie, or Anne Tyler, [that] strikes me as autobiographical to some extent. . . . Stories long or short just don't come out of thin air." Tess Gallagher, in her introduction to *A New Path to the Waterfall*, in several ways invites readers to consider links between Carver's life and his work—most notably by calling attention to Carver's choice of a Robert Lowell line ("Yet why not say what happened?") as the headnote to one of the book's sections, but also by referring to "the poems about his first marriage, and . . . the havoc it had caused." In general, in his last three collections of poetry and in several late stories assembled in *Where I'm Calling From* (1988), Carver seemed to embrace a directness of expression in which the line between life and artifice dwindles to invisibility—works that offer, in Greg Kuzma's memorable phrase about *Ultramarine*, "experience delivered smoldering like new-born calves." But in earlier work as well, particularly the narratives of alcoholism, certainly a portion of the impact derives from the authority of Carver's having "been there" and having determined to write what he knew well.

In 1970, as a result of reorganization at SRA, Carver was laid off. He was able to live for nearly a year on the strength of severance pay, unemployment benefits, and a National Endowment for the Arts Discovery Award. It was a good and fruitful time: his second collection of poetry, *Winter Insomnia* (1970), was published by Kayak Press in Santa Cruz, and he was able, for the first time in his life, to write for long stretches of time. During this year, nearly half of the stories for *Will You Please Be Quiet, Please?* (1976) were drafted. During this year, too, Maryann finished her degree.

Carver's growing regional reputation led in the early 1970's to a temporary teaching position at the University of California at Santa Cruz and a Wallace Stegner Fellowship at Stanford—

developments that boosted his self-esteem, but continued to bemuse him. He told an interviewer, Michael Schumacher, in 1987 that

> never, in my wildest imaginings, could I have seen myself as a teacher. I was always the shyest kid in class—*any* class. I never said anything. So the idea of conducting a class or having anything to say or being able to help students was the furthest thing away from my mind.

In this period, too, he re-established contact with Gordon Lish, a friend from his SRA days. Lish had worked in a textbook firm across the street from SRA before moving to New York to become fiction editor for *Esquire*. One of Lish's first gestures in his new job was to ask Carver for stories—a request Carver immediately responded to, only to receive them back by return mail. Lish, however, was encouraging, and eventually took one, "Neighbors," for which Carver received six hundred dollars. Soon after, James Dickey, then *Esquire*'s poetry editor, took several of Carver's poems for the magazine, and, as Carver wrote in tribute to Lish, "nothing, it seemed to me, would ever be the same."

In a certain respect, Carver later observed of the period following his ascension to national prominence, "things had never seemed better." In 1972 he won the Joseph Henry Jackson award for fiction, and in the fall of 1973 he was invited back to the Iowa Writers Workshop, not as a student but as a teacher. In each of the years from 1973 through 1975, the annual *Prize Stories: The O. Henry Awards* included stories by Carver ("What Is It?," "Put Yourself in My Shoes," and "Are You a Doctor?"). And in 1974 Capra Press of Santa Barbara published a limited-edition chapbook of his stories, *Put Yourself in My Shoes.* Yet the five or six years preceding his repudiation of alcohol on June 2, 1977 also provided some of the grimmest episodes in his life, interludes that even a decade later he would discuss only obliquely. Life after fame, he wrote in "Fires," "soon took another veering, a sharp turn, and then it came to a dead stop off on a siding." To Mona Simpson he said simply, "On occasion, the police were involved and emergency rooms and courtrooms. . . . It's strange. You never start out in life with the intention of becoming a bankrupt or an alcoholic or a cheat and a thief. Or a liar." His account to Simpson of the teaching experience at Iowa emphasized extracurricular activities. John Cheever and he "did nothing *but* drink. . . . I don't think either of us ever took the covers off our typewriters. We made trips to the liquor store twice a week in my car."

Two poems in *A New Path to the Waterfall* preserve images of Carver's domestic life during this period. In "Miracle" a husband and wife fly from Los Angeles to San Francisco after bankruptcy proceedings against them. The couple has been "turned inside out, crucified and left / for dead, . . . dropped like so much / garbage in front of the terminal." Fortified with "doubles" in the airport lounge before they board, they strap themselves in and continue drinking until the woman, without a word, begins to hit her husband, beating him on the head until his nose bleeds. As he is pounded, the man "protects / his whiskey. Grips that plastic glass as if, yes, / it's the long-sought treasure." She stops and goes back to her own drink (because her arms are tired, the man concludes); he looks out the window and then around at the other people in the plane while blood collects in his drink napkin, picturing

> bloody husband
> and wife, both so still and pale they could be
> dead. But they're not, and that's part of
> the miracle. All this is one more giant step
> into the mysterious experience of their lives.

The plane lands, and the two are able to "walk away from this awful fix," but with the speaker's reminder that much remains in store for them—"so many fierce / surprises, such exquisite turnings."

In the other poem, "On an Old Photograph of My Son," Carver remembers family life in 1974, when his son—here described as a "petty tyrant," a "jerk," and a "bully"—terrorized the household by his demands on his mother:

What's for supper, mother dear? Snap to!
Hey, old lady, jump, why don't you? Speak
when spoken to. I think I'll put you in
a headlock to see how you like it. I like
it. I want to keep you on
your toes. Dance for me now. Go ahead,
bag, dance. I'll show you a step or two.
Let me twist your arm. Beg me to stop, beg me
to be nice. Want a black eye? You got it!

Though the speaker is filled with "despair and anger" so potent it threatens to send him back to the bottle, an even worse sensation is the consciousness that his former wife, on seeing this picture, will react only to her son's "youth and beauty," will weep over the image, may even "wish for those days / back again!"

During the academic year 1975–1976 Carver was on appointment at the University of California at Santa Barbara, but was unable to finish the year because of his alcoholism. The next year he was in and out of alcohol rehabilitation centers—"completely out of control and in a very grave place." In May 1977 he met Fred Hills of McGraw-Hill in San Francisco to discuss a contract for a novel. Carver had been drunk for two days before the meeting and had downed a half pint of vodka before driving into the city. In the wake of this meeting—which resulted in an offer of money despite Carver's condition—Carver drove home, kept drinking for another few days, and then stopped for good. Alcoholics Anonymous was an indispensable aid during the first weeks and months; Carver sometimes went to two meetings a day as he began to recover. Some of the sensations of this period found expression in "Rogue River Jet-Boat Trip, Gold Beach, Oregon, July 4, 1977" in *Fires*.

Although the work Carver had published in *Esquire* in the first half of the 1970's led to a certain level of national attention, the bulk of Carver's stories first appeared in little magazines such as the *Chicago Review*, the *North American Review*, and *Sou'wester*, read mainly by people in academic circles. During the years Carver had been, as he put it, "devoting myself to drinking," Gordon Lish had continued to promote Carver in small ways, mainly by reading his work on the radio and at writers' conferences. In 1976 Lish had collected some of the stories and given them to McGraw-Hill, which published them as *Will You Please Be Quiet, Please?* The following year, the book received a National Book Award nomination, and Carver's stature was secured.

Will You Please Be Quiet, Please? is Carver's most eclectic collection of fiction, the stories reflecting changes in style and subject matter over a fifteen-year span. The earliest, "The Father," is a product of Carver's undergraduate days, though it is closer in manner to his mature work than to other apprentice stories. It is a spare, slight narrative: a father listens numbly to a conversation about whom his baby resembles, the talkers concluding eventually that although the baby looks like Daddy, Daddy looks like nobody. The father's face at the end, as if to confirm this unsettling perception, is "white and without expression." The collection is peopled with the characters that became Carver's trademark—waitresses, a mailman, a vacuum-cleaner salesman, mill workers, a mechanic, collectors of unemployment. Although a few of the stories are explicitly set in the rural Northwest, their primary terrain is simply the generic landscape of America's lower-middle class. It is worth noting, however, that the population of Carver country includes professional people as well—such as Arnold Breit in "Are You a Doctor?,'' who carries a briefcase and whose wife travels as a buyer; Myers, the writer of ''Put Yourself in My Shoes''; the student who reads Rilke to his attention-starved wife in ''The Student's Wife''; Harry in ''How About This?,'' a writer-actor-musician who travels with ''a volume of plays by Ghelderode'' in the back seat of his car; and Marian and Ralph Wyman of the title story, teachers whose relationship began in a Chaucer class.

Most of the stories conclude with an implication that things will be worse hereafter. In ''They're Not Your Husband,'' for example, an out-of-work salesman, Earl, visits the restaurant where his wife works as a waitress and overhears two men joke about her weight. Upset in an obscure way (''the feeling started in his face and worked down into his stomach and legs''), Earl imposes a diet on her, with the result that she loses weight and energy both. At the end Earl tries to extract confirmation of Doreen's increased attractiveness from another waitress and a stranger at the restaurant's counter, but instead he himself is exposed as a ''joker.'' Doreen's slow shake of the head and shrug of the shoulders suggest that the scales have fallen from her eyes, and Earl's frozen smile in response to everyone's stare forecasts retreat and further emotional deterioration. A similarly baleful sensation pervades the end of ''Nobody Said Anything,'' in which the young narrator's attempt to defuse a parental argument backfires as the mother and father furiously reject the mutilated steelhead salmon he has caught in a neighborhood creek. Harry and Emily seem to recognize at the end of ''How About It?'' that their dream of renovating their lives by renovating an old house in the country is doomed to failure, and the prayer that closes ''The Student's Wife'' seems unlikely to bring the couple much respite from the weariness that afflicts their moments of closeness or the increasing distance between their emotional worlds.

The possibility of positive change is a note sounded only occasionally in these stories, yet it *is* heard from time to time. The waitress who narrates ''Fat'' seems to take on emotional substance and to become dissatisfied with the insensitivity of others after her encounter with a customer with a gargantuan appetite who refers to himself as ''we.'' Unexpected and mysterious sources of energy become accessible to the couple who imaginatively inhabit the identities of the people across the hall in ''Neighbors'' and to Myers as he listens to Mr. Morgan try to provide him with ''material'' for his writing in ''Put Yourself in My Shoes.'' And at the conclusion of the title story, Ralph Wyman—''marveling at the impossible changes he felt moving over him''—appears able to relinquish the jealousy and feelings of inferiority that earlier prevented him from acknowledging and embracing his wife's sensual nature.

Stylistically, the stories range from the rather full, expository technique of ''Will You Please Be Quite, Please?'' and ''Sixty Acres'' to the dialogue-driven narrative mode of ''What's in Alaska?'' Typically, the language of a Carver story is pared down, curtailed, reflective of the mostly inarticulate people who are his usual subjects. Richard Schetnan has described Carver's voice (which we are to assume is his own although it closely resembles that of some of his fictional characters) as one that ''attempts to gather, extemporaneously, as many details of a story as possible, but [that] also refrains from assembling those details into a complete and immediately meaningful whole to avoid the emotional threats and confusion that connections and relationships between ideas may present.'' This mode is evident in the following passage from one of the latest stories in the book, ''Collectors'' (first published in 1975), in which a man expecting to ''hear from up north'' is unable to prevent a vacuum-cleaner salesman from demonstrating his wares or eventually from leaving with a piece of the narrator's mail:

> He went about his business. He put another attachment on the hose, in some complicated way hooked his bottle to the new attachment. He moved slowly over the carpet, now and then releasing little streams of emerald, moving the brush back and forth over the carpet, working up patches of foam.
>
> I had said all that was on my mind. I sat on the chair in the kitchen, relaxed now, and watched him work. Once in a while I looked out the window at the rain. It had begun to get dark. He switched off the vacuum. He was in a corner near the front door.

The narrator's emotional paralysis permits only direct, indifferent observation of the course of events; short syntactical units, in which the gaze moves randomly from one element of the scene to another and in which all elements remain disjunct, are the primary narrative vehicles.

In 1976 and 1977 Capra Press published two other collections of Carver's work—a third gathering of poems, titled *At Night the Salmon Move,* and *Furious Seasons and Other Stories,* a handful of eight stories not included in the McGraw-Hill collection. With the exception of the title story, all of these stories (some extensively revised and retitled) were later included in other compilations, and in the 1983 volume *Fires,* Carver culled ''fifty poems that I wanted to keep'' from the three small-press books.

In November 1977, estranged from Maryann and his children and still very fragile after five months off alcohol, Carver met the poet Tess Gallagher at a writers' conference in El Paso, Texas. The following year, after Carver had been invited to teach at the University of Texas at El Paso, the two met again while Gallagher was traveling on a Guggenheim Fellowship, and their friendship took root. Early in 1979 Gallagher moved to El Paso, and in the fall they went together to Tucson, where Gallagher taught at the University of Arizona and Carver lived on his own Guggenheim. Gradually, as his strength returned over these years, he was able to resume writing, but he later told William Stull in an interview for the *Bloomsbury Review* (reprinted in *Living in Words,* edited by Gregory McNamee) that it was gift enough simply to have his wits back: ''I'd been brain-dead for such a long time. And suddenly I had this other life, another chance at things. And in this new life it wasn't all that important if I wrote or not. . . . I was patient, and I simply waited to see what would come along, if anything.''

What in due course came along were the stories in *What We Talk About When We Talk About Love* (1981), a collection that pervasively reflects the influence of Gordon Lish and that caused Carver to be viewed as the country's chief practitioner of ''minimalist fiction,'' as critics and reviewers began to call it. It is also Carver's most violence-riddled collection, an assembly of dark narratives in which murder, suicide, sudden death, domestic mayhem, and mute but volatile fury are the rule rather than the exception.

Lish's influence is evident in the unprecedentedly elliptical style of the work. Carver referred to it as ''a much more self-conscious book in the sense of how intentional every move was. . . . I pushed and pulled and worked with those stories before they went into the book to an extent I'd never done with any other stories.'' In the *Bloomsbury Review* interview Carver attributed this impulse to both John Gardner and Lish, but particularly to the latter: ''Gardner said don't use twenty-five words to say what you can say in fifteen. This was the way Gorden felt, except Gordon believed that if you could say it in five words instead of fifteen, use five words.'' In the essay ''On Writing'' (first published in 1981 as ''A Storyteller's Notebook,'' included in *Fires*), Carver also celebrated the tension-producing value of ''the things that are left out, that are implied, the landscape just under the smooth (but sometimes broken and unsettled) surface of things.''

These characteristics are all present in ''So Much Water So Close to Home,'' in which the narrator, Claire, must assimilate the fact that her husband and three buddies have discovered the naked corpse of a young girl in the river adjacent to their fishing camp, but delayed contacting the police until the end of their expedition—this, and the fact that Claire's husband waits until the morning after his return to tell her what has happened. We intuit Claire's horror not through any direct expression of it, but through the clenched-teeth tone of paragraphs like the following:

I was asleep when he got home. But I woke up when I heard him in the kitchen. I found him leaning against the refrigerator with a can of beer. He put his heavy arms around me and rubbed his big hands on my back. In bed he put his hands on me again and then waited as if thinking of something else. I turned and opened my legs. Afterwards, I think he stayed awake.

The grimness characteristic of this volume is also evident in the way this version of the story ends. Claire attends the girl's funeral, vaguely menaced on her drive there by a man who pulls alongside her and looks at her breasts and legs. She returns home to find her husband drinking whiskey at the kitchen table. ''I think I know what you need,'' he assures her, and begins to unbutton her blouse. Able to hear nothing ''with so much water going,'' she capitulates, even urges him on, finding no resources in the face of his impulse toward power except her ability to please.

The version of this story published earlier in *Furious Seasons* is twice as long as the version in *What We Talk About When We Talk About Love*. What Carver believed he could eliminate were mainly passages in which Claire mentally reacts to her husband's behavior, but the two versions differ most markedly in their endings. In the earlier version, Claire, on her return from the funeral, expresses fear, to which her husband responds first with sexual aggression and then (when she is resistant) with physical violence. Two days of alternating repentance and belligerence follow, during which Claire seems gradually to bring her husband to an understanding of the dread and revulsion she has felt. This ending is not unambiguously hopeful, by any means, but it is less ghastly than the image of Claire compelling herself into submission, newly conscious of exactly *how* close to home the ''water'' is.

Other previously published stories that appear in *What We Talk About When We Talk About Love* underwent the same process of paring, such as ''The Third Thing That Killed My Father Off'' and ''Everything Stuck to Him.'' In addition, in this collection Carver's attitude toward the characters seems more compassionate: he appears less willing than he was in the stories in *Will You Please Be Quite, Please?* to exhibit their weaknesses in order to invite scorn. In interviews Carver often disavowed interest in irony, objecting to stories in which the author establishes collusion with the audience at the expense of characters. Still, in such early pieces as ''The Idea,'' ''They're Not Your Husband,'' ''What's in Alaska?,'' ''What Do You Do in San Francisco?,'' and ''Signals,'' it is difficult not to feel a significant gulf between the implied values of the author and those of the narrator or protagonist. In contrast, in *What We Talk About When We Talk About Love* the ironic impulse surfaces clearly only once, in ''Sacks.'' There, the narrator gradually assumes more and more grotesque proportions as he shows himself incapable of responding with understanding to his father's explanation of his divorce. At the story's close, the narrator remembers that he has left behind the small gift of candy his father had given him to take home to his wife, and his dearth of ordinary human sympathy is confirmed in his reaction: "Just as well. Mary didn't need candy, Almond Roca or anything else. That was last year. She needs it now even less."

Irony is often a humor-producing mode, and in 1979, in a long review of *Will You Please Be Quiet, Please?,* David Boxer and Cassandra Phillips argued that "humor, irony, and glimmers of the absurd affirm [Carver's] authority." In *What We Talk About When We Talk About Love,* however, the mood is somber: characters are not handled as opportunities for complicity between writer and reader, but rather as emblems of the ways in which life bears down hard on all of us. These characters find themselves caught in the grip of debilitating paranoia (Dummy in "The Third Thing That Killed My Father Off"), unconscious feelings of entrapment (Jerry in "Tell the Women We're Going," Duane and Holly in "Gazebo"), fear of death (Edith and James Packer in "After the Denim," the nameless mother in "The Bath"), or alcohol-induced rage (Burt in "A Serious Talk," L.D. in "One More Thing").

What We Talk About When We Talk About Love indisputably established Carver as one of the "true contemporary masters," in Robert Towers' words. Yet in an influential review of the volume in *Atlantic Monthly,* James Atlas, while praising the "bleak power" afforded by Carver's masterly narrative sense and "willfully simple style," objected finally to the "lackluster manner and eschewal of feeling." "One is left," he complained, "with a hunger for richness, texture, excess." This theme was taken up by a number of other commentators during the 1980's, notably by writers for *The New Criterion* (a conservative quarterly edited by Hilton Kramer) and by most contributors to a 1985 special double issue of the *Mississippi Review* devoted to the subject of minimalist fiction. The works of Carver and others such as Ann Beattie, Bobbie Ann Mason, and Jayne Anne Phillips were taken as a signal of retreat from the effort to articulate thought and emotion in language. Some went so far as to see this fiction as symptomatic of the neoconservative political temper of the country, a rejection of complexity, intellectualism, experimentation, and "the beauties of amplitude," in Joe David Bellamy's phrase. The Carver of *What We Talk About When We Talk About Love* was chided for a perceived inclination to revere the banal, to relinquish moral authority in his determination to render the lives of average people realistically.

By the time such discussion reached its apex, however, Carver had already cast off certain of the traits that reviewers said distinguished his most clearly "minimalist" stories. His life had assumed an entirely new stability: in 1980 he accepted a permanent position in the writing program at Syracuse University, and he and Gallagher shuttled back and forth between teaching duties in Syracuse and writing stints in Port Angeles, Washington, Gallagher's hometown. After the manuscript for *What We Talk About When We Talk About Love* was in his publisher's hands, Carver wrote nothing for six months. Then came, as if from another realm of experience altogether, the story "Cathedral"—"totally different in conception and execution," Carver told Mona Simpson, "from any stories that [had] come before."

> I experienced this rush and I felt, "This is what it's all about, this is the reason we do this" . . . There was an opening up when I wrote the story. I knew I'd gone as far the other way as I could or wanted to go, cutting everything down to the marrow, not just to the bone.

Previously, it had taken Carver years to amass enough stories for a collection, but all of the stories for *Cathedral,* published in 1983, were written in an eighteen-month period. Between these and earlier stories, Carver said he "felt the difference in every one."

The frequently anthologized title story is the

clearest illustration of the departures in tone and thematic emphasis from *What We Talk About When We Talk About Love*. Initially, much is similar to earlier Carver: the attitudes, speech patterns, and preoccupations of the narrator, "Bub," recall the narrators of "Mr. Coffee and Mr. Fixit" and "Gazebo" and the suspicious husband Wayne who takes his wife out to an elegant dinner in "Signals." What first distinguishes Bub from these others is his sense of humor. He is not happy about hosting a male friend of his wife's—particularly a blind one, whose blindness is a source of both intimidation and intrigue. But Bub's grouchiness expresses itself in wryly amusing ways, as in his comment that "next to writing a poem every year," sending tapes to her blind friend has been his wife's "chief means of recreation," and in his suggestion that for entertainment they all go bowling. The comic note continues in Bub's description of their approach to dinner:

> We dug in. We ate everything there was to eat on the table. We ate like there was no tomorrow. We didn't talk. We ate. We scarfed. We grazed that table. We were into serious eating.

More to the point, however, is the turn the narrative takes after dinner and an evening of increasing sleepiness and marijuana-induced disengagement. As a television documentary about cathedrals drones in the background, Bub suddenly wonders whether the blind Robert has any conception of the scope of such structures. Determined to try to convey something of their magnificence, he begins to sketch one on a shopping bag, with Robert's hand on top of his. Momentum gathers, until Robert finally advises him to close his eyes and just keep drawing. Bub does, and what results is a splendid moment of sympathetic identification between the two: "His fingers rode my fingers as my hand went over the paper. It was like nothing else in my life up to now."

Similar moments occur in several other stories in *Cathedral*. Many critics have drawn attention, for example, to the conclusion of "A Small, Good Thing," a much-expanded version of "The Bath," from *What We Talk About When We Talk About Love*. In the *Cathedral* version, a grieving young couple discover that the source of several unsettling telephone calls they have received in the wake of an accident involving their son is a baker, angry because they have not picked up the cake they ordered for their son's birthday. The two drive to the shopping center in the middle of the night and furiously confront the baker with the news that Scotty has died, whereupon the baker comes to his senses, apologizes, and tries to make amends by offering them coffee and hot rolls. "Eating is a small, good thing in a time like this," he says, and the three talk on into the early morning, the horror of Scotty's death at least temporarily alleviated by their having come together in this fragile, unexpected way.

Such an ending would have been inconceivable in an early Carver story and perhaps exemplifies Carver's own sense that in these narratives he was "breaking out of something I had put myself into, both personally and aesthetically." A positive spirit also informs the stories "Feathers," in which the cavorting of an ugly baby and a peacock causes the narrator to feel "good about almost everything in my life"; "Where I'm Calling From," in which a kiss from a female chimney sweep and a memory of a happy interlude with his wife give the narrator courage to re-establish contact with the world outside of the alcoholic drying-out facility where he has landed more than once; and "Fever," in which the kindness and unassuming proficiency of a grandmotherly babysitter get the protagonist through a difficult time. Not all of the stories reflect Carver's altered outlook—several, in fact, are as bleak in their vision as any in *What We Talk About When We Talk About Love*—but the leaven of the four or five affirmative pieces sharply distinguishes the collection from those that preceded it.

The same, more expansive spirit is evident in the stories in *Fires*. The book's tone is established by its epigraph, from William Matthews' *Flood*:

> And isn't the past inevitable,
> Now that we call the little
> we remember of it "the past"?

For Carver *Fires* was a book of retrievals, a gathering of pieces that deserved preservation or renewal, a paying of debts previously not fully acknowledged. Five of the seven stories appear in earlier collections, two of them ("Distance" and "So Much Water So Close To Home") in both *Furious Seasons* and *What We Talk About When We Talk About Love*. Here, however, what was excised is restored, all of the stories are substantially revised, and several are retitled. "There's not much I like better," Carver told Mona Simpson, "than to take a story I've had around the house for a while and work it over again." Carver's afterword to the Capra Press edition of the book elaborates on his passion for "messing around" with his stories. Carver regularly produced ten or twelve drafts of each piece—sometimes as many as twenty or thirty—before relinquishing it into the hands of publishers, and the textual history of the published work confirms his proclivity for revision even after a story had appeared in a collection.

Most clearly in the reminiscent spirit is "The Cabin," a new version of Carver's 1962 story "Pastoral." The early influence of Hemingway is evident here in the central image of a man trying to escape some sort of unspecified trouble (why doesn't he respond to questions about his wife, Frances?) by returning to a favorite fishing spot. But in the unexpected appearance of several boys in pursuit of a deer they have wounded, the story also nods in the direction of another influence, Flannery O'Connor. Mr. Harrold's confrontation with these menacing intruders recalls moments in a number of O'Connor stories in which a character is brought up sharply by a reminder of his mortality, often delivered in grotesque or frightening forms.

The two previously uncollected stories in *Fires* seem somewhat like exercises, "The Pheasant" an attempt at managing three points of view in a brief space, and "Harry's Death" an experiment in conveying a story behind the story the narrator overtly tells. In the aftermath of Harry's unexpected (and unexplained) death, the narrator begins seeing Harry's girlfriend, Little Judith, one of the pleasures of whose company is the thirty-two-foot Chris Craft boat that Harry had bought with her shortly before he died. On the first extended trip the narrator and Little Judith take, Judith ("who couldn't swim a stroke") mysteriously falls overboard in the middle of the night, her disappearance unnoticed by the narrator and the Mexican crewman until the next morning. Says the putatively grief-stricken narrator:

> That is the truth, so help me, and what I told the police when we put in at Guaymas a few days later. My wife, I told them—for luckily we'd married just before leaving San Francisco.

The tale is told from Mazatlan, "three months later," and now the narrator just plans to "keep going until the money runs out," sure that he is "doing things the way Harry would have wanted."

The fiction in *Fires,* however, is secondary to four prose pieces and to a small anthology of poems. In the essays are to be found most of the precepts about writing that Carver learned from John Gardner and others and then passed along to his own students: "Get in, get out. Don't linger. Go on"; Ezra Pound's injunction that "fundamental accuracy of statement is the ONE sole morality of writing"; "No tricks. Period. I hate tricks"; "A little menace is fine to have in a story." Here, too, in "John Gardner: The Writer as Teacher'' and ''Fires'' are Carver's grateful tributes to his first mentor and to Gordon Lish, as well as his poignant but markedly unsentimental account of the impact of family life on his early years as a writer. Carver's memoir of his father probes even further back, to exhume and examine not just the bare images from those days, but also the power they gave to his narrative impulse and the control they continued to exercise over his attitudes and obsessions.

Many of the poems collected in *Fires* bear the impress of William Carlos Williams, whom Carver idolized as an undergraduate. Carver liked to tell the story of writing to Williams to request a poem for the literary magazine he had started in Chico State and being thrilled when Williams sent him a signed piece, ''The Gossips.'' The obligation is explicitly acknowledged in ''Poem for Hemingway & W. C. Williams.'' The more pervasive, though unstated, influence on these poems of Carver's early and middle years may be the Robert Lowell of *Life Studies* (1959) and *For the Union Dead* (1964). The second section of poems in *Fires* comprises a single long poem, ''You Don't Know What Love Is,'' a tribute to Charles Bukowski, also a forceful voice for Carver in those years.

The year 1983 was a watershed for Carver—two books published, first place in the O. Henry competition for ''A Small, Good Thing,'' a front-page notice in *The New York Times Book Review,* an interview in the *Paris Review,* and, most significantly, the Mildred and Harold Strauss Living Award of thirty-five thousand dollars a year for five years from the American Academy and Institute of Arts and Letters. This award freed him from the need to teach, an enormous relief for a man who had always found that role unnerving. (The clearest picture of Carver as an instructor is Jay McInerney's reminiscence in the August 6, 1989 *New York Times Book Review*: ''The idea of facing a class made him nervous every time. On the days he had to teach he would get agitated, as if he himself were a student on the day of the final exam.'') Finding it increasingly difficult to work uninterruptedly in the house he and Gallagher shared in Syracuse, Carver determined to slip out of the media spotlight by moving to Port Angeles in January 1984.

The Strauss prize had been intended to free Carver to concentrate full time on the writing of fiction, but as he settled into Gallagher's recently built Sky House, he found himself moved toward poetry. He wrote at least a poem a day, and sometimes two or three, for sixty-five days, and by the time the impulse had exhausted itself, he had the manuscript for *Where Water Comes Together with Other Water.* ''I've never had a period in my life that remotely resembles that time,'' Carver told Michael Schumacher in 1987. ''I felt like it would have been all right, you know, simply to have died after those sixty-five days. I felt *on fire.*'' After a lecture tour in Brazil and Argentina with Gallagher, Carver wrote more poems, so that when *Where Water Comes Together with Other Water* appeared in 1985 under the Random House imprint, the collection that became *Ultramarine* (published the next year, also by Random) was complete as well. In retrospect, the whole period seemed ''a great gift,'' and Carver allowed that he would be happy ''if they simply put 'poet' on my tombstone . . . and in parentheses, 'and short story writer.' ''

In 1985 Carver's poems appeared in two issues of *Poetry,* on the strength of which he won the magazine's Levinson Prize. In a brief piece in the seventy-fifth anniversary issue, reprinted in *A New Path to the Waterfall,* he acknowledged the powerful impression the magazine had made on him at a crucial moment in his development; the piece also quietly testifies to the pleasure he took in recognizing himself as one of the august crowd enshrined in its pages.

Carver's late poems taxed friendly reviewers to develop a rhetoric of approval that simultaneously conveyed reservation about the astonishing degree of directness and the conversational quality of the language. ''But are they poems?'' Dave Smith wonders in a review of *Where Water Comes Together with Other Water,* evidently uneasy with ''a tone which has the valueless ease and unprofound quality of ordinary talk.'' But after acknowledging that poet Carver at his weakest could be ''maudlin, sentimental, clunky,'' Smith takes delight in ''the feel of extraordinary experience'' and in Carver's ''unusual talent for poems about happiness.'' Greg Kuzma, in a perceptive and respectful response to *Ultramarine,* praises

> a voice unassuming and yet so empowered that one comes to look at it, to listen in it, for how close it can come to the truth without shaking or breaking, . . . poems both heavy with consequence, things taken head-on at full force, and yet fragile, light, gentle in their modesty, their refusal to pretend or puff up or become self-important.

The ''tombstone'' motif in Carver's comments to Schumacher about writing poetry surfaces in a number of these poems, frequently enough to make one wonder if Carver sensed that the years remaining to him were few. In *Ultramarine,* especially, mortality looms: many poems are about the deaths of friends and acquaintances, and many ruminate on his own death. ''Before long, before anyone realizes, / I'll be gone from here,'' intones the speaker of ''The Cobweb,'' and in ''Evening'' a memory of ''exceptional joy'' is all the more intense for the speaker's being overwhelmed by a ''longing / to be back once more, before I die.'' The sensation of impending death appears more than once, too, in Carver's late stories, most prominently in ''Whoever Was Using This Bed,'' in which disturbing calls late at night lead Jack and Iris into conversation about ''what I'd *do* if something ever happened to you.'' Presentiment may also explain Carver's impulse to gather the best of his previous fiction, augmented by seven uncollected stories, in 1988 under the title *Where I'm Calling From: New and Selected Stories.*

It was, in any case, a timely gesture. In September 1987 cancer was discovered in Carver's lungs, and he underwent immediate surgery. Months of slow recovery followed, but in March 1988 the disease reappeared as a brain tumor, and in June new lesions appeared on his lungs. During intermittent periods of relief from the illness, Carver not only saw his own fiction celebrated, but was confirmed in the confidence he had expressed the previous year (in a note for the *Michigan Quarterly Review*) that ''the resurgence of interest in the short story has done nothing less than revitalize the national literature.'' His role in that revitalization was recognized in his being named to the American Academy and Institute of Arts and Letters, granted an honorary doctorate from the University of Hartford, and awarded the Brandeis Medal of Excellence.

During the last months of his life, Carver worked with Tess Gallagher to complete one final book, and in these labors were concentrated the affection, mutual admiration, and passionately supportive energy that had characterized their relationship for the previous eleven years. The fruits of their happy alliance included a screenplay on Dostoevsky's life (written in 1982 for director Michael Cimino, published by Capra Press with an introduction by Carver in 1985), but were more clearly evident in frequent testimonials by both writers to the profound impact each had had on the other. ''She has a wonderful eye and a way of feeling herself into what I write,'' Carver told Mona Simpson; Gallagher called the relationship ''a beautiful alchemy . . . a kind of luminous reciprocity'' in which everything she gave was returned in Carver's loving attention to her own work. Shortly after the return of the cancer, in June 1988, the two flew to Reno to be married—''as if we'd found an answer to / that question of what's left / when there's no more hope,'' Carver wrote in the poem ''Proposal.''

Many of the individual pieces in *A New Path to the Waterfall* had been completed before the unnerving developments of fall 1987, but in the glare of ''What the Doctor Said,'' the book assumed a new shape. Gallagher's introduction to the volume, an account of the putting-together, is the most intimate view available of the fuels by which Carver's imagination was fired and of the intensity and particularity of their collaborative zest. It also highlights an influence that became increasingly important to Carver—that of Chekhov, passages from whose stories, rendered as Carver-like poems, are woven through the book in tribute to the integral role Chekhov's stories had performed in Carver's and Gallagher's spiritual survival. This device illuminates the conclusion of Carver's last story, ''Errand,'' an account of Chekhov's death and an imagined aftermath. As the widow instructs the young man to carry news of Chekhov's death to the mortician, she adjures him to ''imagine himself as someone moving down the busy sidewalk carrying in his arms a porcelain vase of roses.'' Listening to her, the young man is assumed into her vision, appropriates it (a transformation signaled by a leap to the present tense in the third-to-last paragraph), and is elevated by it as he proceeds on his errand. Awe begets love, and appropriation is its proper expression. Raymond Carver died on August 2, 1988.

''Every great or even every very great writer makes the world over according to his own specifications,'' Carver wrote in 1981. Though his humility prevented him from saying so, that is precisely what Carver did, crafting a clear and startling vision of people and circumstances that the rest of us had somehow overlooked. The best analogue for Carver's work may be Walker Evans' photographs in *Let Us Now Praise Famous Men* (1941)—not James Agee's gorgeous and pain-filled narrative (though the gorgeousness and pain are there in Carver's stories too), but those stark, uncaptioned pictures. Who that looked carefully at them would ever see life the same way again?

Selected Bibliography

WORKS OF RAYMOND CARVER

POETRY

Near Klamath. Sacramento: English Club of Sacramento State College, 1968.

Winter Insomnia: Poems. Santa Cruz: Kayak, 1970.

At Night the Salmon Move: Poems. Santa Barbara: Capra, 1976.

Where Water Comes Together with Other Water: Poems. New York: Random House, 1985.

Ultramarine. New York: Random House, 1986.

A New Path to the Waterfall: Poems. With an introduction by Tess Gallagher. New York: Atlantic Monthly Press, 1989.

SHORT STORIES

Put Yourself in My Shoes. Santa Barbara: Capra, 1974.

Will You Please Be Quiet, Please? New York: McGraw-Hill, 1976.

Furious Seasons and Other Stories. Santa Barbara: Capra, 1977.

What We Talk About When We Talk About Love. New York: Knopf, 1981.

Cathedral: Stories. New York: Knopf, 1983.

Where I'm Calling From: New and Selected Stories. New York: Atlantic Monthly Press, 1988.

SCREENPLAY

Dostoevsky: A Screenplay. With Tess Gallagher. Santa Barbara: Capra, 1985.

COLLECTED WORKS

Fires: Essays, Poems, Stories. Santa Barbara: Capra, 1983; New York: Vintage, 1984.

Those Days: Early Writings by Raymond Carver. Edited by William Stull. Elmwood, Conn.: Raven, 1987.

MANUSCRIPTS AND PAPERS

Manuscripts and letters from 1978 to 1984 are deposited at Ohio State University. Papers from 1984 on are in Tess Gallagher's keeping.

BIBLIOGRAPHY

Stull, William L. "Raymond Carver: A Bibliographical Checklist." *American Book Collector*, 8:17–30 (1987).

BIOGRAPHICAL AND CRITICAL STUDIES

Atlas, James. "Less Is Less." *Atlantic Monthly*, June 1981, pp. 96–98.

Barth, John. "A Few Words About Minimalism." *New York Times Book Review*, December 28, 1986, pp. 1–2, 25.

Beattie, Ann. "Carver's *Furious Seasons*." *Canto*, 2:178–182 (1978).

Bellamy, Joe David. "*Will You Please Be Quiet, Please?*" *Harper's Bookletter*, April 26, 1976.

Boxer, David, and Cassandra Phillips. "*Will You Please Be Quiet, Please?*: Voyeurism, Dissociation, and the Art of Raymond Carver." *Iowa Review*, 10:75–90 (1979).

Brown, Arthur A. "Raymond Carver and Postmodern Humanism." *Critique*, 31:125–136 (1990).

Bugeja, Michael. "Tarnish and Silver: An Analysis of Carver's *Cathedral*." *South Dakota Review*, 24:73–87 (1986).

Chenetier, Marc. "Living On/Off the 'Reserve': Performance, Interrogation, and Negativity in the Works of Raymond Carver." In his *Critical Angles: European Views of Contemporary American Literature*. Carbondale: Southern Illinois University Press, 1986. Pp. 164–190.

Eichman, Erich. "Will Raymond Carver Please Be Quiet, Please?" *New Criterion*, 2:86–89 (1983).

Facknitz, Mark. "Raymond Carver and the Menace of Minimalism." *CEA Critic*, 52:68–73 (Fall 1989–Winter 1990).

Gallagher, Tess. "European Journal." *Antaeus*, no. 61:165–175 (Autumn 1988).

———. "Raymond Carver, 1938 to 1988." *Granta*, 25:165–167 (1988).

———. *Carver Country: The World of Raymond Carver*. Photographs by Bob Adelman. New York: Scribners, 1990.

Howe, Irving. "Stories of Our Loneliness." *New York Times Book Review*, September 11, 1983, pp. 1, 42–43.

Johnson, Greg. "Three Contemporary Masters: Brodkey, Carver, Dubus." *Georgia Review*, 43:784–794 (1989).

Kuzma, Greg. "*Ultramarine:* Poems That Almost Stop the Heart." *Michigan Quarterly Review*, 27:355–363 (1988).

Lonnquist, Barbara. "Narrative Displacement and Literary Faith: Raymond Carver's Inheritance from Flannery O'Connor." *Since Flannery O'Connor: Essays on the Contemporary Short Story*. Edited by Loren Logsdon and Charles W. Mayer. Macomb: Western Illinois University Press, 1987. Pp. 142–150.

McInerney, Jay. "Raymond Carver: A Still, Small Voice." *New York Times Book Review*, August 6, 1989, pp. 1, 24–25.

Meyer, Adam. "Now You See Him, Now You Don't, Now You Do Again: The Evolution of Raymond Carver's Minimalism." *Critique*, 30:239–251 (1989).

Robinson, Marilynne. "Marriage and Other Astonishing Bonds." *New York Times Book Review*, May 15, 1988, pp. 1, 35, 40–41.

Saltzman, Arthur M. *Understanding Raymond Carver*. Columbia: University of South Carolina Press, 1988.

Schetnan, Richard. " 'A Way of Trying to Connect Up': The Style of Raymond Carver's 'My Father's Life.' " *Cimarron Review*, no. 91:83–89 (April 1990).

Shute, Kathleen. "Finding the Words: The Struggle for Salvation in the Fiction of Raymond Carver." *Hollins Critic*, 24:1–10 (1987).

Smith, Dave. Review of *Where Water Comes Together with Other Water*. *Poetry*, October 1985, pp. 38–40.

Solotaroff, Ted. "Raymond Carver: Going Through the Pain." *American Poetry Review*, 18:47–49 (1989).

Stull, William. "Raymond Carver." *Dictionary of*

American Literary Biography: 1984. Edited by Jean W. Ross. Detroit: Gale, 1985. Pp. 233–245.

———. ''Raymond Carver.'' *Dictionary of Literary Biography Yearbook: 1988*. Edited by J. M. Brook. Detroit: Gale, 1989. Pp. 199–213.

———. ''Beyond Hopelessville: Another Side of Raymond Carver.'' *Philological Quarterly*, 64:1–15 (1985).

Towers, Robert. ''Low Rent Tragedies.'' *New York Review of Books,* May 14, 1981, p. 37.

Vander Weele, Michael. ''Raymond Carver and the Language of Desire.'' *Denver Quarterly*, 22:108–122 (1987).

INTERVIEWS

Alton, John. ''What We Talk About When We Talk About Literature: An Interview with Raymond Carver.'' *Chicago Review*, 36:4–21 (1988).

Bonetti, Kay. ''Ray Carver: Keeping It Short.'' *Saturday Review*, September–October 1983, pp. 21–23.

McCaffery, Larry, and Sinda Gregory. ''Raymond Carver.'' In their *Alive and Writing: Interviews with American Authors of the 1980s*. Urbana: University of Illinois Press, 1987. Pp. 66–82.

McElhinny, Lisa. ''Raymond Carver Speaking.'' *Akros Review*, 8/9:103–114 (1984).

O'Connell, Nicholas. ''Raymond Carver.'' In his *At the Field's End: Interviews with Twenty Pacific Northwest Writers*. Seattle: Madrona, 1987. Pp. 76–94, 171–173.

Schumacher, Michael. ''After the Fire, Into the Fire—An Interview with Raymond Carver.'' In his *Reasons to Believe: New Voices in American Fiction*. New York: St. Martin's, 1988. Pp. 1–27.

Sexton, David. ''David Sexton Talks to Raymond Carver.'' *Literary Review* (London) 85:36–40 (1985).

Simpson, Mona. ''The Art of Fiction LXXVI.'' *Paris Review* 25:192–221 (1983). Included in *Writers at Work, Seventh Series*. Edited by George Plimpton. New York: Viking, 1986.

Stull, William ''Matters of Life and Death.'' In *Living in Words: Interviews From The Bloomsbury Review, 1981–1988*. Edited by Gregory McNamee. Portland, Ore.: Breitenbush, 1988. Pp. 143–156.

Stull, William, and Marshall Bruce Gentry, eds. *Conversations with Raymond Carver*. Jackson: University Press of Mississippi, forthcoming.

—GARY WILLIAMS

Frederick Douglass

1818–1895

THE STORY OF Frederick Douglass, an escaped slave who became an abolitionist orator, newspaper editor, writer, and adviser to presidents, is paralleled by the growth of the United States from the inconsistencies of its constitutional declarations about freedom through a succession of amendments that granted civil rights to African Americans and women. With every fiber of his being Frederick Douglass opposed the central problematic incongruities in the practice of American democracy: chattel slavery and racism. In practice, American democracy was extended only to white males, and Frederick Douglass devoted his entire life to eradicating the slavery of blacks and extending the vote to both blacks and women. One of his most powerful "sermons" against the oppression of African Americans was his 1852 Fourth of July oration—an ironic rendition of the traditional kind of speech, usually delivered by prominent orators celebrating the virtues of the new country, among them the opportunity for disenfranchised immigrants to make a new beginning. For these people, the Fourth of July signaled the celebration of their release from bondage, of their emancipation from ghettos and other more subtle forms of European class and ethnic discrimination. In the United States, by contrast, these orators claimed, the visitor could find a veritable "melting pot" of races and ethnic groups, without distinction by class or religion, race or creed. This ideal was eloquently articulated, as early as 1782, by Hector St. Jean de Crèvecoeur, who asked himself, "What is the American, the new man?" and then answered:

> He is either an European, or the descendant of an European, hence that strange mixture of blood, which you will find in no other country. I could point out to you a family whose grandfather was an Englishman, whose wife was Dutch, whose son married a French woman, and whose present four sons have four wives of four different nations. He is an American, who leaving behind him all his ancient prejudices and manners, receives new ones from the new mode of life he has embraced, the new government he obeys, and the new rank he holds. He becomes an American by being received in the broad lap of our great Alma Mater. Here individuals of all nations are melted into a new race of men, whose labours and posterity will one day cause great changes in the world.

Frederick Douglass knew better. He knew that this idealistic millennial vision of the great society had not yet been realized in the United States. Between 1845, when Douglass published the first version of his autobiography, and 1895, when he died a celebrated American hero, American democracy functioned imperfectly, denying freedom, dignity, and citizenship to its black population. Speaking on July 5, 1852, in Rochester, New York, Douglass delivered a jeremiad against the hypocrisy of American democracy (in Blassingame, vol. 2), articulating the sins of the nation against African Americans, many of whom were chattel slaves in the Southern states, part of a vicious system protected nationally by the Fugitive Slave Act, part of the Compromise of 1850, a reinforcement of similar legislation that dated from 1792. Douglass begins by showing that the Fourth of July is

> the birthday of your National Independence, and of your political freedom. This, to you, is what the Passover was to the emancipated people of God. It carries your minds back to the day, and to the act of your great deliverance; and to the signs, and to the wonders, associated with that act, and that day.

But for the slave in that same America, Douglass emphasized, the Fourth of July stood as a gesture of hypocrisy and cynicism, a reminder that only whites were free—and not even the whole race, for white women were also denied the franchise. To Douglass, speaking for his race, the Fourth of July was

> a day that reveals to [the slave], more than all other days in the year, the gross injustice and cruelty to which he is the constant victim. To him, your celebration is a sham; your boasted liberty, an unholy license; your national greatness, swelling vanity; your sounds of rejoicing are empty and heartless; your denunciation of tyrants, brass fronted impudence; your shouts of liberty and thanksgivings, with all your religious parade and solemnity, are to him mere bombast, fraud, deception, impiety, and hypocrisy—a thin veil to cover up crimes which would disgrace a nation of savages.

The strongly spoken message of Douglass' oration was heard around the world. By 1852—the year Harriet Beecher Stowe's *Uncle Tom's Cabin* brought antislavery sentiment to a feverish pitch "at the North" in the United States—Douglass was himself a hero. He had been speaking on the abolitionist lecture circuit for a decade and had published, in 1845, his autobiographical *Narrative of the Life of Frederick Douglass, an American Slave, Written by Himself.* This important contribution to the abolitionist cause contained a letter and an introduction by two leading abolitionists: William Lloyd Garrison, editor of the *Liberator,* the newspaper of the abolitionists, and Wendell Phillips, orator and leader of the movement. Garrison had encouraged Douglass to write an account of his life as a slave and his escape to freedom in the North.

The power of Douglass' narrative is repeated in the flourishes of his oratory, and both his autobiographical writings and his hundreds of speeches and tracts show him to be one of the most articulate spokesmen for human rights in the nineteenth century. He denounced America as a reformer from within, while distancing himself from its cruel hypocrisies, always—as in his Fourth of July speech—citing the audience as "you":

> The existence of slavery in this country brands your republicanism as a sham, your humanity as a base pretense and your Christianity as a lie. It destroys your moral power abroad; it corrupts your politicians at home. It saps the foundation of religion; it makes your name a hissing and a byeword to a mocking earth. It is the antagonistic force in your government, the only thing that seriously disturbs and endangers your Union. It fetters your progress; it is the enemy of improvement; the deadly foe of education; it fosters pride; it breeds insolence, it promotes vice; it shelters crime; it is a curse to the earth that supports it; and yet you cling to it as if it were the sheet anchor of all your hopes.

Douglass knew that America would never be "his" until the slaves were freed and everyone, all free citizens of an egalitarian country, was a voting member of a society in which all were equal. His was a remarkable vision, given the circumstances of his birth and youth. While he did not share the belief in passive resistance held by Henry David Thoreau and Mahatma Gandhi and Martin Luther King, Jr., after him, Douglass advocated a united society, as King later did, with all races and peoples joined together in harmony. Douglass was a Romantic idealist in the best sense of the term. He prophesied greatness for the United States on the completion of its mission, but he denounced its current social order not only for its hypocrisy, but also for interpreting the Constitution so as to allow slavery.

This essay will examine episodes in the life of Douglass that contributed to his development as America's leading abolitionist orator, and will examine his three autobiographical accounts, paralleling them with examples from his speeches and writings.

Frederick Douglass himself extensively chronicled his own life, first, in the 1845 *Narrative of the Life of Frederick Douglass*; then, a decade later, in *My Bondage and My Freedom*; and finally, in a very comprehensive and full retrospective account, published in 1881, *The Life and Times of Frederick Douglass, Written by Himself*. In addition, African American writers and leaders have written biographical studies, notably Charles W. Chesnutt (1899), Booker T. Washington (1907), and Benjamin Quarles (1948). But the life of the subject is best told in his own words, as he examines the past from the perspective of a former slave who is now free—the usual point of view adopted by the authors of slave narratives—or, as in the 1845 narrative, from the perspective of an escaped slave who is not yet free.

The story of Frederick Douglass is truly extraordinary; it is at once a personal tale of suffering and human endurance and the story of America's evolution toward social and racial equality through the turbulent years before the Civil War when the democratic experiment was being watched closely by critics not only in the United States but also in Europe. Those who had read Crèvecoeur's and Alexis de Tocqueville's assessments of America's political experiment now also read Douglass' narratives, in order to understand firsthand America's most serious impediment to realizing its democratic ideals. In this sense, Frederick Douglass became a representative American figure, a literary ambassador. Douglass expanded his 1845 account considerably in the 1855 version; this new version elevated the subject of the biography from the status of escaped slave to a more universal figure in the shaping of American affairs. This emphasis was even more prominent in the 1881 autobiography, which, after all, was written well after Douglass had achieved international prominence and in the wake of his having been an adviser and social acquaintance of Abraham Lincoln. When Ralph Waldo Emerson remarked in his *Representative Men* (1850) that "there is properly no history; only biography," he meant that the lives of eminent persons comprise the only true chronicle of human events, and that dates and battle statistics and political statements have less value than the way in which an individual can embody the values and attitudes of a generation. Frederick Douglass was that kind of "representative man," and his story expresses the conflicts and triumphs of his time.

His first autobiography stands as *the* representative nineteenth-century slave narrative. Slave narratives are, by definition, accounts of the lives of victims, tales of unendurable suffering and torment that alert the reader to a counterculture present in America. The slave story usually follows the pattern of a "before" and "after" structure. Each narrative is focused on the experience of the protagonist, who narrates from the point of view of a free person looking back on the experience of slavery. This structural movement from slavery to freedom, viewed from the perspective of hindsight, gives each narrative a curiously ironic tone: the writer searches the harsh reality of his or her personal experience in order to establish the conditions of slavery from which the later portions of the narrative will illustrate a blessed deliverance. In Douglass' 1845 narrative, however, the deliverance is incomplete—and, in 1845, he has not yet attained his later greatness. Rather, *Narrative of the Life of Frederick Douglass* is a deeply personal account of human suffering and endurance, of triumph over adversity of the most intensely personal kind. All three accounts should be read as an evolving narrative, not unlike Walt Whitman's *Leaves of Grass,* which Whitman began in an 1855 version and expanded and altered until his death in 1892. Both Douglass and Whitman were truly "representative men" in the Emersonian sense of the word, but America in the nineteenth century did not properly recognize either, although Douglass certainly received attention as a representative of the emerging group of freed slaves. Moreover, Douglass' saga is representative of a tension pervading all slave narration: the paradoxical desire to tell the whole story and the necessity to immerse the narrator's persona in the events of the past, when suffering and hardship were paramount and freedom was only a dream. Most slave narratives were composed from 1830 to 1860, the period when the abolitionists challenged the legalized institution of chattel slavery. These accounts were not only intended to recall the cruelties of the past; they were also clearly designed to reform the institution, if not to end it altogether. Like most slave narratives, Douglass' 1845 book was the product of Douglass' composition and the editing of Garrison, whose agenda for reform has been thought to have set the tone for the work.

This is clearly not the case. From the outset, the narrative is a deeply moving, personal account of ascension. Most autobiographies commence with some kind of genealogical address to the audience. Benjamin Franklin begins his *Autobiography,* for example, by addressing it to his "Dear Son," William Franklin, then the governor of New Jersey. Franklin then attempts to establish his family ties with the past, with England, and with tradition. The slave's attempt to establish genealogical identity, however, is often prevented by a total absence of the necessary information. The Douglass' narrative offers a stark contrast to Franklin's opening genealogy. On the first page, Douglass writes:

> I have no accurate knowledge of my age, never having seen any authentic record containing it. By far the larger part of the slaves know as little of their age as horses know of theirs, and it is the wish of most masters within my knowledge to keep their slaves thus ignorant. I do not remember to have ever met a slave who could tell of his birthday. . . . A want of information concerning my own was a source of unhappiness to me even during my childhood.

Moreover, if the slave is the illegitimate progeny of a white owner and a slave woman, his identity may be traceable only to the mother. Douglass suffered enormously over this:

> My father was a white man. He was admitted to be by all I ever heard speak of my parentage. The opinion was also whispered that my master was my father; but of the correctness of this opinion, I know nothing; the means of knowing was withheld from me.

"The means of knowing" was of course his mother, who might have provided the young Douglass with sufficient information about his genealogical identity. But in this case, the whole process of retrieving the self by examining the past was frustrated by his lack of access even to his mother.

My mother and I were separated when I was but an infant—before I knew her as my mother. . . . I never saw my mother, to know her as such, more than four or five times in my life; and each of these times were very short in duration, and at night. She was hired by Mr. Stewart, who lived about twelve miles from my home. She made her journeys to see me in the night, travelling the whole distance on foot, after the performance of her days' work. She was a field hand, and a whipping is the penalty for not being in the field at sunrise. . . . I do not recollect ever seeing my mother by the light of day. She would lie down with me, and get me to sleep, but long before I waked she was gone. Very little communication ever took place between us. Death soon ended what little we could have while she lived, and with it her hardships and suffering. She died when I was about seven years old.

So Frederick Douglass, who was born Frederick Augustus Washington Bailey in February 1818, began life with very powerful memories of his loving mother and complete ignorance of his absent and mysterious father. Throughout the autobiographical accounts, Douglass seems to be searching for this lost father figure, the authority and mentor in his early life who stood only as a dream and an unfulfilled wish. Like most slaves, he assumed a name; he took his from a romantic figure he admired in Sir Walter Scott's *The Lady of the Lake* (1810).

Douglass' emergence from adolescence into manhood was marked by several harsh episodes of transition. Early in his narrative, he tells of his first realization, at the age of seven, that he and the other members of his race were slaves. Mr. Plummer—a "slave-breaker" and overseer who was "always armed with a cowskin [whip] and heavy cudgel," would "cut and slash women's heads so horribly that even master would be enraged at his cruelty, and would threaten to whip him if he did not mind himself"—whipped Douglass' young aunt mercilessly:

He would at times seem to take great pleasure in whipping a slave. I have often been awakened at the dawn of day by the most heart-rending shrieks of an aunt of mine, whom he used to tie up to a joist, and whip upon her naked back till she was literally covered with blood. No words, no tears, no prayers, from his gory victim, seemed to move his iron heart from its bloody purpose. The louder she screamed, the harder he whipped; and where the blood ran fastest, there he whipped longest. He would whip her to make her scream, and whip her to make her hush; and not until overcome by fatigue, would he cease to swing the blood-clotted cowskin.

The 1845 narrative, like many slave narratives, operates on two levels simultaneously. The interior narrative, like a bildungsroman, recounts the narrator's growth from youth to adulthood as he comes to terms with the environment external to his developing self. But the narrative also addresses larger, external issues. Graphic scenes like the brutal whipping of Douglass' aunt alert the reading audience to the evils of slavery as an institution as well as recall an event in the life of the protagonist. Douglass offers a retrospective commentary on this scene, clarifying its personal and sociological purposes:

I remember the first time I ever witnessed this horrible exhibition. I was quite a child, but I well remember it. I shall never forget it whilst I remember anything. It was the first of a long series of such outrages, of which I was doomed to be a witness and participant. It struck me with awful force. It was the blood-stained gate, the entrance to the hell of slavery, through which I was about to pass. It was a most terrible spectacle. I wish I could commit to paper the feelings with which I beheld it. . . . I was so terrified and horror-stricken at the sight, that I hid myself in a closet, and dared not venture out till long after the bloody transaction was over. I expected it would be my turn next. . . . I had never seen anything like it before.

Some of the emotional force of this scene derives from the displacement of the violent and mysterious circumstances of his own conception, a connection suggested by the figure of "the blood-stained gate." An association between these traumas, between his physical birth into slavery and his spiritual and intellectual awakening to his slave condition, is thus forged by his conflation of the two events in his memory.

A second crucial formative event follows the whipping of his aunt, when Douglass is well immersed in the life of the slave, belonging to the Aulds of Baltimore. He writes:

Very soon after I went to live with Mr. and Mrs. Auld, she very kindly commenced to teach me the A, B, C. After I had learned this, she assisted me in learning to spell words of three or four letters. Just at this point in my progress, Mr. Auld found out what was going on, and at once forbade Mrs. Auld to instruct me further, telling her, among other things, that it was unlawful, as well as unsafe, to teach a slave to read. To use his own words, further, he said, "If you give a nigger an inch, he will take an ell . . . If you teach that nigger . . . how to read, there would be no keeping him. It would forever unfit him to be a slave. He would at once become unmanageable, and of no value to his master. As to himself, it could do him no good, but a great deal of harm. It would make him discontented and unhappy." . . . I now understood what had been to me a most perplexing difficulty—to wit, the white man's power to enslave the black man. It was a grand achievement, and I prized it highly. From that moment, I understood the pathway from slavery to freedom.

In these passages, we find two hallmarks of Douglass' style: first, the moment of epiphany, when out of his life experience emerges a recognition that is universal and historic; second, the direct address to the reading audience, which clarifies the philosophical significance of the account of his life. Douglass shows clearly that the gaining of freedom is linked to achievement of literacy, because all three of his narratives—like other slave narratives—carry the burden of bearing witness to the truth, of the past through an act of writing, using language that so often is inadequate to the task. Douglass is attempting, simultaneously, to resist his past and to recapture it in a literary narrative he has had to produce without formal education and with little assistance. Indeed, the veracity and credibility of his narrative had to be reinforced in prefaces written by the white abolitionists Wendell Phillips and William Lloyd Garrison. Mr. Auld was indeed correct: Douglass' becoming literate was indeed his pathway to freedom, enabling him, in his own words, "to write [his] own pass." Toward the end of his narrative, Douglass recalls his understanding of the complex relationships between the fulfillment of the self, the achievement of freedom, and the gaining of literacy. Literacy gained through struggle is remembered even more vividly as liberation. With Douglass, the liberation of the body, the spirit, and the intellect are interconnected. For most slave narrators, the gaining of literacy was overwhelming. The humble apologias that preface antebellum slave narratives are more than conventions of style; rather, they are often sincere statements of doubt and inadequacy, statements of the powerlessness felt by the narrators in the face of their task of communicating truth to a predominantly white audience whom they wish to convince of the illegality, injustice, and brutal cruelty of chattel slavery. This frustration is coupled with the anger of the freed slaves as they recall the past "selves" from which they have been delivered. This tension compels the writers to powerful declarations of selfhood that contrast with the patterns of oppression and suffering that characterize the past.

All of the slave narratives, and Douglass' narratives in particular, contain episodes illustrating the cruelty of white masters, as the narrator either witnesses or experiences torture and abuse by owners. These graphic episodes provide another characteristic of the slave narrative: the depiction of the white culture's attempts to dominate and repress the slave self through physical torture. Whippings were not merely designed to cause pain; they were also used to reduce the slave psychologically to a state of total obedience and humility. As one central purpose of autobiographical writing is to create for the reader a clear sense of the subject's identity, the slave narrators face the enormous task of relating how they have emerged from a state of abject misery into their present free and vocal state of being.

Douglass' early identity was linked to a family he did not even know. Like many slaves, he had to endure the double jeopardy of being both servant and child to his master. Of the mulatto product of a white father and a black slave mother he observes:

Such slaves invariably suffer greater hardships, and have more to contend with, than others. They are, in the first place, a constant offence to their mistress. She is ever disposed to find fault with them; they can seldom do anything to please her; she is never better pleased than when she sees them under the lash, especially when she suspects her husband of showing to his mulatto children favors which he withholds from his black slaves. The master is frequently compelled to sell this class of slaves, out of deference to the feelings of his white wife; and, cruel as the deed may strike anyone to be, for a man to sell his own children to human flesh-mongers, it is often the dictate of humanity for him to do so; for, unless he does this, he must not only whip them himself, but must stand by and see one white son tie up his brother, of but a few shades darker complexion than himself, and ply the gory lash to his naked back; and if he lisp one word of disapproval, it is set down to his paternal partiality, and only makes a bad matter worse, both for himself and the slave whom he would protect and defend.

This passage from the 1845 narrative exemplifies a hallmark of Douglass' writing: the universalizing of his personal circumstances. In the later versions of his autobiography, the expansion of a personal incident or moment to a universal, even philosophical, conclusion, is everywhere apparent.

When still in his teens, Douglass was sent by his master, Thomas Auld, to Edward Covey, a notorious slave-breaker. Slave-breakers like Edward Covey were an essential part of the complex institution of slavery; their brutality usually exceeded that found on the plantations themselves. Operating small concentration camps for defiant slaves, they meted out punishment for disobedience and usually returned slaves to their masters externally, at least, docile and compliant, regardless of what the slaves might have actually felt. This process did not work with Douglass, and the recounting of his experience with Covey occupies a central place in each of the three autobiographies. For almost one full year, Douglass endured weekly whippings for no apparent reason and was worked mercilessly until his strength was almost entirely sapped. After one particularly brutal assault and whipping, Douglass left for his master's place, at great risk to himself, and sought refuge in his master's protection from Covey's brutal inhumanity. But Auld sided with Covey, and returned Douglass to the camp. He writes in the 1881 narrative:

My last hope had been extinguished. My master, who I did not venture to hope would protect me *as a man,* had now refused to protect me *as his property,* and had cast me back, covered with reproaches and bruises, into the hands of one who was a stranger to that mercy which is the soul of the religion he professed.

When Douglass finally returned, Covey attacked him and tried to flog him. But Douglass did not submit.

I was resolved to fight, and what was better still, I actually was hard at it. The fighting madness had come upon me, and I found my strong fingers firmly attached to the throat of the tyrant, as heedless of consequences, at the moment, as if we stood as equals before the law. The very color of the man was forgotten.

There were many observers of the confrontation, and Covey called to a succession of people for assistance, including his slave woman, Caroline. All refused, and Douglass prevailed.

At length (two hours had elapsed) the contest was given over. Letting go of me, puffing and blowing at a great rate, Covey said: "Now, you scoundrel, go to your work; I would not have whipped you half so hard if you had not resisted." The fact was, he had not whipped me at all. He had not in all the scuffle, drawn a single drop of blood from me. I had drawn blood from him, and should even without this satisfaction have been victorious, because my aim had not been to injure him, but to prevent his injuring me.

During the whole six months I lived with Covey after this transaction, he never again laid the weight of his finger on me in anger.

Again, Douglass elaborates the importance of this crucial incident in his early life in relation to his evolution as a free American and a public figure. In the 1881 *Life and Times of Frederick Douglass,* he views the event not in the isolation of the moment, but as the turning point in his life. With characteristic honesty and directness he articulates the developmental significance of the confrontation, elaborating on the theme introduced in his 1845 narrative:

This battle with Mr. Covey, undignified as it was and as I fear my narration of it is, was the turning-point in my "life as a slave." It rekindled in my breast the smouldering embers of liberty. It brought up my Baltimore dreams, and revived a sense of my own manhood. I was a changed being after that fight. I was nothing before—I was a man now. It recalled to life my crushed self-respect, and my self-confidence, and inspired me with a renewed determination to be a free man. A man without force is without the essential dignity of humanity. Human nature is so constituted, that it cannot honor a helpless man, though it can pity him, and even this it cannot do long if signs of power do not arise. . . .

It was a resurrection from the dark and pestiferous tomb of slavery, to the heaven of comparative freedom. I was no longer a servile coward, trembling under the frown of a brother worm of the dust, but my long-cowed spirit was roused to an attitude of independence. I had reached the point at which I was *not afraid to die.* This spirit made me a freeman in *fact,* though I still remained a slave in *form.* When a slave cannot be flogged, he is more than half free.

Douglass here universalizes the episode, compares his resurrection to Christ's, and adopts the rhetorical strategy of the Indian captivity narrative. He also associates manhood with the willingness to fight. He was to return to this theme as a central argument in support of the enlistment of black soldiers during the Civil War.

In all three of Douglass' accounts, the desire for personal freedom is the informing principle of the narrative. The definition of the narrative persona is directly linked to the narrator's impulse for and movement toward personal freedom. This conflation of the desire for freedom and the identity of the subject pervades all slave narratives; indeed, the power of this central theme governs one of the most complex paradoxes in all slave autobiography. As William Andrews, John Sekora, Annette Niemtzow, and other critics have observed, the slave narrators are compelled to recall their former states, their former selves, even as they have reached "the promised land" of freedom and have achieved that purpose toward which the entire objective of their experience has been directed. Niemtzow writes in "The Problematic Self in Autobiography: The Example of the Slave Narrative," "The slave, happily ceasing to be a slave, describes his or her slave self to preserve it just as it is about to cease to be a condition under which the self lives." This tension between the narrator and the narrator's former self as it is represented in the narrative is intensified in slave narration because the "before" and "after" structure of these documents clearly shows an evolutionary development from servile humility to the power of emancipation, and it is particularly important when the narrator provides such clear examples of the moments of transformation as does Douglass in the account of his confrontation with Covey. Thus these episodes assume an epic dimension, and they give the subject mythic proportions by showing the formative development of an already established American hero. This "turning point" led to the immediate and rapid development of Douglass as the central subject.

After his years with Covey, Douglass, though technically still the slave of Auld, was hired out to a succession of surrogate masters, including the relatively gentle William Freeland, William Gardner, and Walter Price, while he worked as a ship's caulker and perfected his trade. The burning urge to be free continued to intensify, as Auld pocketed the earnings of Douglass' rigorous labor. As he had earlier discovered the link between literacy and freedom, Douglass now began to understand how a man's self-esteem was coupled with his work and the earning of wages for his labor. He wrote in *The Life and Times of Frederick Douglass*:

To make a contented slave, you must make a thoughtless one. It is necessary to darken his moral and mental vision, and, as far as possible, to annihilate his power of reason. He must be able to detect no inconsistencies in slavery. The man who takes his earnings must be able to convince him that he has a perfect right to do so. It must not depend upon mere force—the slave must know no higher law than his master's will. The whole relationship must not only demonstrate to his mind its necessity, but its absolute rightfulness. If there be one crevice through which a single drop can fall, it will certainly rust off the slave's chain.

Always the leader of his peers, Douglass developed and implemented an escape plot, departing from Baltimore, slavery, and servitude on September 3, 1838. He was assisted in his escape by Anna Murray, the free black woman he would later marry. Disguised as a sailor and carrying forged papers, Douglass took the train from Baltimore to the Susquehanna River, which he crossed by ferry to Wilmington, Delaware; from there he took a boat to Philadelphia. One day after he had left Baltimore he arrived in New York City, and he was married within the month. These details were withheld from Douglass' reading public until 1873 (when he divulged them in a Philadelphia speech) because he did not wish to endanger his allies.

Technically an escaped slave, Douglass found life "at the North" also disrupted by racial prejudice. Settling in New Bedford, Massachusetts, he sought work as a ship's caulker but soon found that the other caulkers objected to working with a black man, so he performed common labor. It was at this point in his life, sometime in 1838 or 1839, that Frederick Augustus Washington Bailey changed his name to Frederick Douglass. In

1841 the Douglass family moved to Lynn, Massachusetts, and then to Rochester, New York, in 1847. During this decade, Douglass joined forces with William Lloyd Garrison's abolitionist movement, made hundreds of speeches on the lecture circuit for the antislavery cause, and published his *Narrative of the Life of Frederick Douglass* (1845). He was still a slave, but he was living in comparative freedom and enjoyed increasing prominence as a spokesman for the antislavery cause.

Douglass' marriage to Anna Murray was apparently happy, and it lasted forty-four years. The union produced five children: Rosetta (born June 24, 1839); Lewis Henry (born October 9, 1840); Frederick, Jr. (born March 3, 1842); Charles Remond (born October 21, 1844); and Annie (born March 22, 1849). The parents' love for each other extended to the children, who enjoyed close relationships with them. But in August 1882 Anna Douglass suffered some kind of paralysis for several weeks and then died. Douglass remained close to his children and continued to help them financially. In 1884 he married Helen Pitts, his secretary, who was white. Although many objected to the marriage, for Douglass it not only was a second successful and loving relationship but represented his vision of color-blind harmony. As W. E. B. DuBois writes, "he laughingly remarked that he was quite impartial: his first wife 'was the color of my mother, and the second, the color of my father.' " Douglass thus enjoyed two extremely happy marriages.

Douglass' domestic life was tranquil and stable; his public life demanded much travel, best chronicled in the 1881 autobiography *The Life and Times of Frederick Douglass, Written by Himself.* A life-long supporter of women's rights as well as of emancipation and racial harmony, he became one of the century's most powerful speakers and writers. On the day he died, February 20, 1895, he had attended a women's rights convention.

The career of Frederick Douglass as an orator, writer, editor, and public figure commenced almost immediately after his arrival in the North in 1838. In 1841 Douglass attended a convention of the Anti-Slavery Society on Nantucket; there he not only associated with abolitionists, whose sentiments he shared, but was also able to speak to the convention, inaugurating an oratorical career that would eventually take him on a lecture tour of Great Britain from 1845 to 1847, and to the 1848 Women's Rights Convention in Seneca Falls, New York, where he spoke against slavery and against denying the vote to blacks and women. Several themes are prominent in his speeches and his writings, all of which were crafted with precision and wrought with an exactitude that he demanded not only of himself, but also of the contributors to his newspapers, *The North Star* (founded in 1847) and *Frederick Douglass' Paper* (founded in 1851). Douglass found his most effective literary and oratorical voice in the polemic or jeremiad, a sermon form in which the speaker condemns contemporary evil and advocates change. (The term "jeremiad" refers to the ancient Hebrew prophet Jeremiah, who condemned the sins of Israel and advocated a return to God's moral demands.)

The pervasive themes in Douglass' work include: freedom as a natural and inalienable right; the need for political activism as a means of effecting change in society; the moral offense represented by slavery in any form; the rights of women as equals under the law; and the necessity for the equality of all citizens regardless of race, religion, or gender. Douglass was at least a century ahead of his time in arguing eloquently for the civil rights that are only now being implemented as laws in our society. He stood firmly against racism in all its manifestations. He was frequently forced to accept "segregation" even in the North, and his indignation rose to heated anger in his recollection of these episodes, as in the following passage from *The Life and Times of Frederick Douglass*:

My treatment in the use of public conveyances about these times was extremely rough, especially on the Eastern Railroad, from Boston to Portland. On that road, as on many others, there was a mean, dirty, and uncomfortable car set apart for colored travelers called the Jim Crow car. Regarding this as the fruit of slaveholding prejudice and being determined to fight the spirit of slavery wherever I might find it, I resolved to avoid this car, though it sometimes required some courage to do so, . . . and sometimes, I was soundly beaten by conductor and brakemen.

It is important to note that Douglass bases his objection to the Jim Crow car not only on its physical condition but on the tradition of segregation by race, the implication that one race is essentially different from another. Proslavery racism in both the North and the South usually subscribed to the polygenetic theory of evolution, which held that the many races represented on earth were evolved from diverse original races at the time of creation. The antislavery abolitionists usually argued a monogenetic theory, which held that all races were essentially the same because the origin of the species was monogenetic rather than polygenetic. There were many variations on these basic ideas, but Douglass firmly believed in the essential social and racial equality of all and rejected as evil nonsense arguments for the racial inferiority of blacks. One such argument, curiously, came from the mouth of Abraham Lincoln, who, debating with Stephen A. Douglas during the congressional election campaign of 1858, attempted to show that blacks and whites could not live in harmony together. Although Lincoln always opposed slavery as a moral evil, he was in direct conflict with Douglass in what he said about race relations:

I am not, nor ever have been in favor of bringing about in any way the social and political equality of the white and black races . . . I am not nor ever have been in favor of making voters or jurors of negroes, nor of qualifying them to hold office, nor to intermarry with white people; and I will say in addition to this that there is a physical difference between the white and black races which I believe will forever forbid the two races living together on terms of social and political equality. And inasmuch as they cannot so live, while they do remain together there must be the position of superior and inferior, and I as much as any other man am in favor of having the superior position assigned to the white race.

In fairness to Lincoln, who pushed the Emancipation Proclamation through Congress in January 1863, and who was here fighting for his political life, it is important to note that he often wrote about his abhorrence of the institution of slavery, a position which Douglass endorsed.

Douglass reached some of his most eloquent moments in his denunciation of racism, such assumptions about the inferiority of blacks as that endorsed by Lincoln—and, before him, by Thomas Jefferson. Douglass wrote, in the *North American Review* of June 1881, a stunning essay called "The Color Line," which displays his rhetorical powers fully. A philosophical treatise of high merit, "The Color Line" (in Foner, vol. 4) states the case against racism in both moral and logical terms:

Few evils are less accessible to the force of reason, or more tenacious of life and power, than a long-standing prejudice. It is a moral disorder, which creates the conditions necessary to its own existence, and fortifies itself by refusing all contradiction. It paints a hateful picture according to its own diseased imagination, and distorts the features of the fancied original to suit the portrait.

Douglass alerts his reader to his scholarly and learned understanding of the history of racial prejudice by tracing examples from ancient and English history; however, he reserved the full force of his argument against racism for the prejudice to which African Americans were subjected:

> Of all the races and varieties of men which have suffered from this feeling, the colored people of this country have endured most. They can resort to no disguises which will enable them to escape its deadly aim. They carry in front the evidence which marks them for persecution. They stand at the extreme point of difference from the Caucasian race, and their African origin can be instantly recognized, though they may be several removes from the typical African race. They may remonstrate like Shylock—"Hath not a Jew eyes? hath not a Jew hands, organs, dimensions, senses, affections, passions? fed with the same food, hurt with the same weapons, subject to the same diseases, healed by the same means, warmed and cooled by the same summer and winter, as a Christian is?"—but such eloquence is unavailing. They are Negroes—and that is enough, in the eye of this unreasoning prejudice, to justify indignity and violence. In nearly every department of American life they are confronted by this insidious influence. It fills the air. It meets them at the workshop and factory, when they apply for work. It meets them at the church, at the hotel, at the ballot-box, and worst of all, it meets them in the jury-box. . . . When this evil spirit is judge, jury, and prosecutor, nothing less than overwhelming evidence is sufficient to overcome the force of unfavorable presumptions. Everything against the person with the hated color is promptly taken for granted; while everything in his favor is received with suspicion and doubt.

Douglass had himself experienced many forms of prejudice because of his race, from the public-conveyance problem in Boston and New England to segregated seating in houses of worship, particularly in New Bedford, where he therefore affiliated loosely with the African Methodist Episcopal Zionist church. A deeply religious man who often quoted scripture along with Shakespeare, he attacked the institutional Christian church for its segregated practices. In "The Color Line," he devastates the opposing argument with the practiced skills of a mature debater:

> But is this color prejudice the natural and inevitable thing it claims to be? If it is so, then it is utterly idle to write against it, preach, pray, or legislate against it, or pass constitutional amendments against it. Nature will have her course. . . .
>
> If I could talk with all my white fellow-countrymen on this subject, I would say to them, in the language of Scripture: "Come and let us reason together." . . . There are at least seven points which candid men will be likely to admit, but which, if admitted, will prove fatal to the popular thought and practice of the times.

Like Mark Antony in Shakespeare's *Julius Caesar,* Douglass here turns the racists' own arguments against them by revealing them all to be unreasonable, even unreasoning.

In Douglass' fabricated arguments we find a characteristically rich mixture of legal, moral, and evangelical rhetorical strategies. The structure is simple: seven basic lines of argument are stated, and then each is pursued and answered in a longer section. This format follows closely the Puritan sermon structure, where "reasons" and "objections" were anticipated by the minister, who would propose rhetorical questions to his congregation and then respond with fully developed answers. Douglass begins gently enough:

> First. If what we call prejudice against color be natural, *i.e.,* a part of human nature itself, it follows that it must be co-extensive with human nature, and will and must manifest itself wherever the two races are brought into contact. It

would not vary with either latitude, longitude, or altitude; but like fire and gunpowder, whenever brought together, there would be an explosion of contempt, aversion, and hatred.

Second. If it can be shown that there is anywhere on the globe any considerable country where the contact of the African and the Caucasian is not distinguished by this explosion of race-wrath, there is reason to doubt that the prejudice is an ineradicable part of human nature.

Determined to show that human nature and racism are not inextricably linked at the time of creation, but that racism is a product of social engineering, Douglass builds to a crescendo in his final two points, which he elaborates in great detail later in the text:

Sixthly. If prejudice of race and color is only natural in the sense that ignorance, superstition, bigotry, and vice are natural, then it has no better defense than they, and should be despised and put away from human relations as an enemy to the peace, good order, and happiness of human society.

Seventhly. If, still further, this aversion to the Negro arises out of the fact that he is as we see him, poor, spiritless, ignorant, and degraded, then whatever is humane, noble, and superior, in the mind of the superior and more fortunate race, will desire that all arbitrary barriers against his manhood, intelligence, and elevation shall be removed, and a fair chance in the race of life be given him.

Here Douglass introduces an ironic bitterness that is more characteristic of his early style, as exemplified by the 1845 narrative. If the Puritan sermon provided the structure for many of his essays and speeches, his style was often derived from Benjamin Franklin's *Poor Richard's Almanack* and his *Autobiography,* which effectively use irony to control the reader's response to the argument.

In the long final sections of "The Color Line," Douglass argues that color prejudice is a learned condition, and that there is absolutely nothing "natural" about it:

In the abstract, there is no prejudice against color. No man shrinks from another because he is clothed in a suit of black, nor offended with his boots because they are black. . . . Aside from the curious contrast to himself, the white child feels nothing on the first sight of a colored man. Curiosity is the only feeling. The office of color in the color line is a very plain and subordinate one. It simply advertises the objects of oppression, insult, and persecution. . . . The color is innocent enough, but things with which it is coupled make it hated. Slavery, ignorance, stupidity, servility, poverty, dependence, are undesirable conditions. When these shall cease to be coupled with color, there will be no color line drawn.

Douglass understood human nature extremely well, and there is no better example of his profound social reasoning than this mature essay. But his concern with racial equality may be found also in his earliest writings.

After the publication of his 1845 narrative, Douglass clearly was in danger of being returned to slavery. His abolitionist friends encouraged him to leave for England and safety. He sailed on August 16, 1845, aboard the *Cambria,* a Cunard steamer, but was not allowed to stay in the better accommodations because of his race. He arrived in England twelve days later, having lectured on board against racism and slavery, to the distress of some of the Southern passengers. In England, he toured for the abolitionists, spreading the same message as he had in the States: that slavery as an institution was inherently evil, that racism was unnatural rather than natural, and that the Christian church was perpetuating both by refusing to interpret Scripture as God had intended it to be read. In a speech made in 1846 (collected in Foner), he says:

Slavery is a system of wrong, so blinding to all around, so hardening to the heart, so corrupting to the morals, so deleterious to religion, so sapping to all the principles of justice in its immediate vicinity, that the community surrounding it lacks the moral stamina necessary to its removal. It requires the humanity of Christianity, the morality of the world to remove it.

England was something of a paradise for Douglass; he was for once freed from his role as an escaped slave and celebrated as a touring hero, despite the incident on the steamship. But he never lost the consciousness of his race and its unfortunate condition in the United States, which became in his English lectures not a "promised land" of "milk and honey" but a seriously corrupt nation of artifice and fraud. He was given a warm welcome by English reformers, who were proceeding with their own reform acts. A group of these Englishmen raised the money to purchase Douglass' freedom, an act that his abolitionist colleagues in the United States deplored, as it implied that Douglass regarded himself as someone else's property. This was not the case. Douglass was an extremely practical man, and to return to the United States with a bounty on his head was unwise. The sale was consummated. Douglass was legally a free man for the first time in his life; spiritually, he had been one for many, many years.

The years in England altered his view of America considerably, intensifying his attitude toward his country's social evils. He wrote regularly to his mentor and friend William Lloyd Garrison, who as much as anyone represented the lost father figure he had sought since his childhood. (The letters are in Foner, vol. 1.) Although he would later break with Garrison over his right to publish his own abolitionist newspaper, he wrote during his visit to England:

In thinking of America, I sometimes find myself admiring her . . . but . . . when I remember that all is cursed with the infernal spirit of slaveholding, robbery and wrong,—when I remember that with the waters of her noblest rivers, the tears of my brethren are borne to the ocean, disregarded and forgotten, and that her most fertile fields drink daily of the warm blood of my outraged sisters, I am filled with unutterable loathing, and led to reproach myself that anything could fall from my lips in praise of such a land. America will not allow her children to love her.

On his return to the United States in 1847, Douglass set out to edit and publish his own newspaper, *The North Star,* an ambition he had held since first observing the power and influence of Garrison's paper, *The Liberator.* This activity instantly immersed him in political issues, and he was a speaker at the Seneca Falls Convention of 1848, the year in which the women of America united for the first time and articulated their grievances in a "Declaration of Sentiments." The year 1848 was particularly important in the midcentury era of political and social change, with the Paris Commune; *The Communist Manifesto*; and the Seneca Falls Convention, which signaled the emergence of women's rights as a political force in American culture, a movement that Douglass supported fully. The era witnessed an intensification of the division in American society between those who supported and those who opposed slavery as an institution, whether they lived in Atlanta or New York. The decade of the 1840's, when Douglass was beginning his paper, also saw the annexation of Texas, the Mexican War, and the protest of Thoreau against the state of Massachusetts for its support of the federal government in its annexation claims and its passage of the Compromise of 1850. The Compromise's extension of the Fugitive Slave Act gave Douglass and Harriet Beecher Stowe their most fertile ground for protest.

Douglass had always held that the United States Constitution was essentially a proslavery document, defending private property and the rights of owners over the civil rights of their slaves. He engaged in the complex disputes concerning whether slavery should be permitted in the new territories and states (his writings concerning this dispute are collected in Blassingame). His position was unequivocal: slavery as an institution must come to an end.

> The efforts to shut the slave power out of the territories, one by one, will keep the country in a constant commotion with assassinations, incendiarisms, conspiracies, civil wars, and all manner of sickening horrors. The only true remedy for the extension of slavery is the immediate abolition of slavery. For while the monster lives, he will hunger and thirst, breathe, and expand. The true way is to put the knife into its quivering heart.

Douglass was quick to defend Captain John Brown, who had led a raid on Harper's Ferry, Virginia, in October 1859, where there was a federal ammunition arsenal. Brown was condemned to death for his part in the raid, and Douglass, who had been involved in the plot, was once again a wanted man. But more than anything else, he was temporarily vilified in some quarters for his powerful rhetorical support of Brown's terrorist activity:

> He has attacked slavery with the weapons precisely adapted to bring it to the death. Moral considerations have long since been exhausted upon slaveholders. It is in vain to reason with them. . . . Slavery is a system of brute force. It shields itself behind might, rather than right. It must be met with its own weapons. Captain Brown has initiated a new mode of carrying on the crusade of freedom, and his blow has sent dread and terror throughout the entire ranks of the piratical army of slavery. His daring deeds may cost him his life, but priceless as is the value of that life, the blow he has struck, will, in the end, prove to be worth its mighty cost.

Douglass' idealism had a cost, but his extremely practical turn of mind led him not only to develop antislavery, antiracist, and antisegregationist arguments for society, but also to offer some very pragmatic advice to his African American brothers and sisters who sought to free themselves from poverty and degradation.

Always an advocate of literacy as a means to real intellectual and spiritual freedom, he taught African American students in various schools, including several that were attacked and destroyed by white supremacists. Through his writings he urged his brethren not only to become free and literate, but also to develop skills and trades that would make them economically independent. His children were also beneficiaries of this encouragement; all of them worked on *The North Star,* which later became *Frederick Douglass' Paper.* As vice president of the first meeting of the American League of Colored Laborers in 1850, Douglass insisted that his audience recognize that industry and education were as vital as protest to their pursuit of freedom. Douglass' position on this issue was very similar to that espoused by Booker T. Washington nearly forty years later. In an essay in *Frederick Douglass' Paper* for March 4, 1853 (in Foner, vol. 2), the editor did not mince words about the alternatives available to his brothers and sisters:

> These are the obvious alternatives sternly presented to the free colored people of the United States. It is idle, yea, even ruinous, to disguise the matter for a single hour longer; every day begins and ends with the impressive lesson that free negroes must learn trades, or die.

The piece continues with a full development of this central argument, and it shows that occupations formerly held by blacks exclusively, while slaves, are now being usurped by whites:

The old avocations, by which colored men obtained a livelihood, are rapidly, unceasingly and inevitably passing into other hands; every hour sees the black man elbowed out of employment by some newly arrived immigrant, whose hunger and whose color are thought to give him a better title to the place; and so we believe it will continue to be until the last prop is levelled beneath us. . . .White men are becoming house-servants, cooks, and stewards on vessels, at hotels. . . . Formerly, blacks were almost the exclusive coachmen in wealthy families; this is so no longer; white men are now employed, and from aught we see, they fill their servile station with an obsequiousness as profound as that of the blacks. . . . As a black man, we say if we cannot stand up, let us fall down. We desire to be a man among men while we do live; and when we cannot, we wish to die. It is evident, painfully evident to every reflecting mind, that the means of living, for colored men, are becoming more and more precarious and limited. Employments and callings, formerly monopolized by us, are so no longer.

For Douglass, education was the only remedy. He was always a teacher and a student, and he eventually served on the board of trustees of Howard University, after moving his family to Washington, D.C. In the essay's conclusion he stresses the value of educational pursuit as a means to self-development, one of the central themes in all of his writings:

We, therefore, call upon the intelligent and thinking ones amongst us, to urge upon the colored people within their reach, in all seriousness, the duty and necessity of giving their children useful and lucrative trades, by which they may commence the battle of life with weapons commensurate with the exigencies of the conflict.

Douglass' doctrinal differences with other abolitionists had surfaced when he decided, in 1847, to publish his own newspaper, an act that Garrison regarded as just short of betrayal. But Douglass quickly found new allies. Harriet Beecher Stowe was, like Douglass, a believer in the power of education and intellectual development to elevate the individual in society. In a letter dated March 8, 1853 (in Foner), he argues that "the root cause" of African Americans' problems in America was slavery, accompanied by "poverty, ignorance, and degradation, three things that are notoriously true of us as a people." Douglass sought to

deliver them from this triple malady, and to improve and elevate them, by which I mean to put them on an equal footing with their white fellow-countrymen in the sacred right to "Life, Liberty, and the Pursuit of Happiness." I am for no fancied or artificial elevation, but only ask fair play. How shall this be obtained? I answer, first, by establishing for our use schools and colleges. . . . High schools and colleges are excellent institutions, and will, in due season, be greatly subservient to our progress; but they are the result, as well as they are the demand, of a point of progress, which we, as a people, have not yet attained.

He goes on to argue for the establishment of industrial trade schools, which were a special interest of Stowe's. Douglass opposed the efforts of well-meaning supporters to engage the freed blacks in agricultural work, and the allocation of farmland in the West for their use:

Agricultural pursuits are not, as I think, suited to our condition. The reason of this is not to be found so much in the occupation (for it is a noble and ennobling one) as in the people themselves. That is only a remedy, which can be applied to the case; and the difficulty in agricultural pursuits, as a remedy for the evils of poverty and ignorance amongst us, is that it cannot, for various reasons, be applied. We cannot apply it, because it is almost impossible to get colored men to go on the land.

Here, Douglass bases his argument on a fact that Emerson and Thoreau already knew: America was changing from a Jeffersonian, agricultural economy with pastoral landscapes and gentlemen farmers to a more urbanized, industrialized country with the kinds of metropolitan scenes described in Walt Whitman's poetry. Douglass, always seeking to bring his people into the mainstream of American democratic opportunity, understood that it would be in cities and factories, rather than on rural farms, that the greatest opportunities would be:

Another consideration against expending energy in this direction is our want of self-reliance. To go into the western wilderness, and there to lay the foundation of future society, requires more of that important quality than a life of slavery has left us. This may sound strange to you, coming from a colored man; but I am dealing with facts, and these never accommodate themselves to the feelings or wishes of any. . . . Therefore, I look to other means than agricultural pursuits for the elevation and improvement of colored people. Of course, I allege this of the many. There are exceptions. Individuals among us, with commendable zeal, industry, perseverance, and self-reliance, have found, and are finding, in agricultural pursuits, the means of supporting, improving, and educating their families.

But Douglass' grand scheme for the improvement of blacks in America included mechanical and industrial colleges specifically designed for their needs:

We must become mechanics; we must build as well as live in houses; we must make as well as use furniture; we must construct bridges as well as pass over them, before we can properly live or be respected by our fellow men. We need mechanics as well as ministers!

Another problem Douglass addressed was the urging by some of his contemporaries for a program of recolonization, by which the freed blacks would be given incentives for returning to Africa. Even Thomas Jefferson had entertained a scheme by which the problem of slavery would be resolved by sending the blacks back to Africa. By the 1850's, this was being seriously considered at the highest levels. Abraham Lincoln had advocated such a plan when he was a congressman. Despite his continuous criticism of his society's failure to live up to its own ideals, Douglass believed in the American dream; he wished for nothing more than total freedom for his people and their full engagement in the opportunities represented by the Declaration of Independence and the United States Constitution, and for him the recolonization scheme was untenable. In his letter to Stowe, Douglass goes on to say:

There is little reason to hope that any considerable number of the free colored people will ever be induced to leave this country, even if such a thing were desirable. The black man—unlike the Indian—loves civilization. He does not make very great progress in civilization himself but he likes to be in the midst of it, and prefers sharing its most galling evils, to encountering barbarism. Then the love of the country, the dread of isolation, the lack of adventurous spirit, and the thought of seeming to desert their "brethren in bonds," are a powerful check upon all schemes of colonization which look to the removal of the colored people, without the slaves. The truth is, dear madam, we are *here,* and we are likely to remain. Individuals emigrate—nations never.

In this letter to Stowe, presented to the Colored National Convention in Rochester in July

1853, Douglass held firm to his conviction that industrial and mechanical trades and skills would best enable African Americans to advance themselves:

What can be done to improve the condition of the free people of color in the United States? . . . The establishment of an INDUSTRIAL COLLEGE in which shall be taught the several branches of the mechanical arts.

Like Thomas Jefferson proposing the University of Virginia, Douglass proposed an educational institution to resolve the problems of literacy, poverty, and degradation brought about by slavery. Unlike Jefferson, who himself drew up architectural plans for his university and sketched out a curriculum, Douglass confessed:

Never having had a day's schooling in all my life, I may not be expected to map out the details of a plan so comprehensive as that involved in the idea of a college. . . . I leave the organization and administration to the superior wisdom of yourself.

We must recall that this was presented nearly ten years before the Emancipation Proclamation. So Douglass' conclusion returns to his pervasive theme, the eradication of slavery:

The most telling, the most killing refutation of slavery, is the presentation of an industrious, enterprising, thrifty, and intelligent free black population.

Douglass had moved his family to Washington, D.C., in 1853, in order to be more directly involved in the political process of lobbying against slavery, by which an end to injustice and inequality might be achieved; however, he never lost the dynamic speaking and writing style so important to his early work. Several examples from the 1840's and 1850's will make this clear. In a letter (quoted in Andrews) published in *The North Star* on September 8, 1848, after his return from England and the purchase of his freedom, he addressed his ''Old Master,'' Thomas Auld:

I am myself, you are yourself; we are two distinct persons. What you are, I am. You are a man, and so am I. God created both, and made us separate beings. I am not by nature bound to you, or you to me. Nature does not make your existence depend upon me, or mine to depend upon yours. . . .

The grim horrors of slavery rise in all their ghastly terror before me; the wails of millions pierce my heart and chill my blood. I remember the chain, the gag, the bloody whip; the deathlike gloom overshadowing the broken spirit of the fettered bondman; the appalling liability of his being torn away from wife and children, and sold like a beast in the market. Say not that this is a picture of fancy. You well know that I wear stripes on my back, inflicted by your direction, and that you, while we were brothers in the same church, caused this right hand, with which I am now penning this letter, to be closely tied to my left, and my person dragged . . . from the Bay Side to Easton, to be sold like a beast in the market, for the alleged crime of intending to escape from your possession.

The direct personal attack on Auld is subsumed in the rage directed against slavery as an institution, the system that permits one person to ''own'' another. Throughout his career, Douglass drew this distinction precisely and repeatedly. For example, in a lecture he delivered in Rochester on December 1, 1850 (in Blassingame, vol. 2), he returned to a theme first articulated in his 1845 narrative, where he contrasted the poor of Europe—made familiar to his American readers by the writings of Charles Dickens—to the separate and unique condition of slavery.

It is often said, by the opponents of the anti-slavery cause, that the condition of the people of Ireland is more deplorable than that of the American slaves. . . . I must say that there is no analogy between the two cases. The Irishman is poor, but he is not a slave. He may be in rags, but he is not a slave. He is still master of his own body, . . . and poor as may be my opinion of the British parliament, I cannot believe that it will ever sink to such a depth of infamy as to pass a law for the recapture of fugitive Irishmen!!

The lecture circuit provided Douglass with the opportunity to speak out against the institution he held in such contempt; it also honed his rhetorical skills and polished his writing style. In another lecture delivered in Rochester, on December 8, 1850, "An Antislavery Tocsin," he employed the biblical strategy of parallelism and repetition to enforce his moral argument against slavery:

I have shown that slavery is wicked—wicked, in that it violates the great law of liberty, written on every human heart—wicked, in that it violates the first command of the decalogue—wicked, in that it fosters the most disgusting licentiousness—wicked, in that it mars and defaces the image of God by cruel and barbarous inflictions—wicked, in that it contravenes the laws of eternal justice, and tramples in the dust all the humane and heavenly precepts of the New Testament. The evils resulting from this huge system of iniquity are not confined to the states south of Mason and Dixon's line. Its noxious influence can be traced throughout our northern borders.

Concluding this address, Douglass adopts the rhetorical style of an evangelical minister—a posture he often adopted—and warns his audience of impending doom in a jeremiad (in Blassingame, vol. 2) that would be repeated in the concluding pages of Stowe's *Uncle Tom's Cabin*:

I warn the American people, by all that is just and honorable, to BEWARE!! I warn them that strong, proud, and prosperous though we be, there is a power above us that can "bring down high looks; at the breath of whose mouth our wealth may take wings; and before whom every knee shall bow;" . . . without appealing to any higher feeling, I would warn the American people and the American government, to be wise in their day and generation. I exhort them to remember the history of other nations . . . that the time may come when those they now despise and hate, may be needed; when those whom they now compel by oppression to be enemies, may be wanted as friends. . . . The crushed worm may yet turn under the heel of the oppressor. I warn them, then, with all solemnity, and in the name of retributive justice, *to look to their ways;* for in an evil hour, those sable arms that have, for the last two centuries, been engaged in cultivating and adorning the fair fields of our country, may yet become the instruments of terror, desolation, and death, throughout our borders.

The coming of this Armageddon, the American Civil War, gave Douglass a new opportunity, that of witnessing an end to the system he had so long opposed. He was also a direct participant, proposed for a military commission by Lincoln and a very active recruiter of black soldiers for the Union forces. The 54th Massachusetts Regiment, celebrated in the film *Glory* (1989), was created by Douglass; his own sons were among the first of the nearly two hundred thousand black soldiers he helped inspire to enlist. In "Men of Color, to Arms!" (1863, in Foner, vol. 3) Douglass recalls the battle cries of Thomas Paine, whose *Common Sense* (1776) had aroused sentiment against Great Britain at the time of the American Revolution:

Liberty won by white men would lose half its luster. "Who would be free themselves must strike the first blow." "Better even die free, than to live slaves." This is the sentiment of every brave colored man amongst us.

Throughout the Civil War, Douglass visited the White House many times and acted as an adviser to Abraham Lincoln. He continued to write and speak out against slavery. Perhaps his most eloquent testimony came on December 28, 1862, three days before the publication of the Emancipation Proclamation; this speech was printed as "A Day for Poetry and Song" in *Douglass' Monthly,* in January 1863. He begins by enthusiastically noting:

This is scarcely a day for prose! . . . We stand today in the presence of a glorious prospect. . . . Among the first questions that tried the strength of my childhood mind—was first why are colored people slaves, and the next was will their slavery last forever. . . . How long! How long oh! Eternal Power of the Universe, how long shall these things be? This inquiry is to be answered on the first of January, 1863.

Douglass was, however, unrelenting in his contempt for the institution that had robbed him of life and liberty, and that continued to enslave thousands of his African American brothers and sisters, soon to be legally free citizens of the United States:

This is no time for the friends of freedom to fold their hands and consider their work at an end. The price of Liberty is eternal vigilance. Even after slavery has been legally abolished, and the rebellion substantially suppressed . . . there will still remain an urgent necessity for the benevolent activity of the men and the women who have from the first opposed slavery from high moral conviction.

Douglass makes a swift transition from the legalized institution of slavery to those moral and prejudicial forces in human behavior that have permitted it to exist in the first place. For Douglass, it was this malignancy of spirit that would long remain in the public psyche:

Law and sword can and will in the end abolish slavery. But law and the sword cannot abolish the malignant slaveholding sentiment which has kept the slave system alive in this country during two centuries. Pride of race, prejudice against color, will raise their hateful clamor for oppression of the Negro as heretofore. The slave having ceased to be the abject slave of a single master, his enemies will endeavor to make him the slave of society at large.

The rhetorical power that had long characterized Douglass' style as a writer and speaker was in this address perhaps most effectively realized. The country was dealing with a disease, not merely an institution; for racism to be eradicated, a complete change of character would be necessary:

Slavery has existed in this country too long and has stamped its character too deeply and indelibly, to be blotted out in a day or a year, or even in a generation. The slave will yet remain in some sense a slave, long after the chains are taken from his limbs; and the master will retain much of the pride, the arrogance, imperiousness and conscious superiority and love of power, acquired by his former relation of master. Time, necessity, education, will be required to bring all classes into harmonious and natural relations.

This final line contains Douglass' dual message: a realistic assessment of the circumstances under which black people exist in the fragmented and divided United States, and a belief in the possibility of harmonious union and racial equality. Unlike Lincoln, Douglass genuinely felt that the United States might possibly produce an egalitarian society with racial harmony at its center. He also argued the corollary: without such harmony a hostile separation of the races, leading to armed aggression between the races, would ensue.

Following the Civil War, Douglass enjoyed

the life of a celebrated American hero. He was given several governmental posts by grateful presidents. To mention only three, first Grant made him assistant secretary of the commission of inquiry sent to Santo Domingo in 1871; second, Garfield appointed him marshall and recorder of deeds for the District of Columbia in 1881; and then Harrison made him minister to Haiti in 1889, the most prestigious appointment.

Douglass' rise from the abuses of slavery to the prominence and intellectual power of his final years was an enormous achievement. But he was also a great American, one who, in the Emersonian sense, ''represented'' the emerging nation as it experimented with democracy and social ideals. William Andrews, in his introduction to *My Bondage and My Freedom,* suggests some reasons for the pervasive, immense power of the man:

> And the secret of his power, what is it? He is a Representative American—a type of his countrymen. . . . To the fullest extent, Frederick Douglass has passed through every gradation of rank comprised in our national make-up, and bears upon his person and upon his soul everything that is American. And he has not only full sympathy with everything American; his proclivity or bent, to active toil and visible progress, are in the strictly national direction, delighting to outstrip all creation.

Douglass re-created his life in three autobiographical versions even as America was in the process of defining itself. He experienced slavery in its most brutal form, fought against the institution with his body and his soul, witnessed the dissolution of the Union and fought to preserve it, and wrote prolifically about the social and political problems of the emerging nation with a fervent belief in the possibility of America's greatness. Douglass was, with Emerson and Thoreau, also critics of the rising glory of America, one of our nation's most devoted patriots.

Selected Bibliography

The author wishes to acknowledge the superb editing of John Blasingame of Yale University and Philip Foner of Columbia University, who have provided modern readers with authoritative texts of Frederick Douglass' works, as cited below.

WORKS OF FREDERICK DOUGLASS

AUTOBIOGRAPHIES

Narrative of the Life of Frederick Douglass, an American Slave, Written by Himself. Boston: The Anti-Slavery Office, 1845; New York: Penguin Books, 1982.

My Bondage and My Freedom. New York: Miller, Orton & Mulligan, 1855; Urbana: University of Illinois Press, 1987.

The Life and Times of Frederick Douglass, Written by Himself. Hartford: Park Publishing Company, 1881; rev. ed., 1892; New York: Bonanza Books, 1962.

COLLECTED WORKS

The Frederick Douglass Papers, edited by John W. Blassingame. Series I. 3 vols. New Haven: Yale University Press, 1979–1985.

The Life and Writings of Frederick Douglass, edited by Philip S. Foner. 5 vols. New York: International Publishers, 1950–1975.

MANUSCRIPT PAPERS

The papers of Frederick Douglass are in the Yale University Library, New Haven, Connecticut. See also *North Star,* published in Rochester, New York, from 1847 to 1851; *Frederick Douglass' Paper,* published in Rochester from 1851 to 1859; and *Douglass' Monthly,* published in Rochester from 1859 to 1863.

BIOGRAPHICAL AND CRITICAL STUDIES

Andrews, William. *To Tell a Free Story: The First Century of Afro-American Autobiography, 1769–1865.* Urbana: University of Illinois Press, 1986.

Baker, Houston. *The Journey Back: Issues in Black Literature and Criticism.* Chicago: University of Chicago Press, 1980.

Bell, Bernard. *The Afro-American Novel and Its Tradition.* Amherst: University of Massachusetts Press, 1987.

Blassingame, John. *Frederick Douglass: The Clarion Voice.* Washington, D.C.: National Park Service, 1976.

———. *The Slave Community: Plantation Life in the Antebellum South.* New York: Oxford University Press, 1972; rev. and enl. ed., 1979.

Butterfield, Stephen. *Black Autobiography in America.* Amherst: University of Massachusetts Press, 1974.

Chesnutt, Charles W. *Frederick Douglass.* Boston: Small & Maynard, 1899.

DuBois, W. E. B. "Frederick Douglass." In *Dictionary of American Biography.* Vol. 3. New York: Scribners, 1930.

Foner, Philip S. *Frederick Douglass.* New York: Citadel Press, 1964.

Gates, Henry Louis. "Binary Oppositions in Chapter One of *Narrative of the Life of Frederick Douglass, an American Slave, Written by Himself.*" In *Afro-American Literature: The Reconstruction of Instruction.* Edited by Robert Stepto and Dexter Fisher. New York: MLA Press, 1979.

Huggins, Nathan I. *Slave and Citizen: The Life of Frederick Douglass.* Boston: Little, Brown, 1980.

Lowance, Mason. "Biography and Autobiography in Early America." In *The Columbia Literary History of the United States.* Edited by Emory Elliott et al. New York: Columbia University Press, 1988.

Martin, Waldo E. *The Mind of Frederick Douglass.* Chapel Hill: University of North Carolina Press, 1984.

Matlack, James. "The Autobiography of Frederick Douglass." *Phylon,* 40:15–28 (March 1979).

Minter, David. "Conceptions of the Self in Black Slave Narratives." *American Transcendental Quarterly,* 24:62–68 (1974).

Niemtzow, Annette. "The Problematic Self in Autobiography: The Example of the Slave Narrative." In *The Art of the Slave Narrative.* Edited by John Sekora and Darwin Turner. Macomb: Western Illinois University Press, 1982.

Quarles, Benjamin. *Frederick Douglass.* Washington, D.C.: Associated Publishers, 1948.

———. "Abolition's Different Drummer: Frederick Douglass." In *The Anti-Slavery Vanguard: New Essays on the Abolitionists.* Edited by Martin Duberman. Princeton: Princeton University Press, 1965.

———. "Frederick Douglass: Black Imperishable." *Quarterly Journal of the Library of Congress,* 29:159–161 (July 1972).

Sekora, John, and Darwin Turner. *The Art of the Slave Narrative: Original Essays in Criticism and Theory.* Macomb: Western Illinois University Press, 1982.

Stone, Albert E. "Identity and Art in Frederick Douglass' *Narrative.*" *CLA Journal,* 17:192–213 (December 1973).

Washington, Booker T. *Frederick Douglass.* Philadelphia: G. W. Jacobs, 1907.

Yellin, Jean Fagan. *The Intricate Knot: Black Figures in American Literature, 1776–1863.* New York: New York University Press, 1972.

Yetman, Norman R., ed. *Voices from Slavery: Selections from the Slave Narratives Collection of the Library of Congress.* New York: Holt, Rinehart & Winston, 1970.

—*MASON LOWANCE*

Susan Glaspell

1876–1948

"THIS IS THE mysterious law: go beyond." Victor Hugo's exhortation to writers could well have served as the motto for both Susan Glaspell's protagonists and for the writer herself. She was determined to go beyond the limited world of the the Midwest, where the expansive pioneer spirit had shrunk into jingoistic provincialism. From her earliest work for the stage, she aimed to surpass the timid conventions of the popular theater and explored a range of drama—from the concentrated, quiet realism of *Trifles* (1916) through the polemics of *Inheritors* (1921) to the expressionism of *The Verge* (1922). In fiction, Glaspell went from writing local-color, formulaic short stories for popular magazines to producing novels in which both form and theme stretched the limits of the familiar. Above all, in the fiction, drama, and biography she wrote, Susan Glaspell struggled to embody her commitment to an idea of evolution, to moving beyond present human limits toward some new life awareness, perhaps some new life form.

Glaspell's desire to go beyond contributes both to her strengths and to her weaknesses as a writer. The urgency of such central characters as the women in *The Visioning* (1911), *Ambrose Holt and Family* (1931), and *The Verge* to become more than decorative wives generates powerful drives, confrontations, drama. The frustrations of her characters who feel trapped provide many works with powerful openings and vividly detailed pictures of psychological cages. The first third of the novel *Norma Ashe* (1942), for example, with Norma as the owner of a shabby boardinghouse, is one of Glaspell's most concrete pictures of a woman turned into an almost mindless drudge by the struggle to survive. Yet here as in many of her other novels, the dramatic introduction is unfortunately followed by awkward plotting, vague and strained philosophical passages, and a final impression of melodrama and mawkishness. In the tighter form of the play, some of these problems are minimized; nevertheless, Glaspell preferred fiction.

The evolutionary ideal that appears in almost every major work from her second novel through her last is most vividly embodied in *Norma Ashe,* in the image of fish who, driven by some power beyond their own understanding, fling themselves onto the beach in order to become air breathers, land creatures. This idea of an evolutionary urge, certainly not Charles Darwin's, she took from George Cram Cook, her first husband and by far the greatest influence on her life, thought, and work. The Susan Glaspell work we know today was almost all written after she met Cook and is permeated with his influence. She wrote most personally about him in *The Road to the Temple* (1927), and she quoted one of his poems in her last novel, but more important is that a typical figure in her work—the teacher, guide, or mentor—is based on Cook. "Jig," as he was usually called, was also a writer, and although he did not manage to complete much successful work of his own, he inspired many others. It is Glaspell who brought his ideas to life: she was at once his disciple, his critic, and his surpasser.

Susan Glaspell was born on July 1, 1876, in Davenport, Iowa, the daughter of Elmer S. and Alice Keating Glaspell. (C.W.E. Bigsby has persuasively argued that her birthdate is not 1882, as some sources assert.) She attended Drake University in Des Moines, and after her graduation in 1899 became a legislative reporter for the *Des Moines Daily News*. She had begun writing short stories in college, and in 1901 she returned to Davenport determined to be a full-time writer. She quickly became successful as a producer of short stories for women's magazines. Many of her early stories are set in Freeport, a name invented for Davenport by a popular local author, Alice French, in stories published ten years before. Arthur Waterman says of these Freeport stories:

> Miss Glaspell adhered to the values held by her readers. Love and money are the most desirable things in the world, but the greater of these is love. Although social classes exist, class boundaries may be crossed by deserving individuals. Evil is usually overcome by good; suffering builds character.

In 1909, her first novel, *The Glory of the Conquered,* followed a premise similar to that of the short stories. Even more revealing than the title is the subtitle: *The Story of a Great Love.* This romantic, melodramatic tale concerns a woman painter who marries a scientist; he shortly goes blind and dies young. The heroine determines to go on painting in a way that will show the glory of their love.

Although Glaspell had met Cook, and his friend Floyd Dell, in 1907, it was not until 1910, after a year of travel in Europe, that she became an enthusiastic member of the Monist Society, started in Davenport by the two men as a discussion group centering on the works of Friedrich Nietzsche. She found the discussion exhilarating, and she and Cook fell in love. Glaspell saw in Cook an idealist who combined a love of the pioneer past and unhappiness with the growing provincialism of the present, with a dynamic view of the future. He had abandoned a promising academic career to become a farmer and writer. He was dedicated both to ancient Greek literature and to avant-garde ideas. In 1913, Cook divorced his second wife, with whom he had two children, and married Glaspell; they moved to Greenwich Village, determined to succeed as writers. Glaspell's work after 1910 is directly and indirectly a reflection of Cook's idealism and enthusiasm. Her development was profoundly influenced by Cook and their life together; even long after his death, she was still coming to terms with his ideas and ideals.

The first product of this new force in her life was *The Visioning,* Glaspell's second novel. An awkward, often implausible story, this book sets themes that were to occupy her for most of her career. The novel's protagonist is a wealthy orphan in her early twenties, Katherine Wayneworth Jones, and its title has multiple related meanings: Katie's realizations about her own life, her discovery of the world outside the narrow confines in which she has lived, and her visions of how she and society must change. The daughter of a distinguished general, Katie lives a life of privilege on army bases; her brother is an officer at the Rock Island Arsenal, near Chicago. At the start of the novel, Katie sees a young woman about to walk into the river to commit suicide. Katie tricks the young woman into believing that she (Katie) needs help, and takes the near-suicide home with her. Then, at first merely in a spirit of fun, Katie invents a name, Ann, for the other, then a history. Quickly, Ann accepts the role, blossoms under Katie's care, and begins to inform Katie about the world of the poor working woman. By a horrible coincidence, one of Katie's suitors is a man who was once Ann's seducer; encountering him, Ann flees. Searching for Ann, Katie discovers the narrow-minded fundamentalism of Ann's family and the spirit-destroying work open to a single woman in the city. She eventually finds Ann, ill and in despair. But Katie's brother, himself divorced and unhappy about the army, marries Ann, resigns his commission, and becomes a forest ranger. Katie meanwhile falls in love with a wise and magnetic young man who mends boats, Alan Mann. He lends her books on evolution and socialism, then astounds her by revealing that he was an enlisted man (which she considers rabble) who had been court-martialed, imprisoned, and dishonorably discharged for striking a cruel, despotic officer. Her knowledge of Alan's background tests Katie's newfound understanding and tolerance, and at first she cannot accept him. But love and awareness triumph.

Foremost in this melodrama is the growth of the heroine from self-indulgence to self-awareness, from conformist to rebel, from aristocrat to socialist. Of almost equal importance is the figure of the guide—Alan Mann—the wise, loving mentor, obviously based on Cook, who seems self-sufficient yet needs her love and trust to escape the bitterness of his worldview. Many scenes, especially those set in Chicago, are vividly created, but the plot is, for all the psychological and philosophical trappings, a set of variations on the arrival of Mr. Right; Katie's brother and Alan Mann are both wonderfully noble, and all obstacles melt before the power of love. Glaspell's story and her ideas are poorly fitted.

Fidelity, a novel published in 1915, two years after Glaspell's marriage, seems nevertheless to deal with her ambivalence about her affair with Cook. Her heroine, Ruth, yearning to escape small-town life, runs off with a married man. When she has the opportunity to marry him, however, she refuses, preferring to go to Greenwich Village and start a new life, more concerned about fidelity to herself. Told from multiple points of view, *Fidelity* marks an improvement in structure and plausibility, but unfortunately not in depth. The "new" women Ruth expects to meet in New York are shadowy, while the pains of ostracism and guilt are more vivid.

By the time *Fidelity* was published, Glaspell and Cook were living in Greenwich Village. They had begun, almost accidentally, on the next chapter of their lives, the one for which both were best remembered, the creation of the Provincetown Players. Significantly named The Playwrights' Theater in its New York home, but generally referred to according to its Cape Cod origins, the Provincetown Players had a major effect on American theater, an effect out of proportion to the relatively few plays produced and the very few that have remained viable. Its importance lay in the emphasis on new American writers, particularly those working with experimental techniques and unconventional ideas. Other little theaters, such as the Washington Square Players, were more interested in introducing the new drama of Europe. Best remembered for first producing Eugene O'Neill, the Provincetown might be even better identified as the model Greenwich Village theater, fiercely non-commercial and non-traditional. Cook was the guiding force, while Glaspell was by far the most important of the playwrights after O'Neill.

Ferment in the theater was not new in 1915. The little theater movement, reflecting such experimental European models as Die Freie Bühne, had been flourishing. In 1911, in Chicago, Cook and Glaspell had seen the Irish Players (a troupe from the Abbey Theatre), and that group had left a lasting impression. Still, neither of them had thought of becoming a playwright, even though Cook was dedicated to Greek drama. So it was in a lighthearted, satiric spirit that they collaborated on *Suppressed Desires,* a one-act play, not much more than a sketch, mocking the new interest in psychoanalysis and the popular oversimplification of Freudian ideas. Earlier in 1915 they had submitted this little drama to the two-year-old Washington Square Players (later the Theatre Guild), the most advanced group of the time. It was rejected as clever but too special. Cook and Glaspell read it to friends, and in Provincetown the next summer they presented *Suppressed Desires* along with another short comedy, *Constancy,* by Neith Boyce Hapgood, at the Hapgoods' home. The program's reception was enthusiastic, and at the same time they discovered that many of their friends also had written plays. They persuaded Mary Heaton Vorse to rent them her fish house on a pier, which they used for a tiny theater to present two more plays later in the summer.

The success of the first season led Cook to announce another program for the next summer that would include a play by Glaspell, one not yet written or even planned. As she described it, she sat in the theater staring at the small stage until she imagined a kitchen there, and then some characters entering. The setting suggested an incident she had known as a reporter. The result was *Trifles,* Glaspell's best-known and most often produced play. It was staged the next summer along with several other new plays, including one called *Bound East for Cardiff,* written by Provincetown resident Eugene O'Neill. The company was on its way.

Trifles has the structure of a short story. (Glaspell recast it as the story "A Jury of Her Peers" in 1917.) Into the farm kitchen come the sheriff, the county attorney, and a neighbor to investigate the murder of John Wright by his wife; they are searching for the motive. Mrs. Peters, the sheriff's wife, and Mrs. Hale, the neighbor's, come along to clean up and get some things for Mrs. Wright, now in jail. While the men search for clues, the women talk of the loneliness of farm life and notice odd traces of disturbance, among them some bits of erratic sewing and signs of a dead bird. When they point out the sewing, the men dismiss their concern over "trifles." The women come to understand how Mrs. Wright was driven to murder by her isolation and her husband's brutality, but to protect themselves from the men's laughter, and out of sympathy for Mrs. Wright, they say no more. By the end of the play, their sympathy has developed into feelings of guilt for not having helped Mrs. Wright in the loneliness with which they can identify.

Glaspell uses the skill of a local-colorist, and as in many of her plays, there is little action, much discussion, and the main character is offstage. The dead bird is suggestive of August Strindberg's *Miss Julie* (1889); Glaspell, like O'Neill, admired Strindberg.

Suppressed Desires and *Trifles* are the most anthologized and produced of Glaspell's plays. Although they are effective and surprisingly skillful for a neophyte playwright, they are also not very ambitious and are unrepresentative of Glaspell and of the Provincetown Players. Glaspell's distinction lies in her motivation to explore increasingly difficult and complex problems. She did, in fact, move toward newer, more expressionistic forms earlier than did O'Neill. They undoubtedly encouraged and inspired each other. Glaspell's description of the first time O'Neill read a play to the group is often quoted:

> Then we knew what we were for. We began in faith, and perhaps it is true that when you do that "all these things shall be added unto you."

In the winter of 1916–1917 the members of the Provincetown group rented a space in Greenwich Village, which they christened the Playwrights' Theatre and where they repeated their summer programs and continued to produce new works. Under Cook's enthusiastic direction, the Provincetown Players lasted as a company in New York until 1922, although it gave up the summer productions in Provincetown after a few seasons. As the Provincetown grew in success, O'Neill was its chief attraction, but Glaspell was second in importance and popularity. While O'Neill's works would have found their way to the stage in any case, Glaspell's were completely the product of circumstances, of Cook's urging and the needs of the theater for new work. In all, Glaspell wrote seven one-act and four full-length plays while associated with the Provincetown; she also performed, to frequent acclaim, in many of the plays staged by the company.

Two of Glaspell's three plays from 1917, *The People* and *Close the Book,* were thin theatrical exercises. But *The Outside,* her fifth play, produced in December 1917, marked a decisive move toward something new. In *The Outside,* Glaspell turned toward the actual setting of Provincetown and a deeper treatment of the themes of loneliness and bereavement hinted at in *Trifles.* The play takes place in a former Coast Guard lifesaving station that is slowly sinking into the dunes. It is now rented by a wealthy, reclusive woman, Mrs. Patrick. At the start of the play, rescuers have brought a drowned man into the building, where they try to revive him. They fail and carry him off, but not before Mrs. Patrick angrily objects to their invading her privacy. Her anger drives her servant, the otherwise silent Allie Mayo, to speech. The two argue. Mrs. Patrick, abandoned by her husband, is focused on death, watching the sand engulf the plants, even the trees. Mayo, though herself numbed by years of tragedy, rejects that vision and asserts that new growth will triumph over the sand, life winning over death. At the very least, life does not surrender to nothingness. While Mrs. Patrick remains unpersuaded, the play ends with the reawakening of Mayo and the affirmation of hope.

The Outside struggles toward a philosophical, poetic richness. The formerly silent Mayo is meant to achieve a kind of awkward, broken eloquence. Glaspell herself played Mayo in the first production, and one cannot help wondering how much she is echoing O'Neill's semiarticulate characters, like Yank in *Bound East for Cardiff,* a role played by Cook. The result in Glaspell's drama, as often in similar attempts by O'Neill, is more awkward than eloquent, more struggle than achievement. Furthermore, the static situation, the heavy-handed symbolism of the lifesaving situation (the men undeveloped as characters), and the vague resolution work against the play. But the two women are firmly drawn and the strain to make a statement carries its own value.

After *The Outside,* Glaspell stayed with the one-act form two more times. *Woman's Honor,* produced in 1918, is a satiric sketch about a number of women who offered to provide alibis for a noble young man accused of murder. *Tickless Time,* which premiered later the same year, was another collaboration with Cook and revolves around an unconventional couple's failed attempt to do without a clock.

On March 21, 1919, the Provincetown Players presented Glaspell's first three-act play, *Bernice.* Thus far in its history, only Cook's *The Athenian Woman,* produced a year earlier, had been full-length. In Glaspell's play, the title character is dead when the play begins, reportedly a suicide. Believing that she died for him, in grief at his infidelity, Bernice's husband determines to change his life, to become worthy of her sacrifice. Her skeptical friend, however, learns from a servant that the death was from natural causes but that Bernice asked that it be reported as suicide. Although the work is static, and feelings and ideas are presented in abstract terms, it is noteworthy in the way it repeats Glaspell's interest in fidelity and guilt.

Inheritors returns to even more familiar motifs: the setting again is the Midwest, where the old idealism is almost lost in greed and narrow-minded provincialism, and the play foregrounds a fun-loving heroine, Madeline. Like Katie in *The Visioning,* Madeline discovers herself, society's injustice, and the need to sacrifice herself for her principles. In the first act, an early settler, inspired by an exiled Hungarian revolutionary who owns a neighboring farm, decides to found a college. Acts 2 and 3 take place in the present (that is, around 1920) at the college, which is now in need of government support. The president of the college, the Hungarian's son, is attempting to placate a state senator upset by the publications of a liberal professor. The college has also had bad publicity created by students from India demonstrating for independence for their country. The president is determined that nothing must stand in the way of the college's success, while his son, a student at the college, is rabidly intolerant. The "radical" professor reluctantly agrees to silence; he needs to preserve his job and his income in order to provide for his invalid wife. Only Madeline, a descendant of both the college founder and the Hungarian, determines to stand up for the Indians and may even go to jail.

To modern viewers, the play seems diagrammatic and obvious, but many in the original audience were impressed. A decade after the Provincetown Players staged this important work, Ludwig Lewisohn, one of Glaspell's greatest admirers, described its impact on the state of the American theater in 1921:

> It is the first American play in which a strong intellect and a ripe artistic nature grasped and set forth in human terms the central tradition and most burning problem of the national life quite justly and scrupulously, equally without acrimony and compromise. The American drama had not shown . . . anything comparable to Miss Glaspell's dramatic projection of the decadence of the great tradition of American idealism. . . . *Inheritors,* moreover, was more than a stirring play; it was in its day and date, a deed of national import.

Although *Inheritors* has not withstood the test of time, the same cannot be said of *The Verge* (1922), Glaspell's most ambitious stage work and one that most clearly reveals her theme of transcendence. While it is not directly autobiographical, *The Verge* strongly suggests some personal parallels with Glaspell's and Cook's lives at the time it was written.

The heroine, Claire, is a wealthy woman obsessed with developing new plants in her greenhouse, where all the action of the play takes place. These are not merely new varieties of flowers but new life forms with highly symbolic names: the Edge Vine and Breath of Life. They are new stages of evolution. Breath of Life, her most ambitious creation, is about to bloom. Claire herself yearns to transcend her material and materialistic life. She reaches out to Tom Edgeworthy, something of a mystic, another of Glaspell's guide figures. Edgeworthy is planning to go to Asia to lead the life of an ascetic; Claire persuades him to stay, but when she wishes to go beyond their understanding to a physical union, Edgeworthy retreats. In despair, Claire strangles him. At the end of the play, while her assistant is enraptured by the blooming of Breath of Life, Claire is quite insane, falteringly singing "Nearer My God to Thee."

The Verge was written at a point when Cook (and probably Glaspell) was becoming dissatisfied with the Provincetown Players. The commercial success of O'Neill's *Emperor Jones* in 1920 had brought them fame and considerable financial reward, but the earlier enthusiasm and risk-taking had given way to concern over funds and the drifting away of early theater members. At the same time, no single talent other than O'Neill had strongly emerged from the group;

Glaspell was certainly the most important after him, but clearly overshadowed. *The Verge* may have been, at some level, Glaspell's response to a fear of stultification and also an urge to move into the limelight. Like *Emperor Jones,* Glaspell's play was moved to Broadway, but only for a series of unsuccessful matinees.

One wonders also how much the play reveals Glaspell's mixed feelings about Cook. Rachel France says:

> A curious omission from discussions of *The Verge* is the remarkable similarity between Claire and . . . Cook. Even before Glaspell began to write her play, Cook's dream for the Provincetown, his "beloved community of life-givers," was collapsing around him. Claire's reactions to an unsatisfactory reality mirror Cook's own temperament.

Parallels between Edgeworthy and Cook seem even stronger; the one as eager to depart for Asia as is the other for Greece. Even more important, Edgeworthy, like so many of Glaspell's guide figures, is ultimately ineffectual and the heroine's faith in him proves unwarranted.

Other provocative and disturbing elements in *The Verge* likewise reflect the circumstances of Glaspell's own life. One of the most powerful and painful scenes in the play involves Claire's repudiation of her daughter as one who has surrendered to conventional society. Glaspell herself had no children; she had at least two pregnancies that ended in miscarriage. Cook, however, had a son and a daughter, and these children spent considerable time with him and Glaspell. Could she be venting some anger at Cook's children and expressing pain regarding her own childlessness?

A noteworthy element of *The Verge* is its strong echo of the character types in Nathaniel Hawthorne's "The Birthmark," only in Glaspell's play the heroine is herself both the monomaniacal scientist and the victim of the attempt to play God.

Even more outstanding is the influence of Strindberg, especially of *A Dream Play* (1907). In *A Dream Play,* the heroine is the daughter of the Vedic deity Indra, and she must ultimately leave an earth that is too stifling for the spirit. At her death, the mysterious castle flowers and burns. The expressionist form and tone, the importance of flowers, the motif of insanity, a struggle between male and female, and the blending of transcendence, escape, and destruction—all these in *The Verge* seem to echo Strindberg.

Such mingled strains give *The Verge* intense interest, but as with *Inheritors* the form is ultimately inadequate. The symbolism of plants and names is almost cartoonish. The characters are neither realistic nor do they resonate allegorically. The shifts from realism to expressionism are often awkward, and once again the language is in many instances abstract and vague.

In 1922, Cook and Glaspell went to live in Greece. Cook had always thought of Greece as his spiritual home and intensely studied the language and the literature. When the Provincetown Players disappointed him, turning cautious and resisting his leadership, he announced that it was time to go. He and Glaspell lived there for two years, rather simply, in a small town. Cook made friends and was known as a dedicated scholar; Glaspell says little of her experience, but she was apparently writing fiction at the time, not plays. However, Glaspell did leave behind a play, *Chains of Dew,* that was produced after their departure but never published. Only a sense of the plot survives from reviews, but she reused the basic story later in her novel *Ambrose Holt and Family.*

In 1924, Cook died in Delphi. Glaspell reports that he died of some infectious disease caught from a stray dog they befriended, but the details are vague. Traveling in Europe afterward, Glaspell met and married Norman Matson. Together they wrote a short, light comedy, *The Comic Artist* (published in 1927 and produced in 1928), but most of Glaspell's effort turned to *The Road to the Temple,* a biography of Cook. In this structurally intriguing work, Glaspell used, wherever possible, Cook's own words drawn from fragmentary diaries, letters, or simply thoughts jotted down on scraps of paper. The flavor of his thought, his dynamic personality, and his poetic sensibility all come through strongly, but there are also disturbing gaps and confusions. For example, Cook's first wife is barely mentioned, not even named, and the story of his second marriage is blurred.

More serious is Glaspell's failure to probe or analyze. Cook's various shifts in career are presented but not examined. His extraordinary life in Greece appears in idyllic terms, but incompletely. Nor does she acknowledge his failures. Her own feelings are muffled. She wishes to appear little more than an editor, yet her limited appearance is odd. She gives the detailed anecdote of how she came to write *Trifles,* but virtually none of her other work is even mentioned, despite the powerful bond between her writing and her relationship with Cook. Figures resembling Cook appear in her fiction after his death just as they had from the time she met him. Yet there is the murder of Edgeworthy in *The Verge,* there was her precipitate and unsuccessful marriage after Cook's death, and great ambiguity surrounds the guide figures in Glaspell's later novels.

Glaspell and Matson soon separated, and they divorced in 1931. In that same year, she won the Pulitzer Prize for her last play, *Alison's House* (1930), produced by the Civic Repertory Theatre. *Alison's House* was suggested by the life of Emily Dickinson, and the Dickinson parallels probably played some role in the play's brief success, but the center of the play is elsewhere.

Once again the title character is offstage, and once again the focus is on a midwestern town where prudishness and greed have nearly destroyed idealism.

Glaspell's poet, Alison, lived in the Midwest and has been dead some years at the time of the play—significantly, the turn of the century. Alison's brother is preparing to sell the old homestead, while her surviving sister objects and also clings to some unpublished poems. Family quarrels are climaxed by the return of the brother's daughter, who had run off with a married man. When Alison's sister dies, the brother and his daughter read the secreted poems and learn of Alison's frustrated romance. They agree that she knew that true love is greater than conventional morality. The brother forgives his wayward daughter and acknowledges his own secret romance.

Despite the Pulitzer Prize, *Alison's House* was not financially successful, and Glaspell needed to support herself economically with her work. That was certainly one reason she turned to the novel and wrote no other plays except for an unproduced work called *The Big Bozo.* Also, she was no longer involved with a theater group pressing her for new work. Most seriously lacking was Cook's enthusiastic direction. In any case, as her novels published between 1923 and 1945 reveal, Glaspell turned to subjects that were broader, more complex, and more reflective than she had ever attempted on stage. The novels resume the explorations of her earlier fiction. Glaspell's theater work may well have been an exciting interruption, but she apparently did not see herself as a playwright.

During the years of her marriage to Matson, Glaspell published two novels in rapid succession: *Brook Evans* (1928) and *Fugitive's Return* (1929). In *Brook Evans,* which in 1930 was made into a Paramount Pictures film titled *Right to Love,* Glaspell returns to a midwestern setting and to the theme of a love thwarted and twisted but ultimately redeemed. It is Glaspell's most Hollywoodish story, with enormous jumps in time and a logic that depends on almost mystical affinities.

In part 1, Naomi, daughter of poor, pious farmers, falls in love with the son of a wealthy landowner; they make love beside a rippling brook. When her lover is killed in a harvesting machine accident, Caleb Evans agrees to marry the pregnant Naomi and to move with her to another state before the child is born. In part 2, Naomi's daughter, Brook, falls in love with a local boy of mixed Indian and Italian parentage. Caleb disapproves, and when Brook bends to her father's will, Naomi tells her of her real father. Naomi then manipulates matters so that Brook can run off with her lover, but Brook is closer to Caleb and instead runs away with a neighbor woman leaving to do missionary work in the Middle East. In the last part of the novel, Brook, now a widow with a son, Evans, has been swept off her feet by Erik Helge, and she has come to understand Naomi's passion. Evans, confused by his mother's behavior, agrees to go to see his grandfather Caleb, now back in the old hometown. On his first visit to America, Evans finds his grandfather senile and the Midwest rather crude, yet he senses his roots are there, and by the rippling brook, though he does not know its role in his story, he feels at peace.

Fugitive's Return is far more ambitious. At the start of the novel, Irma Schraeder intends to commit suicide; her child has died and her husband has left her. A fortuitous visit from her oldest friend results in her going to Greece, using the name and ticket of a woman whose travel plans have abruptly changed. On board ship Irma is silent, and so she remains for some time in Greece, where she takes up residence in the house of an American classical scholar who is traveling. She becomes involved in the lives of three Greek women: her dedicated servant; a dwarfish shepherd girl who had once been raped by a local man who is now in prison; and a vibrant orphan refugee. Irma's silence is broken when she scolds some boys for tormenting animals. Soon after that the American scholar returns, and he and Irma become romantically involved. Finally, she helps the shepherd girl escape vigilantes after the girl murders her rapist—who had taken up with the refugee girl after his release from prison. In the center of the novel is a long flashback to Irma's childhood and youth in a small midwestern town, where she grew up feeling inferior to more well-to-do girls. She now realizes how, in her insecurity, she drove away her lovers, including her husband. At the novel's end, she returns to the old homestead to find peace.

Glaspell's picture of Greek life is substantially different from Cook's. Her heroine, despite her sympathy for the women around her, is always the outsider. While Irma's long silence is explained by the psychological traumas of her marriage, it may well stand for Glaspell's isolation in Greece. Also, the Greek world she portrays is brutal, and the women suffer most. Even though the rapist spends some time in jail, he returns to rape again. Irma breaks her silence on Easter, and her first words contain a Christian message that stresses the sense of modern Greece as pagan and certainly not noble.

As in *Brook Evans,* the return to home-ground provides a neat but weak closure. A highly provocative opening moves toward a vague, unfocused, "hopeful" ending. The issues raised provide some dramatic scenes but are hardly resolved. The three Greek women, along with Irma's decisive friend, provide a range of alternative personalities and experiences, but when the novel ends they have disappeared into what Waterman aptly calls "too much strained lyricism," as in one of Irma's final thoughts:

> What she would be now was real—as never before. Hard though it was to leave this beauty, she knew now that to move through beauty does not

constitute beauty. Through truth it must come, perhaps through the reality that is service. . . .

Waterman calls *Fugitive's Return* Glaspell's "only try at the Jamesian international novel," with its theme of the innocent American abroad. While the novels of Henry James may have been on her mind, and Waterman points out that Cook was a James admirer, *Fugitive's Return* more clearly focuses on Glaspell's continuing struggle to come to terms with Greece, and by extension with Cook. Though superficially different from *Brook Evans,* the book also deals with the conflict between the foreign, the cosmopolitan, and the heroine's roots.

Glaspell's 1931 novel *Ambrose Holt and Family* repeats many of these issues in a more complex, more successful way. The heroine, Henrietta (but usually called Blossom), is pampered by her wealthy parents, especially her father, and by her husband, Lincoln Holt, a poet and businessman. Lincoln is in charge of his father-in-law's cement business, and he has begun to make a reputation as a modernist poet. (Wallace Stevens comes to mind as a possible model.) He limits his writing to his study, a room apart from the rest of the house; it is situated in a kind of tower between floors. Thus he tries to keep the two aspects of his life separate, for he wishes to be a fine poet and yet have material success. When he is faced with the fact that the cement business is destroying a local forest, he sardonically accepts this as the price of success. When the inner conflict grows too intense, Lincoln goes off for solitary visits to Greenwich Village and his literary friends there. Throughout, Blossom yearns to help him and be something more than a household ornament, but Lincoln prefers to keep her on her pedestal.

At the heart of Lincoln's problem is his father, Ambrose Holt, a successful newspaperman who deserted his family when his son was a boy. He has become a drifter, and Lincoln lives in fear of becoming like him. When Ambrose reappears in town, Blossom is drawn to him. He is unconventional, relaxed, sage, and loving. He has only vague feelings of guilt about his abandoned family. Even his wife admits that his departure gave her the determination to prove herself, and she still loves him.

Lincoln's editor arrives when he is out of town and tells Blossom that Lincoln is not fulfilling himself as a poet; he is holding back from a full emotional commitment. When Lincoln returns he is enraged by his father's reappearance and by the editor's criticism. Ambrose leaves again; he goes to a nearby town, where he commits suicide by not taking his diabetes medicine, but before he dies he sends Blossom an inspiring message. His wisdom and the sacrificial nature of his death become a release for both Lincoln and Blossom. Thus the guide figure returns to Glaspell's fiction, and his idealism triumphs over crass materialism and conformity. Still, Blossom and Lincoln will continue to live well, for there is no reason for their lives to change much. Lincoln will now write better poems and Blossom is emancipated—she even talks firmly to her father—but that denouement is wrapped in lyrical commentary.

The Morning Is Near Us appeared in 1939 after a substantial hiatus in Glaspell's writing. During part of that time, she was the Midwest director for the Federal Theatre Project. While her job involved selecting plays and organizing productions, she did not, apparently, return to playwriting herself.

In *The Morning Is Near Us,* Glaspell builds her tale around a mystery, and structures the book in a highly melodramatic, cinematic way. The heroine, Lydia Chipmann, returns home after many years upon learning that her father has left her the family homestead. Her mother has been dead for many years, and Lydia had lost touch with her father and brother. In fact, she returns only after learning of the bequest by accident. In her early teens, Lydia had been sent off by her parents to live with an aunt, and then her father and mother, especially her mother, found many excuses for her not to return. She never saw her mother again. She became a world-wanderer, first living off a small legacy from the aunt, and later being supported with a generous gift from a mysterious benefactor she encountered during her travels. When she returns home, she assumes, as does the reader, that her father is dead and that she is fulfilling provisions of his will; she is surprised that her father has thought of her. She brings with her two adopted children, a Greek girl and a Mexican boy, as well as a donkey. Though her brother fears that her unconventional behavior will lead to scandal and ostracism, she is soon welcome in town and settles down. Still, she wonders more than ever why, if she was sent away at her father's request, as she believes, he has left the house to her.

Mysteries multiply as she discovers strange clues to her mother's origin. Neighbors comment obliquely about her parents. Then she discovers that her father is not dead, but rather is imprisoned in an asylum for the criminally insane after murdering a man for spreading vicious rumors about Lydia's mother. Lydia goes to visit her father, but he rebuffs her and denies he wants her to have and preserve the house. In despair, she plans to leave, but on her last night—a night of rain and wind—her father arrives, having escaped from the asylum, to tell the true story. She is not his child; her mother is the one who wanted her removed because Lydia was a reminder of her adultery, but always loved her deeply and wants her to stay. Exhausted by his journey and the strain of confession, the father dies.

The story recalls the love of "father" and "daughter" as in *Brook Evans,* with extraordinary complications. When Lydia finds a heartbreaking, unsent letter written by the mother to her lost brother, she discovers that her mother had appeared in Chipmann's life as if from nowhere as a young girl, apparently on the run from some horrendous situation. Taken in by the Chipmann family, the mother feels always that the man she eventually married is more a brother than a lover. Thus is her adultery explained and somewhat justified. Furthermore, the reader is led to deduce that Lydia's benefactor, met abroad, is her real father.

The movement of the novel depends on implausibilities and withheld information. Lydia's brother, who lives in town, is exceptionally reticent. He assumes, quite illogically, that Lydia knows more than she possibly can. He also seems to represent the provincialism of the town, yet Lydia and her strange family have absolutely no trouble in becoming part of the community. Could Glaspell have been hoping for a movie sale? The exotic children, the father's midnight arrival, Lydia's determination to learn how to drive in order to find her father—these and many other details are strongly cinematic.

Glaspell's novels had always featured plots that were convoluted and fantastic, depending on unlikely, even inexplicable, causalities. *The Morning Is Near Us* is probably the most fantastic, with theme and story line awkwardly joined. As in many of her other novels, a good deal depends on flashbacks. Incidental moments, like Lydia's discovery of her mother's letter, are sensitive and moving. On the other hand, attempts to be lyrical often result in vague, purplish passages. France, in describing some of Glaspell's plays, reflects a criticism that also fits most of the novels through *The Morning Is Near Us*.

Her ideas are . . . said to have been shrouded in murky ambiguities. In fact, it is the particular vocabulary of New Thought which pervades. . . . New Thought, an amalgam of beliefs ranging from the ancient Greeks to Eastern mysticism, postulates the unity of all things. . . . (Possibly the best known example of New

Thought still read today is *The Prophet,* 1923, by Kahlil Gibran.)

In Glaspell's last two novels, *Norma Ashe* and *Judd Rankin's Daughter* (1945), she surrendered little of her intensity or concern, but she chose a realistic approach that served her better than did her more ambitious and contrived tales. Both at times still depend on coincidence and slide into the vaguely rapturous, but the groundwork is more secure. World War II contributed much to this new solidity.

The first third of *Norma Ashe* may be Glaspell's finest realistic portrait, the novelistic equivalent of *Trifles*. The setting is a shabby boardinghouse in a midsized Illinois city. Mrs. Utterbach, the landlady, is beset by financial problems, worried about her children, and exasperated by her unpleasant tenants. The scene is unrelievedly gloomy.

Mrs. Utterbach receives a surprise visit from an old college friend, who remembers her as Norma Ashe and has come to her for help. Norma had been the wisest and most promising of a group of followers of an inspiring professor at Pioneer College; now she is dull and nearly defeated, and her former friend leaves in tears because Norma is no longer the life-affirming spirit the visitor had come to find.

The novel moves into a flashback, typical of Glaspell. We follow Norma, the optimistic small-town girl who intends to go to the University of Chicago and fulfill her dream of becoming a teacher like her professor. Instead, a chance meeting leads to a romantic marriage to an ambitious and feckless businessman. They move about the country as the husband's various schemes fail. He dies in debt; the old mansion on which he held a mortgage is Norma's total inheritance, hence the boardinghouse.

The narrative returns to the present: her son's financial and legal problems bring Norma to Chicago, where she finds her way to the university and attends a lecture by one of the old group of disciples. This friend has become a demagogue, using the old teachings in a twisted way to defend his greed and power. The great teacher had emphasized the idea of a life force willing itself toward greater intelligence and freedom; now the demagogue argues a kind of social Darwinism, the survival of the fittest. Norma's argument with him leads to meetings with others of the old group and new disillusion when she learns of her teacher's suicide, but she finds a young student eager to understand her ideas. After a period of working in Chicago, Norma returns to the boardinghouse, which is now successfully operated by her daughter and son-in-law. Soon after, Norma dies feeling that she is passing on some of the hope, some of the ideas of change and development that had once been passed on to her by the professor.

The teacher is one of Glaspell's clearest guide figures, in many ways another reflection of Jig Cook. A small, rural college founded by a visionary farmer and featuring a brilliant, unorthodox teacher is an echo of the situation in *Inheritors* and may also reflect Cook's idea of combining intellectual and rural lives. The image of willed evolution is presented in terms very like those Glaspell quotes from Cook in *The Road to the Temple*. Once again, like the professor in *Inheritors,* the guide is somewhat ineffectual, although this time the fault may lie more with the disciples than with the teacher. One of the people Norma meets again is the country boy who had been the teacher's companion and servant. He is the one who tells her that the teacher's death was a suicide, that though the teacher was kind and concerned, toward the end he had doubts about his ideas. Perhaps he even mocked the disciples for their belief, though this may be only the sardonic reflection of the survivor. At first, Norma is devastated, but ultimately she rises above her disillusionment with the consolation that while change may be slower than hoped for it is inevitable nonetheless.

In the elegiac *Judd Rankin's Daughter,* Glaspell appears to review her own life, though the novel is not directly autobiographical. As World War II moves toward its conclusion, Frances Rankin (referred to by her maiden name throughout), who lives in New York and Provincetown, is faced with the conflict between her father's midwestern conservatism and her husband's eastern, urban liberalism. Judd Rankin, her father, has published a collection of newspaper pieces humorously but sympathetically picturing the isolationism of the Midwest. Frances' husband, a reviewer for a leftist magazine something like *The Nation,* rejects these ideas as anachronistic. Meanwhile, their son returns from combat in the Pacific; he is at first unwilling to come home at all, then, when he does, he quarrels with his father and allies himself with a somewhat fascist editorial enemy of his father. His grandfather's book at first reinforces his desire to lash out at the imperfect world, but eventually it helps him to bring into perspective both his idealism and the cruelties of life. He comes to feel that the war may do very little to change things. Frances remains somewhat divided in her allegiance. She is deeply disturbed by a revelation of the anti-Semitism of one of their Provincetown friends; a visit to her father reminds her of the warmth and humanity of a more rural and isolated world, but she remains in the East with husband and son.

Waterman, who has written the only extended study of Glaspell, concludes that she was essentially a regionalist. One cannot fail to note how frequently the Midwest plays a major part in her work, sometimes as the major setting but more frequently as a place of origin and memory or as a vague type of haven. This soft-focus view suggests that regionalism is not a very useful label or a complete description. The Midwest Glaspell deals with is usually a region that once had a golden age but that is now sadly diminished. Judd Rankin is the best of the contemporary Midwest, yet he refuses to travel east, even for a visit, because he recognizes that his ideas make sense only in the rural heartland; he knows himself to be an anachronism. Glaspell herself settled in the East, in Provincetown and New York.

The regional label explains too little and is inadequate as a term to describe her most impressive works, those which, though usually imperfect, still breathe with intensity, with the struggle to shape a meaning. Among the plays the strongest are *Trifles, The Outside,* and *The Verge;* among the novels, *The Visioning, Ambrose Holt and Family, Norma Ashe,* and *Judd Rankin's Daughter* are the most successful.

Trifles is a wonder, a neat little machine that continues to work perfectly. Its picture of women's isolation in a bleak world is finely drawn, but the strength of the play is in its solidity, in the neat unraveling of the mystery. It is of all Glaspell's work the only one where intent and achievement meet. C. W. E. Bigsby sums up his discussion of the play with the statement that "*Trifles* was a modest but remarkable debut, most especially in the context of a national theatre which had consistently preferred melodrama to psychological truth."

The other two plays, like all of her novels, suffer from the author's struggle to find a form to contain their depth of feeling. While the form is never fully achieved as it is in *Trifles,* the struggle itself becomes the source of power. *The Outside* is the paradigm and a foreshadowing of most of the work to come. At the time it was written it most reflected Glaspell's struggle to find a voice as a playwright. Hindsight reveals that the struggle for voice was Glaspell's lifelong concern, sometimes acknowledged but more often demonstrated in the strain toward lyricism, the urge to give a philosophical veneer to melodramatic situations. In the struggle she took risks and was always experimenting. This is clearest in the plays, but, despite their more conventional form, it is also true of the novels.

Ironically, what first gave her a voice, Cook and the Provincetown Players, also contributed to Glaspell's problem as a writer. Starting with *The Visioning,* Glaspell points to Cook as mentor and illuminator, and in work after work, especially after his death, she continues to create guide figures. But the guides inevitably falter, commit suicide, turn out to be less than promised. Something similar happens with the father figures; notably in two of the works, they are not biological fathers, yet are greatly loved by the heroines. In Ambrose Holt, the two types are combined; Ambrose is the heroine's father-in-law, but closer to her than her own businessman father, and Ambrose is of course a guide. In *Judd Rankin's Daughter* both father and husband-mentor are in conflict for the heroine's soul. The possibility is left open that her son will reconcile the differences.

Ultimately, at the core of most of the plays and novels, the heroine is on her own. The mentor or father can help only so much and may even complicate matters. Glaspell's plays and her later novels deal with themes of isolation, struggle, and rebellion. Cook also dealt with these themes in his writing, as did Glaspell's coworkers, most notably O'Neill. But in Glaspell's work the struggle at its most vivid has a special focus—the need to go beyond a life stifled by convention and dissipated by the failure to find a suitable alternative. For example, in *The Verge,* Claire's husband feels that growing flowers is a most appropriate activity for a woman, totally misunderstanding the significance of her obsession. Unfortunately, her only alternative is madness. Another example is Norma Ashe, carried off on a wave of romantic love into a life of material success, at first, then one of poverty. In either case, the life of the mind and spirit is lost; the struggle destroys Norma even though she finds some solace at the end. Other protagonists, like Blossom Holt, object to the role of wife and mother defined for them, but find no other models. Despite her own independence as a writer, Glaspell most successfully pictures dependence and incompleteness.

When Susan Glaspell died in Provincetown on July 27, 1948, she left behind a body of work that encompassed some four decades. In *The Visioning,* written before World War I, the army appears as a largely useless organization, almost feudal in nature. Katie's brother objects to devoting his time to developing new weapons of doubtful value. On the other hand, Katie's experiences in Chicago focus on social conditions and turn her toward an idealistic socialism. In Glaspell's last novel, *Judd Rankin's Daughter,* written toward the end of World War II, the horrors of war are well understood and a muted, cautious liberalism colors the story. In few other works, however, does Glaspell refer specifically to the changing America in which she played her part. Most of the plays and novels deal with abstract issues, the problems of love and self-discovery, rather than the central social ideas of her time. Glaspell's last novels are more realistic than her earlier ones, and the writing is more mature, with less strain and less "fine" writing; here and there one detects the influence of film. Still, the basic structure, the fundamental themes, and the style changed very little over the course of her career.

Despite the traces in them of social criticism and the elements of feminism, the novels were never treated, even when they first appeared, as startling innovations. Critics often singled out the melodramatic elements of her fiction, and Glaspell was often scolded for vagueness. As a novelist, Glaspell is an intriguing footnote in literary history because her true strength lay elsewhere.

Susan Glaspell's importance is in her theater work, which altogether occupied her for barely fifteen years if one includes *Alison's House,* but only seven if her work with the Provincetown Players is considered alone. It was an astonishing seven years, ranging from regionalist realism to expressionist tragedy, from satiric sketches to allegory. Her plays show surprising mastery from the first, and during those seven years were consistently experimental and daring. They were especially effective when performed for an audience eager for the new. James Agate ranked *Inheritors* with Henrik Ibsen's 1892 play *The Master Builder* (quoted by Bigsby). Most critics compared Glaspell with O'Neill, often to her advantage. Isaac Goldberg wrote in 1922, when her career as a playwright seemed only to be heading for greater heights, that

> Glaspell's intensity of thought . . . induces a straining toward wit, an eminently intellectual process; her humor . . . presupposes persons of sophistication. As O'Neill inclines toward the masterful man, so she leans toward the rebellious woman. Where the author of *The Hairy Ape* spurts out words like the gushing of a geyser, Glaspell is reticent, laconic. . . .

But 1922 is when she and Cook left for Greece, in part because the O'Neill experience had led the Provincetown Players away from the quieter experiments.

After her return from Europe, Glaspell's plays followed more conventional models. Her earlier work quickly faded in the stronger light cast by O'Neill and the crowd of new American dramatists who had begun to appear. Elmer Rice's *The Adding Machine* was produced in 1923, and such playwrights as Robert Sherwood, Sherwood Anderson, Clifford Odets, and Samuel Nathaniel Behrman were dominating the scene, as were larger and more ambitious theater companies, especially the Group Theatre. The Provincetown Players had helped to show the way for a new generation of writers who took to the stage with great vigor and assurance. Their greater control of language, whether the language of the streets as in Sidney Kingsley's *Dead End* (1935) or the language of the salon as in Behrman's *Biography* (1932), reveals Glaspell's shortcomings, the vague lyricism and the old-fashioned hesitations and euphemisms.

In an ironic turn, Glaspell now seemed the epitome of the little theater, once the model for a stage revolution, now the symbol of the amateurish. Still, as Waterman says, "It is safe to say that her work paved the way and that the Provincetown created a climate where original plays by American playwrights were acceptable to the Broadway producers and to the theatre public." Bigsby sums up her contributions as a playwright even more strongly:

> Without her there must be some doubt as to whether the Provincetown Players would ever have been established and certainly whether that crucial organization would have been able to sustain itself as it did. She was, without doubt, one of its two greatest discoveries; and if her plays were imperfect then so, too, were O'Neill's and for much the same reason. In her work, as in her life, she never settled for anything less than total commitment. Sometimes that took her where few others were willing or ready to follow. She chanced more than most of her contemporaries and achieved more than many of them. She deserves more than a footnote in the history of drama.

In the literary ferment of the first quarter of the twentieth century, Susan Glaspell was one of many who helped to shape the modern consciousness. She is a representative figure. Her work speaks of the turmoil, the awakening to new, often disturbing, ideas in psychology, in social and political thought, and in art. As a woman and a midwesterner, she was particularly sensitive to the breakup of older values, and in much of her work there is a nostalgia for a stable, small-town society. Many of her novels, as well as such plays as *Alison's House,* deal with the loss of security. Nonetheless, while the return to the homestead might bring repose, the struggle for the new and the finer remained the driving force, and Susan Glaspell was her own best example of the searcher for deeper understanding. She was not always successful, but always eager, exploring, moving beyond.

Selected Bibliography

WORKS OF SUSAN GLASPELL

PLAYS

Plays. Boston: Small, Maynard & Co., 1920. Collects the one-act plays, *Suppressed Desires* (1915), *Trifles* (1916), *Close the Book* (1917), *The Outside* (1917), *The People* (1917), *Woman's Honor* (1918), and *Tickless Time* (1918), as well as Glaspell's first full-length play, *Bernice* (1919).

Inheritors (1921). Boston: Small, Maynard & Co., 1921.

The Verge (1921). Boston: Small, Maynard & Co., 1922.

Chains of Dew. Produced in April 1922. Unpublished.

The Comic Artist, with Norman Maston (1928). New York: Frederick A. Stokes Co., 1927.

Alison's House (1930). New York: Samuel French, 1930.

Plays by Susan Glaspell. Edited by C. W. E. Bigsby. Cambridge: Cambridge University Press, 1987. Contains *Trifles, The Outside, The Verge,* and *Inheritors* along with an introduction, biographical record, bibliography, and notes.

NOVELS

The Glory of the Conquered. New York: Frederick A. Stokes Co., 1909.

The Visioning. New York: Frederick A. Stokes Co., 1911.

Fidelity. Boston: Small, Maynard & Co., 1915.

Brook Evans. New York: Frederick A. Stokes Co., 1928.

Fugitive's Return. New York: Frederick A. Stokes Co., 1929.

Ambrose Holt and Family. New York: Frederick A. Stokes Co., 1931.

The Morning Is Near Us. New York: Frederick A. Stokes Co., 1939.

Cherished and Shared of Old. New York: Julian Messner, 1940. A brief Christmas story.

Norma Ashe. New York: J. B. Lippincott Co., 1942.

Judd Rankin's Daughter. New York: J. B. Lippincott Co., 1945.

SHORT STORIES

Glaspell published forty-three short stories in a variety of periodicals. C. W. E. Bigsby, in the bibliography to *Plays by Susan Glaspell,* provides the complete list.

MISCELLANEOUS WRITINGS

''Last Days In Greece.'' In *Greek Coins*. Poems by George Cram Cook, edited by Glaspell. New York: George H. Doran Co., 1925.

The Road to the Temple. New York: Frederick A. Stokes Co., 1927.

BIOGRAPHICAL AND CRITICAL STUDIES

Dell, Floyd. *Homecoming*. New York: Farrar & Rinehart, 1933.

Deutsch, Helen, and Stella Hanau. *The Provincetown: A Story of the Theatre*. New York: Farrar & Rinehart, 1931.

Dickinson, Thomas H. *Playwrights of the New American Theater*. New York: Macmillan, 1925.

France, Rachel. ''Susan Glaspell.'' In *Dictionary of Literary Biography*. Edited by John MacNicholas. Vol. 7, *Twentieth-Century American Dramatists*. Detroit: Gale Research, 1981.

Goldberg, Isaac. *The Drama of Transition*. Cincinnati: Stewart Kidd Co., 1922.

Krutch, Joseph Wood. *The American Drama Since 1918*. New York: Random House, 1939.

Lewisohn, Ludwig. *Expression in America*. New York: Harper & Brothers, 1932.

Macgowan, Kenneth. *Footlights Across America: Towards a National Theater*. New York: Harcourt, Brace, 1929.

McGovern, Edythe M. "Susan Glaspell." In *American Women Writers* 2. Edited by Lina Mainiero. New York: Frederick Ungar, 1980. Pp. 144–146.

Meserve, Walter J. "Glaspell, Susan (Keating)." In *Great Writers of the English Language: Dramatists*. New York: St. Martin's, 1979. Pp. 254–256.

Quinn, Arthur Hobson. *A History of the American Drama from the Civil War to the Present Day*. New York: F. S. Crofts, 1927.

———. *American Fiction*. New York: D. Appleton-Century Co., 1936.

Sayler, Oliver M. *Our American Theatre*. New York: Brentano's, 1923.

Sievers, W. David. *Freud on Broadway: A History of Psychoanalysis and the American Drama*. New York: Cooper Square, 1970.

Snell, George. *The Shapers of American Fiction 1798–1947*. New York: E. P. Dutton, 1947.

Vorse, Mary Heaton. *Time and the Town: A Provincetown Chronicle*. New York: Dial, 1942.

Waterman, Arthur E. *Susan Glaspell*. New York: Twayne, 1966.

—MILTON LEVIN

Elizabeth Hardwick

1916–

"IN CERTAIN WAYS, the mysterious and somnambulistic 'difference' of being a woman has been, over 35 years, Elizabeth Hardwick's great subject," Joan Didion wrote in 1979, reviewing Hardwick's acclaimed third novel, *Sleepless Nights*. Didion notes that "no one has written more acutely and poignantly about the ways in which women compensate for their relative physiological inferiority." She cites an essay on Simone de Beauvoir in which Hardwick states that "any woman who has ever had her wrist twisted by a man recognizes a fact of nature as humbling as a cyclone to a frail tree branch." Didion found Hardwick's assertion "at once so explicit and so obscurely shameful that it sticks like a burr in one's capacity for wishful thinking."

Hardwick's insistence that women's physical differences from men amount to a determining inferiority and Joan Didion's suggestion that to think otherwise is wishful thinking now sound antifeminist. But Hardwick wrote from her experience as a woman who built a public career as a liberal intellectual during the late 1940's through the early 1960's, when culture and politics were matters of urgent debate and women's rights were not. Retrospective looks at the personal lives of many of the women writers of her generation make the paucity of feminist discourse during those years seem painfully serious. Women carried on their intellectual labors alongside men—their husbands, lovers, friends—whose careers often overshadowed and threatened to consume their own. These men may have encouraged and supported the women, but in many cases they also used them and indulged in the destructive behavioral excesses sometimes considered the privilege of mad genius. A great mystery of Hardwick's life is her marriage of over twenty years to the poet Robert Lowell. Lowell, who suffered from a cyclic mental illness, regularly dealt emotional abuse to the wife whose nonpossessive caretaking became almost legendary.

Yet Hardwick made her own literary reputation. By the 1960's she was known as a major American critic. Reviewers of her novels and essay collections have consistently praised her deft, ironic style; despite the distanced feeling, the something that remains unsaid in Hardwick's work, her sheer skillfulness bears a ferocious determination to sort, to judge, and to be heard. Limits are real, Hardwick insists, and practical effort counts. Never self-pitying and rarely confessional even in her autobiographical writings, she does not claim that her experiences and the barriers that have shaped them count. Rather the something that remains unsaid gives her sentences a pressing emotional power.

The constraints on women intellectuals were not as severe as those faced by their nineteenth-century forebears, of whom Hardwick wrote with incisive sympathy in *Seduction and Betrayal: Women and Literature* (1974). Indeed, the women of Hardwick's generation are sometimes spoken of as having gained their achievements on the same footing as men. But there were differences, shaped by the pressure of attitudes from a lingering Victorianism.

Style was crucial to women writers of her generation, as Hardwick suggests in *A View of My Own: Essays in Literature and Society* (1962) in an essay on Mary McCarthy, a writer who was her close friend for forty years. Much of what Hardwick wrote about McCarthy's style applies to her own:

> A career of candor and dissent is not an easy one for a woman; the license is jarring and the dare often forbidding. Such a person needs more than confidence and indignation. A great measure of personal attractiveness and a high degree of romantic singularity are necessary to step free of the mundane, the governessy, the threat of earnestness and dryness. . . . With Mary McCarthy the purity of style and the liniment of her wit, her gay summoning of the funny facts of everyday life, soften the scandal of the action or the courage of the opinion.

Elizabeth Hardwick was born on July 27, 1916, in Lexington, Kentucky. Her father, Eugene Allen Hardwick, had a plumbing and heating business for a time, then sold oil furnaces and worked for the city as an inspector, though he preferred to fish. Her mother, Mary Ramsey Hardwick, bore nine children and engaged in the "dreadful labors" required of respectable lower-class homemakers. Elizabeth earned a B.A. and an M.A. in English at the University of Kentucky in Lexington, then at twenty-three left home and the South. Her career as an intellectual and her marriage to Lowell took her to Europe and various parts of the United States, but she became most strongly identified with New York. Her longtime association with *The New York Review of Books* makes finding her listed in *Southern Writers: A Biographical Dictionary* something of a surprise. She wrote in 1976, in a letter to Inge, the author of that listing: "I feel that as a writer I have been formed by the union in myself of my Kentucky background and my skeptical intellectual temperament—what might be called 'the New York' part of my interests and themes." Fifty years after her self-imposed exile, her voice—still heard at public readings and lectures—clearly signaled her southern roots.

Hardwick began the doctoral program in English at Columbia University in 1939 and quit after two years. She stayed in New York and wrote. Her first novel, *The Ghostly Lover,* was published in 1945, and her short stories appeared in literary magazines. Between 1945 and 1949 five of her stories were republished in the annual volumes of the *O. Henry Memorial Award Prize Stories* and *The Best American Short Stories,* and in 1948 she received a Guggenheim grant to work on fiction.

Reviews of *The Ghostly Lover* were mixed but offered encouragement to Hardwick, and shortly after the novel's publication Philip Rahv asked her to write for *Partisan Review,* of which he was an editor. Starting with the spring 1945 issue, her name regularly appeared on the cover along with those of such established writers as Hannah Arendt, Lionel Trilling, Randall Jarrell, Delmore Schwartz, Eric Bentley, Katherine Anne Porter, and Elizabeth Bishop. To write for *Partisan Review,* a major liberal journal, was to join a group of New York intellectuals at the heart of postwar political and cultural thought and action. In 1948 Hardwick was among thirty writers who, sparked by Mary McCarthy, signed a manifesto founding the Europe-America Groups with the aim of providing solidarity and financial aid to European intellectuals isolated "in the face of the extreme polarity of Soviet and American power." Hardwick's association with

Partisan Review also offered her the opportunity to develop her skills as an essayist. Though she continued to write fiction, she became best known for her essays, which she regards as examples of imaginative writing.

Hardwick's fiction of the 1940's reflects a young woman's struggle to differentiate herself from her family, class, and region; to escape their madness and conventionality; and to establish herself as an independent intellectual, freed from the false comforts of mainstream values but finding little to replace them with other than a critical viewpoint. *The Ghostly Lover* follows Marian Coleman from her home in a Southern town to graduate school in New York, an autobiographical story line, though Marian's family configuration differs from Hardwick's. Marian and her homosexual brother, Albert, live with their nearly mute grandmother while their parents travel constantly, in search of work for their father, who, despite many schemes, never prospers. A likely candidate for the lover of the title is introduced on the first page: Bruce, a divorced neighbor ten years older than Marian, holds her in his gaze. But Bruce dwindles in significance as the novel progresses, though their relationship serves, through Bruce's obsessions, to introduce Marian to a world beyond her stifling home. Playing the role of Pygmalion and paying for Marian's year studying music in New York, Bruce is the agent by which the plot of escape unfolds, while the female lead remains baffled and passive.

By the end of the novel it is clear that the haunting love that has shaped all Marian's relationships has been her desire for her absent "ghostly" mother. One reviewer felt this unexpected emotional focus made the book's title false advertising, but the dismantling of romantic passion and the power of the mother-daughter relationship are features that remain of great interest to readers grounded in feminism. After her grandmother's death, Marian visits her down-at-the-heels parents. They ask to borrow the five hundred dollars she has inherited from her grandmother, and she refuses them. In New York Marian has met a new lover, Leo, whose conventional possessiveness seems to destine their relationship for marriage. But having learned that her first, filial love will never be gratified, Marian evades Leo when he comes to meet her at the station on her return to New York. Marriage seems no more possible for Hardwick's heroine than does her reabsorption into the family. At the end Marian is shut out of Eden, left with an "icy ray of light," alienated but comfortlessly enlightened. With nowhere to go and nothing to do—she is too critical of her skills to pursue a music career—she will have to act beyond the novel as she has not within it, and the reader has no way of imagining what she might do. But she has five hundred dollars with which to make a start.

Critical in her reviews of fiction that replayed the 1920's plot of tragic upper-class heroines drawn to the bohemian life, Hardwick gave her characters class backgrounds similar to her own. Of her prizewinning short stories of the 1940's, two are of greatest biographical interest. "The Mysteries of Eleusis" (1946) continues Hardwick's critique of love and marriage. Dreaming of the impoverished rural home she has escaped, a young woman wakes on her wedding day in her rented room in the city. Her freedom exacts a cost: "drudgery was the payment she owed to some unnamed source, her appeal to the revenge that pursued her." Unlike Marian, she is powerless to stop her marriage, compelled toward the ceremony not by any clear feeling about the groom but "by the miraculous fact" of union. Love is absent but necessary: "She dimly perceived that all this world was pitifully dependent upon the steady recurrence of the emotion into which she and the boy were drawn."

"Evenings at Home" (1948) is a funny, mock-gothic autobiographical story. "I am here in

Kentucky with my family for the first time in a number of years and, naturally, I am quite uncomfortable,'' it begins. In unexpected ways, the self-conscious intellectual ''I'' is out of place in her own past. Her family, to her horror, ''is entirely healthy and normal,'' not riddled with the hostilities that her childhood memories, filtered through readings in psychology, have led her to expect. Seeing an old boyfriend, she is humiliated to remember ''what kind of man I first fell in love with'': a ''Neanderthal'' who alternated between stupefaction and anarchic laughter. Her old friends are skeptical of her, not, to her relief, because of this former attachment but because of her radical politics. Packing to return to New York, ''the exile for those with evil thoughts,'' she anticipates visiting her brother's grave, a sentimental moment the narrator undercuts with savage humor. She imagines her mother saying, '' 'Sister, I hate to think of you alone in New York, away from your family. But you'll come back to us. There's a space for you next to Brother. . . .' '' The narrator concludes: ''And so it is, as they say, comforting to have roots.''

The aspect of Hardwick's writing of the 1940's most likely to inspire resistance in contemporary readers is her portrayal of African-American characters. Marian's most active moment in *The Ghostly Lover* occurs when her grandmother's housekeeper, Hattie, quits without notice and Marian searches unsuccessfully for her in the black neighborhood. Both in Marian and Hattie's relationship and in ''The People on the Roller Coaster,'' a 1945 short story, southern white women of modest means expect an intimacy with the black women who work for them. Hardwick undermines these historically rooted fantasies: the maternal qualities of those relationships are illusory—something is changing. Hardwick suggests that southern blacks are rejecting servitude; yet her descriptions of black characters are stereotypical in ways we are apt to find objectionable.

Reviewing Richard Wright's *Black Boy* for *Partisan Review* in 1945, Hardwick praises Wright's characterizations in contrast to the narrow portrayal of blacks by white liberals. ''Where the sympathetic white writers felt compelled to deal only with lovable, suffering Negroes, Richard Wright tackled the problem of a full human being subject to fantastic terrors and desires.'' Hardwick praises Wright for overcoming both the rhetoric of communism and the need to speak for ''the black millions,'' a difficult role which, she felt, ''accounts for the appalling naivete of such writers as Zora Neale Hurston, Langston Hughes and Countee Cullen.'' Stressing ''literary'' qualities universalized across racial lines, she finds no value in the aesthetic concerns that arose from the cultural politics of the Harlem Renaissance.

In 1948, reviewing William Faulkner's *Intruder in the Dust,* Hardwick sympathizes with Faulkner's wish to preserve the autonomy of the South. The novel's plot highlights ''the South's appalled recognition of its sins'' toward African Americans, the need of white Southerners to ''save the Negro'' in order to expiate their guilt, and ''the moral superiority'' that suffering has given the victims of oppression. Hardwick insists that Faulkner's vision of ''the final emancipation of the Negro'' is a ''real and historical'' fact that ''only Stalinists and certain liberals'' perversely underestimate. Reading this passage now, after the decades of the civil rights struggle and the subsequent erosion of gains, one might be struck by Hardwick's failure to understand slavery's persistent legacy or to foresee the difficulties that lay ahead. Her resistance to a more pessimistic view of the future of race relations is conditioned by the agenda urgently expressed throughout *Partisan Review* during this period: a critical attack on totalitarianism, particularly Stalinism, a focus that made the *Partisan Review*'s assessment of the problems within American society less than rigorous.

When *Partisan Review* was founded in 1935, its editorial statement promised opposition to war, fascism, decadent culture, and sectarianism, and defense of the USSR. While representing typical positions of the American Communist party, the *Review* editors, Philip Rahv and William Phillips, resisted the Stalinist line that art should serve as political propaganda, a position they believed debased writing and creativity. In 1936 Rahv and Phillips stopped publication of the *Partisan Review;* the next year they started it again with a new, thoroughly anti-Stalinist policy, opposing both the aesthetics and politics of the party. When Stalin signed a pact with Hitler in 1939 and, later, as revelations concerning the bloody oppression of Stalin's regime reached the United States, the American Communist party was weakened. Some refused to believe the evidence against Stalin, while others struggled to maintain belief in leftist principles while recognizing that the Soviet example had failed; some veered away from the Left. The editors of *Partisan Review* used the printed page to identify and condemn, sometimes with more fervor than discrimination, signs of collaboration with communism among writers who had formerly been their political allies. Hardwick brought to *Partisan Review* her credentials as a "reformed Stalinist," having engaged in radical politics in college. The anticommunist agenda, as well as other aspects of the traumatized leftist conscience, entered her reviews.

In the *Partisan Review* (Summer 1946), she praised *The Bitter Box,* a first novel by Eleanor Clark, describing it as an "answer to those people who pride themselves upon never having taken an interest in politics simply because, by their apathy, they were spared disillusionment." Reviewing Paul Goodman's *The State of Nature,* she commented on the intellectual apathy of most writers, the dullness of Goodman's committed writing, and the tendency of social critics to denounce bad taste as vigorously as they denounce totalitarianism. Of the books Hardwick reviewed (in the July–August 1947 issue) Vladimir Nabokov's *Bend Sinister* came closest to transforming an account of totalitarianism into authentic art, but the achievement called into question such traditional literary values as realism and heroism: "Perhaps the totalitarian truth of the Hitler and Stalin governments is, when translated into art, unconvincing, farcically exaggerated beyond belief and purpose. . . ."

By 1948 Hardwick had gained a reputation as a fearsome critic. Her reviews were witty, often biting, and usually negative; she panned established and new writers alike, making frequent disparaging remarks about the general condition of contemporary letters. Elizabeth Bishop, learning that Robert Lowell's stay at the Yaddo artist colony in Saratoga Springs, New York, in the fall would overlap Hardwick's summer stay by a few days, wrote to Lowell: "I forgot to comment on Elizabeth Hardwick's arrival—*take care.*" Instead Lowell cultivated Hardwick's company. He urged her to return to Yaddo and she did, in the winter.

Yaddo had recently been investigated by the FBI, and one of its occasional guests, writer Agnes Smedley, was suspected of being a spy. She was cleared, but the national hysteria that would launch Senator Joseph McCarthy's infamous anticommunist campaign two years later was rising. Lowell became convinced that the Yaddo director, Mrs. Ames, was a sinister figure and, supported by the other guests, including Hardwick, he presented to the board a case for firing Ames. The board refused, recognizing what Hardwick had missed, that Lowell was suffering from paranoia. His mental condition deteriorating, Lowell visited Allen Tate in Chicago, who wrote to Hardwick warning her that Lowell was homicidal. When Lowell's family put him in a Massachusetts mental hospital in April, however, Hardwick stayed near the hospital for two weeks in June of 1949 and visited him often. On July 6 he wrote: "How would you like to be engaged? Like a debutant. WILL YOU?" (This and subsequent correspondence is quoted in Hamilton, *Robert Lowell.*) Hardwick agreed, and they were married three weeks later at Lowell's parents' house in Boston. Hardwick wore a fashionable black hat that Mary McCarthy loaned her. Lowell sank into another depression shortly afterward and was hospitalized again. That the author of *The Ghostly Lover* and "The Mysteries of Eleusis" might have begun married life in a more conventional way is hardly imaginable.

"He certainly needs someone, but if I were you I wouldn't do it," Lowell's doctor had told Hardwick. Lowell's father, dubious about the forthcoming marriage, had written to his son: "I do feel that both you and she, should clearly understand, that if she does marry you, that *she* is responsible for you." Hardwick sustained this responsibility with exhaustive faithfulness.

By January 1950 Lowell was well enough to take a teaching position at the University of Iowa, and he and Hardwick settled into a tiny apartment in Iowa City for the spring semester. They left for a shoestring stay in Europe the next fall, settling in Florence for seven months. Hardwick began writing a novel based on a sensational murder trial she had followed closely in Iowa City, but several years would pass before she could finish it. In the summer of 1951 Lowell, increasingly anxious and weary of Italy, sent Hardwick to Amsterdam to find them a place to live in a country he felt would be closer to his Protestant New England background. While the move prevented Lowell from developing a full-scale manic episode, Hardwick found Holland "a nightmare," and she was delighted when Lowell accepted an invitation to teach at a summer seminar in American studies in Salzburg, Austria. In the spring of 1952 they took in operas and art museums in Brussels, London, Paris, and Vienna, then in July moved on to the eighteenth-century castle where the seminar was held. Exhausted and manic, Lowell became involved with a young music student, Giovanna Madonia; adultery would accompany his manic phases for many years to come. Near the end of the seminar he barricaded himself in his room and American military police were called to get him out. Hardwick accompanied him to a hospital in Munich, then a sanatorium in Switzerland, where he quickly improved.

A year of productive calm followed. Lowell taught at Iowa again, then accepted a position at the University of Cincinnati for the spring of 1954. As the semester began, his mother suffered a stroke and Lowell immediately flew to Italy. She died before he arrived. After discovering that Giovanna Madonia was still obsessed with him, he announced upon his return to Cincinnati that he and Hardwick were separating so that he could marry Madonia. Hardwick moved back to New York, a little relieved until Lowell's long, abusive phone calls convinced her he was ill again. His colleagues at Cincinnati, caught up in his passion, impeded her intervening on his behalf until his behavior—including an incoherent lecture on Hitler—became clearly psychotic. In April Hardwick went with a friend to Cincinnati; once again the police were called and Lowell was hospitalized. Emotionally exhausted, Hardwick wrote to a friend:

> I knew the possibility of this when I married him, and I have always felt that the joy of his "normal" periods, the lovely times we had, all I've learned from him, the immeasurable things I've derived from our marriage made up for the bad periods. I consider it all gain of the most precious kind. But he has torn down this time everything we've built up. . . . Now everyone knows that Cal goes off, says anything degrading he pleases about me, then comes to and I'm to nurse him back to health. There is nothing petty in my resentment of this. . . .

In September Hardwick and Lowell moved to Boston, where Hardwick finished her second novel, noting in a February 1955 letter to a friend that Lowell was "his old self again."

Reviews of *The Simple Truth* (1955) as with Hardwick's first novel, were mixed. Surprisingly for a murder story, the plot is minimal. A wealthy student, Betty Jane Henderson, is dead of asphyxiation and her lower-class boyfriend, Rudy Peck, is on trial for her murder. The solution to the mystery of how the victim died is delivered whole by the accused at the story's end, not pieced together by a forensic mind. Some reviewers saw the novel as a character study of the two obsessive observers of the trial, Joe Parks and Anita Mitchell; others saw the characterization as subordinate to ideas. Parks and Mitchell represent not so much ideas as sensibilities associated with different strains of modern thought. Parks, a vaguely Marxist would-be writer, blames the murder on class conflict, while Mitchell, a faculty wife preoccupied with psychoanalysis, suspects Henderson's self-destructiveness drove her to her fate.

The two observers agree on nothing but that Peck should be freed and that the townspeople lack the intellectual sophistication to judge him fairly. Both are let down when the jury simply accepts Peck's explanation that Henderson died by accident; the observers' analyses of the event required a murder to have taken place. The malaise of the liberal intellect continues and Hardwick again attempts to bare it: the university's rejection of the town's morality masks a deeper reliance on mainstream values to preserve order. One reviewer found Peck's testimony hard to believe. But to believe it, particularly in relation to Hardwick's life, suggests that the chilling "simple truth" she found behind the Iowa City trial was the extraordinary fragility of the female throat. Without consciously intending her any harm, a man can stop a woman's voice and choke out her life.

In the fall of 1955 Hardwick and Lowell bought a house in Boston. Earlier that year Lowell's cousin Harriet Winslow had given them the use of her summer home in Castine, Maine, which she would leave to Hardwick on her death. Lowell began teaching at Boston University in 1956, and on January 4, 1957, Hardwick gave birth to a daughter, Harriet Winslow Lowell. More settled than they had ever been, they took pleasure in entertaining literary guests. "I do like them," Marianne Moore wrote to Elizabeth Bishop after a tea, "heartfelt, generous, genial, initiate and so prepossessing." Lowell was writing a great deal, changing his style, and Hardwick gave extensive editorial advice on his prose pieces.

In December 1957 Lowell threw an impromptu bash at their house. Seventy-two hours later he was still manically awake, and once again Hardwick had to call the police to restrain him. Again he fell in love, this time with a college student doing fieldwork at the hospital, and was convinced that nothing was wrong with him that divorce and remarriage would not cure. By March, however, Hardwick reported that Lowell was "pretty much himself." She planned a trip to Europe the following spring, but the cycle of Lowell's illness continued, and in April 1959 he was back in the hospital. "I do not know the answer to the moral problems posed by a deranged person," Hardwick wrote to Allen Tate after ten years of marriage, "but the dreadful fact is that in purely personal terms this deranged person does a lot of harm. . . . I feel a deep loyalty and commitment to him; and yet at the same time I don't know exactly what sort of bearable status quo I can establish with him."

For reasons that cannot be blamed entirely on the city, Hardwick and Lowell tired of Boston. In January 1961 they bought an apartment on West Sixty-seventh Street in Manhattan, but by February Lowell was "speeding up" and in love again. His new psychiatrist, taking an existential approach, encouraged his delusions. After six weeks in a hospital, Lowell announced to Hardwick that he was going to live with his new love, a young poet named Sandra Hochman. Hardwick returned to Boston, more depressed by this episode than by any previous one. Lowell soon left Hochman and called his doctor saying, "I want to go home." He spent the summer in Castine with Hardwick and their daughter and in October 1961 the family finally settled in New York.

Hardwick continued her own literary work, and one of her projects in 1961, a volume of William James's correspondence for a great letters series, prompted Lowell to weave quotations from James into his poem "For the Union Dead." Throughout the 1950's Hardwick's essays had appeared in *Partisan Review* as well as *Harper's Magazine, The New Republic, The New York Times Book Review, Kenyon Review,* and *The New Yorker*. In 1962, she published a selection from over a decade's work, her style in these essays less analytical than exploratory. As in *The Simple Truth,* the ideas presented in *A View of My Own* are borne along by sensibilities, and specific subjects take on generalized significance.

One reviewer, in doubt about the long-term worth of many of the essays in *A View of My Own,* most enjoyed Hardwick's "hatchet job" on sociologist David Riesman. Concluding that essay, Hardwick takes a swipe at all of sociology:

> I have come to the belief that there is not merely an accidental relationship between bad writing and routine sociological research, but a wonderfully pure, integral relationship; the awkwardness is necessary and inevitable. . . . It is the extreme fragility of the insights that leads to the debasement of language; the need to turn merely interesting and temporary observations into general theory and large application seems to be the source of the trouble with these incredible compositions.

Written in 1954 with a postscript in 1961, the essay is now of value for its coverage of the transition in social atmosphere between the complacent 1950's and the frightened early 1960's, when the proliferation of nuclear weapons caught the attention of social critics. Hardwick is impatient with Riesman's shifting views; a need for firm critical judgments seems to haunt her essays. William James and Bernard Berenson, humanistic thinkers for whom critical valuations were problematic in different ways, serve as representative figures. In the James essay, reprinted from her introduction to the letters, Hardwick finds James so perfectly liberal that exact thought was repugnant to him. The Berenson memoir recalls Hardwick's and Lowell's visits with him when they lived in Florence. An expatriate American, Berenson had used his extensive knowledge of art for commercial purposes, and a reputation, however undeserved, for dishonest valuations clung to him.

As the title suggests in its echo of Virginia Woolf's *A Room of One's Own,* the book has a feminist cast: for a woman to have formed her own critical opinions about culture and society in spite of the constraints under which she labors is an achievement. One reviewer, Melvin Maddocks of the *Chicago Sunday Tribune,* saw in Hardwick's essays a "purified balance of sympathy" that may be "the special function of the woman writer." Astonishing now, after feminist thought has become a complex established fact, is the vehemence with which Hardwick attacks Simone de Beauvoir's *The Second Sex*. De Beauvoir lists the physiological differences between men and women, but claims "they are insufficient for setting up a hierarchy of the sexes . . . they do not condemn her to remain in a subordinate role forever." Hardwick disagrees, in the essay that Didion found so startling; because of their physical inferiority, "women are 'doomed' to situations that promise reasonable safety against the more hazardous possibilities of nature which they are too weak and easily fatigued to endure. . . . Any woman who has ever had her arm twisted by a man''—and who can doubt that Hardwick speaks from experience—''recognizes a fact of nature as humbling as a cyclone to a frail tree branch. How can *anything* be more important than this?'' Women are restricted from experiencing adventure, war, politics, even depravity because of their weaker bodies and, as a result, they make poorer artists. Experiences such as bearing children and nursing the ill, which Hardwick shared with other women, do not make her list of the experiential materials of art.

Even in writing, where women have excelled, common opinion holds that no female author has matched the greatest male authors, and again Hardwick comes down on the side of established judgment, however anxious it may make her as a woman writer. De Beauvoir's writing on artistic women and the traps that limit them is ''brilliant,'' Hardwick concedes, though not enough is made ''of how 'natural' and inevitable their literary limitations are.'' She closed with a grim panorama:

> Coquettes, mothers, prostitutes and 'minor' writers—one sees these faces, defiant or resigned, still standing at the Last Judgment. They are all a little sad, like the Chinese lyric:
>
> *Why do I heave deep sighs?*
> *It is natural, a matter of course, all*
> *creatures have their laws.*

Hardwick's autobiographical concerns are submerged in the essays but come through indirectly, sometimes in surprising ways. In her gripping critique of the complicity of Dylan Thomas' American colleagues in his self-destruction, written in 1956, one hears the authority of the woman who had rescued another mad poet from his worshipers in Cincinnati two years earlier. The essay already most famous before the book came out was ''Boston,'' first published in *Harper's Magazine* in 1959. Hardwick declares the legendary culture of old Boston long dead: the heirs to its past glory, she writes, are weak amateurs; the real Boston is commercial, shabby, and full of bad restaurants. Its most unforgivable fault, one senses, is that it is not New York. Hardwick's fierce satiric spirit is infectious and thorough. But for a moment at the end, she redeems Lowell's birthplace, the city they would wait another two years to leave:

> The weight of the Boston legend, the tedium of its largely fraudulent posture of traditionalism, the disillusionment of the Boston present as a cultural force makes quick minds hesitate to embrace a region too deeply compromised. They are on their guard against falling for it, but meanwhile they can enjoy its very defects, its backwardness, its slowness, its position as one of the large, possible cities on the Eastern seacoast, its private, residential charm. They speak of going to New York and yet another season finds them holding back, positively enjoying the Boston life. . . .

In the summer of 1962, traveling in South America, Lowell again ''sped up'' and was hospitalized. The exhausting cycle continued. But the move to New York, Hardwick said, ''saved my life.'' When a long newspaper strike shut down *The New York Times Book Review,* a group of writers, including Hardwick, founded *The New York Review of Books* early in 1963. The *Review* would become a leading, controversial intellectual journal.

The need, as the founders saw it, was not just for another journal, but for a different kind of journal. In ''The Decline of Book Reviewing,'' which she wrote in 1959 for a *Harper's* special supplement, ''Writing in America,'' Hardwick outlined the background that would shape the new publication. A survey of book reviews showed that 51 percent were positive, only 4.7

percent were negative, and a startling 44.3 percent were noncommittal. "Sweet, bland commendations fall everywhere upon the scene; a universal, if somewhat lobotomized, accommodation reigns," Hardwick wrote. "A book is born into a puddle of treacle; the brine of hostile criticism is only a memory." The commercial interests of the book trade could not, Hardwick felt, be blamed for the indiscriminate distribution of praise; publicity, not reviews, sold books. Editors lacking literary knowledge had replaced the "drama of opinion" with a blandly democratic idea of "coverage," and reviews lacked the "involvement, passion, character, eccentricity" that constitute literary style. Reviewers for the London *Times Literary Supplement,* in contrast, were intellectually secure, unconcerned that the majority of English citizens might not share their interests.

Hardwick's vision for the literary journal is frankly elitist:

> The communication of the delight and importance of books, ideas, culture itself, is the very least one would expect from a journal devoted to reviewing of new and old works. Beyond that beginning, the interest of the mind of the individual reviewer is everything. Book reviewing is a form of writing. . . . It *does* matter what an unusual mind, capable of presenting fresh ideas in a vivid and original and interesting manner, thinks of books as they appear.

Hardwick granted that superficial literary comment may have its place in small-town papers, but "for the great metropolitan publications, the unusual, the difficult, the lengthy, the intransigent, and above all, the *interesting,* should expect to find their audience."

The first issue of *The New York Review of Books,* pasted up in Hardwick's dining room and financed with a four-thousand-dollar bank loan, was published in February 1963. A roster of forty-four distinguished writers—among them Norman Mailer, Mary McCarthy, Susan Sontag, Gore Vidal, and Robert Penn Warren—appeared under the masthead. Hardwick and Lowell were on the board of directors with the publisher, A. Whitney Ellsworth; Barbara Epstein and Robert Silvers were the coeditors; also included was Epstein's husband Jason. Hardwick was the advisory editor. Over forty thousand copies sold, a phenomenal reception for a little-publicized new "highbrow" publication, and the founders received more than a thousand letters encouraging its continuation. In the following months they sold stock to investors, and published a second special issue in June. Regular biweekly publication began with the third issue, September 26, 1963. Within three years the *Review* was running in the black and its circulation topped eighty thousand in 1968.

Despite its impressive list of associates, the *Review*'s early issues suffered from a shortage of reviewers, and a core group—most of them former *Partisan Review* colleagues—found themselves evaluating one another's books, sometimes with discomfiting consequences. On successive pages R. W. Flint reviewed Adrienne Rich's poems, Rich reviewed Paul Goodman's, and Goodman reported on Toronto. Xavier Prynne lampooned both Mary McCarthy and Norman Mailer, and Mailer panned McCarthy's now best-known novel, *The Group.* Learning that Xavier Prynne was actually Elizabeth Hardwick, McCarthy felt betrayed. The editors, searching for additional talent, turned to Great Britain; the low pay that the *Review* could afford to offer was worth more in London than in New York. By the fifth issue the names of such distinguished British intellectuals as A. J. P. Taylor, V. S. Naipaul, A. Alvarez, and Stephen Spender had begun to appear in the table of contents.

Even in the grief-filled Kennedy memorial issue devoted to "the present crisis in America," the *Review* from 1963 to 1964 expressed guarded optimism: social progress was seen as genuine, if imperfect; and angry, bitter voices such as James were criticized for potentially inciting violence. But a period of massive change had begun, and the multitude of social problems that would make the late 1960's tumultuous found increasing coverage in *The New York Review of Books*. Hardwick visited Selma, Alabama, in 1965 and reported on a civil rights demonstration. An uneasiness about how to evaluate the civil rights movement edges her essay "The Charms of Goodness" (collected in *Bartleby in Manhattan and Other Essays,* 1983), revealing some of the cognitive dissonance that liberal New York intellectuals faced in articulating the issues at stake in the social change of the decade.

> The intellectual life in New York and the radical tone of the Thirties are the worst possible preparation for Alabama at this stage of the Civil Rights Movement. In truth it must be said that the demonstrators are an embarrassment of love and brotherhood and hymns offered up in Jesus' name and evening services after that. Intellectual pride is out of place, theory is simple and practical, action is exuberant and communal. . . .

Articles on Vietnam, civil rights, and student protest increased through 1965 and 1966, and by 1967 every issue reflected the urgency of political and social concerns. At Hardwick's insistence, the *Review* sent Mary McCarthy to Vietnam; her reports began appearing in April 1967. A new split among liberals was widening over Vietnam: the moderate position advocated negotiations for South Vietnamese self-determination but claimed public demonstrations and draft resistance in the United States would "comfort" the enemy, while the radical position advocated such public activism, refusing to take an anticommunist stance. A similar division occurred with relation to the civil rights movement. Its pages full of the drama of opinion, *The New York Review of Books* moved toward the radical position.

The most divisive issue, published on August 24, 1967, included an article by Andrew Kopkind critical of Martin Luther King's pacifism and one by Tom Hayden sympathetic to the frustration in the Newark ghetto that had erupted into riots in July. On the cover was a schematic of a Molotov cocktail. Hardwick contended that the cover was a statement against violence, but its irony was lost on many readers. Some liberals viewed the drawing, in combination with the articles, as editorial support for revolutionary violence. To some the elegantly drawn homemade bomb meant that radicalism had become fashionable and the intelligentsia were keeping step with the times. Journalist Tom Wolfe would describe *The New York Review of Books* as "the chief theoretical organ of radical chic." Advertising for subscribers, the *Review* traded on its controversial reputation. The ad copy under a photograph of a Roman statue thumbing its nose read: "*The New York Review of Books* has been called cliquish, intellectual, opinionated, and snobbish. For $7.50 a year you can be too."

In 1968 the assassinations of Martin Luther King and Robert Kennedy called on the *Review* to eulogize two leaders who had been criticized in its pages for not being sufficiently radical. Hardwick attended the memorial march for King in Memphis, Tennessee, and his funeral in Atlanta. "The political non-violence of Martin Luther King was an act of brilliant intellectual conviction, very sophisticated and yet perfectly consistent with evangelical religion," she wrote in "The Apotheosis of Martin Luther King" (in *Bartleby in Manhattan*), countering the August 1967 writer's denigration of King's pacifism. His death inspired an outpouring of legislative and financial support for civil rights, and also eruptions of mass rage: "In 125 cities there was burning and looting." A new, militant rhetoric, "probably a lasting repudiation of empty courtesy and bureaucratic euphemism,'' was replacing King's style of practical exhortation based on a tradition of spiritual simplicity. Hardwick's conclusion brings to mind her position on the South in the 1948 review of Faulkner: perhaps, she suggests, the funeral in Atlanta marked ''the waning of the slow, sweet dream'' that southern Christianity could save ''the Negro masses'' from oppression.

Over the next two years radical pieces were overbalanced by cautionary analyses in *The New York Review of Books:* revolutionary disruption in the United States would bring on martial law, structural institutional change was needed, violence would not do. In a 1973 interview with Philip Nobile about the *Review*'s politics (in *Intellectual Skywriting*), Hardwick answered ''The politics are very sensible. They're violently antiwar, and that's about it. We all stand for the same thing—civilization.''

Many of Hardwick's essays for *The New York Review of Books* are collected in *Seduction and Betrayal* and *Bartleby in Manhattan*. She also wrote film and book reviews for *Vogue* during this period, and in 1967 she became the first woman to receive the George Jean Nathan Award for drama criticism. Read in the context of the compelling social concerns that preoccupied *The New York Review of Books,* her theater pieces are stunning for their insistence that a production, whether of an old or a new play, should confront its audience with problems of the historical meaning of the present. Her high standards were rarely met. An April 2, 1964, article lambasting the new Repertory Theater at Lincoln Center concluded, with high wit: ''Do not take hope. . . . The gods, parceling out their gifts, clearly do not mean for America to be purged of pity and terror by drama. For that, destiny has sent us TV.''

For the 1965–1966 season the Repertory Theater chose several difficult political plays. Hardwick commended their effort but lamented, ''That the company suffered from a peculiar literalness was a great sadness.'' Hardwick's reviews drew out of the plays the effects that the stagings had failed to produce. Writing for the *Review* on *The Condemned of Altona,* Jean-Paul Sartre's play on German post-holocaust guilt, Hardwick found chilling parallels to the contemporary American conscience:

> Our century . . . seems to be leading us to a true meeting with guilt, leading us to suffering, to acquaintance with the sorrows and mysteries and miseries to which *hubris* and power have led other nations. . . . It appears that we do not—neither director nor actor, neither audience nor critic—understand what is happening here. . . .

As the 1966–1967 season opened, Hardwick attacked the opinion-shaping power of the drama critics of daily newspapers, noting particularly that Walter Kerr of the *Times* disliked experimental theater. The need for theater to challenge the conventions of commercial culture runs through Hardwick's reviews of the season. She found naturalistic acting—playing to the audience's emotions—is inadequate for a drama of historical horrors such as Peter Weiss's *The Investigation,* based on testimony about the Auschwitz death camp, which Hardwick reviewed in November of 1966. In December she attacked sentimentality, which infected even protest dramas. The immediate antidote she found was *Kill for Peace,* a ''wildly funny'' performance by the protest-rock group the Fugs. How, she wondered, could a Broadway lyricist such as Alan Lerner carry on after the Fugs's ''My Baby Done Left Me and I Feel Like Home-Made Shit'' had aired? At the end of the season she praised twenty-three-year-old Sam Shepherd's *La Turista*—both play and production—which she attended despite the company's unconventional refusal to extend formal invitations to drama critics. The sense of order one used to expect from high culture, Hardwick reflected, no longer had a place among serious writers. Order was now a property of commercial culture; what one found in the best experimental work was a disarrayed wealth of "despair and humor."

Hardwick did not cover the 1967–1968 drama season in New York, but in February she reviewed a production in Washington, D.C., of Howard Sackler's *The Great White Hope,* a play based on the life of the black fighter, Jack Johnson, whose winning of the 1908 World Heavyweight Championship humiliated white boxing fans. Real life, old and new theatricality, could not be separated in the boxing world, and the director had "*consciously*—and that is the art of it—been contented to leave it all there, corrupted, sentimentalized, full of the shabbiest folklore." Hardwick's "New York part" looked to Europe for models of high culture, and to this side of her, *The Great White Hope* was puzzling "in the somehow sweet acceptance of the grossest artistic deformations of our immediate past." But she felt that "a longing to see the reality of American experience on the stage attends . . . every entrance into a theater," and this play satisfied that longing. Writing the review brought out her Kentucky side; she was deeply interested in the play's revitalization of the "moribund" materials of popular American culture. Visiting Lexington a year later, she wrote "Going Home in America," an essay she later transformed for her third novel. Erasing the years of exile, "This was, is, truly home to me, not just a birthplace," she began. In the anguish of divisive social turmoil, America, with Hardwick, was searching for itself.

Hardwick was losing interest in drama criticism. Looking back on the season, she wrote in June 1968 in an essay, "Notes on the New Theater," "The most interesting works are not interesting to write about: they are bits and pieces of scene and action. Criticism lives on plot, character, and theme." Avant-garde theater, "rooted in Hippydom—innocent nudity, ingratiating obscenity, charming poverty"—was hard put to keep up with "the far reaches of tragedy and farce" being played out in real life. The theater of alienation was too austere and intellectual for "Hippydom"; instead the new theater worked for audience participation, "a substitution for a loss we are all trying to forget," the loss of coherence in both art and life. *Beard,* a farce on sexual liberation in which Jean Harlow and Billy the Kid meet in the afterlife, "chained in repetition, their minds in eternity fixed on F...ing," Hardwick notes as one of the season's highlights. "In the play's prison of everlasting sex, there is an appallingly genuine metaphysical conception. 'If we don't do what we want, we're not divine,' Billy the Kid says." She also attended two shows in which several roles were played in drag, *When Queens Collide* and *Conquest of the Universe,* and found the staging, acting, and costuming brilliantly imaginative: "The texts are fantastic parodies of politics, drama, history, sex, films and the entertainments have, in the end, the profoundest authenticity." Of traditional theater she wrote simply, "no relief in sight."

Hardwick's marriage continued along much the same pattern as before. Hospitalized shortly after the assassination of President Kennedy, Lowell confided to friends that President Johnson had appointed him to the cabinet. A messy affair with a dancer accompanied a manic episode in January 1965. Again, Lowell's psychiatrist indulged his infatuation. Hardwick resigned herself to his leaving her, but when he wanted to come home she welcomed him. In December he fell in love again, but this time his object was the safely inaccessible Jacqueline Kennedy. There were hospitalizations in January and December 1966. Lithium carbonate, a new treatment for manic-depression, became available in 1967, and it kept Lowell out of the hospital for four years.

When Lowell took a position at Oxford University in the spring of 1970, Hardwick resigned from her teaching position at Barnard College and waited in New York for him to settle their living arrangements. Learning in June that Lowell was living with Lady Caroline Blackwood, Hardwick did not reserve her anger. She sent him stinging cables and letters full of contempt. Lowell was hospitalized in July, and Hardwick, hearing that the conditions at the hospital were poor, flew to London. Finding the hospital satisfactory, she returned to New York, leaving Lowell a note: "If you need me, I'll always be there, if you don't, I'll not be there." Over the fall Lowell's letters vacillated from "I don't think I can go back to you" to "I wonder if we couldn't make it up." Hardwick by year's end was certain: the split was final.

On September 28, 1971, Caroline Blackwood bore a son, Sheridan Lowell. Hardwick and Lowell divorced in October 1972 and Lowell married Blackwood. In July 1973 three books of Lowell's poetry, *History, For Lizzie and Harriet,* and *The Dolphin,* were published. In some of the poems, Lowell had appropriated and rephrased passages from letters Hardwick had written him during their breakup. "The inclusion of the letter poems stands as one of the most vindictive and mean-spirited acts in the history of poetry," Adrienne Rich, by this time radically feminist, wrote for *American Poetry Review.* Hardwick was deeply hurt by the poems' publication. She told Lowell she never wanted to hear from him again and denounced his publishers.

Read in connection with Hardwick's life, *Seduction and Betrayal,* a selection of her essays for *The New York Review of Books* from 1970 to 1974, takes on multiple meanings. As a contribution to the growing body of literary criticism associated with the women's movement, the essays lack the polemical focus of such feminists as Adrienne Rich and Kate Millett. The difference is partly one of style: although anger is everywhere present, it is channeled through Hardwick's oblique and resonant sentences—direct ideological argument is rare. The essays explore the experiences of literary women and heroines, experiences so often resembling Hardwick's own that sentences leap off the page, charged with double entendre. That the book was reprinted as late as 1990 is significant: by then the urgency for a polemical agenda in feminist criticism had lessened and more feminist critics were turning instead to the effort of constructing the history of women as writers and thinkers. *Seduction and Betrayal* enters that history doubly, both as an account of historical and fictional women and as the work of a woman who had built her intellectual career before feminism began to be institutionalized as an academic discipline. The book is also, irresistibly, a piece of imaginative writing with its author's own journey mapped between the lines.

"The sisters seized upon the development of their talents as an honorable way of life and in this they were heroic," Hardwick concludes of the Brontës. Compared with the little that the "real world" offered serious, impoverished women, their confined lives had a kind of freedom which they turned, by a "practical, industrious, ambitious cast of mind," into literary careers. "To be female: What does it mean?" Hardwick finds Henrik Ibsen posing this problem and uses his female characters to discuss women's relations with men. Nora Helmer of *A Doll's House* (1879) is practical and independent, despite her domesticity, taking pride "in having assumed responsibility for her husband's life." Thea in *Hedda Gabler* (1890) finds "purpose for her own intellectual possibilities" by playing nursemaid to the "damaged artist," Lövborg. In *Rosmersholm* (1886) Rebecca West, desperate for both a home and a cause worthy of her high-minded intelligence, lights on a married man. The outcome is sordid, exposing "the pathetic false hopes of the heroines that by possession and appropriation they would possess themselves." The wife, Beata, dead of suicide before the play begins, is an omnipresent moral force in Hardwick's essay. She condemns the adulterous lovers with finality: "nothing will turn out to have been worth the destruction of others and of oneself."

"Living as a sort of twin, as husband and wife, or brother and sister, is a way of survival," Hardwick writes of Zelda Fitzgerald.

In the case of artists these intense relations are curiously ambivalent, undefined collaborations —the two share in perceptions, temperament, in the struggle for creation, for the powers descending downward from art, for reputation, achievement, stability, for their own uniqueness—that especially. Still, only one of the twins is real as an artist, as a person with a special claim upon the world, upon the indulgence of society.

F. Scott Fitzgerald appropriated letters and journals of Zelda's in his writing, and William Wordsworth used his sister Dorothy's journals. Hardwick does not condemn these incursions outright because the women in these unbalanced partnerships could never, she claims, have been great artists: Zelda was an inferior talent despite her strong creative drives, which were pitiably suppressed, and Dorothy's dependency held back her capacity to make meaning of her perceptions, a task her brother executed with brilliance. But the "illusion" of collaborating with William offered Dorothy fulfillments that one should not, Hardwick cautions, downplay. In the marriage of Jane and Thomas Carlyle, "a collaboration of superior, tortured souls," Jane undertook "an original adventure for which credit was due her." The unhappiness of her last years came from her husband's ungrateful neglect: "In the long run wives are to be paid in a peculiar coin—consideration for their feelings. And it usually turns out this is an enormous, unthinkable inflation few men will remit, or if they will, only with a sense of being overcharged."

The last essay in the collection, "Seduction and Betrayal," is a catalog of tragic heroines and an elegy for virtues that are no longer required. Hester Prynne is exemplary for "the striking skepticism of her mind, the moral distance she sets between herself and the hysterias of the time." Bourgeois fiction asks of the heroine a stoicism more complex than passion: "a sense of reality, a curious sort of independence and honor, an acceptance of consequence that puts courage to the most searing test." Her purity is not sexual but "a lack of mean calculations, of vindictiveness, of self-abasing weakness." Female heroism can act as a reproach; when her moving virtues "are called upon, it is usual for the heroine to overshadow the man who is the origin of her torment." Sexual cause-and-effect is the origin of her suffering, and biology is destiny only for girls; "the men do not really believe in consequence for themselves." Today, Hardwick claims, innocence is no longer a value, and contraceptive technology has removed the inevitability of the consequences of sex. Long-suffering heroism "hurts and no one easily consents to be under its rule," Hardwick writes. Stoicism still has its uses, but "improvisation is better, more economical, faster, more promising."

Hardwick's own long-suffering, heroic loyalty has been given its place in literary history by Lowell's critics and biographers. One after another they pause from their scholarly tasks to register incredulity that Hardwick stayed with him for so long. Jeffrey Meyers in *Manic Power: Robert Lowell and His Circle,* offers a range of speculations: "Hardwick's surpassing love, frenetic fidelity, devotion merging into martyrdom, humiliating masochism, unlimited capacity for suffering and endurance made her the tragic heroine of his life."

But one might take *Seduction and Betrayal* as a caution not to underestimate the rewards of Hardwick's "collaboration" with the troubled poet to whom she devoted so much care.

The mystery of Hardwick's relationship with Lowell did not end with their divorce. By the spring of 1976 they were on speaking terms. When Lowell suffered congestive heart failure in January 1977, Hardwick visited him in the hospital. Although Lowell returned to Caroline Blackwood over Easter, he decided their marriage should end. In July he and Hardwick traveled to Moscow as members of an American delegation to the Union of Soviet Writers. They spent the rest of the summer together in Castine, which over the years had become the favored summer retreat of many of their old friends. Visiting Blackwood in early September, Lowell became restless and phoned Hardwick to say he was returning to New York. He died in the taxi from the airport to the apartment on West Sixty-seventh Street.

From its first sentences, Hardwick's third novel, *Sleepless Nights,* shows her continued working out of the changing values she wrote about in *Seduction and Betrayal.* The novel begins on a note of improvisation: "It is June. This is what I have decided to do with my life just now. I will do this work of transformed and even distorted memory and lead this life, the one I am leading today." Virtually all of the critical ideas about change in literary form that Hardwick had developed during the twenty-five-year interim since the publication of her second novel are synthesized in her third. If plot was a weakness in *The Ghostly Lover* and *The Simple Truth,* the repudiation of plot is the strength of *Sleepless Nights.* Carol Simpson Stern suggests that the earlier novels "show a niggling regret on the author's part that the story is not a little more important," but in *Sleepless Nights* "ordinary experience needs no apology." Hardwick's disagreement with Simone de Beauvoir over the limits of female experience remains firm, except that now—as in *Seduction and Betrayal*—that rich experience is worth recording, and the abolition of the conventions of fictional narrative frees writing for the purpose.

"Can it be that I am the subject?" Hardwick (or her narrator, Elizabeth) writes, a little astonished. "True, with the weak something is always happening: improvisation, surprise, suspense, injustice, manipulation, hypochondria, secret drinking, jealousy, lying, crying, hiding in the garden, driving off in the middle of the night. The weak have the purest sense of history. Anything can happen." Books, places, and the people for whom Elizabeth has a "prying sympathy" constitute her experience, which lacks the drama of an adventure on the high seas, "But after all, 'I' am a woman."

Critics have puzzled over how to classify *Sleepless Nights,* at once experimental in form and as stylistically controlled as any of Hardwick's other writing. It is fiction so transparently autobiographical that the category of fiction falls away, replaced by memory, so that the novel resembles a series of personal essays. Although Elizabeth tells her own story only peripherally, she is everywhere in the production of the sentences, much as Hardwick's presence in her essays comes through not from self-description but from her observations, judgments, and arrangements of words. Whereas in Hardwick's critical work self-reflexivity generates double meanings, in *Sleepless Nights* the reflexivity is explicit. Sleeplessly writing to "those whom I dare not ring up until morning and yet must talk to throughout the night," Elizabeth exposes the vulnerabilities behind Hardwick's polished style. She observes that the drunken Canadians who have recently shared a train car with her are not prosperous: "I am sure of that from my unworthy calculations based on the arithmetic of snobbery and shame." The emotional stratum of style is shame: " 'Shame is inventive,' Nietzsche said. And that is scarcely the half of it. From shame I have paid attention to clothes, shoes, rings, watches, accents, teeth, points of deportment, turns of speech." But the emotional stratum of style is also grief. At the end of the novel Elizabeth writes to M., identified with Mary Mc-

Carthy through the novel's dedication: ''Why is it that we cannot keep the note of irony, the jangle of carelessness at a distance? Sentences in which I have tried for a certain light tone—many of those have to do with events, upheavals, destructions that caused me to weep like a child.''

Should *Sleepless Nights* read as biography? Hardwick seems to offer the novel as a counterpoise to the known events of her life, the story that can be garnered from, say, an index to Lowell's biography or a scholarly guide to the events behind his letter poems. Through Elizabeth, she writes: ''Sometimes I resent the glossary, the concordance of truth, many have about my real life, have like an extra pair of spectacles. I mean that such fact is to me a hindrance to memory.'' The book's episodes fill in the textures of different times and places that are part of Hardwick's life, without quite allowing the reader to treat these details as fact. Yet no plot, no message—nothing other than their air of authenticity and the urgency with which Elizabeth tells them—justifies their presence in the book. It is as if Hardwick not only abolishes the convention of plot but also complicates the convention of a persona, a fictional narrator who is not the author, by making her narrator difficult to distinguish from herself. She seems to have used such displacement techniques—identified with postmodern writing—to speak directly while maintaining uncertainty about what the truth is, both preserving and protecting the details of her own life that had not become famous because of her association with Lowell.

In Lexington, a mother with ''fateful fertility,'' assertive in her profound acceptance of nature's dominance, is utterly indifferent to the past. Many brothers and sisters slip in late, ''each one gorged on a petty vanity, the fantasies of being an orphan.'' About the Kentucky Derby, thoroughbreds, gambling, and Dostoyevsky, Elizabeth notes, ''It is true that only one out of a hundred wins, but what is that to me?'' An older man, the one Bruce in *The Ghostly Lover* is based on, introduces Elizabeth to '' 'experience,' and I gathered that what is meant is an attraction to something contrary to oneself, usually a being or habit lower, more dangerous, risky.'' In college, two members of the Communist party in Cincinnati visit Lexington to observe organizing in the South. Elizabeth has read all the pamphlets. A poor Scotch-Irish family from Appalachia replaces all the usual passions with politics, their invalid son swimming in communist texts. In New York Elizabeth wakes up longing for her mother. She lives with a gay friend from home in the sleazy Hotel Schuyler and together they haunt clubs, watching Billie Holiday's ''luminous self-destruction'' up close. She says to herself during these years:

> In my heart I was weasel-like, hungry, hunting with blazing eyes for innocent contradictions, given to predatory chewings on the difference between theory and practice. That is what I had brought from home in Kentucky to New York, this large bounty of polemicism, stored away behind light, limp Southern hair and not-quite-blue eyes.

Sex is ''evangelical,'' to be had, not enjoyed. There is an abortion performed by a cheerful, cigar-smoking practitioner who also runs a funeral home. In Amsterdam couples combine, separate, and recombine under each other's noses because there is nowhere else to go. An elderly roué remarks of his shrewish wife, ''They don't forgive you after all. They have their revenge.'' Back in Castine, Ida hauls the laundry of the summer residents to her bungalow on a hill. She also takes in Herman, a ne'er-do-well who eventually robs her. Elizabeth writes: ''A few hours ago I made the journey to Ida's house, knocked on the latched screen door and felt something close to fright coming over me. Oh, God, there she is, homely, homely, scabby with a terrible skin rash. . . . Her large, muscled arms hold me for a moment in a pounding embrace.''

In the present, Elizabeth greets a bag lady who used to be her neighbor. Phone conversations, visits, parties: ''Divorces and separation—that is the way to get attention.'' Three hundred or more photographs lie in desks, in chests, in marked envelopes, bearing witness to the form of marriage.

Sleepless Nights earned superlative reviews and a National Book Critics Circle Award nomination. To account for the novel's unusual form, Joan Didion described ''The method of the 'I' '' as ''that of the anthropologist, of the traveler on watch for the revealing detail: we are provided precise observations of strangers met in the course of the journey, close studies of their rituals.'' Didion compared *Sleepless Nights* to Claude Lévi-Strauss's *Tristes Tropiques,* an apt comparison reinforced by Hardwick's having written about Lévi-Strauss in ''Sad Brazil,'' a 1974 essay she revised for *Bartleby in Manhattan.* To Hardwick *Tristes Tropiques* is as much a journey of self-discovery as a record of observations. The observable facts, even in remote, primitive parts of the New World, have an air of deterioration, shattered bonds, loss. Lévi-Strauss self-critically questions the coherence and validity of his own position as an investigator, a reflexivity that, like Elizabeth's, is filled with sadness. Another piece in *Bartleby in Manhattan* that supplies critical background to *Sleepless Nights* is ''The Sense of the Present,'' a series of very short essays exploring the changing formal, psychological, and critical issues that define postmodern fiction. She finds that paranoia has replaced guilt as a central character feature, events accumulate randomly with little deference to the conventions of genre, a ''strict ear for banalities'' connects the extreme and the ordinary to form a kind of history. Though we may be happier reading classic nineteenth-century novels, Hardwick writes, ''It is important to concede the honor, the nerve, the ambition'' of writers such as Kurt Vonnegut, Donald Barthelme, Renata Adler, and Thomas Pynchon. What is honorable in their works ''is the intelligence that questions the shape of life at every point.''

The twenty-four essays in *Bartleby in Manhattan* serve as a retrospective of the literary and social concerns—always joined—that Hardwick articulated over the twenty-year span from the founding of *The New York Review of Books* to their publication in book form. The book opens with Hardwick's 1965 and 1968 essays on Selma, Alabama, and on Martin Luther King for the *Review* and includes a selection of her drama criticism. In 1971, at the peak of conservative and moderate attacks on the *Review,* Hardwick wrote ''Militant Nudes,'' an omnibus film review that should have discredited any charges that the *Review*'s attitude toward chic radicalism was uncritical:

> Professor Theodor W. Adorno, at the University of Frankfurt, was, not long before his death, the audience for—or the object of—a striking bit of symbolic action. Adorno, a distinguished philosopher and the teacher of many leftist students, had come to be worried about student zeal for immediate action, about spontaneity, random rebellion, and, of course, the possibility of repressive actions by the government. And how was the sacred old father rebuked? A girl got up in the classroom and took off her clothes.

Hardwick uses the incident to frame her dialectical critique of radical sexuality and militancy. Sexuality has become a political abstraction, the young body ''a class moving into the forefront of history,'' while militant rhetoric has become a mystical and coercive apocalyptic ''program'' that kills ''the uses of reality. . . .'' Like GI's weary of waiting to be sent to Vietnam, young radicals take up compulsive sex and violent activism as ''tours of active duty at last,'' only to compound their alienation. The consequence is moral numbness and indifference to pain. "There is death everywhere," Hardwick writes of *Gimme Shelter,* the documentary film about the Rolling Stones concert at Altamont Speedway, where violence ended the benign dreams of the 1960's counterculture.

> Something pitiless and pathological has seeped into youth's love of itself, its body, its politics. . . . You feel a transcendental joke links us all together; some sordid synthesis hangs out there in the heavy air. No explanation—the nuclear bomb, the Vietnam war, the paralyzing waste of problems and vices that our lives and even the virtues of our best efforts have led us to—explains. Yet it would be dishonorable to try to separate our selves from our deforming history and from the depressing dreams being acted out in its name.

Hardwick vindicated the *Review*'s immersion in contemporary culture: however anguished and inexplicable the historic moment, criticism must not repudiate it but participate.

"Casualties of every spiritual and personal nature lay about us as the legacy of the sixties," Hardwick wrote as the following decade waned. "Domestic Manners," like "Militant Nudes," a strongly dialectical essay, describes the 1970's retreat into intimacy and narcissism, ego validation in private relationships and schemes for self-improvement, in search of "remission of aches of the mind and psyche." The anarchic sexuality of the 1960's had been transformed into a sexual information business whose purpose was to enhance family life, to support, not oppose, social stability. But the family is a meaningless generalization, Hardwick points out, namely "because the classes are so far apart in the scenery in which daily life takes place." In the cities poverty breeds a "dangerous criminal insanity" that randomly victimizes mainly the poor; "a vibrant, ferocious, active, heartbreaking insanity is as much a part of the seventies as intimacy, retreat to the private." And family life has been changing for several decades; the women's movement crystallized the corresponding changes that had occurred both in the inner lives of women and in the roles society needed them to play. The movement's positions on economic equality should be welcomed by a society in which "the wife economy is as obsolete as the slave economy." The "more devastating" challenge to custom is the great critical potential of feminism. Hardwick concludes "Domestic Manners" stating,

> The women's movement is above all a critique. And almost nothing, it turns out, will remain outside its relevance. It is the disorienting extension of the intrinsic meaning of women's liberation, much of it unexpected, that sets the movement apart. It is a psychic and social migration, leaving behind an altered landscape.

"Wives and Mistresses" extends the concerns of *Seduction and Betrayal* and has the same near-transparent quality of being drawn acutely from Hardwick's own life. As in *Sleepless Nights,* the biographer searching for the facts and themes of the life of her subject is caught in self-consciousness: embedded in Hardwick's texts are critical reflections on the problems of producing biography. She opens "Wives and Mistresses" with an epigraph from Boris Pasternak's *Zhivago Poems:*

> For who are we, and where from,
> If after all these years
> Gossip alone still lives on
> While we no longer live?

Hardwick does not shrink from relating the gossip: Countess Tolstoy's campaign to defend herself against her husband's humiliating representations of her, Lady Byron's lifelong campaign to smear a husband of one year, Olga Ivinskaya's restless idealization of Pasternak—in none of these examples does the woman's actions give her an appeal independent of the man's greatness. Yet Hardwick excavates these cases in an attempt to understand the significance of how wives and mistresses are the "footnotes" of great men's lives, selecting women with whom she has in common a central experience, then sorting through the anguishes, dangers, and downfalls of different manifestations of that experience. The essay has a double ending. In the first, Hardwick tells of Nadezha Mandelstam, wife of the Soviet poet Osip Mandelstam, who was murdered in prison. Nadezha writes to him just before she learns of his death: "In my last dream I was buying food for you in a filthy hotel restaurant. . . . When I had bought it, I realized I did not know where to take it, because I do not know where you are. When I woke up, I said to Shura, 'Osia is dead.' . . . It's me, Nadia. Where are you? Farewell." Mandelstam, her memoirs a brilliant "battle against tyranny and death," is more than an exemplary case; her letter supplies Hardwick's essay with a release of grief. But another end follows the letter, a brief postscript on husbands' memoirs of great women—banal, self-serving, no better than most of the female "footnotes" had been.

The emotional clarity of Mandelstam's letter draws attention to the complexity of feeling throughout this powerful essay, inviting an imaginative reading. As usual—to the bafflement of some reviewers—Hardwick does not argue and conclude; the interplay of epigrammatic examples, impressions, and valuations that structure her criticism more often resembles the method of a prose poem or story than an academic essay. Marriage, conflicted and inauthentic feeling, death and mourning, then recomplication: women cannot come into their own by publicizing their suffering in intimacy with great men, nor can they, great themselves, expect men to do justice to their memory; what matters is authenticity of feeling and a critical practice of one's own. While it would be a disservice to reduce any of Hardwick's writing merely to encoded tellings of her own life, in "Wives and Mistresses" she seems to have recorded the difficulties she herself faced in marriage, to have grieved, and to have distinguished herself from the "footnotes," preempting autobiography with critical thought.

Though Elizabeth Hardwick has written infrequently since the early 1980's for *The New York Review of Books* she has remained an advisory editor. When *The Best American Essays* series was founded in 1986, Hardwick was suitably chosen as the editor of the first volume. Her introduction defines the essay form, ancient, prolific, but not quite legitimate, characterized by epigram, comparison, and example. The form differs from journalism in that information is not the object: "We consent to watch a mind at work, without agreement often, but only for pleasure. Knowledge hereby attained, great indeed, is again wanted for the pleasure of itself." The essayist shares with poets and fiction writers a compulsion "to animate the stones of an idea, the clods of research, the uncertainty of memory," but must do this magic without rhyme or assonance, character or plot. And while "the usual miserable battering of the sense of self" is enough to supply the content of a story or poem, the essay requires a mind full of diverse knowledge, particularly of the history of the essay form itself. In "essayistic" writing, an author takes liberties for the sake of expression—"freedoms illicit in the minds of some readers, freedoms not so much exercised as seized over the border." An essayist aggressively assumes "the authority to speak in one's own voice," Hardwick writes. The authority to express oneself is self-justifying, in that a writer earns it by a career of exercising it. In contemporary essays, Hardwick writes, authority divides against itself: buried in the sentences "is an intelligence uncomfortable with dogmatism, wanting to make allowances for the otherwise case, the emendation." Use of the first person is one way writers retract their authority to make room for the reader's participation. Style is another way. As Hardwick suggested of Mary McCarthy, writing that promotes controversial ideas risks being rejected by its audience, a risk that style mitigates: "The mastery of expository prose, the rhythm of sentences, the pacing, the sudden flash of unexpected vocabulary, redeem polemic, and, in any case, no one is obliged to agree." But stylistic mastery selects its audience, who must match the writer's mind in sophistication: "Wit, the abrupt reversal, needs to strike a receptive ear or eye or else the surprise is erased, struck down." Here is the "above all *interesting*" —to quote Hardwick's re-excitement of a tired word—paradox at the heart of a career such as hers that blends feminism into lifelong liberal intellectualism: to publish essays is to cultivate an audience that shares your privileged knowledge of history, culture, and ideas, to constitute an elite. The aggressiveness of the essay form is imperialistic insofar as that elite imposes itself on others it labels its inferiors; subversive insofar as the properties of culture and intellect stand as a critique informing an unjust society that it is wrong and need not remain that way, insofar as it is subversive for women to have taken up the historically patriarchal equipment of criticism.

"Often we read something unexpected by writers whose work we know," Hardwick writes in the introduction to *The Best American Essays 1986*. "Each month, somewhere, one or another will have written about subjects we had not thought to connect them with." For readers who know Hardwick for her novels and criticism, her pieces for *Architectural Digest* and *House & Garden* in the 1980's are likely to be those unexpected finds. These are garden pieces in a particularly New York way, essays about the remnants of Eden's wake as they are represented in large, beautiful books about the histories of gardens in different countries, in an urban museum's exhibition of garden paintings, in the city dweller's summer pilgrimages to the country. While the subject matter may be a surprising one for Hardwick, the concerns are familiar, though here richly framed with color photographs. Concepts that she often worked with as a literary critic turn out to illuminate not only literature but also artistic arrangements and representations of flowers. She applies her understanding of modernity to photographs of Claude Monet's garden in Giverny: "Internationalism and eclecticism are, in landscaping as elsewhere, the definition of a modern sensibility." The rendering of a portrait of a plant is, like poetry or drama, "imbued with cultural history and the drift of each period's changing conception of itself." Paintings of garden scenes also offer her opportunities to take up the themes she wrote about in *Seduction and Betrayal,* the physical constraints on women and the imbalance in women's relationships with male artists. "What a lot of clothes the women are dragging around in these rich-toned landscapes," she remarks. "Hats, sleeves, petticoats, ties at the neck, parasols—a shroud of protection, giving a somewhat fatigued femininity to these lost summer days." In a landscape by John Singer Sargent, a man paints while his companion, a woman, "is reading in a hat like a haystack, a dark skirt, and holding an inevitable lacy umbrella, a thing of no apparent utility unless it be a weapon against a change of his mood there in the erotic sleepiness of a full summer afternoon."

Hardwick's essay on a summer retreat to Castine, Maine, "Puritanical Pleasures," is austere and elegiac. To a reader practiced in searching her prose for its multiple levels, the following passage from early in the essay seems to contain the major themes of Hardwick's life, the emotional strains that accompanied her intellectual career: stoicism and loss, a slightly distanced expressiveness, a man who takes off on an adventure and ultimately does not come back alive, a young woman who leaves for the big city and becomes a part of it.

The splendor of the region always retains a pristine frugality in its messages, a puritanical remnant in its pleasures. Like the blossoms, you are reminded that you can wait—and also you can do without. A lonesome pine, country music drift in the air, long-lost sentiments. He'll never return from the sea (the Merchant Marine) and the blue-eyed girl has gone to the office desks of Connecticut, never to look back.

Selected Bibliography

WORKS OF ELIZABETH HARDWICK

NOVELS

The Ghostly Lover. New York: Harcourt, Brace, 1945.

The Simple Truth. New York: Harcourt, Brace, 1955; Ecco Press, 1982.

Sleepless Nights. New York: Random House, 1979.

CRITICISM

A View of My Own: Essays in Literature and Society. New York: Farrar Straus, 1962.

Seduction and Betrayal: Women and Literature. New York: Random House, 1974.

SHORT STORIES

"The People on the Roller Coaster." In *O. Henry Memorial Award Prize Stories of 1945.* Edited by Herschel Brickell. New York: Doubleday, 1945.

"The Mysteries of Eleusis." In *The Best American Short Stories 1946.* Edited by Martha Foley. Boston: Houghton Mifflin, 1946.

"Evenings at Home." In *The Best American Short Stories 1949.* Edited by Martha Foley. Boston: Houghton Mifflin, 1949.

ESSAYS

"The Decline of Book Reviewing." *Harper's Magazine,* 219:138–143 (November 1959).

"Going Home in America: Lexington, Kentucky." *Harper's Magazine,* 239:78–82 (July 1969).

Bartleby in Manhattan and Other Essays. New York: Random House, 1983.

"Gardens of the World." *Architectural Digest,* 42:264 (October 1985).

"Puritanical Pleasures." *House & Garden,* 158:96–99 (August 1986).

"Introduction." *The Best American Essays 1986.* New York: Ticknor and Fields, 1986.

"The Heart of the Seasons." *House & Garden,* 159:125–128; 230–231 (May 1987).

REVIEWS

"Artist and Spokesman." *Partisan Review,* 12:406–407 (Summer 1945).

"Fiction Chronicle." *Partisan Review,* 13:384–393 (Summer 1946).

"Fiction Chronicle." *Partisan Review,* 14:196–200 (March–April 1947).

"Fiction Chronicle." *Partisan Review,* 14:427–431 (July–August 1947).

"Faulkner and the South Today." *Partisan Review,* 15:1130–1135 (October 1948).

"The Disaster at Lincoln Center." *The New York Review of Books,* 2:1–3 (April 2, 1964).

"Sartre's *The Condemned of Altona* at Lincoln Center." *The New York Review of Books,* 6:6–7 (March 3, 1966).

"Report on the New York Theater." *The New York Review of Books,* 6:8–9 (April 28, 1966).

"*The Investigation* by Peter Weiss." *The New York Review of Books,* 7:5 (November 3, 1966).

"New York Theater." *The New York Review of Books,* 7:14 (December 15, 1966).

"New York Theater." *The New York Review of Books,* 8:6, 8 (April 6, 1967).

"*The Great White Hope* by Howard Sackler." *The New York Review of Books,* 10:4 (February 1, 1968).

"Notes on the New Theater." *The New York Review of Books,* 10:5–6 (June 20, 1968).

BIOGRAPHICAL AND CRITICAL STUDIES

Aaron, Daniel. *Writers on the Left.* New York: Avon, 1965.

Branin, Joseph J. "Elizabeth Hardwick." In *Dictionary of Literary Biography.* Vol. 6, *American Nov-*

elists Since World War II. Second series. Edited by James E. Kibler. Detroit: Gale, 1980. Pp. 133–136.

Didion, Joan. "Meditation on a Life." *New York Times Book Review*, April 29, 1979, pp. 1, 60.

Gelderman, Carol W. *Mary McCarthy: A Life*. New York: St. Martin's Press, 1988.

Hamilton, Ian. *Robert Lowell: A Biography*. New York: Random House, 1982.

Inge, M. Thomas. "Elizabeth Hardwick." In *Southern Writers: A Biographical Dictionary*. Edited by Robert Bain, Joseph Flora, and Louis Rubin. Baton Rouge: Louisiana State University, 1979.

Maddocks, Melvin. Review of *A View of My Own*. *Chicago Sunday Tribune*, September 9, 1962.

Meyers, Jeffrey. *Manic Power: Robert Lowell and His Circle*. New York: Arbor House, 1987.

Nobile, Philip. *Intellectual Skywriting: Literary Politics and The New York Review of Books*. New York: Charterhouse, 1974.

Stern, Carol Simpson. "Elizabeth Hardwick." In *Contemporary Novelists*. Edited by James Vinson. London and Chicago: St. James Press, 1986.

With thanks to Harvey Teres.

—*JANET GRAY*

Jack Kerouac

1922–1969

REGARDED AS THE authentic voice of the Beat Generation in twentieth-century American literature, Jack Kerouac considered himself a storyteller and experimental writer in the literary tradition of Marcel Proust and James Joyce, creating a method of writing that he called "spontaneous prose" and that he was confident would become the prose of the future. Contrary to his expectations, his technique was not taken up by later writers of fiction. In fact, recent decades have shown that his narrative style ran counter to the spirit of his time, as expressed in the ironic "metafictions" of his contemporaries William Burroughs, John Barth, Thomas Pynchon, and other postmodernists.

Yet Kerouac's style and the stories he told in the 1950's of his own adventures and those of his friends had a different kind of influence, one that he had never intended and later disowned. When his books were first published, they were so compelling that their description of an alternative lifestyle contributed to the cultural revolution that swept America and Europe in the late 1960's. In the process, the larger intent and design of Kerouac's literary achievement was obscured by the notoriety associated with his popular status as "the king of the Beats."

Kerouac protested in vain that he was a serious writer. Unlike his friends Allen Ginsberg, William Burroughs, Lawrence Ferlinghetti, and Gary Snyder, he was singularly unskilled at giving interviews to the press, partly because he was met with undisguised hostility but mostly because he did not feel he had to justify what he was doing. Since Kerouac's death on October 21, 1969, the influence of his individual approach to language has been acknowledged by writers as dissimilar as Ken Kesey, who tried to follow in Kerouac's footsteps, and Thomas Pynchon, who went in a different direction as a writer but remembers Kerouac's prose as having been an "exciting, liberating, strongly positive" influence on him. University students in creative-writing programs still read Kerouac and try their own spontaneous prose experiments. Outside the university, Kerouac's works continue to be read by young people, who respond to him as a counterculture hero, a Beat rebel, the archetypal outsider. In the words of the French-Canadian critic Victor-Lévy Beaulieu, "Jack became a hero . . . a wise man who showed you that illumination could reach you only when you broke with the old habits."

Literary historians conventionally attribute the roots of Kerouac's alienation as a Beat writer to the massive changes and dislocations of the postwar society reflected in his autobiographical novels. He himself defined "Beat Generation" for the *Random House Dictionary* as "members of the generation that came of age after World War II who, supposedly as a result of disillusionment stemming from the Cold War, espouse mystical detachment and relaxation of social and sexual tensions.'' But as time distances Kerouac's readers from the cold-war society of the 1950's, and as our cultural awareness broadens to encompass a closer examination of the experiences of minority and immigrant groups in America, his books also tell another, equally powerful story. Kerouac's autobiographical writings are among the most complete, dramatic, and devastating accounts in our country's literature of the high cost of acculturation paid by a sensitive and ambitious first-generation native son.

Kerouac's self-description as ''a French Canadian Iroquois American aristocrat Breton Cornish democrat'' in his book *Desolation Angels* (1965) suggests his heightened awareness of his family background and the complex, uneasy psychological balance in which he held the different parts of his heritage. Kerouac, never completely assimilated into American life, was a writer deeply marked by the different cultural experience of his French-Canadian family. He developed his unique style of writing to create a highly personal language and method of narration that allowed him to capture the emotional experience he had while writing about the events and people in his life. The layers of memories and associations he evoked in the process of creating ''fictions'' left a record of his consciousness in twenty published books, including what he called the ''vast books'' comprising his autobiography, ''The Legend of Duluoz.'' Because the books chronicling the ten-year Beat period in his life are the best known, the larger design of what he considered his major work and the influence of his early French-Canadian immigrant background on all of his writing are usually overlooked.

Considering himself ''an outsider American genius Canuck,'' Kerouac knew from early childhood the feeling of belonging to a different cultural group. His roots were solidly planted in working-class immigrant soil. Kerouac's grandparents first emigrated from Quebec to New Hampshire, members of that population of nearly a million impoverished people who left the farms of French Canada for the factories of New England between 1840 and 1930. In 1891 the French-Canadian chronicler Père Hamon described the background of a typical poor Catholic immigrant family who had left Canada with the hope of finding a better life in America:

> A ''habitant,'' poor in goods and land but rich in children, decides to emigrate to the States. The family arrives in a manufacturing center, Lowell, Holyoke, Worcester, for example; along with the father and mother there are eight or ten children of different ages. . . .Everyone wears clothes made of homespun, that is fabric woven by the housewife. Their ''butin,'' the word the Canadians use to designate their possessions, is wrapped up in bundles that the father distributes to the biggest of his sons while he keeps for himself the ''poche'' which contains what he considers to be his most precious possessions. They arrive at the station. . . . The Americans are there, impassively watching this spectacle with which, however, they are beginning to become familiar. Perhaps they are thinking to themselves: ''Here comes some new personnel for our factories. They're solid and full of life. Who knows, maybe in fifty years the sons of these people might even replace the wornout impoverished Puritan race here in New England?''

Père Hamon's prophecy about ''the sons of these people'' came true in a way he could hardly have expected: sixty years after Hamon's description, Kerouac wrote *On the Road,* and after its publication in 1957 the ''wornout impoverished Puritan'' literary culture of America was never quite the same.

Kerouac's father, Leo, was born in New

Hampshire. His mother, Gabrielle L'Evesque, had emigrated there from Quebec. Before Kerouac's birth his parents moved to Lowell, Massachusetts, a thriving mill town dependent on the labor of generations of immigrant factory workers. Determined to succeed in American life, they kept their family small, just three children: Gerard, Caroline, and Jack, or Ti Jean, as his mother always called him, born Jean-Louis on March 12, 1922. During the Great Depression his parents struggled to make a living: Leo's printing shop failed and Gabrielle worked long hours in a shoe factory.

Along with his family's economic hardships, Kerouac inherited an environment of social marginalization common to the other immigrant groups in Lowell, the Irish and the Greeks. The most tangible asset of the French-Canadian immigrants was their sense of belonging to a large, tightly knit community sharing a different language and religion, the *joual* (Quebecois language) spoken at home by Kerouac's parents, and the Catholicism practiced by his devout mother. *Joual* was Kerouac's first language, and he did not learn English until he started parochial school at the age of six.

Although Leo and Gabrielle Kerouac were members of a poor immigrant community, they told their children that the family possessed an aristocratic heritage. Years later, when Kerouac summarized his background in an author's statement introducing his book *Lonesome Traveler* (1960), he wrote that his nationality was Franco-American and that his

> people go back to Breton France, first North American ancestor Baron Alexandre Louis Lebris de Kérouac of Cornwall, Brittany, 1750 or so, was granted land along the Rivière du Loup after victory of Wolfe over Montcalm; his descendants married Indians (Mohawk and Caughnawaga) and became potato farmers. . . .My father's mother a Bernier related to explorer Bernier—all Bretons on father's side—my mother has a Norman name, L'Evesque.

Through his family's pride in their history, language, and religion, Kerouac's immigrant background made such a profound psychological impression on him that some French-Canadian critics have argued that he can be considered a Quebec writer. If, as the Canadian novelist Margaret Atwood maintains, the test of a Quebec writer is not birthplace but whether he or she is obsessed with the question, What goes on in the coffin? then Kerouac indeed deserves such consideration.

The coffin entered his consciousness with the death of his older brother, Gerard, in 1926, when Kerouac was four years old. Nearly thirty years later, in his book *Visions of Gerard* (1963), he wrote that he regarded his brother's death as the most significant emotional event of his childhood. Ecstatically describing Gerard's funeral in that book, Kerouac was transported back to his earliest memories and most vivid dreams, connecting the funeral with the "Pure Land" of death accessible only to someone in a coffin.

> The whole reason why I ever wrote at all and drew breath to bite in vain with pen of ink, great gad with indefensible usable pencil, because of Gerard, the idealism, Gerard the religious hero—"Write in honour of his death" (Écrivez pour l'amour de son mort) (as one would say, write for the love of God. . . .)

The philosophical riddle of death—why are we born but to die?—was the original riddle Kerouac inherited in childhood. All his life he wrote for the love of God (which he associated with what he regarded as his brother's Christlike martyrdom), so that in this sense all his writing is religious, emanating from Gerard's beloved coffin, "Gerard the religious hero." Kerouac was also obsessed with a second riddle, the question of suffering—how can we love a God who causes

His innocent creatures pain? Stubbornly he tried to answer this riddle throughout his life, later augmenting his Catholicism with the philosophical consolations of Buddhism during the time he was closely associated with the Beat writers.

In its description of Kerouac's boyhood after the death of his brother, Gerard, the second novel in the Duluoz chronology, *Doctor Sax* (1959), following *Visions of Gerard,* is the most dramatic account of the acculturation process that shaped his personality. As Beaulieu writes, this is a novel "which provides the best documentation we possess on Franco-American life in the 1920s and 30s. I was struck by the large number of monsters, idiots, neurotics and depraved people Jack describes in it. (The lot of all societies in the process of losing their culture . . .)." The narrative gains its power from Kerouac's memories of the emotional effects of his mother's Catholicism reflected in his extraordinary childhood fantasies. In this book Kerouac's basic mythological source is the popular religion of Quebec, not the official Catholicism practiced in the churches of Lowell. His family's heritage of folk religion, seen in his mother's devout practice of Catholicism in their home, is marked by vivid fears and symbols of "the night-side of human existence." These instinctive fears are associated with shadows. Louis Rousseau, in his analysis of Kerouac's Catholicism in *Moody Street Irregulars,* points out that in the Kerouac family home these shadows "are impossible to seize; and they come to one unexpectedly. 'Qui a farmez ma porte?' ('Who slammed my door?')—'Nobody' is the answer in *Doctor Sax.*"

When Kerouac wrote *Doctor Sax,* he mingled his boyhood fear of the shadows associated with the religious objects in his home, his mother's stories about martyrs and saints, and his memory of the characters and plots in the pulp magazines that he took as the basis of his own fantasies in the games he played alone and with friends. This amalgam resulted in a rich mixture of cultural influences, but it also contributed some confusion at the end of the book. Rousseau was the first to identify the problem. The folk heritage from which Kerouac drew in his novel contains images relating to death, but as Rousseau points out, the outcome in the popular Quebec legends is never tragic. By ruse, intelligence, and trickery the Quebec legendary figure always wins, and the devil, shadow, or demon always loses.

In contrast, Kerouac's boyhood hero, Doctor Sax, is uncloaked at the end of the book and revealed as an ineffectual poseur, a loser. Kerouac lamely concludes his battle between Sax and the villain snake by having the universe step in to absorb its own evil; Sax cannot accomplish this miracle. The weak ending is an example of the tug-of-war between the Franco-American influences in Kerouac's background and his love of American popular culture. Shortly before concluding the writing of *Doctor Sax* in Mexico City in 1952, Kerouac saw the film *The Wizard of Oz* (1939). He based the ending of his book on the denouement of that film, rather than remaining consistent to the spirit of the popular Quebec religious legends.

Kerouac wrote a third book about growing up as a French Canadian in Lowell, *Maggie Cassidy* (1959), a novel about his success in his senior year of high school as a football player and track star, and his hopeless infatuation with his first girlfriend, the young Irish beauty who his mother fears will trap him into an early marriage. Here we see Kerouac beginning to break free, though still susceptible to his parents' traditional values, afraid that if he marries Maggie instead of going on to college he will jeopardize his future. In the novel he trudges miles from Lowell's French-Canadian neighborhood of Pawtucketville to visit Maggie at her home in the Irish section of town, only to have her mock his lack of sexual experience and his obedience to his mother's command that he act like a "good boy" and respect her virtue.

The rich, surrealistic prose of *Doctor Sax* gives way in *Maggie Cassidy* to a simpler, almost stilted romantic style. *Joual* is absent from Kerouac's writing in this book, almost as if he were struggling to find a language to describe the world outside his home. The emotional legacy of his mother's religious practice and the mystery of his boyhood fantasies about good and evil permeate *Visions of Gerard* and *Doctor Sax,* but with his adolescent love affair in *Maggie Cassidy* Kerouac tries to take a step away from the Franco-American community. Stung by a sense of failure after Maggie takes another boyfriend, Kerouac goes back to his mother. He is left with a dark sense that her description of the hardships endured by the family in Lowell will be a prophecy of his own future. In *Maggie Cassidy* his mother bluntly sums up the family's experience: "We try to manage and it turns out shit."

The turning point that marked Kerouac's unsuccessful attempt to enter mainstream American life is recorded at the end of *Maggie Cassidy* and at the beginning of the next book in the chronology, *Vanity of Duluoz* (1968). Here Kerouac wrote about his departure from Lowell after his high-school graduation to study in New York City, first at the Horace Mann School and then at Columbia College. When Kerouac first left home, his ancestral heritage presented him with a third riddle, the difficult one of social assimilation, the question of how to belong to two different and sometimes radically opposed cultures. In this matter Kerouac tried to follow the example of his father, who stubbornly believed that he could escape the marginality inherent in his immigrant status, or, in the words of Beaulieu, "attain American comfort without leaving the old French-Canadian heritage behind."

Beaulieu's theory clarifies much of Kerouac's life and work. Neither of Kerouac's parents was concerned about the survival of French-Canadian culture in America; like most immigrants they chose to retain their identity only within their own home, realizing that there was no high social status inherent in their heritage. Struggling to survive and to support their family in the worst years of the Great Depression, Leo and Gabrielle Kerouac knew where they stood in America, and they passed on their awareness of their marginal status to their son. It was inconceivable to them to try to interest others outside the Franco-American community in the importance of their own language and religious customs. Uneducated members of the working class, they knew that, for Jack, a college education and assimilation into mainstream culture was the safest road to economic success. As a teenager he dreamed of being a college football star, a wealthy businessman, and a Nobel Prize–winning author—of satisfying the ambitions that his parents had for him.

Kerouac carried the burden of his parents' dreams as well as the legacy of an immigrant culture that opposed the assimilation process. In his autobiographical writings he returns almost compulsively to a troubled period of his life: his brief career as a football player at Columbia and his behavior under stress a short time later as a young navy recruit during the early years of World War II.

When Kerouac wrote about this experience in *Vanity of Duluoz,* near the end of his life, he said that he was constitutionally unable to handle navy discipline, so he managed to secure a psychiatric discharge, apparently with his father's approval. Leo Kerouac held traditional isolationist opinions during World War II, exhibiting the Quebec distrust of wars fought for distant causes in foreign countries. Did twenty-year-old Jack Kerouac share his father's immigrant ideology in 1942? He did not say. Yet when he wrote *Vanity of Duluoz* twenty years later, he said that he saw his "dream of being a real American man" receding from his window in the navy psychiatric ward. As a first-generation American, Kerouac was both witness to and victim of the heat of the melting pot, the difficult assimilation of the different backgrounds of immigrants and their families into a shared, if elusive, national identity.

At the end of World War II, in which Kerouac had participated as a merchant seaman in the North Atlantic, he disappointed his parents by telling them he wanted to be a writer instead of returning to college. Leo Kerouac was dying of cancer. Jack took care of his father at home while his mother worked her factory job, but he spent whatever free time he had with new friends in Manhattan. In 1944 Kerouac met Allen Ginsberg and Lucien Carr through his girlfriend Edie Parker, who had been introduced to Jack by a friend he had made during his year at the Horace Mann School. Edie Parker became his first wife in a marriage that lasted only a few months.

Both Ginsberg and Carr were students at Columbia College, and with them Kerouac shared his enthusiasm for literature. Ginsberg and Carr had been introduced to the poetry of Arthur Rimbaud by their friend William Burroughs and idolized Rimbaud for what they called his "New Vision" of life. Kerouac resisted their enthusiasm for the "New Vision" in Rimbaud's poetry. Since he spoke *joual* at home he did not think that his fluency in French was an intellectual achievement, and he put down what he called his friends' "tedious intellectualness" when he described this period of his life a few years later in *On the Road.* As he said of himself in *Vanity of Duluoz,* "My saving grace in their eyes . . . was the materialistic Canuck taciturn cold skepticism all the picked-up Idealism in the world of books couldn't hide."

Another member of the early Beat group, Carl Solomon, told me about "down-to-earth" Jack at this time: "He was very American when a lot of us were rather Frenchified." While Solomon and the others steeped themselves in the European cultural tradition, excited by the discovery of existential philosophy, classical music, and modernist French poetry, Kerouac, still loyal to his working-class immigrant origins, wrestled with the riddle of cultural assimilation. He espoused American popular culture, championing big-band swing music and bebop jazz, Frank Sinatra, and the novels of Thomas Wolfe, which he came to admire after putting aside earlier enthusiasms for the fiction of William Saroyan and Ernest Hemingway.

Yet, at the same time as Kerouac was playing the role of the hard-boiled "Canuck" to impress his new friends, he had great aspirations as a writer. After his father's death in 1946, he worked for two years on a manuscript, imitating Wolfe in an attempt to write the great American novel. After the publication of *The Town and the City* in 1950, Kerouac acknowledged that the novel had been conceived according to the techniques that Professor Mark Van Doren had been trying to teach his freshmen English class at Columbia. Although Kerouac disguised his Franco-American background in that thinly veiled autobiographical work, recent French-Canadian literary critics have analyzed deeper textual patterns in *The Town and the City* and found a recurrent image of "true North" that is the source of his unfulfilled longing for home in this and subsequent books.

Kerouac's immigrant background also adds a deeper resonance to his next novel, *On the Road* (1957), begun and completed in a three-week burst in April 1951, after he had struggled for years to free himself from the influence of Wolfe in order to find his own voice. Read as autobiography instead of fiction, *On the Road* fits into the larger "Legend of Duluoz" chronology after *Vanity of Duluoz.* Taking the books sequentially, one finds *On the Road* only a partial description of Kerouac's life, but this is also true of earlier books, such as *Visions of Gerard* and *Doctor Sax.* Because the Jack Kerouac who describes his boyhood in these books is a grown man relying on memory for the events of his past, one can accept a more poetic recollection of his life. In *On the Road* Kerouac puts himself on the sidelines in the story of his own life, concentrating on the personality of his friend Neal Cassady, who introduced him to life on the road. Kerouac's French-Canadian identity is completely submerged in the book, as is his identity as an ambitious writer struggling to finish *The Town and the City* and find a publisher for it between his trips with Cassady.

The books Kerouac wrote about his own life are more fiction than autobiography. The "fiction" results not because Kerouac made up characters or events that never existed, but because his point of view as narrator of his life story is so emotionally charged that he makes all the characters and events a reflection of his own feelings. He later said that he wrote *On the Road* to describe his adventures with Cassady to his second wife, Joan Haverty, and that his French Canadian background had nothing to do with the story.

Writing *On the Road,* Kerouac finally found his true subject—the story of his own life as an outsider searching for a place in America. *On the Road* can be read as a quest undertaken by the narrator, Sal Paradise, who sets out to test the reality of the American dream by trying to pin down its promise of unlimited freedom and opportunity. Dean Moriarty (Neal Cassady) is as much on the margins of society as Sal Paradise, but he has no illusions about his future. Envisioning it, he tells the credulous Sal:

> You spend a whole life of non-interference with the wishes of others . . . and nobody bothers you and you cut along and make it your own way. . . .What's your road, man?—holyboy road, madman road, rainbow road, guppy road, any road. It's an anywhere road for anybody anyhow. Where body how?

For Sal Paradise, his friend Moriarty is "Beat—the root, the soul of Beatific," in possession of the key to unlock the door to the mysterious possibilities and richness of experience itself.

Kerouac's description of Dean Moriarty is so compelling that most readers of the novel do not dwell on the fact that the frantic cross-country trips leave Sal exhausted, strung out, penniless, and deserted at the end of the road. The rushing optimism of their search for Dean's father leads nowhere, and their comradery on the highway does not last long after they have parked their battered cars on the streets of San Francisco, New Orleans, and Manhattan. The vitality of Kerouac's descriptions of America and his openhearted belief that the dream he and Dean are chasing will appear just ahead at the end of the road are underscored by Kerouac's poignant sense of their shared mortality. As Sal says at the conclusion of the novel, "Nobody knows what's going to happen to anybody besides the forlorn rags of growing old."

Kerouac's presentation of the rush of events and chaos of personal encounters in *On the Road* moves so swiftly that emotions are bypassed and short-circuited, submerged in Sal's feelings as he narrates his story. The effect on the reader is exhilarating because Sal is so swept up in his presentation of what is happening that one thing follows another without reflection or explanation. Sal chases the dream back and forth on the highways between the east and west coasts, and finds that it has little reality; it is merely a "sad paradise" when he finally catches up with it in New Orleans, Denver, San Francisco, Chicago, and New York. *On the Road* has become a classic because Kerouac, feeling himself on the margins of society, stripped himself of his past and confronted the riddle of the American dream, dramatizing the lure of its elusive promise and its failure to live up to his expectations. Like *The Adventures of Huckleberry Finn* and *The Great Gatsby,* Kerouac's novel has a particular appeal for young readers, who can easily emphathize with the narrator's disillusionment, sympathizing with his dreams and sharing his position outside the mainstream.

Kerouac was nearly thirty when he wrote *On the Road* in April 1951. The previous year his first published novel, *The Town and the City,* had received polite reviews but had had only negligible sales, and his mother continued to work at her factory job. Kerouac knew he always had a home with her, whenever he tired of the company of his New York friends or ran out of money on his trips across the country with Cassady. Encouraged to write as he pleased by Ginsberg and Burroughs, he felt he had nothing to lose by going his own way as a writer. He had been dissatisfied with the way he wrote his first published novel as an imitation of Wolfe, because he wanted to find a prose style that expressed his own sense of language. Writing *On the Road* in a three-week burst on a roll of teletype paper had been an experiment designed to capture the quality of his road trips with Cassady. In that experiment Kerouac had dropped his ''literary'' language and used the style of the letters he was exchanging with Cassady after their trips together, in particular one long letter from Cassady he called ''the Joan Anderson letter.'' Several thousand words in length, it described Cassady's sexual adventures with one of his girlfriends in Denver. Kerouac still was not satisfied that he had discovered what he was searching for as an artist. He was looking for an approach to writing he called ''deep form,'' which would capture the emotional essence of his subject.

Six months later he began to experiment with language in a different way, developing a method of ''sketching'' with words on paper, trying to attain ''deep form'' like a painter or the bebop jazz musicians he admired. French-Canadian literary critics have argued that after years of writing straightforward narrative in the various versions and revisions of *The Town and the City* and *On the Road,* Kerouac's discovery of his method of spontaneous prose in October 1951 freed him to begin exploring his French-Canadian heritage. For example, he found that this method of writing was a way to deal with his bilingualism—the dilemma of how to incorporate the sense of his first and most spontaneous language, *joual,* into the development of a colloquial, American prose style. The Quebec critic Maurice Poteet writes:

> The spontaneity of *Doctor Sax* (''don't stop to think,'' baroque phrasing and form, word-play, bilingual texts, film-book comparisons) permits Kerouac to build bridges to and from a number of inner and local realities which otherwise might not ''become'' American at all. In other words, ''spontaneous'' writing and effect are one answer, at least, to an ethnic situation that in many ways resembles the ''double bind'' of psychology: if a writer cannot be himself in his work (a minority background) he is lost; if he becomes an ''ethnic'' writer, he is off on a tangent. Also, ''spontaneous'' writing, as a technique, reflects a cultural set of values which pins hopes upon the individual (''I had a dream'') who can come up with something original and new. [Translation provided by Poteet.]

''Sketching'' spontaneous prose, Kerouac felt he had found his own voice as a writer at last. Confident he was on the right track, he decided to write experimental books using his unique approach to language as his distinctive literary style. This decision was temperamentally suited to Kerouac's stubborn sense that he could not fit into the mainstream of American society; since he left his second wife after completing *On the Road* and continued to make his home with his mother, he did not have to try.

Kerouac's new prose method left him free to write about anything that excited him. Typically an image in his mind would trigger a spontaneous rush of emotional associations, prompting a flow of language that he could jot down in his notebook to capture his poignant sense of the ephemeral nature of his existence. The most humble details triggered an intense emotional response, such as a lunchroom close to his mother's home in Long Island, described in *Visions of Cody*:

The smell is always of boiling water mixed with beef, boiling beef, like the smell of the great kitchens of parochial boarding schools or old hospitals, the brown basement kitchens' smell—the smell is curiously the hungriest in America—it is FOODY insteady of just spicy, or—it's like dishwater soap just washed a pan of hamburg—nameless—memoried—sincere—makes the guts of men curl in October.

From 1951 to 1957, in a burst of creative energy, Kerouac swam in the heady seas of his own prose, now captured in more than a dozen works. Some would eventually be published, and others are known to have been left in manuscript at his death in 1969; they include, in order of composition (see the bibliography for publication dates): *Visions of Cody* (1951–1952), *Doctor Sax* (1952), "October in the Railroad Earth" (1952), *Book of Dreams* (1952–1960), *Maggie Cassidy* (1953), *The Subterraneans* (1953), "San Francisco Blues" (1954), *Some of the Dharma* (1954, not published), *Mexico City Blues* (1955), *Tristessa* (1955–1956), *Visions of Gerard* (1956), and *Desolation Angels* (1956). Six of these books (*Doctor Sax, Maggie Cassidy, The Subterraneans, Tristessa, Visions of Gerard,* and *Desolation Angels*) were conceived as autobiographical novels that would fit chronologically into his larger scheme of what Kerouac called "The Legend of Duluoz." Others were experimental prose in their initial concept (*Visions of Cody,* "October in the Railroad Earth," *Book of Dreams*), books of poetry ("San Francisco Blues," *Mexico City Blues*), or translations from French Buddhist texts and meditations ("Some of the Dharma"). All were examples of spontaneous "sketching." In most of these works Kerouac's immersion in the torrents of language released by his prose method and the various drugs he used to fuel his inspiration resulted in language that overspills and effervesces on the page.

During the years when he explored his new prose method, Kerouac wrote nearly constantly, keeping notebooks and pencil with him at all times; he even tied them to his bed at home so he could turn on the light at night and record his dreams. Riding a freight train on the California coast in December 1951, for example, he dug a little dime-store notebook out of his jacket pocket to transcribe what he saw and thought. His observations became a sentence in *Lonesome Traveler*:

Ole Jack you are now actually riding in a caboose and going along the surf on the spectralest railroad you'd ever in your wildest little dreams wanta ride, like a kid's dream, why is it you cant lift your head and look out there and appreciate the feathery shore of California the last land being feathered by fine powdery skeel of doorstop sills of doorstep water weaving in from every Orient and bay boom shroud from here to Catteras Flapperas Voldivious and Gratteras, boy.

The linguistic inventiveness and playfulness in Kerouac's books from this period were unprecedented. No prose like this had ever been written in English by a writer in America hoping to earn a living from his work. As expatriates, Gertrude Stein, James Joyce, and Ezra Pound had experimented with language in a similar manner while they lived in France or Italy, but English was not the language of the surrounding culture. Steeped in his Franco-American identity, Kerouac, too, regarded his written language as being different from the everyday language of common discourse. Writing his books in the bedroom or the kitchen of his mother's house, speaking *joual* all the time he was with her, he shaped his prose style on the page to the rhythms and sounds of the language he heard in his mind. These were the words closest to his heart, closest to the language he shared with his mother.

With the discovery of his method of spontaneous prose, Kerouac found not only a way to write his books but also a literary method that justified his sense of isolation. His audience was primarily himself; unlike a bop soloist, he did not perform with other musicians, although he regarded Ginsberg, Burroughs, and a few other sympathetic artists as his "band." In the early months of practicing the new method, he jotted down his impressions, thinking of them as part of one vast book, what he called a "book-movie," capturing the rushing line of his verbal consciousness in words on the page.

The book that was posthumously published as *Visions of Cody*—Kerouac had titled it "Visions of Neal"—collects the separate prose experiments from the period 1951–1952. This is a series of sketches of varying lengths loosely connected around his impressions of Cassady but without a formal plot linking the sections into a chronological narrative. Written during the first months of his prose experiment, Kerouac considered it his second version of *On the Road.* (He liked it so much better than the original version that he read a section of it years later on Steve Allen's television show as if it were the actual published version of *On the Road.*)

Stein eliminated plot in her experimental prose, but Kerouac was essentially a storyteller. In July 1952, several months into his "sketching" method, he started *Doctor Sax,* deciding to abandon his use of Cassady as the central figure in his writing and instead telling the story of his own boyhood. Nevertheless, Kerouac started *Doctor Sax* after having read a few manuscript pages of Cassady's own attempt to write a book about growing up in Denver; in that sense Kerouac was still influenced by Cassady, but once he embarked on *Doctor Sax* Kerouac realized that it would be his own life story. His French-Canadian past was as irresistible to him as his practice of spontaneous prose. While living in Cassady's house in San Francisco, both combined in his dreams, as described in the opening words of *Doctor Sax:*

> The other night I had a dream that I was sitting on the sidewalk on Moody Street, Pawtucketville, Lowell, Mass., with a pencil and paper in my hand saying to myself "Describe the wrinkly tar of this sidewalk, also the iron pickets of Textile Institute, or the doorway where Lousy and you and G. J.'s always sittin and dont stop to think of words when you do stop, just stop to think of the picture better—and let your mind off yourself in this work."

Kerouac's work from this period records his daily activities working on the railroad in California and living with the Cassadys or in a skid-row San Francisco hotel; his memories of trips with Neal and of his boyhood in Lowell; and his dreams, captured in writing only moments after waking up. Dreams and visions were important to Kerouac as pictures leading to an emotional response; when he wrote, he was more interested in his feelings than in his ideas. As his friend John Clellon Holmes understood, Kerouac's intent as a writer encompassed more than a simple chronicle of the events of his life. Holmes explains in *Gone in October* that

> From the beginning, Kerouac wrote about the double evolution of a consciousness, a consciousness that was evolving in the Past the books describe, and is evolving in the Present of their composition. As a result "The Legend of Duluoz" constitutes a prolonged search for a lost identity, for that singleness of vision, that sense of wholeness, that the uprootings of modern life have all but obliterated.

In the summer of 1953, back on Long Island, living with his mother after trips to California to see Cassady and Mexico City to visit Burroughs, Kerouac tried his hand at what he thought of as a more commercial writing project. Kerouac envisioned *Maggie Cassidy* as following *Doctor Sax* in the chronology of his autobiography. Love was his theme in this and three subsequent books, *The Subterraneans, Tristessa,* and *Visions of Gerard.* Kerouac did not plan them in any sequence, just as he did not systematically outline a series of books to chronicle all the years of his life in the larger book he called "The Legend of Duluoz"—"Duluoz," his pseudonym, humorously suggesting his view of himself as "the Louse."

Kerouac conceived his books as spontaneously as he wrote them, but typically he composed them in pairs: he considered "Visions of Neal" (reissued as *Visions of Cody*) to be an in-depth version of *On the Road*; *Doctor Sax* was his response to Cassady's boyhood memoir, titled *The First Third*; and *Maggie Cassidy* became a warm-up for *The Subterraneans* a few weeks later, the story of a brief but tumultuous love affair he had with an African-American woman in Greenwich Village during the summer of 1953. Just as "Visions of Neal" was a "spontaneous" rewriting of *On the Road,* Kerouac returned to his spontaneous style in *The Subterraneans* after trying to write the stiff "commercial" prose of *Maggie Cassidy.*

Like "October in the Railroad Earth," *The Subterraneans* is one of Kerouac's purest examples of spontaneous prose. With the help of the amphetamine Benzedrine, he wrote it in his room in his mother's apartment during three nights in October 1953. In the narrative, Kerouac weaves together past and present thoughts as they enter his mind, almost as if he were delivering a pep talk to himself as both star athlete and coach, urging himself on to greater heights as a writer:

> In other words this is the story of an unself-confident man, at the same time of an egomaniac, naturally facetious won't do—just to start at the beginning and let the truth seep out, that's what I'll do—. It began on a warm summernight—ah, she was sitting on a fender with Julian Alexander, who is. . . .

Sympathetic critics like Warren Tallman, in his early essay "Kerouac's Sound," understood that Kerouac's method of composition in *The Subterraneans* was as much his subject as was the love affair that constitutes the book's plot. The structure and sound of the individual sentences run on like a bop riff, starting with a simple idea and taking off to follow emotional associations as they occur in the writing process. Past narrative and present circumstances mix together in a rich tonality, spun out and returning to the central narrative idea.

> Angels, bear with me—I'm not even looking at the page but straight ahead into the sadglint of my wallroom and at a Sarah Vaughan Gerry Mulligan Radio KROW show on the desk in the form of a radio, in other words, they were sitting on the fender of a car in front of the Black Mask bar on Montgomery Street.

Writing about his love affair with Mardou gave Kerouac more pleasure than the affair itself. As he told Ginsberg and Burroughs, who read the manuscript of *The Subterraneans,* writing prose was a form of sexual activity for him. Kerouac's friends asked him to clarify what he meant, so he wrote down what he called "Essentials of Spontaneous Prose," a short description of his method from start to finish, the most extensive aesthetic statement he ever made:

> SET-UP The object is to set before the mind, either in reality, as in sketching (before a landscape or teacup or old face) or is set in the

memory wherein it becomes the sketching from memory of a definitive image-object.

PROCEDURE Time being of the essence in the purity of speech, sketching language is undisturbed flow from the mind of personal secret idea-words, blowing (as per jazz musician) on subject of image.

METHOD No periods separating sentence-structures already arbitrarily riddled by false colons and timid usually needless commas—but the vigorous space dash separating rhetorical breathing (as jazz musician drawing breath between outblown phrases)—''measured pauses which are the essentials of our speech''—''divisions of the sounds we hear''—''time and how to note it down.'' (William Carlos Williams)

SCOPING Not ''selectivity'' of expression but following free deviation (association) of mind into limitless blow-on-subject seas of thought. . . . Blow as deep as you want—write as deeply, fish as far down as you want, satisfy yourself first, then reader cannot fail to receive telepathic shock and meaning-excitement by same laws operating in his own human mind.

Kerouac hoped for a mystical connection with his reader through what he envisioned as the total spontaneity of his words on the page. His distrust of intellectuality led him to explicitly forbid revision—''no revisions (except obvious rational mistakes, such as names or calculated insertions in act of not writing but inserting).'' For him, spontaneous prose was validated because it was ''confessional''—associated with the act of confession in church and therefore holy. At the same time, it was also sexual release:

write excitedly, swiftly, with writing-or-typing cramps, in accordance (as from center to periphery) with laws of orgasm, Reich's ''beclouding of consciousness.'' Come from within, out—to relaxed and said.

Despite his prohibition on revision, Kerouac did revise when preparing his work for publication. Typically he wrote his novels in small notebooks using the real names of his friends; when he typed these novels for publication, he changed the names so that he would not be sued for libel, and with *The Subterraneans* he also changed the setting of the novel from Greenwich Village to San Francisco as a further precaution against a lawsuit, should the woman he portrays in the book try to sue him. Changes of names and settings did nothing to diminish the ''honesty'' of his account, in Kerouac's view. His method was to present the actual events of his life from his own point of view, softening any unpleasant reality in the process of dramatizing his innocence as a spectator; for example, if a girlfriend couldn't have children after an illegal abortion, Kerouac left out the details of the abortion and merely mentioned in passing that she was sad because she could not conceive. In a note written for the Norwegian edition of *The Subterraneans* years later, he said it was

a full confession of one's most wretched and hidden agonies after an affair of any kind. The prose is what I believe to be the prose of the future, from both the conscious top and the unconscious bottom of the mind, limited only by the limitations of time flying by as our mind flies by with it.

The writer Henry Miller, whose introduction to *The Subterraneans* was included in some editions of the book, observed that Kerouac's prose is as striking as the confession of his inadequacies as a lover. Kerouac's insecurity is naked on the page in *The Subterraneans*; his persona in his books is as innocent as his literary method. His genius as a writer was that his persona was so compelling he could simultaneously write spontaneous prose and keep the reader interested in the story he was telling.

Maggie Cassidy and *The Subterraneans* can be read as two accounts of physical love in the Duluoz chronology. *Tristessa* and *Visions of Gerard,* his next two novels, explore the theme of spiritual love, although they were not conceived schematically, just as Kerouac did not consciously balance every book written about his Beat life with one describing his French-Canadian origins. All his books were conceived as part of "The Legend of Duluoz," and they were also motivated by events occurring at the time: *Tristessa,* set in Mexico City, is the story of his relationship in 1955 with a prostitute who was a morphine addict; *Visions of Gerard,* written a year later, chronicles Kerouac's love for his brother, who died in Lowell in 1926. Kerouac continued pairing experiences from his past with adventures in the present, always presenting his adult self as homeless, out of place, and alone.

When Kerouac began *Tristessa,* he was living in Mexico City, and the experience of writing in a Spanish-speaking country enforced the sense of freedom he felt while using English in his manuscript notebooks. His prose in *Tristessa* and in *Visions of Gerard* also includes Buddhist terminology; he had begun studying and translating Buddhist texts the year before. Despite Tristessa's addiction and her prostitution, Kerouac viewed her as a saint who shared with him the belief that, as she says, "Tomorrar we may be die, and so we are nothing."

In Mexico City during the late summer and early fall of 1955, Kerouac's daily practice of his prose technique also led him to compose poetry. Experimenting with various drugs—he explicitly refers to scotch for the composition of *Tristessa,* Benzedrine for *The Subterraneans,* and wine for "October in the Railroad Earth"—he used morphine while creating a long poem based on the idea of a jazz musician blowing a series of solo variations, each notebook page the limit of each poem, as formally structured as the lyric of a blues piece. *Mexico City Blues* is one of Kerouac's most extraordinary productions. Meant to be read aloud with jazz accompaniment, it is a uniquely successful experiment in jazz poetry. The recordings of Kerouac reading excerpts from the poem give a sense of the work, but true appreciation of *Mexico City Blues* requires a full reading of the 242 choruses. Kerouac writes in tribute to jazz musicians and people close to him, like Ginsberg in the 213th chorus and his mother in the 149th chorus:

> I keep falling in love with my mother,
> I don't want to hurt her
> —Of all people to hurt.
>
> Every time I see her she's grown older
> But her uniform always amazes me
> For its Dutch simplicity
> And the Doll she is,
> The doll-like way she stands
> Bowlegged in my dreams
> Waiting to serve me.
>
> And I am only an Apache
> Smoking Hashi
> In old Cabashy
> By the lamp

At this time of his life, Kerouac was pushing the limits of what his writing could do. Thinking of himself as a stylist similar to James Joyce in his prose experiments, he started "an endless automatic writing piece" titled "Old Angel Midnight" (1959) that is the most radical of his works, a transcription of his stream of consciousness, taking his own mind as raw material. Without question his practice of Buddhist meditation contributed to the idea for this long poem. Although he had been reared as a Roman Catholic, Kerouac's subsequent involvement with Buddhism not only offered a new direction for his religious feelings but also helped him to practice his craft, since he used meditation techniques to help free his mind for spontaneous composition experiments. Kerouac employed the Buddhist technique of "letting go" in the composition of "Old Angel Midnight," annotating the stream of words that ran through his consciousness as he responded to the auditory stimuli around him.

The full text of the "Old Angel Midnight" manuscript is in the Berg Collection of the New York Public Library, and these notebooks attest to Kerouac's dedication to his experiment. Often he lit candles and sat quietly transcribing sounds outside the window before turning within to scribble down his mental images. Since he made no attempt to tell a story in "Old Angel Midnight," he was not held by any narrative line. His associations moved freely through thoughts to images to pure sounds to emptiness.

The intense bursts of writing that produced a dozen books in the years between 1951 and 1957, along with the physical demands of his lifestyle, began to take their toll on Kerouac's health. By the time *On the Road* was published in the fall of 1957, Kerouac was beginning to tire. This was also the period when he was closest to the other writers of the Beat Generation: Allen Ginsberg, William Burroughs, Gregory Corso, and John Clellon Holmes in New York City; Lawrence Ferlinghetti, Gary Snyder, Michael McClure, Philip Lamantia, and Philip Whalen in San Francisco. It was with their encouragement that he immersed himself in his prose experiments, but the book that chronicles his adventures with them, *Desolation Angels,* is one of his thinnest.

In 1960, three years after the publication of *On the Road,* Kerouac rallied again to create a great spontaneous-prose novel, *Big Sur* (1962), the story of his alcoholic breakdown in Ferlinghetti's cabin on the California coast. Kerouac had gone there with a literary project in mind, a transcription of the sounds of the Pacific Ocean, which he included as a series of poems at the end of the book. In this work he mixed *joual* with English at the height of his delirium. *Big Sur* was Kerouac's rueful farewell to his adventures as a Beat wanderer. He abandoned any hope of sustaining a life on his own when he returned to his mother's home and the Catholicism that he shared with her.

In *Big Sur* Kerouac humorously acknowledges the difference between the person he actually was and the "legend" he had become to the readers of his best-selling books. Resting comfortably on the California Zephyr train on his way to California, his rucksack packed by his mother with supplies (like a sewing kit for emergencies while he was away from her), he thinks:

> all over America highschool and college kids thinking 'Jack Duluoz is 26 years old and on the road all the time hitch hiking' while there I am almost 40 years old, bored and jaded in a roomette bunk crashin across that Salt Flat.

Nevertheless, today Kerouac is still best known as the author of three books of Beat adventures—*On the Road, The Subterraneans,* and *The Dharma Bums*—which are permeated by a sense of his reverence for life and have remained in print continuously for more than thirty years.

Read as autobiography, all three of the books are psychologically motivated by Kerouac's sense of alienation from mainstream American life, but read as fiction, the books are a prescription for adventure. As Beaulieu comments:

> A whole generation took it up, young men and girls bought sleeping bags and blue jeans and went hitchhiking all along the American roads, beginning Jack's trip again in their fashion, ending up like him in Mexico or Frisco.

On the Road has become an American classic. Kerouac created a living character in Dean Moriarty, the outsider, the essential drifter—or, in the poet Gary Snyder's term, "the cowboy crashing" after the closure of the western frontier. Kerouac's hero was his spiritual brother because, as Sal Paradise admits, "The only people for me are the mad ones, the ones who are mad to live, mad to talk, mad to be saved, desirous of everything at the same time.''

Two years after this revelation, Kerouac portrayed himself as one of ''the mad ones'' in *The Subterraneans*. The restless, off-balance rush of his spontaneous-prose style is a superb reflection of his own emotional conflicts. The fact that he admits his lack of romantic success is not a deterrent to his readers' view of the pleasures and risks of bohemian promiscuity, because he describes his ideal ''JOY of being and will and fearlessness'' so compellingly that the failure of a love affair seems an acceptable risk.

The third book in the trilogy of Beat life, *The Dharma Bums,* dramatizes Kerouac's adventures in California in 1955, two years after the events in *The Subterraneans*. Kerouac wrote *The Dharma Bums* shortly after the publication of *On the Road,* on the advice of Malcolm Cowley, his editor at the Viking Press, who patronizingly suggested that he try for another best-seller by keeping his prose simple and writing a book describing his adventures with another of his colorful friends. Kerouac chose the poet Gary Snyder, whom he had met in Berkeley a few years before, as his hero in a book he later dismissed as a ''potboiler.'' Snyder is the character Japhy Ryder in *The Dharma Bums,* and Kerouac describes him as ''a great new hero of American culture.'' Snyder represents an alternative to what Kerouac felt was the banality and repression of conventional middle-class American life, with a lifestyle that would be defined as ''counterculture'' in the 1960's.

Kerouac masked his French-Canadian identity in his three best-selling books, but when he described his Beat life in articles after the success of *On the Road,* memories of his Franco-American heritage would enter his thoughts. For example, in ''The Origins of the Beat Generation,'' which he wrote for *Playboy* magazine in 1959, he pointed out that as spokesman of the Beat Generation—''I am the originator of the term, and around it the term and the generation have taken shape''—he knew its true origins: ''It should be pointed out that all this 'Beat' guts therefore goes back to my ancestors who were Bretons who were the most independent group of nobles in all old Europe.'' Kerouac claimed that the spirit of the Beat Generation could also be traced ''back to the wild parties my father used to have at home in the 1920's and 1930's in New England that were so fantastically loud nobody could sleep for blocks around and when the cops came they always had a drink.'' He idealized his memories of the French-Canadian community in his old neighborhood in Lowell because he felt it was the prototype of his vision of a community of Beat friends.

In the 1960's, the last decade of his life, Kerouac made his home with his mother, who refused to let him continue his old friendships with Ginsberg and Burroughs but tolerated his alcoholism. His income from his books was modest but steady. His short-lived second marriage in 1951, to Joan Haverty, resulted in the birth of a daughter, Jan Kerouac, whom he did not acknowledge or support as his child. Living with his mother, Kerouac delved more deeply into the European French traditions that were part of his Franco-American heritage. Most notably, he returned to France to trace his ancestors, a trip short-circuited by his alcoholism; his stumbling adventures are humorously chronicled in *Satori in Paris* (1966). In France he had hoped to complete his sound poem of the voice of the Pacific Ocean begun in California at Big Sur, by transcribing the Atlantic waves off the coast of Brittany, but he was physically unable to complete the project. Kerouac returned to the United States and then, from his new home in Saint Petersburg, Florida, journeyed north to Montreal to do a television interview in *joual*. There he said that he belonged to the international community of writers who wrote in French, in addition to the community of Beat writers usually associated with his name.

Again Kerouac confronted the complex riddle of cultural identification in his own stubbornly independent way. He wrote his books in English, with occasional recourse to *joual* French, but he claimed his ambition was to be considered a storyteller like Honoré de Balzac and Marcel Proust—or, as he phrased it in "Belief and Technique for Modern Prose" in 1959, advising other writers to follow his method of spontaneous prose, "Like Proust be an old teahead of time."

In 1960 Kerouac published, in the magazine *Yugen,* his poem "Rimbaud," an exuberant tribute to the French writer admired fifteen years before by his friends at Columbia. The tone of this poem is intimate, as if Kerouac were bantering with Rimbaud as a member of his own family or as another Beat poet, brilliantly summarizing the events of the French poet's brief, tragic lifetime:

> Arthur!
>   On t'appela pas Jean!
> Born in 1854 cursing in Charle-
> ville thus paving the way for
> the abominable murderousnesses
> of Ardennes.

Kerouac characterizes Rimbaud as a "mad cat" in this poem, a jazz term used there to refer to Rimbaud's impetuosity, which Kerouac admired as a form of spontaneity, along with his independence, his poetic visions, and his language experiments. The poem is stubbornly, humorously anti-intellectual. Kerouac addresses Rimbaud as an equal while sounding at the same time himself "like a peasant writing well." The poem ends, inevitably, with another of Kerouac's Quebec coffin visions:

> So, poets, rest awhile
>   & shut up:
> Nothing ever came
>   of nothing.

In 1964 Kerouac published "Letter on Céline" in *The Paris Review*. This essay is the best glimpse of his view of the French literary tradition, to which he responded in a very personal way. He read his own major theme as a writer—the idea that all life is suffering—into the work of Louis-Ferdinand Céline. He found the process of reading Céline to be like that of watching a movie, a reference to Kerouac's concept of his novels as "bookmovies," a term related to his theory and practice of spontaneous prose.

Toward the end of "Letter on Céline," Kerouac referred to the complex issue of politically committed literature versus uncommitted (that is, apolitical) literature. He concluded by stating his own position on the matter, which was in opposition to that held by Albert Camus. Apolitical, Kerouac ignored the issue of Céline's anti-Semitism and sympathy for the fascists. His letter helps explain his refusal to join the other Beat writers in protest against America's repressive foreign policy in the 1960's.

On this issue Kerouac found himself once again an outsider, describing himself as "a bippie in the middle" in a syndicated newspaper article written in the fall of 1969, shortly before his death. There he said he supported America's participation in the Vietnam War because he was grateful the country had taken in his French-Canadian ancestors. If he had any reservations about his decision, he brushed them off by insisting that writers had better things to do than take sides in political controversy. Throughout his life he remained alienated from both the mainstream and the fringes of American politics. On a rare incursion into the subject in *Maggie Cassidy,* he tosses off something he remembered his father saying during an election campaign in Lowell in the years before World War II: "Get those Democrats outa there before this country goes to hell."

Kerouac died at the age of forty-seven, in a hospital in Saint Petersburg, of a massive abdominal hemorrhage brought on by his alcoholism. With him was his third wife, Stella Sampas, whom he had known earlier in Lowell and had married in 1966 after his mother suffered a stroke that left her bedridden.

Buried in the Edson Cemetery in Lowell, Kerouac was later honored by his hometown as a "native son," with a handsome memorial in downtown Lowell containing sculptures on which are inscribed eloquent passages from his work. The words on his memorial are proof that Kerouac remained close to his roots. His memory of his family life in Lowell, his religion, and his love for *joual* caused him ultimately to resist complete assimilation into the American mainstream.

Every descendant of American immigrants confronts difficult riddles of cultural assimilation, and Kerouac was no exception. He resolved these enigmas more or less successfully but always on his own terms, without compromise. Most readers think of him as a nonconformist, a modern-day Thoreau, the quintessential Beat. Perhaps the final riddle of Kerouac's life lies in his books; they reveal him as an American writer whose life and work commemorate both the vitality and persistence of an ancestral heritage, and the psychological toll this heritage exacted from him as he honored it.

Selected Bibliography

WORKS OF JACK KEROUAC

PROSE

The Town and the City. New York: Harcourt, Brace, 1950.

On the Road. New York: Viking, 1957.

The Dharma Bums. New York: Viking, 1958.

The Subterraneans. New York: Grove, 1958.

Doctor Sax: Faust Part Three. New York: Grove, 1959.

Maggie Cassidy. New York: Avon, 1959.

Excerpts from Visions of Cody. New York: New Directions, 1960.

Tristessa. New York: Avon, 1960.

Book of Dreams. San Francisco: City Lights Books, 1961.

Pull My Daisy. New York: Grove, 1961. Film script and narration.

Big Sur. New York: Farrar, Straus & Cudahy, 1962.

Visions of Gerard. New York: Farrar, Straus, 1963.

Desolation Angels. New York: Coward-McCann, 1965.

Satori in Paris. New York: Grove, 1966.

Vanity of Duluoz: An Adventurous Education, 1935–46. New York: Coward-McCann, 1968.

Pic. New York: Grove, 1971.

Visions of Cody. New York: McGraw-Hill, 1972.

POETRY

Mexico City Blues. New York: Grove, 1959.

"Old Angel Midnight." *Big Table,* 1:7–42 (Spring 1959).

Rimbaud. San Francisco: City Lights Books, 1960.

The Scripture of the Golden Eternity. New York: Totem Press / Corinth, 1960.

Scattered Poems. San Francisco: City Lights Books, 1971.

Trip Trap: Haiku Along the Road from San Francisco to New York, 1959. With Albert Saijo and Lew Welch. Bolinas, Calif.: Grey Fox Press, 1973.

ESSAYS

"Essentials of Spontaneous Prose." *Black Mountain Review,* 7:226–228 (Autumn 1957).

"October in the Railroad Earth." *Black Mountain Review,* 7:30–37 (Autumn 1957).

"Belief and Technique for Modern Prose." *Evergreen Review,* 2:57 (Spring 1959).

"The Origins of the Beat Generation." *Playboy,* 6:31–32, 42, 79 (June 1959).

"Letter from Jack Kerouac on Céline." *Paris Review,* 31:136 (Winter–Spring 1964).

AUTOBIOGRAPHY

Lonesome Traveler. New York: McGraw-Hill, 1960.

BIBLIOGRAPHIES

Charters, Ann. *A Bibliography of Works by Jack Kerouac, 1939–1975*. New York: Phoenix Book Shop, 1975.

Milewski, J. *Jack Kerouac: An Annotated Bibliography of Secondary Sources, 1944–1979*. Metuchen, N.J.: Scarecrow Press, 1981.

BIOGRAPHICAL AND CRITICAL STUDIES

Beaulieu, Victor-Lévy. *Jack Kerouac: A Chicken-Essay*. Translated by Sheila Fischman. Toronto: Coach House Press, 1975.

Berrigan, Ted. "The Art of Fiction, XLI." Interview with Jack Kerouac. *Paris Review,* 43:60–105 (Summer 1968).

Challis, Chris. *Quest for Kerouac*. London: Faber & Faber, 1984.

Charters, Ann. *Kerouac: A Biography*. San Francisco: Straight Arrow, 1973.

———. "Kerouac's Literary Method and Experiments: The Evidence of the Manuscript Notebooks in the Berg Collection." *Bulletin of Research in the Humanities,* 84, no. 4:431–450 (Winter 1981).

———, ed. "The Beats: Literary Bohemians in Postwar America." Parts I and II. *Dictionary of Literary Biography*. Vol. 16. Detroit: Gale Research, 1983.

Clark, Tom. *Jack Kerouac*. New York: Harcourt Brace Jovanovich, 1984.

Cook, Bruce. *The Beat Generation*. New York: Scribners, 1971.

Donaldson, Scott, ed. *On the Road: Text and Criticism*. New York: Viking, 1979.

Eaton, V. J., ed. *Catching Up with Kerouac: Getting Boulder on the Road*. Warren, Ohio: 1984.

Feied, Frederick. *No Pie in the Sky: The Hobo as American Cultural Hero in the Works of Jack London, John Dos Passos, and Jack Kerouac*. New York: Citadel, 1964.

French, Warren. *Jack Kerouac: Novelist of the Beat Generation*. Boston: Twayne, 1986.

Gifford, Barry. *Kerouac's Town*. Berkeley, Calif.: Creative Arts, 1977.

Gifford, Barry, and Lawrence Lee. *Jack's Book: An Oral Biography of Jack Kerouac*. New York: St. Martin's, 1978.

Hipkiss, Robert A. *Jack Kerouac: Prophet of the New Romanticism*. Lawrence, Kans.: Regents Press of Kansas, 1976.

Holmes, John Clellon. *Nothing More to Declare*. New York: Dutton, 1967.

———. *Gone in October: Last Reflections on Jack Kerouac*. Hailey, Idaho: Limberlost Press, 1985.

Hunt, Tim. *Kerouac's Crooked Road: Development of a Fiction*. Hamden, Conn.: Archon, 1981.

Johnson, Joyce. *Minor Characters*. Boston: Houghton Mifflin, 1983.

McNally, Dennis. *Desolate Angel: Jack Kerouac, the Beat Generation, and America*. New York: Random House, 1979.

Montgomery, John. *The Kerouac We Knew: Unposed Portraits, Action Shots*. San Anselmo, Calif.: Fels & Firn Press, 1982.

Nicosia, Gerald. *Memory Babe: A Critical Biography of Jack Kerouac*. New York: Grove, 1983.

Parkinson, Thomas, ed. *A Casebook on the Beat*. New York: Crowell, 1961.

Poteet, Maurice. *Textes de l'exode: Recueil de textes sur l'emigration des Quebecois aux États-Unis, XIXe et XXe siècles*. Montreal, Quebec: Guerin litterature, 1987.

———. "*Le Devoir* Dossier on Kerouac." *Moody Street Irregulars*. Spring–Summer 1982, pp. 14–16.

Tallman, Warren. "Kerouac's Sound." In Parkinson.

Tytell, John. *Naked Angels: The Lives and Literature of the Beat Generation*. New York: McGraw-Hill, 1976.

Walsh, Joy, ed. *Jack Kerouac: Statement in Brown*. Clarence Center, N.Y.: Textile Bridge Press, 1984.

Weinreich, Regina. *The Spontaneous Poetics of Jack Kerouac: A Study of the Fiction*. Carbondale: Southern Illinois University Press, 1987.

Ziavras, Charles E. *Visions of Kerouac*. Lowell, Mass.: Ithaca Press, 1974.

—ANN CHARTERS

Galway Kinnell

1927–

. . . we are not really at home in
our interpreted world. . . .
(Rilke, *The Duino Elegies,*
"The First Elegy")

. . . But listen to the voice of the wind
and the ceaseless message that forms itself out of
silence.
(Rilke, *The Duino Elegies,*
"The First Elegy")

POET, NOVELIST, TRANSLATOR, and occasional poet–critic and writer of children's literature, Galway Kinnell has been called "a kind of evangelist of the physical world," "dishearteningly prolix," "a shamanist, rather than a historicist, of the imagination," and a poet whose "risks are so great, his very lapses seem preferable to the limited successes of many other poets." He has published nine volumes of poetry: *What a Kingdom It Was* (1960), *Flower Herding on Mount Monadnock* (1964), *Body Rags* (1968), *First Poems 1946–1954* (1971), *The Book of Nightmares* (1971), *The Avenue Bearing the Initial of Christ into the New World: Poems 1946–64* (1974), *Mortal Acts, Mortal Words* (1980), *Selected Poems* (1982), and *The Past* (1985).

He has also, like many of his contemporaries, translated the work of artists who captured his imagination. "When you translate a poet," Kinnell remarked in a 1971 interview with Mary Jane Fortunato, "you invite or dare that poet to influence you." Kinnell's translations include René Hardy's novel *Bitter Victory* (1956), *The Poems of François Villon* (1965, and a second version in 1977), Yves Bonnefoy's *On the Motion and Immobility of Douve* (1968), and Yvan Goll's *Lackawanna Elegy* (1970). In addition, he has published one novel, *Black Light* (1966); a selection of interviews, *Walking Down the Stairs* (1978); and a children's book, *How the Alligator Missed Breakfast* (1982).

Applauded as one of the most vibrant voices in contemporary American poetry, Kinnell has received major recognition for his work: the Pulitzer Prize (1983) for his *Selected Poems,* an award from the National Institute of Arts and Letters (1962), two Guggenheim Fellowships (1961–1962, 1974–1975), Fulbright teaching appointments, two Rockefeller Foundation grants (1962–1963, 1968), the Brandeis Creative Arts Award (1969), the Shelley Prize of the Poetry Society of America (1974), the Medal of Merit from the National Institute of Arts and Letters (1975), the Harold L. Landon Translation Prize (1979), the American Book Award (shared with Charles Wright, 1983), and a MacArthur Foundation grant (1984). While Kinnell's awards and honors might suggest that he has relied on the safety and security of the academy, his numerous temporary academic appointments, extensive traveling, and political activities suggest otherwise.

Kinnell received his first tenured position in 1985, when he became the Samuel F. B. Morse Professor of Arts and Science at New York University. Before that, he held temporary appointments in the United States, in Europe, and in Australia. He also had been politically active, particularly during the 1960's, when he took part in anti–Vietnam War poetry readings, and in the 1980's, when he became involved in the antinuclear movement. In addition, he was president of P.E.N. during 1983–1984.

Some of Kinnell's poems refer to his political activities; "The Last River," for example, which appeared in *Body Rags* (1968), chronicles the time he spent in Louisiana in 1963, working in the voter registration campaign for the Congress of Racial Equality, and the week he was jailed there for his activities. It also points up Kinnell's increasing need to personalize his politics, to transcend the historical moment:

Through the crisscross
of bars at the tiny window
I could see the swallows
that were darting in the last light,
late-flying creatures that surpass us in plain
    view . . .
bits of blurred flesh . . .
wavy lines . . .

Nothing's there now but a few stars
brightening
under the ice-winds of the emptiness. . .

Isn't it strange
that all love, all granting of respect,
has no face for its passing expressions but yours,
Death?

Kinnell's meditation in jail does not ground him in the particular moment; instead, he focuses on how such moments are necessarily absorbed by the emptiness around us. The shadow of our mortality is ever present. This posture looks forward to *The Book of Nightmares* and *Mortal Acts, Mortal Words*.

Given Kinnell's prolific canon, made up of some exquisitely compressed short lyrics and some long poems that revitalize the use of rhythm, the short line, and the sentence, it is striking how little his concerns and preoccupations have changed over the decades. Reading through his poems, we encounter, albeit in different poetic forms, the same issues: the poet in a state of exile, "the comfort of darkness," "the sadness of joy," emptiness and silence as a plenitude, the purification afforded by flames, ruins, and ashes, song as redemptive, the inextricable relationship between eros and loss, the search for "the sublime" in an American landscape, a Stevensian celebration of "death [as] the mother of beauty," and a loving attentiveness to, as Kinnell notes, "the things and creatures that share the earth with us."

Thus, the question we are tempted, even compelled, to ask of most artists' work—"Does the aesthetic and poetic vision change and evolve over time?"—must be abandoned. As Lee Zimmerman points out, "Like Yeats, his early master, Kinnell spends his career working the same set of insights, but, predicated on changing experience, these are refashioned at every point." It is the continual refashioning of self, then, in a changing constellation of new and unexpected experiences that we must attend to in Kinnell's work.

Though only occasionally linked with James Merrill, Kinnell shares Merrill's early poetic preoccupation with the "need to make some kind of house / Out of the life lived, out of the love spent" ("An Urban Convalescence"). But, unlike Merrill, Kinnell starts from the premise that he is in a state of exile, "seeking home" but seldom finding such a resting place. For Kinnell the journey, composed of crossings and transitions, is everything. "And yet I can rejoice / that everything changes, that / we go from life / into life" ("Lost Loves"). It is these changes that his poetic project maps and that this essay will trace.

Born in Providence, Rhode Island, on February 1, 1927 (the same year as James Wright, John Ashbery, and W. S. Merwin), Galway Kinnell was the youngest of four children. Both of his parents were immigrants: his mother, from Ireland, and his father, a carpenter and teacher of woodworking, from Scotland. In "The Sadness of Brothers" (in *Mortal Acts, Mortal Words*), Kinnell remembers them, highlighting their differences:

> . . . the serene-
> seeming, sea-going gait
> which took him down Oswald Street in dark of each morning
> and up Oswald Street in dark of each night . . .
> this small, well-wandered Scotsman
> who appears now in memory's memory,
> in light of last days, jiggling
> his knees as he used to do—
> *get out of here,* I knew
> they were telling him, *get out of here, Scotty*—
> control he couldn't control
> thwarting his desires down
> into knees which could only jiggle
> the one bit of advice least useful
> to this man who had dragged himself to the earth's ends
> so he could end up
> in the ravaged ending-earth
> of Pawtucket, Rhode Island; where the Irish wife willed
> the bourgeois illusion all of us dreamed
> we lived, even he, who disgorged
> divine capitalist law
> out of his starved craw
> that we might succeed though he had failed
> at every enterprise but war. . . .

His father, "who had dragged himself to the earth's ends," is an outcast from life's feast, while his mother, more wedded to her dreams, "willed the bourgeois illusion all of us dreamed / we lived."

In a 1990 interview published in *New York Woman,* Kinnell described his childhood to Lois Smith Brady as "almost unbearably lonely." As a child his reading and desire to write gave him access to a private world of his own. He alludes to this in a 1971 interview with A. Poulin, Jr., and Stan Sanvel Rubin:

> As for the impulses that set me writing, I remember I lived a kind of double life: my "public" life with everyone I knew—brother, sisters, parents, friends, and so on—and my secret life with the poems I would read late at night. I found my most intimate feelings were shared in those poems more fully than in the relationships I had in the world.

In 1932 the family moved to Pawtucket, Rhode Island, where Kinnell attended public schools until his senior year of high school, when he was awarded a scholarship to Wilbraham Academy in Massachusetts. In this setting he was encouraged to write and probably was steered toward Princeton, which he entered, along with W. S. Merwin, in 1944. When asked by Wayne Dodd and Stanley Plumly in a 1972 interview if he and Merwin had written poems while at Princeton and shared them with one another, Kinnell replied:

> Yes, we showed each other poems—though mine, by comparison, were crude. Even at nineteen Merwin was writing poems of extraordinary skill and grace. His sense of the richness of English, his ear for its music, were then, and remain now even in his leaner poems, superior to anyone's.

During his junior year Kinnell studied with Charles Bell, who took his early efforts quite seriously; that summer he went to Black Mountain College, where Bell was lecturing. Bell fondly recalls one of their first encounters:

In the winter of 1946–47, when I was teaching at Princeton University, a dark-shocked student, looking more like a prize fighter than a literary man, showed me a poem, maybe his first. I remember it as a Wordsworthian sonnet, not what the avant-garde of Princeton, Blackmur or Berryman, would have taken to—old diction, no modern flair. But the last couplet had a romantic fierceness that amazed me. The man who had done that could go beyond any poetic limits to be assigned. I was reckless enough to tell him so.

At Merwin's insistence, Kinnell began reading Yeats. He frequently alludes to the significance of this influence; for instance, we know from the interview with Dodd and Plumly that Yeats influenced Kinnell's structuring of poems:

In my early twenties I thought Yeats was not only the greatest of all poets, but also in a manner of speaking, poetry itself. In everything I wrote I tried to reproduce his voice. If my poems didn't sound like Yeats, I thought they weren't poetry. . . . Yeats became a more useful mentor when I began to see his limitations, I think my interest in the poem made of sections, of elements that don't come together until the end, probably derives from Yeats, from poems like "Among Schoolchildren." I've always loved how all the materials of that poem come back woven together and transformed.

This remark looks forward to a poem like "Freedom, New Hampshire," which appeared in *What a Kingdom It Was.* The poem is an elegy to Kinnell's older brother, Derry, who died in a car crash when Kinnell was thirty. The poem's first sections, which include memories of their time together on a farm in New Hampshire, contain images of death—"We came to visit the cow / Dying of fever," and "We found a cowskull once; we thought it was / From one of the asses in the Bible. . ."—as well as their vision of birth, a vision that pays homage to the darkness from which we come and to which we return:

That night passing Towle's Barn
We saw lights. Towle had lassoed a calf
By its hind legs, and he tugged against the grip
Of the darkness. The cow stood by chewing
    millet.
Derry and I took hold, too, and hauled.
It was sopping with darkness when it came free.

In the last section, Kinnell moves from the past to a present that acknowledges and makes audible "the abruptly decaying sounds" around us. While he recognizes that at the moment of death "only flesh dies, and spirit flowers without stop," he also realizes that his brother's death, and everyone's, encompasses a certain finality: "When he is dead the grass / Heals what he suffered, but he remains dead, / And the few who loved him know this until they die." The pathos of this impersonal generalization is mitigated a bit by the more personal and particular recognition that only Kinnell, and "the few who loved" Derry, can preserve his memory. As Zimmerman maintains: "Later in his career, Kinnell comes closer to James Merrill's complex but comforting proposition that 'nothing either lasts or ends,' but here his sense of temporariness is fierce. . . ."

After graduating from Princeton in 1948, Kinnell attended the University of Rochester, where he received an M.A. in English in 1949. This was the end of his formal education. After two years as an instructor at Alfred University, Kinnell moved to Chicago, where, between 1951 and 1954, he supervised the liberal arts program at the downtown campus of the University of Chicago.

Kinnell's *First Poems 1946–1954,* those composed at Princeton and during the early 1950's, address "the comfort of darkness" and its relationship to "the feast" of life. In "The Feast," (1954), for example, Kinnell anticipates his 1971 essay "The Poetics of the Physical World," in which, following Rainer Maria Rilke, Wallace Stevens, and Elizabeth Bishop, he makes a virtue of Stevens' assertion in "Peter Quince at the Clavier": "The body dies; the body's beauty lives. / So evenings die, in their green going." "That we last only for a time," Kinnell asserts, ". . . that we know this, radiates a thrilling, tragic light on all our loves, all our relationships, even on those moments when the world, through its poetry, becomes almost capable of spurning time and death." In "The Feast," Kinnell also flirts with the possibility of "spurning time and death":

The sand turns cold—or the body warms.
If love had not smiled we would never grieve.
But on every earthly place its turning crown
Flashes and fades. We will feast on love again
In the purple light, and rise again and leave
Our two shapes dying in each other's arms.

Most of Kinnell's early poems display their indebtedness to his precursors, particularly Yeats, Robert Frost, William Carlos Williams, and Theodore Roethke; the more compelling influences of Walt Whitman and Rainer Maria Rilke come later. In a 1977 *Partisan Review* piece, Alan Helms finds *First Poems 1946–1954* "most remarkable for the unassimilated debts Kinnell incurs"; he also points out that "in *What a Kingdom It Was* (1960) Kinnell pays off some of his debts; [while] in *Flower Herding on Mount Monadnock* (1964) he's in the black, writing his own good poetry, especially in Part II of that book."

Certain poems in *What a Kingdom It Was* are memorable for what they portend in Kinnell's canon: "First Song," with its realization that song can lead to a "fall" into "darkness and into the sadness of joy"; "Freedom, New Hampshire," Kinnell's elegy to his brother, which anticipates "Another Night in the Ruins," in which the poet imagines a world where there is no phoenix but, rather, "the cow / of nothingness, mooing / down the bones"; and "The Supper After the Last," which announces that it is desirable to give up the "Lech for transcendence" in favor of "Intricate and simple things / As you are, created / In the image of nothing." *What a Kingdom It Was* is significant, however, because of the long poem that comprises Part IV: "The Avenue Bearing the Initial of Christ into the New World."

This poem, which many of Kinnell's critics feel is only partially successful, grew out of his experience of living on Avenue C on the Lower East Side of New York from 1957 to 1959. The thirty-year-old Kinnell was one of several poets who took up residence in this neighborhood during the 1950's. According to Lois Smith Brady, "Denise Levertov lived in his building; Allen Ginsberg lived within walking distance; Robert Bly used to come over in the afternoons." In this same interview Kinnell comments on the relationship between this setting and his poetic project, and on Whitman's influence. He began reading Whitman seriously while teaching at the University of Grenoble in 1956–1957, just before he moved to Avenue C.

In those days the Lower East Side was a terribly vivid and active exotic world. I had just discovered Whitman, who wandered around New York with his notebook, looking into butcher shops and blacksmith shops and taking notes, so I did the same. Gradually, I realized I wanted to write a little hymn to this part of the world, and that turned out to be "The Avenue Bearing the Initial of Christ into the New World."

An interview with Ken McCullough in 1976

sheds additional light on Kinnell's project. In it he points out an important distinction between his vision and Whitman's: ''Much of Whitman's poetry is devoted to celebrating ordinary sights and sounds and in this respect the 'Avenue C' poem probably does follow Whitman. But in my poem, time and progress appear as enemies, as they never do in Whitman.'' Despite this important difference in focus, it is clear that Whitman had a profound influence on the form of Kinnell's poem. Thirty years after the poem was written, in the introduction to *The Essential Whitman* (1987), Kinnell described the change that took place in his poetry when he discovered Whitman: ''Under Whitman's spell I stopped writing in rhyme and meter and in rectangular stanzas and turned to long-lined, loosely cadenced verse; and at once I felt immensely liberated.''

Morris Dickstein claims that Kinnell's ''little hymn'' to Avenue C ''is less a poem than a vast poetic notebook that enabled [him]—by a discipline of attention to the world around him—to slough off the artificialities and tired literary devices of the old style.'' Paul Mariani also maintains that Kinnell's subject allowed him to abandon ''earlier formalist techniques'' and

> to pursue new rhetorical models, to see what he could do, for example, with the Whitmanian catalogue, the language of the image, and—unlike Whitman but very much like Villon—with the suppression of a poetic self in favor of allowing the mirror world on the other side of the poet's window to reveal something of the interiority of the human condition.

We can also see Kinnell's kinship with Villon when he identifies with the marginal individual—the transgressor, who might at any time be banished from society. This identification emerges in Kinnell's vision of ''the wiped-out lives—punks, lushes, / Panhandlers, pushers, rumsoaks . . .'' on Avenue C.

Even though the influence of Whitman's catalogs, speech rhythms, and readiness to make observations lurks behind Kinnell's aesthetic and form in the poem, the voice is Kinnell's, perhaps for the first time. It is Kinnell's close observation of the life and energies surrounding these ''wiped-out lives'' that vitalizes the poem. Section 6, for example, focuses on ''the pushcart market, on Sunday,'' where vegetables display a subterranean energy, giving us a vision of how all life comes into the light from darkness:

A crate of lemons discharges light like a battery.
Icicle-shaped carrots that through black soil
Wove away lie like flames in the sun.
Onions with their shirts ripped seek sunlight
On green skins. The sun beats
On beets dirty as boulders in cowfields,
On turnips pinched and gibbous
From budging rocks. . . .

And in section 11 Kinnell describes the fishmarket with its ''Fishes [which] do not die exactly, it is more / That they go out of themselves. . . .'' He allows us to see the fish in their otherness; they are laid out to be sold, but he banishes the consumer by taking us in after hours.

The fishmarket closed, the fishes gone into flesh.
The smelts draped on each other, fat with roe,
The marble cod hacked into chunks on the
  counter,
Butterfishes mouths still open, still trying to eat,
Porgies with receding jaws hinged apart
In a grimace of dejection, as if like cows
They had died under the sledgehammer, perches
In grass-green armor, spotted squeteagues
In the melting ice meek-faced and croaking no
  more,
. . . .
. . . two-tone flounders
After the long contortion of pushing both eyes
To the brown side that they might look up,

Brown side down, like a mass laying-on of
hands,
Or the oath-taking of an army.

Kinnell's metaphors at the end of this section remind us of his own poetic enterprise in the poem. His observations, like Whitman's in "Song of Myself," become a kind of faith healing—"a mass laying-on of hands." Perhaps Kinnell wishes to heal himself: seeing with the inclusiveness of Whitman and cataloging the images around him become means toward redemption, means of temporarily forgetting the historical moment and those "enemies": "time and progress."

But it takes a leap of faith to see such a project as politically viable at this time in our history. As Cary Nelson perceptively points out:

Kinnell's verbal motives require not deftly managed synecdoche but a sense of broad inclusiveness established through accumulated detail. So long as the details are American, the method is patently Whitmanesque, and by now culturally approved and politically safe. Yet our history has soured us for such projects. . . . We can now *see* with Whitman's eyes; the vast poem of America founders all about us. Visually, we can cross the continent in a minute. If the trip takes longer, the poem of community succumbs to the obvious visual evidence of violence and greed.

In *Flower Herding on Mount Monadnock,* Kinnell asks us to make still another leap of faith by beginning with "The River That Is East." We might expect him in this poem, which focuses on the East River rather than the Mississippi, to write off the American dream; instead, Kinnell finds a way, reminiscent of Nick Carraway's vision at the end of Fitzgerald's *The Great Gatsby,* to reinscribe its potency even in the face of the wonderless river "Which drags the things we love, / Processions of debris like floating lamps, / Towards the radiance in which they go out?"

The first section pays homage to the movement of things on the river: the clanging buoys, the tugs, the carfloat, and the "white-winged gulls which shriek / And flap from the water. . . ." Traveling along this working river, we see its shores and the Williamsburg Bridge "That hangs facedown from its strings / Over which the Jamaica Local crawls."

In section 2 Kinnell moves from this concrete and particular perspective, shifting our attention to a boy sitting by the river and trying to conjure up some romance of his own. The poet wonders if the young boy can be linked to others in American literature who had their unrealized, though no less potent, dreams. In this context Kinnell offers a meditation on the male twentieth-century American romance tradition of questing. Orson Welles, F. Scott Fitzgerald, Ernest Hemingway, Thomas Wolfe, and Theodore Dreiser define this tradition. Taking us out of the present moment of section 1, Kinnell, a diehard romantic, looks back at these cultural "heroes":

On his deathbed
Kane remembered the abrupt, missed Grail
Called Rosebud, Gatsby must have thought back
On his days digging clams in Little Girl Bay
In Minnesota, Nick fished in dreamy Michigan,
Gant had his memories, Griffiths, those
Who went baying after the immaterial
And whiffed its strange dazzle in a blonde
In a canary convertible, who died
Thinking of the Huck Finns of themselves
On the old afternoons, themselves like this
boy. . . .

Section 3 focuses on "a man," rather than "a boy," who "has long since stopped wishing his heart were full / Or his life dear to him." Yet despite this disavowal, he still thinks, when he sees "the dirty water," of the possibility of some transcendent moment: "If I were a gull I would be one with white wings, / I would fly out over the water, explode, and / Be beautiful snow hitting the dirty water." This conditional conjecture prepares us for the Nick Carraway-like sentiments in section 4:

And thou, River of Tomorrow, flowing . . .
We stand on the shore, which is mist beneath us,
And regard the onflowing river. Sometimes
It seems the river stops and the shore
Flows into the past. Nevertheless, its leaked promises
Hopping in the bloodstream, we strain for the future,
Sometimes even glimpse it, a vague, scummed thing
We dare not recognize, and peer again
At the cabled shroud out of which it came,
We who have no roots but the shifts of our pain,
No flowering but our own strange lives.

What begins as a critique of why this "River of Tomorrow" is inseparable from "the past" of "leaked promises" turns into a reaffirmation of the Emersonian mythology of "self-reliance"; Emerson's mythology celebrates the possibility of knowing "No flowering but [one's] own strange [life]" and of denying historical contingencies: knowing "no roots but the shifts of [one's] pain." This particular type of "self-fashioning" obviously serves to take us back to Kinnell's allusions to Kane, Gatsby, Nick Adams, Eugene Gant, and Clyde Griffiths in section 2. Most important, it signals Kinnell's increasing concern with being true to "the shifts of [his own] pain" and the "flowering [of his] own strange [life]." Without being confessional in the sense that Merrill and Robert Lowell are, Kinnell turns again and again in his poems to the shape and texture of his life, to the trajectories of the journeys he has taken and will take.

When he moves from the cityscapes in Part I of *Flower Herding on Mount Monadnock* to the rural landscapes of Part II, Kinnell's relationship to the life he is living begins to change as he confronts his own mortality. Charles Molesworth points this out when he maintains that "it is only when Kinnell escapes the city for the country that the possibilities of mortality become positive rather than negative." This impulse is played out in Kinnell's embrace of the darkness and in his Rilkean realization that "we are not really at home in / our interpreted world. . . ." Some lines from "Middle of the Way," a poem about an actual journey through a particular landscape, whose signs cannot be deciphered, illustrate the point: "I love the earth, and always / In its darknesses I am a stranger"; "All I see is we float out / Into the emptiness, among the great stars, / On this little vessel without lights"; "But I know I live half alive in the world, / I know half my life belongs to the wild darkness."

The final poem of the collection, "Flower Herding on Mount Monadnock," is striking in its evocation of Rilke's knowledge of "Things, / which live by perishing . . ." (*The Duino Elegies,* "The Ninth Elegy"). The poet realizes as he looks at this flower that "Its drift is to be nothing." Dropping out of sight in the final end-stopped lines of the poem, Kinnell gives the flower its autonomy, allowing its finitude a visibility and prominence: "The appeal to heaven breaks off. / The petals begin to fall, in self-forgiveness. / It is a flower. On this mountainside it is dying." This relinquishing of the poetic I, but not the poetic eye, is an unfamiliar posture in Kinnell's canon up to this point. More often, he is like Frost's speaker at the beginning of "The Most of It," who "thought he kept the universe alone." Kinnell's desire, like his precursor's, is to have "original response" from his surroundings rather than "copy speech" in return for his efforts to connect to the things of this world.

In 1965, the year Kinnell's translation of Villon was published, he took part in an anti–Vietnam War reading at Town Hall in New York City. During the 1960's Kinnell was an active presence at such readings. "Vapor Trail Reflected in the Frog Pond," which appeared in

Body Rags, captures his virulent antiwar, and by extension anti-American, feelings at this time. In the poem, which some critics have described as a parody of Whitman's "I Hear America Singing," Kinnell listens to the "varied carols" America *now* sings; he hears the dissonance of

crack of deputies' rifles practicing their aim on
 stray dogs at night,
sput of cattleprod,
TV groaning at the smells of the human body,
curses of the soldier as he poisons, burns, grinds,
 and stabs
the rice of the world,
with open mouth, crying strong, hysterical
 curses.

Kinnell mirrors the dissonance of the "singing" in his seemingly arbitrary line lengths and in his convoluted syntax. While we might expect to see the soldier's tortured body language—"open mouth, crying strong, hysterical curses"—before his violent actions, Kinnell disorients us by delaying the description.

In 1965 Kinnell married Inés Delgado de Torres. A year later their daughter, Maud, was born and his novel, *Black Light,* was published. *Black Light,* which Kinnell describes as "closer to a fable than to a novel," grew out of the year he spent in Iran (1959) as a lecturer for six months at the University of Tehran and then as a journalist for an English-language edition of a Tehran newspaper. While working for the newspaper, he traveled around the country, "sometimes with friends who knew Iran very well, more often alone. . . ."

Black Light anticipates *Body Rags,* his third volume of poetry, in dealing with how exile can be empowering. The protagonist, a carpet mender named Jamshid, commits a murder; the circumstances surrounding this action lack a fundamental meaning or logic. We are asked instead to focus on the consequences of this action: Jamshid is forced to leave his village, to wander somewhat aimlessly, and to redefine his relations with others and his past. Paradoxically, he can begin to reconstruct his history only in the moment that he appears most cut off from it. By giving up the possibility of repairing or restoring the rug on which he has been working so that it will be whole again, he can begin to know the painful fragments—a vision of the dissonances—that constitute his life:

He had spent all those years in Meshed weaving closed the gaps, as if he had thought that if you perfected a surface what it was laid upon no longer had to be reckoned with. Now that he had broken through the surface, it seemed he had no choice anymore but to die into the essential foulness of things.

It is no coincidence that two of the poets Kinnell translated—Villon (1965) and Yvan Goll (1970)—also experienced the feeling of being exiled and explored the implications of this state in their work. Villon, who was repeatedly arrested (for street fights and thefts), was finally banished from Paris for ten years. When asked in an interview with Mary Jane Fortunato about his translations of Villon, Kinnell maintained that "When you translate a poet, you invite or dare that poet to influence you. In my case I think one can see Bonnefoy in *Flower Herding* and possibly shades of Villon in *Body Rags.*"

Although Kinnell's interest in Goll's work looks forward to his own poetic vision in *The Book of Nightmares,* it also may be seen as integral to his aesthetic in *Body Rags,* where, like Goll, Kinnell moves steadily toward a recognition of "the permanence of his [own] solitude." Goll, whose French poems captivated Kinnell, left France during World War II and resided in New York City until after the war. In his preface to his translation of the *Lackawanna Elegy,* Kinnell links Goll's creative project to his state of feeling exiled: "The permanence of his solitude was the terrible discovery of his exile: knowing finally that he belonged nowhere. Out of this solitude he wrote this masterpiece, the grave and beautiful poems of the *Lackawanna Elegy.*"

Body Rags, Kinnell's third volume of poems, appeared in 1968, the year his son, Finn Fergus, was born. It moves away from the somewhat pastoral forays of *Flower Herding on Mount Monadnock* toward "the cold, savage thumpings of a heart" ("Going Home by Last Night") that knows the cost of spending "Another Night in the Ruins." As Richard Howard points out, ". . . life for Galway Kinnell [in *Body Rags*] becomes a matter of sacred vestiges, remnants, husks." In a state of perpetual exile—"terrified, seeking home, / and among flowers / I have come to myself empty" ("The Porcupine")—Kinnell tries to see what still remains, what is not lost, what can be recovered from the ruins. In "The Fossils," for example, his survey of prehistoric plant and animal life leads him to affirm: "Over the least fossil / day breaks in gold, frankincense, and myrrh." Kinnell learns in *Body Rags* what Frost's ovenbird "frames in all but words": "what to make of a diminished thing."

Body Rags is probably best known for Kinnell's concluding poems, "The Porcupine" and "The Bear." Many critics have pointed to the poet's need to identify with these animals. The identification is particularly acute in "The Bear": The poet eats a bear "turd sopped in blood," then climbs inside the dead bear's carcass:

I hack
a ravine in his thigh, and eat and drink,
and tear him down his whole length
and open him and climb in
and close him up after me, against the wind,
and sleep.

At this point in the poem, the poet's existence is likened to the bear's; like the bear he lumbers "flatfooted / over the tundra, / stabbed twice from within." And as he absorbs the "ill-digested bear blood" and "the ordinary, wretched odor of bear," he is recalled, momentarily, to the possibility of hearing "a song / or screech, until I think I must rise up / and dance." But this poet's/bear's dance only enables him to wander, wonder, and question, knowing only the certainty of hunger and loneliness.

And one
hairy-soiled trudge stuck out before me,
the next groaned out,
the next,
the next,
the rest of my days I spend
wandering: wondering
what, anyway,
was that sticky infusion, that rank flavor of
blood, that
poetry, by which I lived?

The poet's dance and song have been replaced by "that rank flavor of blood." Associated with the pain of being wounded and hunted, poetry, or the project of writing—finding what will suffice—becomes that "sticky infusion," pulled out of his guts. This dream / descent prepares us for the nourishing nightmares in *The Book of Nightmares.*

Many of the best poems in *Body Rags,* particularly the short lyrics, focus on those moments in which the speaker gains knowledge that allows him to reimagine both his existence and his poetic project. In "Another Night in the Ruins" the poet remembers his brother, Derry, who "used to tell [him]":

"What good is the day?
On some hill of despair
the bonfire
you kindle can light the great sky—
though it's true, of course, to make it burn
you have to throw yourself in . . ."

By the end of the poem Kinnell finds a way to embrace these words, but first he must confront "the eaves of [his] ruins." He must know "the cow / of nothingness, mooing / down the bones" and the rooster who "thrashes in the snow / for a grain. Finds / it. Rips / it into / flames." Kinnell must become the rooster who "Flaps. Crows. / Flames / bursting out of his brow" before he can give up the image of the phoenix:

How many nights must it take
one such as me to learn
that we aren't, after all, made
from that bird which flies out of its ashes,
that for a man
as he goes up in flames, his one work
is
to open himself, to *be*
the flames?

Richard Howard provides a useful frame for Kinnell's purification rite:

The poetry of Galway Kinnell . . . is an Ordeal by Fire. It is fire which he invokes to set forth his plight, to enact his ordeal, and to restore himself to reality. It is fire—in its constant transformations, its endless resurrection—which *is* reality, for Kinnell as for Heraclitus. . . . The agony of that knowledge—the knowledge or at least the conviction that all must be consumed in order to be reborn, must be reduced to ash in order to be redeemed—gives Galway Kinnell's poetry its astonishing resonance. . . .

The notion of purification is reconfigured in different terms in "Lost Loves," in which Kinnell likens his existence, in the face of both "ashes of old volcanoes" and his body's "deathward flesh in the sun," to "the tadpole, his time come, tumbling toward the / slime."

In *Body Rags,* Kinnell repeatedly looks for ways of living without the phoenix. In "How Many Nights," for example, he finds peace in "the frozen world" from an unlikely source:

How many nights
have I lain in terror,
O Creator Spirit, Maker of night and day,

only to walk out
the next morning over the frozen world
hearing under the creaking of snow
faint, peaceful breaths . . .
snake,
bear, earthworm, ant . . .

and above me
a wild crow crying *'yaw yaw yaw'*
from a branch nothing cried from ever in my life.

When asked about the crow in a 1969 interview with William Heyen and Gregory Fitz Gerald, Kinnell responded with a poem that provides an interpretation of the last two lines of "How Many Nights":

I know the line about that crow is puzzling. In fact, when the poem was first published, some friends telephoned me, to ask whether I'd thought of the crow as benign or as an unwelcome presence. I wrote this bit of verse to explicate those last lines. It's called "The Mind."

Suppose it's true
that from the beginning, a bird has been perched
in the silence of each branch.

It is this to have lived—
that when night comes, every one of them
will have sung, or be singing.

I was thinking of those diagrams—I still don't know if they are of the nervous system or of the blood vessels—that show the brain in the shape of a tree. At moments of full consciousness all the birds would be singing. Whether or not the crow's cry is beautiful mattered less to me than that this hitherto mute region comes into consciousness.

Kinnell might have settled for the "faint, peaceful breaths" of the hibernating creatures under the snow. Instead, in a moment reminiscent of Stevens' speaker in ''Autumn Refrain,'' who hears ''some skreaking and skrittering residuum'' of grackles now gone, Kinnell looks up at a single wild crow, who cries ''from a branch nothing cried from ever in my life.'' Like Stevens, Kinnell will never hear the nightingale. But, unlike Stevens, Kinnell finds nothing ''desolate'' in the sound of his wild crow. This crow does not change ''the frozen world,'' but it does begin to affect Kinnell's inner landscape. The crow restores him, in a way that the ''Creator-Spirit'' cannot, to a part of his existence. This unexpected restoration is a kind of grace.

Kinnell's next volume of poetry, *The Book of Nightmares* (1971), is less concerned with such moments of earth-born grace. If possible, Kinnell's journey is still darker and more probing of those ''mute region[s]'' of the self/soul. The most ambitious and most successful of Kinnell's work to date, the poem took four years to write. ''A lot of that time,'' Kinnell notes in a 1972 interview with James J. McKenzie, ''I worked on it day after day.'' When asked about the genesis of the poem, Kinnell replied:

> I began it as a single ten-part sequence. I had been rather immersed in the *Duino Elegies*. In the Ninth Elegy, Rilke says, in effect, ''Don't try to tell the angels about the glory of your feelings, or how splendid your soul is; they know all about that. Tell them something they'd be more interested in, something that you know better than they, tell them about the things of the world.'' So it came to me to write a poem called ''The Things.'' Like the *Elegies* it would be a poem without plot, yet with a close relationship among the parts, and a development from beginning to end. . . . The poem has moved far from its original intention to be about things and now probably does try to tell the angels about the glory of my feelings!

In this long poem modeled upon Rilke's *Duino Elegies,* made up of ten sections of seven parts each, Kinnell confronts death's ''two aspects—the extinction, which we fear, and the flowing away into the universe, which we desire. . . .'' The epigraph from Rilke, which appears underneath the dedication to Kinnell's children, Maud and Fergus, further illuminates his emphasis on death in the poem:

> But this, though: death,
> the whole of death,—even before life's begun,
> to hold it also gently, and be good:
> this is beyond description!

In the 1972 interview with Dodd and Plumly, Kinnell provides a useful commentary on the relationship between the epigraph and the dedication, one that serves to illuminate the poem's concerns as a whole:

> This passage appears after the dedication to Maud and Fergus. From one point of view, the book is nothing but an effort to face death and live with death. Children have all that effort in their future. They have glimpses of death through fatigue, sleep, cuts and bruises, warnings, etc., and also through their memory of the nonexistence they so recently came from. They seem to understand death surprisingly clearly. But now time passes slowly for them. It hardly exists. They live with death almost as animals do. This natural trust in life's rhythms, infantile as it is, provides the model for the trust they may struggle to learn later on. *The Book of Nightmares* is my own effort to find the trust again. I invoke Maud and Fergus not merely to instruct them, but also to get help from them.

In the first section of the poem, ''Under the Maud Moon,'' Kinnell's description of the birth process as a cutting of Maud's ''tie to the darkness'' magnificently captures how close children are to death—to the memory of ''the nonexistence they so recently came from.''

. . . And as they cut

her tie to the darkness
she dies
a moment, turns blue as a coal,
the limbs shaking
as the memories rush out of them. . . .

At the end of this section Kinnell looks toward a future that no longer includes his protective presence and hopes that his book of nightmares, drawing ''from everything that dies,'' will comfort his daughter, who thus far is more familiar with the darkness from which she came:

And in the days
when you find yourself orphaned,
emptied
of all wind-singing, of light,
the pieces of cursed bread on your tongue,

may there come back to you
a voice
spectral, calling you
sister!
from everything that dies.

And then
you shall open
this book, even if it is the book of nightmares.

Kinnell also draws inspiration from Maud in section VII—''Little Sleep's-Head Sprouting Hair in the Moonlight''—when he makes a list of things he might do to protect her from the finality of death that he embraces.

I would blow the flame out of your silver cup,
I would suck the rot from your fingernail,
I would brush your sprouting hair of the dying light,
I would scrape the rust off your ivory bones,
I would help death escape through the little ribs of your body,
I would alchemize the ashes of your cradle back into wood,
I would let nothing of you go, ever. . . .

Later in the same section he encourages Maud to see the relationship between ''enduring love'' and ''the still undanced cadence of vanishing.'' When she is most sure of the permanence of love, she will ''learn to reach deeper / into the sorrows / to come. . . .''

If Kinnell is instructing Maud, and later Fergus, he is also preparing himself for ''the mercy of darkness'' and ''the sorrows / to come.'' In section II, ''The Hen Flower,'' he thinks in a moment of almost mystical union:

. . .—if only
we could let go
like her, throw ourselves
on the mercy of darkness, like the hen,

tuck our head
under a wing, hold ourselves still
a few moments, as she
falls out into her little trance in the witchgrass,
or turn over
and be stroked with a finger

. . . .

. . . until the fatted thing
woozes off, head
thrown back
on the chopping block, longing only
to die.

In a 1976 interview with Margaret Edwards, Kinnell comments on his ''fascination with hens.'' Explaining that his family had ''had a henhouse'' when he was growing up, he remarked:

Though not very personable, hens have an unusual psychic dimension, due, I like to think, to the suppression of their capacity to fly. When you hold their heads under their wings they slump into a strange coma. You might think they think it is the night, except that they do the same thing if you turn them on their backs and stroke their throats.

In "The Hen Flower" Kinnell seems to identify with "the suppression of their capacity to fly": "—and unable / to fly, / and waiting, therefore, / for the sweet, eventual blaze in the genes, / that one day, according to gospel, shall carry [them] back / into pink skies. . . ." He also waits for a future in which he might "let go." Yet the only certainty he has for now is that "these feathers freed from their wings forever / are afraid."

In section III, "The Shoes of Wandering," Kinnell wonders if our wandering "is the last trace in us / of wings?" He returns to the hen who cannot fly:

And is it
the hen's nightmare, or her secret dream,
to scratch the ground forever
eating the minutes out of the grains of sand?

Kinnell desires the certainty of "the great wanderers, who lighted / their steps by the lamp / of pure hunger and pure thirst," but must settle instead for "the Crone's" words:

You live
under the Sign
of the Bear, who flounders through chaos
in his starry blubber:
poor fool,
poor forked branch
of applewood, you will feel all your bones
break
over the holy waters you will never drink.

In the final section of the poem, "Lastness," Kinnell makes his peace with his journey toward his own death. In the first section, he had lit "a small fire in the rain." This fire is now "somewhere behind me":

Somewhere behind me
a small fire goes on flaring in the rain, in the
desolate ashes.
No matter, now, whom it was built for,
it keeps its flames,
it warms
everyone who might wander into its radiance,
a tree, a lost animal, the stones,

because in the dying world it was set burning.

As in section I, Kinnell is still the black bear sitting alone; this time, however, the image leads him to imagine his own death:

. . . a death-creature
watches from the fringe of the trees,
finally he understands
I am no longer here, he himself
from the fringe of the trees watches
a black bear
get up, eat a few flowers, trudge away,
all his fur glistening
in the rain.

This image of the bear frames Maud's birth in section I; in "Lastness" it frames Fergus' birth. The mother and maternal nurturing are curiously absent in both sections of the poem. Kinnell puts the spotlight on himself as father and receiver of life.

When he [Fergus] came wholly forth
I took him up in my hands and bent
over and smelled
the black, glistening fur
of his head, as empty space
must have bent
over the newborn planet
and smelled the grasslands and the ferns.

We next see the poet "walking toward the cliff. . . ." From this vantage point he calls out to "the stone," which "calls back, its voice hunting among the rubble / for my ears." Conjuring up his echo/presence leads him to imagine his death/absence—a world "where the voice calling from stone / no longer answers, / turns into stone, and nothing comes back." Kinnell finds himself back in "the old shoes / flowed over by rainbows of hen-oil,'' ''the whole foot trying / to dissolve into the future.'' And he asks an old question: ''Is it true / the earth is all there is, and the earth does not last?'' The answer is implicit in the end-stopped lines, which strive for a sense of closure in a poem that usually denies such a possibility: ''Stop. / Stop here. / Living brings you to death, there is no other road.'' As Robert Langbaum perceptively points out: ''Stated so baldly, these seem rather banal observations.'' The lines are certainly anticlimactic, if not banal, at this point in the poem, though the case could be made that they are the unsaid chant underlying each section of the poem.

Finally the poem celebrates the poet's struggle to make the ''earthward gesture'' while still trying to be ''the sky-diver''—to be the hen who has forgotten what it might mean to fly:

This poem
if we shall call it that,
or concert of one
divided among himself,
this earthward gesture
of the sky-diver, the worms
on his back still spinning forth
and already gnawing away
the silks of his loves, who could have saved him,
this free floating of one
opening his arms into the attitude
of flight, as he obeys the necessity and falls. . . .

If the poem had ended here, it might seem like the last poem Kinnell would need to write; it ends, however, with some rather flip advice for his son.

On the body,
On the blued flesh, when it is
laid out, see if you can find
the one flea which is laughing.

The stark image of the ''blued flesh'' is muted, or undermined, by the image of one flea laughing. We might, more appropriately, have been given an image of the ghastly ''flesh-fly,'' ''starved for the soul,'' from Kinnell's poem ''The Fly,'' which appeared in *Body Rags*.

Kinnell's next volume of poetry, *Mortal Acts, Mortal Words,* did not appear until 1980. In 1977 his revised version of *The Poems of François Villon* was published. In 1979 he received the Harold L. Landon Translation Prize. In the fall of 1978 he held a Fulbright lectureship in France at the University of Nice. That same year, *Walking Down the Stairs: Selections from Interviews* was published, providing his readers with new insights into his aesthetic. In 1979 Kinnell was a visiting writer in Sydney, Australia, at MacQuarie University. He spent the next two years teaching in Hawaii; in 1980, the year *Mortal Acts* was published, Kinnell returned to New York briefly to visit James Wright, who was dying of lung cancer. Anne Wright describes their last meeting:

Galway came straight from the airport to the hospital. As soon as he saw James he leaned over his bed and hugged him, tubes and all. James couldn't talk but he wrote notes to Galway on a yellow-lined pad. During that visit James was alert, a little bit stronger, well aware his friend was there.

Galway returned in March. When he came to the hospital I had a photocopy of James's manuscript, *This Journey,* for him. Galway had always gone over manuscripts with James and, sick as he was, James urged me to have his latest one ready for Galway.

In ''A Winter Daybreak at Vence,'' the poem Kinnell suggested should complete *This Journey,* Wright remembers the time he and Anne spent with the Kinnells in southern France:

I turn, and somehow
Impossibly hovering in the air over everything,
The Mediterranean, nearer to the moon
Than this mountain is,

Shines. A voice clearly
Tells me to snap out of it. Galway
Mutters out of the house and up the stone stairs
To start the motor. The moon and the stars
Suddenly flicker out, and the whole mountain
Appears, pale as a shell.

In *Mortal Acts,* Kinnell turns away from the dark nightmares of *The Book of Nightmares* and *Body Rags* toward "the singing / of mortal lives, waves of spent existence" ("There Are Things I Tell to No One"). He renews his belief that song can heal: "for those who can groan / to sing, / for those who can sing to heal themselves" ("The Still Time"). He explores, as he had in previous volumes, the inexorable relationship between eros and loss, as the following lines from "The Apple" illustrate:

No one easily
survives love; neither the love
one has, nor the love
one has not; each breaks down
in the red smoke blown up
of the day when all love will have gone on.

Kinnell has not traveled very far from the sentiment expressed in his early poem "The Feast": "If love had not smiled we would never grieve." Nevertheless, there is a kind of faith, absent from his early poems, that he can make the journey "from night / into day, from transcending union always forward into difficult day" ("Flying Home").

Mortal Acts includes some delightfully self-contained lyrics, particularly in Part II, where we find "Daybreak," "The Gray Heron," and "Blackberry Eating." These poems celebrate in uncomplicated ways the things and creatures of the earth. In "Daybreak," Kinnell likens "dozens of starfishes" to "enormous, imperfect stars." As the starfishes sink into the mud, they become invisible, like "the true stars at daybreak." Kinnell sustains his simile without reaching after anything grander than his analogy. In "The Gray Heron" he watches a heron that moves out of sight; he then encounters a three-foot-long lizard whose head reminds him of "a fieldstone with an eye / in it." Still watching, he suddenly realizes he is being watched. The shift in perspective is highlighted by the final lines, in which the possibility emerges that in being watched, he may change shape or evolve into some other form of life: the lizard "was watching me / to see if I would go / or change into something else." And in "Blackberry Eating" finding language to describe the blackberries is as sensuous as the process of devouring the berries:

lifting the stalks to my mouth, the ripest berries
fall almost unbidden to my tongue,
as words sometimes do, certain peculiar words
like *strengths* or *squinched,*
many-lettered, one-syllabled lumps,
which I squeeze, squinch open, and splurge well
in the silent, startled, icy, black language
of blackberry-eating in late September.

For Kinnell grace comes in moments like this when he finds "certain peculiar words" with which to embrace the things of this world.

Mortal Acts is the most autobiographical of Kinnell's works. In "Wait," Kinnell asserts that "the need / for the new love *is* faithfulness to the old." He might have said that going forward requires turning back to the past, to remembering, to reconstructing, to making new stories out of the old. "Distrust everything if you have to. / But trust the hours. Haven't they / carried you everywhere, up to now?" "Time," as Zimmerman points out, is a "palpable presence" in this volume: "Kinnell's efforts 'to reach a new place' in his poetry . . . repeatedly lead, in *Mortal Acts,* to the old places, to the subject and substance of memory."

Perhaps in homage to the final section of *The Book of Nightmares, Mortal Acts* begins appropriately with a poem about Fergus' need "to get out of the shadow" "of this father"; such a perspective leads naturally to his "fall" toward "the blued flesh." Sitting on a branch of a white pine, Fergus sees Bruce Pond in the distance for the first time; "its oldness" and "its old place in the valley" make him feel "heavier suddenly / in his bones / the way fledglings do just before they fly." At this point the branch cracks, Fergus falls, and the poet hears his cry "as though he [Fergus] were attacked." "His face went gray, his eyes fluttered closed a frightening moment. . . ." The pond initiates Fergus into a world where things and people are "gone." Kinnell may also be drawing on the Celtic myth of Fergus, who, in Yeats's poem "Fergus and the Druid," wants to abandon his kingdom for "the dreaming wisdom that is" the Druid's. In this sense Fergus' fall in Kinnell's poem may be a movement away from the possibilities afforded by poetic language or by dreaming.

Kinnell's need to witness his son's fall, reminiscent of his need to attend to people, particularly family members, who are gone, requires a different vision of how the past impinges on the present than that found in *The Book of Nightmares*. Kinnell in a sense gives up "the dreaming wisdom" of his previous volume.

In Part III of *Mortal Acts,* Kinnell writes about his family, finding a language to stress both the connections he feels with them and those he missed. In "52 Oswald Street," he announces that life is "unrepeatable." He also positions himself in the family as one of three "who have survived the lives / and deaths in the old house / on Oswald Street. . . ." Placing himself in the family configuration, rather than beside it, he hopes to find a language to talk about "bodies of mother and father / and three children, and a fourth, / sleeping, quite long ago."

Kinnell's brother, Derry, who appears in Kinnell's poems "Freedom, New Hampshire" and "Another Night in the Ruins," is the initial focus of "The Sadness of Brothers," the first poem in Part III of *Mortal Acts.* In Part 1 of the poem, Kinnell starts from the premise that he can no longer call Derry up from the depths of memory:

He comes to me like a mouth
speaking from under several inches of water.
I can no longer understand what he is saying.
He has become one
who never belonged among us, someone
it is useless to think about or remember.

Then suddenly, "this morning," "twenty-one years too late," he begins to recover his brother; the recovery is about repositioning himself in relation to his brother. He imagines an exchange with his brother and finds that the reaching backward to him is a way of reaching forward:

But this morning, I don't know why,
twenty-one years too late,
I imagine him back: his beauty
of feature wastreled down
to chin and wattles, his eyes
ratty, liver-lighted, he stands
at the door, and we face each other, each of us
suddenly knowing the lost brother.

In Part 2, Kinnell alludes to his brother's dream of being a pilot—a dream he held "until pilot training, 1943, / when original fear / washed out / all the flyingness in him. . . ." Unmoored from himself, Derry wanders:

a man who only wandered
from then on; on roads
which ended twelve years later
in Wyoming, when he raced his big car
through the desert night, under
the Dipper
or Great Windshield Wiper
which, turning, squeegee-ed existence everywhere,
even in Wyoming, of its damaged dream life. . . .

Derry's wandering gives Kinnell access, in Part 3 of the poem, to their father, who also was "well-wandered." A connection between brothers leads to a web of familial connections and divisions.

Finally, in Part 5 Kinnell returns to his brother, imagining an embrace between them now—in the present:

> We embrace in the doorway,
> in the frailty of large,
> fifty-odd-year-old bodies
> of brothers only one of whom has imagined
> those we love, who go away,
> among them this brother. . . .

Conjuring up his brother here, in the present, allows the poet to return to "the memory that came to me this day / of a man twenty-one years strange to me." But this gap is not divisive; rather, it is binding: "we hold each other, friends to reality, / knowing the ordinary sadness of brothers." The adjective "ordinary" is important; for Kinnell "ordinary sadness" is a luxury because it is "commonplace" and "normal" and occurs in the daylight of today. In contrast, at the beginning of the poem his sadness was subterranean, hard to see, and thus his brother was "one / who never belonged among us."

In "The Last Hiding Places of Snow," Kinnell attempts to recover some "ordinary sadness" about not being with his mother when she died. "I was not at her bedside / that final day, I did not grant her ancient, / huge-knuckled hand / its last wish. . . ." Calling up her love—"its light / like sunlight"—Kinnell feels his mother has empowered him to "wander anywhere, / among any foulnesses, any contagions." Yet what follows is a curiously disturbing and threatening image of his mother as a devourer/destroyer:

> My mother did not want me to be born;
> afterwards, all her life, she needed me to return.
> When this more-than-love flowed toward me, it brought darkness;
> she wanted me as burial earth wants—to heap itself gently upon but also to annihilate—
> and I knew, whenever I felt longings to go back,
> that is what wanting to die is. That is why
>
> dread lives in me,
> dread which comes when what gives life beckons toward death,
> dread which throws through me
> waves
> of utter strangeness, which wash the entire world empty.

This passage in the poem might remind us of Maud's birth—her cutting of "the tie to darkness"—in *The Book of Nightmares,* though Kinnell does not in that instance invoke the presence of her mother as an active agent in the birth process. Here, in contrast, the image of Kinnell's "tie to the darkness" is swallowed up by the image of his mother, who rapaciously wills his return to the womb, an image more than a little offensive. As Lorrie Goldensohn points out:

> In this stance, Kinnell is not Antaeus, deriving strength from a reaffirmation of the ground of earth which is his being. While the lines depend on a basic identification of woman as earth-mother, they also follow the traditional misogynist conflation of womb/tomb, where the chthonic female is not muse, but instead the fixedly mortal part: the dread mother who in giving life beckons toward death.

Kinnell avoids confronting his own missed past connection with his mother by focusing instead on a future link he might have with his own children:

> I would know myself lucky if my own children
> could be at my deathbed, to take
> my hand in theirs and with theirs

to bless me back into the world as I leave,
with smoothness pressed into roughness. . . .

By imagining this bond with his own children, he can look back again—this time with a renewed sense of his complicated relation to his mother:

> in an imaginary daybreak, I see her,
> and for that moment I am still her son
> and I am in the holy land
> and twice in the holy land, remembered
> within her, and remembered in the memory
> her old body slowly executes into the earth.

These lines are as close as Kinnell can come to expressing "ordinary sadness" about his mother, a sadness safely placed in the burial ground and consumed by the earth.

Kinnell's *Selected Poems* (1982) contains a generous selection of pieces from all six of his previous collections, spanning his career from 1946 to 1980, when *Mortal Acts, Mortal Words* appeared. *Selected Poems* gives us insights into Kinnell's evolution as a poet; while some of his early derivative poems seem haunted by the influences of Yeats, Roethke, or Frost, the poems from *Body Rags* and *The Book of Nightmares* pay homage to the influences of Villon, Whitman, and Rilke in ways that heighten Kinnell's distinctive and individual poetic voice. Gathering these poems together takes a certain courage and conviction about one's project over time. As Liz Rosenberg notes in a review of *Selected Poems:* "These early poems indicate influences that a poet is later smart enough to hide, or outgrow." Kinnell chooses to show his readers something about the process of outgrowing these influences.

The year *Selected Poems* appeared, Kinnell published a children's book, *How the Alligator Missed Breakfast.* Nancy Tuten maintains that while the book "was written to entertain children, it reflects themes common to Kinnell's other works. For example, when the animal characters . . . endeavor to be something they are not, by nature, meant to be, Kinnell alludes to his disgust with twentieth-century technological man's false sense of dominion over nature."

In 1982 Kinnell helped organize an antinuclear reading, "Poets Against the End of the World," at Town Hall in New York City. His poem "The Fundamental Project of Technology," which appeared in *The Past* (1985), probably dates from this time. Beginning with a reference to the bombing of Hiroshima and Nagasaki in 1945—"A flash! A white flash sparkled!"—Kinnell takes us inside the Nagasaki museum:

> Under glass: glass dishes which changed
> in color; pieces of transformed beer bottles;
> a household iron; bundles of wire become solid
> lumps of iron; a pair of pliers; a ring of skull-
> bone fused to the inside of a helmet; a pair of
>   eyeglasses
> taken off the eyes of an eyewitness, without
>   glass,
> which vanished, when a white flash sparkled.

But such a repository for the visible signs of destruction is no safeguard against future annihilation. Each stanza ends with an image of "a white flash," as if the dropping of the atomic bomb is bound to be repeated. And the poem itself ends on an apocalyptic note; archives, museums, and guardians of "history" are a thing of the past: "no one lives / to look back and say, a flash, a white flash sparkled."

In 1985 Kinnell and his wife, Inés, divorced and Kinnell took a permanent position on the faculty of New York University. In a 1990 interview with Lois Smith Brady, Kinnell mused that "Marriage is like throwing yourself out of an airplane. . . . There's something irrevocable about it. You just sail on forever. You can't say let's stop, as you can in most things. Even after you get divorced, it's irrevocable."

The Past (1985), a collection of new poems written between 1980 and 1985, is a disappointment. There is a falling off of energy, an exhaustion and weariness; old concerns seem old. For the first time Kinnell does not find a way formally or thematically to energize the familiar insights of previous poems. "The Road Between Here and There," for example, employs a Whitmanesque catalog to arrive at some links between "here"—this place—and the past events in the landscape. The place has not changed—a slightly romantic posture in the late twentieth century—but the poet has. There is something self-indulgent and monotonous about the list of past activities and the prosaic, end-stopped lines:

> Here I abandoned the car because of a clonk in the motor and hitchhiked (which in those days in Vermont meant walking the whole way with a limp) all the way to a garage where I passed the afternoon with ex-loggers who had stopped by to oil the joints of their artificial limbs.

As in previous work, Kinnell looks back at himself and his family in two of the poems, but "The Man Splitting Wood in the Daybreak" and "The Frog Pond" are not in any sense autobiographical. They are not about Kinnell's desire to recover a story—untold or told—about his connection to his wife or his children. Rather, in both poems, place is the anchor. In "The Frog Pond," for example, Kinnell describes his particular relation to the pond: "In those first years I came down / often to the frog pond." Then "the frog pond became the beaver pond"; "A few years after I got here, the beavers came." When the family is introduced—"the four / of us would oar, pole, and bale out"—the poet becomes a man sitting on the bank who watches the four people in the boat. The family becomes every family: "the man seems happy, / the two children laugh and splash, / a slight shadow crosses the woman's face." Suddenly, we shift from the past to a future in which Kinnell imagines himself alone—though he is still "the man"—without his children and with "true love broken." The only constant here is his memory of the pond:

> The man who lies propped up
> on an elbow, scribbling in a notebook
> or loafing and thinking, will be older
> and will remember this place held a pond once,
> writhing with leeches and overflown
> by the straight blue bodies of dragonflies,
> and will think of smallest children
> grown up and of true love broken
> and will sit up abruptly and swat
> the hard-biting deer fly on his head,
> crushing it into his hair, as he has done before.

Although Kinnell seems to be saying, "So you see, / to reach the past is easy. A snap" ("The Past"), the past is most accessible in the moments when Kinnell lives at a distance from himself. This signals a departure from his earlier poems. In "The Past" Kinnell wants to be in "the ordinary day the ordinary world / providentially provides" ("The Waking"), but he seems to have lost his way.

Looking back at *Mortal Acts, Mortal Words* and *The Past,* we see a poet who has moved away from the emotional expenditures, the lyric grace, and the search for a mythology that we find in *Body Rags* and *The Book of Nightmares.* Nevertheless, Kinnell continues to be a poet whose vision and risks matter. As his new poems appear, they will be read with care; his ear and eye will be measured against both his past accomplishments and his future writings. Few contemporary American poets are guaranteed this attention, for, as Harold Bloom maintains, Kinnell is "a poet who cannot be dismissed, because he seems destined still to accomplish the auguries of his grand beginnings."

Selected Bibliography

WORKS OF GALWAY KINNELL

POETRY

What a Kingdom It Was. Boston: Houghton Mifflin, 1960.

Flower Herding on Mount Monadnock. Boston: Houghton Mifflin, 1964.

Body Rags. Boston: Houghton Mifflin, 1968.

First Poems 1946–1954. Mt. Horeb, Wis.: Perishable Press, 1970.

The Book of Nightmares. Boston: Houghton Mifflin, 1971.

The Avenue Bearing the Initial of Christ into the New World: Poems 1946–1964. Boston: Houghton Mifflin, 1974.

Mortal Acts, Mortal Words. Boston: Houghton Mifflin, 1980.

Selected Poems. Boston: Houghton Mifflin, 1982.

The Past. Boston: Houghton Mifflin, 1985.

TRANSLATIONS

Bitter Victory, by René Hardy. Garden City, N.Y.: Doubleday, 1956. Novel.

The Poems of François Villon. New York: New American Library, 1965. Rev. ed., Boston: Houghton Mifflin, 1977.

On the Motion and Immobility of Douve, by Yves Bonnefoy. Athens: Ohio University Press, 1968. Poems.

Lackawanna Elegy, by Yvan Goll. Fremont, Mich.: Sumac, 1970. Poems.

PROSE

"Only Meaning Is Truly Interesting." *Beloit Poetry Journal* 4:1–3 (Fall 1953).

Black Light. Boston: Houghton Mifflin, 1966. Rev. ed., San Francisco: North Point, 1980. Novel.

"The Poetics of the Physical World." *Iowa Review* 2: 113–126 (Summer 1971).

"Poetry, Personality, and Death." *Field,* no. 4: 56–77 (Spring 1971).

"Whitman's Indicative Words." *American Poetry Review* 2:9–11 (March/April 1973).

Walking Down the Stairs: Selections from Interviews. Ann Arbor: University of Michigan Press, 1978. All of the interviews quoted in this essay are collected in this volume.

How the Alligator Missed Breakfast. Boston: Houghton Mifflin, 1982. Children's book.

Introduction to *The Essential Whitman.* New York: Ecco, 1987.

BIBLIOGRAPHY

Galway Kinnell: A Bibliography and Index of His Published Works and Criticism of Them. Potsdam, N.Y.: State University College, 1968.

BIOGRAPHICAL AND CRITICAL STUDIES

Altieri, Charles. *Self and Sensibility in Contemporary American Poetry.* New York: Cambridge University Press, 1984.

Bell, Charles G. "Galway Kinnell." In *Contemporary Poets,* 3rd ed., edited by James Vinson. New York: St. Martin's, 1980. Pp. 835–837.

Bloom, Harold. "Straight Forth out of Self: *Mortal Acts, Mortal Words.*" *New York Times Book Review,* June 22, 1980, p. 13.

Brady, Lois Smith. "Poet About Town." *New York Woman,* April 1990, pp. 98–100.

Davie, Donald. "Slogging for the Absolute." *Parnassus* 3:9–22 (Fall/Winter 1974).

Dickey, James. *Babel to Byzantium: Poets and Poetry Now.* New York: Farrar, Straus & Giroux, 1961, 1968; New York: Ecco, 1981.

Dickstein, Morris. "Intact and Triumphant." *New York Times Book Review,* September 19, 1982, pp. 12, 33. Review of *Selected Poems.*

Gallagher,Tess. "The Poem as a Reservoir for Grief." *American Poetry Review* 13:7–11 (July/August 1984).

Goldensohn, Lorrie. "Approaching Home Ground: Galway Kinnell's *Mortal Acts, Mortal Words.*" *Massachusetts Review* 25:303–321 (Summer 1984).

Guimond, James. *Seeing and Healing: The Poetry of Galway Kinnell.* Port Washington, N.Y.: Associated Faculty Press, 1986.

Hall, Donald. "A Luminous Receptiveness." *Nation,* 213:377–378 (October 18, 1971). Review of *The Book of Nightmares.*

———. "Text as Test: Notes on and Around Carruth and Kinnell." *American Poetry Review* 12:27–32 (November/December 1983).

Helms, Alan. "Two Poets." *Partisan Review* 44, no. 2: 284–293 (1977). Review of *The Avenue Bearing the Initials of Christ* and *Book of Nightmares*, pp. 288–293.

Howard, Richard. *Alone with America: Essays on the Art of Poetry Since 1950.* New York: Atheneum, 1969.

———. "Changes." *Partisan Review* 38:484–490 (Winter 1971–1972).

Langbaum, Robert. "Galway Kinnell's *The Book of Nightmares.*" *American Poetry Review* 8:30–31 (March/April 1979).

Mariani, Paul. "Kinnell's Legacy: On 'The Avenue Bearing the Initial of Christ into the New World.' " In *On the Poetry of Galway Kinnell: The Wages of Dying*. Edited by Howard Nelson. Ann Arbor: University of Michigan Press, 1987.

Molesworth, Charles. *The Fierce Embrace: A Study of Contemporary American Poetry*. Columbia: University of Missouri Press, 1979.

Nelson, Cary. *Our Last First Poets: Vision and History in Contemporary American Poetry*. Urbana: University of Illinois Press, 1981.

Nelson, Howard, ed. *On the Poetry of Galway Kinnell: The Wages of Dying*. Ann Arbor: University of Michigan Press, 1987.

Perloff, Marjorie. "Poetry Chronicle: 1970–71." *Contemporary Literature* 14:97–131 (Winter 1973). Review of *Nightmares*, pp. 123–125.

Ricks, Christopher. "In the Direct Line of Whitman, the Indirect Line of Eliot." *New York Times Book Review*, January 12, 1975, p. 2.

Rosenberg, Liz. "A Poet with the Flame of Greatness." *Philadelphia Inquirer*, February 13, 1983, p. R-06. Review of *Selected Poems*.

Tuten, Nancy Lewis. "Galway Kinnell." *Dictionary of Literary Biography Yearbook 1987*. Pp. 257–264. Detroit, Mich.: Gale Research, 1987.

Weston, Susan B. "Kinnell's *Walking Down the Stairs.*" *Iowa Review* 10, no. 1:95–98 (1979).

Williamson, Alan. *Introspection and Contemporary Poetry*. Cambridge, Mass.: Harvard University Press, 1984.

Wright, Anne. "Sitting on Top of the Sunlight." In *On the Poetry of Galway Kinnell: The Wages of Dying*. Edited by Howard Nelson. Ann Arbor: University of Michigan Press, 1987.

Yenser, Stephen. "Recent Poetry: Five Poets." *Yale Review* 70:105–128 (Autumn 1980). Review of *Mortal Acts, Mortal Words*, pp. 123–128.

Zimmerman, Lee. *Intricate and Simple Things: The Poetry of Galway Kinnell*. Urbana: University of Illinois Press, 1987.

—CELESTE GOODRIDGE

Stanley Kunitz

1905–

"THE ONLY ADVANTAGE of celebrity that I can think of is that it puts one in a position to help others," Stanley Kunitz told Chris Busa in a 1977 *Paris Review* interview (collected in *Next-to-Last Things: New Poems and Essays,* 1985). By 1990, working on a new collection of his poems, Kunitz had become one of America's most celebrated poets. Five years earlier, in 1985, even before he was named poet laureate of New York State, his eightieth birthday was commemorated by a series of festivals in New York City; Worcester, Massachusetts, his birthplace; and Provincetown, Massachusetts, where he is a founder of the Fine Arts Work Center, a resident community of emerging writers and visual artists, and where plans are being made to dedicate a building to him. In 1986, poets as diverse as Yehuda Amichai and Kenneth Koch were represented in *A Celebration for Stanley Kunitz on His Eightieth Birthday,* a book of poems, essays, and letters edited by Stanley Moss.

The author of numerous books of poetry, essays, and translations, Kunitz has been the winner of a Pulitzer Prize, a Brandeis University Medal of Achievement, a Senior Fellowship of the National Endowment for the Arts, and a Bollingen Prize. He is a chancellor of the Academy of American Poets, a member of the American Academy of Arts and Letters, and a former consultant in poetry to the Library of Congress. Age has not diminished his zeal for writing, lecturing, and traveling to read his poems to large audiences.

At his home on West Twelfth Street in Manhattan, where he lives with his wife, the painter Elise Asher, Stanley Kunitz is visited frequently by artists, writers, and former students. Many of the student callers were in his classes at Columbia University, from which he has retired as senior professor in the writing program. He is a mentor to painters as well. Even before his marriage to Asher, in 1958, he was drawn to the visual arts, an attraction he traces to his childhood in Massachusetts, where, he told me in 1990, "the Worcester Art Museum was a refuge for me." He mused: "In another life, I would like to be freed of the angst which the visual artist escapes, liberated by the externality of the medium. Gardening is my substitute. I work at it just as I would sculpture or painting."

Kunitz has had close friendships with many innovative New York artists, including Mark Rothko, Robert Motherwell, Willem de Kooning, and Franz Kline. In his essay "Remembering Guston," included in *Next-to-Last Things: New Poems and Essays* (1985), he recalls Philip Guston's admiration for the poetry of Gerard Manley Hopkins. Dore Ashton, art critic and historian, wrote of his affinities to visual artists in "Kunitz and the Painters," collected in *A Cele-*

bration for Stanley Kunitz: ''[The visual artists] . . . were committed to a point of view of existence—an esthetic—that assumed that their place was in a universe created by art and, of necessity, moral.'' And in 1978 *The Nation* published his poem ''The Crystal Cage'' (collected in *The Poems of Stanley Kunitz, 1928–1978,* 1979), dedicated to the artist Joseph Cornell. The poem embodies images and concerns that have been prominent throughout Kunitz' work: the stairway, the ascent, the artist's amazement at the natural world. It begins:

> To climb the belltower,
> step after step,
> in the grainy light,
> without breathing harder;
> to spy on each landing
> a basket of gifts,
> a snowbox of wonders:
> pressed flowers, pieces
> of colored glass,
> a postcard from Niagara Falls,
> agates, cut-outs of birds,
> and dozing in the pile,
> in faded mezzotint,
> Child Mozart at the Clavichord.

Including the poem in *A Joseph Cornell Album,* which she edited, Dore Ashton commissioned Kunitz to create a visual work to accompany the poem. His composition consists of the poem in his handwriting, flanked by a collage that contains a tiny cat, a staircase, children's heads. Another of Kunitz' pieces, exhibited in his apartment, is a wooden box whose compartments contain found objects, each having to do with an image in his poems: stone fossils; a wooden insect; a picture of Celia, the Kunitzes' cat, that appears in the poem ''Route Six''; a waltzing mouse that resembles the rodent in ''The Waltzer in the House''; and a clock that reads five minutes to twelve. The timepiece is a whimsical comment on his poem ''The Science of the Night,'' which ends: ''Each cell within my body holds a heart / And all my hearts in unison strike twelve.''

The Kunitzes live part of the year in Provincetown, where he tends his flowering terraces as he would a sculpture. When I asked him why he lives in the city at all, he spoke of Elise, as well as of his attachments to friends, to the cultural world, and to teaching. ''Apart from that,'' he said, ''the city is not my habitat. I'm always longing for the seaside life. I'm not a nature poet, but I am a poet of the natural world. In writing about what I am, I find the most accurate metaphors in what is called nature.''

Kunitz' identification with the natural world is central to the poems. That profound intimacy is found in ''The Snakes of September,'' a late poem that appeared in *Antaeus* and was collected in *Next-to-Last Things.* It ends with a unification of poet and nature:

> I put out my hand and stroke
> the fine, dry grit of their skins.
> After all,
> we are partners in this land,
> co-signers of a covenant.
> At my touch the wild
> braid of creation
> trembles.

His impact on student writers is widely acknowledged. In *A Celebration for Stanley Kunitz,* Marie Howe, who studied with him in the writing division of Columbia University's School of the Arts, attests to his influence:

> Stanley has managed to do what many of us fear is impossible. He is a poet and he is sane. He is *of* this world and from there he speaks. And he shines even as he turns into dark and deeper dark. When I write, it is his courage and his luminosity that I conjure as much as his poems, which seem born from both rock and water.

When I asked him whether the absence of a father in his youth—the dark motif of the early poems—had anything to do with the generous teacher he became, he replied: "I suppose I've wanted to become the father I never had, and that has been one of the motivations in my life."

The poet was born Stanley Jasspon Kunitz on July 29, 1905, in Worcester, Massachusetts, the only son among three children born to Yetta Helen Jasspon Kunitz. His mother was an immigrant from Lithuania who worked as an operator in the sweatshops of New York's Lower East Side before she moved to Worcester to marry. Her husband, Solomon, Stanley's father, committed suicide some months before Stanley was born. When the boy was eight, his mother remarried. That, too, ended in sadness: her second husband, Mark Dine, died five years later. After his death, Yetta, then forty, opened a dry goods store to support her children. Eventually she became a dress designer and developed a substantial manufacturing enterprise.

For many years, Kunitz remembered his mother as being remote, and as having little time for affectionate contact with her family. He was later to recognize her insight and courage. "She was a woman of formidable will, staunch heart, and razor-sharp intelligence," he recalls in a prefatory note to "My Mother's Story," a memoir included in *Next-to-Last Things*. In it he writes: "She must have been one of the first women to run a large-scale business in this country."

An early source of his concern for human suffering, his mother was conversant with left-wing thought. In the same prefatory note to his memoir of her, he describes Yetta, who died in 1952 at the age of eighty-five, as having been "articulate to the last on the errors of capitalism and the tragedy of existence."

A talented violinist, young Stanley was deeply moved by books in his parents' library, including complete sets of Dickens, Shakespeare, and Tolstoy; the Bible; and an edition of Goethe. He recalls with special delight an edition of Wordsworth's *Collected Poems*. He remembers being attracted to an edition of Dante's *Inferno* with Gustave Doré illustrations. The book inspired his reading of Dante, which led him later to the metaphysical poets, especially John Donne and George Herbert.

Kunitz graduated from Harvard summa cum laude, having won the Garrison Medal for Poetry, among other important prizes. He had majored in English and philosophy. He stayed on to earn an M.A. with the thought of teaching there, but was rejected. To his humiliation and rage, he was told that the English faculty had denied him the position because "Anglo-Saxons would resent being taught English by a Jew." Thereafter, he struggled for years to find a means of survival that would still permit him to write.

After working as a staff reporter for the *Worcester Telegram*, he became assistant Sunday editor, writing a literary column and feature articles. One of his assignments was to report on the aftermath of the guilty verdict in the Sacco-Vanzetti trial of 1927 that resulted in the notorious execution of the two anarchists. He told Chris Busa, in the 1977 *Paris Review* interview:

> I soon saw that a terrible injustice was being perpetrated. My particular assignment was to cover the judge, Judge Webster Thayer, a mean little frightened man who hated the guts of these "anarchistic bastards." He could not conceivably give them a fair trial. I was so vehement about this miscarriage of justice, so filled with it, that around the newspaper office they used to call me "Sacco."

After the execution of Nicola Sacco and Bartolomeo Vanzetti, Kunitz left for New York, having received permission to submit Vanzetti's eloquent letters for publication. Although he took them to many publishers, editors declined, fearful of political implications. The letters appeared only years later, edited by Felix Frankfurter.

At twenty-three, Kunitz, penniless in New York, landed a job with the H. W. Wilson Company, a publishing firm, and founded a reference series for contemporary authors. Working in cramped quarters for forty-two dollars a week, at a time when there was little information about living writers, Kunitz initiated the *Wilson Library Bulletin* and the *Authors Biographical Series*. He was to continue editing standard literary reference works, eventually on a free-lance basis, for more than forty years.

In 1930 Kunitz married Helen Pearce, a poet, and with the first five hundred dollars he saved after coming to New York, he bought a hundred-acre farm on Wormwood Hill in Mansfield Center, Connecticut, which included an eighteenth-century house with a gambrel roof. In the Connecticut home, he fulfilled his love for woodworking and repair by mending or actually installing the heating, running water, and electricity. Although the marriage ended in divorce in 1937, Kunitz enjoyed rural life in Connecticut and, later, in Bucks County, Pennsylvania, where he cultivated acres of ground and felt at peace with the living creatures around him. The Bucks County location was the setting of his poem "River Road," which was collected in *The Testing-Tree* in 1971. Here the poet uses imagery of the natural world to tell of survival; the speaker, a farmer, establishes himself firmly in a fresh, green landscape:

That year of the cloud, when my marriage failed,
I paced up and down the bottom-fields,
tamping the mud-puddled nurslings in
with a sharp blow of the heel
timed to the chop-chop of the hoe:
red pine and white, larch, balsam fir,
one stride apart, two hundred to the row,
until I heard from Rossiter's woods
the downward spiral of a veery's song
unwinding on the eve of war.

There, as in many of his poems of the period, personal disaster is used metaphorically to embody the public tragedy of war. It was a method he shared with several of the Russian poets he translated in the 1960's and 1970's, notably Anna Akhmatova and Andrei Voznesensky. In keeping with his later poems, the images of earth and trees are more benign than in the earlier work. Here their harmony is in sharp contrast to human discord. That treatment of nature is significant, for the development of primary images from desolation to joy is continuous in the poetry of Stanley Kunitz.

In 1930, the year of his marriage to Pearce, Kunitz' first collection of poetry, *Intellectual Things,* was published by Doubleday, Doran, and reviewed favorably by Eda Lou Walton in *The Nation,* Morton Dauwen Zabel in *Poetry,* and William Rose Benét in the *Saturday Review of Literature*. Its title is from the line, "For the tear is an intellectual thing," in William Blake's poem "The Grey Monk." In the poem Blake unifies human emotion with its apparent opposite, conceptual thought, just as Kunitz, in his first book, presents the juxtaposition of feeling and idea.

In the mid 1930's, there began an abiding friendship between Kunitz and his fellow poet Theodore Roethke. Kunitz remembers that their first meeting took place when Roethke visited him in his Pennsylvania home, unannounced, and disclosed his intimate knowledge of Kunitz' first published poems. The two men had similar backgrounds: both were poets haunted by lost fathers and renewed by the garden world; both were committed to the act of seeing in darkness. Both had, as well, a certain innocent simplicity that originated in their attachments to nature. Roethke's "I stay up half the night / To see the land I love" ("Night Journey") is close in tonality to Kunitz' wondrous affirmations (for example, ". . . every stone on the road / precious to me," from "The Layers").

Apart from being a safe harbor in the gale of Kunitz' emotional and financial crises, the friendship led to his first teaching position, at Bennington College, which he held from 1946 to 1949. It began when he succeeded Roethke, who was ill and insisted that Kunitz replace him. After that, Kunitz was poet-in-residence at the University of Washington and at Queens College. By the time he accepted the position at Columbia University, he had established his role as mentor to young poets.

In 1939, two years after his divorce from Pearce, he married Eleanor Evans, the mother of his child, Gretchen, who was born in 1950. When he was nearly thirty-eight, in 1943, he was drafted as a nonaffiliated pacifist with moral scruples against using weapons. Although his understanding with the draft board was that he would be assigned to a service unit, such as the medical corps, that agreement was not honored. Consequently, he went through several sessions of basic training. In one camp he edited and distributed, on his own time, a publication that won an all-army prize, and led to his being assigned to the air transport command headquarters in Washington, D.C. Serving until 1945, declining commission, he was a staff sergeant by the end of World War II.

Under that grim cloud, his second book, *Passport to the War,* was published by Holt in 1944. Although it was reviewed favorably by A. J. M. Smith in *Poetry,* the book was out of print one year later. Moreover, it would be fourteen years before the appearance of *Selected Poems, 1928–1958,* which was rejected by numerous publishers before it was accepted by Atlantic–Little, Brown and then went on to win the Pulitzer Prize. That ambivalent response is characteristic to Kunitz' critical reception to this day: in his poems, the blend of naturalness and heightened intensity, the mixture of idea and sensuous detail, are often misunderstood. Nevertheless, they are factors that contribute to his major achievement.

Although many of the poems in *Passport to the War* were composed before he entered the army, the book's tone is one of rage. The poet is horrified by the violence and greed of his time, as "Welcome the Wrath" attests:

Wrath has come down from the hills to enlist
Me surely in his brindled generation,
The race of the tiger; come down at last
Has wrath to build a bonfire of these rags
With one wet match and all man's desolation.

Anger of that kind pervades the collection, but does not constitute the book's essential impact. To embody this rage in art, the poet constructed a persona and a network of images that would serve as a structure for his pain and terror. That structure, as it evolves in the work, is the basis for any study of the poems of Stanley Kunitz.

"If you understand a poet's images, you have a clue to the understanding of his whole work," Kunitz said in the *Paris Review* interview of 1977, expressing an idea he developed in another of the later essays, "From Feathers to Iron" (collected in *Next-to-Last Things*):

One of my convictions is that at the center of every poetic imagination is a cluster of key images that go back to the poet's childhood and that are usually associated with pivotal experiences, not necessarily traumatic. . . . That cluster of key images is the purest concentration of the self, the individuating node, the place where the persona starts. When fresh thoughts and sensations enter the mind, some of them are drawn into the gravitational field of the old life and cohere to it. Out of these combining elements, the more resistant the better, poetry happens.

In his work, repeated images—water, earth, home, scar, name, sphere, star—change as they are perceived. However vivid those figures are, their function is not to portray the man in his growth. Instead, they are used as the building blocks of a persona that is dramatized, at times mythologized, to recount the events and emotions of the poems. The method is akin to one he analyzed in the essay "At the Tomb of Walt Whitman" (collected in *Next-to-Last Things*). He spoke of it as the "process of transformation" by which the earlier poet transcends the self. "This is the supreme and imperative act of the poetic imagination: to create the person who will write the poems," Kunitz asserts. In a conversation with me he described that process, and the change it involves, as being central to his work: "The self is not a finished thing. It must be renewed through change. I'm talking about process as opposed to stasis, becoming as opposed to being. Becomings are rivers that flow into the sea. Being is the sea, and that's ever-changing."

Kunitz' early poems are shadowed by dark, dank watery images associated with the father lost to suicide before the poet's birth. In actuality, the poet's father died neither in water nor of drowning, but in a public park, by poisoning himself with carbolic acid. Only in late middle age did the poet discover the exact cause of his father's death, on a certificate in Worcester's city hall.

Nevertheless, the water images are linked to that loss. For example, in a poem called "Father and Son," collected in 1944 in *Passport to the War* but composed some time before, he envisions "Him, steeped in the odor of ponds, whose indomitable love / Kept me in chains," and implores the father to " 'teach me how to work and keep me kind.' "

In "Of 'Father and Son,' " an essay collected in *A Kind of Order, A Kind of Folly: Essays and Conversations* (1975), he writes that the origin of the poem, along with that of another poem, "Goose Pond," was

> a small, reputedly bottomless waterhole that I frequented in Quinapoxet [actually Quinnapoxet, as in the poem of that title], outside Worcester, and my memory of it is alive with snakes and pickerel and snapping turtles and pond lilies. . . . As far as I am concerned, the pond in Quinapoxet, Poe's "dank tarn of Auber," and the mere in which Beowulf fights for his life with Grendel and the water-hag are one and the same. It is the pond where I am never surprised to find demons, murderers, parents, poets. Did my father really die there? No, he never even saw it; and I was the one who came closest to drowning.

Characteristically, the pond of "Father and Son" is set against the house, another of the poet's key images. Throughout the work, water recurs in the form of ponds, rivers, reservoirs, slime, ice, and snow. So, too, the house obsession recurs in the guise of doors, windows, halls, walls, attics, gates, and lintels. It is as though the poet is building artistic enclosures to compensate for life's domestic chaos.

An earlier poem, "For the Word Is Flesh," in *Intellectual Things,* typifies the language, manner, and thematic concern of Kunitz' beginnings. Though dense and allusive, it contains those basic figures that indicate clearly "the place where the persona starts." It begins:

O ruined father dead, long sweetly rotten
Under the dial, the time-dissolving urn,
Beware a second perishing, forgotten,
Heap fallen leaves of memory to burn
On the slippery rock, the black eroding heart,
Before the wedged frost splits it clean apart.

In the one long, sweeping sentence, the speaker warns the dead father that only a life in memory can avert a second death. The speaker's admonition, though, falls back on the writer—the literary persona indicated by "fallen leaves of memory." Images of the "slippery rock" and the "wedged frost" are characteristic of the wet chilly pictures Kunitz uses for the lost parent. The final verb, "splits," describing the frost's action, is consistent with the poet's early language of division: "Parting" and "The Separation" are titles in the first book, and in the second is the plaintive line "Heart against mouth is singing out of tune" ("The Guilty Man"). The cumulative effect of such words and phrases is to amplify the central figure's dark self that strives for completion without the father.

In that early poem, decay is, paradoxically, what binds the dead father to the living son who has of him "no syllable to keep, / Only the deep rock crumbling in the deep." The son, pursuing "deeds ephemeral" and "dazzling words," finding in Christian myth a metaphor for the father's abandonment, exclaims, "I hear the fierce / Wild cry of Jesus on the holy tree." The poet's early theme of father as teacher appears here in the final couplet: "Let sons learn from their lipless fathers how / Man enters hell without a golden bough." And, apart from the subject matter that recurs in the early work, "For the Word Is Flesh" has the tone and rhythm of its period: passion strains against the set form, in this case six-line rhymed stanzas in iambic pentameter.

Just as the father of the early poems is presented in images of rot and wetness, the mother is shown as a destructive force linked to a natural world that is cruel and without mercy. "Poem," in *Intellectual Things,* which consists of an address to the heart about a dream, is built on that cold maternal image:

In the year of my mother's blood, when I was
  born,
She buried my innocent head in a field, because
  the earth

Was sleepy with the winter.

As though the poet wished to allay the early fears by coming to terms with them, later poems embody the idea of mother either more gently or in more explicit detail. In "No Word," a poem from *Passport to the War,* the maternal image is milder: the poet writes of "the mothering dark, / Whose benediction calms the sea." "The Portrait," included in *The Testing-Tree,* contains the tragic facts of the father's suicide in a public park and of the mother who "locked his name / in her deepest cabinet."

As for the watery images of the father, they are considerably softer in the later poems. Gentleness increases throughout the work, and in "The Way Down," from *Selected Poems: 1928–1958,* the speaker perceives the awakening of animals sunk "in moss and slime" and cries, "Hail, dark stream!" He calls to a father-god: "Receive your dazzling child / Drunk with the morning-dew." The realization of love for the absent father continues, often in the form of water images that are safe or actually comforting. After 1970, water figures bring forth renewal: water is home to the salmon swimming upstream in "King of the River" (*The Testing-Tree,* 1971); the sea is a refuge for the titular creature of "The Wellfleet Whale" (*The Wellfleet Whale and Companion Poems,* 1983).

And in "Quinnapoxet," collected in *The Poems of Stanley Kunitz: 1928–1978* (1979), the speaker, who is fishing "in the abandoned reservoir," tenderly acknowledges a man who accompanies a woman in mourning:

I touched my forehead
with my swollen thumb
and splayed my fingers out—
in deaf-mute country
the sign for father.

Here the stale water of the early poems is seen as a place where life can flourish, and the cut flesh—another of the central images that soften in the later work—is hardly dangerous. Indeed, it is no barrier to the fisherman's silent gesture of peace.

Stanley Kunitz is by no means the only American writer who has focused on the welter of emotions surrounding a father's suicide. In the twentieth century alone, John Berryman and Ernest Hemingway are among the major writers who were offspring of such fathers. While those two authors themselves died of suicide, however, Kunitz survived—and that grim, arduous resolve to embrace life is enacted in the poems. "I dance, for the joy of surviving, / on the edge of the road," cries the fatherless Solomon Levi of "An Old Cracked Tune," a poem from *The Testing-Tree*. That frenzied dance of life over a precipice is an emblem of Kunitz' valorous struggle. It is, in fact, the basic story of his poems.

In *Stanley Kunitz: An Introduction to the Poetry,* Gregory Orr has written that any study of Kunitz' poems depends on the understanding that the term "father" embodies "the fusion of the *pain* of the beloved stepfather's sudden death with the *imagery* and *mystery* of the biological father's suicide." Orr maintains: "They [the two fathers] are also, and this point is critical, perceived as being actual or potential allies in Kunitz' quest for identity and his related effort to break free of the power of the maternal."

That search for a new image of self is the source of Kunitz' process for transforming personal reality in an effort to call the poems into being. The quest is dramatized in "Open the Gates." Collected in *Passport to the War,* the poem indicates just how the process of self-transcendence—or, in Kunitz' terms, the creation of "the person who will write the poems"—contributes to the power of the later work. A pivotal poem of the early middle period, it remains one of his favorites, according to his assessment in 1990. Here it is given in full:

Within the city of the burning cloud,
Dragging my life behind me in a sack,
Naked I prowl, scourged by the black
Temptation of the blood grown proud.

Here at the monumental door,
Carved with the curious legend of my youth,
I brandish the great bone of my death,
Beat once therewith and beat no more.

The hinges groan: a rush of forms
Shivers my name, wrenched out of me.
I stand on the terrible threshold, and I see
The end and the beginning in each other's arms.

The tone is everything here, and it is Kunitz' unique combination of conversational directness and plangent resonance. It is found here and elsewhere at this stage in his career, and emerges when the passionate diction strains against the form of rhymed quatrains in iambic pentameter.

The title, figuratively "the monumental door" of "the terrible threshold," signifies a terrifying entrance that is, at the same time, a place of discovery. It stands among the mysterious, threatening doorways of *Passport to the War*—"a hundred doors by which to leave," for example, in "The Harsh Judgment," and "the gates of mystery" in "The Tutored Child." It is a variation on the ominous entrances of the earlier *Intellectual Things,* such as, for instance, the entrance to hell at the end of "For the Word Is Flesh." A door of promise here, it predicts the slightly open doors of *Selected Poems* as well as the marvelous doorways of triumph in the later work, such as the gate that leads to heaven for the "nameless painter" of "Words for the Unknown Makers" (collected in *The Poems of Stanley Kunitz*).

In "Open the Gates," the great door groans open for the passage of a new identity: "A rush of forms / Shivers my name, wrenched out of me." Actually, "Open the Gates" is a translation from Hebrew of the *ne'ila* (closing) prayer of the Yom Kippur service, the twilight observance of the Jewish Day of Atonement, for Jews the holiest day of the year. At dusk the gates close, signifying the closing of the temple and of the heavenly gates. The event marks the end of a cycle, and the prayer to stay the closure is an especially poignant one. In 1990 Kunitz told me that he had been unaware of the allusion. Judaism is, however, in his background, and I suspect the knowledge was deeply ingrained—or at least that the naked, prowling "I" of the poem intoned the prayer regularly, even if the author did not. In any case, the central figure of the poem is presented as moving toward a new self in a way that resonates with the new cycle of the year, as in the Jewish ritual. He is shown as accepting the burden of his past and confronting the "curious legend" of his early tragedy.

At the same time, "Open the Gates" is a heightened love poem: in an erotic moment marked by the words "in each other's arms," the speaker has a revelation of "the end and the beginning." Essentially, it is a poem about poetry, for "the end and the beginning" emerges as a metaphor for the artist's vision of continuous time. The self, transcendent now, is no longer bound by static, conventional time, with its sense of endings—separation, loss—as it is in the early poems, with their painful lessons of death and of division. Instead, it is on the way to a new unification.

In addition, "Open the Gates" has a new sonority that recurs in the later work: the bold, ringing tone of "Shivers my name . . . ," in which the speaker's identity is found, recurs for many years in concert with the same image. A notable example is "Passing Through" (collected in *Next-to-Last Things*), a poem composed on the occasion of Kunitz' seventy-ninth birthday, in which the speaker declares: "nothing is truly mine / except my name."

Selected Poems appeared in 1958, the year that Stanley and Eleanor Evans Kunitz were divorced. In that year he married Elise Asher. The book that won him a Pulitzer Prize in 1959 and changed the course of his critical reception, *Selected Poems* appeared after a hiatus of fourteen years, containing only thirty-two new poems. Those pieces, which appear under the section title "This Garland, Danger," suggest that the apparently less productive years actually were years of intense change.

In the new period, the figure of the beloved woman looms as the person with whom the artist identifies in the search for a unified and transcendent self. The section title "This Garland, Danger" is from one of the new poems, "Green Ways," in which the speaker turns to "lift this garland, Danger from her throat / To blaze it in the foundries of the night." The wearer of the endangered wreath, "the moon-breasted sybilline," is one of the exalted images of the beloved woman that appear throughout this group of poems. She becomes, in "The Science of the Night," the "mistress" of "far Magellans"; in "Sotto Voce," the "Huntress of nerves"; and in "The Unwithered Garland," the sufferer "on a distant star." Through the beloved, there is a softening of those figures Kunitz refers to as "key images": even in a domestic quarrel, the "slammed and final door" of "Foreign Affairs" shows signs of giving way. The stagnant water images of the early poems yield to "the liquid language of the moon" in "The Science of the Night." The dangerous earth images become joyful and multiply: "flowers have flowers" in "As Flowers Are." Stars, recurrent also, are associated with remote human beings in the earlier work; here, they are radiant, happy figures, as in "She Wept, She Railed": "And we went out into the night / Where all the constellations shine."

Representing another stage in the transformation of the self, the poems of "This Garland, Danger" embody the Kunitz persona as an active, hopeful counterpart of the earlier man. "The Approach to Thebes," an amazing poem, is also typical of the poet's rhythm. It is freer than the earlier poems, cast in a more varied iambic pentameter, and the approximate rhymes ("pearled"/"gold"; "scorned"/"ordained") are more commensurate with passionate tonality. Here the poet presents the beloved, "who was all music's tongue," as an altering, agile version of the sphinx:

Of shifting shape, half jungle-cat, half-dancer,
Night's woman-petaled, lion-scented rose,
To whom I gave, out of a hero's need,
The dolor of my thrust, my riddling answer,
Whose force no lesser mortal knows. . . .

The woman is dangerous to the speaker; he is a modern Oedipus who is seen by "nervous oracles" to have her for his destiny. She possesses an enchantment that causes him to dim his rational restraint, and brings him freedom that ends in tragedy. The speaker is shattered to the center of his being. In the powerful ending, "Blinded and old, exiled, diseased, and scorned," he is determined to assume responsibility for his fate:

. . . On the royal road to Thebes
I had my luck, I met a lovely monster,
And the story's this: I made the monster me.

The self is an active force now, boldly risking destruction, unwilling to accept a bitter destiny without a vigorous struggle. The speaker knows he is the source of his own turmoil, for he has identified with the sphinx, bringer of "art or magic," and has traded complacency for "the secret taste of her." Moreover, he declares at the climax of this poem that he is "tied to life"—determined to survive in a world of tragic conflict—and this fierce choice is a major theme in Kunitz' later poetry.

The poem is a turning point in the work as a whole. After the fusion of speaker and beloved, the wish to survive is asserted more frequently, often in plangent tones. The persona is more defiant. Along with a more vital image of the self, there is a mellowing of those recurrent images such as water, earth, house, and wound.

Of that mellowing, Kunitz remarked to me: "I became aware of the tragic circumstances of my early life in the very act of unfolding [the harsh images] in my work. There is a triumph in being able to speak of them, to absorb them into the creative process, although they still remain dark in their origin."

Kunitz' debts to Freud and Jung are, of course, evident. A Freudian reading of "The Approach to Thebes" would have Kunitz-Oedipus as the narrator, spurned by the mother-beloved; a Jungian approach would argue the spiritual nature of the quest. Both are viable, both true. Further, Kunitz' images are archetypal, in the Jungian sense of a collective unconscious. At the same time, they are individual. Their power is in that combination of universality and uniqueness. Kunitz, who was never analyzed himself but who did absorb most of the writings of Freud and Jung, assimilated some of their principles into his aesthetic renewal of self-defining images.

That varying of images is at the heart of "The Layers," a poem that appeared in the *American Poetry Review* and was collected in *The Poems of Stanley Kunitz*. In it, a voice in a dream directs the speaker to " 'Live in the layers, / not on the litter.' " The poem concludes:

Though I lack the art
to decipher it,
no doubt the next chapter
in my book of transformations
is already written.
I am not done with my changes.

In a later essay called "The Layers: Some Notes on 'The Abduction' " (collected in *Next-to-Last Things*), Kunitz asserts that the concept of "layering" consists of dredging the memory and artistically mounting "thought on thought, event on event, image on image, time on time." Those images, mined from consciousness, their changes traced, are elements that emerge in and for the poem. The created poem, then, contains "the occult and passionate grammar of a life." Commenting on the last line of "The Layers," Kunitz said to me: "I'm always reinventing those images to find out what they are trying to say to me. The greatest miracle is how the whole baggage of memory is incorporated into one's whole structure of being. The lost souls are those who try to get rid of that baggage.''

The last line of ''The Layers,'' ''I am not done with my changes,'' is a wry, subtle affirmation of the poet's life-sustaining process of metamorphosis. He said to Chris Busa in 1977:

> Anybody who remains a poet throughout a lifetime, who is still a poet let us say at sixty, has a terrible will to survive. He has already died a million times and at a certain age he faces this imperative need to be reborn. . . . He's capable of perpetuation, he turns up again in new shapes.

Kunitz' archetypal images are just such agents of change. They gather strength as they are transformed, changing, in the course of the work, from tragic resignation to tragic joy. And it is the mysterious gift of this poet to shape those images in such a way as to make them resound in the consciousness of all people.

His later poems epitomize this mastery of the art of endurance. ''King of the River,'' in *The Testing-Tree,* is an account of a dying salmon's journey upstream,

> slapping, thrashing,
> tumbling
> over the rocks
> till you paint them
> with your belly's blood. . . .

It has an incantatory force, largely the result of the conditional tense and the suspended main clause: ''If the water were clear enough /. . . you would see yourself.'' Its tone of combined naturalness and passion is typical of Kunitz' late work. The poem reflects the author's turn, in the mid 1950's, from set forms to the adoption of a line that has, normally, three heavy stresses and a varying number of light syllables. The wording is spare, its energy concentrated in nouns and verbs.

In the first two stanzas of ''King of the River,'' the poet establishes so close an identification with the salmon that his intimate address, ''you,'' refers to the fish, to himself, and, beyond that, to all human beings unwillingly changing toward death. The bruised salmon is also seen as being intensely human and mortal:

> A dry fire eats you.
> Fat drips from your bones.
> The flutes of your gills discolor.
> You have become a ship for parasites.

The salmon image illuminates man's active role in his own destiny. The theme was born in ''Open the Gates,'' developed in ''The Approach to Thebes,'' and is apparent throughout the later poems. Here the speaker admonishes the salmon—and himself—to accept mortality. Fighting it would be inappropriate as well as futile, for as the wind tells the creature:

> You have tasted the fire on your tongue
> till it is swollen black
> with a prophetic joy:
> ''Burn with me!
> The only music is time,
> The only dance is love.''

Kunitz' ''key images'' here are presented as pictures of undefeated life even in the face of death. The water is life to the bleeding fish; the doorway, confining in early poems and hopeful in the middle period, here becomes ''the threshold / of the last mystery,'' when

> you have looked into the eyes
> of your creature self,
> which are glazed with madness,
> and you say
> he is not broken but endures,
> limber and firm
> in the state of his shining,
> forever inheriting his salt kingdom,
> from which he is banished
> forever.

In this, one of the great poems of his later years, Kunitz celebrates the drive to endure despite the inevitable process of decay. It is the light that amplifies the endurance: "the state of his shining." That illumination, predicted by tantalizing but subdued moon images of the middle years, is seen frequently in the later poems, as in the "glittering world" in "Journal for My Daughter" (in *The Testing-Tree*) and in the light-kissed roses that lift the writer in "The Round" (in *Next-to-Last Things*). Here, in "King of the River," it consecrates an indomitable life force.

In the 1960's, many American poets translated the work of Russians and Eastern Europeans. Besides admiring the poems, our poets shared the national optimism about peace between the United States and the Soviet Union. Stanley Kunitz, with only rudimentary Russian, rose to the challenge of translation. In the 1960's and 1970's, he worked with Russian scholars to create English versions of poems by Anna Akhmatova, Andrei Voznesensky, and Osip Mandelstam. In the 1980's and into the 1990's, he collaborated in translating other Eastern European poems. To support translation possibilities for other writers, he served on the executive board of the Translation Center, Columbia University. His work as a translator is second only to his teaching as a vital supplement to his own work.

When Kunitz read his Yevgeny Yevtushenko translations in Madison Square Garden, he and the other poets danced on the platform for a curtain call. On June 21, 1967, at Philharmonic Hall in New York, he read his translations in "A Tribute to Andrei Voznesensky," sponsored by the Poetry Center of the Ninety-second Street YM-YWHA. Robert Lowell and William Jay Smith read their versions as well. Because Voznesensky's government did not approve his visit, a vacant chair was placed on the platform and stagehands played a Columbia LP recording of the poet reading in Russian. To an enormous, hushed audience, Kunitz read seven translations of Voznesensky's poems. He also read his versions of Mandelstam's "Tristia," Akhmatova's "Boris Pasternak," and Bella Akhmadulina's "Silence." Those three versions appear in Kunitz' *Poems: 1928–1978*.

At a time when the new wave captured many readers, Kunitz was a leading translator. He was one of seven who rendered the English versions of poems in *Antiworlds* (1966), a book that won public acclaim. It was a bold experiment in its day. Editors Patricia Blake and Max Hayward provided rough literal translations and read the poems aloud in Russian to Kunitz, W. H. Auden, Jean Garrigue, Max Hayward, Stanley Moss, William Jay Smith, and Richard Wilbur.

In the essay "On Translating Akhmatova" (collected in *A Kind of Order, A Kind of Folly*), Kunitz points out that the act of translating the poems of others can stimulate the poet's own work:

> Poets are attracted to translation because it is a way of paying their debt to the tradition, of restoring life to shades, of widening the company of their peers. It is also a means of self-renewal, of entering the skin and adventuring through the body of another's imagination. In the act of translation one becomes more like that other, and is fortified by that other's power.

After the decade of the 1960's, the translation of poetry from languages less known to English readers lost some of its immense appeal. Nevertheless, Kunitz continued his work on Eastern European versions. Notable among the later efforts is his translation of the poems of Ivan Drach; for *Orchard Lamps,* published by Sheep Meadow in 1978, he worked with the Ukrainian language, collaborating with Bohdan Boychuk and others.

His most consequential volume of translations is *The Poems of Anna Akhmatova,* which he rendered from the Russian with Max Hayward. The book was published by Atlantic–Little, Brown in 1973 and since then has been in popular demand. In a 1982 conversation with Daniel Weissbort, Kunitz said that his own poems grew in the process of translating Akhmatova's work, which kept him

> alive to the possibility of translating human situations, conflicts, disturbances into poems that go beyond the personal, that can be read as existential metaphors. She confirmed my image of the poet as witness to history, particularly to the crimes of history

In that interview, collected in *Translating Poetry: The Double Labyrinth* and edited by Weissbort, Kunitz said that he learned specifically "something about transparency of diction, directness of approach to a theme, the possibility of equating personal emotion with historical passion." That equation is fundamental to the poetry of Kunitz as well. The two poets also share a progression throughout their work to freer rhythms, with differences in their methods: Kunitz changed dramatically from received forms to freer cadences; Akhmatova, on the other hand, continued to write in fixed forms, but in verse that was less regular. Both, however, changed in the direction of rhythmic fluidity, and that development was in league with their increasing fusion of personal and public passions.

Kunitz' genius for linking domestic turmoil with human suffering deepens in the later poems. There exists in them simultaneously a reverence for art and a public sensibility, and the successful integration of those concerns is rare in modern poetry. Over and over again he dramatizes the bond between an individual's sadness and a nation's disaster, as in "The Testing-Tree":

> In a murderous time
> the heart breaks and breaks
> and lives by breaking.

Stanley Kunitz is a poet of experience. He has responded to large events of the century, and has played an active role in the lives of students, friends, and colleagues. Nevertheless, in his poetry of this world, a startled innocence prevails and is his mark. It is an untainted purity, a trusting to "the better angels of our nature," as he writes of the president in "The Lincoln Relics." In Kunitz' poems, that quality of innocence is joined to his affinity with natural things. His very personal sense of oneness with living creatures paradoxically gives his work a public authority.

That innocence is the tone of "The Wellfleet Whale," a major poem of the later years. With childlike awe, he presents the creature, immense and exalted, stranded on the beach. He writes also of the people who observe its dying. In wonder, the poet exclaims:

> You prowled down the continental shelf,
> guided by the sun and stars
> and the taste of alluvial silt
> on your way southward
> to the warm lagoons,
> the tropic of desire,
> where the lovers lie belly to belly
> in the rub and nuzzle of their sporting;
> and you turned, like a god in exile,
> out of your wide primeval element,
> delivered to the mercy of time.
> Master of the whale-roads,
> let the white wings of the gulls
> spread out their cover.
> You have become like us,
> disgraced and mortal.

Selected Bibliography

WORKS OF STANLEY KUNITZ

POETRY AND PROSE

Intellectual Things. Garden City, New York: Doubleday, Doran, 1930.

Passport to the War. New York: Holt, 1944.

Selected Poems, 1928–1958. Boston: Atlantic–Little, Brown, 1958.

The Testing-Tree. Boston: Atlantic–Little, Brown, 1971.

The Coat Without a Seam: Sixty Poems, 1930–1972. With illustrations by Leonard Baskin. Northampton, Mass.: Gehenna, 1974.

The Terrible Threshold: Selected Poems, 1940–1970. London: Secker and Warburg, 1974.

A Kind of Order, A Kind of Folly: Essays and Conversations. Boston: Atlantic–Little, Brown, 1975.

The Poems of Stanley Kunitz: 1928–1978. Boston: Atlantic–Little, Brown, 1979.

The Wellfleet Whale and Companion Poems. New York: Sheep Meadow, 1983.

Next-to-Last Things: New Poems and Essays. Boston, New York: Atlantic Monthly Press, 1985.

EDITED OR TRANSLATED WORKS

Poems of John Keats. Edited by Kunitz. New York: Crowell, 1964.

Antiworlds, by Andrei Voznesensky. Translated by Kunitz and others. New York: Basic Books, 1966.

Antiworlds & The Fifth Ace: A Bilingual Edition, by Andrei Voznesensky. Translated by Kunitz and others. New York: Schocken, 1967.

The Poems of Anna Akhmatova. Translated by Kunitz with Max Hayward. Boston: Atlantic–Little, Brown, 1973.

Story Under Full Sail, by Andrei Voznesensky. Translated by Kunitz with others. New York: Doubleday, 1974.

Orchard Lamps, by Ivan Drach. Translated by Kunitz with Bohdan Boychuk and others. New York: Sheep Meadow, 1978.

The Essential Blake. Edited by Kunitz. New York: Ecco, 1987.

EDITED REFERENCE WORKS

Living Authors: A Book of Biographies. New York: H. W. Wilson, 1933.

Authors Today and Yesterday: A Companion Volume to Living Authors. New York: H. W. Wilson, 1933. With Howard Haycraft and Wilbur Hadden.

The Junior Book of Authors. New York: H. W. Wilson, 1934. With Howard Haycraft.

British Authors of the Nineteenth Century. New York: H. W. Wilson, 1936. With Howard Haycraft.

Twentieth-Century Authors. New York: H. W. Wilson, 1942. With Howard Haycraft.

British Authors Before 1800. New York: H. W. Wilson, 1952. With Howard Haycraft.

Twentieth-Century Authors: First Supplement. New York: H. W. Wilson, 1955. With Vineta Colby.

European Authors, 1000–1900. New York: H. W. Wilson, 1967. With Vineta Colby.

INTERVIEWS

Busa, Chris, ed. "Table Talk." *Paris Review*, 83 (Spring 1982). Reprinted with minor changes in *Next-to-Last Things*. Pp. 83–118.

Weissbort, Daniel, ed. "Translating Anna Akhmatova." In his *Translating Poetry: The Double Labyrinth*. London: Macmillan, 1989. Pp. 107–124.

BIOGRAPHICAL AND CRITICAL STUDIES

Arnold, Edmund R. *Stanley Kunitz: A Bibliography and Index*. Potsdam, N.Y.: State University College Library, 1967.

Hénault, Marie. *Stanley Kunitz*. Boston: Twayne, 1980.

"Stanley Kunitz Issue." *Antaeus*, 37 (Spring 1980).

Moss, Stanley, ed. *A Celebration for Stanley Kunitz on His Eightieth Birthday*. Riverdale-on-Hudson, New York: Sheep Meadow, 1986. Essays by Dore Ashton, Roger Skillings, Daniel Halpern, Mark Rudman, and others.

Orr, Gregory, *Stanley Kunitz: An Introduction to the Poetry*. New York: Columbia University Press, 1985.

—*GRACE SCHULMAN*

Denise Levertov

1923–

DENISE LEVERTOV HAS earned praise for her mastery of free verse and other nonmetrical forms, and for her urgent and powerful attempt through her poetry to conflate private and public languages in the grave, calm texture of myth. Though she has been described as more interested in the psychology of the poet than in the resulting poem, most of her admirers consider her commitment to craft and preoccupation with language to be the heart of her poetics. For her, perception is inseparable from the act of making poetry. In *The Poet in the World* (1973), she argues that

> the poet does not see and then begin to search for words to say what he sees: he begins to see and at once begins to say or to sing, and *only in the action of verbalization does he see further*. His language is not more dependent on his vision than his vision is upon his language.

This organic view of the creative process so closely links the psychology of perception with the impulse to make a poem—arguing, in fact, that for a poet, making a poem *is* perception—that they become inseparable. This view also reflects her conviction that the form and the content of a poem must coincide as fully as possible.

Levertov's understanding and articulation of her own poetic has given her a deservedly high reputation as a critic. Her poetry, while sometimes receiving mixed reviews, has earned her a reputation as one of the finest contemporary American poets and almost certainly the best of those committed to the formal ideas of William Carlos Williams and Charles Olson. Kenneth Rexroth in 1961 called her "incomparably the best poet of what is getting to be known as the new avant garde," and in 1970 said, "She . . . resembles Mallarme or Pierre Reverdy, except that she is easily understood." Her work has developed and varied its focus over the five decades of her career, notably providing some of the most controversial public poetry of our time, but her characteristic techniques and concerns give it a consistency and tone peculiarly her own.

Most important is Levertov's aesthetic requirement that the poem form a coherent, cohesive whole, rejecting or reinterpreting the fragmentation and loose association of the poetry of her mentors, William Carlos Williams and Charles Olson. James F. Mersmann points out that "Levertov tries to give her poems the shape and pattern she discovers outside the poem." Perhaps because of this poetic animism, this desire to imitate in the poem the form of its subject, she focuses entirely on the short poem, or on brief sequences of short lyrics, and avoids the larger-scale enterprise of Williams' *Paterson,* Ezra Pound's *The Cantos,* or Olson's *The Maximus Poems*. But rather than limiting her subject matter, her aesthetic program makes available a wide range of content.

The search for poetry of an inner harmony, a harmony of form and content that by 1965 Levertov would call "organic poetry," coincides with her desire for a poetic that would be flexible enough to admit both polemical responses to political and social concerns and the larger abstractions that the imagism of the modernist period generally prohibited. The formal cohesion of the poem, derived from the cohesion of individual perception, makes available any subject of genuine interest to the perceiving mind of the poet. "Organic poetry," she writes in her 1965 essay "Some Notes on Organic Form" "is a *method of apperception,* i.e., of recognizing what we perceive, and is based on an intuition of an order, a form beyond forms, in which forms partake, and of which man's creative works are analogies, resemblances, natural allegories."

Only under the pressure of realized poetic form can these varied perceptions fully cohere and harmonize. Her recognition that poetic form and language tend to allegorize natural imagery has directed Levertov toward myth: not, until recent years, toward the inclusive, narrative mythology of the Bible and the classical period, but rather to a sense of the power of language to transcend the banalities of actuality and to embody, in some small degree, an otherwise elusive ideal or ineffable sense of the presence of spiritual mystery. To Levertov the primary task of the language of poetry is to give voice to the potential myth of natural landscape and the quotidian by asserting the strangeness, the otherness, of the familiar, as in "Matins" (*The Jacob's Ladder*): "The cow's breath / not forgotten in the mist, in the / words." She describes that process of language-discovery, one that actively engages the reader in the making of myth, in "To the Reader," the brief *ars poetica* that opens her 1961 volume, *The Jacob's Ladder*:

As you read, a white bear leisurely
pees, dyeing the snow
saffron,

and as you read, many gods
lie among lianas: eyes of obsidian
are watching the generations of leaves,

and as you read
the sea is turning its dark pages,
turning
its dark pages.

What is happening in this little poem? What sort of questions does it respond to, given that Levertov (in *The Poet in the World*) argues that "what the poet is called upon to clarify is not answers but the existence and nature of questions?" Its most obvious response is to the question, "What happens when we read?" Rather than a direct answer the poem offers a group of mysterious images and directs us toward the source of myth and the process of making it out of nature. The white bear that "leisurely / pees" may seem a slightly satiric figure of the writer, who inscribes the white absence (the blank page) with the effluvia of the mind. But it is also a fairy-tale figure rendered in actual terms, a mysterious white animal (white animals are usually magical) that functions with physiological verisimilitude. This illustrates what Richard Pevear has identified in a review of *Footprints* in the *Hudson Review* (1973) as "a natural piety that tends toward animism," and suggests that for the poet the natural world is not entirely objective but in some way is caught up with our inner lives.

Linking the half-concealed life in nature with the inner world of the self is a primal task for the writer. The critic Northrop Frye has identified this project as the "final cause" of art. But this poem gives the reader the responsibility of making that link, equating reading with the greater temporal process of vegetative succession ("generations of leaves'') and the evolution of order out of chaos, turning the pages of the book as the sea turns its dark pages. The shape of the poem, an unfolding that turns, finally, on the word ''turning,'' mimes with mostly enjambed free-verse lines the larger act of turning pages.

The figure of the reader, according to Levertov's 1968 lecture ''Origins of a Poem'' (in *The Poet in the World*), is half of a dialogue of the artist with herself. She approvingly quotes Ernst Barlach, a German playwright and sculptor, who argues that ''Every art needs two—one who makes it, and one who needs it,'' then extends the argument by postulating a reader within one's self. This reader will respond ''with the innocence you bring to a poem by someone unknown to you.'' Thus the reader-self is a critical buffer between the poet-maker and the unknown, anonymous reader out there somewhere. ''To the Reader'' then addresses both the self, carrying on that inner colloquy Levertov finds at the heart of many of her poems, and the traditional reader.

Levertov's poetics of organic order and natural piety inform even her stridently antiwar poems of the late 1960's and early 1970's. This poetic may derive in part not only from the early influence of Herbert Read and the other British neo-Romantics popular in her youth and from the objectivism learned from Robert Duncan, Robert Creeley, and Charles Olson, but also from her complex family background. Doris Earnshaw argues that as ''granddaughter on her father's side of a Russian Hasidic Jew and on her mother's of a Welsh mystic,'' Levertov ''was fitted by birth and political destiny to voice the terrors and pleasures of the twentieth century.'' Because Levertov so often derives her poems from the immediate or the past events of her life, her biography can usefully inform responses to her poetry.

Levertov's father was a Russian Jew who had immigrated to England and become an Anglican minister. Denise Levertov was born there on October 24, 1923, and grew up in suburban Ilford, Essex. (Sources conflict over whether her city of birth was actually London or Ilford.) Her father, who spelled his name Levertoff, descended from the founder of Habad Hasidism. Some of the characteristics of this sect seem to survive in Levertov's poetry, since she describes it as embodying both ''a very great strain of asceticism'' and ''a recognition and joy in the physical world'' (quoted in Wagner, *Denise Levertov: In Her Own Province*). This seems to describe perfectly a great deal of her own work, though it also suggests that Levertov has chosen to understand this sect on her own terms. Her mother was Welsh and, like Levertov's father, was descended from a religious figure, the preacher-tailor Angel Jones of Mold. Though Levertov's poetry, even her later overtly Christian work, is more pantheistic than conventionally religious in the Judeo-Christian tradition, it is infused with this strongly religious family background.

Levertov did not receive a good deal of formal education (she attended neither grammar school nor a university), but her schooling at home was thoroughly literary. Her mother introduced her to the work of the great Victorian writers, particularly Tennyson, of whom she later said, ''I had him practically stuck under my armpit for several years of my childhood'' (quoted in Wagner, *In Her Own Province*). Through reading at home, through the formal study of ballet, and through exposure to the refugees, artists, and eccentrics her father befriended, she came early in life to believe in the importance of art and its place in her own life.

As Levertov recounts in the introduction to her *Collected Earlier Poems,* at the age of twelve she sent some poems to T. S. Eliot, who responded some months later with a lengthy letter ''full of advice.'' She then recalls that at sixteen she met Herbert Read, whose ideas on art and culture are a major influence on her poetry to the present day. By the time she was nineteen her work was appearing in journals such as *Poetry Quarterly, Outposts,* and *Voices*. During the war Levertov served as a civilian nurse in St. Luke's Hospital in Fitzroy Square, London. There she wrote most of the poems in her first book, *The Double Image,* published in 1946 by the Cresset Press. To achieve this publication, Levertov by her own account walked naively into the office (mistakenly entering through the stockroom) and handed her "ill-typed manuscript" to an editor. Though doubtful, the editor passed the manuscript on to John Hayward, the director of the press, who decided to publish it.

Critics have usually described the poems in *The Double Image* as characteristic of the neo-Romantic mood of British poetry at the time. However, the best poems already display a tendency to defamiliarize the domestic and natural world and emphasize the essentially private way the individual is forced to confront otherness. The second half of "Christmas 1944" illustrates the mixture of Georgian imagery and startling and effective personification ("a dark excited tree," "hearing hatred crackle in the coal") that defines her work of the 1940's:

A painted bird or boat above the fire,
a fire in the hearth, a candle in the dark,
a dark excited tree, fresh from the forest,
are all that stands between us and the wind.
The wind has many tales to tell of sea and city,
a plague on many houses, fear knocking on the
doors;
how venom trickles from the open mouth of
death,
and trees are white with rage of alien battles.
Who can be happy while the wind recounts
its long sagas of sorrow? Though we are safe
in a flickering circle of winter festival
we dare not laugh; or if we laugh, we lie,
hearing hatred crackle in the coal,
the voice of reason, the voice of love.

The free verse is almost as measured as blank verse, and the orderly, fluent syntax and manifest faith in natural epiphany characterize her work at this time. The faith in epiphany is Wordsworthian and will remain with her through a long, productive career, so that even late work like "The day longs for the evening" from *Breathing the Water* (1987) can ask of an almost wholly personified landscape "What is that promised evening?" and find the illumination of faith in natural occurrence.

The poems of *The Double Image* embody a recurring sense of loss, which in the context of Levertov's natural piety requires the ritualizing of death. To defer the bottomless mystery of death, Levertov in "To Death" addresses it directly and offers its personified form the honors due a god. But the poem also invites death to play a role, to be an image rather than an actuality, a sign instead of a referent. "Enter with riches. Let your image wear / brocade of fantasy, and bear your part / with all the actor's art and arrogance." If death does this (that is, if it accepts the role of image and actor) it "will receive, deserve due ritual," and the speaker will be able to address this fictional version of death as "eloquent, just, and mighty one"—praise that otherwise, except for the last modifier, actual death hardly deserves. This Romantic personification of death typifies the early Levertov's withdrawal from the modernist urban imagery of Eliot and Auden and the avoidance of the horrors of the just-concluded war. Later, although retaining the concern with mythmaking, the devices of personification and apostrophe, the natural piety and idealism, Levertov would move sharply in the other direction, embracing the mundane horror of modern war in a language that if anything was too nakedly eager to confront its subject matter. But in doing so she demonstrated how flexible an instrument her early poetic was, and proved that her commitment to an expressive,

Romantic aesthetic by no means limited her range.

Levertov first appeared in an American publication in 1949 in Kenneth Rexroth's anthology *New British Poetry*. By then she had married Mitchell Goodman, an American soldier, novelist, and poet, had moved to New York City, and had produced a son, Nikolai. Sometime during her first few years in New York, Levertov began to read William Carlos Williams, whose influence transformed her poetry and gave her a new idiom that amalgamated her early romanticism with a more hard-edged language of immediate perception. Her interest in two other younger poets confirmed her sense of the importance of Williams. Robert Creeley, who published her work in *Black Mountain Review* and *Origin,* and Robert Duncan became her friends in the early 1950's. Both poets taught at Black Mountain College, under the direction of Charles Olson, and through them Levertov became known as a "Black Mountain" poet. But her poetry cannot be assigned to any school, and while she admires Duncan and Creeley she has always considered her work distinct from theirs. Williams is the common denominator. Though the full effect of exposure to Williams appeared gradually, by 1957 when her second book, *Here and Now,* appeared, the shift from her rich but somewhat Georgian early poetry was complete.

This second book and the third, *Overland to the Islands* (1958), have interesting and overlapping histories. They are so linked that Levertov now thinks they should have appeared as a single volume. Weldon Kees, Levertov reports, had solicited a collection of her work for a small press he planned to start with a friend. Unfortunately for Levertov and American poetry, Kees shortly thereafter leapt from the Golden Gate Bridge. The following year, Lawrence Ferlinghetti, who had obtained the manuscript material in Kees's possession, offered to publish a book, and after sifting through available poems produced *Here and Now*. The following year, Jonathan Williams published *Overland to the Islands,* which according to Levertov consisted of the "rejects" from the earlier volume, and a few more recent poems. In her introduction to *Collected Earlier Poems* Levertov comments that "poems that should really have been in a single book together because of their interrelationships were arbitrarily divided between *Here and Now* and *Overland to the Islands.*" Further, Robert Duncan suggested that both books suffered from a lack of clear ordering. Levertov points out that "to *compose* a book is preferable to randomly gathering one."

Whatever the problems with the ordering of these books, the individual poems display a firmness of imagery, a clarity of language, and the first signs of Levertov's mastery of the "variable foot" of Williams, which would become central to her theory of rhythm and the organic unity of her poetic. In an interview with Walter Sutton (in *Poet in the World*), Levertov describes the source of the variable foot as "a sense of pulse, a pulse in behind the words, a pulse that is actually sort of tapped out by a drum in the poem." She considers this form distinct from free verse, believing that verse requires a regularity, and rejects the "breath-spaced" line as well on the grounds that it attempts to imitate speech, while the poem should reflect an "inner voice" that may not be reproducible in speech. This "inner voice," she argues, "is not necessarily identical with [the poet's] literal speaking voice, nor is his inner vocabulary identical with that which he uses in conversation." By rejecting an easy identification of poetry with speech Levertov distinguishes herself from the less thoughtful imitators of Williams and retains the Romantic-expressive core of her poetic. Despite or perhaps because of her animism there can be no perfect clarity in the relationship between the natural world and the language in which she describes it. The clarity of her rhythms, however, would brilliantly outline that mystery and help give her poems a structural firmness that would more than make up for slack language and occasional vagaries of metaphor.

Levertov's early, pre-Williams poems have the virtues of conventional form as well as a flair for unexpected phrasing. Her primary weakness is an overreliance on symbolic convention and predictably poetic subject matter. By *Here and Now,* though, the example of Williams had begun to free her from conventions, both of form and content, and her poems open themselves to the domestic and commonplace, while embracing a paradoxical sense of both the otherness and the spiritual congeniality of the natural world—a paradox that by the period of *The Jacob's Ladder* would give her poems a rich mythic texture. The poems of *Here and Now* are sometimes too insistently joyful, their language often too decorative, but the grasp of Williams' rhythmic principles lends them a drive and energy that the poems of *The Double Image* lacked. "Jackson Square" illustrates the strengths and weakness of her mid-1950's idiom:

Bravo! the brave sunshine.
A triangle of green green contains
the sleek and various pigeons
the starving inventors and all
who sit on benches in the morning,
to sun tenacious hopes—indeed
a gay morning for hope to feed on
greedy as the green
                and gray
                and purple-preening birds . . .

The repetition of "green," the typographical insistence on the colors of the birds, the poem's tendency toward self-explication ("to sun tenacious hopes . . . a gay morning for hope") echo Williams' weaker mannerisms, but the adroit flexing of syntax against the loose but regular rhythms imposed by the line-breaks shows how well Levertov has grasped his rhythmic principles.

If the language of *Here and Now* sometimes is too ornately pictorial, *Overland to the Islands,* although supposedly made up of rejects from the previous book, often displays a more concentrated focus on the everyday world, less tendency to rhapsodize. The most interesting poems focus on domestic concerns in a fresh, colloquial voice, as in "The Dogwood":

The sink is full of dishes. Oh well.
Ten o'clock, there's no
hot water.
The kitchen floor is unswept, the broom
has been shedding straws. Oh well.

This poem illustrates another lesson well learned from Williams: the clearly defined, colloquial speaking voice gives a necessary life to things not by imposing abstractions upon them but by acknowledging them for what they are. Williams learned this from his early reading of Keats, so it is a lesson perfectly compatible with Levertov's Romantic faith in the sufficiency of the world.

Levertov's next book would be her first by a major publisher. Rexroth, she believes, brought her work to the attention of James Laughlin, and in 1960 New Directions published *With Eyes at the Back of Our Heads.* The title directs the reader to Levertov's concern with indirection, with finding what one wants by avoiding looking directly for it, and her belief that what we see with the physical eye is less essential than what we see with the mind's eye, the unconscious back-of-the-head eye directed by a mind alert to myth. This is the topic of her title poem:

With eyes at the back of our heads
we see a mountain
not obstructed with woods but laced
here and there with feathery groves.

Unlike real mountains, which tend to be obstructed with woods, this one, the sheer bulk of the mythic world available to the imagination, with its "feathery groves" is the background against which we can construct more personal fantasies. The personal fantasy of this poem revolves about a house, perhaps a facade, that is both shelter and garment. Architect and knitter, two functionaries of the imagination, combine their talents to render the house accessible so that we may pass through it and reach the mountain beyond:

> When the doors widen
> when the sleeves admit us
> the way to the mountain will be clear,
> the mountain we see with
> eyes at the back of our heads, mountain
> green, mountain
> cut of limestone, echoing
> with hidden rivers, mountain
> of short grass and subtle shadows.

The imagination, here embodied in the arts of knitting and architecture, bridges the gap between the mind and the exterior world. The house, though only a facade—something that like a sweater we "wear" to define ourselves better—gives admittance to the natural world beyond. Both the created and the natural world in this poem are products of imagination, but art, not their mutual source in the mind, links them. The pleasure Levertov takes in the poetic function, the power of joining self and nature in the common medium of mythic language, shapes this book and gives it an affirmative tone distinct from the ironic, cool, witty, or learned tones of contemporaries such as Creeley, Lowell, Rich, or Olson.

"To the Snake" most clearly points to the source of that joy, the pleasure in working through natural symbol to produce a synthesis between the self and the world. By hanging the green snake around her throat the poet assumes the power of the goddess (the subject of another poem in this volume). She also takes a risk—snakes tempt, lie, and bite—but the poet is willing to assume the full weight of the symbol, and by avoiding the illusion that myth is necessarily either positive or negative she experiences a richer sense of its place in the world:

> Green Snake—I swore to my companions that
> certainly
> you were harmless! But truly
> I had no certainty, and no hope, only desiring
> to hold you, for that joy,
> which left
> a long wake of pleasure, as the leaves moved
> and you faded into the pattern
> of grass and shadow, and I returned
> smiling and haunted, to a dark morning.

This implied definition of the poet's task, to assume the mantle of myth and risk losing one's self in the larger patterns of the natural world, would be refined in *The Jacob's Ladder* (1961), in which Levertov turned to the problem of the proper language of poetry. The first poem (after the poem "To the Reader"), "A Common Ground," sites the poet's work in the "common ground" of agriculture, which is "here and there gritty with pebbles / yet elsewhere 'fine and mellow— / uncommon fine for ploughing.' " The poem's second section turns to the issue of the place of both poetry and nature in the contemporary world of New York's Central Park where "the girls / laugh at the sun, men / in business suits awkwardly / recline" and poetry occupies a secretive, almost subversive role: "Poems stirred / into paper coffee-cups, eaten / with petals on rye in the / sun. . . ." The third section turns to the question of language: "Not 'common speech' / a dead level / but the uncommon speech of paradise," she argues, "a language / excelling itself to be itself."

This book refines that language through the dictates of a more sophisticated and compelling sense of rhythm. "Six Variations" catalogs some of the rhythmic possibilities available to the organic poem with its unified field of imagery. One kind of rhythm (in the third variation) is onomatopoeic in origin:

> Shulp, shulp, the dog
> as it laps up
> water
> makes intelligent
> music . . .

Another section (fourth variation) in the manner of Alexander Pope manipulates vowels to slow the line in imitation of its subject:

> when your answers
> come
>   slowly, dragging
> their feet

But the title poem reminds us that poetry isn't entirely a matter of craft. "The Jacob's Ladder" argues that the humility of the religious suppliant is also a necessary aspect of poetry (its visionary aspect) and argues that whatever the poem envisions it experiences as real:

> A stairway of sharp
> angles, solidly built
> one sees that the angels must spring
> down from one step to the next, giving a little
> lilt of the wings:
>
> and a man climbing
> must scrape his knees, and bring
> the grip of his hands into play. The cut stone
> consoles his groping feet. Wings brush past him.
> The poem ascends.

This poem demonstrates how Levertov's neo-Romantic tendencies have given way to a more vividly mystic aspiration, perhaps derived in part from the work of Robert Duncan and surely linked to the Hasidic tradition of her early years. The idiom of William Carlos Williams, though, helps ground this mysticism in a feeling for actuality. Rather than ecstatic revelation, these poems make ritual encounters with concrete particulars of nature the basis of the relationship between the speaker and the subjects of the poems. Though vague spirit-figures prowl on the fringes, the source of mystery seems to lie in the human ability to bond through imagination the self and the exterior world.

This sense of mystery as something rooted in us haunts Levertov's work to the present. The failure to realize or to respect this essential link with otherness disappoints or even enrages her. The difficulty in effectively directing her frustration with the narrow, unimaginative, inhumane vision of establishment politics is one of the causes of the aesthetic failures of some of her Vietnam War–era poems. She sometimes forgets her own injunction (in *Poet in the World*) that "Insofar as poetry has a social function it is to awaken sleepers by other means than shock." But even in those difficult times her poetry, as we will see, retains its organic ideals of form and rhythm, its faith in individual vision, and its trust in nature as the source of metaphorical and spiritual significance.

The Jacob's Ladder and the two books that followed confirmed Levertov as a distinct, unique, and powerful voice in American poetry. In reviewing *The Jacob's Ladder,* James Wright called her "one of the best living poets in America," and other reviewers, if not always so effusive, accorded her the respect due an important writer. *O Taste and See* (1964) is a more sensuous book, with more imagery of the body, sex, childbirth, and marriage. But the domesticity of the subject matter does not exclude the mystic vision central to *The Jacob's Ladder.* "Eros at Temple Stream" typifies the language of bodily pleasure that permeates this book, and it also demonstrates how these poems work toward transcendence through, not despite, the body and the other material things of this world:

> The river in its abundance
> many-voiced

all about us as we stood
on a warm rock to wash

slowly
smoothing in long
                sliding strokes
our soapy hands along each other's
slippery cool bodies

The poem retains this sensuous materiality but introduces a visionary note as the hands become flames and the entire body becomes "sleek and / on fire." Linking flesh to fire is a way of asserting the immortality of the spirit as something derived from the vitality of the body itself. As nature inspirits language in Levertov's world, so the body now inspirits the soul and will continue doing so through her future work.

In 1965, the year after the publication of *O Taste and See,* Levertov's important essay "Some Notes on Organic Form" appeared in *Poetry* magazine. This is her clearest and most prescriptive comment on her art and has been reprinted several times, most influentially in Stephen Berg and Robert Mezey's anthology *Naked Poetry* (1969). Her description of the poetic process is so concrete and so aptly applies to her own work that it is hard to remember that for other poets the writing experience may be quite different: "I think it's like this: First there must be an experience, a sequence or constellation of perceptions of sufficient interest, felt by the poet intensely enough to demand of him their equivalence in words: he is *brought to speech.*"

Like Wordsworth, she places the origin of poetry in individual experience and gives less importance to the larger, cultural experience that like language itself makes poetry possible. Arguing from the amalgamation (a "constellation") of perceptions, as Eliot does for the metaphysical poets, she makes the poem entirely a product of sense perception and emotion. Though not completely original, her assertion that organic poetry is self-formative, that instead of refusing form it creates a fresh form with every effort, had great appeal and influenced many other poets, particularly those coming to maturity in the 1960's.

By 1965 the Vietnam War was a dominant political and moral issue in American life. Levertov became one of the most outspoken opponents of the war, which contravened her belief in the centrality of nature and the imagination. The war violated nature and betrayed the imagination, denied the spirit and degraded the body. One of her best books, *The Sorrow Dance* (1967), describes in eight carefully arranged sections her growing commitment to political action. The transition from celebration of the natural world of love to poems of social protest was triggered in part by the terrible spectacle of Vietnam (which in many of the poems of *The Sorrow Dance* is represented by the depiction of peace- and nature-loving Buddhists assuming activist roles) and partly by the death of her sister Olga, who had been more committed to political activism than Levertov herself was at this point.

The elegiac sequence entitled "The Olga Poems" is one of Levertov's strongest poems. Levertov depicts her closeness to her sister in the language of nature, as if Olga in death had entered the very being of the world:

Now as if smoke or sweetness were blown my
    way
I inhale a sense of her livingness in that instant,
feeling, dreaming, hoping, knowing boredom
    and zest like anyone
                else—

a young girl in the garden, the same alchemical
    square
I grew in.

Yet perhaps because she was so attuned to nature, Olga was willing to oppose its inertia and stasis and consequently set herself to impossible tasks:

. . . To change,
to change the course of the river! What rage for order
disordered her pilgrimage—so that for years at a time

she would hide among strangers, waiting
to rearrange all mysteries in a new light.

Levertov had begun to realize that praising nature is not enough to shape adequate human ideals. Because the natural order of things does not necessarily correspond to the most desirable human order, one must sometimes "change the course of the river" and place one's self in opposition to impossible forces. Olga would become her model for such opposition, but so would the Buddhists of Southeast Asia and the young people of America who in the late 1960's looked to nature, farming, communal living, and the utter rejection of war as they attempted to make new metaphors for the human community.

By 1967 Buddhist protestors in Vietnam had demonstrated the necessity, the beauty, and the consequences of such opposition. In "The Altars in the Street" Levertov acknowledges their heroism in terms that pit nature against the city, the innocence of natural religion against the spiritual corruption of repressive violence.

Children begin at green dawn nimbly to build
topheavy altars, overweighted with prayers
. . . .
. . . by noon
the whole city in all its corruption,

all its shed blood the monsoon cannot wash away,
has become a temple,
fragile, insolent, absolute.

The next to last section of *The Sorrow Dance,* which includes "The Altars in the Street," is called "Life At War" and contains a poem prophetically entitled "Didactic Poem." The title indicates the direction that much of Levertov's work would take during the next few years.

The poems Levertov wrote in the late 1960's reflected her own involvement in protest and the sacrifices she and her husband made on behalf of the peace movement. She traveled to Hanoi, participated in peace rallies as a featured speaker, and joined with Robert Bly, Galway Kinnell, and other poets in organizing readings against the war. Mitchell Goodman's involvement was even deeper, and eventually he was tried with Benjamin Spock on charges of conspiracy to incite resistance to the draft. The poems concurrent with these activities often are journalistic, fragmentary, apparently disordered.

Most of the reviewers of *Relearning the Alphabet* (1970) and *To Stay Alive* (1971) objected to her rhetoric of protest, finding it an inflexible use of language that discouraged the play of imagery that informed her best work, though some of those reviewers were also sympathetic to the aesthetic as well as the moral necessity behind these poems. Marie Borroff, writing in the *Yale Review,* commented of Levertov that "the time-honored impulse to celebrate, to wonder, to sing is basic in her, and this impulse is, literally, disturbed by the knowledge that an unassimilable evil exists which must be hated and which must be fought on the level of action." Most reviewers seemed aware of and sympathetic to the pressure Levertov felt from what she took to be the forces of evil, the war and its supporters and profiteers.

But the resultant poetry discouraged even many of Levertov's previous supporters. Marjorie Perloff's review of *To Stay Alive* typifies the negative reaction to both the strong rhetorical stance and the dubious formal characteristics of the poems of this period: "Her anti–Vietnam War poems, written in casual diary form, sound rather like a versified *New York Review of Books*—the same righteous indignation, the same uncompromising moral zeal and self-important tone. It is difficult to believe that the poet who, as one of the most promising heirs of William

Carlos Williams, wrote 'The world is / not with us enough / O taste and see,' should now resort to the flat abstractions, the facile polemics, and the careless rhythms of *To Stay Alive.*''

To Stay Alive opens by reprinting ''The Olga Poems,'' and the high quality of those elegies contrasts starkly with the rambling, inefficient journal-poems gathered under the title ''Staying Alive'':

Chuck Matthei
travels the country
                    a harbinger.
(He's 20. His golden beard was pulled and
     clipped
          by a Wyoming sheriff, but no doubt
     has grown
               again
though he can't grow knocked-out teeth.
He wears sneakers even in winter,
to avoid animal-hide; etc.)

One might feel that the journal-world signified by ''etc.'' could continue indefinitely. But worse than the rambling and seemingly disorganized, decidedly inorganic quality of the verse is the trite sentiment that crops up in place of the crisp epiphanies that empowered her earlier poems:

     But Chuck has found in it
a message for all who resist war,
     disdain to kill,
     try to equate
     'human' with 'humane.'

In recent years, however, more scholarly approaches to these poems have partly rehabilitated them. Richard Jackson finds that their journal aesthetic constitutes an interesting problem in the way a text manipulates its subject matter and temporal framework. Nancy J. Sisko finds merit even in the disorderliness of many of the poems, arguing that ''when Levertov accurately records her own struggle she in turn mirrors the struggle of others like her during that era.'' And Bonnie Costello comments that ''*Relearning the Alphabet* was Levertov's most successful effort of identification [empathy with victims], for it showed how history had turned the very tools of the poet—language and imagination—into cruel weapons of distortion.'' With distance these poems have acquired some of the charm history confers on the artifact, but also they seem more clearly now to reveal beneath the sometimes shrill rhetoric Levertov's respect for life as the subtext of her rage.

Footprints, her 1972 volume, returned to her old concerns, but many of the poems seem exhausted and unraveled. Levertov's faith in organic form no longer engenders tightly knit poems like those in *The Jacob's Ladder* and *O Taste and See.* Instead, a looser kind of association and tone of elegiac uncertainty mark the poems of her next few books. ''A Place to Live'' exemplifies both the style and the ethos of her changed voice:

Honeydew seeds: on impulse
strewn in a pot of earth. Now,

(the green vines) wandering
down over the pot's edges:

certainly no room here to lay
the egg of a big, pale,
green-fleshed melon.
                    Wondering

where the hell to go.

Where indeed? Levertov's antiwar poems opened up new possibilities, looser structures, more journalistic ideas of form, but she had not yet found a way to link her evolving formal ideas to her earlier concern with mythmaking and vision.

In *The Freeing of the Dust* (1975) the thematic concern with Vietnam continues with poems about her visit to North Vietnam in 1972, about a trip to Moscow, and about lost, misdirected, or failed personal relationships. In North Vietnam she visited the Bach Mai Hospital and was moved to write poems like "Weeping Woman" as well as the important essay "Glimpses of Vietnamese Life" in *The Poet in the World* (1973). Meanwhile, at home in America, her marriage was dissolving, and the book that resulted, by conflating essentially private grief with a public outrage over Vietnamese war casualties, seems unwittingly to equate these markedly distinct sources of pain.

Though Levertov carefully divided *The Freeing of the Dust* into nine well-considered sections to give it a clearly autobiographical shape that would help justify the inclusion of such different kinds of poems, the impression remains of a poet still somewhat at odds with herself. More journal-like poems ("Conversation in Moscow," "Modes of Being") alternate with poignant though sometimes bathetic brief lyrics of suffering and loss. Strong antiwar poems such as "The Pilots," which attempts to deal with her complex feelings about the participants in the war (and is frank about her sense of moral and class superiority to these American prisoners of war), stand beside poems that lapse into the preachy abstractions of *To Stay Alive*. The best poems in this book, however, such as "Room," call for a renewal of the poetry and aesthetic of celebration. Harry Marten's comment that "the lyrics in *The Freeing of the Dust* . . . represent an expansion of Levertov's range of experience" is correct, but the match between her essentially mystical, visionary sensibility and public and political subject matter remains an uneasy one.

Life in the Forest (1978) is a book of healthy metaphorical vision, of poems in which most personal emotions find objective correlatives, though its more historical or public poems still display a flaccid, sometimes sentimental rhetoric. In its best poems—and this is a book with many fine poems—the dominant sense is of private experience opening into metaphor, and through that language process, of emotion finding correlation in the natural world. Instead of the abstraction into which the weaker poems in *The Freeing of the Dust* lapsed, here imagery shapes the argument of the poems. Partly this is the result of rejecting some aspects of the autobiographical voice as she had established it. In her introduction, Levertov says she wanted to "try to avoid overuse of the autobiographical, the dominant first-person singular of so much of the American poetry—good and bad—of recent years." Many of the poems are, in fact, written in the first person, and many use highly personal subject matter, but her statement may be an indirect way of acknowledging her desire to escape the tendency to moralize and draw abstract conclusions.

As Bonnie Costello argues in a long review, "When Levertov makes myth serve humanity—that idol of prophets and politicians—it is sluggish in its duties. She is a dreamer at heart, and her best moments are stolen, solitary ones, glimpses of a landscape at one A.M. when 'humanity' has long since gone to bed." Her public myths tend toward the polemic, her private ones achieve the luminosity of real vision. For this reason, moralizing for Levertov may be the most anti-autobiographical of acts. If she came to recognize this it would explain why most of *Life in the Forest* breaks so cleanly with the weaker work of her recent past. Also in her introduction, Levertov points to her poems that imitate the manner of Italian poet Cesare Pavese. His poems are actually much like many of those in Levertov's early volumes, so it is not surprising that her discovery of his work prompted a renewal of her own strongest mode. Though *Life in the Forest* uses a variety of voices and strategies, and includes discursive long-lined poems, brief intense imagistic lyrics, and some looser journal-like poems, she brings to all of this variety a greater sureness, a keener sense of language and the poetic line, and most important, a greater faith in imagery and metaphor than her poetry had displayed since *The Sorrow Dance*.

Levertov has often worked with poets whose sensibilities are compatible with her own and whose work in some way points toward her current thematic or structural concerns. The strategy of drawing upon translations to complement and illuminate her own work began with her important, separately published translation of Eugene Guillevic's *Selected Poems* (1969). Guillevic's loosely strung, vaguely political sequence "Interrogation" points toward the journal-poems Levertov would write in protest of the war, while Rilke's mystic vision became in a later work a model for her growing inwardness, her attempts to reconcile the visionary spirit with the limitations and pleasures of the flesh. "Variations on a Theme by Rilke," derived from a poem in his *Book of the Hours,* is one of a pair of translations that frame *Breathing the Water* (1987). Part two of this poem makes explicit Levertov's resignation to contextual human limitations:

There will never be that stillness.
Within the pulse of flesh,
in the dust of being, where we trudge,
    turning our hungry gaze this way and that,
the wings of the morning
brush through our blood
as cloud-shadows brush the land.
What we desire travels with us.
We must breathe time as fishes breathe water.
    God's flight circles us.

But resignation to mortality is not the only mood in Levertov's recent work. A renewed sense of harmony between self and nature, language and feeling, pervades her four books of the 1980's. As her invocation of Rilke suggests, to a great extent this is due to a renewal of her religious and mystical sensibility. Her six-part sequence, "Mass for the Day of St. Thomas Didymus," from *Candles in Babylon* (1982), most fully represents this new awakening to the mysterious otherness of the world. It is utterly frank in acknowledging her inability to link the known to the unknowable and her new inclination to refuse the didacticism and arrogant tone of the poetry of the war years:

We live in terror
of what we do not know,
in terror of not knowing,
of the limitless, through which freefalling
forever, our dread
sinks and sinks,
                or
    of the violent closure of it all.

But the poem takes its consolation where Levertov first found it, in a pantheistic but now increasingly Christian sense of the order of nature:

The name of the spirit is written
in woodgrain, windripple, crystal,
in crystals of snow, in petal, leaf,
moss and moon, fossil and feather . . .

This nature is similar to us in sensibility, so that our attempt to impose order through the word (an attempt she would soon repudiate) bears at least some analogy to the larger order of things:

blood, bone, song, silence,
very word of
very word.

flesh and
vision.

This renewed sense of contact with visionary mystery, and further, an enlarged sense of privilege in sensing or touching such cosmic matters, informs the best poems of *Candles in Babylon, Oblique Prayers* (1984), *Breathing the Water,* and *A Door in the Hive* (1989). One of the dominant notes in these books is submission to natural order, which is not an entirely new idea but one that would be more insistently presented after her profession of Christianity in the early 1980's. This new submissiveness does not represent a repudiation of her rage at the perversion of natural and social order represented by war, but another, more oblique way of approaching the same problem. The rage remains, with its attendant problems of rhetoric and didacticism, as "El Salvador: Requiem and Invocation" in *A Door in the Hive* demonstrates. But the political note no longer dominates. Nor does the raised voice of the revolutionary calling for overt action. Instead the most compelling voice of her recent work argues that the important task is to submit to nature and learn from it, learn not to attempt to force or reshape it to our will (to "interpret" it). This is illustrated by "The Absentee" (from *Breathing the Water*):

> Uninterpreted, the days
> are falling.
>
> The spring wind
> is shaking and shaking the trees.
>
> A nest of eggs,
> a nest of deaths.
>
> Falling
> abandoned.
>
> The palms rattle, the eucalypts
> shed bark and blossom. Uninterpreted.

If we heed this call for the acceptance of death and a meditative refusal of the intellect's urge to imposed order, what will we gain? The answer, unsurprisingly, is faith. Levertov in "A Poet's View" (1984) describes her own coming to faith as "not inevitable" but nearly so, a function of her very existence as a poet, a person dependent on the imagination.

> It must therefore be by the exercise of that faculty [the imagination] that one moves toward faith, and possibly by its failure that one rejects it as delusion. Poems present their testimony as circumstantial evidences, not as closing arguments. Where Wallace Stevens says, "God and the imagination are one," I would say that the imagination, which synergizes intellect, emotion and instinct, is the perceptive organ through which it is possible, though not inevitable, to experience God.

Through the imagination one may experience God and so come to faith. But that faith, though hard earned, is difficult to maintain against the human will to entropy and the relentless numbing routine of the ordinary. And as "The Love of Morning," in Levertov's *A Door in the Hive,* warns us, it is easy to accept God's love on mornings of birdsong when "sunlight's gossamer lifts in its net / the weight of all that is solid," but harder to realize "on gray mornings" when "all incident . . . is hard to love again" and "we resent a summons / that disregards our sloth, and this / calls us, calls us." This is the test.

But Christianity may be a resting place for the imagination, not a stimulus. That God should call us to the love of things when in exhaustion and depression we find little love in ourselves is neither a fresh nor unnoticed problem, and some of these late poems, instead of reaching for the sudden epiphany of a well-turned image, settle for rehashing familiar Christian themes. In such poems the imagery, like "sunlight's gossamer," lacks the vitality of the unexpected yet telling phrase.

On the other hand, poems like "Flying High," "Ikon: The Harrowing of Hell," "Midnight Gladness," and "Praise of a Palmtree," all from *A Door in the Hive,* demonstrate that Levertov remains capable of writing in language of rich ambiguity and producing poems in which rhythmic harmony and sensuous imagery generate convincing visions of the spiritual endowment of the world of things. "Midnight Gladness" exemplifies this unity of vision and imagery with its quiet but dramatic enactment of the act of perception:

The pleated lampshade, slightly askew,
dust a silverish muting of the lamp's fake brass.
My sock-monkey on the pillow, tail and limbs
    asprawl,
weary after a day of watching sunlight
                prowl the house like a wolf.
Gleams of water in my bedside glass.
Miraculous water, so peacefully
waiting to be consumed.

Though in the sixth decade of her career she has become a professed Christian, Levertov in her most alert poetic mode fixes her gaze not on the abstract ideal of paradise but on the things of this world and the embodied spirit that moves them—a spirit that like the transcendentalist world-soul is analogous to our own. Her myth-making now assumes distinctly biblical overtones, but the organic sense of the oneness of language and perception still endows her work with a feeling of wholeness and completion. Public and academic regard for her poetry remains high. A steady flow of scholarly articles testifies to a continuing interest in and respect for her work, and through her readings and teaching she still exerts considerable influence on younger poets. In her most recent books her poems remain clear and satisfying, their aesthetic and rhythmic integrity perfectly in tune with her evolving spiritual vision and admirably principled life.

Selected Bibliography

WORKS OF DENISE LEVERTOV

POETRY

The Double Image. London: Cresset, 1946.

Here and Now. San Francisco: City Lights, 1957.

Overland to the Islands. Highlands, North Carolina: Jargon, 1958.

With Eyes at the Back of Our Heads. New York: New Directions, 1960.

The Jacob's Ladder. New York: New Directions, 1961.

O Taste and See. New York: New Directions, 1964.

The Sorrow Dance. New York: New Directions, 1967.

Relearning the Alphabet. New York: New Directions, 1970.

To Stay Alive. New York: New Directions, 1971.

Footprints. New York: New Directions, 1972.

The Freeing of the Dust. New York: New Directions, 1975.

Life in the Forest. New York: New Directions, 1978.

Collected Earlier Poems 1940–1960. New York: New Directions, 1979.

Candles in Babylon. New York: New Directions, 1982.

Poems 1960–1967. New York: New Directions, 1983.

Oblique Prayers. New York: New Directions, 1984.

Poems 1968–1972. New York: New Directions, 1987.

Breathing the Water. New York: New Directions, 1987.

A Door in the Hive. New York: New Directions, 1989.

PROSE

The Poet in the World. New York: New Directions, 1973. Includes her 1965 essay, "Some Notes on Organic Form."

Light Up the Cave. New York: New Directions, 1981.

TRANSLATIONS

In Praise of Krishna: Songs from the Bengali. Translated by Edward C. Dimock, Jr., and Denise Levertov. Garden City, N.Y.: Anchor Books, 1967.

Selected Poems, by Eugene Guillevic. With an introduction by Denise Levertov. New York: New Directions, 1969.

Black Iris, by Jean Joubert. Port Townshend, Wa.: Copper Canyon Press, 1988.

UNCOLLECTED PROSE

Untitled statement. In *The New American Poetry*, edited by Donald M. Allen. New York: Grove Press, 1960. Pp. 411–412.

"Foreword." In *Where Silence Reigns: Selected Prose by Rainer Maria Rilke*, translated by G. Craig Houston. New York: New Directions, 1978. Pp. iv–vi.

"The Ideas in the Things." In *Ezra Pound and William Carlos Williams: The University of Pennsylvania Conference Papers,* edited by Daniel Hoffman. Philadelphia: University of Pennsylvania Press, 1983. Pp. 313–342.

"Remembering Kenneth Rexroth." *American Poetry Review,* 12, no. 1:18–19 (January–February 1983).

"A Poet's View." *Religion and Intellectual Life,* 1:46–53 (Summer 1984).

"On Williams' Triadic Line: or How to Dance on Variable Feet." *Ironwood,* 12:95–102 (Fall 1984).

"Horses with Wings." In *What Is a Poet?*, edited by Hank Lazer. Tuscaloosa: University of Alabama Press, 1987. Pp. 124–134.

INTERVIEWS

Atchity, Kenneth John. "An Interview with Denise Levertov." *San Francisco Review of Books,* March 1979, pp. 5–8.

Estes, Sybill. Interview with Denise Levertov. In *American Poetry Observed: Poets on Their Work,* edited by Joel Bellamy. Urbana: University of Illinois, 1984. Pp. 255–267.

Hallisey, Joan. " 'Invocations of Humanity.' Denise Levertov's Poetry of Emotion and Belief." *Sojourners,* February 1986, pp. 32–36.

Ossman, David, ed. "Denise Levertov." In *The Sullen Art.* New York: Corinth, 1963. Pp. 73–76.

Packard, Vance. "Craft Interview with Denise Levertov." In his *The Craft of Poetry.* New York: Doubleday, 1974. Pp. 79–100.

Reid, Ian. " 'Everyman's Land': Ian Reid Interviews Denise Levertov." *Southern Review* (Australia), 5:231–236 (1972).

Smith, Lorrie. "An Interview with Denise Levertov." *Michigan Quarterly Review,* 24, no. 4:596–604 (1985).

Sutton, Walter. "A Conversation with Denise Levertov." *Minnesota Review,* 5:322–338 (December 1965).

ARCHIVES AND BIBLIOGRAPHIES

Lockwood Memorial Library Poetry Collection, State University of New York at Buffalo, Buffalo, N. Y. Microfilms of Levertov's worksheets.

Sakelliou-Schultz, Liana. *Denise Levertov: An Annotated Primary and Secondary Bibliography.* New York: Garland, 1988.

Wilson, Robert A. *A Bibliography of Denise Levertov.* New York: Phoenix Book Shop, 1972.

Yale University Library, American Literature Collection, New Haven, Conn. Letters from Levertov to William Carlos Williams.

BIOGRAPHICAL AND CRITICAL STUDIES

Altieri, Charles. "Denise Levertov and the Limits of the Aesthetics of Praise." *Enlarging the Temple: New Directions in American Poetry During the 1960s.* Lewisburg, Pa.: Bucknell University Press, 1979. Pp. 225–244.

Borroff, Marie. "New Books in Review." *Yale Review,* 62, no. 1:81–83 (Autumn 1972).

Breslin, James E. B. *From Modern to Contemporary: American Poetry, 1945–1965.* Chicago: University of Chicago Press, 1984.

Carruth, Hayden. "What 'Organic' Means?" *Sagetrieb,* 4, no. 1:145–146 (Spring 1985).

Costello, Bonnie. " 'Flooded with Otherness.' " *Parnassus,* 8, no. 1:198–212 (Fall/Winter 1979).

Dargan, Joan. "Poetic and Political Consciousness in Denise Levertov and Carolyn Forche." *CEA Critic,* 48, no. 3:58–67 (1986).

Earnshaw, Doris. Review of Levertov's *Collected Earlier Poems 1940–1960. World Literature Today,* 55, no. 1:109–110 (Winter 1981).

Elder, John. *Imagining the Earth: Poetry and the Vision of Nature.* Urbana: University of Illinois Press, 1985.

Felstiner, John. "Poetry and Political Experience: Denise Levertov." In *Coming to Light: American Women Poets in the Twentieth Century,* edited by Diane Wood Middlebrook and Marilyn Yalom. Ann Arbor: University of Michigan Press, 1985. Pp. 138–144.

Gilbert, Sandra M. "Revolutionary Love: Denise Levertov and the Poetics of Politics." *Parnassus,* 12–13, nos. 2–1:335–351 (Spring–Winter 1985).

Glitzen, Julian. "From Reverence to Attention: The Poetry of Denise Levertov." *Midwest Quarterly,* 16:325–341 (1975).

Hallisey, Jane. "Denise Levertov's 'Illustrious Ancestors': The Hassidic Influence." *Melus,* 9, no. 4:5–11 (Winter II 1982).

———. ''Denise Levertov '. . . Forever a Stranger and a Pilgrim.' '' *Centennial Review,* 30, no. 2:281–291 (Spring 1986).

Harris, Victoria. ''The Incorporative Consciousness: Levertov's Journey from Discretion to Unity.'' *Exploration,* 4, no. 1:33–48 (December 1976).

Jackson, Richard. ''A Common Time: The Poetry of Denise Levertov.'' *Sagetrieb,* 5, no. 2:5–46 (Fall 1986).

Juhasz, Suzanne. *Naked and Fiery Forms: Modern American Poetry by Women: A New Tradition.* New York: Harper's, 1976.

Lacey, Paul A. ''The Poetry of Political Anguish.'' *Sagetrieb,* 4, no. 1:61–71 (Spring 1985).

Marten, Harry. ''Exploring the Human Community: The Poetry of Denise Levertov and Muriel Rukeyser.'' *Sagetrieb,* 3, no. 3:51–61 (Winter 1984).

———. *Understanding Denise Levertov.* Columbia: University of South Carolina Press, 1988.

Mersmann, James F. ''Denise Levertov: Piercing In.'' *Out of the Vietnam Vortex: A Study of Poets and Poetry Against the War.* Lawrence, Kans.: University Press of Kansas, 1974. Pp. 77–112.

Middleton, Peter. *Revelation and Revolution in the Poetry of Denise Levertov.* London: Binnacle, 1981.

Mills, Ralph J., Jr. *Contemporary American Poetry.* New York: Random House, 1965. Pp. 176–196.

———. *Cry of the Human: Essays on Contemporary American Poetry.* Urbana: University of Illinois Press, 1975.

Ostriker, Alicia Suskin. *Stealing the Language: The Emergence of Women's Poetry in America.* Boston: Beacon Press, 1986.

Perloff, Marjorie. ''Poetry Chronicle: 1970–71.'' *Contemporary Literature,* 14, no. 1:97–131 (Winter 1973).

Pope, Deborah. ''Homespun and Crazy Feathers: The Split-Self in the Poems of Denise Levertov.'' In *A Separate Vision: Isolation in Contemporary Women's Poetry.* Baton Rouge: Louisiana State University Press, 1984. Pp. 84–115.

Rexroth, Kenneth. ''Denise Levertov.'' In *Assays.* New York: New Directions, 1961. Pp. 231–235.

———. ''Poetry in the Sixties.'' In *With Eye and Ear.* New York: Herder & Herder, 1970. Pp. 69–77.

Sisko, Nancy. *''To Stay Alive:* Levertov's Search for a Revolutionary Poetry.'' *Sagetrieb,* 5, no. 2:47–60 (Fall 1986).

Smith, Lorrie. ''Songs of Experience: Denise Levertov's Political Poetry.'' *Contemporary Literature,* 27, no. 2:213–232 (Summer 1986).

Surman, Diana. ''Inside and Outside in the Poetry of Denise Levertov.'' *Critical Quarterly,* 22, no. 1:57–70 (Spring 1980).

Wagner, Linda Welshimer. *Denise Levertov.* New York: Twayne, 1967.

———. ''Levertov and Rich: The Later Poems.'' *South Carolina Review,* 11, no. 2:18–27 (Spring 1979).

———, ed. *Denise Levertov: In Her Own Province.* With an introduction by Wagner. New York: New Directions, 1979.

Wright, James. ''Gravity and Incantation.'' *The Minnesota Review,* 2:424–427 (Spring 1962).

Younkins, Ronald. ''Denise Levertov and the Hasidic Tradition.'' *Descant,* 19, no. 1:40–48 (Fall 1974).

—*WILLIAM DORESKI*

John McPhee

1931–

THE WORLD WE experience through John McPhee's books can seem odd. In a Georgia wilderness we encounter a dragline operator using an enormous piece of equipment with unexpected delicacy while "reaming a river" and killing snakes. We watch as the Alaskan wilderness meets the largest bulldozer made by Caterpillar, operated by two bush pilots who rearrange another stream to benefit their placer mining operation. McPhee maintains an extraordinary control over his narratives, yet he refuses to tell the reader how to think about the people who work on these huge yellow machines. "A well-written editorial is a good thing—but it's not what I'm out to do," McPhee remarked in an interview for *Sierra* magazine. "I don't want to look at a topic from just one perspective."

John McPhee's career demands a statement that could somehow incorporate the subjects of twenty-one books, a distinctive perspective on reporting and literature, and his connections to his subjects. McPhee would want to start with one simple fact: he writes nonfiction about real people in real places. His books reach beyond the traditional boundaries of informational nonfiction. McPhee is counted among the modern masters of literary journalism.

McPhee loves narrative and characterization. Yet his longest work takes on the world's slowest narrative subject, geology, which is full of rocks and descriptions but short on characters. His triumph has been in making all those effects interesting and artistic. Benjamin DeMott commented after McPhee's thirteenth book, "There is not a bad book among them, seldom indeed a laxly composed page. In short, John McPhee . . . has become the name of a standard by which ambitious magazine journalism is now judged." The same could be said after twenty-one books.

McPhee has been a staff writer at *The New Yorker* since 1965. Almost every word in his books was originally published in that magazine. Remarkably, all his books remain in print.

Tight narrative control has shaped McPhee's prose. He uses an elaborate method of organizing his material and structuring his narratives before he starts writing. This method permits him to range over an unprecedented variety of subjects: basketball and tennis, art and airplanes, the New Jersey Pine Barrens and the wilderness of Alaska, atomic energy and birchbark canoes, oranges and farmers, the Swiss Army and the United States Merchant Marine, the control of nature and the scientific revolution in plate tectonics that created modern geology.

"If you make a list of all the work I've ever done," McPhee said during an interview, "and put a little mark beside things that relate to activities and interests I had before I was twenty, you'd have a little mark beside well over 90 percent of the pieces of writing.'' Before the age of twenty, McPhee actively participated in sports, developed a desire to write, went to canoe camp in Vermont, and attended Princeton University. The relationship with Princeton has continued. He teaches there, prefers to write in his office at the university, and sometimes allows the work of other professors to spark a story idea.

John McPhee's father, Harry, a doctor with a specialty in sports medicine, was born in 1895. For twenty years, he served as the United States physician at the Pan-American Games and the winter and summer Olympics. After a stay at Iowa State University, during which McPhee's brother, Roemer, and his sister, Laura Anne, were born, the family moved to Princeton. His father was the physician for the university athletic teams and a member of the faculty. He died in 1984. McPhee's mother, Mary Ziegler, born in 1897, had been a French teacher in Cleveland before the marriage.

''When I was a child,'' McPhee said, ''I was forever mouthing words, saying them just because they sounded good. Even the name of a commercial product, a proper name, if it had some flavor that appealed to me, I'd repeat over and over again, sometimes out loud. My brother and sister would make fun of me for that.'' This verbal strain might be attributed to his mother's side of the family—her father had been the editor of a book-publishing firm in Philadelphia—but McPhee thinks it derived from his father's Scottish heritage. He remembers his father driving every summer to the Keewaydin canoe camp in Vermont and mumbling words just because he liked the sound of them. McPhee's paternal great-grandparents had married in Scotland in 1858 shortly before they immigrated to the coal mining country of Ohio, and although they had signed the marriage registry with an *X*, McPhee said, ''they could certainly talk.'' He believes the family's Celtic verbality came with them from Scotland. ''There's not so much difference between the Scots and the Irish,'' McPhee said, ''except that the Scots are responsible.''

John Angus McPhee was born on March 8, 1931, in Princeton, New Jersey, then a small town of about seven thousand. His parents' house sat on the edge of town with fields and woods beyond it. Today the site is close to the middle of Princeton, grown to thirty thousand with suburbia filling in the open spaces. McPhee spent his childhood biking around campus and attending football and basketball practices with his father. When he was eight and nine years old, he wore a Princeton football shirt and ran around at the games retrieving the ball after extra points and serving as the team mascot. When older, he practiced with the Princeton basketball team. ''I grew up among the various sports,'' McPhee said. ''That's all I cared about until I finished high school.''

His longtime jogging partner William Howarth, a professor of English at Princeton, says that McPhee's relationship to the community and the university is deeply rooted. ''In the fall his whole family would be at the football games. The president of the university probably knew Johnny McPhee by name. It's remarkable to jog along through town and listen to McPhee. Almost every foot awakens a new story about the town.'' The elementary school at 185 Nassau Street, for instance, which he attended through eighth grade, was later purchased by the university and now houses the creative writing program in which McPhee teaches.

World War II arrived when he was ten. There were blackouts, recycling drives, and ration stamps, but McPhee's contribution was as an air spotter. He took his training at the university; the silhouettes of airplanes were flashed on a screen for one second after which he had to write down the name of the plane. He watched the skies from a little hut on high ground and phoned in the sightings to New

York: "I knew every airplane that flew in anybody's sky in the world. It wasn't difficult to know that then. I knew them all. It was like some kids with cars, only with me it was airplanes." McPhee remains characteristically modest. He typically says he flunked kindergarten, where he stayed for two years, rather than mentioning that he skipped a grade in elementary school and graduated from Princeton High School when he was barely seventeen.

His mother complained that McPhee did not work hard enough in high school, and he agrees. Rather than doing homework after dinner, he shot baskets in the backyard "out of the sheer love of it." The homework got done in school, which must have required real speed because his English teacher for three years, Olive McKee, assigned three pieces of writing a week. "I feel a large and considerable debt to her," he said. "Every piece of writing you turned in had to have a piece of paper on top of it showing the structure. In her case it was roman numerals and that kind of thing." As Ferris Professor at Princeton, teaching one writing course a year, he has adopted her techniques. "When I assign structural outlines with my students, it can be a drawing, but they have to show that they have an idea of the internal structure of the piece." Olive McKee frequently had her students read aloud to the class. Today, before McPhee publishes any piece of writing in *The New Yorker,* he reads it aloud to his wife, Yolanda. In an interview with the author he said,

In hearing that come across my tongue, I not only pick up her reaction but I pick up my own reaction. You start listening more. It certainly was true in Olive McKee's class. Some of the things were entertaining, maybe, and you wanted to get up and hear the other kids laugh or jeer or whatever. It was fun.

Of all the possibilities in nonfiction writing—the different subjects, the characters, the artistic opportunities—McPhee has been most drawn to the complexities in a planned structure. He calls it "the single most important thing for me, other than the final writing itself." Each of McPhee's books is held together by an architectonic plan; internally each book has a design that would impress Olive McKee.

McPhee has an athletic build on a five-foot-seven frame. He has silky brown hair, thinning in back, and wears a grizzled, salt-and-pepper beard. Weathered crow's-feet crinkle behind brown-rimmed glasses. Encounters with McPhee tend to be casual, relaxed, friendly, even when he stares through his glasses directly into your eyes. He answers questions in grammatically correct, carefully worded sentences that can intimidate those who are less articulate. He dislikes interviews because his wording cannot be revised and rewritten. Even so, he allowed me two interviews that are the source of most of his comments quoted in this essay.

Sitting one day in his office in the East Pyne Building at Princeton, McPhee explained the progression of his profiles during the early years at *The New Yorker.* The first was "A Sense of Where You Are" (1965), about the Princeton All-American basketball player Bill Bradley, who would later play for the NBA champion New York Knicks and become a United States senator from New Jersey. Then came "The Headmaster" (1966), a profile of Frank L. Boyden, headmaster of Deerfield Academy, followed by "A Roomful of Hovings" (1967), focused on Thomas Hoving, director-elect of the Metropolitan Museum of Art. Along the way, McPhee wrote about other individuals, including Euell Gibbons, an expert on edible wild foods and the author of *Stalking the Wild Asparagus,* and Robert Twynam, who grew the grass on tennis courts at Wimbledon. These profiles had complex inner structures, but they were focused on a single person. The characters took shape on the page from material surrounding them—the overlapping anecdotes told by old schoolteachers, coaches, parents, and archenemies.

"What developed in my mind for a long while was, 'What if you did the same thing with two people?' If you found two people and did all that for each of them, then things would start going back and forth in there." McPhee drew on a blank piece of paper the structural pattern he was thinking about. There were the two individuals, each surrounded by dots representing the satellite figures in their lives. He drew lines rebounding back and forth among the dots.

One plus one just might add up to more than two. I had this in my mind and I wondered just who these people might be. An architect and his client? An actor and a director? A pitcher and a manager? One day I was watching television, and there were Arthur Ashe and Clark Graebner in the semifinals of the first United States Open Tennis Championship at Forest Hills. Each twenty-five years old. Each an American. So they'd have to know each other very well because you could put all the good tennis players in the country in this room.

McPhee sat down with Ashe and Graebner and watched a film of the match over and over as each of them described his thoughts and feelings. The result was *Levels of the Game* (1969), a profile of two men, filled with portraits of their parents and coaches, and multiple viewpoints on their development as players.

"When *Levels of the Game* worked out," McPhee said, "I got ambitious and thought, 'Well, if it works for two, how about more?' " He put a diagram on his wall that looked like this:

$$\frac{\textbf{ABC}}{\textbf{D}}$$

The plan was to let one person, D, relate to the other three. "This is not a promising way to develop a piece of writing," McPhee said. You don't do it backwards. This is an exception. I had no idea what the basic subject would be here, when this was already up on my bulletin board. But I'm interested in outdoor things and the conservation movement was starting up—this was in 1968. I went to Washington for two weeks, and went around talking to people in conservation organizations and to their "natural enemies," as I put it eventually. That's how *Encounters with the Archdruid* [1971] started out.

The central figure in McPhee's structural plan became David Brower, head of a conservation group called Friends of the Earth and former executive director of the Sierra Club. Brower's natural enemies were Charles Park, a geologist and mineral engineer who wanted to open a copper mine in the Glacier Peak Wilderness; Charles Fraser, a land developer with plans for a resort on Cumberland Island, Georgia; and Floyd Dominy, Commissioner of Reclamation, who wanted dams built in the Grand Canyon. McPhee wrote in *Encounters with the Archdruid*:

In the view of conservationists, there is something special about dams, something—as conservation problems go—that is disproportionately and metaphysically sinister. The outermost circle of the Devil's world seems to be a moat filled mainly with DDT. Next to it is a moat of burning gasoline. Within that is a ring of pinheads each covered with a million people—and so on past phalanxed bulldozers and bicuspid chain saws into the absolute epicenter of Hell on earth, where stands a dam.

The tensions between these men were balanced by McPhee's even-tempered, objective portrayal of their opinions. Brower goes hiking with Park. He stays on Fraser's yacht off Cumberland Island and helps him review environmentally sensitive development plans. He rides a raft down the Colorado River in the Grand Canyon with Dominy.

McPhee launched the participants on those encounters so he would have a narrative and something to describe. ''Participation is a way of finding a narrative,'' he said, ''a way to find something more interesting to report than a *Playboy* interview.''

In his narrow office filled with momentos from recent writing projects, McPhee took out another piece of paper with a complex structure that had once been pinned to the cork above his desk. On it was drawn a swirling line, something like a lowercase *e*. This was the internal structure of ''Travels in Georgia'' (collected in *Pieces of the Frame* [1975]). McPhee traveled eleven hundred miles in the company of Carol Ruckdeschel, a field zoologist who worked for the Georgia Natural Areas Council taking inventory of wild places worth preserving in the state. She also collected the pelts of animals for the state university: weasels, rattlesnakes, mountain lions, snapping turtles, whatever she found dead on the road during her travels. Rather than waste the meat, she ate it.

This practice demanded a structural innovation. As with all of McPhee's structural plans, it arose from the material itself. In our first interview he explained:

There's an immediate problem when you begin to consider such material. The editor of *The New Yorker* [then William Shawn] is practically a vegetarian. That served a purpose, pondering what a general reader's reaction would be. When people think of animals killed on the road, there's an immediate putrid whiff that goes by them. The image is pretty automatic—smelly and repulsive. These things we were picking up off the road were not repulsive. They had not been mangled up. They were not bloody. They'd been freshly killed. So I had to get this story off the ground without offending the sensibilities of the reader and the editor.

One of the creatures that was found actually dying on the road was a snapping turtle. We ate the snapping turtle later on. The Campbell Soup Company cans snapping turtles. They make soup out of them. The snapping turtle was a whole lot more acceptable than the weasel, the muskrat, the rattlesnake. Also, it was an amusing and interesting scene: the snapping turtle where she was about to lay her eggs, and a cop whipping out his pistol and trying to shoot the thing at point-blank range, and missing.

McPhee began in medias res at that point.

Next they went to a stream channelization project, where Chap Causey was sitting on his dragline, a natural riverbed stretching out in front of him and a stripped, barren channel behind. Chap liked to kill water moccasins and leave the snakes on the dragline as a warning. He quietly showed off for Carol, who wasn't afraid of snakes at all. McPhee then digresses from that scene. He spins a marvelously long, rambling background sketch about Carol, and eventually ends up back at the riverbank.

One naturally wonders who this person is who's cleaning up this snapping turtle and taking its eggs and talking this way and dealing with the stream channelization man, so it's a time to cut back to Atlanta, where her home is, and tell about what she does, how she got there, what she studied and what her place looks like with all those wounded and battered animals that she's fixing up. After going through all that we *still* haven't had a weasel. Now, we're two-fifths of the way through the piece. If you've read this far, now we can risk some of these animals. After all, this has either proved itself or not by now as a piece of writing. We then go back to the beginning of the journey—the journey that on page one we were in the middle of—and there's a fresh-killed weasel lying in the middle of the road. And the muskrat follows. When we come to the snapping turtle and the stream channelization project, we just jump over them and keep right on going in the form the journey had. The journey itself became the structure, broken up chronologically in this manner.

Structure has been a creative tool in McPhee's hands. While he stops short of the kind of invention that only fiction can support, he believes that narrative, dialogue, character sketching, and metaphor are "absolutely legitimate" tools in nonfiction. His internal structures—the lowercase *e* in "Travels in Georgia," the articulated *Y* of "A Roomful of Hovings," and the other drawings that have been pinned to his bulletin board during composition—permit creative solutions to the erratic twists that any nonfiction-writing project can take. In *Levels of the Game* and *Encounters with the Archdruid* he created the external structures before he reported the real events. He visualized the work, then went out and found Graebner and Ashe, and Brower and his "natural enemies." In the same way a fiction writer can select any setting for a novel, McPhee has freedom of choice. He is writing about real people in real places and is limited by the demands of nonfiction form, but he selects the events and sometimes, as in sending David Brower down the Colorado River with Floyd Dominy, he creates the events as well. The real people are out there, but McPhee must turn nature to literature before we can read about them.

McPhee was accepted by Princeton University—the only place he applied—after high school. Because he was so young and had grown up in the same town, his parents sent him to Deerfield Academy for an additional year of study before he entered college. He met excellent teachers there: Mrs. Helen Boyden in chemistry, Frank Conklin in geology, and Robert McGlynn in English ("He got me excited about reading in a way I'd never been before").

He also discovered Frank Boyden, who would become the subject of *The Headmaster*. The book had a sentimental tone, appropriate for a former Deerfield boy writing about the headmaster at age eighty-six. It was polished but not critical, in part because it lacked a character who would voice any criticisms. In Boyden, McPhee found a person similar to Bill Bradley. Boyden was a strong personality who had a firm, "straight arrow" moral code, was perhaps the best in the country at what he did, and was a local hero who operated on a national level. Boyden left his mark on the boys in the form of ethical standards, not academics. "His first-hand relationship with his boys has always been extraordinary," McPhee wrote, "and Deerfield students for sixty years have been characterized by the high degree of ethical sensitivity that he has been able to awaken in them." Boyden's ethics seem to have stuck to McPhee. He loved his year at Deerfield, played on the basketball, lightweight football, and lacrosse teams, and completed all the academic assignments. Boyden "believed in wearing the boys out," McPhee wrote, which created an invigorating atmosphere for his year there, but McPhee is not sure he could have stood it any longer. For one thing, attendance was checked seventeen times a day.

At Princeton with the class of 1953, McPhee entered the creative writing program headed by Richard Blackmur, a maverick who had dropped out of high school in Boston and attended so many classes at Harvard, without ever enrolling or even applying, that he could have earned several degrees. McPhee spent his sophomore and junior years in the program, studying with Blackmur, Randall Jarrell, and Tom Riggs. He proposed to write a novel for his senior thesis. "I was an English major and they wouldn't hear of it. I argued all over the place and they finally let me do it."

Having decided at an early age to be a writer, and wanting from the age of eighteen to write for *The New Yorker,* McPhee was not completely satisfied with the fiction program.

If you go back into the years when I was writing a novel for a senior thesis, I was also writing factual articles every week. Princeton had a feast of undergraduate publications, and any young writer ought to know that when you're in college you have an unparalleled opportunity to publish things, see yourself in print, see what it's like, grow in it. That's going to stop dead as a doornail the day you graduate.

McPhee worked for the *Nassau Sovereign,* the *Daily Princetonian,* the *Princeton Tiger,* and the *Nassau Literary Magazine*. In his senior year he wrote a one-page essay every week for the *Princeton Alumni Weekly* and was paid for it. He remembers it as "the single best piece of training I had as an undergraduate."

The *Princeton Tiger* was a humor magazine that had previously been edited by Booth Tarkington and F. Scott Fitzgerald. When McPhee became editor, he transformed it into an imitation of *The New Yorker,* complete with a front section called "Spires and Gargoyles" that looked like "Talk of the Town." This change caught the eye of a *New York Times Magazine* editor, who asked McPhee for an article about college humor publications. Thus his first professional piece of writing, full of adolescent barbs at the other humor magazines, ran in *The New York Times Magazine* in 1952 alongside a response by the Yale humor editor.

After graduation, McPhee began a long experimentation with several forms of writing. "Being out of school at last and knowing you never wanted to do anything but be a writer is a perplexing and bewildering time in life," McPhee recalled. "Saying you want to be a writer isn't the same as being in a training program as an investment broker or something tangible. How the hell do you become a writer? What do you do?"

First, he went to Cambridge University for a year of postgraduate study in English, and while there he played basketball and worked as a stringer for *Time* magazine. Returning to New York, he tried free-lancing and wrote short stories. One day he had an opportunity to watch rehearsals for a live television show in a warehouse on the Upper West Side. Without pay, McPhee watched weeks of rehearsals for "Robert Montgomery Presents," read old scripts, and began writing his own one-hour television plays. "Things went pretty well," he said. "I wrote five plays in one year, of which three were bought and two were produced." But he was frustrated watching his compositions evolve away from him as the plays were produced. He wanted to be more in control. For a while he wrote speeches for W. R. Grace & Company, a Wall Street firm, and did articles for the company magazine.

Still dedicated to his dream of becoming a *New Yorker* writer, McPhee steadily submitted articles. All were rejected. He interviewed for a position as a "Talk of the Town" reporter, one of the few salaried jobs for a writer at the magazine. "It was a way to get young writers started," McPhee said. "Not very many. They hired a couple every ten years. They had me write six trial 'Talk' pieces, not for publication. I gave them to them and heard nothing for six months. Nothing at all." In the meantime, he took a job at Time-Life, writing for a mimeographed house organ called *FYI.* This was a trial—get a job at a company magazine within a year or you were gone. He got a four-week trial at *Time,* writing in the "Hemisphere" section about Canada, and was hired at the end of the period.

From 1957 through 1964 McPhee wrote "back of the book" articles for *Time*—articles about people, art, show business, religion, education, books. He wrote nine cover stories, including profiles of Joan Baez, Richard Burton, Jackie Gleason, Jean Kerr, Alan Jay Lerner and Frederick Loewe, Sophia Loren, Mort Sahl, and Barbra Streisand, as well as the cover story on the

1964 New York World's Fair. The "front of the book" was the political and foreign news. "I did not want to work in the front," McPhee said, "and turned down an opportunity when it came to me. I was invited to go into 'National Affairs.' I said I didn't want to do it, which in effect said, 'I don't want to work here indefinitely, or don't want to be an editor here.' Which I didn't."

He wrote short stories that were published in *Playboy, Reporter* magazine, and the *Transatlantic Review*. He wrote articles, poetry, and short stories in his free time. One day he had a cup of hot chocolate with Harold Hayes, editor of *Esquire*. They agreed McPhee would write an article about playing basketball in England during his postgraduate year at Cambridge.

"I wrote the piece and sent it to him. He said he didn't want it. He was sorry but it disappointed him. I thought, 'Hoooo!' " McPhee said, waving his arm in the air as if to banish the memory. "I was so depressed. Then . . . *The New Yorker* bought it"—his first piece in that magazine. "Basketball and Beefeaters" appeared in 1963. "It didn't make any difference," McPhee said. "I went on working at *Time*. It was the Bradley piece that changed my life."

The book on Bill Bradley started one winter day in 1962 when McPhee's father called him in New York. "There's a freshman basketball player down here who is the best basketball player who has ever been near here and may be one of the best ever," Dr. McPhee said. "You ought to come down and see him." This was rare praise from the Princeton team physician. When John McPhee showed up for the freshman game against Pennsylvania the next night, the stands were filled and his father was holding a seat for him. Three years later, "A Sense of Where You Are" appeared in *The New Yorker*. By the end of 1965, Bradley, a six-foot-five player from Crystal City, Missouri, had been named an All-American, had led his Ivy League team into the Final Four of the NCAA (National Collegiate Athletic Association) tournament, had been named most valuable player in the tournament, and had been the number one draft choice of the Knicks, turning down their lucrative offer in favor of a Rhodes Scholarship. He had also, apparently, restored a writer's faith in the game. In the article on Bradley, McPhee wrote:

> My own feeling for basketball had faded almost to nothing over the years because the game seemed to me to have lost its balance, as players became taller and more powerful, and scores increased until it was rare when a professional team hit less than a hundred points, win or lose; it impressed me as a glut of scoring, with few patterns of attack and almost no defense any more.

His devotion to the game, nurtured in high school and Deerfield, by a freshman season at Princeton and another at Cambridge, was rekindled while watching Bradley work out the fundamental possibilities of play.

In his profile, McPhee built the image of a superior basketball player through a series of incidents that demonstrated Bradley's natural abilities, his effort, and the reactions seen in players and fans. Bradley showed McPhee that the seemingly impossible—shooting without looking at the basket—was only a matter of practice, something Bradley had seen Oscar Robertson and Jerry West do many times. Bradley tossed the ball into the basket while looking McPhee in the eye, and then did it again. "The shot has the essential characteristics of a wild accident," McPhee wrote, "which is what many people stubbornly think they have witnessed until they see him do it for the third time in a row." After you've played the game a while, Bradley explained, "You develop a sense of where you are."

McPhee said Bradley's passing ability, not to mention his knack for making baskets while looking away from the hoop, had given him a reputation for seeing out of the back of his head. McPhee asked a Princeton ophthalmologist to measure Bradley's total field of vision. As a boy in Crystal City, Bradley had tried to expand his view, by window-shopping while looking straight down the sidewalk, for example, although the doctor doubted this would have much effect. His peripheral vision, however, measured fifteen degrees wider on the horizontal, five degrees more straight down, and a full twenty-three degrees more looking upward than the medical profession considered perfect. Bradley was a deadly shot. He made three-quarters of his field goals in his last NCAA tournament game and scored fifty-eight points. Once when he was warming up before a tournament game in Philadelphia, his standard pregame set shots, jump shots, whirling reverse moves, and hook shots with either hand so impressed the crowd that they were "applauding like an audience at an opera." This was before the game began, in a neutral stadium. McPhee took a measurement of his own:

Last summer, the floor of the Princeton gym was being resurfaced, so Bradley had to put in several practice sessions at the Lawrenceville School. His first afternoon at Lawrenceville, he began by shooting fourteen-foot jump shots from the right side. He got off to a bad start, and he kept missing them. Six in a row hit the back rim of the basket and bounced out. He stopped, looking discomfited, and seemed to be making an adjustment in his mind. Then he went up for another jump shot from the same spot and hit it cleanly. Four more shots went in without a miss, and then he paused and said, "You want to know something? That basket is about an inch and a half low." Some weeks later, I went back to Lawrenceville with a steel tape, borrowed a stepladder, and measured the height of the basket. It was nine feet ten and seven-eighths inches above the floor, or one and one-eighth inches too low.

Literary critic Kathy Smith has analyzed the devices McPhee used to create a view of Bradley as a superior player. As she noted in "John McPhee Balances the Act," one device was the way McPhee backed up his assessments with facts. First he said Bradley had extraordinary eyesight, then he asked a doctor to measure Bradley's field of vision.

It appears that these astute *observations* have led to the "discovery" of the *new fact* of Bradley's supernormal field of sight, without which the comment that Bradley "can read the defense as if he were reading Braille" would be merely a pretty metaphor. The focus is on verification; only after the trip to the doctor, and only after having all the collected material and notes at his disposal, does McPhee construct this specific image system.

McPhee did the same in the example quoted above concerning the height of the basket at Lawrenceville School. Bradley's "remarkable sixth sense," Smith writes, gives him a degree of infallibility that is verified by McPhee's tape measure.

Neither objective data nor opinion alone suffices to satisfy McPhee's desire for complete coverage of a situation or subject, so he provides both. But by linking point of view so intimately with observed data, and thereby rendering a type of "proof," McPhee avoids inviting the kind of scrutiny that accompanies the literary journalist's writing adventure when point of view and perspective becomes "too" subjective. This strategy works continuously throughout McPhee's piece. It is repeated as a kind of balancing act, an inconspicuous weighing and meting out of perspective and fact so that the thing itself seems to supply narrative structure and value.

Nonfiction has one steady advantage over fiction, according to Smith: "The match between image and representation tends to be regarded as natural and true.'' Readers assume a level of realism, which in turn ''protects authorial license in acts of representation.'' Character does not form naturally on a page. It is selected, organized, created by an author. Backed by the testimony of an eye doctor and a steel tape, McPhee's representations of Bradley's abilities ward off any doubt in the reader's mind.

By 1965 McPhee's writing had achieved the grace and fluidity that he described in Bradley's basketball game. He was knowledgeable and connected, yet as a narrator he remained soft-spoken. Although he preferred to stand in the shadows as a narrator, McPhee still had a distinctive voice and total control over his narrative. These traits may have appealed to William Shawn, editor of *The New Yorker*, because after ''A Sense of Where You Are'' appeared in the magazine, McPhee was named a staff writer. *The New Yorker* gives him the freedom to write about whatever interests him but pays only for what it publishes. At the end of the year, he gets a 1099 tax form, not a W-2 form; this arrangement is like an institutionalized free-lance position. It provides what he calls ''the financial security of a farmer.''

McPhee had achieved his lifetime goal; his apprenticeship was ended. Years later, in his living room in Princeton, McPhee thought back to the rush of energy that followed his arrival at *The New Yorker:* ''The next thing I did was to get up some ideas. I actually started work on three or four things lined up in a row. One was *The Headmaster,* one was *Oranges,* one was *The Pine Barrens.*'' For McPhee, *Oranges* (1967) became a grandfather tree, one of those huge rain forest trees that falls down and becomes a seedbed for generations of new trees. The shoots that grew out of the idea for *Oranges* became *The Pine Barrens* (1968), *Coming into the Country* (1977), and his recent geology books.

In an interview for this essay, McPhee noted that

> *Oranges* was a whim, the result of a machine at Pennsylvania Station in New York where I went every day when I was commuting. I drank this orange juice and I noticed weird things. Fresh orange juice changes color across the winter. I saw an ad in a magazine that showed four or five identical-looking oranges with different names: Parson Brown, Hamlin, Valencia. I thought, ''That's interesting. Maybe it would make a good short piece—go down there for four or five days, talk to growers and nurserymen and go home. Write a little piece.'' What made *Oranges* longer was when I stumbled into the Citrus Experiment Station at Lake Alfred, where they had forty-four thousand items in their library—books and papers about oranges—and they had men and women in white coats walking around who had Ph.D.'s in oranges. One had a heart-lung machine with oranges breathing in and out of it. I discovered the history of citrus, migrating westward along with the migrations of humankind itself. I scarcely suspected I would learn anything like that. But when I did, it was interesting and I went into it, so it was a longish article.

The research he did at the experiment station resulted in a short book loaded with information, a classic McPhee work. If journalism is in one sense an informational form and in another sense a literary form, *Oranges* combines both. Some writers avoid topics burdened with information, preferring instead a powerful story line drawn from a murder or a historic event. McPhee can structure an interesting narrative about something as commonplace as oranges. His opening in *Oranges* makes information fun. We learn how street vendors in Trinidad and Tobago slice oranges and sprinkle salt on them, that Spain exports more oranges—including blood oranges—than the United States, that Irish kids eat them at the movies, and that orange trees bear fruit in Icelandic greenhouses and in the Bronx soil of the New York Botanical Garden.

One device that carries information in a narrative McPhee calls a set piece. In *Oranges,* for example, McPhee rides into a grove on the back of a tractor, and two pages later the reader is off on a set piece about the history of oranges, starting with the evolution of citrus in the Malay Archipelago about twenty million years ago. It is a stylish prose trip, there on the back of the tractor, but it is set apart as a digression from the narrative. We learn about the name "orange," evolving from Sanskrit into French and eventually into Orange, New Jersey, an unlikely place for oranges. They have a history as a medical product, a food, and an additive to alcoholic beverages. Mistaken assumptions about the history of oranges led the master painters of the Italian Renaissance to portray oranges on the tables at the Last Supper, although, McPhee wrote, "in the time of Christ there were no orange trees in or near the Holy Land." Eventually, each set piece in the book returns to the original narrative, but along the way we learn about the history of oranges in Florida, the great frosts that wipe out the trees every so often, the grafting of certain species like Parson Brown and Valencia onto Rough Lemon or Sour Orange rootstock, and the regional culture that has grown up in the orange-growing districts of Florida.

The central narrative itself revolves around a search. McPhee drives into the state hoping to find a delicious glass of fresh-squeezed juice. Instead, he discovers an industry in love with concentrate. The science of orange juice concentrate leads him to the experiment station and its library. He goes to a plant where fresh juice is reduced to concentrate. "When the evaporators are finished with the juice, it has a nice orange color and seems promising, but if it is reconstituted into 'orange juice' it tastes like a glass of water with two teaspoons of sugar and one aspirin dissolved in it." McPhee finally gets his glass of fresh orange juice from a conveyor belt moments before high-season Valencia juice enters an evaporator.

His plan to spend four or five days in Florida turned into four weeks. He returned to Princeton with boxes of photocopied information and books from the University of Florida in Gainesville. His miniature portrait grew into a "broad canvas" containing a wealth of scientific research, historical sweep, character studies, and personal narrative. A reviewer in *Harper's* (March 1967) wrote:

> You may come to the end of it and say to yourself, "But I *can't* have read a whole book about *oranges*!" But the chances are you will have done so, for Mr. McPhee takes this one simple fruit and makes a compote out of it. He writes like a charm, and without being cute, gimmicky, or in any way dull, he just tells you a lot about oranges.

The idea of a broader canvas grew to regional proportions when McPhee turned to the Pine Barrens, a wild, sandy area encompassing hundreds of square miles of New Jersey that is famous for its abundant water supply and fabled residents. The Pineys were once considered mental defectives, a slanderous label assigned when the psychological sciences were themselves a bit defective. McPhee had grown up in New Jersey and heard the stories. He wanted to investigate, but he had never taken on a region as his subject matter.

In an interview he told me, "I wandered around talking to all kinds of people and I had no idea what to make of it. I hadn't done it before." Pointing to the yard outside his living room windows, McPhee said

> I spent two weeks on a picnic table right outside the window here lying on my back in agony and despair, staring up into the trees. I had no idea how I was going to tell the story of the Pine

Barrens. I had miscellaneous stuff, sketches of people. Nowadays I would have an idea what to do with it.

He opened *The Pine Barrens* with his first visit to Fred Brown, resident of Hog Wallow. Fred Brown had no phone, no electricity. His yard was littered with eight cars, old vacuum cleaners, radios, cranberry boxes, "and maybe a thousand other things." He cooked McPhee a pork chop on a gas stove.

He asked where I was going, and I said that I had no particular destination, explaining that I was in the pines because I found it hard to believe that so much unbroken forest could still exist so near the big Eastern cities, and I wanted to see it while it was still there. "Is that so?" he said, three times. Like many people in the pines, he often says things three times. "Is that so? Is *that* so?"

McPhee asked Fred Brown's permission to fill his jerry can at the pump in the front yard. " 'Hell, yes,' he said. 'That isn't my water. That's God's water. That's God's water. That right, Bill?' " Bill Wasovwich, Brown's friend and neighbor, was also sitting in the kitchen at the time, although he was such a shy person you might not notice him.

"I *guess* so," Bill said, without looking up. "It's good water, I can tell you that."

"That's God's water," Fred said again. "Take all you want."

Fred and Bill became McPhee's guides and informants as to the history and geography of the Pine Barrens. He drove the region with them, crisscrossing the sandy terrain on unpaved, unmarked roads past the former towns that had dotted the Pine Barrens and had now receded into nature. McPhee constantly scribbled in his notebook, recording everything but not sure where it would all lead. One time McPhee was driving and Fred Brown said something interesting. McPhee slammed on the brakes and started writing in his notebook. "Fred," McPhee asked, "do you know what I'm doing?"

"No," Fred said, "and I don't think you do either."

McPhee's hosts came to symbolize the native Pineys, a shy, self-sufficient, and maligned people. Never one to editorialize, McPhee nevertheless left his position clear in *The Pine Barrens.*

They are apparently a tolerant people, with an attractive spirit of live and let live. They seem to like hard work, if not steady work, and they like to brag about working hard. When they say they will do something, they do it. They seem shy, like the people who went before them, but when they get to know an outsider they are not shy and will generously share their tables, which often include new-potato stews and cranberry potpies.

There was much more to the Pine Barrens than its people. McPhee presented set pieces on the vernacular of the region, its folktales, how foxhounds are used in a hunt, the history of the region, and some of the mysteries of the dwarf pines, cranberries, and blueberries that grow there. He explained the fires that continually sweep the Pines, using dramatic and informative language that prefigured descriptions of the great Yellowstone National Park fire of 1988.

Toward the end of the book, McPhee wandered into politics, an unusual topic for him. A proposal was afoot to build a supersonic jetport in the Pines, complete with a city in the wilderness. McPhee traveled through the woods with a planner, Herbert Smith, who could visualize this development laid out in imaginary streets and runways on the sand. McPhee allowed Smith to make his best case; he is treated fairly, objectively, but he doesn't have a chance. Before we get to Smith, we have learned the history of the Pine Barrens, met some natives, learned about its natural wonders, and we love it as it stands.

Smith's jetport seems outrageous. Later research would convince Americans that the supersonic jet itself was a hazard to the ozone layer, and it would be abandoned along with the jetport plans for the Pines. But McPhee ends with the opinion that the Pine Barrens "seem to be headed slowly toward extinction." The region was not threatened by a jetport so much as by a lack of legislation to preserve it. "At the rate of a few hundred yards or even a mile or so each year, the perimeter of the pines contracts."

By 1974, at least three patterns had taken shape in McPhee's writing career. First, he played out a string of profiles that included Bill Bradley and Thomas Hoving, and then took a wild structural leap forward. *Levels of the Game* presented two persons with their satellite characters, and *Encounters with the Archdruid* associated one controversial character with three of his natural enemies. After that, McPhee rarely focused on a single character. One exception was *The Curve of Binding Energy* (1974), which was about physicist Theodore Taylor, a former atomic bomb designer who feared that terrorists could steal weapons-grade nuclear material from private industry and build a bomb in their basement. McPhee used Taylor as a vehicle to explore a complex scientific subject, and he does not consider the book a profile. Another exception was *The Survival of the Bark Canoe* (1975), featuring Henri Vaillancourt, an artist and craftsman who builds authentic birchbark canoes.

Oranges opened two other patterns. At one level, McPhee created a portrait of the orange-growing regions of Florida, as he would do later in *The Pine Barrens*. "Each a broad canvas, lots of people, lots of history and science," he said, describing the two books. *The Pine Barrens,* with its regional focus, became the progenitor of his best-selling book about Alaska, *Coming into the Country*. At another level, *Oranges* began a series of books dominated by scientific concerns, including his geology books. There was considerable overlap between the categories, of course.

Nothing illustrates the trend toward regional portraits better than *The Crofter and the Laird* (1970), which is among McPhee's finest and least-known works. He reports on the culture, history, and mythology of the residents of Colonsay, one of the Hebrides islands off Scotland and home to McPhee's ancestors. Unromantically, he shows the conditions of life among the crofters, or small farmers. The laird is the Baron Strathcona, who owns the whole island and its houses, all of which he rents out in a nearly feudal arrangement with the crofters. The laird plays only a small role in the book. He is royalty, an "incomer" in the vernacular of the place. McPhee is more interested in the commoners. Colonsay was like the village of Wiltshire that W. H. Hudson described from an earlier era, where a resident at one end of town might cut his foot with an axe and the tidings of the accident would fly from mouth to mouth to every other resident almost instantly. The islanders were connected to generation upon generation and had lived on the same rock since the clans began in the eleventh century. McPhee said Colonsay was "less like a small town than like a large lifeboat."

As he does in *The Pine Barrens,* McPhee first draws readers into an unknown world and then forcefully expands their knowledge of it until they leave with a deep appreciation. Novelists do the same with their imaginary worlds. That Colonsay actually exists only complicates the problem of bringing its residents and history to life on paper.

Describing the islanders who play the bagpipes, McPhee wrote in *The Crofter and the Laird:*

Pipers have genealogies, lines of pedagogical ancestry, that are as important to them as bloodlines may be to others. A piper schooled in classical *piobaireachd*—or *ceol mor,* the purest expression of Highland bagpipe music—can listen to another piper and say accurately who his teachers were and who, in turn, taught the teachers.

Much the same is true of literary journalists, although the signatures of the teachers are more disguised. Two schools among literary journalists have been described by literary critic David Eason. In "The New Journalism and the Image-World," he labels them "realist" and "modernist." In nonfiction, the realist group includes John McPhee, Tom Wolfe, Tracy Kidder, and other writers who attempt to represent a real world for the reader.

Realist reports reflect faith in the capability of traditional models of interpretation and expression, particularly the story form, to reveal the real. Although the reports acknowledge cultural relativism in their attention to the various symbolic worlds of their subjects, this awareness is not extended to the process of reporting, which is treated as a natural process.

Referring to the other group of writers including Norman Mailer and Joan Didion, Eason continues, "Modernist reports call attention to reporting as a way of joining together writer and reader in the creation of reality. Narrative techniques call attention to storytelling as a cultural practice for making a common world."

These two schools reach as far back as Daniel Defoe, whose realist accounts of the plague in London may have been the first literary journalism in the English language. Like the music of the pipers on Colonsay, McPhee's reporting has a genealogy that includes Defoe, Joseph Addison and Richard Steele, and in this century such writers as Hemingway, George Orwell, A. J. Liebling, John Hersey, and Lillian Ross. Henry David Thoreau belongs on that list, as McPhee recognized in *Survival of the Bark Canoe.* Thoreau took notes on scratch paper when he was in the Maine woods.

Weeks later, when he returned home to Concord, he composed his journal of the trip, slyly using the diary form, and writing at times in the present tense, to gain immediacy, to create the illusion of paragraphs written—as it is generally supposed they were written—virtually in the moments described. With the advantage of retrospect, he reconstructed the story to reveal a kind of significance that the notes do not reveal. Something new in journalism.

McPhee has used increasingly complicated structures in his work while retaining a strict regard for realist assumptions about journalism. Ronald Weber, whose scholarly work has examined literary journalism from Hemingway to the New Journalists of the 1960's, writes of McPhee's *Coming into the Country,* "The book's roots lie not so much in the effort to emulate the novel as in the attempt to extend the range of journalism while remaining within journalistic forms."

Indeed, McPhee was convinced to pursue nonfiction, as opposed to fiction or playwriting, because it has so many interesting literary possibilities. In one interview for this essay he explained:

Remember the possibilities in nonfiction writing, the character sketching that stops well short of illegitimate invention. There's plenty of room for invention, for "creativity," stopping well short of invading a number of things that only fiction can do. You can use fictional techniques: narrative, dialogue, character sketching, description, metaphor. Above all metaphor.

Things that are cheap and tawdry in fiction work beautifully in nonfiction because they are *true.* That's why you should be careful not to abridge it, because it's the fundamental power you're dealing with. You arrange it and present it. There's lots of artistry. But you don't make it up.

Nobody's making rules that cover everybody. The nonfiction writer is communicating with the reader about real people in real places. So if those people talk, you say what those people said. You don't say what the writer decides they said. I get prickly if someone suggests there's dialogue in my pieces that I didn't get from the source. You don't make up dialogue. You don't make a composite character. Where I came from, a composite character was fiction. So when somebody makes a nonfiction character out of three people who are real, that is a fictional character in my opinion. And you don't get inside their heads and think for them. You can't interview the dead. You could make a list of the things you don't do. Where writers abridge that, they hitchhike on the credibility of writers who don't.

In the mid 1970's, when McPhee began making extended visits to Alaska, he was preparing for a regional portrait of epic proportions. *Coming into the Country*, which actually told three separate stories, was published in *The New Yorker* in eight parts and became his most financially successful work.

The first story told of a canoe and kayak trip in arctic Alaska on the Salmon and Kobuk rivers. In the second story, McPhee accompanied a commission looking for a site for a new Alaskan capital. He went to Alaska for the first time in the summer and early fall of 1975, during which time he conducted the research for the first two stories. The third took longer. He went back to Alaska in the spring of 1976 at breakup time and stayed into the summer in the towns of Eagle, Circle, and Central, Alaska, in the Upper Yukon country northeast of Fairbanks. He returned during the winter of 1977. That portion of the book, itself titled "Coming into the Country," became the longest single piece of writing that McPhee has published.

Coming into the Country sealed McPhee's reputation as one of the premier nature and cultural writers in America. That's fast company, even if limited to *living* writers. Writing in *The New York Times,* John Leonard said the book left him enchanted, dreaming of seal oil, caribou, the Yukon River, and grizzly bears:

The time may come when nobody goes outside, when every American stays home in his "living center," his computerized cocoon, a bionic junkie with programmed dreams. And if it ever occurs to this sloth to wonder about the outside, about what the outside was like when there was an outside, why, all he will have to do is plug a cartridge into his communications console and read, if he can read, a book on his wraparound television screen. The book could be by John McPhee, or Edward Hoagland, or Edward Abbey, or Josephine Johnson—one of the people, anyway, who do our living for us. Remember, the book will say, when there were seasons?

Edward Hoagland called *Coming into the Country* a "masterpiece." He said McPhee must have been looking for a "big, long, permanent book, written while he was still in the midst of life and could go after it, because in peripatetic journalism such as McPhee's there is an adventurous, fortuitous element: where the writer *gets himself* and what he *stumbles on.*" It began with months of research in the country itself, followed by an enormous amount of time spent discovering the history of the state, its natives, the settlement by whites, the gold discoveries, and the oil boom.

Then came the task of structuring all that material into three separate narratives. A reviewer in *Time* said, "Rather than stepping smartly from *A* to *Z*, his plots tend to pick up casually with *N* and then meander back around to *M*. The apparent informality is a ruse.'' Far from informal, the plan to circle from *N* back to *M* had been on McPhee's mind throughout the writing of the first section of the book. Called ''The Encircled River,'' the narrative follows McPhee and four companions from a governmental study team as they travel by canoe and kayak. The story opens on the Salmon River of the Brooks Range above the Arctic Circle. McPhee dips his bandanna into the forty-six-degree water and ties it around his head to fight the blazing sun. It was *N*. They follow the Salmon and Kobuk rivers as McPhee describes his companions and delivers information about the enormous state of Alaska. At the end of Book I, the narrative circles back around to *M*, and McPhee removes the bandanna from his head and trails it in the river.

Ronald Weber felt *Coming into the Country* was ''a distinguished work of literary nonfiction,'' a book that endowed ''the particular with resonant meanings.'' The structure, as Weber explained in *The Literature of Fact,* was in part responsible for the effects in Book I:

> The return to the opening image echoes the circuitous direction of the river journey. A helicopter had taken McPhee and his companions from the village of Kiana a hundred water miles to the upper Salmon River, from where they had drifted to the juncture of the Kobuk River, and then down to Kiana—''closing a circuit,'' McPhee notes—from where they will be flown out by plane. The return to Kiana takes place less than midway through the ninety-page section, and from the return McPhee smoothly shifts the account back in time to describe the helicopter journey and the arrival on the headwaters of the Salmon in ''the most isolated wilderness I would ever see.'' From this point the river journey is again recounted until the reader is brought back nearly to where he began, the bandanna being cooled again in the water.

Back in his office at Princeton University several years later, McPhee drew a circle on a piece of notepaper representing the structure of ''The Encircled River.'' At the point where the narrative begins and ends, where he dips his bandanna in the water, McPhee bisected the circle with a line. The top half of the circle represented the last part of the actual trip. That portion of the text was written in the present tense. A little over halfway around the diagram, he placed another mark. This was near the start of the actual journey but over halfway through the piece of writing. The mark represented an encounter with a bear eating blueberries. The narrative continued, in past tense, toward its starting point. Just before the circle rejoined itself, he encountered another grizzly, four hundred pounds of bear fishing in the river out of sight, sound, and smell of the travelers: ''He picked up a salmon, roughly ten pounds of fish, and, holding it with one paw, he began to whirl it around his head. Apparently, he was not hungry, and this was a form of play. He played sling-the-salmon.'' The bear ambled toward the flotilla of boats. One of them struck a small snag in the river and snapped a stick. The bear froze. He could smell nothing. At first his nearsighted vision failed to reveal the boats on the river. McPhee has a deep-seated fear of grizzly bears. Grizzlies are massive, legendary for their unpredictability, one of the wildest creatures on earth. They are rarely seen, as dramatic as they are dangerous. ''At last, we arrived in his focus. If we were looking at something we had rarely seen before, God help him so was he.'' The bear changed course into a copse of willow. In the next paragraph the boaters entered a flat section of river and McPhee trailed his bandanna in the water.

McPhee had started the narrative moments after this event and circled back around to the same place in order to locate the nearsighted grizzly bear at the end of the story, where his dignity, playfulness, and awesome size could symbolize the wilderness through which they were traveling. He also structured a change of tense into the story, moving from present to past in cyclical form. "When you circle back, you go into the past tense and you stay there," he said.

In the third section of the book, "Coming into the Country," McPhee lived among the residents of the Upper Yukon country. Individualists who find civilization too constricting still migrate to Alaska, looking for land to homestead, a place to build a cabin, gold in the creeks, and the challenge of survival in a cold, hard land.

In most cases, the conditions and the weather drive them away. Ed and Ginny Gelvin, who raised four children in the country near Central, Alaska, population twenty, are the kind of enterprising people who have taken their existence from Alaska in the modern age. Flying above the wilderness in their bush planes and studying old mining records, Ed and his son Stanley located a stream that might contain a placer deposit of gold. Gold erodes out of the mountains and washes down the streams until it collects in alluvial or glacial deposits. Run that gravel through your own sluicebox and you can extract the flakes of gold. The Gelvins wanted to move thousands of tons of gravel, so they drove the largest bulldozer Caterpillar makes, the turbocharged D9, into the wilderness. They choked the stream and created a reservoir, which in turn produced a pressurized stream of water. They bulldozed forty thousand cubic yards of gold-bearing gravels into a metal sluicebox and washed it through using the plume of water. This ecological disturbance was witnessed by McPhee the conservationist:

Am I disgusted? Manifestly not. Not from here, from now, from this perspective. I am too warmly, too subjectively caught up in what the Gelvins are doing. In the ecomilitia, bust me to private. This mine is a cork on the sea. Meanwhile (and, possibly, more seriously), the relationship between this father and son is as attractive as anything I have seen in Alaska—both of them self-reliant beyond the usual reach of the term, the characteristic formed by this country. Whatever they are doing, whether it is mining or something else, they do for themselves what no one else is here to do for them. Their kind is more endangered every year. Balance that against the nick they are making in this land. Only an easygoing extremist would preserve every bit of the country. And extremists alone would exploit it all. Everyone else has to think the matter through—choose a point of tolerance, however much the point might tend to one side. For myself, I am closer to the preserving side—that is, the side that would preserve the Gelvins. To be sure, I would preserve plenty of land as well. My own margin of tolerance would not include some faceless corporation "responsible" to a hundred thousand stockholders, making a crater you could see from the moon.

McPhee located modern-day miners and trappers who inhabit the wilderness, living in the country, ten miles up this or that stream, on a subsistence diet of homegrown vegetables, moose, and fish. Their lives challenged some of McPhee's personal values and his ideals about wilderness.

Dick Cook and Donna Kneeland were living in one such cabin. Dick was an expert in the survival skills needed for backwoods life. He and Donna had divided up their responsibilities in a manner that pioneer families would recognize, but modern women would abhor. McPhee, father of four daughters from his first marriage, heard Donna say, "I'm helping Dick, not doing these things for the sake of being like a man. I can't be like a man. I couldn't haul a soaked moosehide out of the river. It's too heavy. But I haul fish. I cut and sew caribou socks. I train the puppies to pull a sled. Are we going to start planting the garden today?"

''I'll decide that this afternoon,'' Dick replied.

Dick and Donna took McPhee to their cabin. They left the door open when they were gone so grizzlies would make less of a mess getting into the place. ''Bears are on my mind today,'' McPhee wrote, because the next day he had to hike out alone to the Yukon River, where he would be picked up by a boat. He had been ''strongly counselled'' not to go into the woods without a gun. ''Having never hunted, I have almost no knowledge of guns,'' he wrote, and turned down the offer of a gun. On the hike into the cabin, the group passed bear scat. ''Maybe we'll get a bear!'' Donna exclaimed. ''It can happen anytime.'' Dick Cook checked his rifle. Every bear story McPhee had ever heard rushed through his mind.

Here I am about to walk through the woods the distance merely from Times Square to LaGuardia Airport and I am ionized with anticipation—catastrophic anticipation. I may never resolve my question of bears—the extent to which I exaggerate the danger, the extent of the foolishness of those who go unarmed. The effect of it all, for the moment, is a slight but detectable migration of my internal affections from the sneaker toward the bazooka, from the National Wildlife Federation toward the National Rifle Association—an annoying touch of panic in a bright and blazing day.

Dick Cook does not help McPhee's confidence when he tells him to remember that ''the woods are composed of who's killing whom. Life is forever building from death. Life and death are not a duality.'' McPhee begins his two-hour hike to the Yukon River through closed-in willow thickets and soft muskeg.

He thinks as he reaches the river safely,

I can't accept anymore the rationale of the few who go unarmed, yet I am equally loath to use guns. If bears were no longer in the country, I would not have come. I am here, in a sense, because they survive. So I am sorry—truly rueful and perplexed—that without a means of killing them I cannot feel at ease.

Grizzly bears fishing in distant streams, placer mines gouged in the wilderness, gardens planted with ''grass'' and rhubarb, a dogsled sounding over dry snow like ''the rumbling cars of a long freight,'' the sun shining at 11:00 P.M., these things are the real Alaska and emblematic at the same time. They are the things McPhee chose to represent the reality he experienced and the symbols that created Alaska for his readers. Donald Hall, writing in *National Review* (March 31, 1978), said,

It makes no difference what McPhee writes about; his subjects are irrelevant; we love him for his *form*. Oh, how he can shift his feet! Transitions are the *niftiest* things he does, moving from past into present, from present into past, shifting abruptly from one scene or set of characters to another.

McPhee says he spends a lot of time *not* writing those graceful transitions; instead he allows his structures to juxtapose elements that need no bridges to link them together. ''Two parts of a piece of writing, merely by lying side-by-side, can comment on each other without a word spoken.''

McPhee became friends with several of his subjects in Alaska. In standard reporting, a friendship with a subject can be as troubling as a bribe in a police department. City hall reporters are frequently transferred to other assignments so they will not become too familiar with the politicians whose lives and professional conduct they must examine. McPhee's journalism differs. He cannot spend months living in Eagle, Alaska, without admiring some residents and becoming friends with many. Had he avoided such attachments, his writing would be shallow and devoid of feeling.

McPhee has written about only three people whom he knew before they became subjects for his journalism. They were Tom Hoving, director of the Metropolitan Museum of Art; Alan Lieb, a chef; and Frank Boyden, headmaster of Deerfield Academy. "With few exceptions, I meet people for the first time when I seek them out to write about them," McPhee said. "Then, some have become good friends—15 percent or something." He listed Ted Taylor, the bomb designer; Bill Bradley, who asked McPhee to be the godfather of his daughter; Sam Candler in Georgia; and several people in Alaska. He told me in an interview:

> The relationship doesn't begin as someone casually met. It's a relationship with someone with an open notebook. The people know in a general way what I'm going to do. I tell them. You don't get into a "friendship" situation and then run into the bathroom to make notes. If you're there a number of months, yes, friendships do form. But they're forming in a context.

People can never read a text with a single interpretation. Some of the people McPhee wrote about in Scotland thought he "abused their friendship" in *The Crofter and the Laird.* "Maybe I did," he said to me.

> But one thing is for sure. They knew what I was doing and when they spoke to me I had an open notebook in front of them. They knew where the notes were going. Somebody I lionized decided the thing was bad. Somebody I satirized thought it was good. There's no way to predict the reactions. Knowing that, you don't worry about it. If you can't predict the outcome, you're not going to try to shape it.

The article that generated the most controversy in the press was about Alan Lieb, a chef who owned a small restaurant in Pennsylvania. McPhee said the chef had prepared the best meals he had ever eaten. Since he knew him beforehand, and because Lieb did not want to be swamped by crowds from New York City, McPhee promised to keep his name and the restaurant's location a secret. Lieb became "Otto" in the article, "Brigade de Cuisine." Otto proved as admirable in the kitchen as Bradley was on the basketball court. The tantalizing mystery—how could a world-class chef be working within a hundred miles of New York City and remain unknown to the restaurant reviewers?—provoked a manhunt. There was another provocative aspect to the article. McPhee and Otto had dined at Lutèce, a fine restaurant in New York. Otto said he guessed the turbot he ate there had been frozen. Owner André Soltner said that was a fact error—he never served frozen fish—and demanded an apology from *The New Yorker.*

New York Times food critic Mimi Sheraton and wine critic Frank J. Prial tracked Otto down in Shohola, Pennsylvania, and ate at his restaurant. Sheraton called the main course disappointing and the appetizers so-so; Prial thought the wine list "somewhat amateurish." That was it. Behind the minor furor that flashed in the columns of *The New York Times, Time, Newsweek,* and *The Nation* was the suggestion that McPhee had failed to get his facts right. William Shawn, editor of *The New Yorker,* permitted McPhee to keep Otto's identity secret. Shawn said it was the first piece in the magazine's history that was not verified in detail by fact checkers. Actually, the fact checkers restricted their inquiries to matters outside Pennsylvania, leaving McPhee to verify facts with the chef. McPhee quoted Lieb as saying he guessed the turbot was frozen. When McPhee reprinted the article in *Giving Good Weight* (1979), after Otto's remark about the turbot he put a footnote that said: "Otto guessed wrong." It was an accurate quote, but a false accusation. The most obvious fact error in the whole affair was made by Prial and Sheraton in their article for the *Times:* they misspelled Alan Lieb's name.

Henri Vaillancourt, the central figure in *The Survival of the Bark Canoe,* felt McPhee misrepresented his character in the book. Vaillancourt builds canoes using only a few tools and the methods the Indians discovered. McPhee and Vaillancourt took two of the canoes and three friends on a ten-day trip on the West Branch of the Penobscot River in northern Maine, passing through Chesuncook Lake, Umbazooksus Lake, windswept Chamberlain Lake, Churchill Lake, Allagash Stream and Allagash Lake, and ending at the spot in Caucomgomoc Lake where the Keewaydin canoe camp began its life.

Before the trip started, Vaillancourt insisted on discarding much of the gear his companions had brought along, including the maps. Out on the water, trouble started. "A canoe trip is a society so small and isolated that its factions—and everything else about it—can magnify to stunning size. When trouble comes on a canoe trip, it comes from the inside, from fast-growing hatreds among the friends who started," McPhee wrote. Vaillancourt, who McPhee lauded as the best birchbark canoe builder in the country, seemed less of an expert in the woods. The paddlers encountered strong winds that whipped the lakes into heavy chop. The boats took on water. Little headway could be made against the weather. "A suspicion that has been growing comes out in the wind," McPhee wrote. "Henri's expertise stops in 'the yard'; out here he is as green as his jerky." It is one of the few negative character portrayals found in McPhee's work.

"I could see his character did not mesh very well with mine," Vaillancourt said of McPhee. "I was anxious for the trip to end." Afterward, Vaillancourt became uncooperative and discouraged further interviews. Today, he feels McPhee took ethical liberties in quoting his comments about other birchbark canoe builders—of the ones he had seen, his were the best—remarks which he feels made him seem immodest, and which he said were "off the record."

"With McPhee the story is the thing," Vaillancourt said in an interview for this essay.

I had the feeling from his line of questioning that he came with a preconceived idea of how he would develop me as a character, and how the story would go. He wanted to develop the eccentric artist-craftsman. I don't think it reflects what I'm about. I'm eccentric in my own way, but I'm not as obsessed as he portrayed me. When you're writing about real people, you have an obligation to represent them as they are, rather than to portray them as you would like them to be.

"Henri is now a different person than the one I went with," McPhee responded. "I did have a preconception of Henri before I met him: as a man about seventy-five years old. He was twenty-three then. I was surprised. That's the one and only preconception I had. The term 'off the record' never came up between us. I don't think he even knew the term then."

For a writer who came to national prominence in the New Journalism era of the 1960's, McPhee has been extraordinarily shy. He has never relished a public literary controversy. His immersion reporting should have made him a charter member of the New Journalism group. But he could not step in front of the cameras to promote his books—literally. His photograph has never appeared on a dust jacket. So he is rarely mentioned in the context of the New Journalism. The controversies of his career involve frozen turbot and the portrayal of a birchbark canoe builder, all of which McPhee takes very seriously. But these episodes pale in comparison to those involving the New Journalists, who were sometimes accused of making things up and who certainly rode controversy for all it was worth. McPhee gets the facts right, an enormous task in itself.

The longest-running project in McPhee's career has been his four books on the geology of North America. The books grew naturally from his earliest interests, including the geomorphology—the study of the surface features of the earth—he learned from Frank Conklin at Deerfield Academy, and from *Oranges, The Pine Barrens,* and *Coming into the Country.* In an interview with me he said,

I was writing about the gold fields of Alaska up there near the Klondike strike. It suddenly occurred to me: I had no idea how the gold got there. I well understood why it was in the streams. The mountains break apart and there's the gold. Geomorphology, right? But how did the gold get into the mountains in the first place?

McPhee called a Princeton geologist, Ken Deffeyes, who explained thermal hot springs and mineral deposits, and a few lines on the subject appeared in *Coming into the Country.* As McPhee told me, another short phone call to Deffeyes later resulted in a whole series of books on geology.

I called him up and asked if he'd like to find a road cut outside New York City and describe what the world looked like when that rock formed. I meant to do a "Talk of the Town" piece. We could look at the blast-exposed face of the rock, read its history, and tell it in the first-person plural. We planned that, and then I asked, "What if we went north, from road cut to road cut, up the Northway through the Adirondacks?" He said, "Not on this continent. If you want to do that sort of thing on this continent, go west—go across the structure." Then I got this weird idea of going all the way across the continent, all growing out of that "Talk" piece, which was never written. All this happened in three or four days, and the next thing I know I'm in a pickup with Deffeyes in Nevada.

The project deals with one of the most fascinating scientific revolutions of the twentieth century, the theory of plate tectonics and continental drift. Between 1959 and 1967, geologists pieced together the theory of rigid plates moving across the earth, riding over or diving under each other, and in certain places spreading apart. "It was a huge scientific revolution, a first-order scientific revolution, and is, in fact, why I got into the whole thing," McPhee said. "Ten years after plate tectonics came along, it was still very much controversial. I wanted to see how this science had settled down with its new theory."

After his talk with Deffeyes, McPhee envisioned a book about the geology of North America, using road cuts of Interstate 80 as windows into the rock. After a year of research, he had organized the narrative, which jumps around. "It starts in New Jersey and leaps to Nevada because the tectonics in New Jersey two hundred million years ago were much the same as the tectonics in Nevada today." After a year, he realized the project was going to take ten or fifteen years to complete. Instead of one book, it would be four.

The first geology book, *Basin and Range* (1981), presents the theory of plate tectonics, and is a primer in the modern geological sciences. The second book, *In Suspect Terrain* (1983), turns to Anita Harris, a geologist "who's clawing at the theory—not totally disbelieving but irritated with the gross extrapolations onto the continent of plate tectonic ideas to a point where they become, in her view, almost imaginative." In the third book, *Rising from the Plains* (1986), McPhee concentrates on Wyoming and the dean of Rocky Mountain geology, David Love. The scientific focus is on the story of the building, burial, and exhumation of the Rocky Mountains. Love struggles with controversial topics in environmental geology and the economics of minerals, oil, gas, and uranium until, in McPhee's view, he becomes a one-man *Encounters with the Archdruid.* The human focus is on

Love and his mother, a woman who had arrived from the East three-quarters of a century earlier. She had kept a journal in an articulate voice, and Love permitted McPhee to quote extensively from it in *Rising from the Plains.* The human characters here seem a match for the monumental geology. The fourth book in the series is about California, "the only place where this continent has a plate boundary on dry land." As McPhee said this, his right arm was immobilized in a sling. He had dislocated it a couple of weeks earlier while cross-country skiing in the Sierra Nevada, a slight detour from a trip up and down the San Andreas fault.

McPhee's best-selling books have been *Coming into the Country* and *The Control of Nature* (1989). Next in line are the geology books. They have been widely adopted in college courses because they clarify a murky subject. Most readers, according to McPhee, are not students or trained scientists, and they do not necessarily have scientific interests. But they can absorb a scientific narrative and appreciate it.

The reviewers fall into two camps: some feel geology is large and difficult enough to be worthy of McPhee's talents; others are simply bored. Evan Connell wrote a review of *Rising from the Plains* in which he appreciated McPhee's characters and natural description, but then concluded, "You need not have passed Geology 101 to enjoy 'Rising From the Plains,' but it might help." Herbert Mitgang, writing in *The New York Times* (November 10, 1986), marveled at McPhee's handling of complex material:

> It would almost be unfair to make notes while reading one of John McPhee's fascinating books that explore some out-of-the-way corner of the American landscape and its inhabitants. They are comparable to Joseph Mitchell's model writing on the Mohawk Indians or the bottom of New York Harbor or any other subject that he has mined for nuggets of information. Among professional writers, there is an added pleasure in watching how authors in their class construct their factual narratives. By covering New York and America like some foreign country, they set a very high standard of originality for writers *and* readers.

Reviewing *In Suspect Terrain,* Michiko Kakutani wrote, "However gracefully he stitches together his facts, selectivity occasionally gives way to an impulse to be thorough and precise, and the reader's interest begins to numb."

While dismayed by some reviews, McPhee understands his readers. He explained to me,

> People sometimes jump all over me for writing about geology. They're bored with it. They say, "I like your work but I don't like the geology." That used to disturb me more than it does now. The curious thing I note is that it doesn't bore everybody and that there's a bigger audience out there for geology than for most of my work.

Geology as a subject presented unexpected difficulties and apprehensions for the writer.

> One of the frustrations in it is that a writer who seeks the multiple possibilities in a piece of nonfiction writing—character sketching and narrative and dialogue and description—is not well served by a subject like geology, which is extraordinarily demanding in one principal area: description. The pressure, the weight, and the opportunity in description are just out of proportion with everything else. This permits sentences to march along in ways that would seem inappropriate in other forms of writing, but are appropriate to the earth itself.

Something has held McPhee to his original plan, something that seems larger than just completing a task or accomplishing a goal. What has been driving him through the only negative criticism he has received, through a project spanning a dozen years, and through mazes of scientific details and descriptions? His oldest daughter, Laura, said the geology has had a powerful influence on McPhee. "The geology made him think about his own mortality and how brief human life is in relation to the earth."

"It's the only piece of ground that we're ever going to inhabit," McPhee said simply. "I know that my own reflections on living and on being here changed considerably in the past few years. It's a perspective on our own position as a species with respect to space and time." McPhee looked up at the world geologic map on his wall for a moment.

"Dammit, it's the only house we're ever going to have," he said emphatically. "It is some interesting thing, this earth and how it works. I could be somewhat evangelical about ideas in geology. I am permitted to talk about it at home ten minutes a day and no more. That's pretty rigid." Evangelical feelings or not, a topic as complex as geology has been too great a challenge for most literary journalists. It comes laden with scientific detail and description, lacks enough characters to satisfy most writers, and demands a fifteen-year commitment. "The world's slowest narrative subject meets America's best journalist"—that was how another literary journalist, Mark Kramer, described to me McPhee's books on geology.

McPhee's perspective on natural forces comes through even more clearly in *The Control of Nature*. If most people are unaware of the vast geologic history of the planet, they are better able to appreciate rivers, volcanoes, and mountains. When the forces of nature come in conflict with our plans, we try to control them. Three such efforts formed McPhee's text.

The chapters presented efforts to control the Mississippi River, volcanoes in Iceland and Hawaii, and the erosion of the San Gabriel Mountains near Los Angeles. The opening chapter unfolds like *The River*, a Depression-era documentary film by Pare Lorentz. McPhee begins at a single point, the site 300 miles up the river from New Orleans where a distributary called the Atchafalaya River draws off 30 percent of the water from the master stream. The Mississippi River continues from that point down toward New Orleans, through the "American Ruhr," an industrial district of great importance to the nation. The Atchafalaya, however, reaches the Gulf in only 145 miles and has a steeper gradient than the main river. The distributary is poised to change the course of the Mississippi, as has happened many times during the formation of the southern portion of Louisiana, but this time human industry hangs in the balance. In 1963, the Army Corps of Engineers opened a structure called Old River whose job was to maintain a constant 30 percent flow into the Atchafalaya and to guarantee that the main river would continue flowing toward New Orleans.

Controlling the Mississippi River would prove difficult. Like Lorentz, McPhee follows the river until his readers grasp the whole system of control on the Mississippi from the first levee the river encounters down to the control structure at Old River. The reader also understands that the river made Louisiana and knows, as do the Cajuns who operate the structure, that the river is stronger than we are. Somewhere along the way readers almost start wishing for a flood to wash away humanity's hubris, all the while guiltily aware of what a disaster that would be for the American Ruhr, and for poor Morgan City, Louisiana, sitting in a subsiding landscape beside the Atchafalaya like a tumbler in a sink. The conflict seems inevitable. Nature will keep trying to take the shortest route to the Gulf, and the Corps of Engineers will keep trying to hold back the river. At the hands of a flood like the ones in 1927, 1937, or 1973, or when the hundred-year flood hits—the "design flood" engineers expect would destroy the works—the change will be made.

Three million cubic feet of water per second will have its way. Or maybe not. McPhee comes close to prediction, but keeps one step away. Maybe the Corps of Engineers will win a few more battles in this war.

The residents of Los Angeles who have moved up into the San Gabriel Mountains have a similar fight on their hands. The San Gabriels are one of the most shattered, most rapidly rising, and most rapidly eroding mountain ranges on earth. Natural cycles conspire to create cataclysmic events. During the dry season, chaparral grows in tangled thickets. When it burns, the ground beneath is seared and becomes impenetrable to water. Then the winter rains bring five or ten inches of water in a deluge. Broken rock from the mountains washes down in huge, destructive debris flows. The flows rampage through suburban neighborhoods, many of them newly built. Residents expect the city to protect them. The city and nature do battle.

"Strung out along the San Gabriel front are at least a hundred and twenty bowl-shaped excavations that resemble football stadiums and are often as large," McPhee wrote. These basins catch the debris flows coming off the mountains, and generally they work. Fleets of trucks empty the basins as they fill. Once in a while, they overflow, sending rock rivers into suburbia. Because the flows are separated by several years, new residents bask in a false sense of security. New houses go up. Almost no one was around when the last debris flow came roaring down that section of the mountains. The cycle sometimes takes twenty or forty years to repeat. Geologic time meets human time. McPhee wrote in *The Control of Nature:*

House on Bubbling Well, Glendora, $167,000. Mud and flood?

Alosta Realty: "No, no. Oh, years and years ago we had a big flood. They built that dam, and there's no problem there at all."

Silent Ranch Estates, shake-roofed or tile-covered castles, "individually built," in the four-hundred-thousand-to-one-million-dollar range. Possible debris-flow problems?

Realtor: "There are a couple of houses which I would not touch. The others—I don't think so. I haven't heard anything to that effect. Every house you'd see, we'd have to take that into account."

Terrace View Estates, gated community, all view lots, up to one and a half acres at roughly $135,000 an acre. Debris flows?

"No. We went through the whole winter there. We had some very heavy rains and there were no problems."

McPhee calls these lists of voices "gossip ladders." In *The Control of Nature* they illustrate the hopeful blindness that sets in. The San Gabriels sit above the smog with beautiful views and a wildness that seems impossible so close to Los Angeles. Believing the debris catch basins will protect them, new owners keep coming. Problems?

"I don't know. I don't think they have that problem there."

"There was a problem years ago. They have a channel there now."

"It's always possible, but that place is not on enough of a hill."

"Not that I know of."

"That I don't know. You have to check with the City of Los Angeles."

The Corps of Engineers trying to defeat the Atchafalaya's capture of the Mississippi River and the City of Los Angeles trying to hold back the San Gabriel Mountains possess the same symbolism. In a later work, "Looking for a Ship," McPhee quoted Captain Paul Washburn of the United States Merchant Marine, who said it best: "Anywhere in the world, if you fool with Mother Nature she's going to get you. This is not a political statement. It is just a fact." *The Control of Nature* deals with the geomorphology McPhee learned at Deerfield Academy, the generally uncontrollable forces that have shaped the surface of the earth. Crustal plates drift about the globe. California suburbanites, living near a plate boundary, try to keep debris slides out of their bedrooms. As McPhee shifts his narrative from plate tectonics to geomorphology, a certain edginess creeps into his voice.

McPhee's life has been strongly rooted. He built a modernist, rambling, two-story house in an isolated corner of Princeton township in 1963, while working at *Time* magazine, and still lives there today. During his first marriage, with four daughters in the house, he kept his office in the garage. There was a divorce—his first wife, Pryde Brown, said they were "victims of the late Sixties social revolution among the middle-class." In 1972 McPhee married Yolanda Whitman, who had four children by her first marriage. Evidence of the children is everywhere in the house, including stunning photographs of Iceland taken by Laura, who was attracted to the landscape during a trip with her father. Maps of the St. John-Allagash Wilderness and Alaska, an Eastern coyote pelt from Maine, a chart of the structures associated with colliding crustal plates, and hundreds of books fill the walls. The house is surrounded by open land that once was owned by Princeton University but is now slated for development. McPhee often sees deer and even wild turkeys in his backyard. This piece of the New York–Philadelphia megapolis, he noted in *Survival of the Bark Canoe,* has one of the densest concentrations of deer in North America—fifty per square mile, compared to five per square mile in Maine. Some of his neighbors have erected fences to keep them out, but McPhee does not put his garden above nature.

His life as a professional writer has institutional connections that many writers would envy: ties to *The New Yorker,* more than twenty books in print, requests for appearances. Above all, he told me, he wants to keep writing:

Writing is like a river meandering along. It won't through time stay in the same banks. It cuts out new things and fills in other places. Sometimes it jumps across its own meanders. You wonder what you're going to be doing ten or fifteen years hence.

You might say my ambition is to write—as little as possible! My daughter Jenny tells me I overdo the negative aspects. I grunt and groan about how horrible it is and how difficult the whole process is without talking about the good parts. In general, I do not wish to be writing anything different in genre than what I'm writing now. It's not my ambition to win awards. My ambition is to keep on writing.

The conversation turned to symbolic realities, and how nonfiction sometimes creates surfaces that are more deeply meaningful than mere information. McPhee brought up Henri Vaillancourt, the main character in *The Survival of the Bark Canoe.*

I have this set of priorities. The surface of a piece of writing should be very clear water. A young man is making a canoe. The canoe is very beautiful. He is totally and compulsively dedicated to making these canoes. He doesn't use nails, rivets, hammers. He uses four instruments and these canoes don't have a bit of metal in them. That's the surface. There are layers and layers beneath the surface. I mean, what does Henri stand for? He's got high standards, doesn't he? He's *completely* devoted to one thing. He's a monomaniac, a fantastic craftsman, an artist. His temperament is the artist's temperament. Can you excuse somebody who is an artist? What kind of a discount do you give him? You're off into various levels and channels in many themes that are brought up by the surface.

These extra dimensions are what literature is made of and what life is made of. They imply huge complexity. They're ever so important. But in a piece of writing, if they are the surface, the raison d'être, I think you have something stillborn. I want these other things to be there in layers *under* a clear surface.

McPhee ran his hand across a granite countertop in his kitchen. The granite was darkly colored like an old oaken desk. The slab had been quarried from the Canadian shield. It was three billion years old, McPhee said, "and still granite." He spoke with some awe at the stability in that part of the shield. Most rocks of such age have been ground up, melted, transformed into something else. McPhee's hand stroked the granite with a craftsman's feel. The granite connects to the piece of North American geology—Chicago to Cheyenne—left out of his geology books, and he plans a "chaser" on the Precambrian basement buried under more recent rocks in Illinois, Iowa, and Nebraska. He seemed to have a reverential attachment to that piece of granite, a stone so permanent that it brought to mind McPhee's life in Princeton. He was born there in 1931 and acquired his desire to become a writer very early in life. His writing has grown and matured, perhaps in part because it has such bedrock beneath it. "I'm still here," he said, "which my daughters think is funny. They think I'm very provincial, and I guess they're right. But I get around a lot."

Selected Bibliography

WORKS OF JOHN MCPHEE

ESSAYS

A *Sense of Where You Are: A Profile of William Warren Bradley*. New York: Farrar, Straus and Giroux, 1965.

The Headmaster: Frank L. Boyden of Deerfield. New York: Farrar, Straus and Giroux, 1966.

Oranges. New York: Farrar, Straus and Giroux, 1967.

The Pine Barrens. New York: Farrar, Straus and Giroux, 1968.

A Roomful of Hovings and Other Profiles. New York: Farrar, Straus and Giroux, 1968.

Levels of the Game. New York: Farrar, Straus and Giroux, 1969.

The Crofter and the Laird. New York: Farrar, Straus and Giroux, 1970.

Encounters with the Archdruid. New York: Farrar, Straus and Giroux, 1971.

The Deltoid Pumpkin Seed. New York: Farrar, Straus and Giroux, 1973.

The Curve of Binding Energy. New York: Farrar, Straus and Giroux, 1974.

Pieces of the Frame. New York: Farrar, Straus and Giroux, 1975.

The Survival of the Bark Canoe. New York: Farrar, Straus and Giroux, 1975.

Coming into the Country. New York: Farrar, Straus and Giroux, 1977.

Giving Good Weight. New York: Farrar, Straus and Giroux, 1979.

Basin and Range. New York: Farrar, Straus and Giroux, 1981.

In Suspect Terrain. New York: Farrar, Straus and Giroux, 1983.

La Place de la Concorde Suisse. New York: Farrar, Straus and Giroux, 1984.

Table of Contents. New York: Farrar, Straus and Giroux, 1985.

Rising from the Plains. New York: Farrar, Straus and Giroux, 1986.

The Control of Nature. New York: Farrar, Straus and Giroux, 1989.

Looking for a Ship. New York: Farrar, Straus and Giroux, 1990.

"TALK OF THE TOWN" STORIES FROM *THE NEW YORKER*

"Big Plane." February 19, 1966, 28.

"Two Commissioners" (Thomas Hoving). March 5, 1966, 33.

"Coliseum Hour." March 12, 1966, 44.

"Beauty and Horror." May 28, 1966, 28.

"Girl in a Paper Dress." June 25, 1966, 20.

"On the Way to Gladstone." July 9, 1966, 17.

"Ms and FeMs at the Biltmore." July 12, 1966.

"The License Plates of Burning Tree." January 30, 1971, 20.

"Three Gatherings" (Americans). December 25, 1971, 25.
"The Conching Rooms." May 13, 1972, 32.
"Sullen Gold." March 25, 1974, 32.
"Flavors & Fragrances." April 8, 1974, 35.
"Police Story." July 15, 1974, 27.
" 'Time' Covers, NR." October 28, 1974, 40.
"The P-1800." February 10, 1975, 30.
"In Virgin Forest." July 6, 1987, 21–23.
"Release." September 28, 1987, 28–32.
"Altimeter Man." September 25, 1989, 48–50.

OTHER NONFICTION

"It's Collegiate—but Is It Humor?" *New York Times Magazine,* May 25, 1952, 17, 58.
"The People of New Jersey's Pine Barrens." *National Geographic,* January 1974, 52–77.
"The Upper 1." *Vogue,* April 1979, 248, 315.

REPRINTED MATERIALS

Wimbledon: A Celebration. New York: Viking, 1972.
The John McPhee Reader. Edited and with an introduction by William L. Howarth. New York: Farrar, Straus and Giroux, 1976.
The Pine Barrens Illustrated. New York: Farrar, Straus and Giroux, 1981.
Alaska: Images of the Country. San Francisco: Sierra Club Books, 1981.
Outcroppings. Introduction and text by John McPhee, edited by Christopher Merrill. Layton, Utah: Gibbs Smith, 1988.

SHORT FICTION

"The Fair of San Gennaro." *Transatlantic Review,* Winter 1961, 117–128. Reprinted in *Stories from the Transatlantic Review.* Edited by Joseph F. McCrindle. New York: Holt, Rinehart and Winston, 1970. Pp. 223–232.
"Eucalyptus Trees." *Reporter,* October 19, 1967, 36–39.
"Ruth, the Sun is Shining." *Playboy,* April 1968, 114–116, 126, 186.

BIBLIOGRAPHY

Clark, Joanne K. "The Writings of John Angus McPhee: A Selected Bibliography." *Bulletin of Bibliography:* 45–51 (January–March 1981).

BIOGRAPHICAL AND CRITICAL STUDIES

Baker, John F. "John McPhee." *Publishers Weekly,* January 3, 1977, 12–13.
Beem, Edgar Allen. "John McPhee on Maine: Conversation with the Archjournalist." *Maine Times,* November 1, 1985, 14–16.
Brown, Spencer. "The Odor of Durability." *Sewanee Review:* 146–152 (Winter 1978).
DeMott, Benjamin. "Two Reporters: At Peace and War." *The Atlantic,* January 1978, 91–93.
Devouring a Small Country Inn." *Time,* March 12, 1979, 70.
Drabelle, Dennis. "Conversations with John McPhee." *Sierra,* October–November–December 1978, 61–63.
Dunkel, Tom. "Pieces of McPhee." *New Jersey Monthly,* August 1986, 37–39, 41–51.
Eason, David. "The New Journalism and the Image-World." In *Literary Journalism in the Twentieth Century.* Edited by Norman Sims. New York: Oxford University Press, 1990.
Hall, Donald. "Johnny Can Write." *National Review,* March 31, 1978: 412–13.
Hamilton, Joan. "An Encounter with John McPhee." *Sierra,* May–June 1990, 50–55, 92, 96.
Hoagland, Edward. "Where Life Begins Over." *New York Times Book Review,* November 27, 1977: 1, 48–49.
Howarth, William. Introduction to *The John McPhee Reader.* New York: Farrar, Straus and Giroux, 1976.
———. "Itinerant Passages; Recent American Essays." *Sewanee Review*: 633–644 (Fall 1988).
Leonard, John. "Books of The Times." *New York Times,* November 25, 1977, sec. 3,23.
Lounsberry, Barbara. "John McPhee's Levels of the Earth." In *The Art of Fact: Contemporary Artists of Nonfiction.* Westport, Conn.: Greenwood Press, 1990.
Schwartz, Tony. "Establishing the Levels of the Game." *More,* July–August 1976, 38–42.
Shenker, Israel. "The Annals of McPhee." *New York Times,* January 11, 1976, sec. 11, 20–21.
Sims, Norman. "The Literary Journalists." Introduction to *The Literary Journalists.* New York: Ballantine, 1984. Pp. 3–25.
Singular, Stephen. "Talk with John McPhee." *New York Times Book Review.* November 27, 1977, 1, 50–51.

Smith, Kathy. "John McPhee Balances the Act." In *Literary Journalism in the Twentieth Century,* edited by Norman Sims. New York: Oxford University Press, 1990.

Smyth, Jeannette. "John McPhee of The New Yorker." *Washington Post,* March 19, 1978, L1, L5–6.

Weber, Ronald. "Letting Subjects Grow: Literary Nonfiction from *The New Yorker.*" *Antioch Review,* 486–499 (Fall 1978). Reprinted in Ronald Weber, *The Literature of Fact: Literary Nonfiction in American Writing.* Athens Ohio University Press, 1980.

—*NORMAN SIMS*

James Merrill

1926–

IN 1939, WHEN James Merrill was thirteen, his parents divorced. Because his father was a powerful financier, the co-founder of the famous brokerage house of Merrill, Lynch, and the man who had turned down President Roosevelt's request that he become secretary of the treasury, the divorce trial was front-page news, even in *The New York Times*. Its effect on the child was sad but not extraordinary—except insofar as it came to shape one of the most imaginative and esteemed poetic minds in American literature.

James Merrill was born in New York City on March 3, 1926, the son of Charles E. Merrill and his second wife, Hellen Ingram. His privileged childhood was passed in a city brownstone and a Long Island estate. "It strikes me now maybe," he told me in an interview (collected in *Recitative*) in 1982, "that during much of my childhood I found it difficult to *believe* in the way my parents lived. They seemed so utterly taken up with engagements, obligations, ceremonies. . . . The excitement, the emotional quickening *I* felt in those years came usually through animals or nature, or through the servants in the house—Colette knew all about that—whose lives seemed by contrast to make such perfect *sense*." He was sent to St. Bernard's and Lawrenceville, and then enrolled at Amherst College, his father's alma mater. During college, he took a year off to serve in the Army, and graduated with the class of 1947, having written his undergraduate thesis on Proust. He taught at Bard College in 1948, and at various later times has taught briefly at Amherst, the University of Wisconsin, Washington University in St. Louis, and Yale University. Merrill was elected to the American Institute of Arts and Letters in 1971, and raised to the more exclusive Academy in 1989. He has been awarded honorary degrees from Amherst and Yale, and in 1986 was named Poet Laureate of Connecticut. In 1954, he moved with his companion David Jackson to Stonington, Connecticut, a picturesque seacoast village; they purchased a building on Water Street, restored its upper floors, and have lived there ever since. For two decades starting in 1964, Merrill and Jackson spent part of each year in Greece; since 1979 they have wintered in Key West. His different homes, and the displacements and discoveries of his travels, are the subject of many poems. But the domestic focus of his work has at its heart—in ways both overt and implicit, descriptive and symbolic—the wrenching upheaval of his adolescence: the divorce.

It would be absurd to reduce Merrill's genius to any formula. In fact, if any word describes his temperament, it is "mercurial." If any word describes the shape of his career, it is "surprising." Few readers would have anticipated that the author of Merrill's early books, with their exquisite, highly wrought lyrics, would have come to write *The Changing Light at Sandover* (1982), a gigantic and unnerving epic poem. But both those early lyrics and that late epic—along with the narratives and meditations of his middle period—resolve to a phrase used about Merrill's work by Mirabell, one of the characters in the poet's Ouija board trilogy. The strange voice wants to usurp Merrill's, but promises to return him to his "CHRONICLES OF LOVE & LOSS." There is no better description of Merrill's achievement than that, not least because it stresses the autobiographical and narrative thrust of Merrill's work, his sense of a life lived and understood over time, and also because it links this poet's two great themes, love and loss. Love is not fully itself until it is lost, until it becomes memory, becomes art.

Again and again, in small poems and large, Merrill returns to the greatest loss of love in his life—that occasioned by his parents' divorce. It is as if that split threw into stronger relief a personality split in the poet himself. Certainly his mind prefers doubled perspectives, prefers to be "of two minds" about all matters. And the elegant tensions in his work derive from characteristics we may as well call paternal and maternal. Merrill is as much his mother's boy as he is his father's son, as much the heir to Father Time as to Mother Nature. Mind and style, reason and sensation, idea and fact, America and Europe, Connecticut and Athens, German and French, verse and language, legend and realism—the list could be extended through nearly every impulse in the poems, which tingle with such opposition. But Merrill's ambition is not merely to display the two aspects of his personality, but to reconcile them, as the child's fantasy is to reconcile his warring parents. Merrill's own image for this is the Broken Home, and the truest energies of his work derive from his efforts—and they extend from the delicacies of metaphor to the creation of an entire cosmological mythology—to unite or harmonize the sides of his life those opposing tendencies represent. Plato says that Love's child is the son of Need and Resource; just so, both the obsessions and inventions at the heart of Merrill's poetry must be attended to. The poet's homosexuality, which is at times his subject and always an influence on his work, may likewise be viewed as a kind of ambivalence, both a need and a resource. But this is to leap ahead. Little of this was apparent at the start of Merrill's career—or it is apparent only in retrospect. His *First Poems* (1951) were only jeweled examples of the period style; the poet had not yet found his distinctive voice.

On the back of *First Poem*'s dust jacket, the publisher advertised recent books by three of its other authors: John Crowe Ransom, Elinor Wylie, and Wallace Stevens. In retrospect, it does not seem an accidental grouping; though not his most important models and certainly not his most enduring, each of these poets did have a crucial bearing on Merrill's early work. In the late 1940's Ransom was the courtly dean of the New Critics, who insisted that a poem represented an action, that its dramatic effects were extensions of its voice, that it unfolded its meanings not by way of discursive logic but by way of an expressive complex of images. The sort of poem that Ransom favored, indeed that was of the prevailing fashion in which Merrill was schooled, most nearly resembled the creative mind itself: sedulous, self-reflective, allusively cultured, having an aloof integrity and an evident, though not necessarily apparent, continuity between its manifold surfaces and its unconscious depths or motives.

What was clear from the start and has remained a hallmark of Merrill's career is the sensuous allure of his work's textures, the lapidary brilliance of its imagery, the fluent, refined eloquence of its tone—qualities that complement its thought-provoking designs. This is a side, a decorum of his poetry for whose source Merrill himself has pointed to Elinor Wylie, the first of his maternal muses and models. Rather than her sentimental temperament, it was the glazed perfection of her technique that attracted the young Merrill—the miniaturist's adroit prosodic skill, the variety of her gleaming lyric forms. He may even have acquired from Wylie's many expert examples his own enthusiasm for the sonnet form, prominent in his work from his fledgling efforts to the virtuosic instances throughout the trilogy, entitled *The Changing Light at Sandover* (1982). Whatever his individual success with the form, his most interesting use of it is the sonnet sequences that make up longer single poems. Among them are several of his pivotal poems, "The Broken Home" and "Matinees" from *Nights and Days* (1966) and *The Fire Screen* (1969) respectively, and it is curious to note that Merrill returns to the sonnet when dealing with his own childhood, as if he associated the form with its ability both to release and control his autobiographical impulses.

The influence of Wallace Stevens is more difficult to summarize because it is more extensive and profound. Stevens endowed Merrill with the joint legacy of Emerson and the symbolists, along with a vocabulary by turns playful and severe, gaudy and abstract, by means of which a poem might seem both charged with thought and absolved from it. That vocabulary, and the exotic or painterly particulars it attended, gave shape to a world Merrill quickly found himself at home in, a world in which the distinction between idea and image is dissolved in metaphor. Without embarrassment or swagger, Stevens had made the creative acts of the imagination the central subject of art; and throughout his career Merrill, too, has turned to the formalities of art and the dreamy play of language, to the mind and the "theater of trope," as types of what George Santayana called "the primary tendencies of our nature and the ultimate possibilities of our soul."

The title *First Poems* is neither as straightforward nor as modest as it seems. In fact, the book was Merrill's third. The first, privately printed at his father's expense in 1942, was *Jim's Book*—fifteen poems, eight stories and sketches, an essay on Wylie, and two translations of Baudelaire. The work is remarkably precocious for an author just sixteen, displaying a felicity of diction and conceit. If his range is narrow, usually limited to the Great Themes, that is compensated for by a delicate and winning sophistication. Four years later his second book, *The Black Swan,* was privately published in Athens. Five of its twelve poems were reprinted a few years later in *First Poems,* and they are the first manifestation of Merrill's adult voice. There is here a fresh wit that gives a poem surprising depth, but his elaborately devised metrical schemes and the top-heavy momentum of glittering details tend to obscure the motives and meaning of the poems. Still, there is a confidence and polish and intelligence at work that are remarkable for a poet not yet out of college, and several features of the book anticipate Merrill's later interests. The contrast between the perceived and reflected worlds is one recurrent theme. And when the speaker of these poems is not invoking a beloved or lost lyrical "you," he usually addresses a child. It is a role Merrill will himself often assume later, and a figure that fascinates him all along. Here the child stands in for a number of possibilities: the innocent soul, the as-yet-unrealized or idealized self, an image of power, a type of the artist, and the agent of love itself, as Eros. *The Black Swan*'s attention is directed mainly at love and its aftermath: on the necessity and impossibility of love, and on the passage of love into memory and art. Clearly, Merrill chose, or had been chosen by, his principal themes from the beginning.

As a title, then, *First Poems* is a misleading description. But it was never meant to be merely that. Instead, it pays homage by way of allusion, an intentionally doubled echo of Rainer Maria Rilke's *Erste Gedichte* and Stéphane Mallarmé's

Premiers Poèmes. Characteristically, Merrill is turning toward an older heritage and singling out both a French and a German affinity. Temperamentally, Merrill cannot be identified with either of his predecessors. His wry wit has forestalled the stark exaltation of Rilke's "Aufsingen"; his sociable irony and critical intelligence have kept him from assuming a role as ascetic, even as sacerdotal, as Mallarmé's.

The type of poem Merrill first wrote declares his marked preference for—to borrow a distinction from W. H. Auden—"mythological" rather than "occasional" poetry; that is, for poems whose overt subjects are universal and impersonal, and whose personal or historical occasions are latent. Of course, throughout his career, Merrill has been drawn to traditional or local myths, indeed, has been obsessed by certain of them; in his later work he has discovered or devised the archetypal dimensions of his past, and in the trilogy he has elaborated a grand mythology for the life of his mind and heart. But in the literal sense of Auden's term, a "mythological" poetry is a wise preference for the young poet especially, whose private feelings and ideas lack the significance that years of living will earn. The myths Merrill sought in Mallarmé and Rilke—the myth of The Word, and the myth of Experience, the one a transformation of the world into art, the other a transumption of art by the world—together constitute the economy of suffering and wisdom, of loss and transcendence that characterizes *First Poems*. Undoubtedly too Merrill was drawn to Rilke's powers of concentration on the immanent significance of unlikely humble details; it is a quality Merrill later picks out for praise in the work of Eugenio Montale and Elizabeth Bishop. And he learned from Mallarmé's array of exquisite images how to evoke rather than explain: things are known by their essences (as Merrill puts it later, an image is that dream of essence distilled from the flowering field of experience), but defined by their effects. It is evident, too, from the most ambitious of these *First Poems* that he had studied Mallarmé's art of blocking poems into episodes of tone and rhythm on the analogy of musical composition. And although it is more apparent later on—in the hermeticism of *Nights and Days* and *Braving the Elements* (1972), where the world becomes text—even in *First Poems* Merrill fashions a poetic language on the principle that words create rather than record their subject, that poems are suggestive networks of elliptical but complementary images.

Among the most appealing poems in the book are a series of emblematic meditations on the poet's lot: "The Black Swan," "The Parrot," "The Pelican," and "The Peacock." "Transfigured Bird" has the last word on the matter. The poem is a series of four fables, done in terza rima. In the first, a "child fond of natural things"—a literalist, one might call him—discovers "the eggshell of appearance," broken but glowing, pearly within and blue (the imagination's color) without. In the second section, an older child's microscope examines the fertile yolk's "point of blood," which hatches a "throbbing legend" in his mind. These two planes, the discernible and the unseen, the literal and imaginary, are brought together, sharply and unsettlingly, in the long third section with the introduction of Philippa, a "belle dame sans merci"; her beauty is a thoughtless, regressive power:

> . . . I must begin
> To tell her of this music in my touch:
>
> Of God who like a little boy with a pin
> Shall prick a hole in either end of the sky
> And blow it clean away, the thing within,
>
> Away, before it waste, or hatching fly
> Out of his reach in noisy solitude,
> Or kill him with the oracle of its eye;
>
> Blow all away, the yolk with its X of blood,

The shelves of jewels away, this drowsing girl
At whose hand, away, the shapely animals fed;

Till the egg is void of all but pearl-on-pearl
Reflections and their gay meanderings;
Shall, tiring, burst the shell, let the fragments
whirl.

"Transfigured Bird" argues that the world imagined is the ultimate good. That argument, however, is neither justified by much practical testimony nor proposed with any absolute conviction. In part, Merrill has not yet discovered the true scope of its exigencies and cost, and certainly not explored its often wrenching autobiographical entanglements. The majority of poems in this first book, by their very protocols, are designed to inhibit such discoveries. Still, the tensions tell. And the two best poems in this volume, "Variations: White Stag, Black Bear" (a poem dedicated to the poet's father) and "Variations: The air is sweetest that a thistle guards," succeed largely because Merrill loosens his metrical grip and allows himself more leeway to develop the implications of his subject. These are more restless and ambitious poems, and wander closer to psychic currents that churn beneath the surface of *First Poems*.

Eight years elapsed between *First Poems* and the publication of *The Country of a Thousand Years of Peace* (1959), the longest interval between any two of his collections. During that time, Merrill both traveled around the world (and introduced exotic observations into poems) and settled into Stonington, Connecticut, a small coastal village that prompted a more domestic focus in his poems. He had also written a novel and two plays, and this experience helped him toward a more fluent and inflected line, a more credible and versatile address. The poems in this volume translate the play of mind into the feints of a voice now talking to itself, now explaining to a sympathetic listener. Some of the energy and props of fiction support his new work as well. A superior narrative skill braces these poems; rhetorical questions, private jokes, lapses and leaps are combined into episodic, *knowing* accounts that rely on the quirks of character and events, instead of image and hypothesis, to catch up the poem's thematic intentions. There is a technical advance as well in *The Country of a Thousand Years of Peace,* more sparkle and salt, the mercurial play of mind that comes with technical control. There is a corresponding obliquity too; many of the poems are darkly inspired and unyielding. Not until *Water Street* (1962) do his poems show a clear-eyed understanding and ironic appreciation of themselves. But here he seems to hesitate before the new and surprising depths he has discovered.

Despite their alluring or even learned trappings, many poems in this book pursue what one of them calls "the inner adventure." "Fire Poem" is one. It takes up the conflict between passion and intelligence, between ardor and ashes, the song of once-burned innocence and twice-shy experience. At one point the fire itself speaks:

If as I am you know me bright and warm,
It is while matter bears, which I live by,
For very heart the furnace of its form:
By likeness and from likeness in my storm
Sheltered, can all things change and changing
be
The rare bird bedded at the heart of harm.

Merrill is writing here about the symbolic function of language to reclaim and transform phenomena, a point he also makes in "The Doodler," whose speaker idly sketches a world of figures on the page's white void.

The fullest version of this presiding theme is to be found in the several poems that deal with "glassen surfaces." In "The Octopus," for example, the "vision asleep in the eye's tight translucence" is compared to an octopus behind an aquarium's plate glass. In another poem, "Some

Negatives: X. at the Chateau,'' the eye is replaced by a camera lens and its ''images of images.'' On the other side of the looking glass, the life beneath the life is deeply ambivalent and disturbing, a sometimes threatening source of psychological and emotional engulfment. ''In the Hall of Mirrors'' takes up the problem of reproduction, and the mirror as the Edenic, silvery version of the self. But the book's best-known poem, ''Mirror,'' is Merrill's fullest account of the dilemma. The poem is a dramatic monologue in the voice of a tall standing mirror, addressed to the wide-open window opposite. It can be read as a debate between the reflective mind and the perceiving eye, or between a perfected but stale art and natural, generational life. But the poem is too astute to deal exclusively with such standard contrasts. Instead, it is a brooding study of frustration and transfiguration. Instead of taking Merrill's preferred role of vulnerable child or artist, the mirror's disembodied voice is that of a surrogate parent, growing old ''under an intensity / Of questioning looks.'' The question is *''how to live''*—how to come to life, as well as how rightly to live. Between its moralizing prologue and epilogue is a compressed, novelistic account of the mirror's ''children,'' who stand before it with their secrets. As time slowly blisters away the mirror's backing—making it into a sort of window—it yields to a higher power, ''a faceless will, / Echo of mine.'' The self accepts determinism *and* exaltation, experience *and* language. It is increasingly characteristic of Merrill's work, here as in later, more accomplished poems, to work not with a set of opposites but with a series of dissolves. The reader is invited to watch the poem's subject through a constantly shifting framework.

Some critics take *Water Street* to be Merrill's decisive collection, the first evidence of his mature style. That distinction more likely belongs to his next book, *Nights and Days,* but the best poems in *Water Street* brilliantly predict the subsequent shift. Like Marcel Proust, this book's presiding mentor, Merrill here seeks in childhood, in family or domestic scenes, the sources of his poetic strength. There is a new attention to motivation, the use of involuntary memories, a heightened awareness of the imperfection of the present and the transience of the past. *Water Street* is in some ways a slighter book than *The Country of a Thousand Years of Peace,* but its strongest work—''An Urban Convalescence,'' ''A Tenancy,'' and ''Scenes of Childhood''—have an autobiographical emphasis and circumstantial intimacy unlike anything he had written before. The best of his earlier style—its brio, its lavish textures and paradoxes—remains in *Water Street,* but the poet is now less content with intellectual conceits and more dependent on vivid phenomenal details. The poems tend to question their own assumptions, to revise their attitudes toward the very experience they recount. The effect, for all the opportunities it gives the poet to vary a poem's pace and to manipulate a reader's responses, is one of emotional honesty, an openness that belies the very artistry used to achieve it. This becomes a hallmark of Merrill's best work from here on, and his most affecting poems succeed not because of how they expose or suppress the facts of his life, but because they rely on an intellectual scrupulosity while searching out the truths of the heart.

''An Urban Convalescence'' finds the poet out for a recuperative walk during which the city becomes an image of his own past:

Out for a walk, after a week in bed,
I find them tearing up part of my block
And, chilled through, dazed and lonely, join the dozen
In meek attitudes, watching a huge crane
Fumble luxuriously in the filth of years.

The speaker broods on the uncaring ravages of time and of a discontented civilization. That theme with its attendant images of demolition and fragmentation, of convulsive change and wasting, is the theme of modern poetry itself. But Merrill next introduces a series of ghostly images—a building, an engraving, a woman in Paris—to explore how the world becomes internalized and spiritualized for us. The woman is the embodiment of an idealized city, a dreamy Paris of *temps perdu,* so unlike the clangorous brutality of New York. Merrill wants to test in this poem how private experience is shaped by myth, an impulse nowhere more apparent (and resolving) than in the last stanzas, where the underworld of memory yields a rueful wisdom, and the past shelters the present:

. . . back into my imagination
The city glides, like cities seen from the air,
Mere smoke and sparkle to the passenger
Having in mind another destination

Which now is not that honey-slow descent
Of the Champs-Elysées, her hand in his,
But the dull need to make some kind of house
Out of the life lived, out of the love spent.

''An Urban Convalescence'' is not a poem of the Broken Home, whose theme is dispossession, but of the Missing Home, whose theme is self-possession. From ''The House'' in *First Poems* through ''18 West 11th Street'' in *Braving the Elements* to ''The House in Athens'' in *The Changing Light at Sandover,* this series of poems addresses the question of how art stabilizes the passage of time. Style, they tell us, is finally an instrument of discovery and freedom, of reconciliation.

Other poems in *Water Street* orbit these themes. ''A Tenancy'' is about the poet's occupancy of the house in Stonington. Again, a few casual details prompt a deepening recollection until the reverie emerges into a moralizing resolution. But it seems a more elliptical poem than ''An Urban Convalescence.'' The poet strikes a Faustian deal with himself:

That given a few years more
(Seven or ten or, what seemed vast, fifteen)
To spend in love, in a country not at war,
I would give in return
All I had. All? A little sun
Rose in my throat. The lease was drawn.

That ''little sun'' is not a child, but a poem, an effective symbol both of the dawning of poetic song and also of the isolation and sacrifice demanded of that gift. The unborn child dominates another poem, ''Childlessness,'' as well. ''Scenes of Childhood,'' though, is superior for its keen understanding of its own disclosures and equivocations. The family romance is at its troubled heart. The poet and his mother are watching home movies of themselves thirty years before, introjected scenes that reveal to the poet past connections and his present relationships, a tiny oedipal melodrama enacted and witnessed by its protagonists.

The man's
Shadow afflicts us both.
Her voice behind me says
It might go slower.
I work the dials, the film jams.
Our headstrong old projector
Glares at the scene which promptly
Catches fire.

Other poems in *Water Street* seek to house the past and to identify the enclosing shelter of memory with poetry itself. ''Scenes of Childhood'' is a more private attempt to do the same thing, substituting heroic for domestic images. And the poem introduces a series of dilemmas Merrill confronts in later books with increasing confidence but persistent anxiety.

When *Nights and Days* was given the 1967 National Book Award, the judges (W. H. Auden, James Dickey, and Howard Nemerov) cited Merrill for ''his scrupulous and uncompromising cultivation of the poetic art, evidenced in his refusal to settle for any easy or profitable stance; for his insistence on taking the kind of tough, poetic chances which make the difference between esthetic success or failure." Indeed the book displays a range and depth altogether new, and everywhere convincing. It is not a long book; there are only eighteen poems. Five of them remain among his very best. Two of them, "The Thousand and Second Night" and "From the Cupola," are long, demanding, even experimental poems that express the two sides of Merrill's temperament. The first of them is set in Istanbul and Athens, the old world, exotic, seductive, masculine, and at the same time threatening and bracing. The second poem is set in an imagined Connecticut, a world of women and weather, at once demanding, sympathetic, and authoritative.

Like "An Urban Convalescence," "The Thousand and Second Night" opens with an illness. It is "the creative malady" familiar from Proust—and here, in the poet's imagined diary entry, it is a kind of facial paralysis that sends him out into the city in search of a cure. What he finds are other versions of the self—each mosque's dome or hamam's marble cell is another "transcendental skull." This is a poem not so much about faces (though it deals with many sides of the notion of facade, of losing face, of masks and styles) as it is a poem about flesh. Or better, about the flesh and the spirit—an old philosophical bone, and abiding poetic theme. Merrill takes the story of the cruel Sultan and his story-telling slave Scheherazade to be a version of the relationship between flesh and spirit:

And when the long adventure reached its end,
I saw the Sultan in a glass, grown old,
While she, his fair wife still, her tales all told,
Smiled at him fondly. "O my dearest friend,"

Said she, "and lord and master from the first,
Release me now. Your servant would refresh
Her soul in that cold fountain which the flesh
Knows not. Grant this, for I am faint with
thirst."

And he: "But it is I who am your slave.
Free me, I pray, to go in search of joys
Unembroidered by your high, soft voice,
Along that stony path the senses pave."

But this is the poem's end, by which time it is also apparent that the pair are types of the poet's own parents, set apart and reconciled within the poem's own myth. But this image is more dramatically pursued in a later poem, "Lost in Translation" (in *Divine Comedies* [1976]). In "The Thousand and Second Night," Merrill moves—in a brilliant series of maneuvers that vary prose, crisp quatrains, and free-verse rambles—through a lively meditation of the "mind-body problem." Which is master of the self? Which is the god in masquerade? Anecdotes about a meeting with a stranger in an Athens park, or fanning a stack of old pornographic postcards, or lecturing a class of undergraduates speed the poet through perspectives on the question. The poem's "long adventure," like the soul's in flesh, takes to the seas; structures he had previously looked to for shelter, here become a means of transport:

Voyages, I bless you for sore
Limbs and mouth kissed, face bronzed and lined,
An earth held up, a text not wholly undermined
By fluent passages of metaphor.

The poet's distrust here of his own powers bespeaks a desire present throughout *Nights and Days* and perhaps linked with Merrill's having bought a house in Athens, and living in a culture and language foreign to him. It is the desire for unmediated experience, prior to language, or beyond it. This same longing is at the heart of the book's other long, and exceptionally difficult, poem, "From the Cupola." The poem draws on another myth about storytelling, that of Psyche and Eros (as first told by Apuleius). Again, it is a story about a divorced couple, but Merrill's focus here is on the nature of desire. His Psyche is a young New England woman, who lives with her two sisters, Gertrude and Alice, all of them originally from the South. Details from Merrill's own life overlap with this imaginary (or projected) history, and the poet has said that the poem took its start from some mysterious letters he began receiving from an admiring reader. The poem, with its eerie incarnations and vatic messages, is the clearest foreshadowing of Merrill's Ouija board epic. "The history of our loves," Santayana once wrote, "is the record of our divine conversations, of our intercourse with heaven." Sexual ecstasy, like the literary sublime, is a metaphor for this sort of possession. It is also helpful to read this poem as a dialogue between the id (or Eros), ego (or Psyche), and superego (the poet himself, who intervenes in the course of things to address his heroine).

No poem in the book—and not many in his entire output—is so extreme, so entirely a landscape of phrases. Other poems in *Nights and Days* take up the same themes, but in more conventional ways. "Time" is one, a disquisition on the concept played out within a sequence of interconnected metaphors (a game of solitaire, mountain climbing, record spinning). Still easier to read, and more heartbreaking, is "Days of 1964" (the first of a series of "Days of" poems that thread through different books, all of them deriving from Constantine Cavafy's erotic poems of Alexandrian life with that formulaic title). The narrative is clear and compelling enough. The poet, enraptured by a new lover, one day finds his devoted housekeeper Kleo dressed and working as a whore. Shaken, he returns to his own lover, but questions now the role of illusion in love, only to have his question stopped by a kiss:

I had gone so long without loving,
I hardly knew what I was thinking.
Where I hid my face, your touch, quick,
merciful,
Blindfolded me. A god breathed from my lips,
If that was illusion, I wanted it to last long;
To dwell, for its daily pittance, with us there,
Cleaning and watering, sighing with love or pain.

Again a version of the Psyche and Eros story, "Days of 1964" is a poem of consummate narrative skill, its characters and tone vivid, its reflections complex but lightly sketched, wise and surprising.

Nights and Days also includes one of Merrill's signature poems, "The Broken Home," a varied sequence of seven sonnets that tells directly the archetypal story that animates all of Merrill's work: "Father Time and Mother Earth, / A marriage on the rocks." One sonnet characterizes each; others comment on their stormy marriage; still others try to calculate the effect of their lives on the child-poet's own.

I see those two hearts, I'm afraid,
Still. Cool here in the graveyard of good and
evil,
They are even so to be honored and obeyed.

The process of affiliation—of making himself both "time's child" and "earth's no less"—is meant to function as "the unstiflement of the entire story." By making the pain of experience over into art, by distancing his real parents to myth, Merrill again makes a shelter out of the love spent.

The Fire Screen is one of Merrill's overlooked books. With a few exceptions, it seems his most occasional collection. But like the others, it shows him of two minds about matters. The long (156 stanzas) ballad that anchors the book, "The Summer People," though set in a fictional Maine seacoast town (called Caustic!), is based on village life in Merrill's Stonington. (He returns to the ballad form, and even more successfully, in "Days of 1935" in his next book, *Braving the*

Elements [1972], and he may have been inspired to write these poems by the example of Elizabeth Bishop's ballad, "The Burglar of Babylon.") "Figures in a ballad," the poem comments, "Lend themselves to acts / Passionate and simple." But that is precisely what Merrill does not do. He uses the "primitive" form to handle sophisticated subject matter—domestic tangles (including a suicide) among a group of six villagers that is part E. F. Benson, part Lady Murasaki.

If "The Summer People" is set in America, most of the book transpires in Greece. The self-conscious, virtuosic ballad is offset by poems that celebrate the life of the senses. "To My Greek," for instance, a witty tribute to both language and lovers, longs for

Those depths the surfacer
Lives, when he does, alone to sound and sound.

The barest word be what I say in you.

"Sound" here means both to versify and to know. What Merrill wants is, as he has said, meaning relieved of sense. It is to sensuality he looks for that; there are tortured love poems in this volume—"An Abdication," "The Envoys," "Remora." But he also looks to the vitality of the unexamined life, in such poems as the dramatic monologue "Kostas Tympakianakis," or "Ouzo for Robin" (addressed to the poet's nephew Robin Magowan). The most exquisite of these poems is the short lyric "Another August." It is in three sections—the first in prose, the second in free verse, and the third, an envoi, a rhymed quatrain. The effect is musical, like a recitative, arioso, and cabaletta. The poem is Proustian, and takes as its text the old catchphrase "One swallow doesn't make a summer," in order to explore how things change in order to remain the same. The poem opens with a return, to Greece, to "so much former strangeness" the "glaze of custom" by now has made home. The second section remembers a wrenching love affair, but then turns to the self, seeking to efface pain by memory:

Open the shutters. Let variation
abandon the swallows one by one.
How many summer dusks were needed
to make that single skimming form!
The very firefly kindles to its type.
Here is each evening's lesson. First
the hour, the setting. Only then
the human being, his white shirtsleeve
chalked among treetrunks, round a waist,
or lifted in an entrance. Look for him.
Be him.

Having receded into nature, become an unfeeling "type," he can afford the envoi's farewell, spoken to the lover:

Whom you saw mannerless and dull of heart,
Easy to fool, impossible to hurt,
I wore that fiction like a fine white shirt
And asked no favor but to play the part.

Playing a part, the whole sense that life is fiction in disguise, has fascinated Merrill throughout his career. The mythologies of the self dramatized by Proust or Sigmund Freud make sense of these poems, though they cannot be reduced to their formulas. Merrill's poems instinctively recognize the limited repertory of drives we are motivated by, and the roles our emotions assume. It is why the opera has always seemed to him, and been used by him as, a sure model of the inner life—melodramatic, intense, at times ridiculous, at times sublime. Two magical poems about the opera are center stage in *The Fire Screen.* "The Opera Company" concerns the goings-on in another house, especially the professional rivalry of two sopranos, whose voices now, on memory's scratchy old recording, "soar and mix, will not be told apart." Opera for Merrill is a feminine world, a stagy one of outsize "counterfeit emotions," and also of heartbreaking gestures of renunciation for love, and of self-sacrifice. "Matinees," a sequence of eight sonnets, is an enchanting poem about the way a young boy's morals are corrupted by opera—that is to say, brought to maturity by art. It is art that helps us to our emotions, both to have and understand them.

The point thereafter was to arrange for one's
Own chills and fever, passions and betrayals,
Chiefly in order to make song of them.

He is led to these revelations in the poem not just by the performers, but by his mother and a society dowager, Mrs. Livingston, to whose opera box he was invited. There are other maternal muse figures in this book, among them Maria Mitsotáki, the subject of "Words for Maria," and later a central character in the *Sandover* trilogy. But the crucial poem in *The Fire Screen,* and the source of the book's title, is "Mornings in a New House." Like the earlier "Scenes of Childhood," the poem projects the psychic outlines of a mother-and-son relationship, at once operatic (with its overtones of Brünnhilde) and autobiographical. The screen here is no longer a movie screen, but the fire screen on which the poet's mother had stitched *her* mother's house. He stands there

. . . Still vaguely chilled,

Guessing how even then her eight
Years had foreknown him, nursed him, all,
Sewn his first dress, sung to him, let him fall,
Howled when his face chipped like a plate.

This is what Freud would call a "dream screen," the projection of other, fearsome memories. What he most fears is what he seems to celebrate about the opera: the foreknown, the overdetermined. This fear is the subtext of *The Fire Screen*'s other strong poem, "The Friend of the Fourth Decade," another sonnet sequence, this time in couplets. The titular friend is, of course, the poet himself—though other friends are mentioned, along with their advice on how to manage one's boredom with life. One suggests soaking the messages off all his old postcards—the images remain, language is washed away. When the poet tries this with a card from his mother, it does not work:

Chances are it was
Some simple matter of what ink she used,

And yet her message remained legible,
The memories it stirred did not elude me.

I put my postcards back upon the shelf.
Certain things die only with oneself.

This sense Merrill cultivates of being the vessel of experience, of having been imprinted, is important to any understanding of his work. The most obvious instance of it is the Ouija board trilogy, in which the poet literally receives messages, and in which atoms and angels are identical. This kind of wise passivity resonates everywhere, and nowhere more mysteriously than in his most hermetic book, *Braving the Elements*. Rather than attempt any stylistic change, as other poets might (Robert Lowell, say, or James Wright), Merrill has always sought new experience in order to give his work both new material and direction. The landscape of the American Southwest and the ghostly presence of a new lover there loom in this book like the giant rock formations in Monument Valley—"the crazy shapes things take," as the poet puts it in his poem (a rather Frostian parable) about that place. Many of the poems in this collection are private, resolute, abstract, heraldic; they resist the intelligence almost successfully, as Wallace Stevens said. The natural history of America, above all a violent one, manifests itself in Merrill's references to the political terrorism of the 1960's. Loss dominates the book. These poems rise from the ashes; they recount experience "after the fire." Those fires are oedipal or passional, erotic or psychic, and from each the poet withdraws, most often into style itself, the screen of language.

The volume's dedicatory poem is "Log," a prayer that things be brought to light. The next poem is "After the Fire," and recounts a fire in the poet's house in Athens (as another poem in the book, "18 West 11th Street," concerns the bombing of the poet's childhood home). "After the Fire" indicates the start of a new book, of course, after *The Fire Screen* (other of Merrill's book titles are elemental), but the poem also revisits the scene and characters of an earlier poem, "Days of 1964." Merrill's poems do this continually, enacting his basic impulse to revise or reconstitute the past. Again we are introduced to Kleo the housemaid, and now to her aging mother and wastrel son, a sleazy character who, it turns out, during a tryst set fire to the poet's house. As Kleo is a type of the long-suffering mother, her son is a skewed version of the poet himself. Under the guise of a Chekhovian comedy, Merrill can once again explore his themes of love's enriching blindness and knowledge's merciless hindsight.

The snuffed-out candle-ends grow tall and shine,
Dead flames encircle us, which cannot harm,
The table's spread, she croons, and I
Am kneeling pressed to her old burning frame.

Other poems take up old, burned-out loves. "Strato in Plaster" and "Days of 1971" do so humorously; "Flèche d'Or" (the title is that of a train, but also a homonym for "flesh door") does so eerily. A current, diffident lover seems to have been the inspiration behind those poems set in the Southwest: "Under Libra: Weights and Measures," "In Nine Sleep Valley," and the first part of "Up and Down." These and other poems such as "The Black Mesa," where the landscape itself speaks, are as difficult a group of poems as Merrill has ever written, recessed and encoded. He drives his style hard here; its intensities and harmonies are thrilling, and not a little dizzying. The final poem in the book, "Syrinx," can stand in here for a hermeticism that suffuses the book. Syrinx was the nymph pursued by Pan, and turned by Zeus into reeds, from which Pan fashioned his pipe. In Merrill's extraordinary poem she is turned into other things as well, including a mathematical equation and the solfège scale ("Who puts his mouth to me / Draws out the scale of love and dread— / O ramify, sole antidote!"). Pan here is "the great god Pain," and his panpipes become a flute (Debussy's, no doubt, who wrote a solo with the same title)

Whose silvery breath-tarnished tones
No longer rivet bone and star in place

Or keep from shriveling, leather round a stone,
The sunbather's precocious apricot

Or stop the four winds racing overhead

Nought
Waste Eased
Sought

There are, of course, less demanding poems in the book. "Days of 1935," for example, is a bravura ballad about an imaginary kidnapping, another example, as well, of Merrill's circling the oedipal drama. A more direct, and rather more sentimental, version of it occurs in the second section of "Up and Down," called "The Emerald." The poet and his mother descend to her bank vault, where she presents him with a ring. " 'Here, take it for— / For when you marry.' " But, looking at the emerald, the poet thinks

Indeed this green room's mine, my very life.
We are each other's; there will be no wife;
The little feet that patter here are metrical.

And he slips the ring onto her finger. "Wear it for me," the poet silently tells her, "Until— until the time comes. Our eyes meet. / The world beneath the world is brightening." "Dreams

About Clothes'' is likewise about an inheritance, and deals with the father (here disguised as a dry cleaner named Art). The poet's dream-plea is at once a boast about his preference for ''the immaterial,'' and a confession of his doubts:

Tell me something, Art.
You know what it's like
Awake in your dry hell
Of volatile synthetic solvents.
Won't you help us brave the elements
Once more, of terror, anger, love?
Seeing there's no end to wear and tear
Upon the lawless heart,
Won't you as well forgive
Whoever settles for the immaterial?
Don't you care how we live?

The peace the poet tries to make here with his parents, with his past, is a tentative, wary one. But the project Merrill next, and unwittingly, embarks on, finally makes that peace by taking his past up into a grand mythology of memory, a high romance of reconciliation.

Divine Comedies, which was awarded the Pulitzer Prize in 1977, may be the single most resplendent of Merrill's individual collections. Its verse combines the conversational fluency of *The Fire Screen* with the oracular density of *Braving the Elements*. The major poems in the volume's first part bring to perfection his preference for the poem of middle length, between one hundred and three hundred lines, with an elegant maze of narrative, a metrical array, and daunting range of allusions. The four preeminent poems in this first part of *Divine Comedies*—''Lost in Translation,'' ''Chimes for Yahya,'' ''Yánnina,'' and ''Verse for Urania''—are all reminiscences or reveries, their narratives shuttling between past event and present meditation. Their tone is one of autumnal resignation, rather like that of Shakespeare's late harmonic romances. (The publication of *Divine Comedies* coincided with the poet's fiftieth birthday.) Each of the poems involves some sort of trip, literal or figurative, so that their recurring plot is the voyage of self-discovery, during which the poet tours his own past, in settings local or exotic. ''Chimes for Yahya'' opens and closes in Merrill's Athens home, but opens out to and closes in on a recuperative stay in Esfahān, Iran, decades earlier, with a chieftain prince. The poem can be read as a mock nativity ode whose playful epiphany becomes an emblem of ''the pain so long forgiven / It might as well be pleasure I rise in.'' The prince in this poem is a mild, beneficent counterpart to the tyrant Ali Pasha in ''Yánnina,'' both of them types of the father. Screened by metaphors of dream, shadow play, and magician's tent, ''Yánnina'' reconstructs the shifting images of feminine and masculine, each split between the destructive and the seductive. That split informs the broken-home theme, which again is the setting for ''Lost in Translation,'' likely destined to be Merrill's signature poem. The jigsaw puzzle which the young Merrill and his governess piece together—during a time when ''A summer without parents is the puzzle / Or should be''—is a tableau of yet another ''Sheik with beard / And flashing sword hilt,'' attended by ''a dark-eyed woman veiled in mauve.'' The child wonders

. . . whom to serve
And what his duties are, and where his feet,

And if we'll find, as some before us did,
That piece of Distance deep in which lies hid
Your tiny apex sugary with sun,
Eternal Triangle, Great Pyramid!

The way we translate life to art, art to life, as if they were each a language indifferently learned but unhesitatingly spoken, is the animating energy behind this brilliant, affecting work, which resolves itself in language—a scene of instruction in which Rilke puzzles out a translation of Paul Valéry's ''Palme,'' sacrificing felicity for sense:

But nothing's lost. Or else: all is translation
And every bit of us is lost in it
(Or found—I wander through the ruin of S
Now and then, wondering at the peacefulness)
And in that loss a self-effacing tree,
Color of context, imperceptibly
Rustling with its angel, turns the waste
To shade and fiber, milk and memory.

The subject of "Lost in Translation," the poet's relationship to his own past, is slightly deflected in "Verse for Urania" but only in order to provide a still more penetrating and embracing meditation on time. The poem is addressed to the infant daughter of his Greek-born, too-Americanized tenants in Stonington on the occasion of her baptism. She is the poet's godchild, perhaps even a type of the Divine Child that Jung considered the most constant and potent symbol of the self in fullest potentiality, and thus a poignant reminder of one's unfulfilled desires. That this child's name is also that of the muse of astronomy and cosmological poetry allows the poet to roam to other details, both abstruse and homely. Since "the first myth was Measure," the very rhythms of life, like those of verse, "Prevail, it might be felt, at the expense / Of meaning, but as well create, survive it." All things pass—"Such is the test of time that all things pass"—only to return upon themselves, and Merrill would hold with Friedrich Nietzsche that he "who consents to his own return participates in the divinity of the world." That is what this poem finally celebrates. We *are* the time we pass through, in a measured design greater than either, as Merrill tells his godchild:

It was late
And early. I had seen you through shut eyes.
Our bond was sacred, being secular:
In time embedded, it in us, near, far,
Flooding both levels with the same sunrise.

The second half of *Divine Comedies* is entirely taken up with "The Book of Ephraim," a poem of nearly one hundred pages, arranged into twenty-six abecedarian sections to match the letters of the Ouija board. For two decades, Merrill and his companion David Jackson had been sitting down to the Ouija board, enthralled by their conversations with the dead, and especially with their contact or medium, Ephraim, a Greek Jew, born in Asia Minor in A.D. 8, later a favorite of Tiberius on Capri, and killed by the imperial guard at age twenty-eight for having loved the monstrous Caligula. There are precedents among poets for this sort of spiritualism—one recalls Victor Hugo's sessions at the *table parlante* or Yeats's correspondence with his familiar spirit Leo Africanus—but it is a risky subject. Throughout, Merrill incorporates his own sceptical doubts, in order to forestall a reader's. Did Merrill himself "believe" in these voices—or not voices actually, but messages, spelled out letter by letter with a teacup's handle? At one point he is told (in the upper case that transcribes a message)"ALL / THESE OUR CONVERSATIONS COME FROM MEMORY & WORD BANKS / TAPPD IN U." And to an interviewer Merrill once explained:

Well, don't you think there comes a time when everyone, not just a poet, wants to get beyond the self? To reach, if you like, the "god" within you? The board, in however clumsy or absurd a way, allows for precisely that. Or if it's still yourself that you're drawing upon, then that self is much stranger and freer and more farseeing than the one you thought you knew.

Merrill was not aware, when he wrote "The Book of Ephraim," that it was only the first part of a much longer encounter with the spirit world, and that subsequent demands on his credulity and imagination (and on his reader's) would be much greater.

Merrill had hinted at his interest in the Ouija

board before, in such early poems as "Voices from the Other World" (in *The Country of a Thousand Years of Peace*), perhaps "From the Cupola," in his short story "Driver" (1962), and most notably in a long episode in his 1957 novel *The Seraglio*. But in "The Book of Ephraim" we have the whole story. Its telling transpires over the course of a year (1974) which includes both the events of the composition itself and the odd coincidences of a novel, now lost, that Merrill had planned to write—as well as the revelations Merrill and Jackson entertained throughout the twenty years that they used the board. The story began in 1955, when "We had each other for communication / And all the rest. The stage was set for Ephraim." Slowly the formula of the Other World is divulged, a scheme not dissimilar to Orphic, Platonic, or Vedic analogues. This formula holds that, while alive, each of us is the representative of a patron beyond, who attends to us only when, after death, we are recycled into other lives—"the quick seamless change of body-stocking"—which recurs until we are sufficiently purged of life to begin the divine nine-stage ascent, where we assume the age "AT WHICH IT FIRST SEEMS CREDIBLE TO DIE" and, patrons now ourselves, rise in station through degrees of "PEACE FROM REPRESENTATION." None of this becomes dogmatic, as Ephraim tells them, "U ARE SO QUICK MES CHERS I FEEL WE HAVE / SKIPPING THE DULL CLASSROOM DONE IT ALL / AT THE SALON LEVEL." In fact, though his gossip about the greats, from Mozart to Montezuma, is always engagingly witty, Ephraim spells out his answers to guide his devotees toward an understanding of themselves, to prompt them in their parts on the world's stage. For Merrill and Jackson, their life with Ephraim (a psychiatrist in the poem terms it their *folie à deux*) parallels their life with each other—gradually domesticated in two villages (Stonington and Athens), on Grand Tours (for which long passages of the poem provide beautifully detailed views), undergoing the difficult dynamics of intimacy, disillusion, and endurance. Ephraim begins as tour guide, and eventually becomes friend and co-conspirator.

> We were not tough-
> Or literal-minded, or unduly patient
> With those who were. Hadn't—from books, from living—
> The profusion dawned on us, of "languages"
> Any one of which, to who could read it,
> Lit up the system it conceived?—bird-flight,
> Hallucinogen, chorale and horoscope:
> Each its own world, hypnotic, many-sided
> Facet of the universal gem.
> Ephraim's revelations—we had them
> For comfort, thrills and chills, "material."
> *He* didn't cavil. He was the revelation
> (Or if we had created him, then we were).
> The point—one twinkling point by now of thousands—
> Was never to forego, in favor of
> Plain dull proof, the marvelous nightly pudding.

Two references within the poem are important glosses on the significance of "belief." At one point, Merrill reminds us that

> Stevens imagined the imagination
> And God as one; the imagination, also
> As that which presses back, in parlous times,
> Against "the pressure of reality."

But Stevens actually posits the imaginer as God, which might encourage us to read the poem as an intricately displaced hymn of praise to the creative power—at an abstract level, of the imagination itself, and at an autobiographical level, of Merrill's own. The other reference draws us still closer to the poem's deeper purposes. Later in the poem Merrill echoes the earlier citation:

> Jung says—or if he doesn't, all but does—
> That God and the Unconscious are one. Hm.

The lapse tides us over, hither, yon;
Tide that laps us home away from home.

Among the many prospective patrons for this poem—Plato, Dante, Proust, Stevens, Auden—it is Carl Jung who presides, especially the later sage of *Answer to Job* and *Memories, Dreams, Reflections.* Again, Merrill has obscured his source's qualification, for Jung himself says that "strictly speaking, the God-image does not coincide with the unconscious as such, but with a special content of it, namely the archetype of the self." Jung thought of us all as "representatives" of the collective unconscious—what the ancients called the "sympathy of all things" and what Ephraim calls "the surround of the living"—personified in the anima-figure who communicates with consciousness through primordial images that reveal as much of life as has ever been lived or imagined. To that extent, each of us contains and transmits "another world"—the dead living in us. Lost paradises, said Proust, are the only true ones.

Compared with its two massive successors, *Mirabell: Books of Number* (1978) and *Scripts for the Pageant* (1980), "The Book of Ephraim" may be seen as merely a prelude. The sheer delight the poem affords is overbalanced by the sublime instructions of the two subsequent panels of *The Changing Light of Sandover,* which complete the trilogy. But its tone, its verse schemes, its cast of characters, make it the most immediately appealing of the three. The title of the volume, *Divine Comedies,* points to Dante, though the poem's tone often recalls the Pope of the *Dunciad,* the romantic exuberance of a Byron or Auden. The theme of "The Book of Ephraim," says Merrill at the start, is "the incarnation and withdrawal of / A god." The main prop or stage for this process is a Ouija board (its arc of letters a trope for language itself) and a mirror (a trope for the self). Out of such instruments of the imagination, Merrill has made a whole world that alludes to this one, like Plato's definition of time as "a moving image of eternity." No discussion of this poem, or of the entire trilogy, can do justice to its parquetry and prosody. At one point, Merrill compares the give-and-take between realism, ours and Theirs, to the texture of verse itself: the enlightened power of art's own second nature like "rod upon mild silver rod." Auden's *The Sea and the Mirror* comes to mind as a similar, though less ambitious (Merrill's trilogy, after all, comes to seventeen thousand lines), example of a long poem whose cumulative impact derives, in part, from its dramatic variety of styles and verse forms. Blank verse, odes, sonnets, terza rima, couplets, canzones—the trilogy is a virtual anthology of received and invented forms. Merrill's particular genius lies in his use of metrics and darting rhymes to explicate his elaborate syntax, of puns or enjambment to create an enriching lexical ambivalence. His timing, his poise, his instinct for allowing experience to discover itself in language are impeccable.

In a review of *Divine Comedies,* the critic Harold Bloom said (in a *New Republic* review) that "Ephraim" could not be overpraised, "as nothing since the greatest writers of our century equals it in daemonic force," and he predicted that the poetic results of Merrill's occult journey, "should they equal or go beyond 'The Book of Ephraim,' will make him the strangest, the most unnerving of all this country's poets." But few readers could have anticipated—the poet himself did not—what came next. Merrill's association with the occult intensified; unexpected encounters at the Ouija board followed the publication of "Ephraim"; new powers were both revealed to and granted the poet. At two-year intervals, further installments of his epic poem appeared. First came *Mirabell,* its subtitle, *Books of Number,* an indication of its format which, instead of the board's letters, takes its numerals to organize the poem's ten major divisions. The poem is twice as long as "Ephraim," and more than twice as complex. Numbers play a further role in its complications. Two new major characters are introduced: the shades of Auden and Maria Mitsotáki (a friend to Merrill and Jackson in Athens), a pair easily seen as a parental couple. The sessions at the Ouija board are hijacked by fourteen creatures, who appear to the dead as hideous batlike beings and are subsequently revealed to be subatomic particles. One of their number, whom we know as 741, replaces Ephraim as interlocutor, and conducts his listeners, living and dead (the five of them now engaged in what is called their "V WORK"), through a series of seminars on matters that range from creations previous to ours and the chemical composition of humankind, to the nature of the atom, the universe, the fall, the soul, heaven, hell, and earth. Explanations are dense, sometimes contradictory, always astonishing. As a cosmogony, Merrill's far outdoes Milton's and Dante's. He, or his informants, are intent to reveal nothing less than the "FORMULAS GOVERNING HUMAN LIFE." The book is an account of these formulas, and of the receiving and ordering of them by the poet during 1976. That is to say, the poem includes his reluctance, resistance, skepticism, and wonder, thereby making of otherworldly revelation a human drama. And when the discussion comes around to manners, there is a remarkable transformation: 741 turns into a peacock, and is given the name Mirabell by his human friends. There follows another set of lessons on the nature of life and the elements. (Each of the five main characters has assumed the attributes of an element: JM is air, DJ is nature, WHA is earth, MM is water, and 741 is fire.) To demonstrate there is "NO ACCIDENT," but that everything is part of God Biology's scheme, examples are brought forward of various relationships (cause to effect, for instance) and phenomena (DNA, say, or dreamwork). These lessons are as much masque as seminar, and instruction is mingled with villanelle or ode. The poem concludes with ten more revelations, their splendor rising as (in the Stonington house where this all takes place) a hurricane rages—until, at the very end, a strange new and powerful voice commands our attention, and clearly anticipates the next installment.

"Why should we fear to be crushed by savage elements," Emerson asked in his 1852 essay "Fate," "we who are made up of the same elements? Let us build to the Beautiful Necessity, which . . . educates . . . to the perception that there are no contingencies." Nature is Merrill's concern in *Mirabell,* as history was in "Ephraim," and mind will be in *Scripts.* And contingency is his text in *Mirabell,* as power is in "Ephraim," and sense is in *Scripts.* But it may be fairer to say that power drives all three poems. In a literary translation, we are talking about the poet's ascent to the sublime: his encounter with imaginative power at its most uncanny; in Emerson's phrase, "the deep power" that is the soul's own final, enormous claim. This power can be daemonic or divine; it may sometimes be internalized or idealized, and thereby involve the self's compensatory response to loss, as it does throughout Merrill's trilogy—his greatest effort to reconcile, to bring his parental forces back together again. The stillness of the *dictées,* the occult panoply and scared precincts, passages of dread, distortions of time and space, the solemnity of "GREAT ORIGINAL IDEAS"—these all give the trilogy a faintly gothic air, and provide critical moments when the poet is, as he says, imbued with otherness. At the very end of *Mirabell,* for example, after the refrains of doubt and fear, the life-and-death issues, the poem rises to an eerie quiet that modulates from suspense to surrender. There has been a daylong vigil for an angel. In the final minutes of that "hour when Hell shall render what it owes," the sun is about to set, and an emblematic gull rises over the waters.

The message hardly needs decoding, so
Sheer the text, so innocent and fleet
These overlapping pandemonia:
Birdlife, leafplay, rockface, waterglow
Lending us their being, till the given
Moment comes to render what we owe.

The book might have ended here, its final word an echo of the word that had opened the poem (''Oh very well, then''), but it does not. The shapeliness of the poem is broken, and a new voice—a voice whose long, imperious lines we learn belong to the archangel Michael—commandeers the poem, replaces the voice of the poet with an ''epic'' voice totally other than Merrill's, and ends the book on an unprecedented high note of its own:

GOD IS THE ACCUMULATED, INTELLIGENCE IN CELLS SINCE THE DEATH
OF THE FIRST DISTANT CELL.
WE RESIDE IN THAT INTELLIGENCE

. . . .

I AM MICHAEL
I HAVE ESTABLISHED YOUR ACQUAINTANCE & ACCEPT YOU

. . . .

LOOK! LOOK INTO THE RED EYE OF YOUR GOD!

This is one of what Wordsworth named the ''extraordinary calls'' of the sublime. And it could be added that the Ouija board considered as a terrain—and it is by Merrill, who even maps it—is the most compelling trope for the sublime since the rugged mountain heights of Romantic landscape, an occult sublime having replaced a ''natural'' sublime.

This ascent to the upper case of higher meaning, this access to power, comes at a price: the sublimation of the self. At the end of *Mirabell,* Merrill first surrenders himself to the symbolic scene's sheer text, and then surrenders his voice, or poetic control. Such moments of obliteration and exaltation, of withdrawal and incarnation, are deeply ambivalent for this poet. They are both cultivated and resisted. Power terrifies and charges. Merrill's uneasiness helps shape the trilogy. Often the *telling* of the poem, both its plot and its style, depends on tones that counter the sublime, that evade or undermine it. The whole domestic side of the poem does so. When the poem's mythical undertones or divine injunctions elevate the planchette into a holier-than-thou grail, we are quickly reminded of two human hands on a dime-store teacup. Another of these inhibiting tones is the poem's psychological realism, its exhaustions, anxieties, or skepticism. And a third is the beautiful. In Merrill's case, this is synonymous with style itself, with his language's imagistic resistance to ''some holy flash past words.'' His style is willing to try on anything that fits—allusive, witty, ironic, tender; rhetorically intricate and metrically ingenious; extremely composed and sociable—that is to say, always aware of itself addressing a subject, being attended to by an audience. The opposite, in other words, of the egotistical (or narcissistic) sublime; it is a style happier with sensuous detail than with abstract discourse or hieratic utterance.

Merrill can describe his own poem (as he does late in ''Ephraim'') as continually drawing him toward, *and* insulating him from, the absolute, or sublime mode. In a sense, then, Merrill's trilogy is of two minds about itself—the poet's and the poem's. When told of his affinities with the element of air in *Mirabell,* Merrill is further reminded that his true vocation is for

MIND & ABSTRACTION—THE REGION OF STARRY THOUGHT COOLER THAN
SWIFTER THAN
LIGHTER THAN EARTH.

Yet throughout the trilogy he refuses, or wants to refuse, such a calling. His temperamental diffidence in ''Ephraim'' grows into a nagging reluctance in the face of the sublime task in *Mirabell,* until finally resistance itself becomes the subject of *Scripts for the Pageant*—indeed, its very format, YES & NO.

Those two responses, plus the ampersand that both separates and joins them, are the remaining characters on the homemade Ouija board Merrill had been using all along. They provided him with the basis for a final poem, an exploration of themes of acceptance (''Oui-ja,'' after all, is an amalgam of the French and German affirmatives), resistance, and ambivalence. *Scripts for the Pageant* is by far the longest of the trilogy's three parts, and the most resplendent. Its cast is larger, its ambitions ampler, its verse richer. The interlocutors now are the four archangels: Michael, the Angel of Light; Emmanuel, the Water Angel; Raphael, the Earth Angel; and their dark, menacing brother Gabriel, the Angel of Fire and Death. They are in service to the final parents in Merrill's evolving private mythology of the Broken Home—God Biology (known as God B) and his twin, Mother Nature, also known as Psyche and Chaos. The supporting cast includes the nine Muses, Akhnaton, Homer, Montezuma, Nefertiti, Plato, Jesus, Gautama, Mohammed, and Mercury, plus two more recently deceased friends of Merrill's, George Cotzias (a scientist) and Robert Morse (a dilettantish neighbor). And there are cameo appearances by the likes of Maria Callas, Robert Lowell, Gertrude Stein, and W. B. Yeats. Ephraim and Mirabell return, and are joined by a new creature, a unicorn named Unice. The poem, in other words, is dizzyingly crowded, and Merrill as stage manager maneuvers his cast with authority. Again, the thrust of the poem is one of initiation. A series of schoolroom seminars, and then a trial—sides taken, pleas entered and argued—argue the case for humankind, and seek to explain some of our most enduring, intractable ideas. The two main questions are put by Michael and Gabriel. Michael's is this riddling proposition: ''THE MOST INNOCENT OF IDEAS IS THE IDEA THAT INNOCENCE IS DESTROYED BY IDEAS.'' Gabriel, in his turn, speaks for the ''BLACK BEYOND BLACK,'' and announces: ''MY THEME IS TIME, MY TEXT: / OF ALL DESTRUCTIVE IDEAS THE MOST DESTRUCTIVE IS THE IDEA OF DESTRUCTION.'' It is Merrill's task to ''MAKE SENSE OF IT''—that is, both to understand the gnomic revelations and to embody them in images and meanings his readers can understand. At the very end, masks pulled off (so that we learn Ephraim all along was a disguise for Michael, and that Maria and Wystan have returned to earth as elements), there is a ceremony of farewell. A mirror is broken into a bowl of water.

Giving up its whole
Lifetime of images, the mirror utters

A little treble shriek and rides the flood
Or tinkling mini-waterfall through wet
Blossoms to lie—and look, the sun has set—
In splinters apt, from now on, to draw blood,

Each with its scimitar or bird-beak shape
Able, days hence, aglitter in the boughs
Or face-down, black on soil beneath, to rouse
From its deep swoon the undestroyed heartscape

—Then silence. The champagne.
And should elsewhere
Broad wings revolve a horselike form into
One Creature upward-shining brief as dew,
Swifter than bubbles in wine, through evening air

Up, far up, O whirling point of Light—:

In 1982, the three poems were combined into a single long work, now called *The Changing Light of Sandover*. This collected edition was awarded the National Book Critics Circle Prize for that year. To the existing long poems was added a thirty-page coda called ''The Higher Keys,'' a poem that continues and (again) revises the revelations, adds five ceremonies of rebirth for one character, and concludes with an extraordinary section in which the characters all gather to hear the poet read aloud his now completed epic. That all this transpires in "the old ballroom of the Broken Home" is a tribute to the autobiographical impulses that underlie Merrill's vast poem. His effort all along has been less to explain than to reconcile—contending powers, conflicting views. Also in 1982, Merrill's publisher issued a collection of selected poems, *From the First Nine: Poems 1946–1976,* so that it was possible to see, in the nine hundred pages of these two books, the thematic consistency and stylistic bravura of an entire career.

Since then, Merrill has published two more collections. *Late Settings* (1985) seems a little overshadowed by the trilogy. It gathers together a number of smaller poems Merrill had written before and during the trilogy's composition, and adds several longish poems to them; but much of the work is devoted to the same concerns the poet had been exploring over the Ouija board. Poems of reminiscence, such as "The School Play" and "Days of 1941 and '44," have an autumnal plangency. Other poems—"Trees Listening to Bach," "A Day on the Connecticut River," or "An Upset"—put on display his hard-edged, gem-bright flair for invention. The major poems in the book, however, are its three longer ones: "Clearing the Title," "Bronze," and "Santorini: Stopping the Leak." The first of these, taken up with the purchase of a house in Key West (as a sort of domestic and emotional exchange for the one in Athens), can be linked with earlier poems about tenancy, or entitlement. "Bronze," another voyage of discovery and recovery, was occasioned by a visit with a former lover to the great bronze statues at Riace, Italy, and ends with a look at a bronze head made of the poet himself as a child. Images of the self, hardening with age or in art, are given a more fluent context in "Santorini: Stopping the Leak." It is a poem that returns to Greece, and involves a disorder (a plantar wart, troublesome old memories) that leads the poet on through dreamy divagations and temporary solutions.

Awarded the prestigious Bobbitt Prize for Poetry by the Library of Congress in 1990, *The Inner Room* (1988) includes a small play (for puppets), and a prose memoir (with haiku) called "Prose for Departure." It deals in part with the death of a friend, the critic David Kalstone—the same friend memorialized in other poems in the book, "Investiture at Cecconi's" and "Farewell Performance." There is a sense in which the huge *Sandover* trilogy is an anti-elegy; the death of friends, like the waning of affections, is elided by the Ouija board trope: they are all reborn as voices, and the poetic medium itself overcomes any loss. "Farewell Performance" is a more realistic account of the poet's feelings. Written in sapphics, the poem opens with one of Merrill's favorite settings, a theater. We are at a ballet performance—one of Kalstone's favorite pastimes. The fairy-tale transformation of the straw of experience into the gold of art informs this first section, which begins with a truism to be tested:

Art. It cures affliction. As lights go down and
Maestro lifts his wand, the unfailing sea change
starts within us. Limber alembics once more
make of the common

lot a pure brief gold. At the end our bravos
call them back, sweat-soldered and leotarded,
back, again back—anything not to face the
fact that it's over.

The ghosts of these memories return to haunt another sort of ceremony. When the poet describes scattering his friend's ashes at sea, he notices "the gruel of selfhood / taking manlike shape for one last jeté on / ghostly—wait, ah!—point into darkness vanished." And when the poem returns at the end to its opening conceit, the tone has changed. The very distance at which art keeps us from the stark realities of loss is abruptly foreshortened, and the poem concludes on a rare, stricken note:

Back they come. How you would have loved it. We in
turn have risen. Pity and terror done with,
programs furled, lips parted, we jostle forward
eager to hail them,

more, to join the troupe—will a friend enroll us
one fine day? Strange, though. For up close their magic
self-destructs. Pale, dripping, with downcast eyes they've
seen where it led you.

This sense of loss is offset elsewhere in the collection by poems of new love and travel. "A Room at the Heart of Things," for instance, and "Walks in Rome" lightly or mysteriously take up the burden of "actor and lover." Merrill's verse here demonstrates an easy mastery, but he continues to place new demands upon it, "Raw luster, rendering its human guise." "Morning Glory" and "Losing the Marbles" are further examples of Merrill's specialty, the diversified poem of middle length. The first has to do with renewal, the second with age. Though he mocks here his own decline ("Long work of knowing and hard play of wit / Take their toll like any virus."), Merrill has all along been celebrating his losses, turning their leaden echo into poetic gold. One section of "Losing the Marble" offers us the sapphic fragments of a poem left out in the rain, and effaced by the storm. Two sections later, the poem is restored, surprisingly different from what we might have expected it to be. Its conclusion, though, comes as no surprise to the reader attentive to Merrill's abiding themes:

> Humbly our old poets knew to make wanderings into
> homecomings of a sort—harbor, palace, temple, all
> having been quarried out of those blue foothills
> no further off, these last clear autumn days, than infancy.

Selected Bibliography

WORKS OF JAMES MERRILL

POETRY

Jim's Book: A Collection of Poems and Short Stories. New York: privately printed, 1942.

The Black Swan. Athens: Icaros, 1946.

First Poems. New York: Knopf, 1951.

The Country of a Thousand Years of Peace. New York: Knopf, 1959; rev. ed., New York: Atheneum, 1970.

Water Street. New York: Atheneum, 1962.

Nights and Days. New York: Atheneum, 1966.

The Fire Screen. New York: Atheneum, 1969.

Braving the Elements. New York: Atheneum, 1972.

The Yellow Pages. Cambridge, Mass.: Temple Bar Bookshop, 1974.

Divine Comedies. New York: Atheneum, 1976.

Mirabell: Books of Number. New York: Atheneum, 1978.

Scripts for the Pageant. New York: Atheneum, 1980.

The Changing Light at Sandover. New York: Atheneum, 1982.

From the First Nine: Poems 1946–1976. New York: Atheneum, 1982.

Late Settings: Poems. New York: Atheneum, 1985.

The Inner Room. New York: Knopf, 1988.

NOVELS

The Seraglio. New York: Knopf, 1957.

The (Diblos) Notebook. New York: Atheneum, 1965.

PLAYS

The Immortal Husband. In *Playbook: Five Plays for a New Theatre.* New York: New Directions, 1956. First produced in New York in 1955.

The Bait. In *Artists' Theatre: Four Plays.* Edited by Herbert Machiz. New York: Grove Press, 1960. First produced in New York in 1953.

PROSE

Recitative. Edited and with an introduction by J. D. McClatchy. San Francisco: North Point Press, 1986. Essays, interviews, and short stories, including "Driver."

BIBLIOGRAPHIES

Hagstrom, Jack W. C., and George Bixby. "James Merrill: A Bibliographical Checklist." *American Book Collector,* NS, 4:34–47 (November/ December 1983).

Hall, Holly. *James Merrill, Poet.* St. Louis, Mo.: Washington University, 1985. Catalog of exhibit drawn from the extensive collection of Merrill papers and manuscripts in the Modern Literature Collection of Washington University Libraries.

BIOGRAPHICAL AND CRITICAL STUDIES

Baird, James. "James Merrill's Sound of Feeling: Language and Music." *Southwest Review,* 74:361–377 (Summer 1989).

Bloom, Harold, ed. *James Merrill.* New York: Chelsea House, 1985.

Gardner, Thomas. *Discovering Ourselves in Whitman: The Contemporary American Long Poem.* Urbana: University of Illinois Press, 1989.

Howard, Richard: "James Merrill." In his *Alone with America,* rev. ed. New York: Atheneum, 1980.

Keller, Lynn. *Re-making It New: Contemporary American Poetry and the Modernist Tradition.* Cambridge: Cambridge University Press, 1987.

Labrie, Ross. *James Merrill.* Boston: Twayne, 1982.

———. "James Merrill at Home: An Interview," *Arizona Quarterly,* 38:19–36 (Spring 1982).

Lehman, David, and Charles Berger, eds. *James Merrill: Essays in Criticism.* Ithaca, N.Y.: Cornell University Press, 1983.

Materer, Timothy. "Death and Alchemical Transformation in James Merrill's *The Changing Light at Sandover.*" *Contemporary Literature,* 29:82–104 (Spring 1988).

McManus, Kevin and Bruce Hainley, eds. James Merrill Special Issue, *Verse,* 5 (July 1988). Essays by George Bradley, Amy Clampitt, Alfred Corn, Richard A. Grusin, J. D. McClatchy, Robert Polito, and Stephen Sandy.

Moffett, Judith. *James Merrill: An Introduction to the Poetry.* New York: Columbia University Press, 1984.

Perkins, David. "The Achievement of James Merrill." In his *A History of Modern Poetry: Modernism and After.* Cambridge, Mass.: Harvard University Press, 1987.

Sloss, Henry. "James Merrill's *The Book of Ephraim.*" *Shenandoah,* 27:63–91 (Summer 1976), and 28:83–110 (Fall 1976).

Spiegelman, Willard. "The Sacred Books of James Merrill." In his *The Didactic Muse: Scenes of Instruction in Contemporary American Poetry.* Princeton, N.J.: Princeton University Press, 1989.

Vendler, Helen. "James Merrill." In her *Part of Nature, Part of Us: Modern American Poets.* Cambridge, Mass.: Harvard University Press, 1980.

———. "James Merrill." In *The Music of What Happens: Poems, Poets, Critics.* Cambridge, Mass.: Harvard University Press, 1988.

Yenser, Stephen. *The Consuming Myth: The Work of James Merrill.* Cambridge, Mass.: Harvard University Press, 1987.

Zimmerman, Lee. "Against Apocalypse: Politics and James Merrill's *The Changing Light at Sandover.*" *Contemporary Literature,* 30:370–386 (Fall 1989).

—J. D. McCLATCHY

W. S. Merwin

1927–

ALTHOUGH W. S. MERWIN has written successfully in several genres, he has published more than twelve volumes of poetry, the first of which, *A Mask for Janus* (1952), was chosen for the Yale Younger Poets series. *The Carrier of Ladders* (1970), his seventh book of poetry, won the Pulitzer Prize in 1971. Merwin's poetry is rooted in both American history and American literary tradition, and in it his readers have discovered a profound expression of the post–World War II literary imagination. While readers have often written approvingly of Merwin's pessimism, they have also found satisfaction in the way he has advanced and modified the concerns of literary modernism by advancing the free-verse line while asserting a more personal, at times autobiographical, level of imagery. Like T. S. Eliot and Ezra Pound, he has spent a significant part of his life in Europe. As a translator, he has contributed much to the internationalization of literature by translating from several other traditions into English, counting among his favorite poets François Villon and Dante.

Besides his poetry, Merwin has written several books of prose, which are a mix of fable, parable, fairy tale, and autobiography, and several plays. He has also translated over eleven volumes, mostly from the French or Spanish. All told he has published well over thirty volumes. In addition, throughout his career he has regularly written nonfiction prose for leading American periodicals, including *The New Yorker* and *The Nation*.

He graduated from Princeton University in 1948, where, as a student, he became acquainted with R. P. Blackmur, his mentor, and John Berryman, who also taught there. During the same period, he visited Ezra Pound at St. Elizabeth's Hospital in Washington, D.C. Merwin was barely twenty at the time, and Pound advised him to translate. Afterward, Pound wrote Merwin postcards, saying in one, "Read seeds, not twigs" (in Hirsch, "W. S. Merwin XXXVIII"). While at Princeton, he also met Galway Kinnell and William Arrowsmith. Through most of his career, Merwin has stayed away from work in academic institutions, giving his attention to translation and the production of poetry and essays.

Merwin's best poetry is that which is driven by the combination of a desire for wisdom and a broad-based emotional force, both of which are at times historical and political in their scope. His poetry of the late 1960's and early 1970's, namely in *The Lice* (1967) and *The Carrier of Ladders*, responds to the horrors of the Vietnam War as well as to the historical and emotional assumptions about American culture that are rooted in the nineteenth century. Then, in the late 1980's, after Merwin had lived in Hawaii for more than ten years, a similar theme, embodied in a somewhat different tone, returns to his work as he bears witness to the destruction of Hawaii's native culture in *The Rain in the Trees* (1988). In much of his poetry, readers have found an elegiac sensibility tempered by a vision of what poet Richard Howard has called the "via negativa." Although pessimism is dominant in Merwin's tone, his poetry reveals a considerable capacity for wonder and a reverence for language that seeks to approach, even if it can never accurately render, the dark unknown.

Much can be made of Merwin's inverse relation to Walt Whitman, to the optimism of Whitman's "Song of Myself." Merwin has said that he simply does not like Whitman and has never been able to sustain an interest in him. It is clear that Merwin refers to the Whitman whose optimism correlates to progress and the idea that civilization in America, characterized by westward movement and by the consumption of wilderness, is destined to overcome and subdue the native. Merwin stands in firm opposition to Whitman's notions of American optimism and progress. He aligns himself instead with Henry David Thoreau, and in many ways the wilderness ethic embodied in Merwin's writing can be seen as paralleling Thoreau's. Both writers are grounded in the deep recognition of humankind's dependence on the natural world and in the importance of wilderness.

An early poem, "The Wilderness," from *Green with Beasts* (1956), illustrates a number of themes that form a consistent pattern throughout Merwin's career:

Remoteness is its own secret. Not holiness,
Though, nor the huge spirit miraculously
    avoiding
The way's dissemblings, and undue distraction
    or drowning
At the watercourses, has found us this place,

But merely surviving all that is not here,
Till the moment that looks up, almost by chance,
    and sees
Perhaps hands, feet, but not ourselves; a few
    stunted juniper trees
And the horizon's virginity. We are where we
    always were.

The secret becomes no less itself for our
    presence
In the midst of it; as the lizard's gold-eyed
Mystery is no more lucid for being near.

And famine is all about us, but not here;
For from the very hunger to look, we feed
Unawares, as at the beaks of ravens.

By defining wilderness as remote and secret, Merwin requires a reading that is concerned both with the physical part of nature, which is being consumed by human progress, and with the abstraction of the human mind, perceiving fragments of the present and hungering for a glimpse of the "secret." This view of wilderness as being neither "holy" nor "miraculous," in contrast to the philosophy claiming that God resides in the wilderness, renders a kind of counterexistence, capable, perhaps, of perceiving fragments—say, hands or feet—but not a totality of the type which would suggest God. If one could assert, as Whitman seems to, that self emerges as the summation of physical reality, Merwin might counter by asserting that at best one can perceive only fragments of physical reality, and that in hungering for totality, one is hungering for the revelation of self. It is this hunger which defines a sort of counterexistence. In a relative sense, our relationship to the counterexistence is static, for wherever we are, we are always surrounded by where we are not. Thus, absence for Merwin could be called the not-self, and it finds value to the extent that it is sought out, yet remains unknown. When Merwin points to "a few stunted juniper trees / And the horizon's virginity," he concludes that our relationship to this remote and secret counterexistence is essentially static—"We are where we always were." The counterexistence is neither diminished nor revealed; the self hungers for revelation, yet in its inevitable absence, Merwin seems to say, perceiving "famine . . . all about," the self feeds anyway, as if on hunger itself.

In the foreword to *Asian Figures,* his 1973 collection of translations of proverbs, aphorisms, and riddles from Korean, Burmese, Japanese, Philippine, Chinese, Malay, and Lao cultures, Merwin approaches the tenuous matter of defining poetry. Although he focuses primarily on those aspects of poetry that are exemplified by short, Asian literary forms, one can extract his notion of what poetry in general embodies: "an urge to finality of utterance . . . to be self-contained, to be whole . . . related to the irreversibility in the words that is a mark of poetry." Merwin has also said that poetry should center on a concern for the spoken idiom rather than the conventions of writing. This idea goes far in explaining the deemphasis of syntactic convention in Merwin's poetry. To be truly singular and irreducible, a poem may need to be marginally free from the traditions of grammar and punctuation; in this way it can be truer to the idiosyncrasies of spoken language.

William Stanley Merwin was born in New York City on September 30, 1927. Growing up he lived in Union City, New Jersey, and Scranton, Pennsylvania. Merwin recollects his childhood, which he has described as repressed, in *Unframed Originals: Recollections* (1982). His father, a Presbyterian minister, seems to be the subject of numerous poems written in an autobiographical tone, most notably in the first section of *Opening the Hand* (1983).

After completing an undergraduate degree in English at Princeton, Merwin did graduate work there in the department of modern languages. Over thirty years later, writing about Blackmur and his Princeton years, Merwin describes himself as having been "busy being Shelley . . . and a bit of Beethoven, in ill-fitting pieces of discarded army uniform" that had been given to him by his father, who was an army chaplain. Merwin knew he wanted to be a poet and was advised by Anne Fleck, the proprietor of the Parnassus Bookshop on Nassau Street in Princeton, to send some poems to Blackmur. Although Merwin never took a formal course from Blackmur, the two became friends. In a poem about Berryman included in *Opening the Hand,* the older poet advises Merwin,

don't lose your arrogance yet
. . . .
you can do that when you're older
lose it too soon and you may merely replace it
    with vanity

About publishing, Berryman advised Merwin to cover his wall with rejection slips.

After one year at Princeton Graduate School, Merwin left America for Spain and Portugal, where he worked as a tutor: during this period he tutored Robert Graves's son in Majorca. By 1951, Merwin was living in London, writing radio scripts for the British Broadcasting Corporation, including *Rumpelstiltskin, Pageant of Cain, Huckleberry Finn,* and *Robert the Devil.* The BBC also produced Merwin's translation of the anonymous fourteenth-century French drama *Robert the Devil,* as well as his translations of two plays by Lope de Vega. It is during this period that *A Mask for Janus* was published.

W. H. Auden wrote in the preface to *A Mask for Janus* that Merwin seems to present the reader with the "collapse of civilization." Yet, as Auden asserts, for Merwin "this collapse is not final" for "on the other side of disaster, there will be some kind of rebirth, though we cannot imagine its nature." Jarold Ramsey writes in "The Continuities of W. S. Merwin" that in *The Lice* Merwin's vision is one of the continuity of life, specifically of Merwin's own life as a poet and more broadly of humanity in general. In books that follow *The Lice,* this sense of continuity becomes more expansive and considerably less anthropocentric, as life is seen in more fundamentally biological terms. And while any vision of the collapse of civilization must be seen as essentially pessimistic, Merwin's rendering of this collapse becomes more generally life-affirming as his career progresses. Whereas in his early work the "other side of disaster" is most often characterized by considerable ambiguity, images of shadow, blackness, and silence, in *The Rain in the Trees* the poet focuses more on the continuity of life, even though such continuity may exclude human civilization.

Merwin offers his first glimpse of this in *A Mask for Janus,* where images of regeneration seem to emerge at the end of "Cancion y Glosa," with its emphasis on speech, breath, sight, and anonymity; an image of composing, "dry leaves in my hand," suggests that perhaps it is the regenerative process of the earth itself that closes the gaps between pain, desperation, hope, desire, pleasure, and regeneration. This process continues in "A Poem for Dorothy," suggesting the ambiguous peace of death, which contains the past. Remembering the past is an act of regeneration which Merwin associates closely with the fundamental pleasure of kissing.

Sitting on stones we kiss to please
Some stilled remembrance that shares our blood,
And warmth whose shape and name were dead
From ruin moving amends our peace.

In the earliest poems of his first book, Merwin establishes a clear relationship with another of his central themes—the nature of selfhood. In "Anabasis (I)" one finds the transformative self, shrouded in negation, always in proximity to elemental, physical nature. The poem reveals the self as tenuous, "estranged almost beyond response," yet clinging, through thought, dream, and memory, to time, to eternity. The "exhausted leaves" of poplars and beeches, perhaps emblems of selfhood surviving the transformations of time, might be burned, but would remain "unconsumed, / The flame perduring, the still / Smoke eternal in the mind." The self emerges as a shadow in a realm where both philosophical belief and religious faith are uncertain and unsatisfying. The aged man, "stroked always by / The vague extremities of sleep," is entangled in the physical and governed "by euphory and the leaves' dictions." Ironically, the self passes toward its grave "blessed, among the many mansions."

In "Anabasis (II)" Merwin asserts the theme of selfhood directly:

We survived the selves that we remembered;
We have dozed on gradual seas where slowly
The hours changed on the silence, and a word,
Falling, expired in the sufficient day.

Here Merwin explores the fullness of a questioning not-self, caught between dream and "the monstrous fixities of innocence." This is selfhood exiled from dreams of its own certainty; even though the dreams provide "rumors" of self-understanding, the self is like water that has "slipped from an escaping land / all night." Because the self vigorously seeks transformation, it plunges into the poet's metaphor, declaring, "we are tidal and obey." In this context, language itself is a small thing, failing to account adequately for experience in which finally "mind and body lose / The uncertain continent of a name."

Negation, in its relationship to melancholy, figures strongly in much of Merwin's early work. In his concern with the inability of language to reveal truth accurately, his tone is elegiac. In *A Mask for Janus,* this tone emerges obviously in "Ballad of John Cable and Three Gentlemen" and "Dictum: For a Masque of Deluge." In the latter, the narrator of the poem observes the beasts walking "beside their shadows"; rather than coming in pairs, they are observed as "wrought for singularity." As emblems of negation, shadows are the animals' "lean progeny." After the deluge, when the land reappears, the solitary man, unlike the habitué of Plato's cave, must recover speech out of its negation, silence; thus he "moves in an amazement of resurrection, / Solitary, impoverished, renewed." Yet whatever glimmer of hope this might provide is itself negated by "the gestures of time" and "a low portent of rain."

"Tower," the first poem in *The Dancing Bears* (1954), points toward both disillusionment and astonishment at the pain of separation; for example, the separation of head from body:

> I saw my body
> As a smooth alien
> On stones and water walking
> Headless, not noticing

Decapitation finally leads to ironic discovery: rather than leaves of birches or apple trees, the speaker of the poem sees green light while life's untruths are revealed in the song of the mindless magpie, mouthing the cliche, " 'Love, love, oh lover, / Oh King live forever.' " The conclusion of the poem suggests the poet's frustrations with worn-out beliefs, grounded in superstition or religion, regarding immortality. Ultimately it is the poet's careful observation of the natural world that leads him toward self-discovery. Out of this grows a fascination with mirrors and the color white, moonlight, and blindness as in "The Lady with the Heron":

> And my eyes thirst
> On the birdless air;
> Blindness I learned
> At the feet of the heron.

Yet it is a blindness teased with amazement and light, and finally, as in "When I Came from Colchis," a question:

> A stranger up from the sunned
> Sea of your eyes, lady,
> What fable should I tell them,
> That they should believe me?

Thus, in the early poems of the book, begins a major theme that dominates the remainder of the book—the transformative power of language to encompass "breath and knowledge" and the "grammar of return," shot through with "the long light of wonder," as in "You, Genoese Mariner." Merwin, here and in much of his writing during this part of his career, seems in awe of the discoveries that language can lead to, but at the same time he increasingly questions the fundamental truths which language has led to in the past. In "Fable" Merwin's language assumes an almost penitential tone while the narrator considers two heartless lovers. A somewhat questing tone is revealed in which the pilgrim prays "for" folly, as though the journey to wisdom could be navigated by witnessing the grievous weeping of heartless ghosts. In the end, the pilgrim seems to realize the futility of his quest:

> I am a sullen unseemly man—
> Pray now no more for folly—
> Who in the bleak and tolling hour
> Walk like a chime without a tower,
> Rending a story, and complain
> Heartless and foolishly.

The recognition that the quest for wisdom is futile seems to lead to self-discovery, in large part because the poet experiences pain. This pain may result from an unfulfilled quest or from losing something or someone once held close. In "The Passion" Merwin suggests that it is pain which characterizes the common, shared element of experience; the poem concludes by asserting that pain "consumes us by / Dividing infinitely" and suggesting that in the scriptural rendering of Christ's passion one might find eternal truth. Although Merwin here explores the redemptive aspects of spiritual pain, the nature of his allusions to Christianity changes dramatically as his poetic career progresses.

"East of the Sun and West of the Moon," Merwin's longest poem at over five hundred lines, follows five "songs" in *The Dancing Bears*. The songs seem to reach out toward hopefulness, but the smiles that might signify hope in "Song of Three Smiles" are rendered as the triumph of pain. In "East of the Sun and West of the Moon" Merwin retells a Norwegian folktale, exploring the self through a consideration of the nature of metaphor:

What is a man
That a man may recognize, unless the inhuman
Sun and moon, wearing the masks of a man,
Weave before him such a tale as he
—Finding his own face in the strange story—
Mistakes by metaphor and calls his own,
Smiling, as on a familiar mystery?

Later, the moon reveals a white bear, who marries the youngest daughter of a peasant. At night the bear turns into a man who explains she must not see him in the light. After she lights a candle and is overcome with the man's beauty, she kisses him. When drops of tallow from her candle fall on him, he awakes and says that he must depart. She begins a quest for the palace that lies east of the sun and west of the moon, for it is there she will find the prince. When she finally arrives at the castle, she finds that the prince is betrothed to another. The prince then requires that his wife-to-be prove herself by washing the tallow stains out of a white shirt; the peasant's daughter accomplishes this and says, "How should I not, since all pallor is mine." In the final stanzas of the poem, the moon muses about her own existence, diffused as it is among thousands of mirrors. She recognizes that she is merely "a trick of light, and tropically." Because she is a trick, she finds her existence questionable: "unless I go in a mask / How shall I know myself among my faces?" Her magic, she declares, is metaphor, and she acknowledges that the story itself, though "an improvisation," defines the continuum of her own being. Finally, she sings out to the sun to save her from her mirrors, to turn into a white bear and marry her, for she is the daughter of a peasant. The moon's plea contains an air of futility, though. Although the reader could assume that after washing the prince's shirt, the peasant's daughter would marry the prince, the poem stops short of describing the union. For such a union would go against the central proposition of the poem. It is the futility of the moon's desire for the sun that provides the impetus for the turning of the world. The poem concludes by declaring the moon an ultimate trope, or final metaphor, who in her turning creates a world of images.

The closing sequence of the book, a group of three poems, each titled "Canso," extends the book's central theme, the transformational power of language, sounding occasionally like Eliot's *Four Quartets* ("The idiom of order is celebration, / An elegance to redeem the graceless years") and Wallace Stevens' *Notes Toward a Supreme Fiction* ("Fictive, among real familiars, or / Real but immortal among the figurative / But dying"). Containing a strong sense of the futility and painfulness of man's attempts to overcome desire, Merwin's vision here is considerably less hopeful than that in either of these works.

In *Green with Beasts* Merwin shifts in style—there are fewer mythographic poems, the poems are shorter, and in general a more lyric than narrative presentation of themes is demonstrated —yet his themes are much the same as in his first two books of poetry. Concern with nature, language, and self-identity seems to dominate much of the book. Many poems contain names of animals, as the title suggests. "Leviathan," possibly Merwin's most anthologized poem, is the first poem of the collection. The animals of the book are largely threatening and destructive, as Leviathan is chaos itself, like the sea in a storm before creation. The animals occupy a place that Merwin strives to locate in "The Wilderness"—a place that is remote and secret, even if one is near it. Yet it is also a place that is immediate and present, as well as a place that is shared with others. "Leviathan" has something of the quality of a riddle, though the riddle's answer is the poem's title. The images of death that dominate much of the first two books become in *Green with Beasts* images of the unknown, and the device that Merwin uses to approach this realm is the negative.

While much of Merwin's development suggests a movement from cool, abstract perception toward a warm and more concrete engagement of the natural world, a countermovement is just as notable, as the more direct description of the concrete, natural world leads to frustration with the failures of the abstract world. In his earlier work, one can easily see Merwin's identification of language with concrete experience, thus his early experiments with style and traditional poetic forms. In his later work, especially in *The Rain in the Trees,* one can clearly see a more direct engagement with the world of biological experience; that is, the specifics of trees and animals become more concrete. But as this happens, the poet's sense of the inadequacy of human language becomes more pronounced. This linguistic sensibility is described in "Learning a Dead Language," from *Green with Beasts.* The entire poem revolves around the act of learning a dead language, of remembering it by attempting to perceive "the whole grammar in all its accidence" and of ultimately finding "the passion that composed it." Thus, the imagery of the poem is exclusively abstract.

In Merwin's examination of "the other side of disaster" the poet makes a considerable point of describing the tenuousness of existence—partially portentous, partially elegiac—which is characterized by the imminence of disaster; it might be said that Merwin writes much about the side of disaster that is inherent in the human spirit. Although his is a poetry of life that is at times joyous, the poems' tendency toward the muting of desire emphasizes the premonitory and elegiac. Such an approach deemphasizes the present and the immediate perception of self and allows the poet to reach toward the future while grieving for the past. It might be added here that this approach also suggests how the self is aligned with the idea of the concrete moment of experience having a locus defined by the not-self of past and future. This at times prescient tone creates the impression that the poems are foretelling a disaster as inevitable as life itself.

This tone characterizes the entire sequence of sea poems that includes Part Three of *Green with Beasts* and the first twelve poems of *The Drunk in the Furnace* (1960). For example, in "Odysseus," from *The Drunk in the Furnace,* Merwin extends this sense of the inevitable in the figure of Odysseus, who finds himself in a constant state of departure because

> The knowledge of all that he betrayed
> grew till it was the same whether he stayed
> Or went. Therefore he went.

Images of a sea voyage seem to define much of the early part of the book; the mariner is always willing to confront the unknown.

In "The Iceberg," the second poem from *The Drunk in the Furnace,* the landscape of desolation, "the terror / That cannot be charted," finally dissolves into a prescience of apple trees. Although it does not dissolve, "Deception Island" is almost as illusory as an iceberg, "filled with silence," a landscape of the lonely imagination of the sea-weary sailor longing for a place to anchor. Characteristically expressed as negative potential, the landscape is "barren / Of all the vegetation of desire"; thus desire is posited as the immediate relative of absence and memory. In "The *Portland* Going Out" the conversion of absence and memory becomes premonitory, "beyond reckoning," when the narrator remembers the last time a doomed ship was seen before it disappeared in a winter storm:

Yet we keep asking
How it happened, how, and why Blanchard
    sailed,
Miscalculating the storm's course. But what
We cannot even find questions for
Is how near we were: brushed by the same
    snow,
Lifted by her wake as she passed. We could
Have spoken, we swear, with anyone on her
    deck,
And not had to raise our voices, if we
Had known anything to say. And now
In no time at all, she has put
All of disaster between us: a gulf
Beyond reckoning. It begins where we are.

The sequence of marine poems in which the two mentioned above are included begins in Part Three of *Green with Beasts*. Here the sea is seen as consuming, as in "The Fisherman," where those who "carry the ends of our hungers out to drop them / To wait swaying in a dark place we could never have chosen" are depicted. As it is inevitable that the sea consumes the fisherman, it is inevitable that the tone of the poem is elegiac in its evocation of transience (the laying of wreaths on the water) and permanence (the commemoration the poem becomes): "We lay wreaths on the sea when it has drowned them." Although most of Merwin's books contain sea poems of one type of another, beginning with "Anabasis I" and "Anabasis II," the first two poems of Merwin's first book, the sea in this later sequence is itself the subject, uncertain with fog and foreboding, yet, as in "The Shipwreck" full of "elemental violence" and a wisdom so intense that it is associated with death. It is the physical embodiment of wildness, yet in its chaos it is "without / Accident" and "in its rage" it is "without Error."

Following the sea poems, *The Drunk in the Furnace* can be divided into two parts. The first part, beginning with "The Highway" and ending with "The Gleaners," is considerably more concrete than poems in his earlier books. The last part of the book, beginning with "Pool Room in the Lions Club," represents a set of strong autobiographical poems. The book concludes with "The Drunk in the Furnace," which describes how a derelict artifact from the past, possibly part of an old still, can occasionally be rejuvenated. While the mysterious drunk bellows away in the junk heap, the "witless offspring" of the overly pious townspeople "flock like piped rats to its siren." The poet explains the irony of this regeneration in the last lines, as the children, "agape on the crumbling ridge," gather and "stand in a row and learn."

After marrying Dido Milroy, Merwin and his wife collaborated on the verse play *Darkling Child,* which was produced in London in 1956. While living in Boston, the Merwins became acquainted with Sylvia Plath and Ted Hughes. The Merwins returned to England, and in 1960, Plath and Hughes also moved, and the Merwins helped them find a place to live. Later Merwin loaned them the use of his study while he and Dido were at their farm near Lot, France. From 1961 to 1963, Merwin served as Poetry Editor of *The Nation.* Merwin's poetry, translations, reviews, and journalism were published with astonishing regularity in *The Nation,* as well as many other major and minor periodicals in America.

For Merwin's poetry, the decade of the 1960's was a time of great transformation. Richard Howard observes how the poetry that characterizes *The Moving Target* (1963), *The Lice,* and *The Carrier of Ladders* is foreshadowed by Merwin's earlier work as dramatist and translator. Merwin's dramas of this earlier period (*Darkling Child* and *Favor Island,* produced in Cambridge,

Massachusetts, in 1957) and his translations (*Robert the Devil,* an anonymous fourteenth-century French play produced by the BBC in 1954; *Punishment Without Vengeance* and *The Dog in the Manger,* both by Lope de Vega, produced by the BBC in 1954; *The Poem of the Cid,* published in 1959, *The Satires of Persius,* published in 1961; and *Spanish Ballads,* published in 1961) indicate the character of Merwin's vision of human experience and of his metric. The "spooky stoicism," Howard says, of the "relaxed octosyllabics" of the verse epilogue of *Favor Island* is hardened by the emphasis put on the sea, "its never-ending finality, its irreversible otherness." According to Howard, finality and otherness characterize Merwin's work during this period and become the embodiment of "Merwin's capacity to moralize his surround, to win from the not-self an appropriate emblem of what the self intends."

In *The Moving Target,* Merwin's investigation of selfhood seems to operate on two somewhat contrary levels. First is the level of the isolated image, which is increasingly realistic, made up of animals; the natural world is revealed through sensory experience. Second is the level of the psyche, concerned in large part with memory and grief. The essential tension of the poems arises from the conflict between the two levels, which finds expression most often (as many of his earlier poems do) in somewhat of a Keatsian negative capability, as in "Recognition":

> I came home as a web to its spider,
> To teach the flies of my household
> Their songs. I walked
> In on the mirrors scarred as match-boxes,
> The gaze of the frames and the ticking
> In the beams. The shadows
> Had grown a lot and they clung
> To the skirts of the lamps.
> Nothing
> Remembered who I was.

Here is an active nothingness, a silence pregnant with unrealized memory; the poet registers a moment of recognition when the self is revealed momentarily, not as sensory experience, not as the spider itself, not as light, not as hope for the future, but as a premonition of the future projected onto the past: "Tomorrow / Marches on the old walls." The recognition coincides with the imminent arrival of memory, a "coat full of darkness."

By removing the future to the past and shrouding the result in darkness, Merwin emerges as one of this century's great poets of melancholy. It is, however, a melancholy considerably more removed from beauty and desire than that of Keats (although no less aimed at the truth of the imagination) and increasingly more apocalyptic than his own writing of the 1950's. Although explicit in the prose "Letter from Aldermaston" he wrote for *The Nation* about a nuclear disarmament protest march, the imagery of the poems, beginning with *The Moving Target,* increasingly reveals a grim prospect for human survival. In "The Crossroads of the World Etc." Merwin accomplishes a transformation of style, especially of diction and syntax, and the book as a whole finds its culmination in this poem. It is at this point in *The Moving Target* that the poet drops all punctuation, a practice that he continues to employ in his later books and that no doubt contributes to the frequent observation by critics that his work is enigmatic. Whether or not the practice is responsible for this criticism, it has become one of the chief identifiers of Merwin's poetic style. The bare appearance of the lines on the page suggests that a barren, perhaps desolate psychic landscape cannot be far removed. By removing the convention of punctuation, the poet reveals a landscape of woe, where syntactic repetition becomes the funeral march of time.

Commenting in 1969 about the nature of poetic form in "On Open Form" from the anthology *The New Naked Poetry: Recent American*

Poetry in Open Forms, Merwin said it is "the setting down of a way of hearing how poetry happens in words. The words themselves do not make it. At the same time it is testimony of a way of hearing how life happens in time." Thus, in poems like "The Crossroads of the World Etc." time exists only in the dominion of memory, where "In the mirrors the star called Nothing / Cuts us off." Time is a desolate metropolis, being ruined as its inhabitant prepares an elegy for the future:

> Ruin
> My city
> Oh wreck of the future out of which
> The future rises
> What is your name as we fall

Occasionally during his career, Merwin has put great emphasis on animals in his poetry, having planned to publish a bestiary some day. With the publication of *The Lice* in 1967, Merwin discloses his identification of animals with language, particularly insects, which take on the unlikely shape of hope. "The Animals" reflects a rare affirmation of hope in Merwin's entire corpus:

> All these years behind windows
> With blind crosses sweeping the tables
>
> And myself tracking over empty ground
> Animals I never saw
>
> I with no voice
>
> Remembering names to invent for them
> Will any come back will one
>
> Saying yes
>
> Saying look carefully yes
> We will meet again

It is, of course, a tentative affirmation, for one could deduce that since the animals have never been seen, it is unlikely that the poet will meet an actual animal, rather only its deceptive name.

This poem and others appearing late in *The Moving Target* and early in *The Lice* seem to correlate to the relationship between language and human emotion; language disguises emotion, attempting to freeze it in time, to objectify that which is entirely subjective. Although the language that Merwin evokes is tempted by personification, it finds its central force in its effort to bypass the portion of sensory experience associated with sight and transfer what energy, or meaning, one would find there to silence and the pregnant emptiness of listening. This is evident in "The Man Who Writes Ants" from *The Moving Target:*

> Called
>
> By what trumpet
>
> He leaves my eyes he climbs my graves
> I pass the names
>
> He is not followed I am not following him no
>
> Today the day of the water
> With ink for my remote purpose with my pockets
> full of black
> With no one in sight
> I am walking in silence I am walking in silence
> I am walking
> In single file listening for a trumpet

Merwin's poetry in its entirety, but especially in *The Lice,* is part of a tradition of writing about the natural world that echoes back to Carolus Linnaeus, the eighteenth-century Swedish botanist who began systematizing the naming and classification of plants. Particularly during the post-Darwinian era it becomes plausible for the popular mind to conceive of humankind not as the highest form of life and the friendly steward of the life of the planet, but as the destroyer of life. Keenly aware of the part both Linnaeus and

Charles Darwin played in shaping twentieth-century attitudes toward the natural world, Merwin shapes, especially from *The Lice* onward, a kind of misanthropy that becomes increasingly pervasive. By the time he writes *The Rain in the Trees,* he is able to assert that insects are wiser than humans.

In *The Lice* the naming of animals, along with the searching out of them, becomes a primary concern, a concern that in the Edenic tradition is closely associated with the origins of language. Merwin extends this tradition by attempting to remember "names to invent for them," by trying to recover a wisdom associated with the primal creativity of the garden. Yet such wisdom must inevitably confront disaster. In "The Hydra" the notion of naming is associated with death, as though human language, the naming of the natural world, is an attempt to keep that world from dying:

As the grass had its own language

Now I forget where the difference falls

One thing about the living sometimes a piece of
    us
Can stop dying for a moment
But you the dead

Once you go into those names you go on you
    never
Hesitate
You go on

Merwin suggests that wisdom is always receding, like a riddle with an irrational answer, that it is some sort of deity, outside of time and outside of language. If the poems of *The Lice* seem cryptic or enigmatic to some, it is because Merwin locates the poems in a realm where the words appear to have died. The poet's illusion here is that, although he cannot literally make the words vanish, he can present them in such ambiguous contexts that conventional notions of their meanings seem inappropriate. In "I Live Up Here," the poet adopts the tone of a displaced magician, a fugitive from conventional meaning and from life itself, leaning heavily on an irony that is built out of heightened cliches—"It's perfectly fair . . . I give what I can . . . It's worth it"—to parody a view of the world that is above politics and above the actual pain and suffering of the living:

Oh down there down there
Every time
The glass knights lie by their gloves of blood

In the pans of the scales the helmets
Brim over with water
It's perfectly fair

Although this ironic tone runs through much of Merwin's work, a related irony—not condescending or aloof, but one thoroughly engaging the theme of the opposition of self and other—emerges in "My Brothers the Silent." The reader may identify stars, blackness, shepherds, and animals, specifically sheep, with the brothers. Including time and "the invisible," the family of possible associations to the brothers of the title is so far-reaching that it is best described as generalized other. Additionally, the two words, "brother" and "other," are linked by a degree of common spelling and meaning. It is because the speaker of the poem believes so much in words that he can claim an inheritance, although one that he cannot have:

What an uncharitable family
My brothers shepherds older than birth
What are you afraid of since I was born
I cannot touch the inheritance what is my age to
    you
I am not sure I would know what to ask for
I do not know what my hands are for
I do not know what my wars are deciding

It is an "uncharitable family" to which the speaker of the poem claims lineage. The brothers in this poem are emblems of the knowable unknown. Thus, the poem revolves around the ironic notion that while the self finds meaning by establishing relationship to the unknown, wisdom, a kind of inheritance, cannot actually be touched. Finally, in the degree to which it employs negative statement, the poem as a whole seems shot through with the general feelings of isolation and loneliness. Perhaps the poet says, ironically, that like unrequited love for a cold family, the pursuit of self-knowledge is a one-way affair.

In *The Carrier of Ladders,* Merwin continues to use animals as guides to the deepest levels of experience; at the same time one sees the reemergence of his early mythographic style in "The Judgment of Paris" and of a beautiful elegiac tone in "Psalm: Our Fathers." When he reviewed *The Carrier of Ladders,* Richard Howard commented on its intimacy, but claimed that it remains successfully impersonal. To appreciate the poems, according to Howard, is to proceed along the "via negativa," which is the way of the visionary, although a way characterized by negative perception of one's surroundings: in this manner, the self is defined by what the self is not.

If Whitman's project was to take in, to encompass history, to make it part of the self, Merwin's is precisely the opposite; however, in order to empty the self, as Ed Folsom explains in "I Have Been a Long Time in a Strange Country," one must first recognize the elements of history which make up the self. In Merwin's work these are autobiography and mythography. It is the mythographic in "The Judgment of Paris" through which the reader is able to witness that Paris is innocent of the historical consequences of his judgment; in turn, the reader is able to judge Paris.

The central sequence of poems in *The Carrier of Ladders* is one that Folsom has aptly called the American sequence, comparing it to Theodore Roethke's "North American Sequence," Hart Crane's *The Bridge,* Gary Snyder's *Turtle Island,* and William Carlos Williams' *In the American Grain.* The sequence begins with "The Approaches" and ends with "The Removal." In "The Approaches" Merwin begins his recovery of American history. He sets off for the promised land, knowing that there is fighting going on there and that the ruins are still warm. So used to writing about the ancient past, the poet suggests the relatively recent "removal" of Native Americans. The entire sequence emphasizes the tragedy of their treatment, underlined by the irony that as civilization marches west, the promised land is being destroyed:

> no one to guide me
> afraid
> to the warm ruins
> Canaan
> where the fighting is

In terms of the evolution of Merwin's style, one of the most significant poems in the sequence is "Lackawanna." Here he merges recollection of his Pennsylvania boyhood with the developing theme of the sequence, the difficulty of finding one's self in the context of history. Identifying the river with the place the dead drift off to, and thus with history, the narrator remembers its blackness and as a child being "told to be afraid / obedient." Yet the child knows that the river is more than history; it is the truth about history, about the passing of the dead into the past:

> you flowed from under
> and through the night the dead drifted down you
> all the dead
> what was found later no one
> could recognize

From the autobiographical tone of "Lackawanna," the sequence moves forward into biography, with references to William Bartram, the eighteenth-century naturalist who wrote about the American wilderness, and John Wesley Powell, who with one arm led the geologic survey that mapped much of the western American wilderness in the late nineteenth century. It is a mark of Merwin's imagination to make much of absences, and so it is in ''The Gardens of Zuñi'' that Powell's missing arm ''groped on / for the virgin land / and found where it had been.'' In ''Homeland,'' Merwin transforms the western landscape itself into a curse on Andrew Jackson, the American president known for killing Native Americans:

The sky goes on living it goes
on living the sky
with all the barbed wire of the west
in its veins
and the sun goes down
driving a stake
through the black heart of Andrew Jackson

In ''Presidents'' Merwin writes one of his most vicious attacks on the forces that pushed the American frontier forward. Standing also as a good example of how the poet is able to turn a surrealistic tone to political ends (as is Pablo Neruda, many of whose poems Merwin translated), ''Presidents'' abandons logic in favor of dagger-sharp invective:

the president of lies quotes the voice
of God
as last counted
the president of loyalty recommends
blindness to the blind
oh oh
applause like the heels of the hanged
he walks on eyes
until they break

In ''The Removal,'' which is dedicated ''to the endless tribe,'' Merwin shifts to a more elegiac tone. Here the river takes on a lethean form, and the sense of loss extends to the ''lost languages,'' so that the tongue itself ''comes walking / shuffling like breath.'' Shadows and mourners go in on one side of the river, hoping to be healed; then on the other side ''ribbons come out / invisible.'' Immediately following the American sequence, Merwin resumes an autobiographical tone, but it is not until much later in the book, in ''The Thread,'' that the theme of history and the search for self emerges again. Here, the black thread is a song that covers the period of time's beginning to ''beyond your dead.'' Along the way one encounters touchstones of physical identity, the soles of shoes ''standing / out in the air you breathe'' and ''bodies / stacked before them like bottles / generation upon / generation.''

To be sure, in this collection Merwin seems to eschew elegy, ''The Removal'' and several other poems notwithstanding, by locating one of the shortest poems in the English language, ''Elegy,'' in the position next to last. Here is ''Elegy'' in its entirety: ''Who would I show it to.'' In his exhaustive treatment of the poem's seven words, Robert Scholes in his essay ''Reading Merwin Semiotically'' (collected in *W. S. Merwin: Essays on the Poetry*) describes the poem as an anti-elegy. Because the preceding poem ends with ''The darkness is cold / because the stars do not believe in each other,'' one can read ''Elegy'' as doubly ironic, as likely anti-elegiac as it is elegiac. So much of Merwin's writing plays on opposites, as though his works reflect one another, usually canceling one another out, pointing to a vision that is at least marginally solipsistic. If Merwin's work seems dark to many, perhaps it is because the alienated self—and for that matter the poem itself—often seems so rarefied that it stands alone at the center of a universe of its own making.

Nevertheless, like many of Merwin's books, *The Carrier of Ladders* ends with a small ray of hope, in that the poet is able to call out through history for a response. ''In the Time of the Blossoms'' reconciles, for a brief time, life with the forces of darkness:

> Ash tree
> sacred to her who sails in
> from the one sea
> all over you leaf skeletons
> fine as sparrow bones
> stream out motionless
> on white heaven
> staves of one
> unbreathed music
> Sing to me

Charles Altieri explains in ''Situating Merwin's Poetry Since 1970'' (collected in *W. S. Merwin: Essays on the Poetry*) that in such reconciliation ''the fullness of life is never far from the realities of death and judgment.'' ''In the Time of the Blossoms'' returns to a myth-time out of which the poet wishes to invoke the ''great language'' that held the ash tree to be sacred and that is large enough to describe how closely ''death participates even in the fullest moments of natural blossoming.''

Merwin's next book, *Writings to an Unfinished Accompaniment* (1973), begins with a sequence of lyrics, some of which can be read as answers to the ''Sing to me'' of the closing poem of *The Carrier of Ladders*. ''The Silence Before Harvest'' contains the idealized sound suggested in ''In the Time of Blossoms'' by ''staves of one / unbreathed music''; as a harvest poem, it, too, reaches back into myth-time, depicting sounds received from ''somewhere else.'' It suggests that the reconciliation of opposites is possible—the sound arrives as light, while the hands that play the harp are dark:

> The harps the harps
> standing in fields
> standing
> and dark hands
> playing
>
> somewhere else the sound
> sound
> will arrive
> light from a star

Charles Molesworth in ''W. S. Merwin: Style, Vision, Influence,'' however, reading the opening sequence of the book as a ''self-contained and self-glossing set of texts,'' has characterized Merwin's poetic as one ''that inevitably turns one emotion into its opposite and then is left with only absence to celebrate.'' Molesworth finds, for example, in ''Looking Back,'' reference to such an immense frame of time—from ''before the first cell''—the poem ''renders details insignificant and turns hope into something furtive and numbing.'' He points to ''Words'' and ''The Unwritten,'' later in the book, as further examples of ''an aesthetic dead end,'' citing ''Words'' as a version of Frost's ''Fire and Ice.'' What Molesworth objects to is Merwin's movement toward unbounded generalization. In ''Words,'' the ''pain of the world finds words'' that ''sound like joy.'' And in ''The Unwritten,'' the tension of ''words that have never been written'' crouching ''inside this pencil'' gives way to the supposition ''that there's only one word / and it's all we need'' and finally ''every pencil in the world / is like this.''

On the other hand, some critics, notably Cary Nelson and Ed Folsom, editors of the important collection *W. S. Merwin: Essays on the Poetry* (1987), suggest that readers not look at the books as self-contained units; rather, they should look at the larger movement of style and theme. For example, Nelson says, ''All the poems from *The Moving Target* to *Writings to an Unfinished Accompaniment* may be read as though they were written simultaneously—in the winter of an eternal present.'' For many readers Merwin's poems seem to represent problems of interpretation because the poet maintains a considerable distance from conventional diction and syntax; however, in the broad view of his writings over several decades, he succeeds in establishing a poetic that is, as he described it in "On Open Form," "something that would be like an echo except that it is repeating no sound." The poem should communicate "something which always belonged to it: its sense and its conformation before it entered words."

While Merwin's next two books, *The Compass Flower* (1977) and *Finding the Islands* (1982), are in many ways the ones in which the poet comes closest to the aesthetic he admires in Thoreau, they are also the books in which he seems to elude many of his critics. Contrary to his earlier books, these replace the "rhetoric of absence" with a pastoralism that celebrates the presence of landscape. In this way, Merwin, like Thoreau, meticulously observes the quality of his day-to-day experience in the context of a profound participation in the life of the place in which he lives. When it appeared in his earlier work, Merwin's pastoralism was often qualified by a subtle misanthropy; however, in these books human companionship and an energetic eroticism mediate the pastoral, contributing to the tone of affirmation. Altieri explains that as Merwin moves away from the rhetoric of absence and the "taut surreal logic" that characterize his earlier work, his lyrics "become less moments of discovery than examples of a faith." In this way, Altieri says, they fail to provide a necessary level of dramatic immediacy.

It needs to be said, however, that through the late 1970's Merwin was becoming increasingly interested in Zen Buddhism and that Altieri's criticism is part of a common Western response to Zen-inspired art. To appreciate fully the intensity of observation that these delicate poems show, one must remember the tradition of Japanese haiku. Dating from the fifteenth century, *hokku,* as it was originally called, is a form made up of seventeen syllables that aims at the direct presentation of experience itself. In its early use, the form introduced a series of linked short poems. Although Merwin makes it clear in his 1984 interview with David L. Eliot that the short poems of *Finding the Islands* are not intended to be haiku, it seems evident that the poems represent the same sort of union of aesthetic and spiritual experience that the early haiku writers cultivated. Merwin's attraction to Zen may be related to something that is fundamental to his aesthetic: the rendering of an appropriate interaction with nature. This interaction is in some respects different from that defined by American romanticism, which sometimes failed to register objections to the nature-destroying capacities of industrialization.

Nonetheless, the ethic of utilitarian simplicity and harmony with the forces of nature that Thoreau describes is one that Merwin obviously emulates. A similar ethic can be found in the writings of Musō Soseki, the twelfth-century Zen teacher whose poetry Merwin has translated in collaboration with Sōiku Shigematsu. In his introduction to that volume of translations, titled *Sun at Midnight* (1989), Merwin writes of Musō's accomplishments as a builder of gardens. In describing the garden at Tenryū-ji, which Musō planned, Merwin observes a combination of "a great sweep of landscape and a feeling of space with one of intimacy and simplicity." In all his teaching Musō emphasized a "vision of emptiness" that comes out of his ability to balance, as Merwin puts it, "convention and control, on the one hand, and spontaneity on the other."

In *Opening the Hand,* Merwin moves back toward the "rhetoric of absence" that characterizes so much of his work before *Compass Flower* and *Finding the Islands;* by restoring this source of tension in his poetry, Merwin makes an important contribution to his active examination of humankind's relationship to the natural world. This is especially true if *Opening the Hand* is seen in conjunction with *The Rain in the Trees,* the book that follows it. In addition, *Opening the Hand* introduces a technical device, the variable caesura, and it contains an important sequence of autobiographically oriented poems.

As Edward Brunner has pointed out in "*Opening the Hand:* The Variable Caesura and the Family Poems," Merwin's use of the device seems related to, yet distinct from, the caesura found in works that he has translated, specifically medieval Spanish and French poetry. Among Merwin's contemporaries, the caesura is also found in the work of James Dickey and Adrienne Rich, although, as Brunner points out, Dickey uses it to slow the line down and Rich uses it for punctuation. Instead, Merwin uses the open space of the caesura to create lines with patterns of hesitation. As Merwin himself has explained regarding the line generally in the interview " 'Fact Has Two Faces,' " "it's making a continuity of movement and making a rhythm within a continuity. It's doing these two things at the same time." It is, in a sense, creating a line within a line, along with the feeling of ambiguity and at times contradiction.

In the first section of *Opening the Hand,* Merwin presents a set of poems centered for the most part on the theme of the father. This sequence is especially significant because it provides a commentary on the qualities of relationship between father and child that contribute to a sense of the poetic imagination, as in "A Pause by the Water":

After the days of walking   alone in the
    mountains
between cities and after the nights   again
    under dripping trees
coming down I kept seeing   in my mind the
    ocean
though I knew it would not be   like anything
    I imagined

after hearing of the old man's   dying and
    after the burial
between rainy morning and rainy
    evening   the start of a cold summer
coming down the misted path alone   I kept
    finding
in my thought the ocean   though I told myself
step by step that it could never   be at all like
    that

Thus, it is the child's sense of wonder at the interaction of his imaginings and the actual world outside that moves the poem forward. The caesura causes the reader to feel the hesitation and uncertainty that attend the child's movement toward the conclusion of the final line. In "The Houses," the father scolds his son when the child reports seeing two houses in the woods; even as he later sees similar houses, the son passes through a period of denying both the reality of his original sighting and his own imagination. However, all the while it seems inevitable that the son's vision will triumph, and "after the father / is dead the son sees the two houses." "The Houses" points to a theme that is central to all autobiography, the simultaneity of memory and experience. Later in the section, in "Talking," Merwin addresses the theme explicitly:

Whatever I talk about is yesterday
by the time I see anything it is gone
the only way I can see today
is as yesterday

. . . . . .

I tell parts of a story
that once occurred
and I laugh with surprise at what disappeared
though I remember it so well

The middle section of *Opening the Hand* is decidedly focused on an urban landscape, although it occasionally comments on a deteriorating Hawaiian landscape, for example in "Questions to Tourists Stopped by a Pineapple Field." The contradiction between the urban and the rural, which this particular poem centers on, foreshadows the movement of the last section of the book in which poems like "The Palm" and "The Black Jewel" point to the major theme of *The Rain in the Trees*. Both poems describe a source of knowledge and truth that resides in nature; it is a knowledge of which humanity for the most part is oblivious.

Merwin's 1988 collection, *The Rain in the Trees,* uses plants and insects as its central metaphors. But the book is about language, especially the failure of language to transcend direct sensory experience. Early in the book, "West Wall" establishes a major motif, absence, in describing the disappearance of shadows and branches of a tree while leaves and apricots become more vivid. In the second stanza, the apricots themselves vanish as the experience of eating transforms them into taste, the taste of apricots then transforming into the taste of the sun:

I might have stood in orchards forever
without beholding the day in the apricots
or knowing the ripeness of the lucid air
or touching the apricots in your skin
or tasting in your mouth the sun in the apricots.

This sense of transformation makes up an important part of Merwin's rhetoric of absence because the transformation results in leaving something behind. Consequently, this process often becomes elegy, and as such is the occasion for a celebration of the fundamental tension between hope and despair. Much of the poetry in *The Rain in the Trees* carries this elegiac sense. For example, "Night Above the Avenue" links "the point of birth" and "the point of death" in an abstract "somebody" surrounded "in pain and in hope." The poem suggests that everybody plays a part in some vast transformative dialectic that defines the terms of being. The first-person speaker of the poem, sounding a bit like Eliot's J. Alfred Prufrock, sits up late at night and becomes like an antenna receiving the paired messages that make up the news:

and I have sat up late
at the kitchen window
knowing the news
watching the paired red lights
recede from under the windows down the
  avenue
toward the tunnel under the river
and the white lights from the park rushing
  toward us
through the sirens and the music
and I have wakened in a wind of messages

The early poems in the book operate with an autobiographical style characterized by a first-person speaker who at times is in dialogue with father and mother. In "Native Trees" and "Touching the Tree" the parental figures are agents of negation when they forget the names of trees and stop the speaker from entering the magical world of the tree. In other poems it is the urban world generally that is associated with negation and the destruction of nature, as in the sequence beginning with "Touching the Tree" and ending with "Shadow Passing." In some ways these poems recall the negativity of *The Lice* (of special note is the relation between "Shadow Passing" and "The Last One"), yet the later poems suggest occasional movements toward hope as the poems shift from an emphasis on urban landscape to rural, more pastoral settings. For example, in "Summer of '82" the speaker and a companion move away from the dirty streets of the city:

and in the evening we alone
took the streetcar to the rain forest

followed the green ridge in the dusk
got off to walk home through the ancient trees

Throughout the book trees become the enduring figures for that wisdom which the urban world either destroys or ignores. The poems represent a seeking out of this wisdom, while rain and wind become metaphors of the process that includes the acquiring of knowledge and the use of language. The poems occasionally call out to a muse that is in some ways omniscient, yet always close to language, to forgetfulness, and to primal origins. In ''The Sound of Light'' the speaker simultaneously hears the sounds of a pastoral world and forgets those of the urban world. In ''Sight'' the speaker personifies a one-cell organism, which is the first to perceive light and therefore the first to create sight. Then transforming into bird, goat, and fish, the first-person narrator of the poem finally becomes a generalized ''I'' seeking relationship with ''you'':

> I
> look at you
> in the first light of the morning
> for as long as I can

In later poems, the speaker seeks to displace time by emphasizing a longing for human companionship, as in ''The Solstice'':

at the thought of the months I reach for your
  hand
it is not something
one is supposed
to say

we watch the bright birds in the morning
we hope for the quiet
daytime together
the year turns into air

In this and in poems like ''Coming to the Morning,'' it is as if the speaker strives to give himself totally to otherness, so that creation itself is the result of listening and remembering: ''and our ears / are formed of the sea as we listen.''

The idea of listening also recalls Merwin's work as a translator of medieval poetry engaged in the remembering of language that much of modern culture has neglected. When Merwin writes ''After the Alphabets,'' in which he is ''trying to decipher the language of insects,'' he describes a paradigm for language that cuts through all abstraction, language that is not limited by time or grammar, and that points toward a grim human future, for after all, the insects ''are the tongues of the future.''

Much of the remainder of *The Rain in the Trees* moves as an elegy for a lost Hawaiian culture. ''Strangers from the Horizon'' establishes the point of view of Hawaiians meeting the first European ships. ''Chord'' parallels Keats's life with the removal of sandalwood forests in the Hawaiian Islands; as the trees are removed the Hawaiian language itself is lost. ''Losing a Language'' depicts the slow, almost imperceptible destruction of the native language:

when there is a voice at the door it is foreign
everywhere instead of a name there is a lie

nobody has seen it happening
nobody remembers

In ''Term'' Merwin brings a similar sensibility to bear on a protest against the proposed closing of an old road to make way for a development. The developers, of course, are not Hawaiian, and Merwin remains pessimistic, as he had been much earlier when writing about the destruction of Native American culture in *The Carrier of Ladders:*

> where the thorny
> kiawe trees smelling
> of honey
> dance in their shadows along the sand

the road will die
and turn into money at last
as the developers
themselves hope to do

In the closing poems of the book Merwin writes as if he were seeing through the eyes of a botanist. He is searching for the ancient wisdom of the natural world by engaging in the recovery of that which is dying the fastest. In Merwin's poems the act of raising plants seems to cohere with the act of writing, as well as the acts of remembering the past and creating the future, as in "The Archaic Maker":

But here is ancient today
itself
the air the living air
the still water

In general terms W. S. Merwin's career can be divided into at least three periods. During the first period, delineated by his first four books, his interest in medieval poetry and in a certain rhetorical firmness emphasizes a search for selfhood. For much of this part of his career, Merwin lived in Europe, making a living by tutoring and translating, as well as writing radio scripts and book reviews. Although his tone never approached the confessional style characteristic of many poets of the period, Merwin began writing sequences of poems that are autobiographical.

With the publication of *The Moving Target* in 1963, Merwin broke with his earlier inclination toward formalism and began writing free verse characterized by the absence of all punctuation and the use of irregular meter. The generally negative sensibility of his earlier poetry continued to expand as the subjects of his poems shifted from mythographic to political. During this second period Merwin lived in New York City, on a farm near Lot, France, and in Mexico. He became more politically active, participating in protests against the Vietnam War and writing poems critical of that part of American culture associated with progress and the destruction of the primitive.

In a statement printed in *The New York Review of Books* following the announcement that he had been awarded the 1971 Pulitzer Prize for *The Carrier of Ladders,* Merwin said:

I am too conscious of being an American to accept public congratulations with good grace, or to welcome it except as an occasion for expressing openly a shame which many Americans feel, day after day, helplessly and in silence.

He asked that the prize money be given to Alan Blanchard, a painter in Berkeley, California, who had been blinded by a police weapon, and to the Draft Resistance.

The third period of his career began roughly with the publication of *The Compass Flower* in 1977. As had been the case throughout his career, Merwin traveled throughout the United States giving poetry readings. By 1978, after several visits to Hawaii, he decided to live at Haiku on the island of Maui. During this period Merwin began to study Buddhism seriously, and *The Compass Flower* and *Finding the Islands* (1982) develop a more affirmative aesthetic, which seems related to his religious studies.

In the late 1980's and early 1990's Merwin increasingly withdrew from a life of travel, prefering instead to work at his home in Hawaii. Throughout the 1980's and into the 1990's, Merwin campaigned vigorously for the preservation of native Hawaiian flora and fauna. His poetry recovered some of the "rhetoric of absence" that had fueled his writing during the 1960's and early 1970's. The absence, as it had been in some poems of the earlier periods, is his own past, and this is reflected in the return to an autobiographical mode. However, the absence in these later poems is also associated with environmental degradation.

Selected Bibliography

WORKS OF W. S. MERWIN

POETRY

A Mask for Janus. New Haven: Yale University Press, 1952.

The Dancing Bears. New Haven: Yale University Press, 1954.

Green with Beasts. New York: Knopf, 1956.

The Drunk in the Furnace. New York: Macmillan, 1960.

The Moving Target. New York: Atheneum, 1963.

The Lice. New York: Atheneum, 1967.

The Carrier of Ladders. New York: Atheneum, 1970.

Writings to an Unfinished Accompaniment. New York: Atheneum, 1973.

The First Four Books of Poems. New York: Atheneum, 1975. Collects *A Mask for Janus, The Dancing Bears, Green with Beasts,* and *The Drunk in the Furnace.*

The Compass Flower. New York: Atheneum, 1977.

Finding the Islands. San Francisco: North Point Press, 1982.

Opening the Hand. New York: Atheneum, 1983.

The Rain in the Trees. New York: Knopf, 1988.

Selected Poems. New York: Atheneum, 1988.

PROSE

The Miner's Pale Children. New York: Atheneum, 1970.

A New Right Arm. Albuquerque, N. Mex.: Road Runner Press, 1970.

"On Being Awarded the Pulitzer Prize." In *New York Review of Books,* 16:41 (June 3, 1971).

"On Open Form." In *The New Naked Poetry.* Edited by Stephen Berg and Robert Mezey. Indianapolis: Bobbs-Merrill, 1976. Pp. 276–278. Also in *Regions of Memory: Uncollected Prose,* 1949–1982. Edited by Ed Folsom and Cary Nelson. Urbana: University of Illinois Press, 1987. Pp. 298–300.

Houses and Travellers. New York: Atheneum, 1977.

Unframed Originals: Recollections. New York: Atheneum, 1982.

Regions of Memory: Uncollected Prose, 1949–1982. Edited by Ed Folsom and Cary Nelson. Urbana: University of Illinois Press, 1987.

DRAMA

Rumpelstiltskin. BBC television production, 1951.

Pageant of Cain. BBC Third Programme, 1952.

Huckleberry Finn. BBC television production, 1953.

Darkling Child. Arts Theatre production, London, England, 1956.

Favor Island. Cambridge, Massachusetts: Poets' Theater production, 1957. BBC Third Programme, 1958. Act I appears in *New World Writing,* 12:154. (1957).

The Guilded West. Coventry, England: Belgrade Theatre production, 1961.

TRANSLATED WORKS

Robert the Devil. BBC Third Programme, 1954; Iowa City, Iowa: Windhover Press, 1981.

Punishment Without Vengeance [Lope de Vega]. BBC production, 1954.

The Dog in the Manger [Lope de Vega]. BBC production, 1954.

The Poem of the Cid [*El poema del mio Cid*]. New York: Las Americas, 1959; New York: New American Library, 1962, 1975.

The Satires of Persius. Bloomington: Indiana University Press, 1961; Port Washington, New York: Kennikat Press, 1973.

Spanish Ballads. New York: Doubleday, 1961.

The Life of Lazarillo de Tormes: His Fortunes and Adversities. New York: Doubleday, 1962.

The Song of Roland. In *Medieval Epics.* New York: Modern Library, 1963; Vintage, 1970.

Yerma [Federico García Lorca]. Lincoln Center production, New York, 1966.

Selected Translations 1948–1968. New York: Atheneum, 1969.

Twenty Love Poems and a Song of Despair [Pablo Neruda]. London: Cape, 1969; New York: Grossman, 1969; Penguin, 1976.

Products of the Perfected Civilization: Selected Writings of Chamfort [Sebastien-Roch-Nicholas Chamfort]. New York: Macmillan, 1969; San Francisco: North Point Press, 1984.

Voices [Antonio Porchia]. Chicago: Follett, 1969.

Transparence of the World: Poems by Jean Follain. New York: Atheneum, 1969.

Asian Figures. New York: Atheneum, 1973. Proverbs, aphorisms, and riddles from various Asian cultures.

Osip Mandelstam: Selected Poems. New York: Atheneum, 1974. Translated with Clarence Brown.

Sanskrit Love Poetry. New York: Columbia University Press, 1977. Translated with J. Moussaieff Masson. Reprinted as *The Peacock's Egg: Love Poems from Ancient India*. San Francisco: North Point Press, 1981.

Vertical Poetry [Robert Juarroz]. Santa Cruz, Calif.: Kayak, 1977.

Euripides: Iphigeneia at Aulis. New York: Oxford University Press, 1978. Translated with George E. Dimock, Jr.

Selected Translations 1968–1978. New York: Atheneum, 1979.

Four French Plays. New York: Atheneum, 1985. Includes *Robert the Devil;* Alain-René Lesage's *The Rival of His Master* and *Turcaret;* and Pierre de Marivaux's *The False Confessions*.

From the Spanish Morning. New York: Atheneum, 1985. Includes *Spanish Ballads;* Lope de Rueda's *Eufemia;* and *The Life of Lazarillo de Tormes*.

Soseki, Musō. *Sun at Midnight: Poems and Sermons*. San Francisco: North Point Press, 1989. Translated with Sōiku Shigematsu.

BIOGRAPHICAL AND CRITICAL STUDIES

Altieri, Charles. "Situating Merwin's Poetry Since 1970." In *W. S. Merwin: Essays on the Poetry*. Edited by Cary Nelson and Ed Folsom. Urbana: University of Illinois Press, 1987. Pp. 159–197.

Brunner, Edward. "*Opening the Hand:* The Variable Caesura and the Family Poems." In *W. S. Merwin: Essays on the Poetry*. Edited by Cary Nelson and Ed Folsom. Urbana: University of Illinois Press, 1987. Pp. 276–295.

Christhilf, Mark. *W. S. Merwin the Mythmaker*. Columbia: University of Missouri Press, 1986.

Clark, Tom. *The Great Naropa Poetry Wars*. Santa Barbara, Calif.: Cadmus Editions, 1980.

Davis, Cheri. *W. S. Merwin*. Boston: Twayne, 1981.

Folsom, Ed. " 'I Have Been a Long Time in a Strange Country': W. S. Merwin and America." In *W. S. Merwin: Essays on the Poetry*. Edited by Cary Nelson and Ed Folsom. Urbana: University of Illinois Press, 1987. Pp. 224–249.

Howard, Richard. "W. S. Merwin." In his *Alone with America*. Enlarged edition. New York: Atheneum, 1980. Pp. 412–449.

Molesworth, Charles. "W. S. Merwin: Style, Vision, Influence." In *W. S. Merwin: Essays on Poetry*. Edited by Cary Nelson and Ed Folsom. Urbana: University of Illinois Press, 1987. Pp. 145–158.

Nelson, Cary. "The Resources of Failure: W. S. Merwin's Deconstructive Career." *Boundary*, 2:573–598. (Winter 1977). Revised version in *W. S. Merwin: Essays on the Poetry*. Edited by Cary Nelson and Ed Folsom. Urbana: University of Illinois Press, 1987.

Nelson, Cary, and Ed Folsom, eds. *W. S. Merwin: Essays on the Poetry*. Urbana: University of Illinois Press, 1987. This volume contains an extensive bibliography of Merwin's collected and uncollected works through 1985 and an excellent summary of the contents of the W. S. Merwin Archive at the University of Illinois at Urbana-Champaign.

Ramsey, Jarold. "The Continuities of W. S. Merwin: 'What Has Escaped Us We bring with Us.' " *Massachusetts Review*, 14:569–590 (1973). Also in *W. S. Merwin: Essays on the Poetry*. Edited by Cary Nelson and Ed Folsom. Urbana: University of Illinois Press.

Scholes, Robert. "Semiotics of the Poetic Text." In his *Semiotics and Interpretation*. New Haven: Yale University Press, 1982. Pp. 37–56. Also in *W. S. Merwin: Essays on the Poetry*. Edited by Cary Nelson and Ed Folsom. Urbana: University of Illinois Press, 1987.

INTERVIEWS

"A Conversation with W. S. Merwin." *Audience*, 4:4–6 (1956).

Clifton, Michael. "W. S. Merwin: An Interview." *American Poetry Review*, 12:17–22 (July/August 1983).

Eliot, David L. "An Interview with W. S. Merwin." *Contemporary Literature*, 29:1–25 (Spring 1988). A 1984 interview.

Folsom, Ed, and Cary Nelson. " 'Fact Has Two Faces': Interview." In W. S. Merwin, *Regions of Memory: Uncollected Prose*. Edited by Cary Nelson and Ed Folsom. Urbana: University of Illinois Press, 1987. Pp. 320–361.

Gerber, Philip L., and Robert J. Gemmett. " 'Tireless Quest': A Conversation with W. S. Merwin." *English Record*, 19:9–18 (February 1969).

Hirsch, Edward. "The Art of Poetry XXXVIII: W. S.

Merwin.'' *The Paris Review,* 29:56–81 (Spring 1987).

Jackson, Richard. ''Unnaming the Myths.'' In his *Acts of Mind: Conversations with Contemporary Poets*. University of Alabama Press, 1983. Pp. 48–52.

MacShane, Frank. ''A Portrait of W. S. Merwin.'' *Shenandoah,* 21:3–14 (Winter 1970).

Myers, Jack, and Michael Simms. ''Possibilities of the Unknown: Conversations with W. S. Merwin.'' *Southwest Review,* 68:164–180 (Spring 1983).

Ossman, David. ''W. S. Merwin.'' In his *The Sullen Art*. New York: Corinth Books, 1967. Pp. 65–72.

Pettit, Michael. ''W. S. Merwin: An Interview.'' *Black Warrior Review,* 8:7–20 (Spring 1982).

—*JIM KRAUS*

Toni Morrison

1931–

Toni Morrison was born Chloe Anthony Wofford on February 18, 1931, in the poor, multiracial steel town of Lorain, Ohio. She was one of four children of Ramah Willis Wofford, a homemaker who sang in the church choir, and of George Wofford, who held a variety of jobs, including car washer, steel mill welder, and road construction and shipyard worker.

From her parents and grandparents Morrison received a legacy of resistance to oppression and exploitation as well as an appreciation of African American folklore and cultural practices. Her maternal grandparents emigrated from Alabama to Ohio in hopes of leaving racism and poverty behind and finding greater opportunities for their children. Her father likewise left Georgia to escape the racial violence that was rampant there. Morrison often tells the story of her mother's letter to Franklin D. Roosevelt protesting the maggot-infested flour that was given to her family during a time when they received public assistance.

Despite these struggles, Morrison recalls the ubiquitousness of African American cultural rituals in her childhood and adolescence; the music, folklore, ghost stories, dreams, signs, and visitations that are so vividly evoked in her fiction have been prevalent and empowering forces throughout her life.

The influence of these presences in her early life informs Morrison's commitment to inscribing the characteristics of modes of black cultural expression in her prose. In an essay titled "Rootedness: The Ancestor as Foundation," she describes the importance of orality and call-and-response in her fiction:

> [Literature] should try deliberately to make you stand up and make you feel something profoundly in the same way that a black preacher requires his congregation to speak, to join him in the sermon, to behave in a certain way, to stand up and to weep and to cry and to accede or to change and to modify to expand on the sermon that is being delivered. In the same way that a musician's music is enhanced when there is a response from the audience. Now in a book, which closes, after all—it's of some importance to me to try to make that connection—to try to make that happen also. And, having at my disposal only the letters of the alphabet and some punctuation, I have to provide the places and spaces so that the reader can participate. Because it is the affective and participatory relationship between the artist or the speaker and the audience that is of primary importance, as it is in these other art forms I have described.

In addition to the tropes and forms of African American cultural expression, the geography of her childhood years figures centrally in Morrison's work. In an interview with Claudia Tate she remarks:

Only *The Bluest Eye,* my first book, is set in Lorain, Ohio. . . . I am from the Midwest so I have a special affection for it. My beginnings are always there. No matter what I write, I begin there. . . .

The northern part of [Ohio] had underground railroad stations and a history of black people escaping into Canada, but the southern part of the state is as much Kentucky as there is, complete with cross burnings. Ohio is a curious juxtaposition of what was ideal in this country and what was base. It was also a Mecca for black people; they came to the mills and plants because Ohio offered the possibility of a good life, the possibility of freedom, even though there were some terrible obstacles. Ohio also offers an escape from stereotyped black settings. It is neither plantation nor ghetto.

Literature was an important presence in Morrison's childhood and youth. She was the only child in her first grade class who knew how to read when she entered school. As an adolescent she read widely in a variety of literary traditions, counting the classic Russian novelists, Flaubert, and Jane Austen among her favorites. However, she was not exposed to the work of previous generations of black women writers until adulthood. Her delayed introduction to the work of those earlier writers does not, to her mind, mean that she writes outside that tradition. Rather, the connections between her work and theirs confirms her notion that African American women writers represent their characters and landscapes in certain specific, identifiable ways. She remarked in a conversation with Gloria Naylor:

[People] who are trying to show certain kinds of connections between myself and Zora Neale Hurston are always dismayed and disappointed in me because I hadn't read Zora Neale Hurston except for one little short story before I began to write. I hadn't read her until after I had written. . . . [The] fact that I had never read Zora Neale Hurston and wrote *The Bluest Eye* and *Sula* anyway means that the tradition really exists. You know, if I had read her, then you could say that I consciously was following in the footsteps of her, but the fact that I never read her and still there may be whatever they're finding, similarities and dissimilarities, whatever such critics do, makes the cheese more binding, not less, because it means that the world as perceived by black women at certain times does exist, however they treat it and whatever they select out of it to record, there is that.

Susan L. Blake quotes Morrison's remark that although the books she read in her youth "were not written for a little black girl in Lorain, Ohio . . . they spoke to me out of their own specificity." During those years Morrison had hopes of becoming a dancer; nevertheless, her early reading later inspired her "to capture that same specificity about the nature and feeling of the culture I grew up in."

After graduating with honors from Lorain High School, Morrison attended Howard University, from which she graduated in 1953 with a major in English and a minor in classics. She describes the Howard years, during which she changed her name to Toni, with some measure of ambivalence. Evidently she was disappointed with the atmosphere at the university, which, she has said, "was about getting married, buying clothes and going to parties. It was also about being cool, loving Sarah Vaughan (who only moved her hand a little when she sang) and MJQ [the Modern Jazz Quartet]." To offset the influence of these sorts of preoccupations, she became involved in the Howard University Players and traveled with a student–faculty repertory troupe that took plays on tour throughout the South during the summers. As Blake suggests, these trips illustrated for Morrison the stories of injustice her maternal grandparents told about their lives in Alabama.

In 1955 Morrison received an M.A. from Cornell University, where she wrote a thesis on the theme of suicide in the works of William Faulkner and Virginia Woolf. She then taught English at Texas Southern University from 1955 to 1957 and at Howard from 1957 to 1964. At Howard she met and married Harold Morrison, a Jamaican architect; they had two sons, Harold Ford and Slade Kevin. Morrison says little about her marriage but has remarked upon the sense of frustration she experienced during that period: "It was as though I had no judgment, no perspective, no power, no authority, no self—just this brutal sense of irony, melancholy and a trembling respect for words." During this time she joined a writers' group and wrote a story about a young black girl who wanted blue eyes. From that story came *The Bluest Eye,* her first novel.

Morrison divorced her husband around the time she left Howard. With her two young sons she returned to Lorain for eighteen months and subsequently began to work in publishing, first as an editor at L. W. Singer, the textbook subsidiary of Random House in Syracuse, New York, and then as senior editor at Random House's headquarters in New York City. While living in Syracuse she worked on the manuscript of what was to become *The Bluest Eye*. In her conversation with Gloria Naylor, she suggests that she resumed work on this novel almost as if to write herself back into existence:

> And so it looked as though the world was going by and I was not in that world. I used to live in this world, I mean really lived in it. I knew it. I used to really belong here. And at some point I didn't belong here anymore. I was somebody's parent, somebody's this, somebody's that, but there was no me in this world. And I was looking for that dead girl and I thought I might talk about that dead girl, if for no other reason than to have it, somewhere in the world, in a drawer. There was such a person. I had written this little story earlier just for some friends, so I took it out and I began to work it up. And all of those people were me. I was Pecola, Claudia. . . . I was everybody. And as I began to do it, I began to pick up scraps of things I had seen or felt, or didn't see or didn't feel, but imagined. And speculated about and wondered about. And I fell in love with myself. I reclaimed myself and the world—a real revelation. I named it. I described it. I listed it. I identified it. I recreated it.

She sent part of a draft to an editor, who liked it enough to suggest that she finish it. *The Bluest Eye* was published in 1970.

Although Morrison was not familiar with much writing by other African American writers when she began her first novel, she has had a profound impact upon the careers of a range of other black authors. As senior editor at Random House, Morrison brought a number of black writers to that publisher's list, including Toni Cade Bambara, Angela Davis, Henry Dumas, and Gayl Jones. Gloria Naylor eloquently describes the impact that Morrison's work had on her as a young author:

> *The presence of [The Bluest Eye] served two vital purposes at that moment in my life. It said to a young poet, struggling to break into prose, that the barriers were flexible; at the core of it all is language, and if you're skilled enough with that, you can create your own genre. And it said to a young black woman, struggling to find a mirror of her worth in this society, not only is your story worth telling but it can be told in words so painstakingly eloquent that it becomes a song.*

From 1967 until 1988 Morrison taught at colleges and universities including Yale, Bard, the

State University of New York at Purchase, and the State University of New York at Albany. Since 1988 she has held the Robert F. Goheen Professorship of the Humanities at Princeton University.

As of 1990 Morrison has published five novels, each of which has enjoyed critical acclaim and sustained scholarly attention. In addition to *The Bluest Eye,* her work includes *Sula* (1973); *Song of Solomon* (1977), which received the National Book Critics' Circle Award in 1978; *Tar Baby* (1981), a best-seller; and *Beloved* (1987), which won the 1988 Pulitzer Prize for fiction.

In each of her novels Morrison boldly reveals the silences and undermines the presuppositions, assumptions, hierarchies, and oppositions upon which Western, hegemonic discourse depends and which legitimate the oppression of people of color, women, and the poor. Her prose simultaneously invokes the lyrical and the historical, the supernatural and the ideological; she seeks to show the place of "enchantment" for people like the ones among whom she grew up, even as she explores the complex social circumstances within which they live out their lives. She said in an interview with Christina Davis:

> My own use of enchantment simply comes because that's the way the world was for me and for the black people that I knew. In addition to the very shrewd, down-to-earth, efficient way in which they did things and survived things, there was this other knowledge or perception, always discredited but nevertheless there, which informed their sensibilities and clarified their activities. . . .
>
> I grew up in a house in which people talked about their dreams with the same authority that they talked about what "really" happened. They had visitations and did not find that fact shocking and they had some sweet, intimate connection with things that were not empirically verifiable. . . . Without that, I think I would have been quite bereft because I would have been dependent on so-called scientific data to explain hopelessly unscientific things and also I would have relied on information that even subsequent objectivity has proved to be fraudulent. . . .

The Bluest Eye centers on a young black girl, Pecola Breedlove, who goes mad because of the combined weight of her feeling of ugliness (confirmed by her family, neighbors, and schoolmates) and the experience of being raped by her father. Narrated for the most part by her friend Claudia MacTeer, the novel illustrates the destructive potential of a culture overinvested in rigid conceptions of beauty, propriety, and morality. The novel specifically addresses the psychological and political implications of black people's commitment to a standard of beauty (the blond-haired, blue-eyed ideal) and order (the life described in the Dick and Jane primer) that is unattainable. It also might be seen as a meditation upon the nature of desire itself, directed as it always is to a goal that can never be achieved.

The novel begins with a passage from the familiar Dick and Jane primer by means of which many of us learn to read. The passage teaches simple vocabulary as well as a normative vision of the nuclear family and capital accumulation. In the context of the novel the reader is made aware that even this basic text is ideologically coded. The passage is then repeated twice; in the first repetition the account is single-spaced and lacks capital letters. In the second repetition the space between lines is even further compressed and the spaces between words have disappeared. This linguistic degeneration into pandemonium reflects the fragility of the Dick and Jane story and anticipates the chaos of Pecola's family that the novel goes on to describe.

The structure of *The Bluest Eye* underscores the proliferation of stories and of narrative voices within the novel. The body of the text is divided into four chapters that are, in turn, subdivided.

Each begins with an episode, usually involving Pecola, told from the point of view of Claudia the child but shaped by her adult reflections and rhetoric. Claudia's stories then yield to one or two stories told by an apparently objective, omniscient narrator. This narrator usually recalls information to which Claudia would not have had access: she tells stories from Pecola's life that involve other characters and weaves flashbacks from these other lives into Pecola's story. In addition, in each chapter several garbled lines from the primer separate Claudia's voice from that of the omniscient narrator and foreshadow the tensions contained within the story that follows.

The chapters counterpoise a past before the narrative present, the eternal present of the primer, and the narrative present of Pecola's story as told by Claudia. The different narratives in each chapter provide variations on a specific theme; these stories address with splendid and various obliquity the consequences of desiring qualities and possessions that are inevitably inaccessible. By using this technique of repetition with a difference, Morrison reveals the interconnectedness of past and present and the myriad ways in which human beings are implicated in each other's circumstances. The form implies that the meaning of Pecola's story may be understood only in relation to broad social practices and beliefs. "Winter," the second chapter, illustrates the interplay of the three narrative voices that both elaborates upon a particular theme and reveals the links between discrete moments in time.

At the beginning of "Winter," Claudia recalls the images of security that she and her family associate with that season. Her memories invoke the presence of her father and the home remedies that kept the threat of cold away:

Wolf killer turned hawk fighter, he worked night and day to keep one from the door and the other from under the windowsills. A Vulcan guarding the flames, he gives us instructions about which doors to keep closed or opened for proper distribution of heat, lays kindling by, discusses qualities of coal, and teaches us how to rake, feed, and bank the fire. . . .

Winter tightened our heads with a band of cold and melted our eyes. We put pepper in the feet of our stockings, Vaseline on our faces, and stared through dark icebox mornings at four stewed prunes, slippery lumps of oatmeal, and cocoa with a roof of skin.

Ironically, the events Claudia and the omniscient narrator present in this chapter recall pneumonia weather—warmth that turns abruptly cold—rather more fully than these characteristics of winter. Claudia describes a day on which she is doubly disappointed; the omniscient narrator tells of the way in which Pecola is wounded by a woman she admires.

Their triumph over a gang of bullies briefly binds the MacTeer sisters, Pecola, and Maureen Peal together. Their camaraderie is striking, since Claudia and Frieda MacTeer usually scorn Maureen, "the high-yellow dream child with long brown hair." True to form, shortly after they bond, the girls begin to fight with each other. The MacTeer sisters cannot forgive Maureen the possessions and characteristics they envy: her wealth, worldliness, long hair, and fair skin. And when they begin to taunt her, she makes explicit her contempt for their dark skin: "I *am* cute! And you ugly! Black and ugly black e mos. I *am* cute!"

The MacTeer girls arrive home that afternoon and are cheered by their parents' boarder, Mr. Henry, who gives them money for candy and ice cream. For the second time that day their delight turns to sadness, however, for they discover that Mr. Henry has sent them off not out of generosity but out of self-interest: he wants to be free to entertain a pair of prostitutes. Both incidents reveal the potential for cruelty and insensitivity that underlies even the most appealing and inviting facades.

In this chapter the omniscient narrator describes Pecola's encounter with Junior, one of her black middle-class schoolmates, and his mother, Geraldine. The episode centers on Geraldine, who, like Maureen and Mr. Henry, represents a false spring. The section begins with the narrator's description of Geraldine's upbringing as a young girl in the South; she is raised to be meticulous, religious, sexless, and unemotional:

> These particular brown girls from Mobile and Aiken are not like some of their sisters. They are not fretful, nervous, or shrill; they do not have lovely black necks that stretch as though against an invisible collar; their eyes do not bite. These sugar-brown Mobile girls move through the streets without a stir. They are as sweet and plain as buttercake. Slim ankles; long, narrow feet. They wash themselves with orange-colored Lifebuoy soap, dust themselves with Cashmere Bouquet talc, soften their skin with Jergens Lotion. They smell like wood, newspapers, and vanilla.

The narrator describes Geraldine as if she were a type, not an individual, in order to emphasize the extent of her assimilation; she is so thoroughly socialized and commodified that nothing unique remains.

The ensuing flashback from Geraldine's point of view explains the vehemence with which she throws Pecola out of her house. Geraldine's adulthood has been a slow process of eradicating "the funk," the kind of disorder that blackness exemplifies for her. In Pecola's face she confronts the image of all she has tried to escape, and feels as if her private territory has been invaded.

> She had seen this little girl all of her life. Hanging out of windows over saloons in Mobile, crawling over the porches of shotgun houses on the edge of town, sitting in bus stations holding paper bags and crying to mothers who kept saying "Shet up!" Hair uncombed, dresses falling apart, shoes untied and caked with dirt. They had stared at her with great uncomprehending eyes. Eyes that questioned nothing and asked everything. Unblinking and unabashed, they stared up at her. The end of the world lay in their eyes, and the beginning, and all the waste in between. They were everywhere. . . . And this one had settled in her house.

The garbled version of the primer separates Claudia's story from that of the omniscient narrator. Here, as in each of the chapters, these lines comment ironically on the content of the chapter. In "Winter" we read: "SEETHECATITGOES-MEOWMEOWCOMEANDPLAYCOMEPLAY-WITHJANETHEKITTENWILLNOTPLAY-PLAYPLA." The correctly punctuated version of these lines might evoke the cliché of the coy household pet too finicky to play. But the scenario at Geraldine's house to which the lines refer is as jumbled as the lines are themselves. For one thing, as the narrator tells us, the cat has replaced both Geraldine's husband and her son in her affections. Moreover, the cat is central to the episode the chapter describes. Junior lures Pecola into his house by promising to let her play with his cat. He tortures and perhaps kills the cat when he finds that it and Pecola are drawn to each other. So if Geraldine's cat will not play, it may well be because it is dead.

This chapter thus shows some of the forms that overinvestment in an alien cultural standard may take. Like Pecola, Maureen and Geraldine yearn to be white. Pecola's aspirations are entirely unattainable, since they take the form of a desire for blue eyes. Maureen and Geraldine aspire to intermediate goals that are more easily accessible. But their desires spring from a hatred of what they are that is as profound as Pecola's. By juxtaposing these and other stories to Pecola's, Morrison displays the dimensions of her protagonist's condition.

In her interview with Claudia Tate, Morrison says that she knew she was a writer when she wrote *Sula,* her second novel:

I've said I wrote *The Bluest Eye* after a period of depression, but the words "lonely, depressed, melancholy" don't really mean the obvious. They simply represent a different state. It's an unbusy state, when I am more aware of myself than of others. The best words for making that state clear to other people are those words. It's not necessarily an unhappy feeling; it's just a different one. I think now I know better what that state is. Sometimes when I'm in mourning, for example, after my father died, there's a period when I'm not fighting day-to-day battles, a period when I can't fight or don't fight, and I am very passive, like a vessel. When I'm in this state, I can hear things. . . . Ideas can't come to me while I'm preoccupied. . . . It happened after my father died, thus the association with depression. It happened after my divorce. It has happened other times, but not so much because I was unhappy or happy. It was that I was unengaged, and in that situation of disengagement with the day-to-day rush, something positive happened. I've never had sense enough to deliberately put myself in a situation like that before. At that time I had to be put into it. Now I know how to bring it about without going through the actual event.

Deborah E. McDowell describes *Sula* as a work that questions the existence and construction of a unitary self defined in opposition to an "other." Indeed, at every turn in the text, Morrison interrogates the ground upon which individual and collective identity are constructed. The novel begins with a brief account of The Bottom, the community within which the novel is set. The narrator establishes that the novel is set during the moment in the life of the town when it was animated by black people's music, stories, dance, and rituals. That time is now gone; places such as the Time and a Half Pool Hall, Irene's Palace of Cosmetology, and Reba's Grill have been leveled to make room for the Medallion City Golf Course and the suburbs. *Sula* is thus situated in a place associated with change and loss.

The narrator goes on to describe the way in which the hill community ironically called The Bottom received its name. The story is, in her words, "a nigger joke." A white farmer promises his slave freedom and a piece of bottomland in exchange for his doing some very difficult chores. When the time comes for the farmer to make good on his word, he tricks the slave into believing that by "bottomland" he meant land in the hills. That land may be high up from a human perspective, the farmer says, but from God's perspective it is "the bottom of heaven." The narrator remarks that the land in The Bottom was really quite beautiful; so much so, in fact, that some people wonder if it really is the bottom of heaven.

As a tale that white people tell about black people and blacks tell about themselves, the story comments upon the history of oppression and the strategies of resistance that inflect the conditions under which African Americans have lived. It suggests the ways in which blacks have made meaning from practices that seek to disenfranchise and oppress them. Indeed, it anticipates an observation that Morrison makes in an interview with Bessie W. Jones about the place of irony in her writing. Morrison here indicates that irony defines the quality of blackness in her work:

Any irony is the mainstay [for black people]. Other people call it humor. It's not really that. It's not sort of laughing away one's troubles. And laughter itself for black people has nothing to do with what's funny at all. And taking that which is peripheral, or violent or doomed or something that nobody else can see any value in and making value out of it or having a psychological attitude about duress is part of what made us stay alive and fairly coherent, and irony is a part of that—being able to see the underside of something as well.

In addition to emphasizing the place of irony in African American cultural practice, the account of The Bottom introduces the issue of the instability of meanings that is central to the text as a whole. This introductory section is followed by the story of Shadrack, a mad World War I veteran who has lost his ability to live with the unexpected aspects of life after seeing fellow soldiers shot in battle. He conquers his fears only by creating National Suicide Day, the day of the year devoted to death to keep everyone safe the rest of the time.

The relationship between Shadrack's story and Sula's is not immediately evident. Indeed, the title character does not appear in the novel until it is almost one-third over. That her story is deferred until the reader is introduced to the town, to Shadrack, to her good friend Nel and Nel's family, as well as to Sula's own family, suggests that, like Pecola's story, Sula's is at once individual and collective, part of the fabric of the communal lore of The Bottom.

Nel and Sula are constructed as complementary opposites. Of the two, Nel is the more restrained and conservative, Sula the more adventurous. Early in their friendship, the two enjoy an intense closeness that might be read as eroticized. However, the novel suggests that the world in which they live cannot sustain their intimacy; Sula leaves town to make her own way, while Nel chooses the safe haven of marriage and family.

Both options separate Nel and Sula from each other. Nel's marriage to Jude and her friendship with Sula are destroyed by Jude's infidelity with Sula; Sula's attempts to define the terms of her life outside of communal standards of women's behavior are unproductive, and she dies at a young age.

Years after Sula's death, Nel realizes that the sense of longing which has characterized her life after Jude's departure is really a response to losing Sula. By showing the complementarity of the two women's identities, Morrison explores the creative possibilities of women's friendship. She problematizes the spectrum by means of which communities assess human action, suggesting that distinctions between socially acceptable and socially unacceptable practices are arbitrary. Additionally, she undermines the centrality of the myth of heterosexual romantic love.

Song of Solomon tells the story of Milkman Dead's unwitting search for identity. Milkman appears to be destined for a life of self-alienation and isolation because of his commitment to the materialism and the linear conception of time that are part of the legacy from his father, Macon Dead. However, during a trip to his ancestral home, Milkman comes to understand his place in an emotional and familial community and to appreciate the value of conceiving of time as a cyclical process.

The Deads exemplify the patriarchal, nuclear family that has traditionally been a stable and critical feature not only of American society but also of Western civilization in general. The primary institution for the reproduction and maintenance of children, ideally it provides individuals with the means for understanding their place in the world. The degeneration of the Dead family and the destructiveness of Macon's rugged individualism symbolize the invalidity of American—indeed, Western—values. Morrison's depiction of this family demonstrates the incompatibility of received assumptions with the texture and demands of life in black American communities.

Pilate Dead, Macon's younger sister, provides a marked contrast to her brother and his family.

While Macon's love of property and money determines the nature and quality of his relationships, Pilate's disregard for status, occupation, hygiene, and manners enables her to affirm spiritual values such as compassion, respect, loyalty, and generosity.

Pilate introduces a quality of "enchantment" into the novel. The circumstances of her birth make her a character of supernatural proportions. She delivered herself at birth and was born without a navel. Her smooth stomach isolates her from society. Moreover, her physical condition symbolizes her thorough independence from others. Her self-sufficiency and isolation prevent her from being trapped or destroyed by the decaying values that threaten her brother's life.

Before Milkman leaves his home in Michigan, he perceives the world in materialistic, selfish, unyielding terms that recall his father's behavior. Indeed, the search for gold that sends him to Virginia reveals his belief that escaping from his past and responsibilities, and finding material treasure, will guarantee him a sense of his own identity.

Milkman's assumption that his trip south holds the key to his liberation is correct, although it is not gold that saves him. In his ancestors' world, communal and mythical values prevail over individualism and materialism; when he adopts their assumptions in place of his own, he arrives at a more complete understanding of what his experience means.

Milkman's development rests partly on his comprehending the ways in which his life is bound up with the experiences of others, and partly on his establishing an intimate connection with the land for which his grandfather died. These accomplishments attend his greater achievement: learning to complete, understand, and sing the song that contains the history of his family. Milkman comes to know fully who he is when he can supply the lyrics to the song Pilate has only partially known. The song, which draws on African and African American stories of blacks who escaped slavery by flying back to Africa, explains Milkman's lifelong fascination with flight. When Milkman learns the whole song and can sing it to Pilate as she has sung it to others, he assumes his destiny. He understands his yearning toward flight as a way in which his ancestral past makes itself known and felt to him.

Milkman's sense of identity emerges when he allows himself to accept his personal and familial past. His quest critiques the faith in self-sufficiency for which his father stands. Through his story Morrison discards Western, individualistic notions of selfhood in favor of more complex, fluid constructions of identity.

Song of Solomon was enthusiastically received and widely reviewed. Its publication catapulted Morrison into the ranks of the most revered contemporary writers. In addition to the National Book Critics' Circle Award, this novel received an American Academy and Institute of Arts and Letters Award. In 1980 President Jimmy Carter appointed Morrison to the National Council on the Arts, and in 1981 she was elected to the American Academy and Institute of Arts and Letters.

The title of *Tar Baby* invokes the African American folktale that, with some variation, is told and retold in African communities and throughout American black communities, and was popularized among nonblacks by Joel Chandler Harris and Walt Disney. In the classic tar baby story, a trickster figure such as Brer Rabbit meets a tar baby that has been placed on the road by a white farmer or by other animals. Brer Rabbit greets the tar baby, and when it fails to respond, he strikes it and then becomes stuck to it. Brer Rabbit escapes when he convinces his captors that he is terrified of being thrown in the briar patch, which is really his home. He is able to free himself by playing on their underestimation of his character and runs away, taunting them.

This novel addresses the kinds of deceptions in which human beings participate to maintain the illusion of harmony and psychological tranquillity. Craig H. Werner argues that in *Tar Baby,* Morrison explores the variety of ways in which characters understand and use myths in their lives. Two characters in particular, Son and Jadine, are represented in terms of the tar baby story. For Morrison, Werner demonstrates, the myth of safety, by which characters seek to protect themselves from the complexities of human interaction, becomes a trap from which they cannot escape.

The novel opens in the household of Valerian and Margaret Street on the Caribbean island of Isle des Chevaliers. The larger community is inhabited primarily by wealthy white Americans and the indigenous blacks whose labor they exploit. The Street household is composed of the Streets; their longtime, devoted black servants, Sydney and Ondine Childs; and occasionally by Jadine Childs, the Streets' protégée and Sydney's niece. One Christmas season the tranquillity of their paradise is interrupted when Son Green, an African American fugitive, is discovered hiding in Margaret's bedroom closet. The Streets and the Childses are repelled by him, but they cannot avoid his touch; his presence forces them to confront secrets they had previously ignored. Once they acknowledge the silences upon which their complacency depends, they can no longer deny them.

Valerian has taken early retirement from his family's candy business in Philadelphia so that he can enjoy a simple and self-indulgent life on the island. Margaret, twenty years his junior and a former beauty queen, is unwilling to share his self-imposed exile, spending six months of each year in the United States and urging him to return there to live. Sydney and Ondine are self-styled "Philadelphia Negroes," a term coined by W. E. B. DuBois that celebrates their class background and aspirations. They have reconciled themselves to the peacefulness of the island, and value their security and Valerian's generosity to them and to Jadine. Orphaned at the age of twelve, Jadine is a fashion model, a student of art history, and the object of many men's desires.

When the novel opens, the family awaits the homecoming of Michael, the Streets' son, at Christmas. They find themselves entertaining Son Green instead. His presence is profoundly disruptive. Margaret's terror reflects the extent to which the myth of the black rapist has invaded her imaginative life, notwithstanding her longstanding, ostensibly cordial relationship with Sydney. Valerian's graciousness toward Son—he entertains him royally and allows him to sleep upstairs in the guest room—prompts Sydney and Ondine to recognize the ways in which Valerian has condescended to them. Son does his best to placate Sydney, Ondine, and Margaret, and to establish an intimate relationship with Jadine. However, when Michael and all the other guests fail to appear at the fateful Christmas dinner, the collective submerged anger erupts.

In anticipation of Michael's long-awaited visit, Margaret disturbs the organization of her household in order to construct an ideal family holiday. Although she entirely lacks culinary skills, she insists on fixing a traditional Christmas meal. Ondine is angry at being displaced from her kitchen and having surreptitiously to fix a dinner to replace Margaret's unfinished one. Sydney and Ondine become enraged when they learn that Valerian has fired Gideon and Thérèse, the two local people who assist with gardening and household tasks, for stealing, rightly feeling that his high-handed insensitivity reflects the contempt with which he sees them. The accusations intensify until Ondine reveals the secret upon which the Street family life is built, that Margaret abused Michael when he was a child. In the wake of this revelation, Valerian agonizes over the vision of his son's suffering, and Margaret admits the extremes to which she was driven by her own boredom.

Son might therefore be read as a tar baby to the extent that the other characters cannot escape his touch and are transformed by it. But he refers to Jadine as a tar baby as well, a figure created by white men's institutions to trap black men. Despite, or perhaps because of, their differences, Son and Jadine find themselves in a passionate affair; the very differences that would seem to divide them bear an erotic charge in their respective imaginations. Son is seduced by Jadine's cosmopolitan beauty and sophistication; Jadine is compelled by his earthy sensuality. Yet when they escape the turmoil of life on Isle des Chevaliers and move back to the United States together, each is threatened by the other's world. Son cannot fit into Jadine's life in New York:

> He needed the blood-clot heads of the bougainvillea, the simple green rage of the avocado, the fruit of the banana trees puffed up and stiff like the fingers of gouty kings. Here prestressed concrete and steel contained anger, folded it back on itself to become a craving for things rather than vengeance.

Jadine feels reproached by the communal mores of black people she meets in Son's hometown of Eloe, Florida. Her discomfort with them is made especially evident by the fact that when she is left on her own, she cannot sustain a conversation with them. She can relate to them only by photographing them, commodifying these people who are ostensibly her own in much the same way that she, as a model, is commodified by professional photographers:

> Jadine was squatting down in the middle of the road, the afternoon sun at her back. The children were happy to pose, and so were some of the younger women. Only the old folks refused to smile and glared into her camera as though looking at hell with the lid off. The men were enjoying the crease in her behind so clearly defined in the sunlight, click, click. Jadine had remembered her camera just before she thought she would go nuts, trying to keep a conversation going with Ellen and the neighbor women who came in to see Son's Northern girl. They looked at her with outright admiration, each one saying, "I was in Baltimore once," or "My cousin she live in New York." They did not ask her what they really wanted to know: where did she know Son from and how much did her boots cost. Jadine smiled, drank glasses of water and tried to talk "down home" like Ondine. But their worshipful stares and nonconversation made Son's absence seem much too long. She was getting annoyed when she remembered her camera. Now she was having a ball photographing everybody. Soldier's yard was full. "Beautiful," she said. "Fantastic. Now over here," click click. "Hey, what'd you say your name was? Okay, Beatrice, could you lean up against the tree?" click, click. "This way. Beautiful. Hold it. Hoooold it. Heaven," click click click.

Moreover, in Eloe, Jadine is haunted by the specter of the Caribbean and Southern black women who are constructed in the novel as being more female than their cosmopolitan counterparts. After a night of lovemaking with Son, she dreams that a group of significant black women from her own and Son's past challenge her with their sexuality:

> [They] each pulled out a breast and showed it to her. Jadine started to tremble. They stood around in the room, jostling each other gently, gently—there wasn't much room—revealing one breast and then two and Jadine was shocked. . . .
>
> "I have breasts too," she said or thought or willed, "I have breasts too." But they didn't believe her. They just held their own higher and pushed their own farther out and looked at her. All of them revealing both their breasts except the woman in yellow. She did something more

shocking—she stretched out a long arm and showed Jadine her three big eggs. It scared her so, she began to cry.

Shortly thereafter, Jadine and Son return to New York, where Jadine hopes to convince Son to get an education and become a professional. Her efforts to change him are no more successful than his attempts to have her fit in at Eloe; Jadine flees first to Isle des Chevaliers and then to Paris. In the Street household Valerian and Margaret seem to have reached a tentative accord with each other and with the Childses. At the end of the novel, Son arrives on the island in pursuit of Jadine, although it remains unclear whether any reconciliation between them is possible.

The novel exposes the nature of the safe havens people create for each other and the consequences of willed ignorance. It explores the variant meanings and constructions of blackness. Moreover, it considers the consequences of the mythicizing or exoticizing of blackness in which whites and African Americans alike participate.

Beloved is Morrison's most celebrated work to date. Based on the true story of Margaret Garner, a slave woman who killed her own child rather than sell her into slavery, *Beloved* is one of a number of contemporary novels by African American authors that retell the story of slavery. As is the case with works such as *Jubilee* (1966) by Margaret Walker, *Flight to Canada* (1976) by Ishmael Reed, *Kindred* (1979) by Octavia Butler, *The Chaneysville Incident* (1981) by David Bradley, *Oxherding Tale* (1982) and *Middle Passage* (1990) by Charles R. Johnson, and *Dessa Rose* (1986) by Sherley Anne Williams, Morrison's novel explores the implications of representing slavery both for the former slaves and for their cultural descendants. In addition, like these other works, *Beloved* explores the ways in which both the documentary materials of history and the free play of the imagination are necessary to capture the unspeakable horrors of slavery.

Beloved reflects Morrison's interest in recovering the slave's experience, given the paucity of available materials from the slave's own perspective. Her sensitivity to the relationship between history and fiction is evident throughout her fiction: to name but two examples, the experience of World War I shapes the life of Shadrack in *Sula,* and the legacy of slavery and the civil rights movement informs the world of *Song of Solomon*.

Morrison remarks in an interview with Marsha Darling that the process of writing the book required her to complement historical research with the craft of fiction writing; only then could she get at the story of the infanticide of a slave child from the child's perspective:

> I did research about a lot of things in this book in order to narrow it, to make it narrow and deep, but I did not do much research on Margaret Garner other than the obvious stuff, because I wanted to invent her life, which is a way of saying I wanted to be accessible to anything the characters had to say about it. Recording her life as lived would not interest me, and would not make me available to anything that might be pertinent. I got to a point where in asking myself who could judge Sethe adequately, since I couldn't, and nobody else that knew her could, really, I felt the only person who could judge her would be the daughter she killed.

Although *Beloved* is based on a real-life incident, Morrison altered the original account in order to make a political point. Her protagonist left her husband in slavery, escaped to freedom, and remained free with her living children. In the original, however, Morrison said to Marsha Darling:

> Margaret Garner escaped with her husband and two other men and was returned to slavery. . . . [Garner] wasn't tried for killing her child. She

was tried for a *real* crime, which was running away—although the abolitionists were trying very hard to get her tried for murder because they wanted the Fugitive Slave Law to be unconstitutional. They did not want her tried on those grounds, so they tried to switch it to murder as a kind of success story. They thought that they could make it impossible for Ohio, as a free state, to acknowledge the right of a slave-owner to come get those people. In fact, the sanctuary movement now is exactly the same. But they all went back to Boone County and apparently the man who took them back—the man she was going to kill herself and her children to get away from—he sold her down river, which was as bad as was being separated from each other. But apparently the boat hit a sandbar or something, and she fell or jumped with her daughter, her baby, into the water. It is not clear whether she fell or jumped, but they rescued her and I guess she went on down to New Orleans and I don't know.

Set in Cincinnati in 1873, eight years after the end of the Civil War, *Beloved* is nevertheless a novel about slavery. The characters have been so profoundly affected by the experience of slavery that time cannot separate them from its horrors or undo its effects. Indeed, by setting the novel during Reconstruction, Morrison invokes the inescapability of slavery, for the very name of the period calls to mind the havoc and destruction wrought during the antebellum period.

A complex novel such as this one does not lend itself easily to summary. It is a work that explores, among other topics, the workings and the power of memory; to represent the inescapability of the past, Morrison eschews linear plot development for a multidirectional narrative in which the past breaks in unexpectedly to disrupt the movement forward in time. The novel begins at 124 Bluestone Road, in the household that Sethe, a former slave, shares with her daughter, Denver, and the ghost of the daughter she killed. Number 124 had once been home also to Baby Suggs, Sethe's mother-in-law, and to Howard and Buglar, Sethe's two sons; but Baby Suggs has died and the two boys have run away from the baby ghost.

The trajectory of the plot begins when Paul D, one of Sethe's friends from the Sweet Home plantation, arrives unexpectedly at her home. They quickly renew their friendship, become lovers, and decide to live together. Paul D attempts to rid the house of the presence of the baby ghost, but his attempt at exorcism triggers her return in another form, as a ghost made flesh in the form of a young woman.

Sethe and Paul D are both haunted by memories of slavery that they wish to avoid. Sethe tries to block out the experience of being whipped and having her breast milk stolen by the nephews (or sons?) of Schoolteacher (her master's cruel brother-in-law); of killing her daughter to prevent her from being taken back into slavery; and of exchanging sex for the engraving on that same daughter's tombstone. Paul D wants desperately to forget having seen the physical and psychological destruction of his fellow Sweet Home men; having been forced to wear a bit; and having endured the hardships of the chain gang.

The former slaves' desire for forgetfulness notwithstanding, the past will not be kept at bay. The slightest sensation triggers memories that overwhelm them. Moreover, the novel turns on the embodiment and appearance of Beloved, the daughter Sethe killed in order to prevent her return to slavery. In the intensity of their connections with each other, and in their various encounters and engagements with Beloved, the characters explore what it means for them to confront the history of their suffering, and learn to move beyond that past. Additionally, through the use of the incarnate ghost, the novel considers the place of black bodies in the construction of narratives of slavery.

Early in her life in freedom, Baby Suggs becomes a preacher—unchurched, uncalled, unrobed, and unanointed—one who brings a message of salvation to the black fugitives and former slaves outside Cincinnati. Her message, which transforms the Christian message of self-abnegation and deliverance after death, is meant to heal the broken and suffering bodies of those who endured slavery. As she herself—with legs, back, head, eyes, hands, kidneys, womb, and tongue broken by slavery—has resolved to use her heart in the service of her vast congregation, she preaches to restore the bodies of those battered by their enslavement:

''Here,'' [Baby Suggs] said, ''in this here place, we flesh; flesh that weeps, laughs; flesh that dances on bare feet in grass. Love it. Love it hard. Yonder they do not love your flesh. They despise it. They don't love your eyes; they'd just as soon pick em out. No more do they love the skin on your back. . . . So love your neck; put a hand on it, grace it, stroke it and hold it up. And all your inside parts that they'd just as soon slop for hogs, you got to love them. The dark, dark liver—love it, love it, and the beat and beating heart, love that too. More than eyes or feet. More than lungs that have yet to draw free air. More than your life-holding womb and your life-giving private parts, hear me now, love your heart. For this is the prize.''

Readers may be inclined to read Baby Suggs's use of the word ''heart'' metaphorically, to assume that by ''heart'' she means compassion. But in the context of this litany of broken body parts, one is reminded that the word ''heart'' refers to an organ as well as to an emotional capacity. In this context it becomes more difficult to make the leap from the corporeal referent to the metaphysical; such an erasure of the corporeal may be read as analogous to the expendability of black bodies under slavery.

The variety of meanings that attach to Baby Suggs's use of the word ''heart'' questions the familiar distinction between body and spirit. This process of interrogation, by which the body is reclaimed and sanctified, is of profound importance within a text that responds to the meanings of slavery. It first reflects the suspicion of received hierarchies and dichotomies that characterizes most of Morrison's writing. Moreover, it critiques the hierarchical system of racial differentiation in which blacks are associated with bodily labor; whites, with spiritual and intellectual gifts. Thus, by questioning the dichotomy between spirit and flesh, the novel also interrogates the basis of the system of slavery.

The focus on bodies in the novel is clear both in the predominance of scenes of physical suffering and scarred bodies and in the characters' sensory experience of their past. During their lives as slaves, Sethe, Paul D, and Baby Suggs know psychological and emotional humiliation. For instance, Paul D is shamed by the knowledge that the barnyard rooster possesses more autonomy than he does. Sethe is deeply threatened by the research that Schoolteacher does on her own and her fellow slaves' racial characteristics. And Sethe and Baby Suggs are acutely sensitive to the power that slavery has over the bonds between kin. Yet despite the recognition of these sorts of philosophical and emotional deprivations, *Beloved* seems especially engaged with the havoc wrought upon black bodies under slavery: the circular scar under Sethe's mother's breast and the bit in her mouth; the bit in Paul D's mouth; Sethe's stolen breast milk and the scars on her back; the roasting body of Sixo, one of the Sweet Home men, to name but a few.

Despite her attempts to forget her enslavement, Sethe's memories come to her through her body; sensory perceptions set flashbacks in motion. When washing some stinging chamomile sap off her legs, the scent and the sensation propel her back into the past:

The plash of water, the sight of her shoes and stockings awry on the path where she had flung them; or Here Boy lapping in the puddle near her feet, and suddenly there was Sweet Home rolling, rolling, rolling out before her eyes, and although there was not a leaf on that farm that did not make her want to scream, it rolled itself out before her in shameless beauty.

Sethe's body is also linked to the past by virtue of the hieroglyphic nature of the scars on her back. She wears on her body the signs of her greatest ordeal at the Sweet Home plantation. The story of the brutal handling she endured under slavery—the stealing of her breast milk and the beating that ensued—are encoded in the scars on her back. Their symbolic power is evident in the variety of ways that others attempt to read them. For Baby Suggs, the imprint from Sethe's back on the sheets looks like roses of blood. And Paul D, who cannot read the words of the newspaper story about Sethe's act of infanticide, reads her back as a piece of sculpture: "the decorative work of an ironsmith too passionate for display." Paul D further reads the suffering on her body with his own body:

He rubbed his cheek on her back and learned that way her sorrow, the roots of it; its wide trunk and intricate branches. . . . [He] would tolerate no peace until he had touched every ridge and leaf of it with his mouth, none of which Sethe could feel because her back skin had been dead for years.

Paul D registers in an incessant trembling the humiliation he felt before Brother, the rooster, and the indignity of being forced to wear leg irons and handcuffs. No one knew he was trembling, the narrator tells us, "because it began inside:"

A flutter of a kind, in the chest then the shoulder blades. It felt like rippling—gentle at first and then wild. As though the further south they led him the more his blood, frozen like an ice pond for twenty years, began thawing, breaking into pieces that, once melted, had no choice but to swirl and eddy.

Insofar as the characters feel suffering through their bodies, they are healed through the body as well. Sethe is three times cured by healing hands: first by those of Amy Denver (the young white woman who helps deliver Denver), then by those of Baby Suggs, and finally by those of Paul D. Indeed, one might read Beloved's sexual relations with Paul D as a bodily cure. Paul D refuses to speak too fully the pain of his suffering in slavery. This refusal reflects his sense that his secrets are located in what remains of his heart: "in that tobacco tin buried in his chest where a red heart used to be. Its lid rusted shut." However, when Beloved, ghost made flesh, compels him to have sexual relations with her—in other words, to encounter her physically—she tells him, in language that recalls Baby Suggs's earlier speech, "to touch her on the inside part." The description of this scene suggests that the act of intercourse with Beloved restores Paul D to himself, restores his heart to him:

She moved closer with a footfall he didn't hear and he didn't hear the whisper that the flakes of rust made either as they fell away from the seams of his tobacco tin. So when the lid gave he didn't know it. What he knew was that when he reached the inside part he was saying, "Red heart. Red heart," over and over again.

In a number of ways, then, Morrison calls attention to the suffering that bodies endured under slavery. The project of the novel, much like Baby Suggs's project, seems to be to reclaim those bodies, to find a way to tell the story of the slave body in pain.

In "Unspeakable Things Unspoken," Morrison writes that she hoped that from the opening lines of *Beloved* her readers' experience of the novel would approximate the slaves' sense of dislocation. Of course, however evocatively Morrison renders human suffering in *Beloved,* ultimately the reader experiences only narrative representations of human suffering and pain. To speak what is necessarily and essentially and inescapably unspoken is not to speak the unspoken; it is only to speak a narrative or speakable version of that event or thing.

Beloved thus indicates a paradox central to any attempt to represent the body in pain; one can never escape narrative. The figure of Beloved herself most obviously calls into question the relationship between narrative and the body. As a ghost made flesh, she is literally the story of the past embodied. Sethe and Denver and Paul D therefore encounter not only the story of her sorrow and theirs; they engage with its incarnation. Beloved's presence allows the generally reticent Sethe to tell stories from her past. Once Sethe realizes that the stranger called Beloved and her baby Beloved are one and the same, she gives herself over fully to the past, and to Beloved's demand for comfort and curing. Indeed, so complete are her attempts to make things right with Beloved that she is almost consumed by her. Without Denver's and her neighbors' and Paul D's interventions pulling her back into the present, she would have been annihilated.

The very name "beloved" interrogates a number of oppositions. Simultaneously adjective and noun, the word troubles the distinction between the characteristics of a thing and the thing itself. To the extent that the title of the book is an unaccompanied modifier, it calls attention to the absence of the thing being modified. Additionally, the word "beloved" names not only the girl baby returned; in the funeral service the word addresses the mourners of the dead. The word thus names at once that which is past and present, she who is absent and those who are present.

Finally, the word "beloved" calls attention to the space between written and oral, for until readers know the context from which her name comes, they do not know how to speak that name: with three syllables or two. In the terms the novel offers, Beloved might be understood to exemplify what Sethe calls "rememory," something that is gone, yet remains. Recalling both "remember" and "memory," "rememory" is both verb and noun; it names the process of remembering and the thing remembered.

The reader confronts the unnarratability—indeed, the inadequacy of language—perhaps most powerfully in the passages of interior monologue told from Sethe's, Denver's, and Beloved's points of view. After telling Paul D about Sethe's murder of her daughter, Stamp Paid, the man who conveyed the family to freedom, is turned away from 124 Bluestone Road by the "undecipherable language . . . of the black and angry dead." Mixed with those voices are the thoughts of Sethe, Denver, and Beloved—"unspeakable thoughts, unspoken." In the four sections that follow, we read the unspeakable and unspoken thoughts of the three women, first separately, then interwoven. Here, from Sethe's perspective, are her memories of killing her daughter, of being beaten, of being abandoned by her mother. Largely addressed to Beloved, Sethe's words convey recollections she could never utter to another. Likewise, in her section, Denver expresses her fear of her mother and her yearning to be rescued by her father—anxieties that, for the most part, had been hidden in the novel.

Beloved's is the most riveting and most obscure of the monologues. In it is represented the preconscious subjectivity of a victim of infanticide. The words that convey the recollections and desires of someone who is at once in and out of time, alive and dead, are richly allusive. The linguistic units in this section—be they sentences, phrases, or individual words—are separated by spaces, not by marks of punctuation. Only the first-person pronoun and the first letter of each paragraph are capitalized. This arrangement places all the moments of Beloved's sensation and recollection in a continuous and eternal present.

From the grave Beloved yearns to be reunited with her mother: "her face is my own and I want to be there in the place where her face is and to be looking at it too." But, in addition to her feelings and desires from the grave, Beloved seems to have become one, in death, with the black and angry dead who suffered through the Middle Passage: "In the beginning the women are away from the men and the men are away from the women—storms rock us and mix the men into the women and the women into the men." In the body of Beloved, then, individual and collective pasts and memories seem to have become united and inseparable.

By representing the inaccessibility of the suffering of former slaves, Morrison reveals the limits of hegemonic, authoritarian systems of knowledge. The novel challenges readers to use their interpretive skills, but finally turns them back upon themselves. By representing the inexpressibility of its subject, the novel asserts and reasserts the subjectivity of the former slaves and the depth of their suffering. It reminds us that, our critical acumen and narrative capacities notwithstanding, we can never know what they endured. We can never enjoy a complacent understanding of lives lived under slavery. To the extent that *Beloved* returns the slaves to themselves, the novel humbles contemporary readers before the unknown, and finally unknowable, horrors the slaves endured.

The story of Beloved reflects Morrison's commitment to representing some measure of the range of atrocities slaves underwent: separation from loved ones, physical abuse, murder, and so on. Moreover, by giving voice to a victim of infanticide, the novel reveals Morrison's concern to make evident what seems inaccessible. In a profoundly persuasive and influential essay published shortly after *Beloved,* "Unspeakable Things Unspoken: The Afro-American Presence in American Literature," Morrison addresses analogous issues within a literary critical context. Here, she explores the significance of silence around the topic of race in the construction of American literary history.

Morrison begins by posing a series of questions about what a canon is or ought to be, and interrogates the presupposition of whiteness that the American canon inscribes. She considers the notion that in recent debates about the canon of American literature, arguments about the exclusion of black writers on the basis of race are often resisted because race remains an unspeakable topic in American culture:

For three hundred years black Americans insisted that "race" was no usefully distinguishing factor in human relationships. During those same three centuries every academic discipline, including theology, history, and natural science, insisted "race" was *the* determining factor in human development. When blacks discovered they had shaped or become a culturally formed race, and that it had specific and revered difference, suddenly they were told there is no such thing as "race," biological or cultural, that matters and that genuinely intellectual exchange cannot accommodate it.

To Morrison, the custodians of the canon retreat into specious arguments about quality and the irrelevance of ideology when defending the critical status quo against charges of being exclusionary. She is, however, skeptical about arguments based on the notion of critical quality, since the term is so frequently self-justifying and fully contested. Those who defend the canon seek to dismiss those who would challenge it by arguing that "the destabilizing forces" operate from political, rather than aesthetic, motives, all the while failing to acknowledge that their own positions are politically motivated.

Morrison then considers the ways that recent approaches to African American literary study respond to critical opinions that delegitimate black literary traditions. In response to those who deny that African American art exists, African Americanist critics have rediscovered texts that have long been suppressed or ignored, have sought to make places for African American writing within the canon, and have developed ways of interpreting these works. Morrison argues that those who would argue that African American art is inferior—"imitative, excessive, sensational, mimetic . . . and unintellectual, though very often 'moving,' 'passionate,' 'naturalistic,' 'realistic' or sociologically 'revealing' "—often lack the acumen or commitment to understand the work's complexity. In response to these labels, African Americanist critics have devised such strategies as applying recent literary theories to black literature so that these noncanonical texts can participate in the formation of current critical discourse and debate.

Morrison problematizes most fully those who condescend to African American art by calling superior those works which coincide with the universal criteria of Western art. She argues that such comparisons neutralize the significance of cultural difference, thereby sustaining the power of hegemonic culture. Moreover, critics of African American works who conceive of them exclusively in terms of their relation to Eurocentric criteria fail to do justice to the indigenous qualities of the texts and the tradition of which they are a part.

In response to these ways of marginalizing African American art and literature, Morrison describes three subversive strategies. To counteract such assaults, she first proposes that critics develop a theory of literature which responds to the tradition's indigenous qualities: "one that is based on its culture, its history, and the artistic strategies the works employ to negotiate the world it inhabits." Second, she suggests that the canon of classic, nineteenth-century literature must be reexamined to reveal the ways in which the African American cultural presence makes itself felt in these ostensibly white texts. Third, she argues that contemporary mainstream and minority literary texts must be studied for evidence of this presence.

Morrison's essay centers on the second and third strategies because of her apparent fascination with the meaningfulness of absence. She eloquently writes (in terms that resonate for our understanding of *Beloved* as well):

> We can agree, I think, that invisible things are not necessarily "not-there"; that a void may be empty, but it is not a vacuum. In addition, certain absences are so stressed, so ornate, so planned, they call attention to themselves; arrest us with intentionality and purpose, like neighborhoods that are defined by the population held away from them. Looking at the scope of American literature, I can't help thinking that the question should never have been "Why am I, an Afro-American, absent from it?" It is not a particularly interesting query anyway. The spectacularly interesting question is "What intellectual feats had to be performed by the author or his critic to erase me from a society seething with my presence, and what effect has that performance had on the work?" What are the strategies of escape from knowledge? Of willful oblivion?

Morrison's incisive reading of Herman Melville's *Moby Dick* as a critique of the ideological power of whiteness exemplifies the second strategy she describes and indicates the subtext around the discourse of race in that classic text that critics have long ignored. She then discusses the opening of each of her novels to show the kinds of ways in which African American culture inscribes itself in black texts. Morrison's analyses of her own prose reverberate and shimmer. They reveal anew the resonance and texture of her narrative prose; moreover, they display the acuity of her critical sensibility. Whether describing the intimacy of "Quiet as it's kept" (*The Bluest Eye*), the "seductive safe harbor" of the first sentence of *Sula,* the mock journalistic style of the opening lines of *Song of Solomon,* or the tentativeness in the meaning of safety in the first words of *Tar Baby,* Morrison indicates the care with which her prose is constructed. Her analyses show how the opening words of each work capture the myriad levels of tone and meaning that pervade the work as a whole.

Morrison's analysis of the beginning of *Beloved* is perhaps most thrilling, for here she shows how much meaning of her representation of slavery is contained in the two sentences with which the novel opens: "124 was spiteful. Full of a baby's venom." Morrison writes that by beginning with numbers she allows her characters—former slaves—to lay claim to an address. This technique also introduces the aural quality of her written language. Perhaps most powerfully, it allows her to pull the reader violently into the text:

> [The opening] is abrupt, and should appear so. No native informant here. The reader is snatched, yanked, thrown into an environment completely foreign, and I want it as the first stroke of the shared experience that might be possible between the reader and the novel's population. Snatched just as the slaves were from one place to another, from any place to another, without preparation and without defense. No lobby, no door, no entrance—a gangplank, perhaps (but a very short one). And the house into which this snatching—this kidnapping—propels one, changes from spiteful to loud to quiet, as the sounds in the body of the ship itself may have changed.

As Morrison demonstrates in this essay, in a variety of ways the historical ideological relations that play themselves out in African American lives find artistic expression in the language of her fiction. By her own example she seeks to set up a dynamic relationship between reader and text, for the enterprises of critics and of writers are deeply linked:

> For an author, regarding canons, it is very simple: in fifty, a hundred or more years his or her work may be relished for its beauty or its insight or its power; or it may be condemned for its vacuousness and pretension—and junked. Or in fifty or a hundred years the critic (as canon builder) may be applauded for his or her intelligent scholarship and powers of critical inquiry. Or laughed at for ignorance and shabbily disguised assertions of power—and junked. It's possible that the reputations of both will thrive, or that both will decay. In any case, as far as the future is concerned, when one writes, as critic or as author, all necks are on the line.

Whether as novelist, critic, professor, editor, or mentor to other writers, Toni Morrison has had a profound impact upon the literature and culture of the twentieth century, both in the United States and around the world. Her narratives of loss and rediscovery, longing and renewal, make visible stories that might otherwise have been lost, and eloquently represent the complex workings of oppression, resistance, and enchantment in African American communities past and present.

Selected Bibliography

WORKS OF TONI MORRISON

NOVELS

The Bluest Eye. New York: Holt, Rinehart and Winston, 1970.

Sula. New York: Knopf, 1973.

Song of Solomon. New York: Knopf, 1977.
Tar Baby. New York: Knopf, 1981.
Beloved. New York: Knopf, 1987.

ARTICLES, ESSAYS, AND REVIEWS

"What the Black Woman Thinks About Women's Lib." *New York Times Magazine*, August 22, 1971, pp. 14–15, 63–64, 66.

"Cooking Out." *New York Times Book Review*, June 10, 1973, pp. 4, 16.

"Behind the Making of *The Black Book*." *Black World*, February 23, 1974, pp. 86–90.

"Rediscovering Black History." *New York Times Magazine*, August 11, 1974, pp. 14, 16, 18, 20, 22, 24.

"Reading. Toni Morrison on a Book She Loves: Gayle Jones' *Corregidora*." *Mademoiselle*, 81:14 (May 1975).

"Slow Walk of Trees (as Grandmother Would Say) Hopeless (as Grandfather Would Say)." *New York Times Magazine*, July 4, 1976, pp. 104, 150, 152, 160, 162, 164.

"Memory, Creation, and Writing." *Thought*, 59:385–391 (December 1984).

"Rootedness: The Ancestor as Foundation." In *Black Women Writers (1950–1980): A Critical Evaluation*. Edited by Mari Evans. Garden City, N.Y.: Doubleday, 1984. Pp. 339–345.

"Unspeakable Things Unspoken: The Afro-American Presence in American Literature." *Michigan Quarterly Review*, 28:1–34 (Winter 1989).

BIBLIOGRAPHIES

Fikes, Robert, Jr. "Echoes from Small Town Ohio: A Toni Morrison Bibliography." *Obsidian*, 5:142–148 (Spring–Summer 1979).

Martin, Curtis. "A Bibliography of Writings by Toni Morrison." In *Contemporary American Women Writers: Narrative Strategies*. Edited by Catherine Rainwater and William J. Scheick. Lexington: University Press of Kentucky, 1985. Pp. 205–207.

BIOGRAPHICAL AND CRITICAL STUDIES

Awkward, Michael. *Inspiriting Influences: Tradition, Revision, and Afro-American Women's Novels*. New York: Columbia University Press, 1989.

Bischoff, Joan. "The Novels of Toni Morrison: Studies in Thwarted Sensitivity." *Studies in Black Literature*, 6:21–23 (1976).

Blake, Susan L. "Toni Morrison." In *Dictionary of Literary Biography*, vol. 33. Edited by Thadious M. Davis and Trudier Harris. Detroit: Gale Research, 1984. Pp. 187–199.

Butler-Evans, Elliott. *Race, Gender, and Desire: Narrative Strategies in the Fiction of Toni Cade Bambara, Toni Morrison, and Alice Walker*. Philadelphia: Temple University Press, 1989.

Christian, Barbara. *Black Women Novelists: The Development of a Tradition, 1892–1976*. Westport, Conn.: Greenwood, 1980.

Darling, Marsha, and Toni Morrison. "In the Realm of Responsibility: A Conversation with Toni Morrison." *The Women's Review of Books*, 5:5–6 (March 1988).

Fick, Thomas H. "Toni Morrison's 'Allegory of the Cave': Movies, Consumption, and Platonic Realism in *The Bluest Eye*." *Journal of the Midwest Modern Language Association*, 22:10–22 (Spring 1989).

Holloway, Karla, and Stephanie Dematrakopoulos. *New Dimensions of Spirituality: A Biracial and Bicultural Reading of the Novels of Toni Morrison*. New York: Greenwood, 1987.

Homans, Margaret. " 'Her Very Own Howl': The Ambiguities of Representation in Recent Women's Fiction." *Signs*, 9:186–205 (1983).

Jones, Bessie W., and Audrey L. Vinson. *The World of Toni Morrison: Explorations in Literary Criticism*. Dubuque, Iowa: Kendall/Hunt, 1985.

Lee, Dorothy H. "The Quest for Self: Triumph and Failure in the Works of Toni Morrison." In *Black Women Writers (1950–1980): A Critical Evaluation*. Edited by Mari Evans. Garden City, N.Y.: Doubleday, 1984. Pp. 346–360.

Lubiano, Wahneema. *Messing with the Machine: Four Afro-American Novels and the Nexus of Vernacular, Historical Constraint, and Narrative Strategy*. Ph.D. dissertation, Stanford University, 1987. Ann Arbor: UMI, 1987. No. 8800980.

McDowell, Deborah E. " 'The Self and the Other': Reading Toni Morrison's *Sula* and the Black Female Text." In *Critical Essays on Toni Morrison*. Edited by Nellie Y. McKay. Boston: G. K. Hall, 1988. Pp. 77–90.

McKay, Nellie Y., ed. *Critical Essays on Toni Morrison*. Boston: G. K. Hall, 1988.

Miner, Madonne M. "Lady No Longer Sings the Blues: Rape, Madness, and Silence in *The Bluest Eye.*" In *Conjuring: Black Women, Fiction, and Literary Tradition.* Edited by Marjorie Pryse and Hortense Spillers. Bloomington: Indiana University Press, 1985. Pp. 176–189.

Mobley, Marilyn E. "Narrative Dilemma: Jadine as Cultural Orphan in Toni Morrison's *Tar Baby.*" *Southern Review,* n.s. 23:761–770 (Autumn 1987).

Smith, Valerie. "The Quest for and Discovery of Identity in Toni Morrison's *Song of Solomon.*" *Southern Review,* n.s. 21:721–732 (July 1985).

Stepto, Robert. " 'Intimate Things in Place': A Conversation with Toni Morrison." *Massachusetts Review,* 18:473–489 (Autumn 1977).

Tate, Claudia, ed. *Black Women Writers at Work.* New York: Continuum, 1983.

Werner, Craig. "The Briar Patch as Modernist Myth: Morrison, Barthes and Tar Baby As-Is." In *Critical Essays on Toni Morrison.* Edited by Nellie Y. McKay. Boston: G. K. Hall, 1988. Pp. 150–167.

Willis, Susan. *Specifying: Black Women Writing the American Experience.* Madison: University of Wisconsin Press, 1987.

INTERVIEWS

Davis, Christina. "Interview with Toni Morrison." *Présence africaine,* 145:141–150 (1988).

Naylor, Gloria, and Toni Morrison. "A Conversation." *Southern Review,* n.s. 21:567–593 (July 1985).

—VALERIE SMITH

Walker Percy

1916–1990

"A GOOD DEAL of my energy as a novelist comes from *malice*—the desire to attack things in our culture, both North and South," Walker Percy told Ashley Brown in a 1967 interview (collected in *Conversations with Walker Percy*). Although Percy's courteous Southern manner and the antic charm of his six novels would seem to belie his confession, a closer look demonstrates that his work is indeed fueled by anger, the wrath of a latter-day prophet exhorting a deaf and recalcitrant postmodern society through satire. What Percy failed to mention, though, is the importance of love, however tentative and vulnerable, in his fiction. Good Catholic writer that he was, his works follow the biblical motion from the Old Testament's anger, judgment, and retribution to the New Testament's faith, hope, and charity.

Percy's background would seem to belong to a writer of neo-Faulknerian tragedies rather than of Christian comedies. He was born in Birmingham, Alabama, on May 28, 1916, the eldest of the three children of LeRoy Pratt Percy, a lawyer, and Martha Susan Phinizy. Through both parents, he was the scion of old Southern families: the Phinizys of Athens, Georgia, and the Percys of Greenville, Mississippi. He spent his youth in the New South of Birmingham, which he would comically invoke in his novel *The Last Gentleman* (1966). The doom-laden Old South called, however, with the suicide of his father on July 9, 1929, when Walker was thirteen, and the move of the widow and her three sons to Greenville in 1931 after a brief residence in Athens. There, as if stalked by Southern Furies, the family was once more struck by tragedy when Walker's mother was killed in an automobile accident on April 2, 1932.

In interviews, Percy said very little about these painful events, but they surfaced in modified form in his fiction. The protagonists' mothers are dead or marginalized, leaving the sons to confront the legacy of what Percy called in his novel *The Second Coming* (1980) the "death-dealing" father. In *The Last Gentleman,* young Will Barrett must overcome his amnesiac lapses and confront the memory of his father's suicide, but not until he is middle-aged, in *The Second Coming,* does Will realize that his father wanted him to accompany him in death. Will must decide whether to follow his father's example or find a new way. Like the elder Barrett, the father of Binx Bolling in *The Moviegoer* (1961) cannot face the fallen condition of the modern world and also seeks his death, in this instance through becoming a casualty of war. A central theme of Percy's fiction is the son's attempt not only to reject the father's way of death but also to establish his own meaningful way of life.

When Percy and his brothers moved to Greenville, he was faced with the Southern legacy and legend of the Percys. Colonel William Alexander Percy (1834–1888), known as the Gray Eagle of the Delta, was a planter and Confederate war hero. Colonel Percy's son LeRoy (1860–1929), Walker's great uncle, was a lawyer and a United States senator renowned for his courage in fighting the Ku Klux Klan, despite attempts on his life, and for his persistence in battling nature by obtaining and maintaining a reliable levee system along the Mississippi River. Percy says little about this Southern heritage in interviews and essays, but it, like the deaths of his parents, permeates his fiction. The title character of his novel *Lancelot* (1977) sits in a restored plantation house, losing himself in drink and television, and muses about his ancestors: "We lived from one great event to another, tragic events, triumphant events, with years of melancholy in between." The Percy protagonist, trapped in the banality of the postmodern world, cannot look forward to the external stimulation of great events to lift him out of his melancholy, but must learn to live a mundane life without despair.

After the death of his mother, Percy and his brothers, LeRoy and Phinizy, were adopted and raised in Greenville by their cousin William Alexander Percy (1885–1942), son of Senator LeRoy Percy. "Uncle Will" provided Walker with a means of ameliorating, if not eliminating, the burden of his Southern past by introducing him to art. In addition to practicing law, William Alexander Percy was a noted poet who is better known today as the author of a classic Southern autobiography, *Lanterns on the Levee* (1941). He shared with his three orphaned cousins his passion for the literature of Shakespeare and Keats and for the music of Beethoven, Brahms, and Mozart. In *The Last Gentleman* and *The Second Coming,* such music is found wanting as a way of providing meaning for life, because in both novels it is associated with the suicide of the protagonist's father.

Despite an active civic and literary life, William Alexander Percy suffered from a sense of belatedness, a feeling that the great days of the past were gone forever. Walker Percy has characterized his cousin's philosophy as a Southern variety of "Greco-Roman Stoicism, in which a man doesn't expect much in the world and does the best he can and tries to make one place a little better and . . . knows that he'll probably be defeated in the end." In *The Moviegoer,* Binx's aunt Emily is the Bolling family's Stoic standard-bearer when she tells him that although this civilization has "enshrined mediocrity as its national ideal," the Bollings "live by our lights, die by our lights, and whoever the high gods may be, we'll look them in the eye without apology." As she speaks, Aunt Emily waves a sword-shaped letter opener that she has taken from a miniature knight on her desk; Percy's sense of Southern stoicism as a dead end is evident as he repeatedly notes that the tip of the blade she brandishes is bent and blunted.

Another aspect of Percy's heritage came from a friend of his uncle Will's, the great Mississippi novelist William Faulkner: the sense of a Southern literary tradition. Percy denies the importance to himself of that tradition; as he told Ashley Brown, "I didn't care about this so-called Southern thing, the myths, the story-telling, the complex family situations . . ."; but he protests too much. As a college freshman, he was seduced by Faulkner's style, as he told Ashley Brown in 1967: "I took the qualifying English test in Faulknerian style (I had been reading *The Sound and the Fury*). I wrote one long paragraph without punctuation. The result of that was that I was put in a retarded English class." In a 1974 interview with Barbara King, collected in *Conversations with Walker Percy,* he commented that Faulkner "was a great writer but he's also been a great burden." In an attempt to resist this anxiety of influence, the young Percy went so far as to avoid meeting Faulkner by remaining in the car while a friend visited the novelist at his home.

Although Percy's novels are permeated by "the myths, the story-telling, the complex family situations," Percy is accurate in denying Faulkner as a primary influence, except in the sense that he noted Faulkner's themes in order to transform them. As he had rejected his uncle Will's stoicism, so he rejected Faulkner's tragic vision. In *Conversations with Walker Percy,* he told Jo Gulledge in 1984, "I would like to think of starting where Faulkner left off, of starting with the Quentin Compson [of Faulkner's *The Sound and the Fury*] who *didn't* commit suicide. Suicide is easy. Keeping Quentin Compson alive is something else."

The story of Percy's young manhood, like that of his fictional protagonists, is not only a rejection of the past's fatal attraction to resignation and death but also a quest to find a positive means of staying alive spiritually as well as physically. In high school Percy toyed with letters, poetry as well as the high school gossip column. In college he explored his fascination with movies as the popular art of the day in that they became almost a substitute for religion as a way of providing role models and firm beliefs. In a 1935 article for *Carolina Magazine,* "The Movie Magazine: A Low 'Slick,' " (collected in Coles), he wrote of movie magazines as a kind of Bible: "Every movie interview and feature embodies one or all of three motives: to reconcile the peculiarities and weaknesses of a movie star with the ideal held by the fans, to trace the star from his honkytonk days to his Hollywood pinnacle, and to give the world the star's philosophy of life." In *The Moviegoer,* Percy sympathetically mocked this use of the movies to avoid the self through Binx Bolling, who can act only when he envisions himself as one of his favorite movie stars.

As a young man, Percy was also seeking certainty in less nebulous areas than art. Although he was well-to-do and would inherit more upon his uncle Will's death, he followed the Percy family tradition of learning and working at a profession. Unlike the Percys, however, he chose medicine instead of law and majored in chemistry at the University of North Carolina at Chapel Hill. After graduating in 1937, he went north to New York City, where he obtained his M.D. from Columbia University in 1941. In *Walker Percy: An American Search,* Robert Coles quotes the mature Percy about his fascination with science: "It was a religion for me; I believed that any problem, anything wrong, could be solved by one or another of the sciences." In his novels *Love in the Ruins: The Adventures of a Bad Catholic at a Time near the End of the World* (1971) and *The Thanatos Syndrome* (1987), Percy characterizes such beliefs as Faustian overreaching, through the comic pratfalls of his protagonist, Dr. Thomas More, who futilely tries to find a scientific cure for the human condition.

For three years in New York Percy also sought mental certainty and surcease through the "science" of Freudian psychoanalysis. He later evaluated his analysis as negatively as his interest in physical science: "There's a tendency in this culture to treat psychiatry as a religion—thrilling that you can get your salvation from it, that the answer is there if you can just find the right analyst, the right group, react to the right group dynamics." In *The Last Gentleman,* displaced Southerner Will Barrett tries years of analysis in New York City, only to find that his analyst, Dr. Gamow, "served his patients best as artificer and shaper, receiving the raw stuff of their misery and handing it back in a public and acceptable form." After his analysis Will is right back where he began, "alone in the world, cut adrift from Dr. Gamow, a father of sorts, and from his alma mater, sweet mother psychoanalysis."

Percy's sense of physical and psychic "disease" took tangible form upon the death of William Alexander Percy on January 21, 1942 and his own contraction of tuberculosis in that same year, from performing autopsies while an intern at Bellevue Hospital. He spent the next three years in sanatoriums, first in the Adirondacks, then, after a relapse, in Connecticut. He had lost his young man's faith in his own immortality, his belief in science, and "a father of sorts" through his uncle Will's death. In his essay "The Delta Factor" (collected in *The Message in the Bottle,* 1975) he later wrote:

> Science cannot utter a single word about an individual molecule, thing, or creature in so far as it is an individual but only in so far as it is like other individuals. . . . It comes to pass then that the denizen of a scientific-technological society finds himself in the strangest of predicaments: he lives in a cocoon of dead silence, in which no one can speak to him nor can he reply.

During the seclusion his illness required, Percy broke through that silence by his intensive reading of existentialist authors, particularly the novelists Fyodor Dostoyevsky, Jean-Paul Sartre, and Albert Camus, and the philosophers Gabriel-Honoré Marcel, Martin Heidegger, Karl Jaspers, and Søren Kierkegaard. From them, he learned that a sense of dis-ease was not unacceptable in man, something that had to be cured by the right medicine or psychological theory; instead, it was an intrinsic part of the human condition. They challenged him to accept a feeling of alienation as a part of being human; as opposed to an endless questing for panaceas, they posited a commitment to a way of life. This interpretation of life would become central to all of Percy's novels.

After his physical cure in 1945, Percy left the crowded Northeast and the practice of medicine for the desert of New Mexico, where he lived on a ranch for several months with his Greenville friend Shelby Foote, who later became a great Civil War historian. The brevity of their stay suggests that the sojourn in the wilderness was not a complete success. In *The Last Gentleman* Percy uses the New Mexican desert's almost terrifying emptiness as the setting for failed physician Sutter Vaught's attempted suicide and his tempting of his dying brother Jamie and the questing Will Barrett to follow his example. Sutter is too disillusioned to commit himself to anything and risk further hurt, so he ends up anesthetized by the endless process of television watching in *The Second Coming.*

Percy returned to Greenville, where he began a series of commitments to life. On November 7, 1946, he married Mary Bernice ("Bunt") Townsend, a nurse whom he had met on an earlier vacation in Greenville. They moved to the summer place at Sewanee, Tennessee, that Walker had inherited from William Alexander Percy. After intensive reading and thought, they converted to Catholicism and moved to New Orleans in 1947; from there they moved in 1950 to Covington, Louisiana, where they raised two daughters and where Percy resided until his death on May 10, 1990. The protagonists of Percy's novels, despite many wrong turns and backslidings, follow a similar pattern of alienation, solitude, and wandering that ends in commitments, however tentative, to a person or persons, to a place, and to God.

Percy did not become a published novelist until 1961, when he was forty-five years old. In the preceding decade, he neither practiced medicine nor led the active civic life of his Percy forebears. Since his inheritance freed him from the burden of earning a living, he was able to prepare for his work as a novelist, and Percy was the type of novelist who particularly needed such preparation. Not only did he have the usual apprentice task of refining his craft, but since he was a didactic novelist in the best sense of the term, he needed to formulate his message in a series of published essays.

To Percy, postmodern man's central problem is alienation, an "impoverishment and loss of sovereignty." Our bodies follow the rut of our routines, our eyes are so inured to what is before them that they really see nothing, and our minds are co-opted by the theories and definitions of society so that we do not really think. Although Percy's philosophical fathers are the European existentialists, in his concern with man's loss of sovereignty he is the heir of the nineteenth-century New England transcendentalists. In his essay "Nature," Ralph Waldo Emerson, the seminal transcendental thinker, wrote, "The foregoing generations beheld God and nature face to face; we, through their eyes. Why should not we also enjoy an original relation to the universe?" He further asserted, "The invariable mark of wisdom is to see the miraculous in the common." Like Emerson, Percy wanted to perceive the divine in the mundane but, unlike Emerson, he did not believe man can do so through his own strength or self-reliance, but only with God's help.

In his essays of the 1950's, some of which were collected in *The Message in the Bottle*, Percy defined postmodern man's problem and proposed solutions. He also experimented with terms and situations that would recur in his fiction. In "The Loss of the Creature," he presents a tourist gazing at the natural wonder of the Grand Canyon, but the tourist's response is not wonder, nor is it a response to the natural. He does not really see the Grand Canyon: "The highest point, the term of the sightseer's satisfaction, is not the sovereign discovery of the thing before him; it is rather the measuring up of the thing to the criterion of the preformed symbolic complex." He may respond with exclamations of ostensible delight, such as "This is it" and "Now we are really living," but all these phrases merely mean "that now at last we are having the acceptable experience." *The Moviegoer*'s Binx Bolling finds himself plunged into "a deep melancholy" in a similar situation when he is at a campfire with a group of couples. The young men so anxiously comment, " 'How about this, Binx? This is really it, isn't it, boy?', that they were practically looking up from their girls to say this."

In his essay "The Man on the Train" (collected in *The Message in the Bottle*), Percy explores the two ways that people often attempt to escape this plight. He borrows the terms "rotation" and "repetition" from Kierkegaard, but uses them to illumine the condition of postmodern man. Percy defines rotation as "the quest for the new as the new, the reposing of all hope in what may lie around the bend"—Don Quixote moves on to the next adventure; the bored homemaker turns the page of another prepackaged romance novel. Percy's fiction is filled with latterday knights-errant questing for the new, moviegoers who seek rotation vicariously, and even those who, like Dr. Thomas More in *Love in the Ruins,* use a series of women for rotations. Needless to say, rotation is only a temporary solution; the new becomes old, and ennui once again sets in.

Repetition at first seems more promising than rotation, since the quester in this instance "voyages into his own past in the search for himself." If his repetition is merely "aesthetic," he is simply enjoying the experience in a frivolous way, as does *The Moviegoer*'s Binx Bolling when he sits in the same seat of the same theater and sees the same movie he saw years before. In an existential repetition, one really asks about the meaning of the past, as does Will Barrett in *The Last Gentleman* and *The Second Coming*. Though neither rotation nor repetition provides ultimate solutions, an existential repetition at least involves a serious questioning that furthers the search.

The plight of postmodern man is further complicated by the fact that not only situations but *words* have become worn-out, devoid of meaning. As Emerson wrote in "Nature," "The corruption of man is followed by the corruption of language." In his essay "Metaphor as Mistake" (collected in *The Message in the Bottle*), Percy explores this problem by citing the poet Thomas Nash's somewhat obscure line "Brightness falls from the air.'' If Nash had written ''Brightness falls from the hair,'' his meaning would be clearer, yet the line would be less satisfactory because ''in the presence of the lovely but obscure metaphor, I exist in the mode of hope, hope that the poet may mean such and such, and joy at any further evidence that he does.'' In *The Second Coming,* when Allison Huger, a recovering amnesiac, hears many common clichés, they sound as fresh and interesting to her as Nash's metaphor because the language is new to her, not a series of hackneyed phrases. Unusual metaphors also provide a measure of relief from what Percy, following Heidegger, calls ''everydayness.''

Unfortunately, rotation, repetition, evocative metaphors, and other devices can provide only temporary respite from everydayness. In his essay, ''The Message in the Bottle,'' Percy proposes what he considers the only relevant response to man's loss of sovereignty over life and language. Following Heidegger, Percy sees man as a castaway on an island remote from his true spiritual home. The castaway seeks news of that home, but true news must meet certain criteria: it must be relevant to the castaway's predicament, its bearer must have the proper credentials, and the news must be possible. For Percy, Christ's news of salvation is the message in the bottle that the castaway needs. The language of salvation is meaningful because it is relevant to the human situation, the credentials of the bearer are impeccable, and the news can be considered possible only through a Kierkegaardian leap of faith beyond the scientific. Receiving this news does not make earth a paradise, but it does render a human being's life more authentic:

> He should be a castaway and not pretend to be at home on the island. To be a castaway is to be in a grave predicament and this is not a happy state of affairs. But it is very much happier than being a castaway and pretending one is not.

Percy sees his protagonists and readers as such castaways; the novelist does not usurp the role of Christ as message bearer, but tries to bring the message to the attention of the castaways. The novelist is like the priest in *The Last Gentleman* who baptizes the dying Jamie Vaught and answers his questions by saying, ''It is true because God Himself revealed it as the truth. . . . If it were not true, . . . then I would not be here. That is why I am here, to tell you.''

As Percy formulated his philosophy through his essays of the 1950's, he also refined his technique. He had to learn such basic lessons as showing rather than telling as a hallmark of good fiction. He sent the lengthy manuscript of his first novel, *The Charterhouse,* to his fellow Southern novelist and Catholic convert Caroline Gordon, an experienced teacher of creative writing, who responded with thirty pages of single-spaced commentary. *The Charterhouse* was never published, but slowly, through another unpublished novel, Percy mastered the techniques of fiction.

Percy did, however, face a problem that many novice writers do not: since he was a didactic novelist, how was he to convey his message without alienating his readers by delivering a sermon or boring them by endlessly repeating the same message? Although Percy's critics differ about the degree to which he overcame this handicap, Percy himself was aware of the challenge from the beginning of his writing career; indeed, it was one of the reasons he became a novelist, rather than writing solely as a philosophical essayist. A didactic writer must have an audience, and, as he commented to Judith Serebnick in 1961, ''people would rather read a novel than an article.'' He also wanted to avoid becoming like a modern scientist who cannot speak to the individual because he can only generalize; instead Percy wanted to speak to individuals about an individual. In a 1968 interview with Carlton Cremeens (collected in *Conversations with Walker*

Percy), he stated that his first novel, *The Moviegoer*, "was conceived by putting a young man in a certain situation."

The Moviegoer's protagonist and narrator, John Bickerson ("Binx") Bolling, appears to be a young man in the conventional situation of rebellion against family values. Instead of living with his distinguished paternal relations in the aristocratic Garden District of New Orleans and following a respected profession like law or medicine, Binx chooses to live in the bland suburb of Gentilly and run a branch office of a brokerage firm. He seems firmly ensconced in his mundane existence; as he puts it, "For years now I have had no friends. I spend my entire time working, making money, going to movies and seeking the company of women."

Binx does not see himself as mired in the quotidian, for he believes he is pursuing a "horizontal search," in which "what is important is what I shall find when I leave my room and wander in the neighborhood." He asserts that the horizontal search is better than the "vertical search" that he had tried earlier, in which "[he] stood outside the universe and sought to understand it." Whether questing in the realm of the details of daily life or the abstractions of books, the goal of Binx's search is the avoidance of the "malaise," what Percy calls man's "loss of sovereignty" and Binx defines as "the pain of loss. The world is lost to you, the world and the people in it."

Although Binx believes he is pursuing a search, he is really avoiding coming to terms with himself and his place in the world. He uses "working, making money, going to movies and seeking the company of women" as rotations. Each new deal, new film, or new secretary holds the promise of novelty but soon becomes worn-out, and the malaise once again descends. In the early part of the novel, Binx plays with aesthetic repetitions but avoids an existential repetition's true examination of his past.

Unlike Percy, Binx refuses to acknowledge his anger at a postmodern society in which, as he puts it, "all the friendly and likable people seem dead to me; only the haters seem alive." After hearing some saccharine professions of faith on a maudlin radio program called "This I Believe," Binx is moved to send in his own credo: "I believe in a good kick in the ass." Such expressions of disgusted wrath are rare for Binx, who usually maintains his facade of the slightly muddled but sweet Southern gentleman. At the end of Mardi Gras, however, Binx has a series of experiences that jolt him out of his complacency and into self-examination and penance appropriate to the Lenten season.

Binx's subconscious seems to be telling him that it is time to wake up when he has a dream about his being wounded in the Korean War and observes that "what are generally considered to be the best times are for me the worst times, and that worst of times was one of the best." He remembers that "six inches from my nose a dung beetle was scratching around under the leaves. As I watched, there awoke in me an immense curiosity." His proximity to death startled Binx into regaining sovereignty for a moment and actually seeing what was before him. This is an example of the extreme sort of rotation, from wars or hurricanes or automobile wrecks, that Percy favors to push his characters out of the malaise. Any rotation, however, dissipates, and so even in the "best times," as in Binx's city where "the good times roll," the malaise redescends.

Binx needs an existential repetition, a true examination of his past, before he can change his life in a meaningful way. For him, such a repetition involves coming to terms with memories of his dead father. The elder Bolling, a physician, seemed to be on an eternal vertical search; Binx concludes, "That's what killed my father, English romanticism, that and 1930 science." The elder Bolling went from scientific fad to scientific fad, from taking his rest on sleeping porches to taking long hikes on the levee, but to no avail; he became so uninterested in life that he could bring himself to eat only when fed by his wife, who distracted him by reading aloud a murder mystery's pseudo-meaningful events. After a while he could no longer eat, but was saved by World War II, which gave him the opportunity to envision himself as the English poet Rupert Brooke and die in the "wine dark sea." Binx may think he understands his father, but that understanding means nothing until he realizes that to his father he was just one more rotation; he thus alleviates his guilt about his father's despair.

On a trip to Chicago, Binx experiences an existential rotation when he remembers a childhood journey there with his father:

> I turned and saw what he required of me . . . he staking his everything this time on a perfect comradeship—and I, seeing in his eyes the terrible request, requiring from me his very life; I, through a child's cool perversity or some atavistic recoil from an intimacy too intimate, turned him down, turned away, refused him what I knew I could not give.

On the one hand, Binx knows that his father was asking too much from him, a perfect relationship impossible in a fallen world. On the other hand, the memory makes Binx see how he has spent most of his life avoiding intimacy or commitment, a seemingly nice guy whom no one—family, friends, or lovers—can ever pin down.

What saves Binx from his father's romantic belief in earthly perfection and his ultimate despair is his heritage from his mother, an earthy Cajun nurse whom the Bollings regard as beneath them. Here Percy is directly in the Southern literary tradition in which character is often determined by bloodlines. Binx's mother tells him, "You know, you've got a little of my papa in you—you're easy-going and you like to eat and you like the girls." She has remarried into what the Bollings would regard as her class and is raising a large, mass-attending Catholic family. As Binx notes, the Smiths "would never dream of speaking of religion," but they believe, and they practice their faith.

The oldest surviving Smith child is Lonnie, a fourteen-year-old confined to a wheelchair by an illness that eventually will kill him. Because he daily confronts the possibility of death, he retains sovereignty over his life. No malaise lurks in his consciousness, and Percy uses him as an example of someone for whom words as well as events have retained their meaning. Binx comments, "I have only to hear the word God and a curtain comes down in my head," but Lonnie can discuss his faith with sincerity and without embarrassment. Lonnie also provides Binx with the important example of someone who can express his feelings, particularly love, without self-consciousness or anxiety about the beloved's response. He keeps this ability alive in Binx, who observes that Lonnie's "words are not worn out. It is like a code tapped through a wall. Sometimes he asks me straight out: do you love me? and it is possible to tap back: yes, I love you."

The most important person with whom Binx must come to terms, however, is Kate Cutrer, his aunt Emily's stepdaughter. Percy's major women characters usually serve as complementary opposites for the protagonists or as exaggerated doubles. Kate belongs in the latter category. Her life as debutante, parade queen, and dutiful daughter has been so trite that she has turned to psychoanalysis, drink, and drugs. Her fiancé was killed in an automobile accident in which she was a passenger, and she informs Binx, "it gave me my life. That's my secret, just as the war is your secret." She also tells him, "You're like me, but worse. Much worse." Considering the tragedy, pathos, and boredom of Kate's life, her statement seems surprising. In the context of the novel, though, Kate is correct. Percy's epigraph for *The Moviegoer* is from Kierkegaard's *The*

Sickness unto Death: ". . . the specific character of despair is precisely this: it is unaware of being despair." Kate indicates in her statement Binx's refusal to acknowledge his own plight.

Kate also perceives one aspect of the solution to Binx's predicament. She suggests, "It is possible, you know, that you are overlooking something, the most obvious thing of all." She has the wisdom to refrain from identifying it for him because he could not yet recognize or act upon it; as Kate tells him, "you would not know it if you fell over it." Kate is referring to love, in particular the love for her that Binx is afraid to acknowledge. In his desire to avoid feeling and worn-out words, his first proposal to her sounds like a business proposition about running a service station: "We could stay on here at Mrs. Schexnaydre's [his landlady's]. It is very comfortable. I may even run the station myself. You could come sit with me at night, if you liked. Did you know you can net over fifteen thousand a year on a good station?" In a backhanded way, Binx is acknowledging his love for Kate, since he does not demean her by spouting the romantic clichés he uses on his secretaries: "You and your sweet lips. Sweetheart, before God I can't think about anything in the world but putting my arms around you and kissing your sweet lips." Binx is also subconsciously realizing that he is still putting the distractions of pleasure "before God."

As Ash Wednesday and Binx's thirtieth birthday approach, he is forced to recognize his despair. On a business trip to Chicago with Kate, their attempt to have a solely sexual relationship, like those he has had (imaginatively, anyway) with his secretaries, fails miserably because "flesh poor flesh now at this moment summoned all at once to be all and everything, end all and be all, the last and only hope—quails and fails." Upon their return to New Orleans, Binx's aunt Emily, the representative of Southern stoicism, upbraids Binx for his failure to maintain the family values, particularly those of Southern chivalry, in his relationship with Kate. She asks Binx, "What do you love? What do you live by?" He has no answer and remains silent.

Binx finally realizes the depth of his despair on his birthday: "Now in the thirty-first year of my dark pilgrimage on this earth . . . knowing less than I ever knew before, having learned only to recognize merde when I see it." As he sits on a bench near a Catholic church and watches a man come out with ashes on his forehead, he remembers that it is Ash Wednesday and that the faithful are acknowledging that they come from dust (or from merde) and they will return to dust. Unlike his father, Binx does not seek death as surcease from despair over the human condition. Instead, as is fitting on the first day of Lent, he makes a resolution: "There is only one thing I can do: listen to people, see how they stick themselves into the world, hand them along a ways in their dark journey and be handed along, and for good and selfish reasons." Binx's resolution is also appropriately small and possible; he has rejected the megalomania of horizontal and vertical searches and the inflated sense of self-importance that led to his father's death.

In the epilogue to *The Moviegoer* Binx, a little over a year later, has continued on the path of helping others and himself in the small, everyday ways that make life bearable. He is attending medical school. He has married Kate, who depends on him for the direction that alleviates her despair. In the novel's final scene, he and Kate are outside the hospital where Lonnie is dying. Binx is able to find words that are not worn-out to answer his stepsiblings' questions about death directly and sincerely. He seems to have reached what Marcel would call "intersubjectivity," in that he recognizes human beings as individuals, not as parts of categories, and so can interact with them on a meaningful basis. The last lines of the novel are suitably understated, since intersubjectivity is as difficult to maintain as to obtain in the dehumanizing postmodern world. Binx sees Kate, and comments, "I watch her walk toward St Charles, cape jasmine held against her cheek, until my brothers and sisters call out behind me."

The Moviegoer was the surprise winner of the 1962 National Book Award for fiction. Percy's late-blooming career as a novelist was off to a remarkable start. His later novels would become popular as well as critical successes, often appearing on the best-seller lists.

Percy's second novel, *The Last Gentleman,* is different from *The Moviegoer* in a number of ways. Instead of the concentrated time, place, and cast of characters of the first book, Percy created a sprawling picaresque novel in which his protagonist, Will Barrett, journeys throughout the country and provides Percy with innumerable targets for satire.

Percy also exchanged focused, first-person narration for the detached, ironic voice of an omniscient third-person narrator. The reason for this choice is evident. Unlike Binx Bolling, Will Barrett can neither define nor articulate his plight. He has fled north to New York City, where he lives a homogenized life in the YMCA and works as a "humidification engineer" at Macy's. He suffers from bouts of amnesia. Because he has not come to terms with his personal, family, and regional pasts, he has no real identity. He is a chameleon, an Ohioan with Ohioans, a conservative Southerner with conservative Southerners, and the perfect analysand for his psychoanalyst. Although he suffers from the existential predicament of malaise, which he calls "noxious particles," he believes that science can provide a cure. He vows, "I shall engineer the future of my life according to the scientific principles and the self-knowledge I have so arduously gained from five years of analysis."

A catalyst for Will's development is provided by the Vaught family, "Yankee sort of Southerners" who are the prosperous denizens of the New South. Each of the four children and one former spouse represent a possible way of life for Will. The youngest, Jamie, doomed by disease, seems to represent Will's present in that he is an unformed character always restlessly traveling in an attempt to find happiness before his death. Kitty, as her name suggests, is a diminished version of *The Moviegoer*'s Kate. She wants the mindless world of sororities and the house in the suburbs that plunged Kate into despair. If Will marries her, he will live a cliché, as he indicates by his repeated desire to "hold her charms in his arms." Jamie and Kitty's older sister, Val, has become a nun who teaches language to deprived black children in Georgia. Although she has the excitement of watching those for whom language is not worn-out, like Percy himself she keeps her animus against postmodern society; she describes herself as "a good hater." Rita, the ex-wife of the eldest son, Sutter, is a secular humanist who spouts platitudes about living a life of beauty and joy.

Sutter is the most significant Vaught for Will Barrett because his old-fashioned clothes and his suicide attempt remind Will of his own father and his suicide. Sutter is a pathologist; as he phrases it, "I study the lesions of the dead." Only one letter separates "lesions" from "legions," and indeed Sutter is obsessed with diagnosing a dead society; but the dead are beyond cure and he has given up on himself as well. Will, though, keeps turning to Sutter for advice, as if he could replace his father; the irony is that both Sutter and Will's father knew only how to die, not how to live.

Through Will's travels with all or some of the Vaughts, Percy takes aim at what he sees as the foibles of the 1960's. He encounters the significantly named Mort Prince, who writes books with more orgasm counts than plots. In Levittown, Pennsylvania, Yankees who claim not to be bigoted start to riot when they think a black might buy a house on their block. The New South appears to be "happy, victorious, Christian, rich, patriotic and Republican,'' but Will sees arrested civil rights workers detained in an old Civil War fort and is knocked unconscious in a campus riot reminiscent of the one that occurred when James Meredith became the first black student at the University of Mississippi.

At the end of *The Last Gentleman,* Will's status is ambiguous, as befits his location in the New Mexican desert, the ''locus of pure possibility.'' On the positive side, he resists Sutter's invitation to join him in suicide, possibly because in his travels he has confronted the memory of his father's suicide. The other evidence is less hopeful, however. Although he hears a priest give the sacraments to the dying Jamie, he does not seem to have received the message of salvation himself. He cares enough about another human being to try to prevent Sutter's suicide, but his words to Sutter, ''don't leave me,'' are those he futilely addressed to his father before *his* suicide. When Sutter decides to stop his car and pick up Will, the last line of the novel suggests that Will may still be following his father's and Sutter's way of death: ''The Edsel waited for him.''

For Percy, the allure of death is typical of the postmodern world. In an essay entitled ''Notes for a Novel About the End of the World'' (1967–1968, collected in *The Message in the Bottle*), he writes, ''The hero of the postmodern novel is a man who has forgotten his bad memories and conquered his present ills and who finds himself in the victorious secular city. His only problem now is to keep from blowing his brains out.'' Mankind suffers from ''angelism-bestialism,'' and is ''divided into two classes: the consumer long since anesthetized and lost to himself in the rounds of consumership [bestialism], and the stranded objectivized consciousness, a ghost of a man who wanders the earth like Ishmael [angelism].''

The protagonist of Percy's third novel, *Love in the Ruins*, is suicidal, despite what seems like an ideal secular life-style, and suffers from angelism-bestialism. Dr. Thomas More is representative of his time and place, the southern United States near the close of the twentieth century. He lives in the ironically named Paradise Estates with scientists and Christians, but beyond that enclave, the society is in disarray or, as Dr. More says of it, alluding to William Butler Yeats's poem ''The Second Coming,'' the ''center did not hold.''

Beyond Paradise Estates lies Fedville, where the scientists watch couples' sexual relations in the Love Clinic and advocate euthanasia for oldsters in the Geriatrics Center. Social dropouts, such as black ''Bantu guerrillas'' and hippies, dwell in the Honey Island Swamp. The shopping center, the heart of the materialistic society, was burned down by the Bantu guerrillas in a Christmas riot five years before, and the Rotary Club ''banner is rent, top to bottom, like the temple veil.'' In a Faulknerian passage, Percy, through Dr. More, blames the state of the South, which God had provided as a ''new Eden,'' on the failure of one test: ''here's a helpless man in Africa, all you have to do is not violate him.''

Spiritual life is equally moribund. St. Michael's Church stands empty, and Catholicism has divided itself into three: the American Catholic church, which celebrates Property Rights Sunday; the Dutch schismatics, ''who believe in relevance but not God''; and a small number of old-style Catholics.

As his physician's title combined with his saint's name suggests, Dr. Thomas More believes he can provide not only physical but spiritual healing for this sick society. It is, however, more a case of ''physician, heal thyself,'' for Dr. More is just as susceptible as the next man. He states, ''I believe in God and the whole business but I love women best, music and science next, whiskey next, God fourth, and my fellowman hardly at all.'' His bestialism is particularly evidenced by his need for three women, Lola,

Moira, and Ellen, whom he treats as interchangeable parts but who represent possible lives for him. Lola suggests a phony return to the values of the Old South with her imitation Tara and her belief that "the only thing we can be sure of is the land." Moira, who works at the Love Clinic, represents the secular values of the New South glossed over by a nostalgia for a false past. Ellen is his necessary complement because she does not believe in God but in her fellow human beings, the Golden Rule, and doing right.

Dr. More blames his lapses on the death of his only child, Samantha, from a neuroblastoma, and the subsequent desertion and death of his wife, a dabbler in spiritual trends. His favorite whiskey, Early Times, indicates the intoxicating nature of his nostalgia. The reader knows that he is rationalizing, because as he himself indicates, he had failed to follow the Golden Rule even before these tragic events. He recalls receiving communion and "rejoicing afterwards, caring nought for my fellow Catholics but only for myself and Samantha and Christ swallowed, remembering what he promised me for eating him."

Dr. More's angelism verges on megalomania. He considers himself a latter-day Christ. After his suicide attempt, he sees himself as "crucified" on his hospital bed. In the mirror over a bar, he later perceives his reflection on "the new Christ, the spotted Christ, the maculate Christ, the sinful Christ. . . . [who] shall reconcile man with his sins." In reality, Dr. More is more Faust than Christ. He has invented a device called a lapsometer, which, as its name suggests, can diagnose the degree of a person's fall into angelism-bestialism, but he is not satisfied. He wants to cure the human condition, so that "man could reenter paradise, so to speak, and live there both as man and spirit, whole and intact man-spirit." He meets his Mephistopheles in the diabolic Art Immelmann, who has an attachment that makes the lapsometer work, and Dr. More signs his contract, or pact, with the devil.

When Dr. More realizes that the Bantus are about to attack again and that Immelmann will use his device to set off a deadly heavy sodium reaction as the president of the United States is delivering a Fourth of July address nearby, he tries to get the lapsometer back in a series of antic adventures. After he is captured by the Bantus, who imprison him in the rectory of St. Michael's Church, he seizes a sword from a statue of St. Michael. Unlike the letter-opener sword of Binx's aunt Emily in *The Moviegoer,* this blade is not bent, and Dr. More uses it to unscrew the grate of an air-conditioning duct and escape. The duct is described as a "cave of winds, black as the womb," foreshadowing his rebirth.

Dr. More cannot achieve this new life until he renounces his hubristic independence; as an old friend has asked him, "You never did like anybody to help you, did you, Doc?" In the moment of peril, when Immelmann's victory seems imminent, Dr. More swallows his pride and prays to his ancestor Saint Thomas More, who had resisted the lure of secular power at the price of his life. Dr. More and his society are saved.

Five years later, the Bantus have won and taken over Paradise Estates, while Dr. More lives in the old slave quarters: the patterns of life seem virtually the same; only the players have switched roles. Dr. More has married the virtuous Ellen, and they have two children. In the sacrament of penance, he has confessed to the sin of "loving myself better than God and other men." Dr. More has certainly improved but, as Percy shows us, as a man he remains a denizen of a fallen world and can always lapse into old sins. Dr. More still indulges in his Early Times and asserts, "I still believe my lapsometer can save the world." The last scene of the novel provides some hope, for it occurs on Christmas Eve, suggesting that Christ's birth provides the means of rebirth for people, however many times they fall.

For many of Percy's characters, hate seems preferable to the anesthetized, mindless content of the postmodern consumer, and so it seems to Lancelot Lamar, the narrator and protagonist of Percy's fourth novel, *Lancelot*. The scion of an old Louisiana family and heir to their plantation house, Belle Isle, Lance has fallen into the deceptively beautiful insularity of reading detective novels, drinking, and watching the evening news in the "pigeonnier," a miniature Belle Isle separated from the life of the main house. He learns that no man is an island when, as he says, "I discovered my wife's infidelity and five hours later I discovered my own life." This sounds like the typical Percy plot in which a discovery or rotation propels the protagonist into a more authentic existence. Lance appears to find a new life as he attempts to prove his wife's infidelity, but in reality he is merely following his obsessions with sex and violence to their logical conclusion in death.

Lance always regarded life in terms of strict, mutually exclusive categories: men are saints or scoundrels; women are ladies or whores. He is unable to accept the ambiguity, the highs and lows of mankind in a fallen world. Because his father had taken a kickback, Lance thinks of him as a total failure. If his mother really did have an affair, to Lance she would be a whore. Lance's first wife was the ethereal Lucy, the emblem of Southern ladyhood, and so Lance seems to want to fit Margot, his second and current wife, into the opposite category.

In Lance, Dr. Thomas More's comic hubris reaches its tragic extreme: playing on his name as belonging to one of King Arthur's Round Table knights, he considers himself, in an ironic inversion, a "Knight of the Unholy Grail" on a "quest for true sin." Dr. More's reliance on the technology of the lapsometer is like Lance's dependence on hidden cameras to spy on Margot. He believes he is a latter-day Philip Marlowe, Raymond Chandler's detective hero, righting wrongs, so he cannot recognize that Margot's sin is less than his own in that he turns sex into sacrament: "my communion . . . that sweet dark sanctuary guarded by the heavy gold columns of her thighs, the ark of her covenant." He thinks he has the godlike power to execute a death sentence, and therefore slits the throat of his wife's lover and blows up Belle Isle.

At the beginning of the novel, after the violence at Belle Isle, which is revealed through flashbacks, Lance is in an institution, talking to his old friend Percival, a priest too doubtful of his vocation to wear clerical garb. As Percival encourages Lance to talk through his memories, Lance remains unrepentant. He refuses to see himself as a sinner among sinners, preferring to believe that he is a sort of messiah who will bring about a new world order because, as he pridefully puts it, he and his followers "will not tolerate this age." His attitude toward women has not changed either; he tells Percival that the "New Woman" will "be free to be a lady or a whore" and that "God's secret design for man is that man's happiness lies for men in men practicing violence upon women and that woman's happiness lies in submitting to it." He is even surprised when Anna, the rape victim in the next room, refuses to accompany him to his new order in Virginia.

Lancelot is by far Percy's darkest vision of life in the postmodern world, but even the satanically proud Lancelot is offered a ray of hope. As Lancelot speaks, his childhood friend Percival, the true Grail knight, claims his identity as Father John, associated with the evangelist of the gospel of love, and opposes his old friend's doctrine of hate. Father John dons his clerical collar and reaffirms his commitment to take a mundane parish in Alabama: no Third Revolution for him. In one of Percy's most fascinating narrative techniques, the reader is dependent on Lance's monologue for news of Percival's appearance and questions; we do not hear Father John speak until the end of the novel, when he has asserted his vocation. In the novel's final pages, to Lance's many questions he can answer yes and counter Lance's horrific negativity. If Lance listens to what Father John tells him, there will be hope for him, too. Lance asks, "Is there anything you wish to tell me before I leave?" and in the last line of the novel, Father John replies, "*Yes.*"

This sense of final affirmation also lingers in *The Second Coming*. In this, his fifth novel, Percy brings his characteristic themes to fruition while eschewing the relatively spare prose of his early works and providing a dense texture, rich with allusions to William Shakespeare, Carson McCullers, Flannery O'Connor, Vladimir Nabokov, William Blake, Dylan Thomas, and many others. The primary allusion, however, is to Yeats's "The Second Coming." Although the novel's title refers to the reappearance of *The Last Gentleman*'s Will Barrett as a wealthy, middle-aged widower, it also points to the world Will now inhabits, where, in Yeats's words, "The best lack all conviction, while the worst / Are full of passionate intensity," and the new Messiah, the Second Coming, could be a "rough beast" which "Slouches towards Bethlehem to be born."

Faulkner's presence also permeates the novel, in that *The Second Coming* seems to be a direct response to the Faulknerian theme of the burden of the past, or the sins of the fathers, leading to the death of the sons. Even the language of Will's stream of consciousness is reminiscent of Faulkner, as he addresses his dead father:

> Ever since your death, all I ever wanted from you was out, out from you and from the Mississippi twilight, and from the shotguns thundering in musty attics and racketing through funk-smelling Georgia swamps, out from the ancient hatred and allegiances, allegiances unto death and love of war and rumors of war and under it all death and your secret love of death, yes that was your secret.

Instead of allowing the doom-laden past to overwhelm him, Will confronts the memory of his father's suicide attempt in a Georgia swamp, and "the meaning of his present life became clear to him." When he further realizes that his father meant to kill him as well, in order to spare him life in a diminished world, Will renounces his dependency on his father, and his father's avatar Sutter Vaught, because of "the total failure, fecklessness, and assholedness of people in general and in particular just those people I had looked to."

Will Barrett is certainly no Quentin Compson, but when he rejects Quentin's fatalistic acquiescence, he ricochets to the other extreme, that of hubristic action. Will decides that suicide is necessary, but that his suicide, unlike that of his father, will not be "wasted." Like Dr. Thomas More attempting to cure the human condition or Lancelot Lamar seeking the Unholy Grail, Will Barrett designs what he calls a "scientific experiment." He will enter a local cave, take some sleeping pills, and, as he states in a letter to Sutter,

> wait for God to give a sign. If no sign is forthcoming I shall die. But people will know why I died: because there is no sign. The cause of my death will be either his nonexistence or his refusal to manifest himself, which comes to the same thing as far as we are concerned.

His arrogance gets its comic comeuppance when he staggers from the cave, vanquished not by demons but by toothache and nausea, intimations of his human frailty.

He does receive a sign, though, in the sense that his weakened condition causes him to fall into a greenhouse occupied by his perfect complement, Allison Huger, the daughter of his former sweetheart Kitty Vaught and Kitty's husband, a fiercely smiling dentist. Allie, an escapee from a mental institution, has little memory left after her shock treatments—in contrast with Will, who is plagued by remembrance of everything. She has learned to hoist heavy equipment into her greenhouse and can exercise her new skill on Will, who keeps falling down. Words are worn-out for Will, but Allie, like a child learning language, plays with words; she says of their relationship, "A fit by chance is romance."

Allie is attempting to evade her rapacious parents, who want to have her declared mentally incompetent so they can control the valuable real estate she has recently inherited. Will's increasing involvement in helping her leads to love, and this love calls him back from the brink of two more suicide attempts. Earlier, Will had confused the message bearer with the message when, intent on self-destruction, he seemed uninterested in a trendy chaplain's comment that he had discovered God "in other people." After finding Allie, Will, like *The Moviegoer*'s Binx Bolling, can resolve to "take care of people who need taking care of."

Will is no longer the megalomaniac who waited in a cave for a sign exclusively for him, and he can now accept the message despite the human foibles of the messenger. In the last lines of the novel, he looks at Allie and a feeble old priest, the aptly named Father Weatherbee, and meditates, "Is she a gift and therefore a sign of the giver? Could it be that the Lord is here, masquerading behind this simple silly holy face? Am I crazy to want both, her and Him? No, not want, must have. And will have." With these words, Will decisively rejects the "death-dealing" Southern past of his father and affirms life, in this world and the next.

Although Percy's first five novels are eminently accessible, his next two works strive to convey his ideas about the plight of postmodern man in popular forms that verge on parody. *Lost in the Cosmos: The Last Self-Help Book* (1983) attempts to present the complicated philosophical and semiotic ideas of *The Message in the Bottle* to the general reader. As its title suggests, Percy does so through the use of a best-selling genre that appeals to the American obsession with self-reliance. He includes a "Twenty-Question Multiple-Choice Self-Help Quiz," a space odyssey, and an antic version of the Phil Donahue show. Percy's ideas are more readily comprehensible in the humorous *Lost in the Cosmos* than in the serious *The Message in the Bottle,* but at the risk of seeming to deprecate his audience as well as its predicament.

Ostensibly a thriller or adventure story, *The Thanatos Syndrome,* Percy's sixth novel, represents a second coming for Dr. Thomas More. At the end of *Love in the Ruins,* the diagnosis for Dr. More was ambiguous: he was still drinking and thinking of his lapsometer even though he was happily at home with his family on Christmas Eve. At the beginning of *The Thanatos Syndrome,* Dr. More, the narrator, seems to have lapsed badly. After serving time for selling drugs at a truck stop, he has returned home to find his wife, Ellen, obsessed with bridge but signaling her despair in her sleep by mentioning the Azazel convention, a distress signal in bridge. His children, Tommy and Margaret, treat him like "a certain presence in the house which one takes account of, steps around, like a hole in the floor." The children's baby-sitter tells him, "You too much up in your head. You don't even pay attention to folks when they talking to you." He has started sipping his whiskey again, and avoids St. Michael's Church and his saintly friend Father Rinaldo Smith. The status of his medical license, probationary, seems to mirror the precarious state of his soul.

Dr. More remains far from perfect, but he does seem to have learned from his errors. In *Love in the Ruins* he had confessed to loving his fellow men "hardly at all," but in *The Thanatos Syndrome* he remarks, "I still don't know what to make of God, don't give Him, Her, It a second thought, but I make a good deal of people, give them considerable thought.'' He has renounced his Faustian reliance on technology because he now considers his patients more than stimulus-response organisms: ''Time was when I'd have tested their neurones with my lapsometer. But there's more to it than neurones. There's such a thing as the psyche, I discovered. I became a psyche-iatrist, . . . a doctor of the soul.'' Although Dr. More sounds as if he believes he has the power to cure the soul, his description of his method shows that he no longer considers physicians godlike: ''Long ago I discovered that the best way to get in touch with withdrawn patients is to ask their help.''

Dr. More certainly needs to be as improved as possible, because the world he confronts seems to have deteriorated during his spell in prison. In *The Thanatos Syndrome,* Percy returns to the broad social satire of the futuristic *Love in the Ruins,* but the comedy is blacker, the humor more desperate. Dr. More seems to be describing Percy's method when he mentions ''the trick of Louisiana civility'' in which ''one doesn't launch tirades over bourbon in the locker room. One vents dislikes by jokes.''

Dr. More's world is far from likable. Fedville is continuing its role in ''gereuthanasia,'' and has now added the killing of malformed or diseased infants, ''pedeuthanasia,'' because the Supreme Court has set the age of personhood above eighteen months. Dr. More's women patients seem content but exhibit sexual behavior more characteristic of primates than of humans and have lost the ability to use language contextually. AIDS patients are quarantined like lepers of old. Crime has mysteriously declined in Feliciana Parish, particularly the slums of Baton Rouge, and people no longer approach Dr. More with their old depressions, terrors, and anxieties, yet everyone seems strangely vacant. Dr. More ponders, ''They're not on medication. They are not hurting, they are not worrying the same old bone, but there is something missing, not merely the old terrors, but a sense in each of her—her what? her self.''

In his investigations, Dr. More discovers that people are losing not only their predicaments as human beings but their very humanity because a maverick scientist at Fedville has dosed most of the parish's water supply with heavy sodium. Through a series of adventures in which Percy continues his social satire, Dr. More foils the Fedville thought controllers; gets a clinic for the terminally ill, the very old, and sick or crippled infants; and disbands a group of child abusers, high on heavy sodium, at the school his children attend. In the process, he must resist his personal temptations as well—the seductive charms of his cousin, ''the sweet heavy incubus'' Lucy Lipscomb, and the bribe of a high-paying job at Fedville.

By the end of *The Thanatos Syndrome,* Dr. More has restored the selves or humanity of his Feliciana neighbors, but the state of his own soul remains in doubt. His family relations have improved, but he seems unable to relate to Ellen's newfound born-again Christianity or her desire to send the children to a creationist academy. When Father Rinaldo Smith exhorts the community to ''keep hope and have a loving heart and do not secretly wish for the death of others'' so that ''the Great Prince Satan will not succeed in destroying the world,'' Dr. More wonders if he is suffering from ''presenile dementia.'' Father Smith keeps luring Dr. More to serve mass for him when he supposedly cannot get others to do so, but Dr. More's motivation seems more philanthropic than devout. The last words of the novel are Dr. More's ''Well well well,'' which can be interpreted as either a hopeful sign or the sounds one utters when one does not know what to make of something or someone.

Percy's fiction is usually criticized on two grounds: that the novels offer no resolution and that the plots and themes are repetitive. These ostensible failings are inextricable from Percy's view of the human condition. About the conclusions of his novels, Percy told Charles E. Claffey, "A novelist can't come out with pat answers, with everything resolved, the search resolved." For a Catholic, no resolution is possible in this imperfect world. To the charge that Percy's novels are repetitious, in that his protagonists follow the same search and often lapse to search once more, the words of Dr. Thomas More in *The Thanatos Syndrome* seem to provide a reply: "It looks as if real failure is unspeakable. TV has screwed up millions of people with their little rounded-off stories. Because that is not the way life is. Life is fits and starts, mostly fits. Life doesn't have to stop with failure." The novelist's task is to make us aware of our human predicament, not to provide what Percy would regard as spurious temporal solutions, for "the search is the normal condition."

Selected Bibliography

WORKS OF WALKER PERCY

NOVELS

The Moviegoer. New York: Knopf, 1961.

The Last Gentleman. New York: Farrar, Straus, & Giroux, 1966.

Love in the Ruins: The Adventures of a Bad Catholic at a Time near the End of the World. New York: Farrar, Straus, & Giroux, 1971.

Lancelot. New York: Farrar, Straus, & Giroux, 1977.

Bourbon. Winston-Salem, N.C.: Palaemon, 1979.

The Second Coming. New York: Farrar, Straus, & Giroux, 1980.

The Thanatos Syndrome. New York: Farrar, Straus, & Giroux, 1987.

COLLECTED ESSAYS

The Message in the Bottle: How Queer Man Is, How Queer Language Is, and What One Has to Do with the Other. New York: Farrar, Straus, & Giroux, 1975.

Lost in the Cosmos: The Last Self-Help Book. New York: Farrar, Straus, & Giroux, 1983.

BIBLIOGRAPHIES

Dana, Carol G. "Walker Percy." In *Andrew Lytle, Walker Percy, Peter Taylor: A Reference Guide.* By Victor A. Kramer, Patricia A. Bailey, Carol G. Dana, and Carl H. Griffin. Boston: G. K. Hall, 1983.

Hobson, Linda Whitney. *Walker Percy: A Comprehensive Descriptive Bibliography.* Introduction by Walker Percy. New Orleans: Faust, 1988.

Wright, Stuart T. *Walker Percy, a Bibliography, 1930–1984.* Westport, Conn.: Meckler, 1986.

BIOGRAPHICAL AND CRITICAL STUDIES

Allen, William Rodney. *Walker Percy: A Southern Wayfarer.* Jackson: University Press of Mississippi, 1986.

Baker, Lewis. *The Percys of Mississippi: Politics and Literature in the New South.* Baton Rouge: Louisiana State University Press, 1983.

Bloom, Harold, ed. *Walker Percy: Modern Critical Views.* New York: Chelsea House, 1986.

Brinkmeyer, Robert H., Jr. *Three Catholic Writers of the Modern South.* Jackson: University Press of Mississippi, 1985.

Broughton, Panthea Reid, ed. *The Art of Walker Percy: Stratagems for Being.* Baton Rouge: Louisiana State University Press, 1979.

Claffey, Charles E. "Walker Percy: The Novelist as Searcher." *Boston Sunday Globe,* January 22, 1984, p. A27.

Coles, Robert. *Walker Percy: An American Search.* Boston: Little, Brown, 1978.

Hardy, John Edward. *The Fiction of Walker Percy.* Urbana: University of Illinois Press, 1987.

Hawkins, Peter S. *The Language of Grace: Flannery O'Connor, Walker Percy, and Iris Murdoch.* Cambridge, Mass.: Cowley, 1983.

Hobson, Linda Whitney. *Understanding Walker Percy.* Columbia: University of South Carolina Press, 1988.

Lawson, Lewis A. *Following Percy: Essays on Walker Percy's Work.* Troy, N.Y.: Whitston, 1988.

Luschei, Martin. *The Sovereign Wayfarer: Walker Percy's Diagnosis of the Malaise.* Baton Rouge: Louisiana State University Press, 1972.

Poteat, Patricia Lewis. *Walker Percy and the Old Modern Age: Reflections on Language, Argument, and the Telling of Stories.* Baton Rouge: Louisiana State University Press, 1985.

Spivey, Ted R. *The Writer as Shaman: The Pilgrimages of Conrad Aiken and Walker Percy.* Macon, Ga.: Mercer University Press, 1986.

Sweeney, Mary K. *Walker Percy and the Postmodern World.* Chicago: Loyola University Press, 1987.

Taylor, Jerome. *In Search of Self: Life, Death and Walker Percy.* Cambridge, Mass.: Cowley, 1986.

Tharpe, Jac. *Walker Percy.* Boston: Twayne, 1983.

———, ed. *Walker Percy: Art and Ethics.* Jackson: University Press of Mississippi, 1980.

INTERVIEW

Conversations with Walker Percy. Edited by Lewis A. Lawson and Victor A. Kramer. Jackson: University Press of Mississippi, 1985.

—*VERONICA MAKOWSKY*